Lecture Notes in Computer Science 12233

More information about this series at http://www.springer.com/series/7408

Emil Sekerinski · Nelma Moreira ·
José N. Oliveira et al. (Eds.)

Formal Methods

FM 2019 International Workshops

Porto, Portugal, October 7–11, 2019
Revised Selected Papers, Part II

 Springer

Editors
Emil Sekerinski (iD)
McMaster University
Hamilton, ON, Canada

Nelma Moreira (iD)
University of Porto
Porto, Portugal

José N. Oliveira (iD)
University of Minho
Braga, Portugal

Workshop Editors *see next page*

ISSN 0302-9743   ISSN 1611-3349   (electronic)
Lecture Notes in Computer Science
ISBN 978-3-030-54996-1   ISBN 978-3-030-54997-8   (eBook)
https://doi.org/10.1007/978-3-030-54997-8

LNCS Sublibrary: SL2 – Programming and Software Engineering

This Springer imprint is published by the registered company Springer Nature Switzerland AG
The registered company address is: Gewerbestrasse 11, 6330 Cham, Switzerland

Workshop Editors

AFFORD
Daniel Ratiu
Argo Ai
Munich, Germany
dratiu@argo.ai

DataMOD
Riccardo Guidotti
University of Pisa
Pisa, Italy
riccardo.guidotti@di.unipi.it

FMAS
Marie Farrell
University of Liverpool
Liverpool, UK
marie.farrell@liverpool.ac.uk

Matt Luckcuck
University of Liverpool
Liverpool, UK
m.luckcuck@liverpool.ac.uk

FMBC
Diego Marmsoler
University of Exeter
Exeter, UK
d.marmsoler@exeter.ac.uk

FMIS
José Campos
University of Minho
Braga, Portugal
jose.campos@di.uminho.pt

HFM
Troy Astarte
University of Newcastle
Newcastle upon Tyne, UK
t.astarte@ncl.ac.uk

NSAD
Laure Gonnord
Claude Bernard University
Lyon, France
laure.gonnord@ens-lyon.fr

OpenCert
Antonio Cerone ⓘ
Nazarbayev University
Nur-Sultan, Kazakhstan
antonio.cerone@nu.edu.kz

Overture
Luis Diogo Couto
Forcepoint
Ireland
ldcouto@gmail.com

Refine
Brijesh Dongol
University of Surrey
Guildford, UK
b.dongol@surrey.ac.uk

RPLA
Martin Kutrib
University of Giessen
Giessen, Germany
kutrib@informatik.uni-giessen.de

SASB
Pedro Monteiro
University of Lisbon
Lisbon, Portugal
pedro.tiago.monteiro@tecnico.ulisboa.pt

TAPAS
David Delmas
Airbus Operations S.A.S.
Toulouse, France
david.delmas@lip6.fr

Preface

The Third World Congress on Formal Methods (FM 2019) took place during October 7–11, 2019, in Porto, Portugal. The congress comprised nine conferences: the 23rd International Symposium on Formal Methods (FM 2019); the 29th International Symposium on Logic-Based Program Synthesis and Transformation (LOPSTR 2019); the 13th International Conference on Mathematics of Program Construction (MPC 2019); the 21st International Symposium on Principles and Practice of Declarative Programming (PPDP 2019); the 19th International Conference on Runtime Verification (RV 2019); the 26th International Static Analysis Symposium (SAS 2019); the 13th International Conference on Tests and Proofs (TAP 2019); the 7th International Symposium on Unifying Theories of Programming (UTP 2019); and the 13th International Conference on Verification and Evaluation of Computer and Communication Systems (VECoS 2019). The conference also included a Doctoral Symposium, an Industry Day, 2 festschrifts, 16 workshops, and 5 tutorials. In total there were 630 registered participants from 43 countries, 381 presentations from 821 authors, 44 invited speakers, and 13 tool exhibitors. The 16 workshops emerged out of 18 workshop proposals. Three workshops, the Second International Workshop on Dynamic Logic, New Trends and Applications (DaLí 2019), the Third International Workshop and Tutorial on Formal Methods Teaching (FMTea 2019), and the 5th Workshop on Formal Integrated Development Environment (F-IDE 2019), had their proceedings published separately. This two-volume book consists of the proceedings of the other 13 workshops.

Volume 1:

AFFORD 2019
    The Third Workshop on Practical Formal Verification for Software Dependability
DataMod 2019
    The 8th International Symposium From Data to Models and Back
FMAS 2019
    The First Formal Methods for Autonomous Systems Workshop
FMBC 2019
    The First Workshop on Formal Methods for Blockchains
FMIS 2019
    The 8th International Workshop on Formal Methods for Interactive Systems

Volume 2:

HFM 2019
    The First History of Formal Methods Workshop
NSAD 2019
    The 8th International Workshop on Numerical and Symbolic Abstract Domains

OpenCERT 2019
  The 9th International Workshop on Open Community Approaches to Education,
  Research and Technology
Overture 2019
  The 17th Overture Workshop
Refine 2019
  The 19th Refinement Workshop
RPLA 2019
  The First International Workshop on Reversibility in Programming, Languages, and
  Automata
SASB 2019
  The 10th International Workshop on Static Analysis and Systems Biology
TAPAS 2019
  The 10th Workshop on Tools for Automatic Program Analysis

The diversity of the workshop themes reflects the evolution that formal methods of software development have taken since the first World Congress on Formal Methods in 1999 (Toulouse, France) and the second in 2009 (Eindhoven, The Netherlands). Each workshop has its unique history and style that was left up to the workshop organizers to maintain. We are pleased to have four workshops for the first time: FMAS, FMBC, HFM, and RPLA. In total, 123 papers were accepted after a first round of reviewing for the presentation at FM 2019. Of those, 108 were submitted for a second round of reviewing after the congress and 68 selected for inclusion in these proceedings. The workshop organizers ensured that all papers received at least three reviews. Nine invited abstracts, two invited papers, and one workshop summary are included as well.

We are grateful to the workshop authors, the workshop organizers, the Program and Organizing Committee members of the workshops, the local organizers, the sponsors of the congress, and everyone else involved in the 34 events of the congress for the concerted effort in putting together such a rich program.

Finally, we thank Springer for their immediate willingness to publish the collected FM 2019 workshop proceedings in the LNCS series and their support in the editing process.

May 2020   Emil Sekerinski
                                                                    Nelma Moreira
                                                                  José N. Oliveira

Organization

General Chair

José N. Oliveira — University of Minho, INESC TEC, Portugal

Program Chairs

Maurice H. ter Beek — ISTI-CNR, Italy
Annabelle McIver — Macquarie University, Australia

Industry Day Chairs

Joe Kiniry — Galois Inc., USA
Thierry Lecomte — ClearSy, France

Doctoral Symposium Chairs

Alexandra Silva — University College London, UK
Antónia Lopes — University of Lisbon, Portugal

Journal First Track Chair

Augusto Sampaio — Federal University of Pernambuco, Brazil

Workshop and Tutorial Chairs

Emil Sekerinski — McMaster University, Canada
Nelma Moreira — University of Porto, Portugal

Organizing Committee

Luís Soares Barbosa — University of Minho, INESC TEC, Portugal
José Creissac Campos — University of Minho, INESC TEC, Portugal
João Pascoal Faria — University of Porto, INESC TEC, Portugal
Sara Fernandes — University of Minho, INESC TEC, Portugal
Luís Neves — Critical Software, Portugal
Ana Paiva — University of Porto, INESC TEC, Portugal

Local Organizers

Catarina Fernandes	University of Minho, INESC TEC, Portugal
Paula Rodrigues	INESC TEC, Portugal
Ana Rita Costa	INESC TEC, Portugal

Web Team

Francisco Neves	University of Minho, INESC TEC, Portugal
Rogério Pontes	University of Minho, INESC TEC, Portugal
Paula Rodrigues	INESC TEC, Portugal

FME Board

Ana Cavalcanti	University of York, UK
Lars-Henrik Eriksson	Uppsala University, Sweden
Stefania Gnesi	ISTI-CNR, Italy
Einar Broch Johnsen	University of Oslo, Norway
Nico Plat	Thanos, The Netherlands

Contents – Part II

Overture 2019 - 17th Overture Workshop

Refine 2019 - 19th Refinement Workshop

RPLA 2019 - Workshop on Reversibility in Programming, Languages, and Automata

SASB 2019 - 10th International Workshop on Static Analysis and Systems Biology

TAPAS 2019 - 10th Workshop on Tools for Automatic Program Analysis

Contents – Part I

FMAS 2019 - 1st Formal Methods for Autonomous Systems Workshop

FMBC 2019 - 1st Workshop on Formal Methods for Blockchains

FMIS 2019 - 8th Formal Methods for Interactive Systems Workshop

HFM 2019 - History of Formal Methods Workshop

HFM 2019 Organizers' Message

This collection of papers is the result of a workshop held on 11th October 2019, as part of the FM'19 conference, in Porto, Portugal. The workshop was on the history of formal methods: mathematical or logical techniques for modelling, specifying, and reasoning about aspects of computing. The aim was to bring together historians of computing, technology, and science with practitioners in the field of formal methods to reflect on the discipline's history. It was the first workshop to bear this name and represented an early attempt to turn the eye of history towards formal methods specifically. The conference web pages can be found at https://sites.google.com/view/hfm2019/ where they will hopefully remain long after the site becomes a historical artefact itself. Here, the pre-conference abstracts can be seen, as well as the slides for each talk.

My own involvement in the workshop came through a rather roundabout route. José Oliveira, the FM'19 chair, got in touch with my PhD supervisor Cliff Jones to ask him if he wanted to chair a workshop on the history of formal methods at the upcoming conference. Cliff said "No, but you could ask Brian Randell." Brian said "Yes, but only if I have a junior partner (to do most of the work)!" At that time I was just wrapping up work on my thesis, on the history of formal semantics, and jumped at the chance to get involved with organising something so relevant to my research interests. Now, a year and a half later, the last efforts have finally made it over the finish line, and the proceedings are complete. It has taken rather a lot of energy and work to get here, but Brian and I—and indeed everyone involved—are very proud of what we all managed to achieve.

There is a long history of mathematical (as well as scientific and engineering) influence on computing, especially due to the large number of trained mathematicians working with the early electronic computers. This is one reason for a community concerned with mathematising aspects of computing: mathematicians brought the tools and agendas of mathematics with them and developed a number of theories of computation. At the same time, growing concerns amongst programmers about the difficulty of determining the correctness of programs, especially as programs took on a more central and vital role in human society, led to the 'Software Crisis' of the late 1960s. Part of the response to that was the development of specialised tools and approaches for designing, specifying, and reasoning about, programs. Many of these concepts and ideas evolved over the years into what are now called 'formal methods'—the term often connoting a desire to find tools for practical problems that apply and use theoretical notions. Research on formal methods has been instrumental in developing fundamental understanding of computation and providing techniques for rigorous development of software, but has not always had the impact on practical and industrial computing that FM proponents might have desired[1].

---

[1] This topic was explored in more detail in a reflective session at the end of the workshop, reported on in 'What have formal methods ever done for us? An audience discussion', found in this volume.

The workshop was aimed at being accessible to people without any historical background. It attracted a wide audience, including a great many current researchers in formal methods. The workshop and the papers resulting contained herein are a valuable source for further analysis and synthesis by historians of science whose work covers formal aspects of computing. One particularly important source is the collection of IFIP WG 2.1 papers, held in the Braga District Archive—the curation of which is discussed in 'From Manuscripts to Programming Languages' by Vidal, Meneses, and Sousa. They are also of great use to current researchers: we firmly believe understanding the history of the field brings greater clarity to technical research. The workshop saw efforts from early stage researchers trying their hand at historical reflection and building an idea of the field's grounding (see, for example, the talk 'The History and Evolution of B and Event-B' by Krings et al.); contributions from historians of computing which provided context and background to formal methods (see 'Flow Diagrams, Assertions, and Formal Methods' by Priestley); and most of all reflections from researchers who have worked in formal methods considering their own contributions and those of their colleagues (for example 'Specification with Class' by Duke and Smith, and 'Formal Specifications and Software Testing, a Fruitful Convergence' by Gaudel).

What follows is a selection of papers resulting from work presented at the workshop, as well as extended abstracts representing the talks which were not able, for various reasons, to result in full papers in this volume.

February 2020   Troy Kaighin Astarte

Organization

General Chair

Troy Kaighin Astarte   Newcastle University, UK

Program Committee Chairs

Troy Kaighin Astarte   Newcastle University, UK
Brian Randell   Newcastle University, UK

Program Committee

Gerard Alberts   University of Amsterdam, The Netherlands
Dan Berry   University of Waterloo, Canada

Jonathan Bowen	London South Bank University, UK, & Southwest University, China
Liesbeth De Mol	Université de Lille, France
Helena Durnová	Masaryk University, Czechia
Cliff Jones	Newcastle University, UK
Matt Luckuck	University of Liverpool, UK
Simone Martini	Università di Bologna, Italy
Elisabetta Mori	Middlesex University London, UK
Peter Mosses	Delft University of Technology, The Netherlands
Olaf Owe	University of Oslo, Norway
Tomas Petricek	University of Cambridge, UK
Davide Sangiorgi	University of Bologna, Italy
John Tucker	Swansea University, UK
Jim Woodcock	University of York, UK
Jeffrey Yost	University of Minnesota, USA

Additional Reviewers

Jeremy Gibbons
Adrian Johnstone
Philipp Körner
Sebastian Krings

Sponsor

Sponsored by the Commission
for the History and Philosophy of Computing,
http://www.hapoc.org.

HaPoC

Extended Abstract

The Prehistory and History of RE (+ SE) as Seen by Me: How My Interest in FMs Helped to Move Me to RE and to Teach Me Fundamental Impediments to Using FMs in SW Systems Development

Daniel Berry

Cheriton School of Computer Science, University of Waterloo, Waterloo, ON,
N2L 3G1 Canada
dberry@uwaterloo.ca

Abstract. This talk builds on Berry's personal professional history as it attempts to explain why formal methods are not being used to develop large-scale software-intensive computer-based systems by appealing to the Reference Model for Requirements and Specifications by Gunter, Gunter, Jackson, and Zave.

Keywords: Formal methods • Requirements engineering •
Requirements engineering reference model • Software development

Extended Abstract

Berry very briefly weaves the twin peaks of (1) his life with interests in computing, programming, programming languages, software engineering, formal methods, electronic publishing, and requirements engineering with (2) the almost concurrent development of the fields of Programming Languages (PLs), Software Engineering (SE), and Requirements Engineering (RE).

He then describes his participation in the field of Formal Methods (FMs), how it stimulated his eventual move to RE at the same time he was becoming more and more disillusioned about the usefulness and effectiveness of formal methods.

What he learned while doing RE research, in particular, the RE reference model [2], allows him to understand and explain why formal methods cannot be as effective as formal methodologists had hoped. His own work on the importance of ignorance in RE [1, 3] suggests that what does help is the presence of formal methodologists in a software development project.

Berry's slides, both those actually covered in the regular one-half-hour slot (0_5hrHyperTrimmedHistoryOfMe_SE_FMs_RE_focusFMs.pdf) and a two-hour version (2hrHistoryOfMe_SE_FMs_RE_focusFMs.pdf), and other materials can be found at https://cs.uwaterloo.ca/~dberry/FTP_SITE/lecture.slides/HistoryOfMe_SE_FMs_RE/. Attached to the end of the two-hour version is a complete bibliography listing the sources of the claims made in the slides; citations to these sources have been added in blue to the relevant slides in this version.

Acknowledgments. Daniel Berry's work was supported in part by a Canadian NSERC grant NSERC-RGPIN227055-15.

References

1. Berry, D.M.: The importance of ignorance in requirements engineering. J. Syst. Softw. **28** (1995)
2. Gunter, C.A., Gunter, E.L., Jackson, M.A., Zave, P.: A reference model for requirements and specifications. IEEE Softw. **17**(3), 37–43 (2000)
3. Niknafs, A., Berry, D.M.: The impact of domain knowledge on the effectiveness of requirements engineering activities. Empirical Softw. Eng. **22**(4), 2001–2049 (2017). https://rdcu.be/6gYF

Babbage's Mechanical Notation

Adrian Johnstone and Elizabeth Scott

Royal Holloway, University of London
A.Johnstone@rhul.ac.uk

Extended Abstract

Charles Babbage (1791–1871) was Lucasian Professor of mathematics in Cambridge from 1828–1839. He displayed a fertile curiosity that led him to study many contemporary processes and problems in a way which emphasised an analytic, data driven view of life. In popular culture Babbage has been celebrated as an anachronistic Victorian engineer. In reality, Babbage is best understood as a figure rooted in the enlightenment, who had substantially completed his core investigations into 'mechanisation of thought' by the mid 1830s: he is thus an anachronistic Georgian: the construction of his first difference engine design is contemporary with the earliest public railways in Britain.

A fundamental question that must strike anybody who examines Babbage's precocious designs is: how could one individual working alone have synthesised a workable computer design, designing an object whose complexity of behaviour so far exceeded that of contemporary machines that it would not be matched for over a hundred years?

We shall explore the extent to which the answer lies in the techniques Babbage developed to reason about complex systems. His Notation which shows the geometry, timing, causal chains and the abstract components of his machines, has a direct parallel in the Hardware Description Languages developed since 1975 to aid the design of large scale electronics. These modern languages typically have a geometry facet in which the arrangement of electronic components in space is specified; a register transfer facet which emphasises the interconnection of functional units and registers; and a behavioural facet which describes sequences as state machines or in software-like notations. The interlaced facets present different abstractions to the design engineer: the separation of concerns underpins our ability to design complex systems. Babbage's notation has a 'trains' facet which captures the chain of cause and effect within a system, a timing facet which displays state and a zforms' facet which shows geometry.

In this presentation, we shall provide a basic tutorial on Babbage's notation showing how his concepts of 'pieces' and 'working points' effectively build a graph in which both parts and their interactions are represented by nodes, with edges between part-nodes and interaction-nodes denoting ownership, and edges between interaction-nodes denoting the transmission of forces between individual assemblies within a machine. We shall give examples from Babbage's Difference Engine 2 (DE2) for which a complete set of notations was drawn in 1849, and compare them to a design of similar complexity specified in 1987 using the Inmos HDL.

We shall show that early drafts of the DE2 notations use hierarchy to manage complexity. We shall discuss whether Babbage's notation is sufficiently formal and complete to allow symbolic simulation of a system such as DE2. We shall conclude by examining the role of abstraction in Babbage's design process, with special reference to Reuleaux's 1876 criticism of Babbage's notation that "It is at once evident, however, that under this system mechanisms of completely different constructions might be represented by one and the same set of symbols" [1].

Reference

1. Reuleaux, F.: Kinematics of Machinery. London: Macmillan and Co. (1876)

The History and Evolution of B and Event-B

Philipp Körner[1] (ID), Sebastian Krings[1] (ID), Michael Butler[2] (ID),
Thierry Lecomte[3], Michael Leuschel[1] (ID), Luis-Fernando Mejia[4],
and Laurent Voisin[5] (ID)

[1] Institut für Informatik, Universität Düsseldorf, Universitätsstr. 1, D-40225,
Düsseldorf, Germany
{rp.koerner,sebastian.krings,leuschel}@hhu.de
[2] University of Southampton, University Road, Southampton, SO17 1BJ, UK
mjb@ecs.soton.ac.uk
[3] CLEARSY, 320 avenue Archimède, 13100, Aix en Provence, France
thierry.lecomte@clearsy.com
[4] Alstom Transportation Systems, 48 rue Albert Dhalenne, 93400, Saint-Ouen,
France
luis-fernando.mejia@alstomgroup.com
[5] Systerel, 1090 rue René Descartes, 13100, Aix-en-Provence, France
laurent.voisin@systerel.fr

Extended Abstract

The B method for software and systems development together with the specification language B and its successor Event-B offer a rich history. Method, language and tools have been influenced by research stemming from other communities, but also have driven research in formal methods themselves. At the same time, the B method has been successfully used in industry, in particular in the railway domain.

B has originally been developed as a successor to Z by Jean-Raymond Abrial in the 1990s, focusing on two key concepts: using refinement to gradually develop models and tool support for proof and model checking. At the time of writing, three classes of industrial applications of B have been established, which evolved from the original ideas:

- B for software (classical B) [4]: refine specifications until B0, a low-level subset of B, is reached and apply code generators
- B for system modelling (Event-B) [5]: verify critical properties, understand why a system is correct
- B for data validation: express properties in B and check data (possibly using a second tool-chain)

In our talk, we will first give a primer on B and Event-B, introducing the main language features and how they are used. Afterwards, we will describe the history of B, starting with B's genesis as a tool for software validation [2, 3, 11], discussing industrial applications of B in projects such as train speed control [10] and signalling [13] and other projects with RATP and SNCF performed by Alstom, Line 14 (Meteor) [14] or Canarsie [15].

Following, we will focus on the evolution of B into Event-B and from software to systems modelling, again focusing on industrial applications such as the flushing line NY [23], OCTYS [12], GIK/Railground [9], the HL3 standard [16] and cooperations with Peugeot. Additionally, we will discuss ventures of using B in other domains such as smart cards [8, 17].

The latest language evolution, B for data validation, will again highlight B's prevalence in the railway domain, discussing its use for Paris Line 1 [22] and the (subway) trains in Barcelona, Amsterdam, Calcutta, Cairo, Singapore and many more locations.

Additionally, we will briefly present other data validation projects and how they influenced language and tool evolution, e.g., projects by RATP using Ovado with predicateB as first and ProB as secondary tool chain [1, 7] and projects by Alstom using B for their URBALIS 400 CBTC system in 2014 using a tool based on ProB called DTVT developed by CLEARSY for various lines, e.g., in Mexico, Toronto, São Paulo and Panama [18]. While discussing B for data validation, we will also take a brief glance at minor language evolutions, where some parties extended the B language in order to increase usability and flexibility.

Language evolution aside, we want to discuss tool evolution in the B ecosystem. Both B and Event-B are supported by a range of tools, from provers to animators to model checkers. We want to give an overview over the B-method tools currently in use and their development and history, such as the B-Toolkit [19, 24], Atelier-B [11], ProB [20, 21] as well as to Rodin [6]. As not all tools are still available, we will also honorably mention the ones that disappeared or never really appeared.

In addition to industrial success stories, the academic reception of the B-method and its tools is notable as well and will be a distinct part of the talk. Starting with the B User Workshop, to the ZB conference and further to the ABZ conference series, which brings together researchers working on different specification languages.

Switching from history and evolution to outlook, we want to discuss new language features such as extensions and customisations on top of classical B and Event-B as understood by Rodin or ProB. Furthermore, we intend to discuss new areas of application both for B as a language as well as for the B-method tools.

Acknowledgments. We would like to express our gratitude to Jean-Raymond Abrial, who provided us with sources, discussions, insider information and knowledge from his personal experiences developing B and Event-B.

References

1. Abo, R., Voisin, L.: Formal implementation of data validation for railway safetyrelated systems with OVADO. In: Proceedings SEFM 2013. LNCS, vol. 8368, pp.221–236. Springer (2014)
2. Abrial, J.R.: The b tool (abstract). In: Bloomfield, R.E., Marshall, L.S., Jones, R.B. (eds.). Proceedings VDM. pp. 86–87. Springer (1988)

3. Abrial, J.R., Lee, M.K.O., Neilson, D.S., Scharbach, P.N., Sørensen, I.H.: The bmethod. In: Prehn, S., Toetenel, H. (eds.). Proceedings VDM. pp. 398–405. Springer (1991)
4. Abrial, J.R.: The B-Book. Cambridge University Press (1996)
5. Abrial, J.R.: Modeling in Event-B: System and Software Engineering. Cambridge, University Press (2010)
6. Abrial, J.R., Butler, M., Hallerstede, S., Voisin, L.: An Open Extensible Tool Environment for Event-B. In: Proceedings ICFEM. LNCS, vol. 4260, pp. 588–605. Springer (2006)
7. Badeau, F., Doche-Petit, M.: Formal data validation with Event-B. CoRR abs/1210.7039, proceedings of DS-Event-B 2012, Kyoto (2012)
8. Benveniste, M.: On Using B in the Design of Secure Micro-controllers: An Experience Report. ENTCS 280, 3–22 (2011)
9. Butler, M.J., Dghaym, D., Fischer, T., Hoang, T.S., Reichl, K., Snook, C.F., Tummeltshammer, P.: Formal Modelling Techniques for Efficient Development of Railway Control Products. In: Proceedings RSSRail. LNCS, vol. 10598, pp. 71–86. Springer (2017)
10. Carnot, M., DaSilva, C., Dehbonei, B., Mejia, F.: Error-free software development for critical systems using the B-Methodology. In: Proceedings ISSRE. pp. 274–281. IEEE (1992)
11. ClearSy: Atelier B, User and Reference Manuals. Aix-en-Provence, France (2009). http://www.atelierb.eu/
12. Comptier, M., Déeharbe, D., Perez, J.M., Mussat, L., Thibaut, P., Sabatier, D.: Safety Analysis of a CBTC System: A Rigorous Approach with Event-B. In: Proceedings, RSSRail. LNCS, vol. 10598, pp. 148–159. Springer (2017)
13. Dehbonei, B., Mejia, F.: Formal methods in the railways signalling industry. In: Proceedings FME. LNCS, vol. 873, pp. 26–34. Springer (1994)
14. Dollé, D., Essamé, D., Falampin, J.: B dans le transport ferroviaire. L'expérience de Siemens Transportation Systems. Technique et Science Informatiques 22(1), 11–32 (2003)
15. Essamé, D., Dollé, D.: B in Large-Scale Projects: The Canarsie Line CBTC Experience. In: Proceedings B. LNCS, vol. 4355, pp. 252–254. Springer (2007)
16. Hansen, D., et al.: Using a Formal B Model at Runtime in a Demonstration of the ETCS Hybrid Level 3 Concept with Real Trains. In: Proceedings ABZ. LNCS, vol. 10817, pp. 292–306. Springer (2018)
17. Lanet, J.L.: The use of B for Smart Card. In: Proceedings FDL (2002)
18. Lecomte, T., Burdy, L., Leuschel, M.: Formally Checking Large Data Sets in the Railways. CoRR abs/1210.6815, proceedings of DS-Event-B 2012, Kyoto (2012)
19. Lee, M., Sørensen, I.H.: B-tool. In: Proceedings VDM. LNCS, vol. 551, pp. 695–696. Springer (1991)
20. Leuschel, M., Bendisposto, J., Dobrikov, I., Krings, S., Plagge, D.: From Animation to Data Validation: The ProB Constraint Solver 10 Years On. In: Formal Methods Applied to Complex Systems: Implementation of the B Method, chap. 14, pp. 427–446. Wiley ISTE (2014)
21. Leuschel, M., Butler, M.J.: ProB: an automated analysis toolset for the B method. STTT 10 (2), 185–203 (2008)
22. Leuschel, M., Falampin, J., Fritz, F., Plagge, D.: Automated Property Verification for Large Scale B Models. In: Proceedings FM. LNCS, vol. 5850, pp. 708–723. Springer (2009)
23. Sabatier, D.: Using Formal Proof and B Method at System Level for Industrial Projects. In: Proceedings RSSRail. LNCS, vol. 9707, pp. 20–31. Springer (2016)
24. Sorensen, I., Neilson, D.: B: Towards zero defect software. In: Winter, V.L., Bhattacharya, S. (eds.) High Integrity Software, pp. 23–42. Springer (2001)

History of Abstract Interpretation

Roberto Giacobazzi[1] and Francesco Ranzato[2]

[1]University of Verona, Italy
roberto.giacobazzi@univr.it
[2]University of Padova, Italy

Extended Abstract

We trace the roots of abstract interpretation and its role as a fundamental theoretical framework to understand and design program analysis and program verification methods. Starting from the historical roots of program verification and formal methods, from A.M. Turing to C.A.R. Hoare, we show how abstract interpretation fits this mainstream in perfect continuity and how this theory shaped the literature and the practice in program analysis in the last 40 years, providing powerful methodologies for designing static program analyzers, automatic verifiers of software/hardware systems, type systems, security protocol analyzers, analyzers of machine learning models, algorithms for formal languages.

We also trace the beginning of the industrialization of abstract interpretation from the very first systematic use in verification of embedded systems to the nowadays widespread use in high-end static program analysers. Noteworthy examples include: (1) Polyspace is a static analyzer for C/C++/Ada programs, fully conceived and designed by abstract interpretation and successfully commercialized by MathWorks, USA; (2) Astrée is a C static analyzer, envisaged and designed from scratch by Patrick and Radhia Cousot's research group on abstract interpretation at École Normale Supérieure Paris, marketed by AbsInt GmbH, Germany, and used in the defense/aerospace (Airbus, Honda), electronic (Siemens), and automotive industries (Daimler); (3) Infer and Zoncolan are static analysis tools developed by Facebook; Infer detects memory safety and concurrency bugs in Java/C/C++/Objective-C code, Zoncolan finds security and privacy violations in Facebook's Hack codebase; both Infer and Zoncolan are firmly based on abstract interpretation and routinely used by Facebook software engineers.

The top five most cited articles at the ACM Symposium on Principles of Programming Languages (POPL, the top-tier and oldest conference in programming languages) include three articles on abstract interpretation, in particular the most cited article, which according to Google scholar has more than 7500 citations. We survey the birth and evolution of abstract interpretation starting from the celebrated Cousot and Cousot's POPL77 paper and landing, through a 40+ years journey, to the current state-of-the-art of this research discipline. We also give some personal hints on the main future challenges faced by abstract interpretation research.

Flow Diagrams, Assertions, and Formal Methods

Mark Priestley[(⊠)]

The National Museum of Computing, Bletchley Park, UK
m.priestley@gmail.com

Abstract. This paper examines the early history of the flow diagram notation developed by Herman Goldstine and John von Neumann in the mid-1940s. It emphasizes the motivation for the notation's mathematical aspects and the provision made for formally checking the consistency of diagrams. Goldstine and von Neumann's introduction of assertion boxes is considered in detail. The practical use of flow diagrams is considered briefly, and the paper then reads Turing's 1949 essay on "Checking a large routine" in the light of his likely knowledge of the Goldstine/von Neumann notation. In particular, his different use of the term "assertion" is considered, and related to the earlier work.

Keywords: Flow diagrams · Assertions · Formal methods

1 Introduction

Flowcharts are one of the defining visual representations of modern computing. Introduced in 1947 by Herman Goldstine and John von Neumann as part of a comprehensive methodology for what they called the "planning and coding of problems", they were a ubiquitous aid to the development of computer programs for at least the next two decades. A wide variety of notations was used, but all forms of the diagrams contained boxes representing operations and decision points, linked by directed line segments representing the flow of control [18].

Despite this ubiquity, historians have questioned the role of flowcharts. Rather than being a significant part of the development process, they were criticized as being burdensome and misleading documentation produced only at the behest of bureaucratically-minded project managers. Ensmenger [5] describes them as *boundary objects* whose value lay in their ability to mediate between managers and developers while meaning something different to the two groups.

Given this, it comes as something of a surprise to realize that, for Goldstine and von Neumann, flow diagrams provided not only a graphic representation of program structure but also a sophisticated mathematical notation. They defined a number of formal conditions, akin to what we would now call proof rules, for

I thank Troy Astarte and Brian Randell for the invitation to give the talk at the HFM 2019 workshop on which this paper is based.

ⓒ Springer Nature Switzerland AG 2020
E. Sekerinski et al. (Eds.): FM 2019 Workshops, LNCS 12233, pp. 15–34, 2020.
https://doi.org/10.1007/978-3-030-54997-8_1

demonstrating the consistency of a diagram. It is not unreasonable, if slightly anachronistic, to describe the original diagrams not simply as a design notation but as an early attempt to define a formal method for software development.

Computer scientist Cliff Jones [16,17] cited the 1947 diagrams as a precursor of Alan Turing's 1949 paper on "checking a large routine" [21,24]. Jones focused on the term "assertion": Turing defined a number of assertions to be checked by the programmer, and the Goldstine/von Neumann notation included a feature called "assertion boxes" which appeared to allow arbitrary logical formulas to be inserted into the diagram. This appears, in turn, to look forward to the work of Robert Floyd in the mid-1960s: in a paper widely regarded as a milestone in the development of formal methods, Floyd attached propositions to the line segments in flowcharts to provide a basis for constructing formal proofs about the correctness of the program represented by the diagram [6].

This gap of almost 20 years should make us pause and wonder whether the resemblance between early and later work is simply a superficial similarity, or whether there are deeper and more meaningful connections. This paper focuses on the development of the Goldstine/von Neumann notation and examines the motivation for its development and the problems it was supposed to solve. The notation is then used to analyze Turing's 1949 flow diagram, highlighting the similarities and the differences between the two approaches.

2   Block Diagrams

Von Neumann's collaboration with Goldstine began in 1944, when the latter was the US Army's representative on the ENIAC project [12]. Along with ENIAC's designers Presper Eckert and John Mauchly, the pair worked on designs for a successor machine, EDVAC, the first so-called "stored-program" computer. By 1946, however, the team had split up and Goldstine followed von Neumann to the Institute for Advanced Study to work on the electronic computer project there. Flow diagrams were first described in a 1947 project report [11], and Goldstine later gave an outline history of their development:

> In the spring of [1946] von Neumann and I evolved an exceedingly crude sort of geometrical drawing to indicate in rough fashion the iterative nature of an induction. At first this was intended as a sort of tentative aid to use in programming. Then that summer I became convinced that this type of *flow diagram*, as we named it, could be used as a logically complete and precise notation for expressing a mathematical problem, and indeed that this was essential to the task of programming. Accordingly, I developed a first, incomplete version and began work on the paper called *Planning and Coding* [...] Out of this was to grow not just a geometrical notation but a carefully thought out analysis of programming as a discipline [9, pp. 266–7].

As far as the surviving evidence allows us to judge, this account is quite accurate. A "first, incomplete" version of the notation appears in an unpublished draft of the *Planning and Coding* reports [10]. At this stage, the notations were called *block diagrams* but by the time the first report was published in 1947, significant syntactic and semantic modifications had taken place, and the terminology had changed [11].

They were not the first graphical representations of computer programs. A wide range of notations had been used to document ENIAC programs, including "master programmer diagrams" [12]. Named for the machine's high-level control unit, these box-and-arrow diagrams represented the "steppers", devices which counted loop iterations and controlled the execution of straight-line blocks of operations shown as simple boxes. The diagrams therefore presented the high-level organization of a program, and were capable of showing complex structures of nested loops and conditional branches.

So-called "flow sheets" had been in use since the late nineteenth century to show the flow of materials in processes in industries such as milling [22], and in the 1920s more general "process charts" were proposed as part of a methodology for describing and improving industrial and commercial processes [7]. A 1947 standard [1] distinguished operation from flow process charts, the latter showing the events affecting some material in an industrial process. Ensmenger [5] notes that flow diagrams are sometimes said to have come to computing through this route, thanks to von Neumann's undergraduate studies in chemical engineering, though similar "flow charts" had been independently used on the ENIAC project to describe the processing of decks of punched cards [19].

However, the fact that the diagrams were originally called "block diagrams" suggests an alternative source, namely the use of block diagrams in electronics. These provided a high-level view of the structure of a circuit, and Goldstine and von Neumann's block diagrams similarly presented a high-level view of the problem-specific organization of a computer's memory. As there was no physical flow of material between processes being illustrated, the use of the term "flow" may not have immediately suggested itself (the metaphor of a "flow of control" seems to postdate the adoption of the diagrams). The change in terminology may reflect the evolution, described below, from a kind of memory map to a more abstract representation of the structure of a computational process. In 1946, Haskell Curry and Willa Wyatt [3] had drawn what they called a "flowchart" to describe the structure of an ENIAC program, in which electronic pulses did flow through the machine's wires to control the order of processing, a usage which may have helped legitimize the term "flow diagram".

The ultimate aim of the diagrams was to effect a division of labour in the process of preparing problems for automatic computation:

> We have attempted [...] to standardize upon a graphical notation for a problem in the hope that this symbolism would be sufficiently explicit to make quite clear to a relatively unskilled operator the general outline of the procedure. We further hope that from such a *block-diagram* the operator will be able with ease to carry out a complete coding of a problem [10].

The process described in the final report was much more complex, but the aim was the same: to bring the work to a point from which the code could

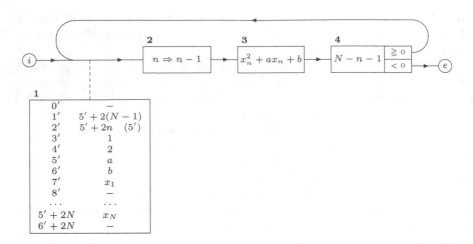

Fig. 1. Block diagram describing the computation of N values of a polynomial [10]. x_n is found in location $5' + 2n$ and the value of $x_n^2 + ax_n + b$ is stored in location $6' + 2n$.

be generated in a straightforward way. The reports contain a range of example problems that are described and coded in detail with the aid of the new diagrams.

In the summer of 1945, von Neumann coded a number of problems to test the code he was designing for the EDVAC. One of these survives, namely a routine to merge two sequences of data [19]. Von Neumann used the familiar technique of "definition by cases" to describe the general outline of the procedure, including alternative courses of action. The introduction of diagrams in 1946 might have been motivated by the belief that diagrams were intrinsically clearer than text for complex problems or that they would be more accessible to "relatively unskilled operators". It may not be a coincidence that ENIAC's first operators recalled using the block diagrams of the machine's electronics as a way coming to understand it well enough to program it.

Figure 1 shows the first diagram from the draft report, a program to calculate and store N values of the polynomial $x_n^2 + ax_n + b$. Each box in the diagram represents a contiguous area of memory. Box 1 is a *storage box* describing the data manipulated by the program: $0', 1', \ldots$ are symbolic addresses of memory locations whose contents are described using the mathematical vocabulary in which the problem is stated. Boxes 2, 3, and 4 represent instructions whose effect is specified by the expressions in the boxes. The program consists of a simple loop controlled by what Goldstine and von Neumann referred to as the "induction variable" n. Box 2 represents the code that increments the value of n, box 3 represents the calculation of the polynomial's value for the current value of n (but doesn't state where that value is to be stored), and the *alternative box* 4 represents the test for loop termination. The initial value $n = 0$ must be inferred by comparing the initial $(5')$ and the general $(5' + 2n)$ values given in box 1 for storage location $2'$. The expression $n \Rightarrow n - 1$ in box 2 denotes the change in the value of n from one iteration to the next.

Address	Order	Result	Comment
2.1	$2'$	$A : 5' + 2(n-1)$	Clear A and add
2.2	$4'$ h	$A : 5' + 2n$	Add to A
2.3	$2'$ S	$2' : 5' + 2n$	Store
2.4	3.1 Sp	$3.1 : (5' + 2n)$ R	Store address field
2.5	3.2 Sp	$3.2 : (5' + 2n) \times$	Store address field
2.6	3.4 Sp	$3.4 : (5' + 2n)$ R	Store address field
2.7	$3'$ h	$A : 6' + 2n$	Clear A and add
2.8	3.8 Sp	$3.8 : (6' + 2n)$ S	Store address field
3.1	$5' + 2n$ R	$R : x_n$	Load register
3.2	$5' + 2n \times$	$A : x_n^2$	Multiply
3.3	$0'$ S	$0' : x_n^2$	Store
3.4	$5' + 2n$ R	$R : x_n$	Load register
3.5	$5' \times$	$A : a x_n$	Multiply
3.6	$0'$ h	$A : x_n^2 + a x_n$	Add to A
3.7	$6'$ h	$A : x_n^2 + a x_n + b$	Add to A
3.8	$6' + 2n$ S	$6' + 2n : x_n^2 + a x_n + b$	Store
4.1	$2'$ −	$A : -(5' + 2n)$	Clear A and subtract
4.2	$1'$ h	$A : 2N - 2 - 2n$	Add to A
4.3	2.1 Cc	$N - n - 1 \geqq 0$	Conditional transfer
4.4	e C		Jump to next order e

Fig. 2. Symbolic code for the polynomial program (after [10]). Three blocks of memory contain the instructions corresponding to boxes 2, 3, and 4 in Fig. 1. The instruction code is defined in [2]. Each order contains a memory reference (in some cases to a location in the table itself) and a code symbol. The result column shows the effect of transfer and arithmetic orders by giving the updated contents of the accumulator (A), the register (R), or a particular memory location, as appropriate. "Sp" orders copy data from the accumulator to the address field of the specified location.

Figure 2 shows the code corresponding to the operation boxes 2, 3, and 4 in Fig. 1. Von Neumann thought of computer memory as a symbolic space consisting of addressable locations in which *words* were stored. *Number words* held coded numbers and *order words* held coded instructions. Most instructions included a numeric field, the address of the memory location on which the instruction was to operate. The purpose of executing instructions was to bring about changes in the contents of memory, a process that von Neumann described as a kind of substitution. Newly calculated numbers could replace the entire contents of a number word or the address field within an order word. The code also seems to allow for the substitution of entire order words, but none of Goldstine and von Neumann's examples use this capability, and the block and flow diagrams provided no way to represent its effect. This capability would prove to be crucial in the automation of coding through such tools as assemblers but, apart from a rather unconvincing discussion of subroutine relocatability, the *Planning and Coding* reports did not cover this topic.

A block diagram can therefore be interpreted in two very different ways. At one level, it is an abstract map of part of a computer's memory. Each block in the diagram corresponds to an area of memory and the directed lines joining them represent what Goldstine called the "itinerary" of the control organ as it executes the program. In this respect, the diagrams are abstract representations of machine-specific hardware, just as ENIAC's master programmer diagrams were. But at the same time the new diagrams aspired to be, in Goldstine's words, "a logically complete and precise notation for expressing a mathematical problem". An important theme in the evolution of the notation was trying to find a way to reconcile these rather different aims.

3   Describing Iterative Processes

In Goldstine's account, the use of diagrams began as an attempt to "indicate [...] the iterative nature of an induction". The most problematic aspect of this was finding a way to describe the changing value of the inductive variable; as this section will explain, Goldstine and von Neumann reached for the concept of substitution to manage this relationship, but it proved less than straightforward to devise a way to make this work.

The loop in Fig. 1 is controlled by the induction variable n. The value of n is not explicitly stored, however, and it only appears in the definition of the contents of location $2'$, namely the address of the location storing x_n. The code in Fig. 2 corresponding to box 2, then, must first increment the value in $2'$ by 2 (instructions 2.1 to 2.3), and then write this new value into the address fields of the instructions which retrieve x_n (3.1, 3.2, and 3.4) and the instruction which stores the new value of the polynomial (3.8). So while the diagram shows a loop controlled by a simple induction variable, the code corresponding to the mathematical operation of incrementing that variable performs a range of quite different tasks.

The annotations given in the code help us understand the way in which the substitution is expressed. The variable n, where $1 \leq n \leq N$, defines the current iteration of the loop. At the point where the dashed line attaches the storage box to the control flow line, then, the values held in storage correspond to the value $n - 1$, as they have not yet been updated by the box 2 code. At this point, the value in $2'$ is $5' + 2(n-1)$, recorded as the accumulator contents after instruction 2.1. Adding 2 to this gives the required value of $5' + 2n$ and the substitution $n \Rightarrow n - 1$ describes the algebraic change.

The notation is rather unfortunate, however, in that the diagram suggests that location $2'$ holds the value $5' + 2n$ at the point of attachment, i.e. before box 2, which appears to increment the value of n. In a hand-written insertion on the typescript, von Neumann commented as follows:

> An alternative procedure would be this: Attach the storage box in its initial form, i.e. with a $5'$ opposite the memory location number $2'$, outside the n-induction loop, i.e. between $\textcircled{i}$ and the first $\longrightarrow$. Attach at the

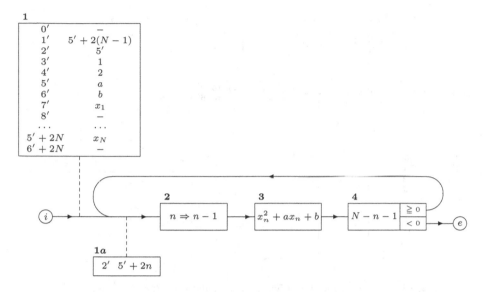

Fig. 3. Block diagram with distributed storage boxes

storage box's present location, i.e. within the n-induction loop, a small storage box which indicates only the change that takes place during the induction: $\boxed{2' \; : \; 5' + 2n}$. At present the simpler notation of the text will be used, however there are more complicated situations (e.g. multiple inductions) where only a notation of the above type is unambiguous [10].

The block diagram with these changes is shown in Fig. 3. This diagram clearly distinguishes the initial value of $2'$ from the more general value given in terms of the inductive variable that it has while the loop is executing.

It looks as if we should be able to do more: the value stored in $2'$ is changed when n is incremented, and it is tempting to insert another storage box after box 2 describing the updated contents of $2'$ as $5' + 2(n+1)$. However, this would make the diagram inconsistent: neither box 3 nor box 4 changes the value of n, so when the loop reenters just before box 2, $2'$ must still hold the value $5' + 2(n+1)$. But at this point, box 1a states that its value is $5' + 2n$.

The root of the problem is an ambiguity in the treatment of n. On the one hand it is the inductive variable, recording the ordinal number of the current loop iteration, but on the other hand, it helps define a stored quantity which is updated at a particular point within the loop. It is therefore unclear exactly when n is incremented, and it seems to be impossible to reconcile these two aspects and to indicate consistently and usefully the point at which the mathematical variable is incremented.

In the flow diagram notation, Goldstine and von Neumann addressed this problem by making a cleaner separation between mathematics and code, and altering and clarifying the semantics of substitution. The flow diagram in Fig. 4 shows one way of representing the polynomial program in the later notation.

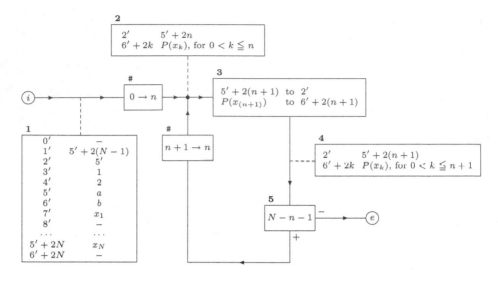

Fig. 4. Flow diagram for the polynomial calculation $(P(x) = x^2 + ax + b)$

The boxes in the diagram now fall into two different categories. As in the block diagrams, operation, alternative and storage boxes correspond to areas of storage containing number or order words, as appropriate. Operation boxes now explicitly show the memory location that a calculated value will be stored in and alternative boxes have a new syntax. However, substitution boxes, marked with **#**, no longer represent areas of storage. Thus in Fig. 4, the substitution box containing the formula $n + 1 \to n$ does not represent the coded instructions that will increment the value of n; these are now carried out as part of box 3.

If substitution boxes no longer stand for coded words, what is their meaning? The best way to approach this question is by considering the general conditions that Goldstine and von Neumann defined for checking the consistency of a flow diagram. The aim of these conditions was to show that the values recorded in storage boxes were consistent with the operations described in the diagram.

For example, box 4 in Fig. 4 states that location $2'$ holds the value $5' + 2(n + 1)$. The preceding box, operation box 3, calculates that very value and stores in it $2'$, so in this respect the diagram is consistent. The general form of a consistency condition for this situation is shown graphically on the left-hand side of Fig. 5, and was expressed by Goldstine and von Neumann as follows (a "constancy interval" can be taken to be a region of a diagram containing a storage box):

The interval in question is immediately preceded by an operation box with an expression in it that is referred "to ..." this field: The field contains the expression in question ... [11].

Fig. 5. Conditions on storage boxes preceded by operation (left) and substitution (right) boxes. The configuration on the right must satisfy the condition $P'[f \rightarrow i] = P$

A similar consistency condition was given for the situation where a storage box was immediately preceded by a substitution box. The right-hand side of Fig. 5 shows the general case and the condition was expressed as follows:

> Replace in the expression of the field every occurrence of every such i by its f. This must produce the expression which is valid in the field of the same storage position at the constancy interval immediately preceding this substitution box [11].

(It is striking that Goldstine and von Neumann's rule applies the substitution to the expression in the storage box following the substitution, a move formally related to the later notion of a weakest precondition).

For example, consider location $2'$ in box 2 in Fig. 4. Box 2 is preceded by the substitution $0 \rightarrow n$. Substituting 0 for n in the expression $5' + 2n$ in box 2 gives the expression $5'$ as the preceding value of $2'$, as recorded in box 1. Box 2 is also preceded, along a different path in the flow diagram, by the substitution $n + 1 \rightarrow n$: substituting $n + 1$ for n in $5' + 2n$ gives $5' + 2(n + 1)$, the expression recorded for $2'$ in storage box 4. The consistency of the diagram at this point follows from these two observations and the following structural rule:

> If the interval in question contains a merger (of several branches of the flow diagram), so that it is immediately preceded by several boxes [. . .], then the corresponding conditions [. . .] must hold with respect to each box [11].

4 Assertions

The previous section showed how, by using storage boxes and substitutions, Goldstine and von Neumann found a way of describing in mathematical terms the step-by-step operation of computations, and in particular the behaviour of typical iterative loops. The flow diagram notation also included *assertion boxes*, however, and these have been seen as foreshadowing later uses of assertions in formal methods [16]. To evaluate this claim, it is useful to look at the role of assertion boxes in flow diagrams and the reasons for their introduction.

Assertion boxes were a late addition to the notation, introduced to solve a problem that arose in describing the result of computing $\sqrt{x}$ by the Newton-Raphson method. In the draft report this was coded in a form which limited the

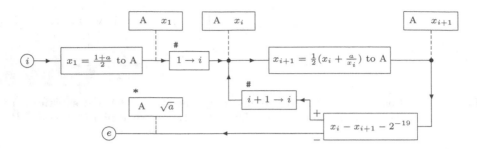

Fig. 6. Von Neumann's initial flow diagram for the calculation of $\sqrt{x}$

process to three iterations, and in early 1947 von Neumann was attempting to develop a more general approach where the loop terminated when the difference between two successive approximations became sufficiently small.

He initially drew a flow diagram similar to the one shown in Fig. 6 [23]. The storage box * at the end of the diagram records where the computed value of $\sqrt{a}$ is stored. However, Goldstine pointed out that this conflicted with the previous storage box that gave the value stored in A as x_{i+1}. Von Neumann then proposed adding the substitution box shown in Fig. 7, where i_0 is defined as the first value of i for which $x_i - x_{i+1} < 2^{-19}$, giving x_{i_0} as the desired approximation to $\sqrt{a}$. He hoped that this would allow the two storage boxes in Fig. 7 to be "reconciled", but soon realized that this solution would not work:

> I must have been feeble minded when I wrote this: $\boxed{i_0 \rightarrow i}$ will reconcile $\boxed{A \;\; \sqrt{a}}$ with a *succeeding* $\boxed{A \;\; x_i}$, but not with a *preceding* one. I.e. one needs something new.
>
> One might play with new entities like $\boxed{i \rightarrow i_0}$, but I think that the best modus procedendi is this:
>
> Let us introduce a new type of box, called *assertion box*. It can be inserted anywhere into the flow diagram, and it contains one or more relations of any kind. It expresses the knowledge that whenever C gets there, those relations are certainly valid. It calls for *no* operations. It reconciles a storage box immediately after it with one immediately before it (and referring to the same storage position), if the expressions in these are equal by virtue of its relations. It is best to mark assertion boxes, say with a cross #.

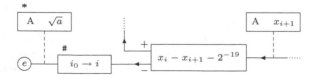

Fig. 7. Von Neumann's "feeble-minded" attempt, using a substitution box

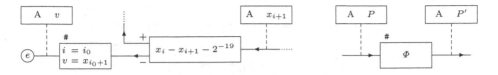

Fig. 8. The final version of the diagram with an assertion box (left-hand side). The general configuration on the right must satisfy the condition $\Phi \Rightarrow P' = P$.

Figure 8 shows the corresponding portion of the diagram from the published report. The two equations in the assertion box imply that $x_{i+1} = v$ and hence reconcile the expressions defining the contents of A in the two storage boxes. The fact that v is the required approximation to $\sqrt{a}$ was stated in the preamble.

The formulas written in assertion boxes were not meant to be proved. They often represent an injection of knowledge into the diagram (such as the fact that at the end of a Newton-Raphson iteration the value computed is $\sqrt{a}$) or allow the introduction of new symbols with given properties. As with substitution boxes, their structural role in the notation is to reconcile preceding and succeeding storage boxes, according to the general schema given in Fig. 8. Goldstine and von Neumann expressed this condition as follows:

It must be demonstrable, that the expression of the field [i.e., A] is, by virtue of the relations that are validated by this assertion box, equal to the expression which is valid in the field of the same storage position at the constancy interval immediately preceding this assertion box [11].

In some cases there was no succeeding storage box, in which case the assertion box has a purely documentary role.

5   Flow Diagrams in Practice

It is outside the scope of this paper to analyze in detail the corpus of flow diagrams surviving from the years following the publication of the first *Planning and Coding* report. The overall picture is one of great notational diversity, united only by the use of a directed graph to depict the "flow of control" between boxes representing operations of various kinds. At the same time, the text in the boxes became increasingly informal. This section briefly describes the fate of the more formal aspects of the notation in three significant areas.

5.1   The *Planning and Coding* reports

The three *Planning and Coding* reports contain examples of the application of flow diagrams to a variety of problems. It is striking that, despite the very general way in which they were described, substitution and assertion boxes are sparingly used, and for a rather limited range of purposes.

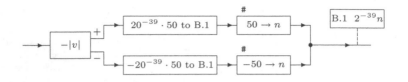

Fig. 9. Substitution boxes uniting different values of a variable

Substitution boxes were almost exclusively used to record the changing values of the induction variables in loops, as shown in Fig. 4. Occasionally they were used in straight-line code to assign a new value to a variable. Figure 9 shows an application of this where n is given different values on the two branches of a conditional structure.

Assertion boxes were most commonly used at the end of loops. If termination was controlled by an explicit test of the inductive variable, the assertion restated and possibly strengthened the loop termination condition. For example, if an alternative box terminating a loop contained the formula $j - J \geqq 0$, it might be followed by a box asserting $j = J$. If the test terminating a loop did not involve the inductive variable, however, an assertion box might introduce a new variable to denote its final value, as in Fig. 8 above.

Assertions boxes were also used with variable remote connections. In one example, an assertion before the connector stated the conditions under which a variable had one of three possible values, and in another case assertions stated properties of certain variables just after a remote connection.

5.2 The Monte Carlo Flow Diagrams

The flow diagram notation was put to the test in the development of the first program to use the Monte Carlo method, a simulation of neutron diffusion in fissile material run on ENIAC in April and May, 1948 [12]. This project took place in the same timeframe as, and most likely inspired, plans to use ENIAC as an interpreter for an EDVAC-style code. Accordingly, the program design graduated from a generic computing plan to large and complex flow diagrams drawn using the notation of the *Planning and Coding* reports. Two complete diagrams have been preserved. The first was drawn up by von Neumann himself in the summer or early autumn of 1947, and the second dates from December of the same year.

Von Neumann's diagram consisted of about 70 operation boxes, 25 storage boxes, 20 substitution boxes, and no assertion boxes. There were six loops, including a nested pair of loops defining the large-scale structure of the program. Storage boxes were not included every time a new value was stored in memory. The program was divided into 10 sections, and storage boxes were typically, though not exclusively, placed at the end of a section to record the location of a significant new value calculated in that section. Many storage boxes immediately followed an operation box assigning a value to the location of interest, perhaps with an intervening substitution box to reconcile notation or introduce a new variable in an obvious way. As a result, the conditions that would need to be checked to be assured that the diagram was well adjusted were largely trivial.

Von Neumann's original design went through an extensive series of changes, but by December it had stabilized and was documented by Adele Goldstine in a second complete flow diagram. This had basically the same structure as von Neumann's, although a couple of sections had been rewritten with alternative algorithms. Storage boxes were used in much the same way as in von Neumann's diagram but notated slightly differently, while the use of substitution boxes in the annotation of loops was rather different.

In this project, we can watch the flow diagram notation evolving in practice. Diagrams were not fully annotated, and became increasingly informal under the twin pressures of application to a large and complex problem and adaptation to the needs of a variety of users. There is no evidence that the conditions for well-adjustedness were recorded or formally checked anywhere. In most cases, these were so trivial that this may not have been felt to be necessary.

5.3   Flow Diagrams Cross the Atlantic

Two British mathematicians were in direct contact with Goldstine and von Neumann as the flow diagram notation was being developed. In January 1947, Alan Turing represented the National Physical Laboratory at a computing symposium at Harvard and then spent a couple of weeks with Goldstine and von Neumann. On his return to the UK he noted that "[t]he Princeton group seems to me to be much the most clear headed and far sighted of these American organizations, and I shall try to keep in touch with them" [20]. There are no records of the discussions, but it is likely that one topic would have been the approaches to programming being considered at Princeton and the NPL.

The mathematical physicist Douglas Hartree had a long-standing interest in computing machinery, and had visited Philadelphia in 1946 to run a problem on ENIAC. He kept in touch with Goldstine, and was sent a copy of the first *Planning and Coding* report soon after its publication. He took it on a family holiday in the west of England, but unexpectedly good weather left him with little time for reading, as he explained to Goldstine:

> So although I was very glad to get your report with von Neumann on coding, and have looked at it rather superficially, I haven't studied it seriously yet. My first impression was that you had made it all seem very difficult, and I wondered if it was really as difficult as all that?! [13].

Goldstine's reply was rather waspish:

> You suggest that possibly our report on coding seems very difficult. Of course it is very hard for me to be objective about it, but I thought, on the contrary, it was fairly simple. Van Wijngaarden, who is now here with us, spent three days studying the text and was then able to code problems

with a reasonable degree of proficiency. I hope that after you have had a
chance to look at the report in more detail you will agree with his opinion
[8].

Hartree's reservations persisted, and he exhibited a continuing preference for
ENIAC-style notations. His 1949 book [14] on computing machines, based on
lectures given the previous year, included a single flow diagram presented in
parallel with an ENIAC master programmer diagram for the same problem. The
flow diagram incorporated a number of modifications to the *Planning and Coding*
notation. In a 1952 textbook [15], he even described something that looked very
similar to an ENIAC diagram as a flow diagram.

This was typical of British uses of the notation, which seemed to treat it
more as a vehicle for exploration than a finished product. At a conference in
Cambridge in 1949, five papers presented flow diagrams of one form or another,
but about all they had in common was the use of a directed graph. In particular,
the mechanism of storage boxes, substitutions, and assertions that enabled the
consistency of a diagram to be checked was almost universally ignored. The sole
exception was a paper by Turing himself on "Checking a large routine" [21, 24].

6   Checking a Routine

As we have seen, Goldstine and von Neumann defined a number of conditions
that had to be checked to ensure that a diagram was consistent. They explained
the connection between the satisfaction of these conditions and the correctness
of the diagram as follows:

> It is difficult to avoid errors or omissions in any but the simplest problems.
> However, they should not be frequent, and will in most cases signalize
> themselves by some inner maladjustment of the diagram, which becomes
> obvious before the diagram is completed [11].

The worked examples in the *Planning and Coding* reports do not, of course,
include any maladjusted diagrams. To get a sense of what this might have meant
in practice and how the notation might have worked as a formal method, we need
to look at a different example.

Turing's 1949 paper [21, 24] included a flow diagram for computing factorials
and discussed how to reason about the correctness of the program. At first
sight, Turing's notation is rather different from Goldstine and von Neumann's.
Nevertheless, Turing's diagram contains operation and alternative boxes linked
by directed line segments, and we will assume that the resulting structure has
the same meaning as in the Goldstine/von Neumann notation. For example, in
language that could almost have been copied from *Planning and Coding*, Turing
writes that "[e]ach 'box' of the flow diagram represents a straight sequence of
instructions without changes of control".

Rather than attaching storage boxes at different points around the diagram,
Turing presented a single table whose columns were labelled with letters cross-
referencing locations on the diagram, a presentation option that had also been

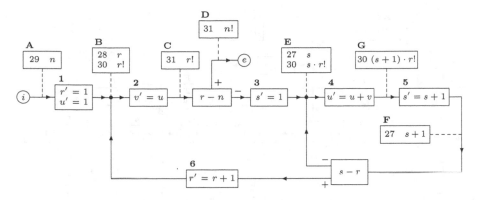

Fig. 10. Turing's flow diagram expressed using the notation of the *Planning and Coding* report. The lettered storage boxes correspond to the sections of Turing's storage table. Operation boxes have been numbered for ease of reference.

described in the *Planning and Coding* report. The table listed the five storage locations used by the program and described their contents using mathematical notation. Turing also associated a unique variable with each storage location:

$$
\begin{aligned}
\text{location 27:} \quad & s \;-\; \text{inductive variable for inner loop}\\
28: \quad & r \;-\; \text{inductive variable for outer loop}\\
29: \quad & n \;-\; \text{routine parameter}\\
30: \quad & u \;-\; \text{accumulates } (r+1)\cdot r! \text{ in inner loop}\\
31: \quad & v \;-\; \text{stores } r!
\end{aligned}
$$

(The variables u and v do not appear in the storage table). The sections of the storage table describe the contents of memory just before the boxes to which their labels are attached and so can be represented as storage boxes attached to the flow line immediately before the relevant box. Figure 10 shows a transcription of Turing's diagram into the Goldstine/von Neumann notation.

Turing's most significant notational deviation was in the operation boxes. Rather than specifying the location where a value is stored, he used primed variable names to indicate what he described as "the value at the end of the process represented by the box". Box 5, for example, contains the expression $s' = s + 1$, indicating that at the end of the box the value of s has increased by 1. Turing does not state when this value is written into the storage location corresponding to s. However, storage box F gives the content of storage location 27 as $s + 1$, implying that the memory update has taken place by the end of the box. The contents of box 5 will therefore be translated as "$s + 1$ to 27" in the Goldstine/von Neumann notation.

As well as storing the new value, Turing's explanation suggests that the value of the variable s has been incremented by the end of box 5. Showing the change

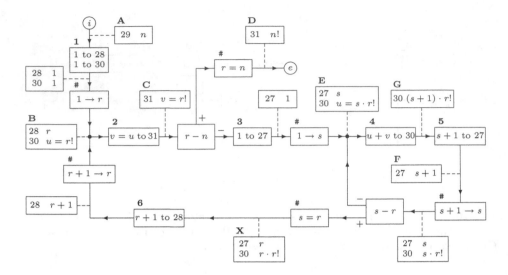

Fig. 11. Turing's diagram with operation boxes rewritten, variables added to storage boxes, and substitution and assertion boxes added. The diagram is "maladjusted", as the substitution $r + 1 \to r$ does not reconcile location 30 in storage boxes X and B.

of value of a variable, as opposed to a storage location, is the reason Goldstine and von Neumann introduced substitution boxes. Adding these to the diagram, we arrive at the diagram shown in Fig. 11 as a full translation of Turing's flow diagram into the Goldstine/von Neumann notation.

Unfortunately, this diagram is "maladjusted", to use von Neumann's term. At the end of the outer loop, the expression describing the contents of location 30 changes from $r \cdot r!$ to $r!$ in the passage between storage boxes X and B. This change should be reconciled by applying the substitution $r + 1 \to r$ to the expression in box B: however, this gives $(r + 1)!$, which is not equal to the value $r \cdot r!$ given in box X. Morris and Jones [17] describe this as a "discrepancy", commenting that "Turing chooses to regard [$s' = s + 1$] as having no effect on the values of his variables"; they correct Turing's diagram by changing the expression being tested at the end of the inner loop to $s - 1 - r$, commenting further that Turing appears to give "no clear rule about when the addition of a prime to a letter makes a difference".

This interpretation differs from the natural reading of Turing's explanation adopted above. The root of the problem is that Turing blurred the distinction between storage locations and mathematical variables by associating a variable with each location. As a result, his notation leaves the temporal relationship between updating a variable value and updating a storage location unspecified. We can make this explicit in the Goldstine/von Neumann notation, and Fig. 12 shows an alternative way of making Turing's diagram consistent. Interestingly, separating the operation box that updates location 27 from the substitution

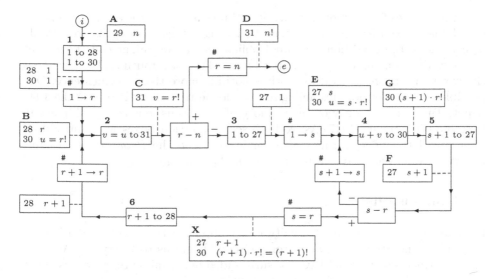

Fig. 12. A "well-adjusted" version of Turing's flow diagram

box that updates the variable s results in a more idiomatic use of the notation, similar in style to the examples in *Planning and Coding*.

Two assertion boxes have been added in Figs. 11 and 12 to make explicit all the conditions necessary to prove the diagram's consistency, but the identities they state were left implicit in Turing's diagram. Turing himself used the term "assertion" in the following, rather different, sense:

> In order to assist the checker, the programmer should make assertions about the various states that the machine can reach.

Unlike assertion boxes, Turing's assertions were not a notational feature. They were written in the columns in the storage table, and their function is to explicitly relate each storage box to its successor, giving additional information about the conditions under which transitions occur and the values of certain variables. For box B, for example, Turing's assertion reads simply "to C", and he paraphrased the argument that the checker would make as follows:

> From the flow diagram we see that after B the box $v' = u$ applies. From the upper part of the column for B we have $u = r!$. Hence $v' = r!$ i.e. the entry for v i.e. for line 31 in C should be $r!$. The other entries are the same as in B.

This is similar in intent to the condition that Goldstine and von Neumann gave for verifying the contents of storage boxes after operation boxes containing "to" (see Fig. 5). The most striking difference is that Turing argues "forwards" from box B to box C, while Goldstine and von Neumann's condition for substitution boxes works "backwards", as explained above.

Turing's use of "assertion", then, has nothing to do with the assertion boxes of the Goldstine/von Neumann notation. In Turing's usage, assertions are roughly equivalent to the conditions, or proof obligations as we might call them, that the flow diagram imposes on the person checking the routine. The fact that the word "assertion" is used for both is nothing more than a coincidence. One possible explanation for this ambiguity would be that when he wrote the 1949 paper, Turing relied solely on his memory of the discussions that took place in Princeton in January 1947. As we have seen, assertion boxes were introduced after this date, and if Turing had never in fact read the *Planning and Coding* report, he would not have been aware of the later usage.

7   Conclusions

Flow diagrams emerged from a culture of computing that made extensive use of graphical notations. From electronic circuit diagrams to Curry and Wyatt's more abstract flowchart, ENIAC was surrounded by visual representations of the machine and the computations set up on it.

As programs were set up on ENIAC in a very immediate and physical way, by plugging wires and setting switches, diagrams of program structure could also be read as pictures of the machine. Less obviously, the same is true of the diagrams introduced by Goldstine and von Neumann. EDVAC-type machines replaced ENIAC's physical connectivity with more transient connections made in a large multi-purpose memory, and the boxes in a block diagram provide a map of memory usage for a particular problem. By implication, the unmarked white surface of the paper represents the computer's memory, a striking image for the logical space defined by the ambitiously large and functionally undifferentiated storage units planned for the new machines.

Crucially, the new machines also made possible programs that modified their own code. This was a central feature of even the elementary polynomial example described above. Eckert and Mauchly [4] noted that diagrams had been used for "laying out the procedure" for programs on ENIAC but, after making explicit reference to the first *Planning and Coding* report, went on to comment:

> The important point, however, is that [...] the instructions may themselves be altered by other instructions. Therefore the particular program that is chosen may not remain the same during successive traverses of it. Because of this feature, it becomes increasingly difficult to follow the course of more complicated problems unless some systematic procedure is adopted. The flow chart just referred to is the basis for such a procedure.

Flow diagrams, in other words, were a direct response to a new generation of computers with a distinctive architecture demanding a new approach to program planning. The development of the notation was driven by the specific challenge of adequately describing the behaviour of a simple loop controlled by an inductive variable. Simple counted loops could be modelled perfectly well with existing notations, such as the ENIAC's master programmer diagrams, but even in the polynomial example, the inductive variable n does not just count loop iterations but is involved in updating the address field of a coded instruction in order to specify where the next function value will be stored.

In order to describe this situation precisely, Goldstine and von Neumann developed a formidable formal notation which described a computation on both physical and symbolic levels and provided a way to check the consistency of diagrams. It is striking, then, that users of the notation, themselves included, made little use of its full capabilities. It was either ignored, simplified, or heavily modified for use in particular circumstances. The most faithful user, Turing, applied it not in practical program development but in a conference paper which emphasized precisely its capabilities for checking correctness.

It is beyond the scope of this paper to consider in detail the relationship between the work described here and Floyd's 1967 paper [6]. Floyd, apparently unaware of the earlier work, described an "interpretation" of a flowchart as the association of a proposition with each of its edges. Syntactically, this could be achieved in the Goldstine/von Neumann notation by placing the proposition in an assertion box at the appropriate point in the diagram, though the pragmatics of the two notations are rather different. Floyd intended to give a "semantic definition" of the notation rather than a practical tool for program development, though his definitions would enable proofs of properties of flowcharts to be given. The relationship between such proofs and the consistency conditions put forward in the *Planning and Coding* report remains a topic for future research.

The reasons for the lack of uptake of the formal aspects of the original flow diagram notation remain underexplored. The earliest application of the notation, the evolution of the diagrams for the Monte Carlo program from von Neumann's original diagram to the final, less formal version, provides a good case study. This passage of work is characterized by the fact that a wide range of people with different skills, interests, and responsibilities became involved with the project. The second diagram was drawn by Adele Goldstine and the code produced and later maintained by Klara von Neumann. Neither had a background or training in logic, and the program used address modification only to control the return from a subroutine [12]. In these circumstances, the formal aspects of flow diagrams may have seemed an overhead that added little to solving the problem at hand or, more importantly perhaps, to the stated aim of enabling operators to produce code *from* the diagrams.

References

1. ASME Standard: Operation and flow process charts. American Society of Mechanical Engineers (1947)
2. Burks, A.W., Goldstine, H.H., von Neumann, J.: Preliminary discussion of the logical design of an electronic computing instrument. The Institute for Advanced Study, 28 June 1946
3. Curry, H.B., Wyatt, W.A.: A study of inverse interpolation of the Eniac. Ballistic Research Laboratories Report No. 615. Aberdeen Proving Ground, MD (1946)

4. Eckert, J.P., Mauchly, J.: First draft report on the UNIVAC. Electronic Control Company, Philadelphia, PA. Herman Goldstine papers, Hampshire College, box 3 (1947)
5. Ensmenger, N.: The multiple meanings of a flowchart. Inf. Cult. **51**(3), 321–351 (2016)
6. Floyd, R.W.: Assigning meanings to programs. In: Schwartz, J.T. (ed.) Mathematical Aspects of Computer Science. Proceedings of Symposia in Applied Mathematics, vol. XIX, pp. 19–32. American Mathematical Society (1967)
7. Gilbreth, F.B., Gilbreth, L.M.: Process charts. American Society of Mechanical Engineers (1921)
8. Goldstine, H.H.: Letter to Douglas Hartree. Herman Goldstine papers, American Philosophical Society, box 3, 16 September 1947
9. Goldstine, H.H.: The Computer from Pascal to von Neumann. Princeton University Press, Princeton (1972)
10. Goldstine, H.H., von Neumann, J.: unpublished draft of [11]. John von Neumann papers, Library of Congress, box 33, folder 7 (1946)
11. Goldstine, H.H., von Neumann, J.: Planning and coding problems for an electronic computing instrument, Part II, vol. 1. The Institute for Advanced Study (1947)
12. Haigh, T., Priestley, M., Rope, C.: ENIAC in Action: Making and Remaking the Modern Computer. MIT Press, Cambridge (2016)
13. Hartree, D.R.: Letter to Herman Goldstine. Herman Goldstine papers, American Philosophical Society, box 3, 7 September 1947
14. Hartree, D.R.: Calculating Instruments and Machines. The University of Illinois Press, Urbana (1949)
15. Hartree, D.R.: Numerical Analysis. Oxford University Press, Oxford (1952)
16. Jones, C.B.: The early search for tractable ways of reasoning about programs. IEEE Ann. Hist. Comput. **25**(2), 26–49 (2003)
17. Morris, F.L., Jones, C.B.: An early program proof by Alan turing. Ann. Hist. Comput. **6**(2), 139–143 (1984)
18. Morris, S.J., Gotel, O.C.Z.: Flow diagrams: rise and fall of the first software engineering notation. In: Barker-Plummer, D., Cox, R., Swoboda, N. (eds.) Diagrams 2006. LNCS (LNAI), vol. 4045, pp. 130–144. Springer, Heidelberg (2006). https://doi.org/10.1007/11783183_17
19. Priestley, M.: Routines of Substitution: John von Neumann's Work on Software Development, 1945-1948. Springer, Heidelberg (2018). https://doi.org/10.1007/978-3-319-91671-2
20. Turing, A.M.: Report on visit to U.S.A., 1st–20th January 1947. Mathematics Division [NPL], 3 February 1947
21. Turing, A.M.: Checking a large routine. In: Report of a Conference on High Speed Automatic Calculating Machines, 22–25 June 1949. pp. 70–72. University Mathematical Laboratory, Cambridge (1949). Reprinted in [24], pp. 3–164
22. Voller, W.R.: Modern Flour Millling, 3rd edn. D. Van Nostrand Company, New York (1897)
23. von Neumann, J.: Letter to Herman Goldstine. Herman Goldstine papers, American Philosophical Society, box 20, 2 March 1947
24. Williams, M.R., Campbell-Kelly, M. (eds.): The Early British Computer Conferences. Charles Babbage Institute Reprint Series for the History of Computing, vol. 14. The MIT Press, Cambridge (1989)

The School of Squiggol
A History of the Bird–Meertens Formalism

Jeremy Gibbons[(⊠)]

University of Oxford, Oxford, UK
Jeremy.Gibbons@cs.ox.ac.uk

Abstract. The Bird–Meertens Formalism, colloquially known as "Squiggol", is a calculus for program transformation by equational reasoning in a function style, developed by Richard Bird and Lambert Meertens and other members of IFIP Working Group 2.1 for about two decades from the mid 1970s. One particular characteristic of the development of the Formalism is fluctuating emphasis on novel 'squiggly' notation: sometimes favouring notational exploration in the quest for conciseness and precision, and sometimes reverting to simpler and more rigid notational conventions in the interests of accessibility. This paper explores that historical ebb and flow.

1   Introduction

In 1962, IFIP formed Working Group 2.1 to design a successor to the seminal algorithmic language Algol 60 [4]. WG2.1 eventually produced the specification for Algol 68 [63,64]—a sophisticated language, presented using an elaborate two-level description notation, which received a mixed reception. WG2.1 continues to this day; technically, it retains responsibility for the Algol languages, but practically it takes on a broader remit under the current name *Algorithmic Languages and Calculi*. Over the years, the Group has been through periods of focus and periods of diversity. But after the Algol 68 project, the period of sharpest focus covered the two decades from the mid 1970s to the early 1990s, when what later became known as the Bird–Meertens Formalism (BMF) drew the whole group together again. It is the story of those years that is the subject of this paper.

BMF arose from the marriage of the work of Richard Bird (then at the University of Reading) in recursive programming [14,15] and of Lambert Meertens (then at the Mathematisch Centrum in Amsterdam) in programming language design, notably ABC [34,48].[1] The motivation for the BMF is *transformational programming*: developing an efficient program by starting with an obviously correct but possibly hopelessly inefficient—maybe even unexecutable—initial specification, then applying a series of meaning-preserving transformations to yield an extensionally equivalent but acceptably efficient final program. In other words,

---

[1] Guido van Rossum, who worked on the ABC project in Amsterdam, was mentored by Meertens and went on to design Python [55] based on some of the ideas in ABC.

© Springer Nature Switzerland AG 2020
E. Sekerinski et al. (Eds.): FM 2019 Workshops, LNCS 12233, pp. 35–53, 2020.
https://doi.org/10.1007/978-3-030-54997-8_2

the approach follows Christopher Strachey's First Law of Programming: "Decide what you want to say before you worry about how you are going to say it" [5].

The essence of the formalism is a concise functional notation. The functional approach ensures referential transparency, and admits the straightforward manipulation technique of substitution of equals by equals, as in high school algebra. Concision is necessary in order to make such manipulations feasible with just pen and paper. In particular, like APL [36], BMF embraced funny symbols such as a slash for reduction ("$+/$" sums a sequence of numbers), arrows for directed folds and scans ("$\rightarrow$" and "$\not\rightarrow$", now called "foldl" and "scanl" in Haskell), and banana brackets ("$([\ldots])$") for homomorphisms; this tendency led to the notation being nicknamed *Squiggol*. Little emphasis was placed on executability: the notation was 'wide-spectrum' [7], accommodating convenient specification notations such as inverses and intersection as well as a sublanguage with an obvious correspondence to executable code.

The BMF research paradigm consisted of establishing a body of theorems about recurring problem structures and corresponding solution techniques. Typical examples are *fusion* properties (combining two traversals over a data structure into one), *scan lemmas* (replacing the independent reductions of overlapping parts of a data structure with a single accumulation across the whole), and *Horner's Rule* (exploiting distributivity, as for products over sums in polynomial evaluation). These three formed the core of a beautiful derivation of a linear-time solution to the Maximum Segment Sum problem [23], a central example in the BMF canon. The effort culminated in Bird and de Moor's book *The Algebra of Programming* [10], with a collection of theorems expressed in a relational notation providing greedy and dynamic-programming solutions to optimization problems.

WG2.1's passion for the approach started to fade after Bird and de Moor's book appeared, and the group's focus diversified again. Partly this was due to falling out of love with the Squiggolly notation, which may be convenient for aficionados but excludes the unfamiliar reader; later work favours more conventional syntax. It was also partly due to dissatisfaction with the relational approach, which seems necessary for many optimization problems but is too complicated for most readers (and even for writers!); in fact, Bird is returning in a forthcoming book [24] to tackling many of the same 'Algebra of Programming' optimization problems but using a nearly completely functional approach. The purpose of this paper is to pick out some of the lessons from this ebb and flow of enthusiasm.[2]

---

[2] From its start, my own research career has been intimately entwined with WG2.1 and the BMF, although I came somewhat late to the party. Bird supervised my DPhil dissertation (1987–1991) [35], and Meertens was my external examiner. I have worked on and off with Bird ever since, and most of my research has been inspired by the BMF; I am Bird's co-author on his forthcoming book [24]. I served as secretary of WG2.1 for thirteen years (1996–2009), during the Chairmanships of Doug Smith and Lambert Meertens, and then succeeded Meertens as Chair myself for the following six years (2009–2015).

2   Abstracto

The history of the development of Algol 68 has been well reported [37,38,53], and we will not dwell on it here. After 1968, WG2.1 spent a few years making small improvements to the language and clarifying its description, leading to the publication of the Revised Report [64] in 1974.[3] The Group then entered a brief 'what next?' phase, setting up a *Future Work* subcommittee chaired by Robert Dewar. This subcommittee in turn organized two conferences on *New Directions in Algorithmic Languages* in 1975 and 1976, with proceedings [56,57] edited by Stephen Schuman. These conferences were public, intended to collect input from the broader community about research topics in algorithmic languages.

After that short period of scanning the horizon, the Group decided to focus again on specific topics. Robert Dewar, as Chair of the Future Work Subcommittee, wrote a letter to members in July 1977, in advance of Meeting #23 of the Group in Oxford in December of that year, explaining:

> *We have decided to break with our two year old 'tradition' of holding conferences with invited outside participants. These conference have been helpful in exploring ideas, but now it is time to get back to the work of our working group and concentrate on the resources of our membership.* [30]

The decision was for the Group to focus for the time being on two topics: programming languages for beginners, and "Abstracto". The former direction led to Meertens's development of ABC [34,42,43,54] and hence eventually to Python [55]; but it is the latter that is of interest to us here.

The name *Abstracto* arose through a misunderstanding:

> *The first author [Geurts], teaching a course in programming, remarked that he would first present an algorithm "in abstracto" (Dutch [sic] for "in the abstract") before developing it in Algol 60. At the end of the class, a student expressed his desire to learn more about this Abstracto programming language.* [33]

Abstracto itself is defined in Dewar's letter as follows:

> *We have taken the name to describe a programming language some of whose features we know:*
> 1. *It is very high level, whatever that means.*
> 2. *It is suitable for expressing initial thoughts on construction of a program.*

---

[3] It is fair to say that the Reports did not meet with universal acclaim. One reason for the mixed reception was the use of van Wijngaarden's two-level grammar notation for describing the language, whereby a possibly infinite language grammar is generated by a finite meta-grammar. The Algol 68 experience has engendered a keen interest in notational issues within the Group ever since.

As to (S2), this fits (f) with the assertion $z \cdot x^y = x^Y$ for p and $y \neq 0$ for b. For the mapping O we can. simply take the identity, since the "goal" is to get y to 0. We thus refine (S2) to

$$*(y \neq 0 \rightarrow z,x,y := z',x',y' \mid z',x',y':$$
$$z \cdot x^y = X^Y \ \& \ y \neq 0 \supset z' \cdot x'^{y'} = X^Y \ \& \ y' < y).$$

Using (g), this may again be refined to

$$*(y \neq 0 \rightarrow z,x,y := z',x',y' \mid z',x',y',r:$$
$$z' = z \cdot x^r \ \& \ x' = x \cdot x \ \& \ y = 2y' + r \ \&$$
$$(r=0 \ \vee \ r=1)).$$

If operations / and % are available, satisfying y = 2(y/2)+(y%2) and (y%2=0 ∨ y%2=1), the use of the unit list u = ZZ,x·x,y/2,y%2 in (d) of Lemma 2, where ZZ is shorthand for (y%2=0→z 〚 y%2=1→z·x), allows to simplify this to

$$*(y \neq 0 \rightarrow z,x,y := ZZ,x \cdot x,y/2).$$

Fig. 1. Abstracto 84 [41]

3. *It need not be (and probably is not) executable. This arises either from efficiency considerations, or even non-effective dictions, say those involving infinite sets.*
   Abstracto is not a specification language as such since it is still concerned with how to do things and not just what is to be done, but it allows the expression of the 'how' in the simplest and most abstract possible way. [30]

So Abstracto was envisioned as an *algorithmic language*: for describing the algorithmic steps in a computation, not just the input–output relation or similar behavioural specification. But it was still envisaged as an exploratory medium, a pen-and-paper notation, a 'tool of thought', rather than primarily an implementation language.

A representative example of Abstracto is shown in Fig. 1. This is part of the development of a 'fast exponentiation' algorithm: given natural numbers X and Y, compute $z = X^Y$ using only $O(\log_2 Y)$ iterations. The first program shows a 'while' loop, with invariant $z \times x^y = X^Y$, variant y, and guard $y \neq 0$. The second program factors out $r = y \bmod 2$, refining the nondeterminism in the first program to a deterministic loop. Thus, Meertens' vision for Abstracto is a kind of refinement calculus for imperative programs, as later developed in much greater depth by Ralph Back [1,2] and Carroll Morgan [49,50].[4]

---

[4] Indeed, the loop body in the first exponentiation program is a 'specification statement' in Morgan's sense [49], albeit one without a frame.

Although it was intended as a focus for the whole Group, the work on a notation named Abstracto was mainly undertaken by Meertens and his group at the Mathematisch Centrum (later CWI) in Amsterdam, and the few published papers [33,41] are written by them. (In 1987, Meertens very helpfully collected these papers—and other papers of his on BMF—into a reader [46] for WG2.1, interspersed with a retrospective commentary on the background to the original publications.)

However, other members of the Group were conducting parallel projects with similar goals. Fritz Bauer's group at the Technical University in Munich, including Helmuth Partsch, Bernhard Möller, and Peter Pepper, were working on the Computer-Aided, Intuition-Guided Programming (CIP) project [6–8], developing a wide-spectrum language to encompass both abstract specifications and efficient implementations of programs. Jack Schwartz, Robert Dewar, and Bob Paige at New York University designed SETL [51,58,59] as a language that accommodated the gradual transformation of specifications using high-level set-oriented dictions such as comprehensions into lower-level programs by instantiating abstract datatypes with concrete implementations and by applying 'strength reduction' [52] to loops. These are just two of the larger projects; there were many smaller ones as well.

3   Disillusionment and Enlightenment

For some of the subsequent meetings of the Group, members were set specific problems to work on in advance [31], so that approaches and solutions could be presented at the meeting—applications such as a text editor and a patient monitoring system, and more technical problems such as string matching and longest upsequence. Meertens observed in the introduction to the Algorithmics paper [45] included in the Abstracto Reader [46]:

> Using the framework sketched in [41], I did most of the examples from the problem sets prepared for the Brussels meeting of WG2.1 in December 1979 [Meeting #26] and the meeting in Wheeling WV in August 1980 [Meeting #27]. On the whole, I was reasonably successful, but I nevertheless abandoned the approach. [46]

To illustrate Meertens' disillusionment, consider the two programs shown in Fig. 2. The problem is to find the (assumed unique) oldest inhabitant of the Netherlands, where the data is given by a collection dm of Dutch municipalities, and an array $mr[-]$ of municipal registers of individuals, one register per municipality. The program on the left combines all the municipal registers into one national register; the program on the right finds the oldest inhabitant of each municipality, and then findest the oldest among these "local Methuselahs". Provided that no municipality is empty of inhabitants, these programs have equivalent behaviour. However, one cannot reasonably expect precisely the transformation from one to the other to be present in any catalogue of transformations; the development should proceed by a series of simpler steps that

```
                          input dm, mr;
                          slm := 0;
                          for m ∈ dm do
    input dm, mr;            alm := -∞;
    gdb := 0;                for i ∈ mr[m] do
    for m ∈ dm do             if i·age > alm then
      gdb := gdb ∪ mr[m]         lm, alm := i, i·age
    endfor;                    endif
    aoi := -∞;               endfor;
    for i ∈ gdb do    ⇒     slm := slm ∪ {lm}
      if i·age > aoi then   endfor;
        oi, aoi := i, i·age  aoi := -∞;
      endif                 for i ∈ slm do
    endfor;                   if i·age > aoi then
    output oi.                  oi, aoi := i, i·age
                              endif
                            endfor;
                            output oi.
```

Fig. 2. The oldest inhabitant, in Abstracto [45]

themselves are present in a smaller and more manageable catalogue of more general-purpose transformations. But what would those atomic general-purpose transformations be?

Meertens continued:

> *The framework is, in fact, largely irrelevant: finding the theorems to be applied is the key to the development [...] If the Abstracto dream is to come true [...] the key 'transformations' are the mathematical theorems and not the boring blind-pattern-match manipulations that I looked upon until now as being 'the' transformations.* [46]

The breakthrough was to abandon the imperative Algol-like language and the corresponding refinement-oriented approach of Abstracto, and to switch to a more algebraic, functional presentation. Meertens continued:

> *Then came the Nijmegen meeting [Meeting #28] in May 1981, at which Richard Bird entered the stage[5] and presented a paper entitled "Some Notational Suggestions for Transformational Programming".[6] It used an applicative (functional) style [...] There were notations for high-level concepts, and just the kind of manipulations, at the right level, that you would*

---

[5] In fact, Bird and Meertens had both been present at Meeting #27 in Wheeling in August 1980, although the meeting of minds evidently had to wait a bit longer.

[6] Meertens' preface in the Abstracto Reader, Meertens' contemporary papers, and the WG2.1 minutes all record Bird's paper under the title "Some Notational Suggestions..." [17]; but the technical report [16] is entitled "Notational Suggestions...".

(i)   <u>Dot rules</u>

Δ1.   f•g•S => (f g)•S

Δ2.   f••g•S => (f•g)•S

Δ3.   f•g••S => (f g•)•S

(iv)   <u>Pulling functions to the left</u>

Δ10.   P:f•S => f•(P f):S

Δ11.   any f•S => f any S

Δ12.   (max\f) g•S => g•(max\f g) S

Δ13.   sub f•S => f••sub S

Fig. 3. Notational Suggestions for Functional Programming [16]

want to see [...] Investigating this led to a whole lot of other discoveries (the applicability to 'generic' structures [...]), and I was very excited about this. [46]

Some of Bird's suggested notations are shown in Fig. 3: "$f \cdot S$" for mapping function f over collection S, "$P : S$" for filtering collection S to retain only elements satisfying predicate P, "<u>any</u> S" for choosing an arbitrary element of (nonempty) collection S; "$(\underline{\text{max}}\backslash f)$ S" for the element of collection S that maximizes function f; "<u>sub</u> S" for the powerset of collection S; juxtaposition for function composition; and so on. Thus rule $\Delta 1$ is what became known as "map fusion"[7] and $\Delta 10$ as "filter promotion"[8].

The equivalent transformation for the problem of the oldest inhabitant using Bird's suggestions [45] is:

$$\uparrow_{age}/ +/mr \cdot dm = \uparrow_{age}/(\uparrow_{age}/mr) \cdot dm$$

The left-hand side takes the oldest in the union of the registers of each of the municipalities, and the right-hand side takes the oldest among the oldest inhabitants of each of the municipalities. (Here, "$\oplus/$" reduces a collection using binary operator $\oplus$, absent from Bird's suggestions; "$+$" is binary union; "$\uparrow_f$" chooses

---

[7] Applying g to every element of S and then f to every element of the result is the same as applying g then f to every element of S in a single pass.

[8] Applying f to every element and then filtering to keep the results that satisfy P is the same as filtering first, using the predicate "P after f", then applying f to every element that will subsequently satisfy P.

here are three rules that correspond to the above in the case of generalized union $\cup \{s1, s2, \ldots\} = s1 \cup s2 \cup \ldots$:

$$p : \cup X = \cup ((p:) * X)$$
$$f * \cup X = \cup ((f*) * X)$$
$$\max (\cup X) = \max(\max * X).$$

The second rule, for example, says that the application of f to each member of the union of a collection of sets gives the same result as taking the union of the collection of sets in which f is applied to each member. The rule is easy enough to justify:

$$\cup ((f*) * X) = \cup \{f * x \mid x \in X\}$$
$$= \cup \{\{fa \mid a \in x\} \mid x \in X\}$$
$$= \{fa \mid a \in \cup X\}$$
$$= f * \cup X.$$

Fig. 4. The Promotion and Accumulation Strategies [18]

which of two arguments has the greater f-value; "$g*$" maps function g over a collection; and function composition is indicated by juxtaposition.)

Clearly the BMF presentation is an order of magnitude shorter than the Abstracto one. It is also easier to see what form the small general-purpose transformation steps should take—just the kinds of equation shown in Fig. 3.

4 Evolution

The BMF notations evolved through use, and through interactions at subsequent WG2.1 meetings. The Algorithmics paper [45] was presented at the Symposium on Mathematics and Computer Science in November 1983, when the Mathematisch Centrum in Amsterdam changed its name to the Centrum voor Wiskunde en Informatica (CWI).[9]

Bird and Meertens produced another working paper [12] for IFIP WG2.1, trying to converge on notational conventions such as operator precedence and semantic considerations such as indeterminacy for an "as yet unborn Science of Algorithmics". This was done together with Dave Wile, whose PhD thesis [65] had been on "a closely related approach to language design" [46]; although Wile was also a member of WG2.1, he could only contribute by post whereas Bird and

---

[9] Publication of the proceedings of this conference seems to have taken frustratingly long: in a 1984 working paper [44] using the same notation, Meertens cites the Algorithmics paper [45] as appearing in the year "[]/ $(1984\leq)\triangleleft \cup$", that is, the arbitrary choice of any number at least 1984. The same joke appears in a 1985 working paper [12] but with a 1985 lower bound.

There are a number of algebraic laws relating the operators introduced so far. The seven which follow are all easily proved from the definitions above:

(L1) $f * g * S = (f \circ g) * S,$

(L2) $P : g * S = g * (P \circ g) : S,$

(L3) $f \downarrow g * S = g * (f \circ g) \downarrow S,$

(L4) $f * A \cup B = (f * A) \cup (f * B),$

(L5) $P : A \cup B = (P : A) \cup (P : B),$

(L6) $f \downarrow A \cup B = f \downarrow (f \downarrow A) \cup (f \downarrow B),$

(L7) $f \downarrow f \downarrow A = f \downarrow A.$

Fig. 5. Transformational Programming and the Paragraph Problem [20]

Meertens met twice in person, so "his influence [...] has probably been much less than it otherwise would have been" [46].[10]

Bird used his version of the notation in journal papers published in 1984 [18] and 1986 [20], extracts from which are shown in Fig. 4 and Fig. 5 respectively. Note that Bird has switched to Meertens' convention of using an asterisk rather than a centred dot for 'map',[11] but still has no general 'reduce' operator. The latter only came with a series of tutorial papers [19,21,22], produced in quick succession and with very similar notation, two being lecture notes from Marktoberdorf and one from the University of Texas at Austin Year of Programming; an example, the calculation for the Maximum Segment Sum problem, is shown in Fig. 6. Now the centred dot is used for function composition, and juxtaposition (not shown) is used only for function application; moreover, filter (also not shown) is written with a triangle "◁" rather than a colon.

Around the time of Bird's three sets of lecture notes, presumably during one of Bird's presentations at WG2.1, Robert Dewar passed a note to Meertens which has one word on it, "Squigol", making a pun with language names such as Algol, Cobol, and Snobol [47]. The name first appears in the minutes of Meeting #35 in Sausalito in December 1985. However, it has come to be written "Squiggol", perhaps to emphasise that the pronunciation should be 'skwɪgɒl ("qui") rather than 'skwaɪgɒl ("quae").

---

[10] Nevertheless, Wile's 'sectioning' notation (giving a binary operator one of its two arguments, as in the positivity predicate "(>0)" and the reciprocal function "(1/)") was discussed, and it persists today in Haskell.

[11] In fact, Meertens says that he deliberately used a very small asterisk for 'map', looking from a distance or on a poor photocopy like a ragged dot, so as not to have to choose between the two notations.

$$
\begin{aligned}
mss &= \text{definition} \\
&\quad \uparrow/ \cdot +/* \cdot segs \\
&= \text{definition of } segs \\
&\quad \uparrow/ \cdot +/* \cdot +\!\!+/ \cdot tails * \cdot inits \\
&= \text{map and reduce promotion} \\
&\quad \uparrow/ \cdot (\uparrow/ \cdot +/* \cdot tails) * \cdot inits \\
&= \text{Horner's rule with } a \circledast b = (a + b) \uparrow 0 \\
&\quad \uparrow/ \cdot \circledast \not\!/_0 * \cdot inits \\
&= \text{accumulation lemma} \\
&\quad \uparrow/ \cdot \circledast \not\!\!/_0
\end{aligned}
$$

Fig. 6. Constructive Functional Programming, showing Maximum Segment Sum [22]

5   Generic Structures

An important practical concern for a calculus of program transformations is that the body of transformations is not only large enough and sufficiently general to cover lots of applications, but also small enough and sufficiently structured to be easy to navigate. In his preface to the Algorithmics paper [45], Meertens writes:

> My main worry was the scope of applicability. Would I find that I needed more and more primitive functions and corresponding rules as I did more examples? So I started doing some problems this way. First I found that I indeed had to invent new functions and laws all the time, which was disappointing. I put it down for some time, but took it up again while I was visiting NYU in '82/'83, since it still looked like the most promising line of research. Then I suddenly realized that there was a pattern in the new functions and laws. [46]

The pattern Meertens noticed is that several of the core datatypes (namely lists, bags, and sets) form a hierarchy of algebraic structures, and many of the core operations (such as maps, filters, and reductions) are homomorphisms from these algebras. Specifically, each of these three datatypes is generated from an empty structure, singleton structures, and a binary combination operation— for example, the empty list, singleton lists, and list concatenation—and differ only in terms of the algebraic laws (associativity, commutativity, idempotence) imposed on the binary operation. Meertens called these 'generic structures' in the Algorithmics paper, as shown in Fig. 7.

Meertens used the same names for all three datatypes ("0" for the empty structure, "ˆx" for a singleton structure containing element x, "+" for the binary operation), disambiguating by context. In contrast, Bird introduced different names for the different datatypes, as shown in Fig. 8. One might also impose no laws on the binary operation, yielding a kind of binary tree as a fourth member of the hierarchy, as in the following table:

Let us start with algebraic structures that are about as simple as possible. Using the notation of MCCARTHY [17], we have

$$S_D = D \oplus S_D \times S_D.$$

This defines a domain of "D-structures", each of which is either an element of the (given) domain D (e.g., numbers, or sequences of characters), or is composed of two other D-structures.

The diligent reader will have noticed an important difference between the structures defined now, and the S-expressions as used for LISP. The value **nil** is missing. We can introduce it by writing (using "0" instead of "**nil**"):

$$S_D = D \oplus \{0\} \oplus S_D \times S_D.$$

It becomes more interesting if we impose an algebraic law: $s + 0 = 0 + s = s$. This gives about the poorest-but-one possible algebra. Now we have a more dramatic deviation from the S-expressions, for it is certainly not the case that, e.g., $\mathrm{cons}(s, \textbf{nil}) = s$.

Fig. 7. Generic structures, from the Algorithmics paper [45] (reference [17] in the figure is to McCarthy's 1963 paper "A Basis for a Mathematical Theory of Computation")

type	empty	singleton	binary	laws
tree	$\langle\rangle$	$\langle\cdot\rangle$	$\pm$	identity
list	$[\,]$	$[\cdot]$	$+\!\!+$	... and associativity
bag	$\{\!\{\,\}\!\}$	$\{\!\{\cdot\}\!\}$	$\uplus$	... and commutativity
set	$\{\,\}$	$\{\cdot\}$	$\cup$	... and idempotency

(although there is no consensus on the naming conventions for trees).

Crucially, each datatype is the *free* algebra on the common signature with a given set of equations, generated by a domain of individual elements; that is, there exists a unique homomorphism from the datatype to any other algebra of the same kind. Therefore to define a homomorphic function over one of the datatypes in the hierarchy, it suffices to identify the target algebra. This leads to the canonical definition scheme (see Fig. 8)[12], as used for example for defining

---

[12] Essentially the same canonical scheme is commonly used today in modern functional programming languages like Haskell:

$$\begin{aligned} map\ f\ [\,] &= [\,] \\ map\ f\ (x : xs) &= f\ x : map\ f\ xs \end{aligned}$$

but for the signature of asymmetric 'cons' lists, rather than symmetric 'cat' lists. This again depends on lists being a free algebra, so the equations have a unique solution, namely the function being defined.

In order to specify functions over lists we need one more assumption, namely that $([\alpha], +\!\!+, [\,])$ is the free monoid generated by α under the assignment $[\cdot] : \alpha \to [\alpha]$. This algebraic statement is equivalent to the assertion that for each function $f : \alpha \to \beta$ and associative operator $\oplus : \beta \times \beta \to \beta$, the three equations

$$
\begin{aligned}
h[\,] &= id_\oplus \\
h[a] &= f\,a \\
h(x +\!\!+ y) &= h\,x \oplus h\,y
\end{aligned}
$$

specify a unique function $h : [\alpha] \to \beta$. In the case that $id_\oplus$ is not defined, the last two equations by themselves determine a unique function $h : [\alpha]^+ \to \beta$.

A similar algebraic statement about freeness holds for bags and sets as well as lists. We assume that $(\langle\alpha\rangle, \uplus, \langle\,\rangle)$ is the free commutative monoid generated by α under the assignment $\langle\cdot\rangle : \alpha \to \langle\alpha\rangle$. Similarly, $(\{\alpha\}, \cup, \{\,\})$ is the free commutative and idempotent monoid generated by α under the assignment $\{\cdot\} : \alpha \to \{\alpha\}$. In the case of bags this means that for each $f : \alpha \to \beta$ and associative and commutative operator $\oplus : \beta \times \beta \to \beta$, the equations

$$
\begin{aligned}
h\langle\,\rangle &= id_\oplus \\
h\langle a\rangle &= f\,a \\
h(x \uplus y) &= h\,x \oplus h\,y
\end{aligned}
$$

define a unique function $h : \langle\alpha\rangle \to \beta$. Similar remarks apply to sets, except that we also require $\oplus$ to be idempotent.

Fig. 8. Generic structures, from "Constructive Functional Programming" [22]

maps:

$$
\begin{aligned}
f * [\,] &= [\,] \\
f * [a] &= [f\ a] \\
f * (x +\!\!+ y) &= f * x +\!\!+ f * y
\end{aligned}
$$

filters:

$$
\begin{aligned}
p \triangleleft [\,] &= [\,] \\
p \triangleleft [a] &= [a], \quad \text{if } p\ a \\
&= [\,], \quad \text{otherwise} \\
p \triangleleft (x +\!\!+ y) &= p \triangleleft x +\!\!+ p \triangleleft y
\end{aligned}
$$

and reductions:

$$
\begin{aligned}
\oplus / [\,] &= 1_\oplus \\
\oplus / [a] &= a \\
\oplus / (x +\!\!+ y) &= \oplus / x \oplus \oplus / y
\end{aligned}
$$

This hierarchy of datatypes has become known as the 'Boom Hierarchy'—a neat pun. The hierarchy was introduced by and named after Hendrik Boom [26]; but Hendrik Boom is Dutch, and 'boom' is also Dutch for 'tree'. Stephen Spackman was a local observer at Meeting #37 hosted by Boom in Montreal in May 1987, and gave a presentation [61] involving the Boom Hierarchy. Spackman was studying for a Master's degree at Concordia University at the time, supervised by Boom and by Peter Grogono. Spackman recalls:

My recollection of how the name came about is that it was Peter Grogono's coinage, that Hendrik instantly said, "what, because it's about trees?", that I laughed, and the name stuck from that moment. My contribution was the appreciation of the joke, not the naming! [60]

Backhouse [3] presents a detailed study of the Boom Hierarchy, and a comparison to the quantifier notation introduced by Edsger Dijkstra and colleagues at Eindhoven. Like Meertens and unlike Bird, Backhouse uses a common naming scheme for all members of the Hierarchy, albeit a different one from Meertens': "1_{+}", "τ", and "$+$".

6   Retrenchment

The concern about whether or not to use a single notation for all the members of the Boom Hierarchy gets to a key issue: a novel, rationalized notation can help to reduce the number of definitions and laws and organize the theory, but by disregarding mathematical convention it can make the presentation less accessible to outsiders. In his preface to the 1984 working paper [44], Meertens recalls:

You can perhaps imagine my disappointment when I heard from Richard that he had dropped this whole approach because he found it was generally ununderstandable to audiences. Subsequent presentations of the Algorithmics paper at WG2.1 meetings strongly suggested the same to me. [46]

But the convenience of a rational notation is seductive. In the preface to the 1985 working paper [12] (which was written jointly with Bird and Wile), Meertens continues the story:

Somehow or other Richard picked up interest in my 'squiggles' again (really his, if he had not disowned them). It cannot have been the general acclaim they met with at my presentations that made him do so. Maybe it was the ease with which I kept pulling functions and operators to the left or pushing them to the right (while writing the formulas upside-down) over a beer, even after many beers, that convinced him of the continued value of this approach. [46]

Similar concerns apply more widely to the choice of notation. The 1985 working paper itself reports a difference of opinion with Wile:

Whereas RB and LM feel that the predefined infix operators should preferably be single symbols, DW prefers longer operator names. Moreover, LM does not like predefined names that are English words. [12]

In a journal paper published in 1989 [23], Bird revisited the Maximum Segment Sum problem he had tackled in earlier Marktoberdorf lectures [22]. But he abandoned the squiggles and reverted to mostly alphabetic identifiers, perhaps under pressure from the journal editor; compare the development in Fig. 9 with the earlier one shown in Fig. 6. Bird wrote in the paper:

$$
\begin{aligned}
\mathsf{mss} &= \text{definition} \\
&\quad \mathsf{max \cdot map\, sum \cdot segs} \\
&= \text{definition of segs} \\
&\quad \mathsf{max \cdot map\, sum \cdot concat \cdot map\, tails \cdot inits} \\
&= \text{map promotion (7)} \\
&\quad \mathsf{max \cdot concat \cdot map(map\, sum) \cdot map\, tails \cdot inits} \\
&= \text{definition of max and fold promotion (8)} \\
&\quad \mathsf{max \cdot map\, max \cdot map\,(map\, sum) \cdot map\, tails \cdot inits} \\
&= \text{map distributivity (3)} \\
&\quad \mathsf{max \cdot map\,(max \cdot map\, sum \cdot tails) \cdot inits} \\
&= \text{Horner's rule, with } x \otimes y = (x+y)\!\uparrow\!0 \\
&\quad \mathsf{max \cdot map\,(foldl\,(\otimes)\,0) \cdot inits} \\
&= \text{scan lemma (12)} \\
&\quad \mathsf{max \cdot scanl\,(\otimes)\,0} \\
&= \text{fold-scan fusion (13)} \\
&\quad \mathsf{fst \cdot foldl\,(\odot)\,(0,0)}
\end{aligned}
$$

where $\odot$ is defined by

$$(u,v) \odot x = (u\!\uparrow\!w, w) \quad \text{where} \quad w = (v+x)\!\uparrow\!0$$

Fig. 9. Algebraic Identities for Program Calculation, and Maximum Segment Sum [23]

In order to make the material as accessible as possible, we shall use the notation for functional programming described by Bird and Wadler. This is very similar to that used in Miranda. (Our preferred notation [19] is rather different. For a start, it is more concise and mathematical [...]) [23]

7   The Book on Algorithmics

A recurring theme in the Abstracto papers is the idea of an imagined textbook on algorithmics:

Suppose a textbook has to be written for an advanced course in algorithmics. Which vehicle should be chosen to express the algorithms? Clearly, one has the freedom to construct a new language, not only without the restraint of efficiency considerations, but without any considerations of implementability whatsoever. [33]

The textbook theme is frequently mentioned in the minutes of discussions at WG2.1 meetings around this time, and becomes a central desideratum for Squiggol. It is alluded to in the title "Two Exercises Found in a Book on Algorithmics" of a short paper by Bird and Meertens [25], another paper with a long gestation period (discussed at Meeting #34 in Utrecht in April 1985, presented at the TC2 Working Conference on Program Specification and Transformation in Bad Tölz in April 1986, and eventually published in 1987).

About a decade later, Bird published the book "The Algebra of Programming" [10] together with Oege de Moor. This book develops general theorems

Theorem 7.2 If S is monotonic on a preorder R°, then

$$(\![min\ R \cdot \Lambda S]\!) \subseteq min\ R \cdot \Lambda(\![S]\!).$$

Proof. We reason:

$$(\![min\ R \cdot \Lambda S]\!) \subseteq min\ R \cdot \Lambda(\![S]\!)$$

$\equiv$ {universal property of min}

$$(\![min\ R \cdot \Lambda S]\!) \subseteq (\![S]\!) \quad \text{and} \quad (\![min\ R \cdot \Lambda S]\!) \cdot (\![S]\!)^\circ \subseteq R$$

$\equiv$ {since $min\ R \cdot \Lambda S \subseteq S$}

$$(\![min\ R \cdot \Lambda S]\!) \cdot (\![S]\!)^\circ \subseteq R$$

$\Leftarrow$ {hylomorphism theorem (see below)}

$$min\ R \cdot \Lambda S \cdot FR \cdot S^\circ \subseteq R$$

$\Leftarrow$ {monotonicity: $FR \cdot S^\circ \subseteq S^\circ \cdot R$}

$$min\ R \cdot \Lambda S \cdot S^\circ \cdot R \subseteq R$$

$\Leftarrow$ {since $min\ R \cdot \Lambda S \subseteq R/S^\circ$; division}

$$R \cdot R \subseteq R$$

$\equiv$ {transitivity of R}

true.

Fig. 10. The Algebra of Programming [10]

and specific constructions for solutions to optimization problems: greedy algorithms, dynamic programming, and so on. Bird and de Moor discovered that
this class of problem really calls for a calculus of *relations* rather than one of
functions, because many problems are most naturally expressed in terms of converses, intersections, orderings, and other notions that are awkward to handle
using pure functions alone. Moreover, in the quest for crisp statements of general
results, the book followed Grant Malcolm's lead [39,40] in bringing in ideas from
category theory such as functors, natural transformations, and initial algebras.
Thus, it has more squiggles, and different ones, such as superscript circles for
converses, inclusions, relational divisions (a kind of weakest prespecification), as
shown in Fig. 10.

The Algebra of Programming book is many things: a work of art, and a tour
de force, and perhaps even a coup de grâce for Squiggol. But one thing it is
not: an easy read. The relational algebra is very elegant, and unquestionably the
idealist's tool for this class of problems; but it is inherently complicated, because
there are simply a lot of laws to remember.

Bird envisioned this work as fulfilling the promise of the legendary textbook
on algorithmics [9], although the book does not actually present itself that way.
In fact, it follows closely the approach taken by de Moor in his doctoral thesis
[29], which itself drew on Freyd and Scedrov's work on allegories as a categorical
axiomatization of relations [32], and Bird now says that "it turned out very
different to the book I had envisaged" [9].

8   Conclusions

The story of Squiggol is one of an ebb and flow of enthusiasm for the squiggly notation. The notation is intended as a *tool of thought* more than a programming language; so there is the freedom to experiment, to invent new operators, to capture newly-observed recurring patterns, unfettered by the need to keep all the paraphernalia of an automated tool chain up to date. But that freedom is a mixed blessing, and it is all too easy to disappear down a rabbit-hole of private scribbling; the notation should also be a *tool of communication*—with other people, and even with one's future self—and undisciplined invention blocks that communication channel.

The supplementary website [11] for the Algebra of Programming book describes it as an "introductory textbook", which is rather optimistic: few people have read the book all the way through, and fewer still have assimilated and can remember all the laws it presents. With a few honourable exceptions, almost everybody who was involved has abandoned the relational squiggles. De Moor soon left this field and moved into work on programming tools, eventually leaving academia to found the company Semmle. Bird also quickly gave up on the squiggly notation, succumbing to his 1989 critics [23] and doing almost everything since the book in a purely functional (Haskell) notation.

Bird and the present author are putting the finishing touches to a new book "Algorithm Design with Haskell" [24], addressing essentially the same material as the Algebra of Programming book with no squiggles at all. This latest approach definitely represents a compromise: a small excursion out of the world of pure functions is required in order to accommodate nondeterministic choice [13]. Only time will tell whether the balance is better this time, with greater accessibility compensating for the loss of expressive power.

Acknowledgements. I am especially indebted to Richard Bird and Lambert Meertens: for much discussion about this work, and correcting some of my misunderstandings, but more importantly for being the inspiration for essentially my entire research career. I would also like to thank Doaitse Swierstra, Hendrik Boom, and Stephen Spackman for answering my many questions, and Cezar Ionescu, Dan Shiebler, the members of IFIP WG2.1, the participants at the workshop on the History of Formal Methods in Porto in October 2019, and the anonymous reviewers for their helpful comments and enthusiastic feedback.

References

1. Back, R.-J.: On correct refinement of programs. J. Comput. Syst. Sci. **23**(1), 49–68 (1981)
2. Back, R.-J., von Wright, J.: Refinement Calculus: A Systematic Introduction. Graduate Texts in Computer Science. Springer, Heidelberg (1998). https://doi.org/10.1007/978-1-4612-1674-2

3. Backhouse, R.: An exploration of the Bird-Meertens formalism. In: International Summer School on Constructive Algorithmics, Hollum, Ameland. STOP project: Also available as Technical report CS 8810, p. 1988. Groningen University, Department of Computer Science (1989)

4. Backus, J.W., et al.: Report on the algorithmic language ALGOL 60. Numer. Math. **2**(1), 106–136 (1960)

5. Barron, D.W.: Christopher Strachey: a personal reminiscence. Comput. Bull. **2**(5), 8–9 (1975)

6. Bauer, F.L.: Programming as an evolutionary process. In: International Conference on Software Engineering, pp. 223–234. IEEE (1976)

7. Brauer, F.L., et al.: The Munich Project CIP, Volume I: The Wide Spectrum Language CIP-L. LNCS, vol. 183. Springer, Heidelberg (1985). https://doi.org/10.1007/3-540-15187-7

8. Bauer, F.L., et al.: The Munich Project CIP, Volume II: The Programme Transformation System CIP-S. LNCS, vol. 292. Springer, Heidelberg (1987). https://doi.org/10.1007/3-540-18779-0

9. Bird, R.: "Algebra of Programming" as the textbook on Algorithmics. Private email to JG, February 2020

10. Bird, R., de Moor, O.: Algebra of Programming. Prentice-Hall, Upper Saddle River (1997)

11. Bird, R., de Moor, O.: Website for The Algebra of Programming (1997). http://www.cs.ox.ac.uk/publications/books/algebra/

12. Bird, R., Meertens, L., Wile, D.: A common basis for algorithmic specification and development. IFIP WG2.1 Working Paper ARK-3 (1985)

13. Bird, R., Rabe, F.: How to calculate with nondeterministic functions. In: Hutton, G. (ed.) MPC 2019. LNCS, vol. 11825, pp. 138–154. Springer, Cham (2019). https://doi.org/10.1007/978-3-030-33636-3_6

14. Bird, R.S.: Improving programs by the introduction of recursion. Commun. ACM **20**(11), 856–863 (1977)

15. Bird, R.S.: Notes on recursion elimination. Commun. ACM **20**(6), 434–439 (1977)

16. Bird, R.S.: Notational suggestions for transformational programming. Technical report RCS 144, University of Reading, April 1981

17. Bird, R.S.: Some notational suggestions for transformational programming. Working Paper NIJ-3, IFIP WG2.1 (1981)

18. Bird, R.S.: The promotion and accumulation strategies in transformational programming. ACM Trans. Program. Lang. Syst. **6**(4), 487–504 (1984)

19. Bird, R.S.: An introduction to the theory of lists. Monograph PRG-56, Programming Research Group, University of Oxford, October 1986. Published in [27]

20. Bird, R.S.: Transformational programming and the paragraph problem. Sci. Comput. Program. **6**, 159–189 (1986)

21. Bird, R.S.: A calculus of functions for program derivation. Monograph PRG-64, Programming Research Group, University of Oxford, December 1987. Published in [62]

22. Bird, R.S.: Lectures on constructive functional programming. Monograph PRG-69, Programming Research Group, University of Oxford, September 1988. Published in [28]

23. Bird, R.S.: Algebraic identities for program calculation. Comput. J. **32**(2), 122–126 (1989)

24. Bird, R.S., Gibbons, J.: Algorithm Design with Haskell. Cambridge University Press, Cambridge (2020, to appear)

52   J. Gibbons

25. Bird, R.S., Meertens, L.: Two exercises found in a book on algorithmics. In: Meertens, L. (ed.) Program Specification and Transformation, pp. 451–457. North-Holland (1987)
26. Boom, H.: Further thoughts on Abstracto. Working Paper ELC-9, IFIP WG2.1 (1981)
27. Broy, M. (ed.): Logic of Programming and Calculi of Discrete Design. NATO ASI Series F, vol. 36. Springer, Heidelberg (1987). https://doi.org/10.1007/978-3-642-87374-4
28. Broy, M. (ed.): Constructive Methods in Computer Science. NATO ASI Series F, vol. 55. Springer, Heidelberg (1988). https://doi.org/10.1007/978-3-642-74884-4
29. de Moor, O.: Categories, relations and dynamic programming. Ph.D. thesis, Programming Research Group, Oxford, April 1992. Available as Technical Monograph PRG-98
30. Dewar, R.: Letter to members of IFIP WG2.1, 26 July 1977. http://ershov-arc.iis.nsk.su/archive/eaindex.asp?did=29067
31. Dewar, R.: Letter to members of IFIP WG2.1, 19 September 1979. http://ershov-arc.iis.nsk.su/archive/eaindex.asp?did=29096
32. Freyd, P., Scedrov, A.: Categories, Allegories. Mathematical Library, vol. 39. North-Holland, Amsterdam (1990)
33. Geurts, L., Meertens, L.: Remarks on Abstracto. ALGOL Bull. **42**, 56–63 (1978). Also in [46]
34. Geurts, L., Meertens, L., Pemberton, S.: The ABC Programmer's Handbook. Prentice-Hall, Upper Saddle River (1990). ISBN 0-13-000027-2
35. Gibbons, J.: Algebras for tree algorithms. D. Phil. thesis, Programming Research Group, Oxford University (1991). Available as Technical Monograph PRG-94. ISBN 0-902928-72-4
36. Iverson, K.E.: A Programming Language. Wiley, New York (1962)
37. Koster, C.H.A.: The making of Algol 68. In: Bjørner, D., Broy, M., Pottosin, I.V. (eds.) PSI 1996. LNCS, vol. 1181, pp. 55–67. Springer, Heidelberg (1996). https://doi.org/10.1007/3-540-62064-8_6
38. Lindsey, C.H.: A history of Algol 68. In: HOPL-II: The Second ACM SIGPLAN Conference on History of Programming Languages, pp. 97–132, April 1993
39. Malcolm, G.: Algebraic data types and program transformation. Ph.D. thesis, Rijksuniversiteit Groningen, September 1990
40. Malcolm, G.: Data structures and program transformation. Sci. Comput. Program. **14**, 255–279 (1990)
41. Meertens, L.: Abstracto 84: the next generation. In: Proceedings of the 1979 Annual Conference, pp. 33–39. ACM (1979)
42. Meertens, L.: Draft proposal for the B programming language. Technical report, Mathematisch Centrum, Amsterdam (1981)
43. Meertens, L.: Issues in the design of a beginners' programming language. In: de Bakker, J.W., van Vliet, H. (eds.) Algorithmic Languages, pp. 167–184. Elsevier North-Holland, New York, July 1981
44. Meertens, L.: Some more examples of algorithmic developments. IFIP WG2.1 Working Paper ADP-7 (1984)
45. Meertens, L.: Algorithmics: towards programming as a mathematical activity. In: de Bakker, J.W., Hazewinkel, M., Lenstra, J.K. (eds.) Proceedings of the CWI Symposium on Mathematics and Computer Science, pp. 289–334. North-Holland (1986). https://ir.cwi.nl/pub/20634
46. Meertens, L.: An Abstracto reader prepared for IFIP WG 2.1. Technical report CS-N8702, CWI, Amsterdam, April 1987

47. Meertens, L.: Squiggol versus Squigol. Private email to JG, September 2019
48. Meertens, L.G.L.T., Pemberton, S.: Description of B. SIGPLAN Not. **20**(2), 58–76 (1985)
49. Morgan, C.: The specification statement. ACM Trans. Program. Lang. Syst. **10**(3), 403–419 (1988)
50. Morgan, C.: Programming from Specifications. Prentice Hall, Upper Saddle River (1990)
51. Paige, R.: Transformational programming: applications to algorithms and systems. In: Wright, J.R., Landweber, L., Demers, A.J., Teitelbaum, T. (eds.) Principles of Programming Languages, pp. 73–87. ACM (1983)
52. Paige, R., Koenig, S.: Finite differencing of computable expressions. ACM Trans. Program. Lang. Syst. **4**(3), 402–454 (1982)
53. Peck, J.E.L.: Aad van Wijngaarden and the mathematisch centrum: a personal recollection. In: Alberts, G. (ed.) Conference on the History of ALGOL 68, volume AM-HN9301. CWI, Amsterdam (1993)
54. Pemberton, S.: A short introduction to the ABC language. SIGPLAN Not. **26**(2), 11–16 (1991)
55. Python Software Foundation. Python website (1997). https://www.python.org/
56. Schuman, S.A. (ed.): New directions in algorithmic languages. Prepared for IFIP Working Group 2.1 on Algol, Institut de Recherche d'Informatique et d'Automatique (1975)
57. Schuman, S.A. (ed.): New directions in algorithmic languages. Prepared for IFIP Working Group 2.1 on Algol, Institut de Recherche d'Informatique et d'Automatique (1976)
58. Schwartz, J.T.: On programming: an interim report on the SETL project. Technical report, New York University (1974)
59. Schwartz, J.T., Dewar, R.B.K., Dubinsky, E., Schoenberg, E.: Programming with Sets: An Introduction to SETL. Texts and Monographs in Computer Science. Springer, Heidelberg (1986). https://doi.org/10.1007/978-1-4613-9575-1
60. Spackman, S.: Boom and Abstracto. Private email to JG, October 2019
61. Spackman, S., Boom, H.: Foop, poof, and parsing. Working Paper 560 COR-15, IFIP WG2.1 (1987)
62. Turner, D.A. (ed.): Research Topics in Functional Programming. University of Texas at Austin, Addison-Wesley, Boston (1990)
63. van Wijngaarden, A., Mailloux, B.J., Peck, J.E.L., Koster, C.H.A.: Report on the algorithmic language ALGOL 68. Numer. Math. **14**(2), 79–218 (1969)
64. van Wijngaarden, A., et al.: Revised report on the algorithmic language Algol 68. Acta Inform. **5**(1–3), 1–236 (1975). https://doi.org/10.1007/BF00265077. Also appeared as Mathematical Centre Tract 50, CWI, Amsterdam, and published by Springer Verlag in 1976
65. Wile, D.S.: A generative, nested-sequential basis for general purpose programming languages. Ph.D. thesis, Department of Computer Science, Carnegie-Mellon University, Pittsburgh, Pennsylvania, November 1973

Reasoning About Shared-Variable Concurrency: Interactions Between Research Threads

Cliff B. Jones[✉]

School of Computing, Newcastle University, Newcastle upon Tyne, UK
cliff.jones@ncl.ac.uk

Abstract. Most research on concurrency involves either communication-based approaches or accepts the shared-variable model. This paper addresses the latter approach and traces the research from Hoare's axiomatic approach, through Sue Owicki's work up to separation logics and rely/guarantee methods. Researchers in these last two approaches have been involved in a friendly rivalry and cooperation. The focus is on the insights that have arisen rather than technical details.

1 Introduction

This paper addresses the important topic of reasoning formally about concurrent computer programs that execute with variables that are shared between threads. The attempt to trace the key **insights** that have shaped the research. There have been some relatively linear sequences of ideas where research contributors build on preceding work; there have also been periods of strong interaction and friendly competition between adherents of different approaches.

Where dates are useful, they are normally related to publication dates. In addition to publications, there have been a number of places where real progress has been made with researchers interacting face-to-face: the most influential venue might have been IFIP's Working Group WG2.3 on *Programming Methodology*,[1] further venues include meetings of lecturers at the Marktoberdorf Summer Schools, Schloss Dagstuhl and the UK *Concurrency Working Group*.

Some avenues of concurrency research focus on the avoidance of shared variables—*Process Algebras* and other approaches not addressed in the body of this paper are mentioned in Sect. 5.2. Despite the challenges that shared-variable concurrent programs present to developers, such programs are both historically important and remain in widespread use.

Even with primitive operating systems, the attempt to keep a CPU busy –whilst slower external devices consumed or delivered data– required care in program design. When there was a single CPU, programs could switch between threads in a way that gave rise to most issues about shared variables. As

---

[1] With respect to the topics considered in this paper, the most productive period was probably the 1970s/80s but the whole history of WG2.3 deserves closer study.

© Springer Nature Switzerland AG 2020
E. Sekerinski et al. (Eds.): FM 2019 Workshops, LNCS 12233, pp. 54–72, 2020.
https://doi.org/10.1007/978-3-030-54997-8_3

input/output processors became more independent from the CPU, flags could be set, interrupts generated and buffers filled independently of the program actually written by a developer.

Concurrency issues have become more important over time because of the creation of full-blown time-sharing systems, the emergence of applications that interact with a world external to the computer and multi-core hardware.[2]

Developing concurrent software poses many challenges including data races, deadlock and "livelock"[3]—the common cause of these issues is interference: the behaviour of the thread of the program about which the programmer would like to reason is influenced by external activities.

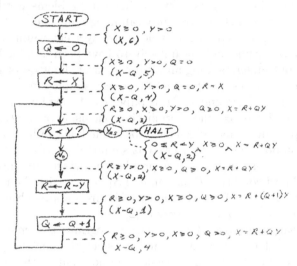

Figure 5.

Algorithm to compute quotient Q and remainder R of X ÷ Y, for integers X≥0, Y>0.

Fig. 1. Floyd's hand drawn flowchart (with assertions) of division by successive subtraction

1.1 Refresher on Reasoning About Sequential Programs

The key steps in research on reasoning about sequential (non-concurrent) software are described in [49]: Hoare's *Axiomatic basis* paper [33] is taken as key;[4] Hoare acknowledges the influence of Floyd [29], van Wijngaarden [89] and

---

[2] More recently, so-called "weak memory" hardware with thread-local caches has added further difficulty—a paper that links with the material below is [56].

[3] This term is attributed to Ed Ashcroft whose contributions are covered in Sect. 2.1.

[4] Hoare is one of the most highly cited computer scientists—although his CSP paper [36] has even more citations, [33] has over 7,000 (GS) citations and has maintained an almost constant level for many years.

Naur [69]. The trace in [49] back to Turing [86] and von Neumann [30][5] shows a surprising hiatus in progress of this research area between 1949 and 1967.

Figure 1 comes from a mimeographed draft of Floyd's 1967 seminal paper;[6] it shows that his annotations were attached to arcs in flowcharts. In contrast, Hoare introduced judgements –now referred to as "Hoare triples"– (now written as $\{P\}$ S $\{Q\}$) in which P and Q are assertions (predicates) and S is a program text; Q is a post condition that expresses what the program text S achieves providing the pre condition P holds before execution and S terminates normally.

One reason that the move away from flowcharts was so important is that it points towards a top-down development method instead of a way of checking completed programs. Hoare's approach lends itself to starting with a specification and decomposing it into progressively smaller sub-problems until each can be achieved by statements of the desired programming language.[7, 8] This top-down description might be viewed as idealistic in today's environment where most programs evolve over time and are unlikely to have been designed initially in a systematic way but understanding an ideal can throw light on other methods.

Hoare axioms (or rules of inference) for a very simple language are given in Fig. 2; the issues in the remainder of this paper can be explained by focusing on the first rule. Such inference rules permit the conclusion of the triple below the horizontal line providing any judgements above the line can be proved. The rule for sequential composition can be viewed as supporting problem decomposition, it can inform the decomposition of the problem below the line indicated by pre condition P and post condition R into finding S_1 and S_2 with their respective pre and post conditions. A useful early survey of Hoare's approach is given in [3, 4] a comprehensive and up-to-date survey is [2].

Crucially Hoare's approach for sequential programs is *compositional* in the sense that the developer of S_1 need only consider the specification P/Q—no awareness is needed of the sibling specification nor that of the overall context. Later sections below make clear that compositionality is not easily achieved for concurrent programs precisely because of interference between threads. But, for

---

[5] Mark Priestly's invited talk at the 2019 *History of Formal Methods* workshop in Porto suggests a revision of the assessment of von Neumann's contribution. In particular, Priestly's archive research has precisely identified the letter to Goldstine in which von Neumann proposes *assertion boxes*.

[6] Floyd acknowledges Gorn and Perlis as the originators of the ideas—Knuth suggested that this was overly modest.

[7] This only became clear in the published version of [35]: an early draft offered a *post facto* proof of the final program and these proofs were extremely hard to check— Hoare revised the paper to exhibit a stepwise development that was much more convincing (the title of the paper was not changed).

[8] It is worth noting that Hoare argued at the 1964 *Formal Language Description Languages* conference at Baden-bei-Wien [84] for a language definition style that could leave things undefined. Also [33, §6] talks about language definition. It could be argued that what has become the cornerstone of 50 years of research into formal development of programs was found during an attempt to solve a different problem (i.e. that of writing a semantic description of a language).

$$\boxed{;} \quad \frac{\begin{array}{c} \{P\}\ S_1\ \{Q\} \\ \{Q\}\ S_2\ \{R\} \end{array}}{\{P\}\ S_1;\ S_2\ \{R\}}$$

$$\boxed{\leftarrow} \quad \overline{\{P[e/x]\}\ x \leftarrow e\ \{P\}}$$

$$\boxed{\text{if}} \quad \frac{\begin{array}{c} \{P \wedge b\}\ S_1\ \{Q\} \\ \{P \wedge \neg b\}\ S_2\ \{Q\} \end{array}}{\{P\}\ \textbf{if}\ b\ \textbf{then}\ S_1\ \textbf{else}\ S_2\ \textbf{fi}\ \{Q\}}$$

$$\boxed{consequence} \quad \frac{\begin{array}{c} P' \Rightarrow P \\ Q \Rightarrow Q' \\ \{P\}\ S\ \{Q\} \end{array}}{\{P'\}\ S\ \{Q'\}}$$

$$\boxed{\text{while}} \quad \frac{\{P \wedge b\}\ S\ \{P\}}{\{P\}\ \textbf{while}\ b\ \textbf{do}\ S\ \textbf{od}\ \{P \wedge \neg b\}}$$

Fig. 2. Hoare's axioms

sequential programs, pre and post conditions suffice: they record everything that the developer of a (sub-)program needs to achieve.

For concurrent programs, non-compositional methods were discovered first and they have a significant role in providing tools that analyse finished code. Apart from the ideal of top-down problem decomposition, compositional methods indicate how descriptions of complex systems can be decomposed into understandable pieces. Ideas from compositional methods can also provide useful abstractions for bottom-up approaches.

1.2   Useful Background Reading on Concurrency

There are many technical challenges that have to be faced when designing concurrent programs. These include data races, atomicity, deadlocks, livelocks and fairness. Various programming language constructs have been proposed to help overcome these challenges. Semaphores were an early idea and higher level constructs such as conditional critical sections have been put forward. Readers unfamiliar with these ideas would learn enough from [10] to follow the rest of the current paper; [5,83] or [60] go much further into formal material.

1.3   Beyond the Sequential Case

Following on from the success of [33], Hoare and colleagues looked at a range of extensions to the axiomatic approach (e.g. [17,34]). His first foray into applying the approach to parallel programs resulted in [39]. Looking back at the rule for sequential combination discussed in Sect. 1.1, the dream would be to find a rule that permitted some simple combination of the pre and post conditions of two threads such as:

$$\boxed{?} \quad \frac{\begin{array}{c} \{P1\}\ S_1\ \{Q1\} \\ \{P2\}\ S_2\ \{Q2\} \end{array}}{\{P1\ \textbf{and}\ P2\}\ S_1 \| S_2\ \{Q1\ \textbf{and}\ Q2\}}$$

As one would expect, Hoare gives a clear outline of the issues and notes that the above rule works (with logical conjunction in the conclusion) providing that S_1 and S_2 refer only to disjoint variables. The paper [39] goes on to investigate ways in which interference can be ruled out (notably by *critical regions*); tackles a number of examples (including a bounded buffer, *dining philosophers* and a parallel version of Quicksort); and includes an effusive acknowledgement to the stimulus of Edsger W. Dijkstra.

The first **insight** then is that separation limits interference—with hindsight this might sound obvious but, in addition, an ideal form of parallel inference rule is given against which other proposals can be judged.

This sets the scene for an interesting split in research directions:

- one line of research is to look at explicit ways of reasoning about interference—this avenue is discussed in Sect. 2;
- alternatively, researchers have investigated reasoning about separation even in the more complicated arena of heap variables—Sect. refSspssep reviews this approach.

Both approaches are clearly important and have spheres of applicability; Sects. 2 and 3 discuss the two avenues in roughly historical order; Sect. 4 outlines fruitful interactions between researchers pursuing the two avenues.

2   Reasoning About Interference

Only with the benefit of hindsight did the criterion of compositionality became a key issue (see [20]) but, since there is also a historical development, the distinction is used to separate Sects. 2.1 and 2.2. Sections 2.3 and 2.4 mention two important –but somewhat orthogonal– detailed issues.

The phrase "non-compositional" might sound negative but bottom-up methods that work with finished code have given rise to many useful tools (see Sect. 4)—part of the attraction of tools that work with finished programs is that they can do useful work relatively automatically.

2.1   Non-compositional Approaches

A first step[9] towards reasoning formally about interfering threads was made by Ed Ashcroft and Zohar Manna in [7].

Ashcroft had done his PhD at Imperial College (London) under the supervision of John Florentin.[10] Ashcroft was also known for his work on the Lucid language with Bill Wadge.[11] Manna's PhD was supervised by Floyd (which fact

---

[9] A reader who is tempted to view this section in particular as too linear should remember that in the 1970s there were fewer active researchers than there are today. Furthermore, this paper is deliberately limited to shared-variable concurrency—subjects such as process algebras were progressing in parallel (see Sect. 5.2).

[10] Florentin and this paper's author had extensive contacts during the 1960s/70s when the latter worked for IBM.

[11] Interestingly, Ashcroft supervised Matthew Hennessy's PhD—Hennessy's main research area is process algebras.

is important below). Manna made huge contributions to many areas[12] including Temporal Logics. A beautiful technical obituary is [21].

The 1971 paper was preceded by a Stanford Tech Report [6]. The ideas build mainly on the Floyd approach including the use of flowcharts for the programs to be justified. There is, in fact, a rather offhand reference to "see also [33]". Manna proposed the idea of non-deterministic programs in [63][13] and the 1971 paper translates concurrent threads into such a non-deterministic program. The state of a computation is essentially the memory plus a program counter. As the authors of [7] concede, this program can be exponentially larger than the original concurrent text because it has to handle all mergings of the threads ([7, p. 37] gives some actual sizes for the examples).

The approach is non-compositional in the sense that it does not support development from specifications because it relies on having full texts (flowcharts) of all threads. Furthermore, it makes the assumption that assignment statements can be executed atomically (this point is returned to below).

A number of ways of limiting the size of the generated non-deterministic program are explained in [7, Part 3]:

- nested parallelism is not allowed;
- blocks are used to increase *granularity*;
- so-called "protected bodies" can be marked on the flowchart by dotted lines.

The examples covered are all abstract programs rather than solutions to specified problems.

The **insight** is that shared-variable concurrency (without separation) creates huge non-determinacy because of the potential interleaving of statements in threads. Furthermore, a specific way of representing such (equivalent) non-deterministic programs is described.

The next step was taken by Ashcroft alone in [8]. The paper starts with the prescient observation that reasoning formally about programs will become more popular with concurrency (because concurrent programs defeat a programmer's mental ability to consider all possible mergings).

Ashcroft commented on the exponential number of proof obligations required by the approach in [6] and set out to tackle this issue. He proposed employing *control states* which record the statements to be executed in each concurrent thread.[14]

Ashcroft's 1975 approach reduces the proof obligation count to the product of the control points. It is still the case that the approach is non-compositional

---

[12] This paper's author was present at the 1968 *Mathematical Theory of Computation* conference at IBM Yorktown Heights where John McCarthy strongly advocated Manna's developments of Floyd's approach.

[13] Since this paper was published in an AI journal, the examples are mainly about search algorithms but McCarthy's *91 function* is also tackled.

[14] As an aside, this bears a strong resemblance to the Control Trees that are part of the "grand state" in early Vienna operational descriptions of the semantics of programming languages (see [59] for more on VDL and [50] for a discussion of the problems with these descriptions).

because it is based on complete flowcharts of all threads and it retains the unrealistic assumption that assignment statements can be executed atomically. In contrast to the 1971 joint paper, Ashcroft's 1975 paper tackles a rather ambitious Airline Reservation System example.

The next step is comparatively far more widely known (than the foregoing) and was made by Susan Owicki—her thesis is [72] and a more accessible source is the paper co-authored with her supervisor David Gries [73].[15] Commonly referred to as the "Owicki-Gries" approach, a proof rule is given for an **await** statement (see rule 3.2 in Fig. 3). Furthermore the approach offers a semblance of compositionality. The first step in the *Owicki-Gries* approach is to prove that the threads satisfy their individual pre and post conditions. It is important for the next phase that these proofs contain complete proof outlines with assertions between every statement. The rule labelled 3.3 in Fig. 3 looks close to the ideal rule in Sect. 1.3. The snag is that the *interference free* proof obligation (elsewhere *einmischungsfrei*[16]) requires proving that no assignment in one thread invalidates any proof step in another thread.

The Owicki-Gries method contributes the **insight** that interference can be judged by its impact on the proof steps of other threads and it proposes a specific proof obligation as a check.

$$(3.2) \quad \textbf{await} \quad \frac{\{P \wedge B\}\, S\, \{Q\}}{\{P\}\, \textbf{await}\, B\, \textbf{then}\, S\, \{Q\}}$$

$$(3.3) \quad \textbf{cobegin} \quad \frac{\{P_1\}\, S_1\, \{Q_1\},\, \dots,\, \{P_n\}\, S_n\, \{Q_n\} \text{ are interference-free}}{\{P_1 \wedge \dots \wedge P_n\}\, \textbf{cobegin}\, S_1\, //\, \dots\, //\, S_n\, \textbf{coend}\, \{Q_1 \wedge \dots \wedge Q_n\}}$$

Fig. 3. Proof rules from [73]

In addition to a small technical example, [73] introduces a *FindPos* example that employs two threads to find the least index of an array A such that some predicate p holds at $p(A(i))$; a producer/consumer problem is also addressed.

As indicated in [20], this approach is non-compositional because the correctness of each thread can only be established with respect to the finished code of all threads. It would clearly be possible that all threads were developed according to their specifications but that the final *einmischungsfrei* proof obligation fails and the development has to be completely restarted.

The [73] paper contains a specific acknowledgement to IFIP Working Group WG2.3: Gries first observed[17] at the meeting in December 1974 and was elected

---

[15] This paper indicates that it was intended to be "Part I" but there is no trace of subsequent parts and a recent private contact with Owicki confirmed that none was written.

[16] Gries obtained his PhD from what is now known as "Technische Universität München" under supervision of Bauer which is the explanation of a German adjective for the key proof obligation in the approach.

[17] IFIP working groups have a process of inviting observers (sometimes several times) before considering people for membership.

a member in September 1975; Owicki was an observer at the July 1976 meeting. These contacts possibly increased the incentive to relate the Owicki-Gries approach to [33] but it is easy to see the Owicki-Gries approach as more strongly linked to the flowcharts of [29]. Owicki's thesis [72] provides soundness proofs for the proof obligations and cites Peter Lauer's research with Hoare [38].

A more subtle objection to the Owicki-Gries approach is the assumption that single statements can be executed atomically (recall that this is also the case with the two approaches above). The problem is that this assumption does not hold for any reasonable compiler. There is an argument given that the assumption holds if there is only one shared variable per assignment.[18] This would prompt splitting any assignment $x \leftarrow x + 1$ into two assignments using a temporary variable but this still leaves the programmer needing to reason about the interference between the statements.[19]

Another interesting discussion concerns *auxiliary* (or *ghost*) variables – this topic is taken up in Sect. 2.4.

2.2 Recovering Compositionality

It is clear that finding a compositional approach to the design of concurrent programs is challenging: because threads interfere, they can potentially be affected by statements in environmental threads; the code of all threads provides maximal information but is not available at the point when a developer suggests a split into parallel threads. Although it would be judgemental to class the need for availability of program code in the methods described in Sect. 2.1 as a flaw, it must be conceded that it makes it impossible to achieve the sort of top-down separation that was observed in Sect. 1.1 for the sequential composition of statements.

One challenge therefore was to find a useful level of abstraction that faced up to interference without having the code of all threads. The key step in the Rely/Guarantee approach [43–45] was to characterise interference by relations.[20] Figure 4:

- shows pre and (relational) post conditions as in their standard VDM use;
- marks that any environment interference can be thought of as an interfering step that satisfies a rely condition—it functions like a post condition of the interfering state transition; and
- shows that the guarantee condition is also a relation and records the interference that the component being specified will inflict on the environment.

---

[18] This is sometimes referred to as "Reynolds' rule" but John Reynolds disowned it in a conversation with this paper's author.

[19] Another venue where useful exchanges on these topics occurred was Schloss Dagstuhl: there were two events on *Atomicity* in April 2004 [15,48] and spring 2006 [18].

[20] VDM had consistently employed relations as post conditions—in fact, this goes back to before the name "VDM" was coined [41]. Use of data abstraction was also a key arrow in VDM's quiver [40] with [42] being an early book to emphasis its use. This becomes important with Rely/Guarantee ideas—see Sect. 2.3.

$$\overbrace{\sigma_0}^{pre} \quad \cdots \quad \overbrace{\sigma_i \; \sigma_{i+1}}^{rely} \quad \cdots \quad \underbrace{\sigma_j \; \sigma_{j+1}}_{guar} \quad \cdots \quad \sigma_f$$

$$\underbrace{\phantom{\sigma_0 \cdots \sigma_i \sigma_{i+1} \cdots \sigma_j \sigma_{j+1} \cdots \sigma_f}}_{post}$$

pre/*rely* are assumptions the developer can make
guar/*post* are commitments that the code must achieve

Fig. 4. A trace of states made by execution of a component and its context

The pre, rely, guarantee and post conditions fit into the generic picture in Fig. 4 and this moves the discussion on to finding an appropriate proof rule that can be used to justify steps of development that introduce concurrency. Pre, rely, guarantee and post conditions can be written in a quintuple wrapped around the program text that is to be executed: $\{P, R\} \; S \; \{G, Q\}$.[21] To indicate how the rely/guarantee rules relate to the non-interfering version of the parallel rule at the beginning of Sect. 1.3, a slight simplification of the actual rule can be written:[22]

$$\boxed{|| - R/G} \quad \frac{\begin{array}{c} \{P_1, R \vee G_2\} \; S_1 \; \{G_1, Q_1\} \\ \{P_2, R \vee G_1\} \; S_2 \; \{G_2, Q_2\} \end{array}}{\{P_1 \; \& \; P_2, R\} \; S_1 || S_2 \; \{G_1 \vee G_2, Q_1 \; \& \; Q_2 \; \& \; \cdots\}}$$

One example of the use of R/G in development can be based on the *Sieve of Eratosthenes* for finding all primes up to some specified number. The specification of the interesting part of the algorithm is to remove all composite numbers from a set. Several papers [32, 46] show how to tackle the design decision to achieve this by executing instances of $Rem(i)$ processes concurrently. The example indicates how the formulation of rely and guarantee conditions interacts with post conditions.

The prime sieve example above uses symmetric (Rem) processes but the proof rule also caters for examples in which concurrent threads have different specifications (e.g. producer/consumer processes have asymmetric specifications).

Proof rules of the above form are proved sound with respect to a model-oriented semantics in [19, 43, 76]. The oldest of these proofs is fairly ugly having been based on a VDL semantics; Coleman's soundness argument is much nicer but is not machine checked; Prensa-Nieto's proof is checked on Isabelle but does not cover nested concurrency. Peter Aczel introduced a form of trace (now referred to as "Aczel traces") as a semantic model [1]; they are employed in [20].

There are many examples of Rely/Guarantee developments in the literature including Owicki's *FindPos*, a concurrent cleanup addition to the Fisher-Galler

---

[21] This quintuple version of rely-guarantee obviously follows Hoare triples (see Sect. 1.1). There are other ways of conveying the same information (see Sect. 5.2).

[22] The simplification is that a stronger post condition can use information from the guarantee conditions.

implementation of *Union-Find*, Simpson's *four slot* algorithm, the *Treiber stack* and the concurrent prime sieve.

The **insight** here is that interference can be specified and reasoned about if relations are used to abstract information about interference; based on this, inference rules for parallelism can avoid the need for access to the code of contextual threads.

There are over twenty PhD theses related to the Rely-Guarantee approach they include:

- [85,91] which both consider progress arguments;
- [64] uses Temporal Logic to encode rely and guarantee conditions;
- Dingel's [22] is an early attempt to combine refinement calculus ideas with the Rely/Guarantee approach;
- · - [75] tackles the challenging task of producing a clear formal development of the implementation by Hugo Simpson of *Asynchronous Communication Mechanisms*;
- Hongjin Liang's [23] thesis [58] proposes RGSim whose interference predicates also address ownership.

There are related approaches described in [20] under names such as *assume-commit*.

The research described in this section sounds sufficiently linear that historians might fear a retrospective tidying up of the story. Two points are worth remembering: the linearity concerns only this narrow thread of research and Sect. 5.2 widens the viewpoint; strong interaction with other threads of research have arisen more recently and are mentioned in Sect. 4.

2.3   Role of Data Abstraction/Reification

Abstract objects make it possible to write specifications which are far shorter than if the same task was specified in terms of the restricted data types of a programming language. Specifications can also postpone much algorithmic detail by employing data types that match the problem rather than trying to achieve efficient implementation. The process of (formally) designing a representation is referred to variously as "refinement" or "reification" (making concrete). The use of data abstraction in the specification of systems can be studied as a subject quite separate from concurrency; its origins are traced in [80] and related to other aspects of program specification and development in [49].

The reason for adding this subsection to the discussion of reasoning about interference is that the use of abstract data types appears to be particularly important in specifying and developing concurrent programs. The **insight** that nearly all examples of Rely/Guarantee developments benefit from the use of abstract data types was first recorded in [47]. To mention one specific example,

---

[23] Hongjin Liang's doctoral research was supervised by Xinyu Feng whose own research on SAGL is mentioned below.

Simpson's *four slot* implementation of *Asynchronous Communication Mechanisms* is tackled in [53] where an abstract object of many slots is a shared variable but the rely conditions on this abstraction facilitate working out exactly what constraints need to be respected on Simpson's (four) race-free slots.

2.4 Auxiliary Variables

An issue that clouds a number of specifications and designs of concurrent programs is the use of *auxiliary* (or *ghost*) variables. The idea is that variables can be inserted into a thread that do not influence its behaviour but make it easier to reason about a thread because the auxiliary variables record some information about the environment. In the extreme, such auxiliary variables could record everything about the environment including the steps to be taken by other threads. This would clearly subvert compositionality. Most uses of auxiliary variables are less detailed and this paper's author has argued that nearly all cases can be avoided if a more appropriate abstraction is found. In some cases, the notation of *possible values* developed in [51] obviates the need for auxiliary variables.

The fact that recourse to auxiliary variable is so common suggests that not everyone would count avoiding them by finding abstractions as an **insight**. Furthermore a delicate (in the sense of tricky) *on-the-fly garbage collector* is studied in [55] and the tentative conclusion there is that the intimate connections between the mutator and collector threads force the use of an auxiliary variable. At the time of writing that paper, the authors were unaware of [31] which might throw further light on the topic.

3 Avoiding or Constraining Interference

This section outlines the background of –and research in– what are termed "Concurrent Separation Logics" (CSL). There are in fact many forms of separation logic making this a large subject; here only the central points are covered so as to facilitate the discussion in Sect. 4 on the interaction between research threads.

There are two distinguished parents of CSL research: John Reynolds' work on Separation Logic and Hoare's study [39] of how variable separation admits the use of the idealised parallel rule from the beginning of Sect. 1.3.[24]

A key summary of Reynolds' work on Separation Logic is [79] in which he looks at the tricky topic of reasoning about programs that use dynamically allocated heap variables. Such programs are notoriously difficult to design and debug because mistakes can have effects that range far beyond the immediate code.

Many presentations of reasoning about such programs start with the code itself (rather than an abstract specification). Although they are in a formal

---

[24] Peter O'Hearn emphasised the debt to [39] during his talk in Cambridge honouring Tony Hoare in April 2009.

system, the discussions tend to be bottom-up in that they abstract a specification from code. (Recall that the point is made above that this offers a route to useful tool support for detecting errors in finished code.)

CSL itself also focusses on programs that employ heap variables. In a concurrent context, interaction between threads often involves them exchanging ownership of addresses between threads. To take the more obvious case of controlling which thread has ownership to write to an address, data races are avoided by making sure that only one thread has write ownership at any point in time but the logic must make it possible to reason about exchange of ownership between threads.[25]

The key reference to CSL is [70] which records a talk given by Peter O'Hearn at the 2005 MFPS-XXI in honour of John Reynolds. A detailed and personal history of the evolution of CSL is available as [14].

Arranging that assertions cover heap addresses requires an extension of the idea of the state of a computation to include a mapping from addresses to values. Based on this it is then possible to build the notion of two assertions as having disjoint heap accesses: $P1 * P2$ can only hold if the addresses in $P1$ and $P2$ are disjoint but otherwise the asterisk functions as a logical conjunction. It is therefore easy to relate the following central CSL rule:

$$\boxed{\| - CSL} \quad \frac{\{P1\} \; S_1 \; \{Q1\} \quad \{P2\} \; S_2 \; \{Q2\}}{\{P1 * P2\} \; S_1 \| S_2 \; \{Q1 * Q2\}}$$

to the idealised rule at the beginning of Sect. 1.3 but it is important to remember that Hoare's rule dealt with (normal) stack variables and that the key to the above $\| - CSL$ is handling heap variables.

Another rule that is considered important for CSL is the *frame rule* that makes it possible to apply an assertion on a limited set of variables to a larger state providing the variables are disjoint. This can be compared with the way that frames are defined for stack variables in Morgan's *refinement calculus* [67] or even VDM's keyword oriented definition of read and write variables.

Having attributed the insight about separation to Hoare in Sect. 1.3, it could be thought that CSL "only" contributes its employment on heap variables. The current author's view is that the key **insight** is actually that CSL makes it possible to reason about ownership of heap addresses.

One issue with studying or reporting on separation logics for concurrency is their proliferation—a point made by Matthew Parkinson in the title of [74] ("The next 700 Separation Logics"). O'Hearn reproduces in [70, Fig. 1] a chart (generated by Ilya Sergey) of developments that relates many of these logics. More recently, Parkinson and colleagues have proposed *Views* [23] as a common semantic underpinning of such logics. This at least reduces the burden of establishing the soundness of the many logics.

---

[25] At the MFPS-XXI conference referred to below, this paper's author suggested that the adjective "ownership" might describe the logic better than using "separation". The link back to Reynolds' research was too strong for this suggestion to be followed.

Research related to CSL has led to extremely successful tools that are applied in industry. Notably, O'Hearn and colleagues formed a company called "Monoidics" that was then acquired by FaceBook and reports of the impact of their tools (e.g. [24]) are extremely encouraging.

4   Productive Interactions Between Groups

The title of this paper mentions interactions between research groups and it is only for simplicity of presentation that the separation is made to appear strong between Sects. 2 and 3. (Furthermore, the focus in this paper on shared-variable concurrency sidesteps discussion of many research avenues some of which are touched on in Sect. 5.2).

Researchers have benefited from many interactions including:

- Both Peter O'Hearn and this paper's author spoke at MFPS-XXI in honour of John Reynolds—O'Hearn's [70] tried to distinguish between CSL as reasoning about race freedom and Rely/Guarantee as tackling "racy programs";[26] Jones' contribution to the proceedings is [47].
- A predominantly UK based *Concurrency Working Group* has met about once every nine months for over a decade.
- Several of the prominent researchers involved in CSL(s) have been awarded prestigious Fellowships by the *Royal Academy of Engineering*—this paper's author has been the official mentor of most of the CSL-related awards and has found it an invaluable way of keeping in touch. In particular there were many fruitful visits to Cambridge to see Matthew Parkinson and his doctoral students.

Specific fruits of these interactions include:

- A friendly rivalry around getting clear specifications and justifications of Simpson's four slot implementation of Asynchronous Communication Mechanisms—see [12,13,51–53].
- Important attempts to bring Rely/Guarantee and CSL ideas into one framework [27,87,88].
- Deny-Guarantee reasoning [25].
- Local Rely/Guarantee reasoning [26].
- RGITL [82] which combines Moszkowski's [68] *Interval Temporal Logic* with Rely/Guarantee ideas.

---

[26] The current author suspects that the negative flavour of the adjective was no accident. Furthermore it is contradicted by the fact that there are examples where an early stage of design allows races on abstract variables as a stepping stone to designing a race free representation—see [53].

5 Concluding Comments

This paper has focussed on shared-variable concurrency and has identified key insights that have shaped 50 years of research in this arena. This is only one aspect of the broader subject of concurrency and this concluding section pinpoints some of the items that remain to be covered.

5.1 Recent References

This brief sub-section leaves some recent markers for researchers who might be tempted to extend this study. The work on Views [23] is referenced earlier but its full impact has yet to be worked out—for example Matthew Windsor's PhD [90] looks at direct tool support for Views.

Section 2.3 discusses the use of data abstraction and reification in developing concurrent programs. A more recent paper [54] makes the point that many cases of separation can be handled by viewing separation *as* an abstraction. Two examples are presented where abstract variables that can be thought of as normal (disjoint) stack variables that can then be reified onto heap structures with the obligation that the disjointness must be established on the representation. It would be fruitful to examine many more examples.

Recent collaboration with Australian colleagues centred around Ian Hayes has led to a complete reformulation of the Rely/Guarantee approach that emphasises its algebraic properties—see [32] and the references therein.

5.2 Further Topics

There are many aspects of research on concurrency that have not been addressed in the body of this paper. These include:

- Process Algebras such as CSP [37], CCS [66], ACP [9] and the π-calculus [65,81]—Hoare credits discussions with Dijkstra at the Marktoberdorf summer schools for some of the inspirations that led to CSP.
- Temporal Logics [28,61,62] including TLA+ [57].
- model checking—see [16].
- considerations of real time.
- Petri net theory [11,71,77,78].

The Leverhulme grant received by this paper's author will hopefully make it possible to cover many of these avenues.

Acknowledgements. This paper is a post-conference version of the talk given at the *History of Formal Methods* meeting in Porto in October 2019. The author is grateful to the organisers for the event and the audience for their feedback. Furthermore, Troy Astarte kindly commented on a draft of this paper. I am extremely grateful for the perceptive and helpful input received from anonymous referees.

Past research has been funded by the EPSRC *Strata* Platform grant and earlier EPSRC responsive mode funding of the Rely/Guarantee research. On the purely technical front, I am a Partner Investigator on Ian Hayes' ARC grant which is closely related to my concurrency research.

The Leverhulme grant (2019–2020) awarded to this paper's author will provide funding to address more topics in the history of concurrency research.

References

1. Aczel, P.H.G.: On an inference rule for parallel composition (1983). (Private communication) Manuscript, Manchester
2. Apt, K., Olderog, E.R.: Fifty years of Hoare's logic. Formal Aspects Comput. **31**(6), 751–807 (2019)
3. Apt, K.R.: Ten years of Hoare's logic: a survey–part I. ACM Trans. Program. Lang. Syst. **3**(4), 431–483 (1981)
4. Apt, K.R.: Ten years of Hoare's logic: a survey–part II: nondeterminism. Theoret. Comput. Sci. **28**(1–2), 83–109 (1983)
5. Apt, K.R., Olderog, E.R.: Verification of Sequential and Concurrent Programs. Texts and Monographs in Computer Science. Springer, New York (1991). https://doi.org/10.1007/978-1-4757-4376-0
6. Ashcroft, E.A., Manna, Z.: Formalization of properties of parallel programs. Technical report AIM-110, Stanford Artificial Intelligence Project, February 1970. Published as [7]
7. Ashcroft, E.A., Manna, Z.: Formalization of Properties of Parallel Programs. In: Meltzer, B., Michie, D. (eds.) Machine Intelligence, vol. 6, pp. 17–41. Edinburgh University Press, Edinburgh (1971)
8. Ashcroft, E.A.: Proving assertions about parallel programs. J. Comput. Syst. Sci. **10**(1), 110–135 (1975)
9. Baeten, J.C.M., Weijland, W.P.: Process Algebra. Cambridge University Press, Cambridge (1990)
10. Ben-Ari, M.: Principles of Concurrent and Distributed Programming. Prentice Hall International Series in Computer Science. Prentice Hall, Upper Saddle River (1990)
11. Best, E., Devillers, R., Koutny, M.: Petri Net Algebra. Monographs in Theoretical Computer Science An EATCS Series. Springer, Heidelberg (2001). https://doi.org/10.1007/978-3-662-04457-5
12. Bornat, R., Amjad, H.: Inter-process buffers in separation logic with rely-guarantee. Formal Aspects Comput. **22**(6), 735–772 (2010). https://doi.org/10.1007/s00165-009-0141-8
13. Bornat, R., Amjad, H.: Explanation of two non-blocking shared-variable communication algorithms. Formal Aspects Comput. **25**(6), 893–931 (2013)
14. Brookes, S., O'Hearn, P.W.: Concurrent separation logic. ACM SIGLOG News **3**(3), 47–65 (2016)
15. Burton, J.I., Jones, C.B.: Atomicity in system design and execution. J. Univ. Comput. Sci. **11**(5), 634–635 (2005). http://www.jucs.org/jucs_11_5/atomicity_in_system_design/managing.html
16. Clarke, E.M., Henzinger, T.A., Veith, H., Bloem, R.: Handbook of Model Checking, vol. 10. Springer, Cham (2018). https://doi.org/10.1007/978-3-319-10575-8
17. Clint, M., Hoare, C.A.R.: Program proving: jumps and functions. Acta Informatica **1**(3), 214–224 (1972)

18. Coleman, J.W., Jones, C.B.: Atomicity: a unifying concept in computer science. J. Univ. Comput. Sci. **13**(8), 1042–1043 (2007). https://eprints.ncl.ac.uk/file_store/production/161042/DCEAA1B2-B87B-4B2D-8227-31DAE51FC776.pdf
19. Coleman, J.W.: Constructing a tractable reasoning framework upon a fine-grained structural operational semantics. Ph.D. thesis, Newcastle University School of Computer Science, January 2008
20. De Roever, W.P., et al.: Concurrency Verification: Introduction to Compositional and Noncompositional Methods. Cambridge University Press, Cambridge (2001)
21. Dershowitz, N., Waldinger, R.: Zohar Manna (1939–2018). Formal Aspects Comput. **31**(6), 643–660 (2019)
22. Dingel, J.: Systematic parallel programming. Ph.D. thesis, Carnegie Mellon University (2000). cMU-CS-99-172
23. Dinsdale-Young, T., Birkedal, L., Gardner, P., Parkinson, M., Yang, H.: Views: compositional reasoning for concurrent programs. In: Proceedings of the 40th Annual ACM SIGPLAN-SIGACT Symposium on Principles of Programming Languages, pp. 287–300. ACM (2013)
24. Distefano, D., Fähndrich, M., Logozzo, F., O'Hearn, P.W.: Scaling static analyses at Facebook. CACM **62**(8), 62–70 (2019)
25. Dodds, M., Feng, X., Parkinson, M., Vafeiadis, V.: Deny-guarantee reasoning. In: Castagna, G. (ed.) ESOP 2009. LNCS, vol. 5502, pp. 363–377. Springer, Heidelberg (2009). https://doi.org/10.1007/978-3-642-00590-9_26
26. Feng, X.: Local rely-guarantee reasoning. In: Proceedings of the 36th Annual ACM SIGPLAN-SIGACT Symposium on Principles of Programming Languages, POPL 2009, New York, NY, USA, pp. 315–327. ACM (2009). https://doi.org/10.1145/1480881.1480922
27. Feng, X., Ferreira, R., Shao, Z.: On the relationship between concurrent separation logic and assume-guarantee reasoning. In: De Nicola, R. (ed.) ESOP 2007. LNCS, vol. 4421, pp. 173–188. Springer, Heidelberg (2007). https://doi.org/10.1007/978-3-540-71316-6_13
28. Fisher, M.: An Introduction to Practical Formal Methods Using Temporal Logic. Wiley, Chichester (2011)
29. Floyd, R.W.: Assigning meanings to programs. In: Proceedings of Symposium in Applied Mathematics. Mathematical Aspects of Computer Science, vol. 19, pp. 19–32. American Mathematical Society (1967)
30. Goldstine, H.H., von Neumann, J.: Planning and coding of problems for an electronic computing instrument. Technical report, Institute of Advanced Studies, Princeton (1947)
31. de Gouw, S., Rot, J.: Effectively eliminating auxiliaries. In: Ábrahám, E., Bonsangue, M., Johnsen, E.B. (eds.) Theory and Practice of Formal Methods. LNCS, vol. 9660, pp. 226–241. Springer, Cham (2016). https://doi.org/10.1007/978-3-319-30734-3_16
32. Hayes, I.J., Jones, C.B.: A guide to rely/guarantee thinking. In: Bowen, J.P., Liu, Z., Zhang, Z. (eds.) SETSS 2017. LNCS, vol. 11174, pp. 1–38. Springer, Cham (2018). https://doi.org/10.1007/978-3-030-02928-9_1
33. Hoare, C.A.R.: An axiomatic basis for computer programming. Commun. ACM **12**(10), 576–580 (1969)
34. Hoare, C.A.R.: Procedures and parameters: an axiomatic approach. In: Engeler, E. (ed.) Symposium on Semantics of Algorithmic Languages. LNM, vol. 188, pp. 102–116. Springer, Heidelberg (1971). https://doi.org/10.1007/BFb0059696
35. Hoare, C.A.R.: Proof of a program: FIND. Commun. ACM **14**(1), 39–45 (1971). https://doi.org/10.1145/362452.362489

36. Hoare, C.A.R.: Communicating sequential processes. Commun. ACM **21**, 666–677 (1978)
37. Hoare, C.A.R.: Communicating Sequential Processes. Prentice-Hall, Upper Saddle River (1985)
38. Hoare, C.A.R., Lauer, P.E.: Consistent and complementary formal theories of the semantics of programming languages. Acta Informatica **3**(2), 135–153 (1974). https://doi.org/10.1007/BF00264034
39. Hoare, C.A.R.: Towards a theory of parallel programming. In: Hansen, P.B. (ed.) The Origin of Concurrent Programming, pp. 231–244. Springer, New York (1972). https://doi.org/10.1007/978-1-4757-3472-0_6
40. Jones, C.B.: Formal development of correct algorithms: an example based on Earley's recogniser. SIGPLAN Notices **7**(1), 150–169 (1972)
41. Jones, C.B.: Operations and formal development. Technical report TN 9004, IBM Laboratory, Hursley, September 1972
42. Jones, C.B.: Software Development: A Rigorous Approach. Prentice Hall International, Englewood Cliffs (1980). http://portal.acm.org/citation.cfm?id=539771
43. Jones, C.B.: Development methods for computer programs including a notion of interference. Ph.D. thesis, Oxford University, June 1981. Printed as: Programming Research Group, Technical Monograph 25
44. Jones, C.B.: Specification and design of (parallel) programs. In: Proceedings of IFIP 1983, North-Holland, pp. 321–332 (1983)
45. Jones, C.B.: Tentative steps toward a development method for interfering programs. Trans. Program. Lang. Syst. **5**(4), 596–619 (1983). https://doi.org/10.1145/69575.69577. https://doi.acm.org/10.1145/69575.69577
46. Jones, C.B.: Accommodating interference in the formal design of concurrent object-based programs. Formal Methods Syst. Des. **8**(2), 105–122 (1996). https://doi.org/10.1007/BF00122417
47. Jones, C.B.: Splitting atoms safely. Theoret. Comput. Sci. **375**(1–3), 109–119 (2007). https://doi.org/10.1016/j.tcs.2006.12.029
48. Jones, C.B., Lomet, D., Romanovsky, A., Weikum, G.: The atomic manifesto. J. Univ. Comput. Sci. **11**(5), 636–650 (2005). https://doi.org/10.3217/jucs-011-05-0636. http://www.jucs.org/jucs_11_5/the_atomic_manifesto
49. Jones, C.B.: The early search for tractable ways of reasoning about programs. IEEE Ann. Hist. Comput. **25**(2), 26–49 (2003). https://doi.org/10.1109/MAHC.2003.1203057. https://doi.ieeecomputer.society.org/10.1109/MAHC.2003.1203057
50. Jones, C.B., Astarte, T.K.: An Exegesis of four formal descriptions of ALGOL 60. Technical report CS-TR-1498, Newcastle University School of Computer Science, September 2016
51. Jones, C.B., Hayes, I.J.: Possible values: exploring a concept for concurrency. J. Log. Algebr. Methods Program. (2016). https://doi.org/10.1016/j.jlamp.2016.01.002
52. Jones, C.B., Pierce, K.G.: Splitting atoms with rely/guarantee conditions coupled with data reification. In: Börger, E., Butler, M., Bowen, J.P., Boca, P. (eds.) ABZ 2008. LNCS, vol. 5238, pp. 360–377. Springer, Heidelberg (2008). https://doi.org/10.1007/978-3-540-87603-8_47. http://www.springerlink.com/content/d63746175654u503/fulltext.pdf
53. Jones, C.B., Pierce, K.G.: Elucidating concurrent algorithms via layers of abstraction and reification. Formal Aspects Comput. **23**(3), 289–306 (2011). https://doi.org/10.1007/s00165-010-0156-1. http://www.springerlink.com/content/e52509k41r31g880/

54. Jones, C.B., Yatapanage, N.: Reasoning about separation using abstraction and reification. In: Calinescu, R., Rumpe, B. (eds.) SEFM 2015. LNCS, vol. 9276, pp. 3–19. Springer, Cham (2015). https://doi.org/10.1007/978-3-319-22969-0_1

55. Jones, C.B., Yatapanage, N.: Investigating the limits of rely/guarantee relations based on a concurrent garbage collector example. Formal Aspects Comput. **31**(3), 353–374 (2019). https://doi.org/10.1007/s00165-019-00482-3. Online April 2018

56. Lahav, O., Vafeiadis, V.: Owicki-Gries reasoning for weak memory models. In: Halldórsson, M.M., Iwama, K., Kobayashi, N., Speckmann, B. (eds.) ICALP 2015. LNCS, vol. 9135, pp. 311–323. Springer, Heidelberg (2015). https://doi.org/10.1007/978-3-662-47666-6_25

57. Lamport, L.: Specifying Systems: The TLA+ Language and Tools for Hardware and Software Engineers. Addison-Wesley Longman Publishing Co., Inc., Boston (2002)

58. Liang, H.: Refinement verification of concurrent programs and its applications. Ph.D. thesis, USTC, China (2014)

59. Lucas, P., Walk, K.: On the formal description of PL/I. Ann. Rev. Autom. Program. **6**, 105–182 (1969)

60. Magee, J., Kramer, J.: State Models and Java Programs. Wiley, Hoboken (1999)

61. Manna, Z., Pnueli, A.: Temporal Logic of Reactive Systems. Springer, New York (1991). https://doi.org/10.1007/978-1-4612-0931-7

62. Manna, Z., Pnueli, A.: Temporal Verification of Reactive Systems. Springer, New York (1995). https://doi.org/10.1007/978-1-4612-4222-2

63. Manna, Z.: The correctness of nondeterministic programs. Artif. Intell. **1**(1–2), 1–26 (1970)

64. Middelburg, C.A.: Syntax and semantics of VVSL: a language for structured VDM specifications. Ph.D. thesis, PTT Research, Leidschendam, Department of Applied Computer Science, September 1990

65. Milner, R., Parrow, J., Walker, D.: A calculus of mobile processes. Inf. Comput. **100**, 1–77 (1992)

66. Milner, R.: Communication and Concurrency. Prentice Hall, Upper Saddle Rive (1989)

67. Morgan, C.: Programming from Specifications. Prentice-Hall, Upper Saddle River (1990)

68. Moszkowski, B.: Executing temporal logic programs. In: Brookes, S.D., Roscoe, A.W., Winskel, G. (eds.) CONCURRENCY 1984. LNCS, vol. 197, pp. 111–130. Springer, Heidelberg (1985). https://doi.org/10.1007/3-540-15670-4_6

69. Naur, P.: Proof of algorithms by general snapshots. BIT Numer. Math. **6**(4), 310–316 (1966)

70. O'Hearn, P.W.: Resources, concurrency and local reasoning. Theoret. Comput. Sci. **375**(1–3), 271–307 (2007)

71. Olderog, E.R.: Nets, Terms and Formulas: Three Views of Concurrent Processes and Their Relationship, vol. 23. Cambridge University Press, Cambridge (2005)

72. Owicki, S.S.: Axiomatic proof techniques for parallel programs. Ph.D. thesis, Department of Computer Science, Cornell University (1975). Published as technical report 75–251

73. Owicki, S.S., Gries, D.: An axiomatic proof technique for parallel programs I. Acta Informatica **6**, 319–340 (1976)

74. Parkinson, M.: The next 700 separation logics. In: Leavens, G.T., O'Hearn, P., Rajamani, S.K. (eds.) VSTTE 2010. LNCS, vol. 6217, pp. 169–182. Springer, Heidelberg (2010). https://doi.org/10.1007/978-3-642-15057-9_12

75. Pierce, K.: Enhancing the useability of rely-guaranteee conditions for atomicity refinement. Ph.D. thesis, Newcastle University (2009)
76. Prensa Nieto, L.: Verification of parallel programs with the Owicki-Gries and rely-guarantee methods in Isabelle/HOL. Ph.D. thesis, Institut für Informatic der Technischen Universität München (2001)
77. Reisig, W.: Petri Nets: An Introduction, vol. 4. Springer, Heidelberg (2012). https://doi.org/10.1007/978-3-642-69968-9
78. Reisig, W.: Understanding Petri Nets: Modeling Techniques, Analysis Methods, Case Studies. Springer, Heidelberg (2013). https://doi.org/10.1007/978-3-642-33278-4
79. Reynolds, J.C.: Separation logic: a logic for shared mutable data structures. In: Proceedings of 17th LICS, pp. 55–74. IEEE (2002)
80. de Roever, W.P., Engelhardt, K.: Data Refinement: Model-Oriented Proof Methods and Their Comparison. Cambridge University Press, Cambridge (1999)
81. Sangiorgi, D., Walker, D.: The π-calculus: A Theory of Mobile Processes. Cambridge University Press, Cambridge (2001)
82. Schellhorn, G., Tofan, B., Ernst, G., Pfähler, J., Reif, W.: RGITL: a temporal logic framework for compositional reasoning about interleaved programs. Ann. Math. Artif. Intell. **71**(1–3), 131–174 (2014)
83. Schneider, F.B.: On Concurrent Programming. Springer, New York (1997). https://doi.org/10.1007/978-1-4612-1830-2
84. Steel, T.B.: Formal Language Description Languages for Computer Programming. North-Holland, Vienna (1966)
85. Stølen, K.: Development of parallel programs on shared data-structures. Ph.D. thesis, Manchester University (1990). Published as technical report UMCS-91-1-1
86. Turing, A.M.: Checking a large routine. In: Report of a Conference on High Speed Automatic Calculating Machines, pp. 67–69. University Mathematical Laboratory, Cambridge, June 1949
87. Vafeiadis, V.: Modular fine-grained concurrency verification. Ph.D. thesis, University of Cambridge (2007)
88. Vafeiadis, V., Parkinson, M.: A marriage of rely/guarantee and separation logic. In: Caires, L., Vasconcelos, V.T. (eds.) CONCUR 2007. LNCS, vol. 4703, pp. 256–271. Springer, Heidelberg (2007). https://doi.org/10.1007/978-3-540-74407-8_18
89. van Wijngaarden, A.: Numerical analysis as an independent science. BIT Numer. Math. **6**(1), 66–81 (1966)
90. Windsor, M.: Starling: a framework for automated concurrency verification. Ph.D. thesis, University of York (2019)
91. Xu, Q.: A theory of state-based parallel programming. Ph.D. thesis, Oxford University (1992)

Specification with Class: A Brief History of Object-Z

Graeme Smith[1]([⊠]) and David J. Duke[2]

[1] School of Information Technology and Electrical Engineering,
The University of Queensland, Brisbane, Australia
smith@itee.uq.edu.au
[2] School of Computing, University of Leeds, Leeds, UK
duke.j.david@gmail.com

Abstract. The end of the 1980s saw a growing interest in object orientation as both a design and programming methodology with the advent of programming languages like C++ and Eiffel. The trend was taken up by some in the formal methods community, including a team of researchers in Australia. Their contribution was a formal specification language, Object-Z, which had immediate industrial impact, gained rapid international recognition, and then two decades later began to fade, along with some of its contemporaries, from the formal methods scene. This paper details the rise and fall of Object-Z from the perspective of two of its original developers.

1 Introduction

The formal specification language Object-Z [20,30,34,78] grew from an alliance of two trends in computer science in the late 1980s. The first was an increasing interest in *model-oriented* formal specification languages as a means to specify important properties, resolve ambiguities and detect design errors early in system development. Unlike algebraic languages such as Clear [18] and OBJ [38], model-oriented languages provided explicit models of systems. This tended to result in specifications which were easier to read and understand; particularly as the languages built on the standard mathematics of set theory and predicate logic that were part of the vocabulary of most programmers. Some of these languages were *state-based*, including an explicit state as part of the model; notable examples include VDM [54], Z [83] and B [1]. Others were *event-based*, describing transitions, or events, without explicit reference to a state; in particular the process algebras CSP [46], CCS [68] and ACP [11]. While this interest mainly arose in academia, some industry sectors also followed the trend. In particular, the state-based languages SDL [10] and Estelle [49], and the event-based language LOTOS [14], were standardised for use in the telecommunications industry; an industry grappling at the time with the increasing sophistication of its protocols and services.

© Springer Nature Switzerland AG 2020
E. Sekerinski et al. (Eds.): FM 2019 Workshops, LNCS 12233, pp. 73–86, 2020.
https://doi.org/10.1007/978-3-030-54997-8_4

The second trend was the rise of object orientation as a dominant programming paradigm. Object orientation originated in the 1960s with the programming language Simula 67 [12], but re-emerged in the programming language community in the 1980s following the advent of Smalltalk-80 [39]. Several object-oriented languages were developed including the C extensions, C++ [86] and Objective-C [21], and the Lisp extensions, LOOPS [13] and Flavors [19]. There were also new languages developed following the object-oriented paradigm including FOOPS [37], POOL [6] and Eiffel [66]. This trend was driven by the need to be able to handle complexity in large-scale software systems: object orientation offered a modular approach to programming where components, i.e., classes, could be understood in isolation and reused to build other classes, and systems understood in terms of interactions between instances of classes, i.e., objects.

Scalability was also a major concern for the formal methods community in the late 1980s. While there had been some industrial success stories, such as the formalisation of parts of IBM CICS in Z [43], the inability to cope with the complexities of large-scale systems was recognised as a barrier to wider adoption of formal methods: the VDM community, for example, explored modules [9], as did the RAISE project [70]. Hence, a natural response to the aforementioned trends was the incorporation of object orientation in model-oriented specification languages. This was led by those working with the standardised languages of the telecommunications industry. An object-oriented approach to specification in SDL was published in 1987 [69], and object-oriented approaches for Estelle and LOTOS in 1988 [63, 75]. The LOTOS approach showed that process algebras offered an intuitive model of the behaviour of objects, and object-oriented notions such as subtyping could be captured using the extension relation defined for LOTOS by Brinksma et al. [16].

At the same time as these developments, Stephen Schuman and David Pitt of the University of Surrey developed a specification language that captured a more intuitive notion of a class by more directly capturing the structure of a class in an object-oriented programming language [74]. Their language was a variant of Z in which classes are specified by a single state schema and an associated set of operation schemas related to the state schema by their headers: the header of each operation schema was prefixed by the state schema's name. This relationship meant that there was no need to explicitly include the state schema's variables in both a pre- and post-state form in each operation, as is done in Z. Semantically, a class was represented by a set of operation histories. This oft-overlooked work was a precursor of things to come.

This paper recounts the rise and fall of Object-Z from the point of view of two of its original developers. It reflects on factors that led to its initial success, and what later caused its loss in popularity. We begin in Sect. 2 by describing the setting in which Object-Z was conceived, a collaboration between the University of Queensland and the Overseas Telecommunication Commission of Australia. In Sect. 3, we detail the initial development of Object-Z, along with the initial successes in both academia and industry. In Sect. 4, we step back and look at the intentional context in which the research was done. We discuss Object-Z's relative success, and reflect on the factors that led to this. In Sect. 5, we examine how Object-Z adapted to meet additional challenges, and to contribute to a change in focus of the international research community. We also conjecture that a further change of focus, to which Object-Z was unable to adapt, ultimately led to it being left behind. Communities of practice are groups of people involved in the development of a particular body of knowledge. In Sect. 6, we use this concept to compare Object-Z with the similar, but more popular, notations Z and B. In Sect. 7, we conclude with a brief summary of Object-Z's contributions to the formal methods discipline.

2   A Suggestion from Industry

The Z notation, on which Object-Z was based, was developed by the Programming Research Group at the Oxford University Computing Laboratory from initial ideas of Jean-Raymond Abrial [3]. One of those involved in the work, driving Z's application to CICS and editing the first book on Z [45], was the Australian computer scientist Ian Hayes. Hayes returned to Australia in 1985 joining the Department of Computer Science at the University of Queensland (UQ), primarily to work with Gordon Rose who had become interested in Z while visiting Oxford on sabbatical the previous year. In 1986, Rose and Hayes set up a collaboration with the Overseas Telecommunications Commission (later Corporation) of Australia (OTC) to improve the state of the art in the use of formal methods in the telecommunications industry. The focus of their work was on using Z. Roger Duke, a National Research Fellow at UQ, joined the collaboration, later taking on a leading role.

The funding from OTC supported two PhD students, Paul King (commencing in 1987) and Anthony Lee (commencing in 1988), and a research assistant, Graeme Smith (commencing in 1988). The initial task was to compare the standardised languages, SDL, Estelle, and LOTOS, with other formalisms. As part of this work, various communications protocols and services were specified using Z [29,31,44,72,76]. This work was well-accepted by OTC, who agreed that Z was suitable for specifying communications systems. The second task, beginning in mid-1988, was to apply Z to a full-scale industrial design provided by OTC. The chosen system was a fault-tolerant communications processor (FTCP) being implemented by OTC as a basis for more flexible and reliable telecommunications services. The system comprised a number of network-layer processors connected to a shared memory which provided fault-tolerant storage, in case one of the processors went down, as well as mutual exclusion and synchronisation for the processors. In particular, the system ran a custom cache coherence protocol, a scaled-down version of which is specified in [80].

Smith took on the role of producing a Z specification from OTC's design documents which were mostly in English with accompanying tables and diagrams, and comprised both high-level functional detail, e.g., invariant properties of the shared memory, and low-level implementation detail, such as bit allocation.

To resolve ambiguities and avoid misunderstandings required an extended visit to OTC (which was in Sydney, over 900 km from UQ), followed by email communication and occasional face-to-face meetings with OTC software engineers. There were no particular technical problems in producing the specification, but even at a high-level of abstraction, the specification started getting large – 37 schemas – and the size was growing considerably as more details of the design were added. The OTC engineers were finding the specification, which was considerably larger than those they had been previously presented with, difficult to navigate and understand. This issue was discussed during a visit by Rose to OTC in late 1988. One of the engineers familiar with C++, the language they were using to implement the FTCP, asked why the Z specification could not be structured like a C++ program. This comment, from a software engineer at OTC, was the seed from which Object-Z was to grow.

3   First Steps

When Rose returned to UQ following the OTC visit, he gathered Smith and Duke in front of a whiteboard and presented his idea for adding a notion of a class to Z: a large Z-like schema in which a state, initial state and several operation schemas were nested. That afternoon, Smith applied the idea to a simple case study, the alternating bit protocol, which he and Duke had previously specified in Z [35]. Specifying the classes for the protocol was straightforward; there was a transmitter, a receiver and two lossy channels, one for messages and one for acknowledgements. The challenge was how to combine the classes to specify the system. Being more familiar with LOTOS than object orientation at the time, Smith specified a system class in which operations of the various component classes were combined using LOTOS's parallel operator.

The conflation of classes and processes in this first specification was one to which Smith, along with other members of the international research community, would return almost a decade later (see Sect. 5). For the immediate needs of OTC, however, a more object-oriented approach was required. The programming languages C++ and Eiffel were examined for inspiration, and it was Bertrand Meyer's excellent book, *Object-Oriented Software Construction* [66], which became the main reference for further development of the notation into Object-Z.

This development occurred over the following year with help from two newcomers: David Carrington joined the group after taking on an academic position at UQ, and Duke took on a PhD student David Duke (no relation) to develop a semantics for the new notation. After the name OZ – a colloquialism for Australia which also appeared in the domain of Australian email addresses at the time – was rejected as not being serious enough, the name Object-Z was adopted. Work progressed in parallel on the syntax, the semantics and the application of the new notation to the FTCP. The close link with the requirements of the OTC engineers encouraged a conservative approach to language design. Throughout Object-Z's design, the team at UQ were keen to relate specification constructs to the emerging practice of object-oriented programming, leading to extensive agonising over (then) topical issues such as co- vs contra-variance in subtyping (see, for example, the work of Roger Duke's PhD student Cecily Bailes [7]), and how best to support multiple inheritance. This concentrated effort resulted in a number of rapid successes.

Papers on Object-Z were published in two major international conferences on formal methods (their presentation aided by the new LaTeX style file, oz.sty, developed by Paul King [58]). The first paper on Object-Z was published in FORTE '89 [20]. This paper introduced the new specification language using case studies to illustrate object instantiation, inheritance and polymorphism. Roger Duke presented the paper in Vancouver in December, 1989. This was followed by a paper on a history semantics of classes for Object-Z in VDM '90 [28].[1] This paper built on the Z semantics in J.M. Spivey's *Understanding Z* [82]. It was presented by David Duke in Kiel in April, 1990.

As well as these academic successes, Object-Z was also well received by the engineers at OTC [33]. When the specification of the FTCP was completed, Roger Duke and Smith attempted a proof of cache coherence which was regarded as the critical property for reliable, fault-tolerant behaviour. A proof carried out over several days on the whiteboard in Roger Duke's office revealed three errors in the cache coherence protocol developed by OTC. Without the Object-Z specification and proof, these errors would not have been discovered until much later in the development, if at all. This validation of the effectiveness of Object-Z led OTC to continue using it internally on other projects [73]. OTC also continued to fund UQ's research on Object-Z, in the form of a PhD scholarship for Smith, until 1992 when the Australian government decided to merge it with Telecom Australia, and OTC ceased to exist.

4 Riding the Wave

Object-Z's publication in 1989 turned out to be very timely. Four other approaches to object-oriented formal specification based on Z were published in 1990 – three in the 1990 Z User's Meeting [59,65,88] and one in VDM '90 [42] – and two more the following year in ECOOP '91 [4,22]. A good survey of the object-oriented varieties of Z from this time was provided by Susan Stepney, Rosalind Barden and David Cooper [84], a summary of which appears in [85]. Another was provided by Kevin Lano and Howard Haughton [60].

Of all these approaches, however, it was Object-Z that grew most in popularity over the next decade. There was interest from individuals in Bellcore and Motorola in the United States where it was used internally on projects, it was considered for use in the ODP (Open Distributed Processing) standard, and endorsed for use in the PREMO (Presentation Environment for Multimedia Objects) standard in 1994 [27]. There was also much interest from universities and research institutes worldwide where it was used in both teaching and

---

[1] The VDM series of conferences, of which VDM '90 was a part, transformed into the FME series (in 1993) and later (in 2005) the current FM conference series.

research. By the year 2000, two books on Object-Z were published. Smith, who had become the default contact for questions about Object-Z, decided a language definition was needed and produced *The Object-Z Specification Language* [78] modelled on J.M. Spivey's *The Z Notation* [83]. Roger Duke and Rose, who had been teaching Object-Z at UQ for almost a decade, produced a textbook based on their teaching material entitled *Formal Object-Oriented Specification using Object-Z* [32]. These books were followed in 2001 by a book by John Derrick and Eerke Boiten of the University of Kent at Canterbury, *Refinement in Z and Object-Z* [23], covering their research on refinement for Object-Z; research done independently of its original developers.

We can only speculate about what pushed Object-Z ahead of its peers. One possibility is that, designed to suit industry needs, Object-Z was a practical language which was easy to use and understand. The notion of an explicit class construct, Rose's original idea, was to aid OTC's software engineers who had trouble navigating pages of Z schemas. Other approaches to object-oriented Z did not have such an explicit notion of class. For example, Hall [42] presented conventions for using standard Z in an object-oriented style, and Schumann and Pitt [74], as mentioned in Sect. 1, only approximated the notion of a class with naming conventions. Whysall and McDermid [88], on the other hand, explicitly represented classes by accompanying a Z specification with an algebraic specification of the class's behaviour. This was aimed, however, at aiding the process of refinement rather than readability. While their approach achieved this aim, the overall specifications were arguably more complex to read and understand.

Another reason may be that it remained syntactically and semantically close to the well-accepted Z language on which it was based. Lano's Z++ [59], for example, adopted a more ASCII-based syntax. Also, Schuman and Pitt [74] adopted a notion of *historical inference* which meant each operation made the minimal change allowed by its specification. This semantic difference to Z, removed the ability to use nondeterminism for abstraction.

These reasons suggest that Object-Z's relative success reflected modest ambition – this may well be true. The UQ team did not set out to provide a formal foundation for object-oriented development, but to take ideas that were found useful in one setting and ask whether, and how, they could be reconstructed in a different setting. A final reason may simply have been that the language was kept alive by continuing research (see Sect. 5). This was not the case for the approaches of Hall, Schuman and Pitt, and Whysall and McDermid, nor for those of Cusack [22] and Alencar and Goguen [4]. While research did continue on Z++ and Meira and Cavalcanti's MooZ [65], it was not to the same extent as that on Object-Z which, at the end of 1992, was about to undergo a major transformation.

5   Changing Times

One of the original aims of Object-Z was to facilitate the refinement of formal specifications into object-oriented programs. Towards the end of 1992, Rose and

Roger Duke decided that it was time to face this challenge. Their idea was to give Object-Z a reference semantics. Until that time, Object-Z had a value semantics in which classes were denoted by a set of values; each value representing an object at some stage of its evolution. The reference semantics would instead denote Object-Z classes by a set of references, or pointers, to values representing its objects. Semantically, this would be a major departure from Z. It would allow *object aliasing*, where more than one variable could reference (and hence share) a given object. It would allow an operation of an object to change, not just its own state, but that of a referenced object. Ultimately, however, it would enable specifications to be directly mapped to object-oriented programs.

Smith, who had just completed his PhD, argued that this would hinder the abstract specification of systems and hence unnecessarily complicate reasoning and refinement. Weekly meetings at UQ became animated as arguments for and against a reference semantics were vigorously discussed.

At the beginning of 1993, Smith left UQ for a post-doctoral position in Europe. During a workshop at ECOOP '93 in Kaiserslautern, he discussed the issue with Alan Wills who had developed an object-oriented version of VDM called Fresco [89]. Together they decided that it would be desirable to refine from a value-based specification to a reference-based one, which could then be further refined to object-oriented code. However, almost ten years passed before Smith eventually published this idea [79].

Meanwhile at UQ, Rose worked with a research assistant, Wendy Johnston, on manually converting Object-Z to C++ [53], and took on a final-year undergraduate student, Alena Griffiths, to develop a reference semantics for Object-Z. Griffiths, continued this work in her PhD [41] which she began in 1994, and additionally investigated refinement between Object-Z and Eiffel [40]. Another PhD student, Jin Song Dong, who was supervised by Roger Duke, used Griffith's semantics to add self and mutually recursive operations and classes to Object-Z [25]. Dong's work, which also included a mechanism called *containment* for explicitly restricting object aliasing [26], constituted the final changes to be made to the language.

By the late 1990s, the formal methods community's focus on specification languages was being replaced by a focus on language integration – combining different specification languages to exploit the strengths of each in a single specification. Notable research in this direction included Helen Treharne and Steve Schneider's work on CSP∥B [87], and Tony Hoare and He Jifeng's *Unifying Theories of Programming* [48], which was the basis of Jim Woodcock's and Ana Cavalcanti's work on the Circus specification language [90].

Object-Z was particularly suited to the trend. In 1996 and 1997, Smith worked at the Technical University of Berlin on an integration of Object-Z and CSP [77] – returning to the idea that a class could be viewed like a process to integrate the languages semantically. At the same time, 400 km away in Oldenburg, Clemens Fischer was developing his own integration of Object-Z and CSP, CSP-OZ [36]. Another 700 km away, across the English channel in Canterbury, John Derrick, Eerke Boiten and others were looking at how to integrate

Object-Z and LOTOS [24]. At the 1st International Conference on Integrated Formal Methods (IFM '99) held in York in 1999, six out of the 22 accepted papers used Object-Z. Work on these and other integrations, including several with UML [5,56,57,67,71], fuelled research on Object-Z over the next five years. Then the formal methods community's focus was replaced by another one to which Object-Z was less suited.

In the early 2000s, tool support for analysis of formal specifications became increasingly important. While it had always been considered a necessity for the wider adoption of formal methods, advances in technology meant that it could no longer be ignored. This was perhaps underlined by Tony Hoare's Verifying Compiler Grand Challenge in 2003 [47]. At that time, tool support for Object-Z was minimal; essentially just a type checker developed by Wendy Johnston called Wizard [52].

In response to this new direction, Smith investigated encoding Object-Z in both the CSP model checker FDR [55] and the theorem prover Isabelle/HOL [81]. However, these approaches could not compete with new developments for highly automated static verification of object-oriented programs using specification languages like JML [17] and Spec# [8], which were directly embedded in code. By 2007, when Smith's PhD student, Tim McComb, completed his thesis on refactoring Object-Z specifications [64], active research on the language had effectively ceased.

6   Communities of Practice

A community of practice (CoP) is a collection of people developing a body of knowledge for a particular professional domain. The concept first appeared in a book by cognitive anthropologist Jean Lave and educational theorist Etienne Wenger in 1991 [61]. A CoP can be seen as moving through five stages as it develops:

1. Potential – a common interest is shared among a group of individuals
2. Coalescing – the group establishes goals based on an understanding of existing knowledge in the field
3. Maturing – the initial goals are realised, the group's context is widened, and a body of knowledge (BoK) is created
4. Stewardship – the group's momentum is maintained, and the knowledge it is developing is kept relevant and up-to-date
5. Transformation – the group takes on a new form, or comes to the end of its useful lifetime

The CoP concept has been used to discuss the evolution of Z [15]. It is interesting to use it to compare Object-Z with other specification languages of the time. Table 1 shows the stage of evolution reached by Object-Z and its contemporary languages Z and B.

Object-Z arose from a shared interest between researchers at UQ and software engineers at OTC in exploring the marriage of object orientation and formal

Table 1. CoP evolution for Object-Z, Z and B

	Object-Z	Z	B
Potential	Yes	Yes	Yes
Coalescing	Yes	Yes	Yes
Maturing	Yes	Yes	Yes
Stewardship	No	Yes	Yes
Transformation	No	No	Yes

specification. After the initial language was defined and applied in industry, it developed further and eventually became useful for integrating different specification paradigms (state-based, event-based, and diagrammatic techniques like UML). The books on Object-Z constituted its body of knowledge. Hence, we see Object-Z's CoP as having reached the "Maturing" stage. However, interest in Object-Z was not maintained once it reached this level of maturity, mainly (as mentioned in Sect. 5) due to its lack of tool support for analysis.

In contrast, interest in Z was maintained after it reached maturity in the late 1980s by the Z User Group, formed in 1992, which ran regular conferences, and the Z Standardisation Committee which developed an ISO standard for the language [50]. Hence, its CoP reached the "Stewardship" stage. However, like Object-Z there was a distinct drop in interest in Z in the early 2000s. This can again be linked to a lack of tools for analysis. Andrew Martin of Oxford University started a Community Z Tools initiative in 2001, but the resulting effort, led largely by Mark Utting of the University of Waikato, did not extend far beyond syntax and type checking [62]. Both Z and Object-Z were designed to be expressive languages, to help users write specifications which were easy to read and understand. Part of the price of such expressiveness was that it was difficult to develop sophisticated analysis tools for them. Furthermore, many of those involved in the development of both languages were theoreticians who were less inclined to work on support tools.

B, on the other hand, was a language that was designed from the start with tool support in mind. It also underwent a major transformation in the early 2000s into Event-B [2] (its CoP reaching the "Transformation" stage). This spurred a new wave of research on both language issues and tools, and has seen Event-B, and B, maintain their relevance to this day.

7   Conclusion

Although interest in Z has waned since the start of the century, this does not negate its impact and importance. The exploration of state-based specification carried out by research on the language played a major influence on current tool-supported specification languages such as Alloy [51] and Event-B (through B). Similarly, Object-Z has had some influence: for example, Daniel Jackson, the developer of Alloy, consulted Graeme Smith when developing its object-oriented features. Object-Z also allowed us, the formal methods community, to examine and gain a better understanding of the relationship between formal specification and object-oriented programming, between state-based and event-based specification paradigms, and between formal and diagrammatic techniques for communicating and understanding object-oriented designs. But being a language, like Z, designed for expressiveness rather than tool support, it has since accepted its place in the history of formal methods and politely stepped back to make way for the next generation of formal techniques.

References

1. Abrial, J.R.: The B-Book: Assigning Programs to Meanings. Cambridge University Press, New York (1996)
2. Abrial, J.R.: Modeling in Event-B: System and Software Engineering. Cambridge University Press, New York (2010)
3. Abrial, J.R., Schuman, S., Meyer, B.: Specification language. In: McKeag, R., Macnaghten, A. (eds.) On the Construction of Programs: An Advanced Course. Cambridge University Press, New York (1980)
4. Alencar, A.J., Goguen, J.A.: OOZE: an object oriented Z environment. In: America, P. (ed.) ECOOP 1991. LNCS, vol. 512, pp. 180–199. Springer, Heidelberg (1991). https://doi.org/10.1007/BFb0057022
5. Amálio, N., Polack, F.: Comparison of formalisation approaches of UML class constructs in Z and Object-Z. In: Bert, D., Bowen, J.P., King, S., Waldén, M. (eds.) ZB 2003. LNCS, vol. 2651, pp. 339–358. Springer, Heidelberg (2003). https://doi.org/10.1007/3-540-44880-2_21
6. America, P.: Issues in the design of a parallel object-oriented language. Formal Aspects Comput. 1(4), 366–411 (1989)
7. Bailes, C., Duke, R.: The ecology of class refinement. In: Morris, J.M., Shaw, R.C. (eds.) 4th Refinement Workshop, pp. 185–196. Springer, London (1991). https://doi.org/10.1007/978-1-4471-3756-6_10
8. Barnett, M., Leino, K.R.M., Schulte, W.: The Spec# programming system: an overview. In: Barthe, G., Burdy, L., Huisman, M., Lanet, J.-L., Muntean, T. (eds.) CASSIS 2004. LNCS, vol. 3362, pp. 49–69. Springer, Heidelberg (2005). https://doi.org/10.1007/978-3-540-30569-9_3
9. Bear, S.: Structuring for the VDM specification language. In: Bloomfield, R.E., Marshall, L.S., Jones, R.B. (eds.) VDM 1988. LNCS, vol. 328, pp. 2–25. Springer, Heidelberg (1988). https://doi.org/10.1007/3-540-50214-9_2
10. Belina, F., Hogrefe, D.: The CCITT-specification and description language SDL. Comput. Netw. ISDN Syst. 16(4), 311–341 (1989)
11. Bergstra, J., Klop, J.: Process algebra for synchronous communication. Inf. Control 60, 109–137 (1984)
12. Birtwistle, G., Dahl, O.J., Myhrhaug, B., Nygaard, K.: Simula Begin. Auerbach, Philadelphia (1973)
13. Bobrow, D., Stefik, M.: LOOPS: an Object-Oriented Programming System for Interlisp. Technical report, Xerox PARC (1982)
14. Bolognesi, T., Brinksma, E.: Introduction to the ISO specification language LOTOS. Comput. Netw. ISDN Syst. 14, 25–59 (1987)

15. Bowen, J.P., Reeves, S.: From a community of practice to a body of knowledge: a case study of the formal methods community. In: Butler, M., Schulte, W. (eds.) FM 2011. LNCS, vol. 6664, pp. 308–322. Springer, Heidelberg (2011). https://doi.org/10.1007/978-3-642-21437-0_24
16. Brinksma, E., Scollo, G., Steenbergen, C.: LOTOS specifications, their implementations and their tests. In: Sarikaya, B., von Bochmann, G. (eds.) Protocol Specification, Testing, and Verification, VI. North-Holland (1987)
17. Burdy, L., et al.: An overview of JML tools and applications. Int. J. Softw. Tools Technol. Transf. (STTT) **7**(3), 212–232 (2005)
18. Burstall, R., Goguen, J.: An informal introduction to specifications using Clear. In: Boyer, R., Moore, J. (eds.) The Correctness Problem in Computer Science, chap. 4. International Lecture Series in Computer Science. Academic Press (1981)
19. Cannon, H.: Flavors. Technical report, MIT Artificial Intelligence Laboratory (1980)
20. Carrington, D., et al.: Object-Z: an object-oriented extension to Z. In: Vuong, S. (ed.) Formal Description Techniques, II (FORTE 1989), pp. 281–296. North-Holland (1989)
21. Cox, B.: Object-Oriented Programming: An Evolutionary Approach. Addison-Wesley, Reading (1986)
22. Cusack, E.: Inheritance in object oriented Z. In: America, P. (ed.) ECOOP 1991. LNCS, vol. 512, pp. 167–179. Springer, Heidelberg (1991). https://doi.org/10.1007/BFb0057021
23. Derrick, J., Boiten, E.: Refinement in Z and Object-Z. Foundations and Advanced Applications. Springer, London (2001)
24. Derrick, J., Boiten, E., Bowman, H., Steen, M.: Translating LOTOS to Object-Z. In: 2nd BCS-FACS Northern Formal Methods Workshop. Workshops in Computing. Springer (1997)
25. Dong, J.S., Duke, R., Rose, G.: An object-oriented denotational semantics of a small programming language. Object Oriented Syst. **4**, 29–52 (1997)
26. Dong, J.S., Duke, R.: The geometry of object containment. Object-Oriented Syst. **2**(1), 41–63 (1995)
27. Duce, D.A., Duke, D.J., ten Hagen, P.J.W., Herman, I., Reynolds, G.J.: Formal methods in the development of PREMO. Comput. Stand. Interf. **17**(5–6), 491–509 (1995)
28. Duke, D., Duke, R.: Towards a semantics for Object-Z. In: Bjørner, D., Hoare, C.A.R., Langmaack, H. (eds.) VDM 1990. LNCS, vol. 428, pp. 244–261. Springer, Heidelberg (1990). https://doi.org/10.1007/3-540-52513-0_14
29. Duke, R., Hayes, I.J., King, P., Rose, G.: Protocol specification and verification using Z. In: Aggarwal, S., Sabnani, K. (eds.) Protocol Specification, Testing, and Verification, VIII, pp. 33–46. North-Holland (1988)
30. Duke, R., King, P., Rose, G., Smith, G.: The Object-Z specification language. In: Korson, T., Vaishnavi, V., Meyer, B. (eds.) Technology of Object-Oriented Languages and Systems: TOOLS 5, pp. 465–483. Prentice Hall International (1991)
31. Duke, R., Rose, G.: Specifying a sliding-window protocol. In: Proceedings 11th Australian Computer Science Conference (ACSC-11), pp. 352–361. Australian Computer Science Association (1988)
32. Duke, R., Rose, G.: Formal Object-Oriented Specification Using Object-Z. Macmillan, Basingstoke (2000)
33. Duke, R., Rose, G., Smith, G.: Transferring formal techniques to industry: a case study. In: Formal Description Techniques (FORTE 1990), pp. 279–286. North-Holland (1990)

34. Duke, R., Rose, G., Smith, G.: Object-Z: a specification language advocated for the description of standards. Comput. Stand. Interf. **17**(5–6), 511–533 (1995)
35. Duke, R., Smith, G.: Temporal logic and Z specifications. In: Proceedings 12th Australian Computer Science Conference (ACSC-12), Appendix, pp. 32–42. Australian Computer Science Association (1989)
36. Fischer, C.: CSP-OZ - a combination of CSP and Object-Z. In: Bowman, H., Derrick, J. (eds.) Formal Methods for Open Object-Based Distributed Systems (FMOODS 1997), pp. 423–438. Chapman & Hall (1997)
37. Goguen, J., Meseguer, J.: Unifying functional, object-oriented, and relational programming with logical semantics. In: Shriver, B., Wegner, P. (eds.) Research Directions in Object-Oriented Programming, pp. 417–477. MIT Press (1987)
38. Goguen, J., Tardo, J.: An introduction to OBJ: a language for writing and testing software specifications. In: Gehani, N., McGettrick, A. (eds.) Software Specification Techniques, pp. 391–420. Addison-Wesley (1985)
39. Goldberg, A., Robson, D.: Smalltalk 80: The Language and its Implementation. Addison-Wesley, Reading (1983)
40. Griffiths, A.: From Object-Z to Eiffel: a rigorous development method. In: Mingins, C., Duke, R., Meyer, B. (eds.) Technology of Object-Oriented Languages and Systems (TOOLS 18), pp. 293–308. Prentice Hall (1995)
41. Griffiths, A.: An extended semantic foundation for Object-Z. In: 1996 Asia-Pacific Software Engineering Conference (APSEC 1996), pp. 194–207. IEEE Computer Society Press (1996)
42. Hall, A.: Using Z as a specification calculus for object-oriented systems. In: Bjørner, D., Hoare, C.A.R., Langmaack, H. (eds.) VDM 1990. LNCS, vol. 428, pp. 290–318. Springer, Heidelberg (1990). https://doi.org/10.1007/3-540-52513-0_16
43. Hayes, I.J.: Applying formal specification to software development in industry. IEEE Trans. Softw. Eng. SE **11**(2), 169–178 (1985)
44. Hayes, I.J., Mowbray, M., Rose, G.: Signalling System No. 7: the network layer. In: Aggarwal, S., Sabnani, K. (eds.) Protocol Specification, Testing, and Verification, IX. North-Holland (1989)
45. Hayes, I.J. (ed.): Specification Case Studies. Series in Computer Science, 2nd edn. Prentice Hall International, London (1993)
46. Hoare, C.A.R.: Communicating Sequential Processes. Series in Computer Science. Prentice Hall International, London (1985)
47. Hoare, T.: The verifying compiler: a grand challenge for computing research. In: Böszörményi, L., Schojer, P. (eds.) JMLC 2003. LNCS, vol. 2789, pp. 25–35. Springer, Heidelberg (2003). https://doi.org/10.1007/978-3-540-45213-3_4
48. Hoare, C.A.R., He, J.: Unifying Theories of Programming. Series in Computer Science. Prentice Hall International, Englewood Cliffs (1998)
49. ISO TC97/SC21: Estelle - A Formal Description Technique Based on an Extended State Transition Model (1988). International Standard 9074
50. ISO/IEC 13568:2002: Information Technology - Z Formal Specification Notation-Syntax, Type System and Semantics (2002)
51. Jackson, D.: Software Abstractions - Logic, Language, and Analysis. MIT Press, Cambridge (2006). Revised 2011
52. Johnston, W.: A Type Checker for Object-Z. Technical report 96–24, Software Verification Research Centre, The University of Queensland (1996)
53. Johnston, W., Rose, G.: Guidelines for the Manual Conversion of Object-Z to C++. Technical report 93–14, Software Verification Research Centre, The University of Queensland (1993)

54. Jones, C.: Systematic Software Development Using VDM. Series in Computer Science. Prentice Hall International, Englewood Cliffs (1986)
55. Kassel, G., Smith, G.: Model checking Object-Z classes: some experiments with FDR. In: 8th Asia-Pacific Software Engineering Conference (APSEC 2001), pp. 445–452. IEEE Computer Society Press (2001)
56. Kim, S.-K., David, C.: Formalizing the UML class diagram using Object-Z. In: France, R., Rumpe, B. (eds.) UML 1999. LNCS, vol. 1723, pp. 83–98. Springer, Heidelberg (1999). https://doi.org/10.1007/3-540-46852-8_7
57. Kim, S.-K., Carrington, D.: A formal mapping between UML models and Object-Z specifications. In: Bowen, J.P., Dunne, S., Galloway, A., King, S. (eds.) ZB 2000. LNCS, vol. 1878, pp. 2–21. Springer, Heidelberg (2000). https://doi.org/10.1007/3-540-44525-0_2
58. King, P.: Printing Z and Object-Z LaTeX Documents (1990)
59. Lano, K.: Z++, an object-orientated extension to Z. In: Nicholls, J. (ed.) Z User Workshop, Oxford 1990. Workshops in Computing. Springer, London (1990). https://doi.org/10.1007/978-1-4471-3540-1_11
60. Lano, K., Haughton, H.: Object-Oriented Specification Case Studies. Prentice Hall International, New York (1994)
61. Lave, J., Wenger, E.: Situated Learning: Legitimate Peripheral Participation. Cambridge University Press, Cambridge (1991)
62. Malik, P., Utting, M.: CZT: a framework for Z tools. In: Treharne, H., King, S., Henson, M., Schneider, S. (eds.) ZB 2005. LNCS, vol. 3455, pp. 65–84. Springer, Heidelberg (2005). https://doi.org/10.1007/11415787_5
63. Mayr, T.: Specification of object-oriented systems in LOTOS. In: Turner, K. (ed.) Formal Description Techniques (FORTE 1988), pp. 107–119. North-Holland (1988)
64. McComb, T., Smith, G.: A minimal set of refactoring rules for Object-Z. In: Barthe, G., de Boer, F.S. (eds.) FMOODS 2008. LNCS, vol. 5051, pp. 170–184. Springer, Heidelberg (2008). https://doi.org/10.1007/978-3-540-68863-1_11
65. Meira, S., Cavalcanti, A.: Modular object-oriented Z specifications. In: Nicholls, J. (ed.) Z User Workshop, Oxford 1990. Workshops in Computing. Springer, London (1990). https://doi.org/10.1007/978-1-4471-3540-1_12
66. Meyer, B.: Object-Oriented Software Construction. Series in Computer Science. Prentice Hall International, Englewood Cliffs (1988)
67. Miao, H., Liu, L., Li, L.: Formalizing UML models with Object-Z. In: George, C., Miao, H. (eds.) ICFEM 2002. LNCS, vol. 2495, pp. 523–534. Springer, Heidelberg (2002). https://doi.org/10.1007/3-540-36103-0_53
68. Milner, R.: Communication and Concurrency. Prentice Hall, Upper Saddle River (1989)
69. Narfelt, K.: SYSDAX - an object oriented design methodology based on SDL. In: SDL 1987: State of the Art and Future Trends. North-Holland (1987)
70. Nielsen, M., Havelund, K., Wagner, K.R., George, C.: The RAISE language, method and tools. In: Bloomfield, R.E., Marshall, L.S., Jones, R.B. (eds.) VDM 1988. LNCS, vol. 328, pp. 376–405. Springer, Heidelberg (1988). https://doi.org/10.1007/3-540-50214-9_25
71. Roe, D., Broda, K., Russo, A.: Mapping UML models incorporating OCL constraints into Object-Z. Technical report, Department of Computing, Imperial College London (2003)
72. Rose, G., Duke, R., Hayes, I.J.: Specifying communications services and protocols. In: Proceedings 2nd Australian Software Engineering Conference (ASWEC 1987), pp. 161–170. The Institution of Radio and Electronics Engineers Australia (1987)

73. Rosenberg, K.: The adoption of formal methods within OTC. In: Parker, K., Rose, G. (eds.) Formal Description Techniques, IV (FORTE 1991), pp. 91–98. Elsevier (1992)

74. Schuman, S., Pitt, D.: Object-oriented subsystem specification. In: Meertens, L. (ed.) Program Specification and Transformation, pp. 313–341. North-Holland (1987)

75. Sijelmassi, R., Gaudette, P.: An object-oriented model for Estelle. In: Turner, K. (ed.) Formal Description Techniques (FORTE 1988), pp. 91–105. North-Holland (1988)

76. Smith, G.: A formal specification of Signalling System No. 7 Telephone User Part. In: Proceedings 1989 Singapore International Conference on Networks (SICON 1989), pp. 50–55. IEEE Singapore Section (1989)

77. Smith, G.: A semantic integration of Object-Z and CSP for the specification of concurrent systems. In: Fitzgerald, J., Jones, C.B., Lucas, P. (eds.) FME 1997. LNCS, vol. 1313, pp. 62–81. Springer, Heidelberg (1997). https://doi.org/10.1007/3-540-63533-5_4

78. Smith, G.: The Object-Z Specification Language. Advances in Formal Methods Series. Kluwer Academic Publishers (2000)

79. Smith, G.: Introducing reference semantics via refinement. In: George, C., Miao, H. (eds.) ICFEM 2002. LNCS, vol. 2495, pp. 588–599. Springer, Heidelberg (2002). https://doi.org/10.1007/3-540-36103-0_60

80. Smith, G., Duke, R.: Modelling a cache coherence protocol using Object-Z. In: Proceedings 13th Australian Computer Science Conference (ACSC-13), pp. 352–361. Australian Computer Science Association (1990)

81. Smith, G., Kammüller, F., Santen, T.: Encoding Object-Z in Isabelle/HOL. In: Bert, D., Bowen, J.P., Henson, M.C., Robinson, K. (eds.) ZB 2002. LNCS, vol. 2272, pp. 82–99. Springer, Heidelberg (2002). https://doi.org/10.1007/3-540-45648-1_5

82. Spivey, J.M.: Understanding Z: A Specification Language and its Formal Semantics, Cambridge Tracts in Theoretical Computer Science, vol. 3. Cambridge University Press, Cambridge (1988)

83. Spivey, J.M.: The Z Notation: A Reference Manual. Series in Computer Science, Prentice Hall International, Englewood Cliffs (1989). 2nd edn. 1992

84. Stepney, S., Barden, R., Cooper, D.: Object Orientation in Z. Workshops in Computing. Springer, London (1992). https://doi.org/10.1007/978-1-4471-3552-4

85. Stepney, S., Barden, R., Cooper, D.: A survey of object orientation in Z. Softw. Eng. J. 7(2), 150–160 (1992)

86. Stroustrup, B.: The C++ Programming Language. Addison-Wesley, Boston (1986)

87. Treharne, H., Schneider, S.: Using a process algebra to control B operations. In: Araki, K., Galloway, A., Taguchi, K. (eds.) IFM 1999, vol. 1945, pp. 437–456. Springer, London (1999). https://doi.org/10.1007/978-1-4471-0851-1_23

88. Whysall, P., McDermid, J.: An approach to object oriented specification using Z. In: Nicholls, J. (ed.) Z User Workshop, Oxford 1990. Workshops in Computing. Springer, London (1990). https://doi.org/10.1007/978-1-4471-3540-1_13

89. Wills, A.: Capsules and types in Fresco. In: America, P. (ed.) ECOOP 1991. LNCS, vol. 512, pp. 59–76. Springer, Heidelberg (1991). https://doi.org/10.1007/BFb0057015

90. Woodcock, J., Cavalcanti, A.: The semantics of *Circus*. In: Bert, D., Bowen, J.P., Henson, M.C., Robinson, K. (eds.) ZB 2002. LNCS, vol. 2272, pp. 184–203. Springer, Heidelberg (2002). https://doi.org/10.1007/3-540-45648-1_10

Formal Specifications and Software Testing, a Fruitful Convergence

Marie-Claude Gaudel[✉]

LRI, Université Paris-Sud, Orsay, France
marieclaude.gaudel@gmail.com

Abstract. This paper gives some account of the evolution of ideas and the main advances in the domain of software testing based on formal specifications and reports some personal anecdotes on my activity in this field. Going back to the seventies, being slightly caricatural, software testing was perceived, on the one hand, by its actors as an empirical activity that had nothing to gain from formal methods, on the other hand, by the advocates of these methods as doomed to disappear based on the belief that in the long run programs will be correct by construction. Currently, these two communities haven't yet reached a complete consensus. But fortunately there have been some significant moves from both sides and various success stories that allow saying that there is a fruitful convergence toward testing methods based on formal specifications.

Keywords: Formal methods · Software testing · History

1 Introduction

Software testing based on formal specifications has a slightly troubled history. In the seventies, most actors of both fields considered that they had nothing to bring to each other. Even worse, some influential scientists from both sides emitted mutual doubts on the pertinence of these fields: from the side of the software-testing research community, one can cite De Millo et al. [13]; and from the side on the formal-approaches-to-software-engineering community, one can cite the famous Dijkstra curse against testing [15], which definitely deserves to be quoted:

> Program testing can be a very effective way to show the presence of bugs, but is hopelessly inadequate for showing their absence. The only effective way to raise the confidence level of a program significantly is to give a convincing proof of its correctness

Another Dijkstra's quotation, more directly relevant to the topic of this paper, is:

> A common approach to get a program correct is . . . by subjecting the program to numerous test cases. From the failures around us we can derive ample evidence that this approach is inadequate. To remedy the situation

© Springer Nature Switzerland AG 2020
E. Sekerinski et al. (Eds.): FM 2019 Workshops, LNCS 12233, pp. 87–94, 2020.
https://doi.org/10.1007/978-3-030-54997-8_5

it has been suggested that what we really need are "automatic test case generators" by which the pieces of program to be validated can be exercised still more extensively. But will this really help? I don't think so. (EWD303, year unknown[1])

Fifty years later, the idea of software testing methods based on formal specifications is accepted as respectable, among the numerous existing approaches to software testing [12], and some powerful tools exist. Most formal specification methods come with some notion of test derivation, submission, verdict and there is a number of success stories. Moreover, the complementarity of tests and proofs in software validation and verification is the subject of active research activities, attested by numerous publications and the fact that an international conference "Tests and Proofs" has taken place annually since 2007. There is an excellent survey by Hierons et al., titled "Using Formal Specifications to Support Testing", published in 2009 in ACM Computing Surveys [22].

Therefore, it is of interest to look back at this evolution towards convergence of two research fields that were originally so distant.

2   Software Engineering, Formal Methods, and Testing in the Seventies and the Beginning of the Eighties

A possible subtitle of this section could be: Why formal? Why testing?.

In the seventies, formal approaches to software development, validation, and verification were not considered as credible by the majority of software engineers and software testers. Symmetrically as mentioned above, many supporters of formal approaches considered that software testing was an ineffective activity doomed to disappearance after the generalisation of formal methods.

My interest in testing based on formal specifications arose during my Ph.D. whose topic was compiler generation based on formal semantics of the source and target languages. I needed examples of source programs to test the generated compilers and my attention was drawn to a work by Houssais on the verification of an Algol 68 implementation [24] and on a little-known subsequent research report of the Université de Rennes 1, titled "Un générateur de tests commandé par les grammaires". Since testing compilers was not the main focus of my Ph.D., I didn't spend much time on fully exploiting Houssais ideas. However, I used them as guidelines, which turned out to be useful.

I had noticed some similarities between programming language definitions and algebraic data types. In both cases, there is a syntax (for algebraic data types, the signature), and some constraints (contextual rules for programming languages, axioms for algebraic data types). This led me to propose as Ph.D. subject to Luc Bougé the generation of test from algebraic specifications. The thesis was defended in 1982 [3], followed by four other ones at the end of the

---

[1] This note can be seen at https://www.cs.utexas.edu/users/EWD/ where it has no date. But one can bracket it between two dated EWDs: EWD 292, 31 Aug 1970, and EWD 306, 16th March 1971 (thanks to Jeremy Gibbons for the hint).

eighties. It was the origin of successful developments, including industrial applications, that are summarised in [20]. At that time, it was not easy to publish on this subject. Dijkstra's curse was very present in the mind of researchers in formal methods. Our first publication in an international conference was in 1985 [4]. However, these ideas turned out to be a rather good selling point of formal methods to industry: in October 1981, I was hired to create a research group on the use of such methods for software engineering in the research laboratory of the Compagnie Générale d'Electricité.[2]

At the same time, i.e. 1981–1983, several research works were led on exactly the same topic, namely testing based on algebraic abstract data types: Gannon, McMullin, and Hamlet in the U.S. [19], and Jalotc in India [26]. A lot of technical questions were still open, but the fundamental ideas were well stated. Among the open issues at that time, there were:

- the determination of equality between two test results, the difficulty coming from the difference of levels of abstraction between the specification and the implementation under test[3].
- the occurrence of partial operations in the specification, with two causes of partiality: either the result is mathematically undefined, or it is not specified, the specification allowing some freedom to the implementation.
- the possibility of non-determinism in the specification or in the implementation.

Note that these issues are not due to the use of formal specifications. They arise in any testing method that is specification-based. For some hints on the way they have been formally treated later on, one can see [20] and [22].

Meanwhile, another research community had been very active in the domain with very strong motivations: the researchers in telecommunication protocols.

3   The Area of Telecommunication Protocols at the Beginning of the Eighties

Communicating systems use well-defined formats for exchanging messages. Each message has an exact role and corresponds to a range of possible answers.

---

[2] During my stay there (1981–1983) I interacted with a group of engineers who developed the software of a telephone switching system. I was impressed by their professionalism. They motivated me to pursue this line of research.

A (not so funny) anecdote is that some years later, being back as a professor in a university, I visited the same place with a Ph.D. student, searching for challenging case studies. Mood and people had changed and the head of the group explained that their goal was to be first on the market and their development strategy was "quick an dirty". To that the Ph.D. student replied that "dirty we can do, but quick I am not sure". The meeting was unproductive...

[3] This is similar to the issue of lifting computational types and values to the logical level in Hoare's logic.

The specification of the protocol is independent of how it may be implemented and exploited by the telecommunication operators. Besides, testing can be based on the specifications only (i.e. it's black-box testing), as manufacturers generally don't disclose implementation details.

Since communication protocols must be agreed upon by various entities such as international agencies, operators, or developers, technical standards, formal or not, have been developed very early for their definitions (see for instance [9]) as well as for conformance testing methodologies [25]. Certification is performed via standard abstract test sets.

In such a context, research projects and publications on specification-based testing of such protocols had flourished (see [33] among the early ones). Note that this paper was published in 1984, at the 2nd IFIP International Workshop on Protocol Specification, Verification and Testing (IWPTS), which has occurred yearly since, modulo a few changes of names[4]. Since 2007, under the name TESTCOM this conference merged with the FATES workshop[5] and has gathered together researchers working on specification-based testing, independently of the kind of considered software: communication protocols or others.

The characteristics of the approaches developed for communication protocols was: the formal specification languages, such as SDL, ESTELLE, LOTOS, were standardised, with some semantics based on Finite State Machines or Labelled Transition Systems that are well-suited for the description of non-terminating processes; the notions of conformance, abstract test specifications, certification, were standardised as well.

In contrast, the approaches developed in the community of formal software engineering, or those that were on the verge to be developed, were based on specification languages designed by research groups, with notations inspired from logic, and semantics based on axioms satisfaction (algebraic data types) or predicate transformers (Z, VDM).

4   What Happened in the Nineties and Later

The end of the eighties and the beginning of the nineties were a turning point for the topic of testing based on formal specifications. Within five years a lot of well-founded testing methods were established and validated for the main formal specification methods. It's impossible to cite all of them. Let us just mention three sets of works[6].

Tests derivation from formal specifications with semantics based on labelled transition systems, such as LOTOS or SDL, started to be abundantly studied at

---

[4] IWPTS: 1983–1996; IWTCS: 1997–1999, TESTCOM: 2000–2009, ICTSS: 2010-now.

[5] This series of workshops (Formal Approaches to Testing of Software) took place in 2001–2007.

[6] A notable omission here is the corpus of research on testing based on FSM (Finite State Machines), which has been considerably influential since the sixties both in hardware and in software testing. For an excellent survey with some historical indications see [28].

the end of the eighties [5,32,38]. Later, in 1996, Tretmans introduced the *ioco* conformance relation [36], which turned out to be quite pertinent for testing those systems that are input-enabled, i.e. they are always ready to accept some input. It has been at the origin of several tools such as TGV [27], TorX [10] and more recently TorXakis [37].

For the VDM specification method, Dick and Faivre presented in 1993 a testing method [14] at the Formal Method Europe Conference (FME'93). It must be observed that this work was performed in an industrial context, namely Bull Information Systems in the UK and its Corporate Research Centre in France, and that it has strongly influenced the subsequent researches on testing based on model-based formal specifications. At the same time, Stocks and Carrington proposed Test Templates, a test method based on Z specifications [35], which was published at the International Conference on Software Engineering (ICSE 15). Both software formalists and software engineers recognised the interest of testing methods based on model-based formal specifications.

In my group, we pursued the work on testing based on algebraic specification. In 1991, with Bernot and Marre we published a case study on the test of binary search trees [2], and in 1993 Dauchy and Marre successfully applied the method and the tool to critical parts of the software of an automatic subway [11]. Since then, our approach has been generalised to other formal methods: full LOTOS [21], Lustre and Esterel [30] with applications to nuclear control systems certification, CSP [7] and *Circus* [8].

One observes that since the mid-nineties, test derivation from formal specifications has become a popular research topic, well accepted both in conferences and journals devoted to formal methods and in conferences and journals devoted to software engineering and testing. New formal specification methods are almost systematically enriched by some test derivation methods: for instance, it was the case for the B method [29,34], and ASMl, the Abstract State Machine Language [1] and its companion testing environment SPEC EXPLORER [39] developed at Microsoft Research.

Moreover, the cultural gap between researchers from the telecommunication world and from the formal software engineering community is much less pronounced. Most theories, methods, and tools are of common use or unified, even if the telecommunication universe remains much more dependent on standards.

5   Conclusion

Despite Dijkstra's curse, the convergence of formal methods and software testing has happened. Definitely, one of the antidotes to Dijksta's curse has been an invited conference and paper by Tony Hoare at the FME Symposium in 1996 titled "How Did Software Get So Reliable Without Proof?" [23]. There, he underlined the effectiveness of software engineering techniques, among which testing, and the fact that formal methods

provide a conceptual framework and basic understanding to promote the best of current practice, and point directions for future improvement.

As mentioned above, nowadays, most formal specification methods come with some notion of test derivation, submission, verdict. There is a number of significant success stories. A majority of them are in link with academia, but a number of them took place in industry. Testing based on formal specification is now one of the recognised resources in the arsenal of software testing methods.

At present, theorem provers and model checkers make use of tests [16,31], and testing tools make use of theorem provers [6,17] and model checkers [18]. The Test and Proof (TAP) series of conferences and the Verified Software: Theories, Tools, Experiments (VSTTE) series of workshops are well established. They attract both communities, provide a forum for meetings and talks, ensuring the development of research activities integrating formal methods and testing.

Acknowledgment. I am grateful to Burkhart Wolff and the members of the LRI Test Club who gave me the idea to talk and write on this topic.

References

1. Barnett, M., Grieskamp, W., Nachmanson, L., Schulte, W., Tillmann, N., Veanes, M.: Towards a tool environment for model-based testing with AsmL. In: Petrenko, A., Ulrich, A. (eds.) FATES 2003. LNCS, vol. 2931, pp. 252–266. Springer, Heidelberg (2004). https://doi.org/10.1007/978-3-540-24617-6_18
2. Bernot, G., Gaudel, M.C., Marre, B.: Software testing based on formal specifications: a theory and a tool. Softw. Eng. J. **6**(6), 387–405 (1991)
3. Bougé, L.: Modeling the notion of program testing; application to test set generation. Theses, Université Pierre et Marie Curie - Paris VI, October 1982. https://tel.archives-ouvertes.fr/tel-00416558
4. Bougé, L., Choquet, N., Fribourg, L., Gaudel, M.C.: Application of PROLOG to test sets generation from algebraic specifications. In: Ehrig, H., Floyd, C., Nivat, M., Thatcher, J. (eds.) TAPSOFT 1985. LNCS, vol. 186, pp. 261–275. Springer, Heidelberg (1985). https://doi.org/10.1007/3-540-15199-0_17
5. Brinksma, E.: A theory for the derivation of tests. In: Proceedings of 8th International Conference on Protocol Specification, Testing and Verification, pp. 63–74. North-Holland (1988)
6. Brucker, A.D., Wolff, B.: On theorem prover-based testing. Formal Asp. Comput. **25**(5), 683–721 (2013)
7. Cavalcanti, A., Gaudel, M.-C.: Testing for refinement in CSP. In: Butler, M., Hinchey, M.G., Larrondo-Petrie, M.M. (eds.) ICFEM 2007. LNCS, vol. 4789, pp. 151–170. Springer, Heidelberg (2007). https://doi.org/10.1007/978-3-540-76650-6_10
8. Cavalcanti, A., Gaudel, M.C.: Testing for refinement in *Circus*. Acta Inf. **48**(2), 97–147 (2011)
9. CCITT: Functional specification and description language (SDL), Recommendation Z.100–Z.104 (1984)
10. Chaudron, M.R.V., Tretmans, J., Wijbrans, K.: Lessons from the application of formal methods to the design of a storm surge barrier control system. In: Wing, J.M., Woodcock, J., Davies, J. (eds.) FM 1999. LNCS, vol. 1709, pp. 1511–1526. Springer, Heidelberg (1999). https://doi.org/10.1007/3-540-48118-4_30

11. Dauchy, P., Gaudel, M.C., Marre, B.: Using algebraic specifications in software testing: a case study on the software of an automatic subway. J. Syst. Softw. **21**(3), 229–244 (1993)
12. DeMillo, R.A.: Software testing. In: Encyclopedia of Computer Science, pp. 1645–1649. John Wiley and Sons Ltd., GBR (2003)
13. DeMillo, R.A., Upton, R.J., Perlis, A.J.: Social processes and proofs of theorems and programs. Math. Intell. **3**(1), 31–40 (1980). https://doi.org/10.1007/BF03023394
14. Dick, J., Faivre, A.: Automating the generation and sequencing of test cases from model-based specifications. In: Woodcock, J.C.P., Larsen, P.G. (eds.) FME 1993. LNCS, vol. 670, pp. 268–284. Springer, Heidelberg (1993). https://doi.org/10.1007/BFb0024651
15. Dijkstra, E.W.: The humble programmer. Commun. ACM **15**(10), 859–866 (1972)
16. Dubois, C., Giorgetti, A.: Tests and proofs for custom data generators. Formal Aspects Comput. **30**(6), 659–684 (2018). https://doi.org/10.1007/s00165-018-0459-1
17. Feliachi, A., Gaudel, M.-C., Wenzel, M., Wolff, B.: The *Circus* testing theory revisited in Isabelle/HOL. In: Groves, L., Sun, J. (eds.) ICFEM 2013. LNCS, vol. 8144, pp. 131–147. Springer, Heidelberg (2013). https://doi.org/10.1007/978-3-642-41202-8_10
18. Fraser, G., Wotawa, F., Ammann, P.: Issues in using model checkers for test case generation. J. Syst. Softw. **82**(9), 1403–1418 (2009)
19. Gannon, J.D., McMullin, P.R., Hamlet, R.G.: Data-abstraction implementation, specification, and testing. ACM Trans. Program. Lang. Syst. **3**(3), 211–223 (1981)
20. Gaudel, M.-C., Le Gall, P.: Testing data types implementations from algebraic specifications. In: Hierons, R.M., Bowen, J.P., Harman, M. (eds.) Formal Methods and Testing. LNCS, vol. 4949, pp. 209–239. Springer, Heidelberg (2008). https://doi.org/10.1007/978-3-540-78917-8_7
21. Gaudel, M.C., James, P.R.: Testing algebraic data types and processes: a unifying theory. Formal Asp. Comput. **10**(5–6), 436–451 (1998)
22. Hierons, R.M., et al.: Using formal specifications to support testing. ACM Comput. Surv. **41**(2), 9:1–9:76 (2009)
23. Hoare, C.A.R.: How did software get so reliable without proof? In: Gaudel, M.-C., Woodcock, J. (eds.) FME 1996. LNCS, vol. 1051, pp. 1–17. Springer, Heidelberg (1996). https://doi.org/10.1007/3-540-60973-3_77
24. Houssais, B.: Verification of an Algol 68 implementation. ACM SIGPLAN Not. **12**(6), 117–128 (1977)
25. ISO: Conformance testing methodology and framework. International Standard IS-9646 (1991)
26. Jalote, P.: Specification and testing of abstract data types. In: IEEE International Computer Software and Applications Conference COMSAC, pp. 508–511 (1983)
27. Jard, C., Jéron, T.: TGV: theory, principles and algorithms. Int. J. Softw. Tools Technol. Transf. **7**(4), 297–315 (2005)
28. Lee, D., Yannakakis, M.: Principles and methods of testing finite state machines-a survey. Proc. IEEE **84**(8), 1090–1123 (1996)
29. Legeard, B., Peureux, F.: Generation of functional test sequences from B formal specifications-presentation and industrial case study. In: 16th IEEE International Conference on Automated Software Engineering (ASE 2001), Coronado Island, San Diego, CA, USA, 26–29 November 2001, pp. 377–381. IEEE Computer Society (2001)

30. Marre, B., Blanc, B.: Test selection strategies for Lustre descriptions in GATeL. Electr. Notes Theor. Comput. Sci. **111**, 93–111 (2005)
31. Petiot, G., Kosmatov, N., Botella, B., Giorgetti, A., Julliand, J.: How testing helps to diagnose proof failures. Formal Aspects Comput. **30**(6), 629–657 (2018). https://doi.org/10.1007/s00165-018-0456-4
32. Pitt, D.H., Freestone, D.: The derivation of conformance tests from LOTOS specifications. IEEE Trans. Software Eng. **16**(12), 1337–1343 (1990)
33. Sarikaya, B., von Bochmann, G.: Some experience with test sequence generation for protocols. In: Protocol Specification, Testing and Verification, Proceedings of the IFIP WG6.1 Second International Workshop on Protocol Specification, Testing and Verification, Idyllwild, CA, USA, 17–20 May 1982, pp. 555–567. North Holland (1982)
34. Satpathy, M., Butler, M., Leuschel, M., Ramesh, S.: Automatic testing from formal specifications. In: Gurevich, Y., Meyer, B. (eds.) TAP 2007. LNCS, vol. 4454, pp. 95–113. Springer, Heidelberg (2007). https://doi.org/10.1007/978-3-540-73770-4_6
35. Stocks, P., Carrington, D.A.: Test templates: a specification-based testing framework. In: Proceedings of the 15th International Conference on Software Engineering, Baltimore, Maryland, USA, 17–21 May 1993, pp. 405–414. IEEE Computer Society/ACM Press (1993)
36. Tretmans, J.: Test generation with inputs, outputs and repetitive quiescence. Softw. Concepts Tools **17**(3), 103–120 (1996)
37. Tretmans, J., van de Laar, P.: Model-based testing with TorXakis. In: Proceedings of 30th CECIIS, the Central European Conference on Information and Intelligent Systems, Varaždin, Croatia, 2–4 October 2019, pp. 247–258 (1987)
38. Ural, H.: A test derivation method for protocol conformance testing. In: Protocol Specification, Testing and Verification VII, Proceedings of the IFIP WG6.1 Seventh International Conference on Protocol Specification, Testing and Verification, Zurich, Switzerland, 5–8 May 1987, pp. 347–358. North-Holland (1987)
39. Veanes, M., Campbell, C., Grieskamp, W., Schulte, W., Tillmann, N., Nachmanson, L.: Model-based testing of object-oriented reactive systems with Spec Explorer. In: Hierons, R.M., Bowen, J.P., Harman, M. (eds.) Formal Methods and Testing. LNCS, vol. 4949, pp. 39–76. Springer, Heidelberg (2008). https://doi.org/10.1007/978-3-540-78917-8_2

From Manuscripts to Programming Languages: An Archivist Perspective

Alexandra Vidal[1]([⊠]), Ana Sandra Meneses[2]([⊠]), and António Sousa[2]([⊠])

[1] Faculty of Documentación, Univ. Complutense Madrid, Madrid, Spain
alexsilv@ucm.es
[2] Arquivo Distrital de Braga, Univ. Minho, Braga, Portugal
{anameneses,asousa}@adb.uminho.pt
https://documentacion.ucm.es/
http://www.adb.uminho.pt

Abstract. This paper presents the archival treatment of documentation produced by IFIP Working Group 2.1, *Algorithmic Languages and Calculi* as kept by former chairman Willem van der Poel (1962-69) and Chris Cheney. It highlights the importance of archival treatment based on standards such as *International Standard for Archival Description—* ISAD(G) and the *International Standard Archival Authority Record (Corporate Bodies, Persons and Families)*—ISAAR-(CPF) both issued by the International Council on Archives, the Portuguese *Guidelines for Archival Description* ODA and *Encoded Archival Description* EAD.

The archived collection enables dissemination and effective access to the information for research and in-depth knowledge of computer history and specifically programming languages and formal methods.

The paper also addresses the issues of the long-term preservation of archival records produced today in their various formats and the importance of contributing to preserving collective memory and enriching the knowledge about the human society.

Keywords: History of software · Archival standards · Digital preservation

1 Introduction

In 2017, some archival documentation from Working Group 2.1 - *Algorithmic Languages and Calculi*, dating to the period when Willem Van der Poel was chairman, was deposited in the Braga District Archive (ADB). This collection is only a part of the documentation produced by the group, presumably from a relevant period of its past. Perhaps something unusual, a technical working group is concerned with the preservation *"for future memory"* of its activity, not only by preserving the documents that highlight it, but also by promoting its accessibility.

ADB is a cultural unit of the University of Minho (UMinho). Having as main mission the archival heritage of the region, it could not miss this opportunity

© Springer Nature Switzerland AG 2020
E. Sekerinski et al. (Eds.): FM 2019 Workshops, LNCS 12233, pp. 95–102, 2020.
https://doi.org/10.1007/978-3-030-54997-8_6

to contribute to the preservation, enhancement and access to an archive closely related to computing, a relevant scientific area of research at UMinho. The collection is an important archive for the history of programming languages and information technology, contributing to our understanding of the evolution of programming technology, either on the technical side, or issues resulting from their impact on society and even the economic and political constraints that may have interfered in the group's activity.

WG2.1 started its activity in the post WW-II period when there was an exponential growth in the use of information and, consequently, in the production of archival documents.[1] These decades led the archival community to eventually rethink its role and the way of looking and acting upon its object: the management of the archival information/document not only in its final stage of life but since its production (as a record) by the individual or collective entity that created or received it. Each archival item is a document produced or received by an individual or a legal person in the exercise of their functions. It shows this activity and is an express proof of a will, action or decision.

This is also the period when information technology begins to develop and impose itself, eventually leading to its current omnipresence in one's everyday life through email, mobile phones, web sites and so on. The same advances in technology have provided archivists with working tools for organizing, describing and disseminating the contents of their archives, including the digital representation of documents. Tools have been created for the management of archival information (information systems), allowing for information dematerialization, thus entering directly into the area that archivists are chiefly dedicated to!

2   The Treatment of the WG2.1 Archive

2.1   The Project: How We (Archivists) Do Our Work

Following the standard practice, the treatment of the WG2.1 collection consisted of its cleaning and packaging, archival organization and description (in Portuguese and in English) and the digitization of an important and relevant part of it. Both the description and digital representations are available from the ADB search interface.[2]

Organization and description of the archives are the heart of our activity to support their preservation and communicability. The organization of archival information is based on respect for the principle of provenance and the original order of the documents. Thus, its organization does not reflect a thematic structure (as in librarianship) or a particular, subjective criterion of the collection (as in museums). It is an organization that reflects the organics and the functions of the entity that produces the archive.

---

[1] Document replication was facilitated by technologies that became increasingly accessible, culminating in the widespread use the photocopier.

[2] URL: http://pesquisa.adb.uminho.pt/.

These principles, combined with the analysis of the contents of the documents, the identification of the authors/producers and the organic-functional context of the production, are characteristic aspects always present in archival treatments. This is supported by rules for describing the documents and their context and for the reference to the entities producing and intervening in the acts.

Archival description instruments such as inventories and catalogs, as we will see in the present case, are effectively a touchstone for the dissemination of information. The idea of the archivist as a document keeper does not characterize the whole job. At present, the information professional has as their main objective also to give access to the information they work on. For this access to be effective, we are guided by norms as the *International Standard for Archival Description—ISAD(G)* [5] and the *International Standard Archival Authority Record (Corporate Bodies, Persons and Families)—ISAAR-(CPF)* [6] both issued by the International Council on Archives. We also use the Portuguese *Guidelines for Archival Description* (ODA) [2]. All these standards are compliant with the Encoded Archival Description (EAD).[3]

These rules and guidelines define a structure of information elements that allow to represent the contents of the documents and the informational structure (organic and/or functional) of the producer of the archive. Thus, we also have information about the context of the production and use of documents.

The use of such standards is very important for access and dissemination of the information based on scientific procedures. In this way, one unveils not only the organic aspects of IFIP, of its Technical Committee TC2 and of WG 2.1, but also the relationships among them and main protagonists such as Heinz Zemanek, Niklaus Wirth and many others.

Standards and guidelines for other purposes are used by Archeevo, a package of software from Keep Solutions[4] used at ADB for describing the documents, managing them and their digitized images and for remote access and interoperability.

The archival treatment results in the instruments that describe contents, offer "finding aids" and allow for the dissemination of document metadata and the associated digital reproduction when available. Information sciences and technology allows any user to access these remotely through the internet.

Archival Description. The adopted archival description is multilevel, ranging from the top level – description of the archive producer – to the level of the most basic unit, the document itself. These are organized according to the functions to which they refer – series – and framed in the organic structure of the producing entity – sections. Both series and section are also subject to description and subject to subdivisions.

For the present case, the WG2.1 documentation belongs to the International Federation for Information Processing (IFIP) archive, where it is an "archival"

---

[3] URL: https://www.loc.gov/ead/.
[4] URL: https://www.keep.pt/en.

subsection of its Technical Committee 2. The description made of the referred documentation, resulted in this simplified structure (its series are detailed in the next section):

- **Fonds**: International Federation for Information Processing (IFIP)
- **Section**: Technical Committee 2
- **Subsection**: Working Group 2.1 - Algorithmic Languages and Calculi
- **Series**:
  - 001 Meeting minutes
  - 002 Correspondence
  - ...

It is within the scope of each series that documents are described. Each item described has a unique identifier that is framed within those that represent its hierarchical position. For instance, the document *"Unconfirmed minutes of the third meeting of IFIP/TC2-'P/L'-Oslo with appendix"* bears identifier 01411, so its reference code is PT/UM-ADB/ASS/IFIP/TC2-WG2.1/001/01411, that is, it is prefixed by identifiers for the country and institution where the document is located and a non-mandatory management code (ASS, for association).

2.2   The Contents of the WG2.1 Archive

Series identification is essential to classify, describe, select, access and disseminate the documentation. It helps to organize the documents and present users with the type of documents they can use in their research. In the ISAD Standard (G), the notion of a *series* is defined as follows:

> *"Documents organized according to an archiving system or conserved forming a unit as a result of the same accumulation, of the same archival process, or of the same activity; that have a particular form; or as a consequence of any other relationship derived from its production, reception or use"*

Theodore Schellenberg, a well-known American archivist, defined *series* as *"a group of documents, files or dossiers that have been gathered together for a specific activity"* [7].

In the present case study we detected ten types of documentary series, and this is where we were able to reveal what IFIP's activity was, the advances and setbacks in relation to the Algol initiative and the pioneering spirit of so many researchers who are now world authorities in computing:

- **Series 001**—Meeting minutes (1962–1995): Minutes, approved and informal minutes on organizational and administrative matters. "Minutes" also include the date of the meeting and the names of all members present or absent, but focus more on summarizing key discussion points and listing all action items to be performed by individuals or the group.

- **Series 002**—Correspondence (1959–1996): The correspondence series (received and dispatched) corresponds to most of the documentation kept by this archive. The vast majority of letters are related to the activity of Willem van der Poel as chairman of WG2.1, mostly concerning the development and study of Algol, directed and received from researchers, university and business institutions from different parts of the world. Within this typology we find telegrams, telefax, aerogram and telex conversations.
- **Series 003**—Proposals (1967–1987): Proposals and also drafts of proposals for the algorithmic language—Algol 68, creation of a metalanguage and its implementation.
- **Series 004**—Technical Notes (1963–1986): Produced at meetings as a result of investigations that had been or were being carried out, discussed or under discussion: memoranda and drafts of comments, informal documents in circulation that might be published.
- **Series 005**—Reports (1962–1981): This series includes the following diversity: activity reports from Technical Committee 2 and Working Group 2.1; copies of reports; preliminary reports; drafts of activity reports; drafts of revised reports and revised reports, as such. There are also proposals for reports, final drafts, evaluation reports and a "minority report" (the result of a non-majority vote by group members).
- **Series 006**—Decisions: Formal resolutions taken by the group and meeting resolutions, corresponding to the final product of the meetings.
- **Series 007**—Meeting dossiers (1962–1995): Support documentation of the meetings: copies of IFIP statutes, meeting notes, memos, lists of group members, participants and observers, WG2.1 membership forms, appendices/annexes, work schedules, syntax lists, errata, meeting programs, votes for decisions at meetings. Also follow-up of meetings, scientific communications to review and so on.
- **Series 008**—News from the press: Newspaper news about the group's activity.
- **Series 009**—Scientific Communications (1962–1998): Published scientific communications, drafts, abstracts and copies of abstracts on the Algol language.
- **Series 010**—Management documents (1959–1997): Support documents for the management of the overall group.

The relative size of each particular document series can be perceived in the chart of Fig. 1.

If a particular item is to be chosen as most representative of the collection, one could select the following dossier, which is catalogued under number 01456:[5]

Dossier with copies of working documents of IFIP WG2.1: "On certain Basic Concept of Programming Languages by Niklaus Wirth" (1–32); Report of Fraser Duncan to the members of WG2.1 about Algol X and Y with an appendix and other reports on Zandvoort, Munich and Amsterdam meetings (33–86); Jack N. Merner sends to WG2.1 members a report

---

[5] Complete reference code: `PT/UM-ADB/ASS/IFIP/TC2-WG2.1/004/01456`.

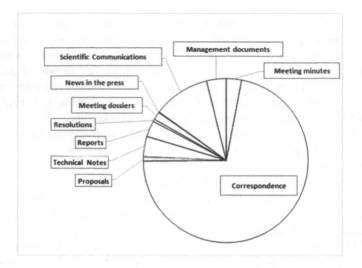

Fig. 1. Relative distribution of documents per series in the WG2.1 archive.

of the Algol-X-I-O Subcommittee (1966-07-26) (87–114); General remarks on the [WG2.1 Warsaw] meeting by A. Mazurkiewicz (115–115); Copy of Notice of the 7th meeting of WG2.1 on Algol by Willem van der Poel (1966-06-04) (116–116); Members mailing list of IFIP/WG2.1 on Algol (1966) (117–123); Copy of letter of C.A.R. Hoare (Tony) to Willem van der Poel about Willem's chairman report (1966-09-28) (124–126); Copy of letter of Niklaus Wirth to Willem van der Poel explaining his position concerning the developments within WG2.1 (1966-09-27) (127–128); Manuscript copy of Willem van der Poel to Andrei Ershov (129–129); Comments on "A contribution to the Development of Algol" by T. Simauti (130–137); Recursive definition of Syntax and semantics by A. Van Wijngaarden presented in IFIP working conference in Vienna (Formal Language Description Language) (138–147); Assigning meaning to programs by Robert W. Floyd (148–167); Record Handling by C.A.R. Hoare (Tony) (a series of lectures to be delivered at the 1966 NATO Summer School) (168–191).

The dossier contains not only administrative but also technical documentation about the vibrant Algol activity of the time, in particular work on its definition as a programming language (and of its "dialects"). More than this, it contains preliminary versions of pioneering papers that would become very relevant in the future, in particular in the field of formal methods, for instance [3].[6]

---

[6] See also PT/UM-ADB/ASS/IFIP/TC2-WG2.1/002/001164, a letter sent by Tony Hoare to Willem van der Poel in December 1968 containing his paper "The axiomatic method, program execution", a precursor of [4]. The letter refers to a previous version that had been distributed at the North Berwick meeting (July/August 1968).

3   Conclusions

Archives are unique and irreplaceable heritage passed from one generation to another. Archives are managed to preserve documents' value and meaning. They are authoritative sources of information underpinning accountable and transparent administrative actions. They play an essential role in the development of societies by safeguarding and contributing to individual and community memory. Open access to archives enriches our knowledge of human society, promotes democracy, protects citizens' rights and enhances the quality of life.

The preservation of Willem van der Poel's collection of documents concerning the period he was chairman of WG2.1 has widened the scope of the Braga District Archives (ADB). For the first time, heritage belonging to a recent technology[7] was studied, analysed and classified by staff working at ADB. For some of us, computing ('informatics') meant little more than using computer tools to record, organize and analyse information. We learnt a lot, from the understanding of the problem domain to the more mundane terminology of compilers, interpreters, syntax, semantics and so on and so forth.

The initiative was also new to us from another facet: it was sponsored by a software house, Primavera Software, telling that not only academics and archivists are interested in preserving the past history of software, but also entrepreneurs in the information technology field support the idea.

4   Future Work

Is this the beginning of a new (possibly never ending) story? Programming languages are the main way of producing computing software. Studying their history and the evolution of the associated programming methodologies seems to be a relevant area for research in the broader field of the history of technology.

It would be interesting to add to the WG2.1 collection under ADB's custody more documentation in the same field, possibly coming from the same or other related TC2 working groups. Moreover, cross-checking information with other on-line archives (e.g. the Ershov archive[8]) is much needed, complementing each other. A possible international network of software archives could be set up.[9]

Using standards, as ADB always does, can but help in this respect. This said, information technology presents new challenges for an old science, as the traditional use of paper as the main document medium is being replaced by computer files, in many different formats. Moreover, preserving large information systems and their metadata is even more challenging. Such dematerialization

---

[7] Recent is the right word here: one of us stepped from work on medieval seals straight into the Algol programming language!

[8] URL: http://ershov.iis.nsk.su/en.

[9] Contributions to these challenges are welcome. The Committee on the Archives of Science and Technology of the Section on University and Research Institutions Archives (https://www.ica.org/en/suv) of the International Council on Archives, of which ADB is a member, can be of help.

will deprive archives in the future of their traditional raw material, and this represents a major challenge for archival science.

In particular, and again taking WG2.1 as working example, is the archival science prepared to preserve its last (say) 20 years bulk of emails, text source files (written in a myriad of different, constant evolving markup conventions or editor formats), PDFs, websites and so on, when compared to the "classical" archival techniques applied to van der Poel's collection?

This brings us into the field of digital preservation, defined by the American Library Association as a combination of *"policies, strategies and actions that ensure access to digital content over time"* [1]. Authenticity is an issue: policies and security procedures should be used to provide evidence that the contents of the archived electronic records has not been altered while in the archives' custody. The economic impact of digital preservation is also great.

We believe digital preservation should be elected as a main topic to address in the field of archival science, further to strategies to soften the significant investments in equipment and staffing required by preservation programs. Perhaps the history of formal methods could be used as case study encompassing the old and the new digital sources of information.

Acknowledgements. ADB and the University of Minho are very grateful to the generosity of Primavera Software. The authors would like to thank the interest of WG2.1 member J.N. Oliveira in bringing the WG2.1 collection into ADB custody. His comments on the current version of the paper are also gratefully acknowledged.

References

1. American Library Association: Definitions of digital preservation. http://www.ala. org/alcts/resources/preserv/defdigpres0408. Accessed 30 Jan 2020
2. DGARQ: Orientações para a descrição arquivística (2007). Direcção Geral de Arquivos, Grupo de trabalho de normalização da descrição em arquivo, 325 p. http://arquivos.dglab.gov.pt/wp-content/uploads/sites/16/2013/10/oda1-2-3.pdf
3. Floyd, R.: Assigning meanings to programs. In: Schwartz, J. (ed.) Mathematical Aspects of Computer Science, vol. 19, pp. 19–32. American Mathematical Society (1967). Proc. Symposia in Applied Mathematics
4. Hoare, C.: An axiomatic basis for computer programming. CACM **12**(10), 576–580, 583 (1969)
5. ICA: ISAD(G): General international standard archival description (1999). International Council on Archives. Adopted by the Committee on Descriptive Standards, Stockolm, Sweden, 19–22 September 1999, 2nd edn. Ottawa: ICA/CDS (2000). http://tiny.cc/suwdjz
6. ICA: ISAAR(CFP): International standard archival authority records for corporate bodies, persons and families (2002). Prepared by the Committee on Descriptive Standards, Rio de Janeiro, Brazil, 19–21 November 2002. http://tiny.cc/eswdjz
7. Schellenberg, T.R.: Modern archives; principles and techniques. Society of American Archivists, Chicago (1996). http://hdl.handle.net/2027/mdp.39015071452539. xv, 247 p. Reprint of the 1956 edn. Includes bibliographical references and index

What Have Formal Methods Ever Done for Us? An Audience Discussion

Troy Kaighin Astarte[✉][iD]

Newcastle University, Newcastle upon Tyne, UK
troy.astarte@ncl.ac.uk

Abstract. The History of Formal Methods 2019 workshop ended with a discussion reflecting on the discipline of formal methods. An initial prompting question, "What have formal methods ever done for us?", was presented, but the discussion evolved from there into consideration of applicability, education, and even Star Trek. The session was chaired and curated by Troy Astarte, who has also prepared this summary of the discussion. It is not a perfect transcription but rather a report on the interesting and stimulating conversation that resulted.

Keywords: Formal methods · History of computing

1 Introduction

At five o'clock on Friday 11th October 2019, contributed talks at the *History of Formal Methods 2019* workshop drew to a close. The day was not yet over, however.

Since the very first discussions about the idea of the workshop, my co-chair Brian Randell and I[1] had wanted to include some form of guided discussion and to write it up for the proceedings. We were inspired by the 1964 IFIP Working Conference on *Formal Language Description Languages* [10], and others of its time, whose proceedings included a detailed reporting of discussions which took place after each talk.[2] These conversations were often as illuminating as the papers themselves—perhaps, for the historian, even more so. We decided in the end that it would be too complicated to do this for every talk, and that the nature of academic conferences had somewhat changed in the intervening fifty-five years, but that a guided and curated discussion would serve rather well instead.

The discussion was somewhat like a panel session, but one in which the whole audience was equally free to participate. We thought it would be a good idea

---

Supported by EPSRC.

[1] Throughout this text, I will refer to myself in the first person when I contributed to the discussion.

[2] I am grateful to Jeremy Gibbons for pointing out that in certain circles, such as IFIP Working Conferences, this tradition persisted for some time. See the 2002 conference on Generic Programming [3].

© Springer Nature Switzerland AG 2020
E. Sekerinski et al. (Eds.): FM 2019 Workshops, LNCS 12233, pp. 103–113, 2020.
https://doi.org/10.1007/978-3-030-54997-8_7

to start with a provocative question—indeed, in early versions of our plans, the session would be guided not by a chair but a *provocateur*—and then let the discussion grow organically from there. We had counted on a diverse set of historical perspectives to have been laid before the audience so that there would be plenty of fuel for a pleasantly warm discussion; and the day did not disappoint.

Here, then, is the report of the discussion. It is based on a recording made by the FM'19 conference volunteers, for which they have our gratitude. It is not a verbatim transcription, being edited for clarity and concision. There are an additional series of footnotes which provide extra details or references.

2   Provocation

"What have formal methods ever done for us?"[3]

3   Industry

The first direction the discussion went in was consideration of formal methods within industry.

Opening the contributions was Graeme Smith, from the University of Queensland. He explained that Amazon Web Services has begun using formal methods in their workflow to cope with significantly increased user numbers.[4] They employ TLA+ and associated tools to avoid releasing any code they're not sure about.

Brian Randell, from Newcastle University, continued the theme. A phrase he learnt in the States many years ago was "technology is most easily transferred on the hoof." Randell thought it would be interesting to see some comprehensive data on movements of people between academia and industry, through various research partnerships and projects—rather than just on the exit trajectories of PhD students, a commonly-cited statistic for engagement. Believable statistics that were more than the current collection of anecdotes would be useful, and industrial companies have indicated their interest in such work.[5] Computing companies have a certain percentage of their workforce with appropriate experience, but there is only anecdotal evidence about transmission of ideas.

Taking up the theme, Ursula Martin, of Oxford and Edinburgh Universities, explained that the origin of formal methods at Facebook was in a very dynamic group of people led by Peter O'Hearn. They started up a company called Monoidics Ltd., which was then bought by Facebook along with its engineering team. Byron Cook at Amazon Web Services is another example of ex-academics using formal methods in industry. She made the point, however, that

---

[3] The inspiration for this question is, of course, the classic scene from *Monty Python's Life of Brian*.

[4] See a report authored by a number of people from the company on their use of formal methods [6].

[5] One example of a study that addressed this was reported in [12].

Facebook buying up a formal methods company is rather different from there being a general cultural of understanding the maths involved. Another route to formal methods in industry came from companies developing their in-house versions.

Martin continued that one can look back in history and see evidence of industrial and academic interaction. In 2016 there was a workshop at Oxford celebrating a hundred years since the birth of Christopher Strachey,[6] and there, Martin said, she was surprised to hear just how many people from companies were coming to visit Oxford's Programming Research Group on a regular basis. People tend to talk as though university–industry interaction is something that was invented ten years ago, but in fact it was always happening.

I added to this that I had seen some specific evidence of interaction about (what would today be called) formal methods in the Strachey archive. In 1971, a member of Oxford University whose job was to engage with industry went to speak to the IBM facility at Hursley and showed them examples of all the various kinds of computing research going on at Oxford. Strachey's formal semantics work had taken their interest most of all.

Jeremy Gibbons, also of Oxford University, now joined the conversation. One thing that concerned him about companies like Amazon and Facebook was that they were hiring lots of very clever people, and sometimes those employees did get to keep doing work related to their research background, such as formal methods, but very often they would be hired just because they were clever. They would then be put to work on other kinds of projects doing other things, sometimes working with quite unsophisticated tools. That might be helpful for the company, and indeed lucrative for the employees, but we researchers might have hoped for loftier goals: better communication with the research community about the techniques developed and the problems experienced in industry.

Wrapping up this particular discussion, independent scholar and HFM2019 keynote speaker Mark Priestley entered the conversation. He remarked that J Robert Oppenheimer, theoretical physicist and one of the developers of the atomic bomb, said that the best way to send information from one place to another is to wrap it in a human being. Priestley observed that this comment, while humorous, makes the point that the kind of information which can be transmitted in a paper or lecture is only a fragment of the practical experience and tacit knowledge that a person can take with them—equally valuable information.

4 Hardware

Priestley then introduced a new topic of conversation, noting that this was a question from an outsider to the world of formal methods. He observed that the vast majority of talks given at HFM2019, his own included, had been about applications to software and programming. He wondered: is there anything to say about

---

[6] The webpages can be found at https://www.cs.ox.ac.uk/strachey100/ which includes a link to recordings of all the talks.

hardware? Have formal methods succeeded differentially in hardware compared to software, or been more accepted by the hardware design community?

Earlier in the day, Adrian Johnstone, of Royal Holloway, had mentioned in his talk about Charles Babbage's mechanical notation [5] that some similarity could be observed with modern-day hardware description languages. It seemed appropriate to turn to him to answer this question.

Johnstone began with a caution that he is not a hardware expert, but does have some knowledge about the area. The British electronics firm Racal-Redac developed an early hardware description language (HDL) called ISIS, which they turned into a heavily marketed product. This HDL was quite radical, argued Johnstone, and precipitated a major shift in the design of circuitry. Prior to ISIS, nearly all integrated circuit design was done at the level of schematics. Designers would draw coloured graphs of transistor circuitry, and print it at a very large scale on acetate. They would then spend a long time literally crawling all over the floor with this huge picture of the chip, making sure that artefacts like wires were not so close to each other that they could not be manufactured with precision.

This design practice was common as late as the mid-1980s, being used, for example, by Motorola for the 6800 chip which powered the original Apple Macintosh computer. So, Johnstone indicated, this was not archaic 1950s behaviour, it was relatively modern. What happened in the late 1980s was a wholesale shift from that essentially graphical mode of design to a textual version: HDLs.

This was a welcome change, explained Johnstone, who said he used to stand up in conferences and say "If God had intended us to use schematic entry[7] we would still be writing in hieroglyphs." One time, however, he noticed he was speaking to an audience comprising mostly Japanese people, and the joke became somewhat unfortunate.

ISIS HDL never really caught on, though, and neither did an HDL called Ella which was rooted in ALGOL 68 functional notions and was a very interesting system. The languages that did make it, continued Johnstone, were Verilog and VHDL. They remain in use today and the majority of current hardware is designed using one of the two. VHDL in particular is worth noting for its similarities to the programming language Ada.

Apart from the notation used, there was a particular design philosophy espoused by Racal-Redac and used as the marketing slogan for the ISIS system: "Correct by construction". By this they meant that you wrote an abstract specification and the system could compile your hardware from that. Johnstone explained that this seemed intuitive to many programmers, who are used to writing Java or C programs and without worrying too much about the underlying compiler. Even so, the ISIS system was not as abstract as is used today in the heavily synthesised piece of hardware from, for example, synopsis VHDL.

---

[7] Schematic entry is the particular part of the electronics design process that involves drawing diagrams.

Wrapping up, Johnstone said that there are indeed formal methods for the hardware design process; and many early successes in verification were in the hardware universe. He remembered being told once by a researcher in this area that hardware was easier to verify than software, a comment Johnstone knows is broadly agreed upon, but does not quite understand. It seems strange given that hardware is something of an open and unconstrained zoo, whereas much software is sequential.

Dan Berry, of the University of Waterloo, wished to provide a comment. He told us he remembered asking a committee of verification people whether the microcode for a computer's instruction set is a small program. At that point, in the 1980s, the general view amongst verificationists was that any small program should be tractable enough for complete verification. Indeed, the formal methods people were (perhaps consequently) arguing that *all* programs should be small. So, wondered Berry, would a reduced instruction set architecture computer's instruction set be small enough for complete verification? The finiteness of the instruction set should have led to a manageable state size, but whether this was actually the case was unclear.[8]

5   Expression

We now moved to a new topic, on the original question, and a thoughtful message from José Oliveira, of INESC TEC, University of Minho. He explained that he felt a lot of the real formal methods impact was implicit rather than explicit—as the previous discussion had considered. Oliveira observed that he felt people always expressed themselves more clearly after attending formal methods events like the FM conferences.

A while ago, Oliveira continued, he bought a book—the only copy remaining at a Springer conference stand—that changed the way he thought about science. The book was written by physicist and linguist Lucio Russo and was called *The Forgotten Revolution: How Science Was Born in 300 BC and Why it Had to Be Reborn* [9]. This book was interesting because it argued that, using evidence and documents still extant, the Ancient Greeks were much better at science than the Ancient Romans. This was arguable despite much more evidence surviving from the Roman era. Russo's linguistics background led him to state that a reason for this is that the Greeks had better terminology. They could say in one word what the Romans said in three. This meant that their understanding of problems was superior—and, in the same way, Oliveira argued, formal methods give us the language to express ourselves better.

Oliveira also told us about another reading experience: he went through a book of mathematics written in 1567 by a Portuguese mathematician, Pedro Nunes [7]. Oliveira read the book—supported by a modern description—and compared the language used in the 16th Century with that used for the same

---

[8] Berry later added by email that he was particularly thinking here of Patterson's PhD thesis [8].

theorems nowadays. He observed quite a difference, and suggested that maths has evolved and improved significantly.[9]

Finally, Oliveira mentioned that he had been recently examining the standard for the patent of the stack concept; the very existence of a patent for something that seems like a fundamental concept was interesting in itself. Furthermore, he found it hard, looking through this patent, to understand exactly how they were defining the stack.[10] Oliveira thought it would be an interesting exercise to write the same standard using a formal methods approach: surely the result would be a much briefer specification. These days, he explained, we teach students the concept of a stack in two minutes; but in the historic standard one had to read very carefully for a much longer time in order to find what the stack is. So, modern formal methods gives us the tools for considerably more precise expression: a great thing.[11]

6 Inconsistency

The discussion now switched towards a critique of formal methods, courtesy of Dan Berry.[12] He came on the stage in order to use a flip chart to illustrate his points.

Recently, explained Berry, he published a paper with Hadar and Zamansky about dealing with inconsistency in requirements specification [4]. A core part of that work discussed how, as you develop a new system and do not yet have full information, your specification is bound to contain inconsistencies. Berry and his co-authors found, from interviews with software engineering practitioners who had experience of requirements specification, that these people had difficulty dealing with inconsistencies and would feel they had to resolve every one.

Here Berry drew a diagram on the flip chart, reproduced in Fig. 1. He explained: specification of the system entails the requirements: $D, S \vdash R$. D and R are written in the vocabulary of the environment and S is written in the

---

[9] The history of maths community would reproach me if I did not comment that mathematical works must be appreciated within their historical context. One handbook for doing this has been written by Wardaugh [11].

[10] A further editorial note courtesy of Berry: patents are often written in a confusing way in order to play up the non-obviousness of the proposed "invention".

[11] Expanding this point, Gibbons remarked in a later email: "Yes, a formal methodist can make a more precise specification than someone who doesn't know maths, e.g. for writing a technical specification. The problem is that the specification must also be *readable* by people who don't know maths. Rick Hehner used to tell a nice story about arguing with his lawyer while trying to write a will: how to specify the class of related people to whom your assets will be distributed. The lawyer had a long piece of text about cousins, and second cousins, and third, etc. Rick had a much shorter specification in terms of the transitive closure of a small relation. Rick lost the argument, because the reader of the will is not someone like Rick, but someone like Rick's lawyer".

[12] Earlier in the workshop, Berry had given a talk about his own shift in research emphasis away from formal methods and towards requirement engineering [2].

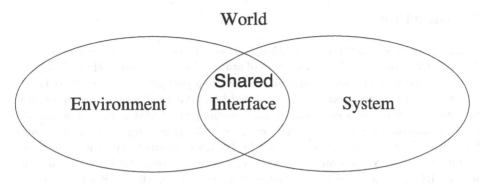

Fig. 1. Berry's World Views diagram, originally from [13].

vocabulary of the interface. So, while the code of the system might be formal, anything about the environment is about the real world and is informal. Thus, in this view, the whole formula becomes hopelessly informal.

Berry gave us an example scenario. Consider some system engineers designing a traffic system. A key safety requirement is that there should be no perpendicular collisions. The specification of a traffic light permits focus on the condition that prevents these collisions: a green light should not be shown in two perpendicular directions simultaneously.

However, Berry continued, that might not be enough. This system makes the assumption that drivers obey the light *and* that the cars obey the drivers. If this assumption is forgotten and the specification is followed to the letter, there could be some inconsistency. Berry argued that sometimes it is necessary to tolerate an inconsistency temporarily until it can be resolved. In the traffic light example, the main thing is that the driver obeys the lights. It might not be necessary to tolerate that permanently, but there is no way to make the software force the driver to obey the lights. Berry reported that when situations like this were described in interviews, practitioners were prepared to accept that there could be some inconsistencies that could not fixed, and would instead have to be tolerated.

The situation might seem different, however, with self-driving cars. One might think "Great! Maybe the light should control the vehicle." This would obviate the need for drivers to obey the lights. One of the aspects of the real world (here Berry indicated the appropriate part of the diagram) has been moved over into the specification, which tells the system it now has to be obeyed. Of course, the vehicle still has to obey the system. This way of framing the situation, Berry and his co-authors found in interviews, was more acceptable to practitioners: it became something they could deal with. So, an informal version of a formal method was able to help people deal with something they couldn't have dealt with when it was completely informal.

7   Direction

Ursula Martin joined the conversation, and suggested an opening up of the discussion, with, in particular, a question of stakeholders. She noted that in Berry's example, there was a tacit community of involved parties: everyone who drives a car, walks on the pavement hoping to avoid being hit by a car, or sits on a train. She was interested in a clarification and opening up of this group. Who should able to prioritise the next line of research questions coming for historians and formal methods people? Should it be the technical community? Industry practitioners? The next generation of students? Martin wondered by whom and in which direction the research question should be developed; she was particularly concerned with this in regards to teaching formal methods to undergraduate students.

8   Education

This led us into our next discussion topic, education, on which topic Jeremy Gibbons had a contribution to make. He wished to highlight Carroll Morgan's talk at the Formal Methods Teaching workshop, the topic of which was hidden formal methods. Gibbons linked this to what Berry had been saying: the idea was to gloss the *intention* of the formal method to make it more appealing and memorable. This approach might avoid people thinking "Formal methods are a theory thing, only for theoreticians. I'm a programmer or engineer, so I don't need to know this formal methods stuff." Formal methods should not be sold as something purely theoretical, Gibbons argued, but rather as a tool of thought. These methods aid in thinking the right things, thinking them clearly, and expressing them well—goals which are of use to everyone. So finding ways to prevent students switching off is very important.

Coming in next on the subject of education, Elizabeth Scott, head of Computing at Royal Holloway, felt that for the three hundred students at her institution, formal methods seemed just too hard. The way of learning them did not match with what the students wanted: they wanted a practical experience. So, trying to find a good angle to sell formal methods was vital. Acknowledging that she was not particularly part of the formal methods community, Scott nevertheless had an intriguing suggestion for this.

What if, she proposed, there was a Star Trek episode in which they travelled to an alternate universe in which formal methods had won? Dana Scott and Christopher Strachey[13] revered—how would that world look different? There was a particular Star Trek episode called 'A Piece of the Action' in which the crew went to a planet on which a book describing the 1920s American gangster scene had fallen. The planet's inhabitants had shaped their whole culture around this. In the fictional universe where formal methods had landed in this way, what would the practitioners be doing? How would the world be different if formal

---

[13] These two worked together on denotational semantics in the 1970s; for an account of their work see Chap. 4 of [1].

methods had been embraced in the way its proponents wished? If we could work that out, Scott suggested, we might present it to students and industry as a selling point.

This was a novel suggestion, and flipped the initial question on its head—not "What have formal methods done for us?" but "What *could* they do for us?"

9 Proliferation

Brian Randell took the microphone, expressing a heartfelt sentiment that what the FM community could do with is more historians. They could provide more *accurate* stories and analyses of who really did what and what really happened. He admitted he knew historians dislike being used as a source of ideas for what should be done next, but Randell said he strongly believed in George Santayana's line "He who forgets the past is forced to relive it".

That led Randell to what was, to him, the really irritating point: why the hell are there so many different formal methods? Never mind so many thousands of different programming languages. Acknowledging that he might just be seeing greener grass, Randell said he felt that the disease was nothing like as strong in the hardware world. He could imagine reasons for some of those constraints, but thought that some good sceptical historians could give formal methods—and many other fields in computer science—quite a strong dose of reality.

I had a response to the question of why there are so many different formal methods, programming languages, and technologies generally. It was mentioned to me that morning while I was talking to another workshop attendee, who was no longer present by the afternoon session. She had told me about her experience of working on a tough problem in an industrial setting: they understood the problem to a reasonable degree of detail, but were not able to shape it easily into a form that could be addressed by an existing language. In that case, they felt, the easiest thing to do was just design a new approach.

I observed further that perhaps a reason for the current success of domain-specific languages was because they enabled a more problem-oriented viewpoint. In a world where there are, say, five formal methods, then one has to be able to state every single problem in at least one of those five different methods. Whereas, if the problem-first perspective is taken, one might design a way to state the problem sufficiently precisely that a solution becomes easy to find.

10 Communication

I took the opportunity to make another observation about education. I had recently started teaching by taking over a module previously taught by Cliff Jones on the subject of semantics of programming languages. In that class, the techniques are illustrated on a language that is neither full-scale and very complicated, nor only trivial. Many students stated in their reflection at the end of the module that they experienced a sudden moment of clarity. They would have been sitting through the lectures, unable to make sense of the concepts—seeing only a jumble of confusing notations—and then suddenly something would click and everything would fall into place. It was even my own experience when I took the module as an undergraduate.

Once that moment had happened, the students became able to look at programming languages in a different way. They were then able to see that what they had thought of as distinct entities actually had a lot more similarity and shared notions. Students reported that it had helped them think about real issues in programming and even designing things like protocols.

In conclusion, I thought one of the real values of formal methods is that they give us ways of discussing fundamental concepts in computing and transmitting these to the next generation. A lot of the tools in formal methods assist in getting to the important ideas and expressing them. Perhaps not always in the *most* intuitive way, but in a way that is somehow precise and useful. This, of course, linked back to what José Oliveira had said earlier—and indeed he was nodding in agreement.

11   Concluding

This took us towards the end of the session. One final remark was made by Dan Berry, who took up the thread of multiplicity of formal methods mentioned by Randell. He indicated his diagram (Fig. 1), and noted that the specification and the system are both formal models of the real world. Every part of the real world was inevitably going to require different formal models, he argued. This can be seen in physics, too: there is a formal model of the macro world which is totally different from—and inconsistent with—the formal model of the quantum world. The reason we have trouble with these formal methods, asserted Berry, is that we are building systems for different parts of the real world, which will need different models, and hence different formal methods.

I now handed the microphone to Brian Randell for a penultimate word from the co-chair. He said he couldn't disagree more with the point Berry had made, and said that to express worries that there are too many languages is not the same as saying "Why don't we all use the same language?" Randell repeated a quotation from Tony Hoare "If you've got a new problem, by all means invent a new language; but for Pete's sake don't write a compiler for it!" Randell noted that he would also add "Don't start writing textbooks for it, and don't start proselyting around, unless you've got a very good reason!" It was almost like a conservation issue to him. Every new language and every new method has disadvantages through its very existence.

That brought the workshop to a close. All the attendees were thanked for a great collection of talks with some very stimulating discussion, and a balanced viewpoint on the effects of formal methods. I suggested we leave the final verdict on whether formal methods had been a good thing or not to the thriving future community of formal methods historians. Perhaps at the next HFM19, in one hundred years' time, decisions about what formal methods had done for us could be made. Until then, everyone was left with a suggestion that reflection on one's work, and on one's discipline, is always a good and healthy thing.

References

1. Astarte, T.K.: Formalising meaning: a history of programming language semantics. Ph.D. thesis, Newcastle University, June 2019
2. Berry, D.M.: The prehistory and history of RE (+SE) as seen by me: how my interest in FMs helped to move me to RE and to teach me fundamental impediments to using FMs in SW systems development (abstract). In: Moreira, N., Sekerinski, E. (eds.) FM 2019 Workshops Proceedings, LNCS. Springer (2020)
3. Gibbons, J., Jeuring, J. (eds.): Generic Programming. In: Proceedings of the IFIP TC2 Working Conference on Generic Programming, Schloß Dagstuhl, July 2002. Kluwer Academic Publishers (2003). ISBN 1-4020-7374-7
4. Hadar, I., Zamansky, A., Berry, D.M.: The inconsistency between theory and practice in managing inconsistency in requirements engineering. Empir. Softw. Eng. 24, 3972–4005 (2019)
5. Johnstone, A., Scott, E.: Babbage's mechanical notation (abstract). In: Moreira, N., Sekerinski, E. (eds.) FM 2019 Workshops Proceedings, LNCS. Springer (2020)
6. Newcombe, C., et al.: Use of Formal Methods at Amazon Web Services, September 2014. http://lamport.azurewebsites.net/tla/formal-methods-amazon.pdf
7. Nunes, P.: Libro de Algebra en Arithmetica y Geometria. Original edition by Arnoldo Birckman (Anvers) (1567)
8. Patterson, D.A.: Verification of microprograms. Ph.D. thesis, University of California, Los Angeles (1976)
9. Russo, L., et al.: The Forgotten Revolution: How Science was Born in 300 BC and Why it had to be Reborn. Springer, Heidelberg (2013). https://doi.org/10.1007/978-3-642-18904-3
10. Steel, T.B.: Formal Language Description Languages for Computer Programming. North-Holland, Amsterdam (1966)
11. Wardhaugh, B.: How to Read Historical Mathematics. Princeton University Press, Princeton (2010)
12. Woodcock, J., Larsen, P.G., Bicarregui, J., Fitzgerald, J.: Formal methods: practice and experience. ACM Comput. Surv. 41(4) (2009)
13. Zave, P., Jackson, M.: Four dark corners of requirements engineering. ACM Trans. Softw. Eng. Methodol. (TOSEM) 6(1), 1–30 (1997)

NSAD 2019 - 8th Workshop on Numerical and Symbolic Abstract Domains

NSAD 2019 Organizers' Message

This volume contains the post-proceedings of the 8th International Workshop on Numerical and Symbolic Abstract Domains (NSAD 2019), held on 8 October 2019 in Porto, Portugal, as part of the Third World Congress on Formal Methods.

The series of Workshops on Numerical and Symbolic Abstract Domains are intended to promote discussions and exchanges of experience in the design of abstract domains: semantic choices, data-structures and algorithmic aspects, and implementation decisions, as well as classical or less classical applications.

Previous workshops were held in Perpignan, Venice, Deauville, Munich, Edinburgh and New York.

The Program Committee (PC) received 6 submissions, which covered a large number of topics, which significately increased the traditional audience of the NSAD workshop.

Each paper was evaluated using a multi-phase review process. In the first phase, each paper received independent reviews from 3 PC members. All 6 submissions were accepted for presentation:

- Farah Benmouhoub, Pierre-Loic Garoche and Matthieu Martel *Improving the Numerical Accuracy of Parallel Programs by Data Mapping.*
- Vincenzo Arceri, Michele Pasqua and Isabella Mastroeni *An abstract domain for objects in dynamic programming languages.*
- Ghiles Ziat, Alexandre Maréchal, Marie Pelleau, Antoine Miné and Charlotte Truchet *Combination of Boxes and Polyhedra Abstractions for Constraint Solving.*
- Guillaume Cluzel and Cezara Drăgoi *Towards an abstraction for data structures that implement cooperation mechanisms.*
- Maxime Jacquemin and Franck Vedrine, *A Dividing Method Minimizing the Linearization Term in Affine Arithmetic.*
- Solène Mirliaz and David Pichardie, *Flow Insensitive Relational Static Analysis.*

The acceptation email also proposed to all papers to resubmit their paper to the postproceeding phase, with clear hints on how to improve the submission to fit the postproceeding standards.

In addition, the program also featured 3 invited talks, shared with the Tenth Workshop on Tools for Automatic Program AnalysiS (TAPAS 2019):

- *Transforming Development Processes of Avionics Software with Formal Methods*, by Pascal Lacabanne (Airbus, France);
- *Establishing Sound Static Analysis for Integration Verification of Large-Scale Software in Automotive Industry* by Bernard Schmidt (Bosch, Germany);
- *Some thoughts on the design of abstract domains*, by Enea Zaffanella (University of Parma, Italy).

Finally, revised versions of some of the presented papers were submitted after the workshop, and the reviews of the PC were updated accordingly. These post-proceedings enclose the two regular contributions to NSAD 2019 selected for formal publication, as well as the abstracts of one invited talk. The abstract of the two other invited talks may be found in the post-proceedings of TAPAS 2019.

We would like to thank everyone involved in the organization of the workshop, and especially David Delmas, chair of TAPAS, which clearly helped a lot in the overall organisation of our two friend worshops. We are very thankful for the members of the Program Committee for their evaluation work, and for all the discussions on the organization of the event. We would like to give a particular acknowledgment to the Organizing Committees of the FM Week and the Static Analysis Symposium (SAS), in particular José Nuno Oliveira (FM General Chair), Nelma Moreira and Emil Sekerinski (FM Workshop and Tutorial Chairs), Bor-Yuh Evan Chang (SAS PC Chair), and Antoine Miné (SAS PC member), for their great support to the organization of satellite events such as TAPAS 2019. We would also like to thank Isabella Mastroeni and Antoine Miné for giving us the opportunity to organize NSAD 2019.

Finally, we would also like to thank the authors and the invited speakers for their contributions to the program of NSAD and TAPAS, as well as Springer for publishing these post-proceedings.

December 2019   Laure Gonnord

Organization

Program Committee Chair

Laure Gonnord   Université Claude Bernard Lyon1, France

Steering Committee

Isabella Mastroeni   Università di Verona, Italy
Antoine Miné   Université Pierre et Marie Curie, Paris

Program Committee

Clément Ballabriga   Université de Lille, France
Mehdi Bouaziz   Nomadic Labs, Paris, France
Matthieu Martel   Université de Perpignan, France
Isabella Mastroeni   Università di Verona, Italy
Pascal Sotin   Université de Toulouse, France
Charlotte Truchet   Univ Nantes, France

Some Thoughts on the Design of Abstract Domains (Invited Talk)

Enea Zaffanella

University of Parma, Italy
enea.zaffanella@unipr.it

Abstract. The Abstract Interpretation framework provides invaluable guidance for the design of abstract domains to be used in static analysis tools. Nonetheless, the development of an adequate abstract domain can be a challenging task: besides the mandatory correctness requirements, also its precision and efficiency need to be properly considered. Drawing mainly from past experience, we show a few examples of the problems that an abstract domain developer may be facing. We rediscuss the tradeoffs that could be adopted while working through the solutions, somehow confirming known rules of thumb, possible exceptions to the rules of thumb and other interesting relationships between correctness, precision and efficiency.

Combination of Boxes and Polyhedra Abstractions for Constraint Solving

Ghiles Ziat[1(✉)], Alexandre Maréchal[1,2], Marie Pelleau[3], Antoine Miné[1],
and Charlotte Truchet[4]

[1] Sorbonne Université, CNRS, LIP6, 75005 Paris, France
ghiles.ziat@gmail.com
[2] Univ. Grenoble Alpes, CNRS, VERIMAG, 38000 Grenoble, France
[3] Université Côte D'Azur, CNRS, I3S, 06100 Nice, France
[4] LS2N, UMR 6004, Université de Nantes, 44300 Nantes, France

Abstract. This paper investigates the use of abstract domains from Abstract Interpretation (AI) in the field of Constraint Programming (CP). CP solvers are generally very efficient on a specific constraint language, but can hardly be extended to tackle more general languages, both in terms of variable representation (discrete or continuous) and constraint type (global, arithmetic, etc.). For instance, linear constraints are usually solved with linear programming techniques, but non-linear ones have to be either linearized, reformulated or sent to an external solver. We approach this problem by adapting to CP a popular domain construction used to combine the power of several analyses in AI: the *reduced product*. We apply this product on two well-known abstract domains, Boxes and Polyhedra, that we lift to constraint solving. Finally we define general metrics for the quality of the solver results, and present a benchmark accordingly. Experiments show promising results and good performances.

1 Introduction

Constraint programming (CP) is a paradigm of declarative programming, in which problems are described in mathematical terms involving constraints (*i.e.* first-order logic formulas) over variables, and then solved using a constraint solver. Solvers often focus on a few *constraint languages*, which are families of constraints such as linear (in)equalities over the reals, over the integers, polynomial constraints, real constraints with mathematical functions (sin, cos, log...), integer cardinality constraints, etc. Yet, most solvers share two common ingredients: first, they use propagation algorithms to reduce the search space by reasoning on the constraints, without losing solutions. Second, they usually feature a branching process that consists in adding hypotheses (e.g. variable instantiation or domain splitting) to the problem. If the new problem is proved infeasible, the solver backtracks on the current hypotheses and makes new ones to explore other parts of the search space. In classic CP solvers, the variables are always considered independent, the only relations between them being the constraints. In practice, solvers thus work in the Cartesian product of the variables domains,

© Springer Nature Switzerland AG 2020
E. Sekerinski et al. (Eds.): FM 2019 Workshops, LNCS 12233, pp. 119–135, 2020.
https://doi.org/10.1007/978-3-030-54997-8_8

which can be real intervals with floating point bounds, integer intervals or finite integer sets. Each of these domain representations comes with specific propagators, such as Hull consistency [3] for real domains or bound-consistency [18,23] for integer intervals, to name a few.

Abstract domain has been introduced for over-approximating sets of interests (traces of programs) in order to capture specific properties. Previous works [17] showed how to unify the core constraint solving methods by re-defining a generic notion of abstract domain, augmented with CP-oriented operations.

A generic solving process based on abstract domains has been introduced in [16], and implemented in the AbSolute abstract solver. Given an abstract domain (e.g. the Cartesian products of real intervals, also called *boxes*), the solver combines propagators and branching operators well defined for this abstract domain (for instance on boxes: Hull consistency propagation and interval splitting). An important feature of this solving method is its modularity: the same formal method can be parametrized with different abstract domains. The main properties of the solver, which are termination, completeness, and soundness, depend on the properties of the abstract domain it uses.[1]

In this fashion, a solver can benefit from the many abstract domains that have already been defined in Abstract Interpretation (AI) to tackle specific program properties: Intervals [6], Polyhedra, etc. For instance, Octagons [14,15] have been adapted to constraint solving with *ad-hoc* propagation and exploration heuristics [17]. Abstract domains feature different precision and costs: for example, Octagons are costlier than Intervals but more precise. Also, some domains such as Ellipsoids are designed to capture very specific properties and ignore other ones, or propose very coarse approximations for them. Choosing which domain to use is not a trivial task as these facts must be taken into account.

In addition, AI defines a set of abstract domain transformers, building upon one or several abstract domains to improve or combine their precision. Such transformers are very useful as they create more expressive combined domains in a modular and generic way. For example the Trace Partitioning transformer [19] partitions execution traces of a program according to the control flow (*e.g.*, which branch of a conditional statement was taken), leading to a path sensitive analysis. It focuses on the abstraction of the control flow and delegates the value analysis to another domain (generally a numeric one), whose accuracy will benefit from the partitioning. In the following, we will extensively use the Reduced Product [7], another very popular domain transformer. It combines two domains to represent conjunctions of properties from both of them. Operations in the reduced product apply a reduction operator to communicate information between the base domains, thus improving the precision.

Contribution. In this article, we first present a Constraint Programming version of the Box and Polyhedra abstract domains [8]. We then introduce a version

---

[1] Contrarily to AI, in CP the term completeness refers to an algorithm which does not lose solutions (over-approximating the solution set), while soundness means that the solver under-approximates the solution set. This vocabulary can be misleading. In the following, we will use "over/under-approximation" to avoid any ambiguity.

of the Reduced Product domain transformer adapted to CP purposes, and we detail a constraint attribution operators for the Box-Polyhedra reduced product. Finally, we present an implementation in the AbSolute solver and experiments made on the Coconut benchmark [22].

To be usable in a CP framework, we will have to define on each abstract domain (1) a *split* operator, to implement the branching process; (2) a *size* function, to determine when the solver finishes; (3) and *propagators* for given constraint languages. Compared to the classic reduced product of AI, our version introduces a hierarchy between the domains, one of them being specialized to a certain kind of problems only, in order to avoid a redundancy of information between the two components of the product.

This paper is organized as follows: Sect. 2 recalls the definitions and results on abstract domains needed afterwards, in particular the generic notion of abstract domain for CP. Section 3 introduces the Box and Polyhedra abstract domains. Section 4 then explains how to build Reduced Products domains for CP, and details the Box-Polyhedra reduced product. Section 5 presents experiments using AbSolute with the new Box-Polyhedra domain. Finally, Sect. 6 concludes.

Related Works. The links between CP and AI have already been highlighted in previous works. The seminal work of Apt [1] expresses the propagation loop which consists in propagating the unfeasible set of some constraints as chaotic iterations in a well-chosen lattice. In the same spirit, [2] defines propagators, whether discrete or continuous, in a similar framework. Later, [20] keeps the same idea and weakens the conditions on the propagators while keeping the convergence of the propagation loop. All these works focus on propagation. We go one step further by expressing the splitting and size operators in the same framework, thus taking into account the whole solving process.

A work more related to ours is [21], which also investigates the use of abstract domains in CP and also mainly focuses on propagation. The key difference is the way we build the abstract domain. [21] defines abstractions solely through Galois connections, which is an important restriction as it bans interesting abstractions such as polyhedra or zonotopes [10]. On the contrary, we can support a larger set of abstractions, including those for which there is no Galois connection.

2   Abstract Constraint Solving

This section introduces the core notions of CP solving, and the extension of abstract domains to the CP context.

2.1   Constraint Programming Background

Constraint solvers can deal with problems written as Constraint Satisfaction Problems (CSP), where *variables* represent the unknowns of the problem. Each variable takes its value from a given set, usually called *domain*, and constraints express the relations between the variables. The variables, domains and constraints are given by the user to represent the problem to solve, and the triplet of these make a Constraint Satisfaction Problem. Note that the domains defined in CP are not abstract domains as defined in AI. Next section will clarify this.

Definition 1. *A Constraint Satisfaction Problem is a triplet $(\mathcal{V}, \mathcal{D}, \mathcal{C})$, where n and m are respectively the number of variables and the number of constraints of the problem:*

- $\mathcal{V} = (v_1, ..., v_n)$ *are variables representing the unknowns of the problem,*
- $\mathcal{D} = (d_1, ..., d_n)$ *are domains for the variable, such that $v_k \in d_k, \forall k \in [1, n]$,*
- $\mathcal{C} = (c_1, ..., c_m)$ *are constraints over the variables.*

Constraints of a CSP are defined in a given constraint language, *i.e.* a family of first-order logical formulæ. For simplicity, we focus in this section on the case of real variables, where the domains are real intervals with floating-point bounds, and the constraints can be written using arithmetic operators, common mathematical functions (sin, cos, log, and any function which can be computed on intervals), and a relation operator within $\{=, \neq, <, \leq\}$. The corresponding abstract domain will be formally defined in Sect. 3.1. Many constraint languages exist in the literature, in particular on finite domains.

We call an *instance* a total mapping $\mathcal{V} \to \mathcal{D}$ from variables to their domain. A solution of a CSP is an instance that satisfies all of the constraints. In the case of finite domains, a solution is given as an instance, *i.e.* values in the domains for the variables, such that the constraints are satisfied when substituting the variables by their corresponding values. If the solutions are not computer-representable, as it is the case with variables taking real values, then solving the CSP means finding, for each variable, subpart of its domains which are either entirely solutions (all the instances inside the domains satisfy the constraints), or are smaller than a given precision (on interval domains for instance, the size of the domain is the interval length). Figure 1 illustrates an example of such a resolution.

The search space is usually either too large (in the discrete case, its size is exponential in the number of variables) or infinite (in the continuous case, solutions for real variable may not be computer-representable) to be explored exhaustively. A key ingredient of constraint solving is the notion of propagation, which relies on the constraints to reduce the search space.

Definition 2. *Let $(\mathcal{V}, \mathcal{D}, \mathcal{C})$ be a CSP, and let $c \in \mathcal{C}$ be a constraint. A propagator ρ for c is a function from $\mathscr{P}(\mathcal{D})$ to itself such that:*

- $\forall \mathcal{D}' \in \mathscr{P}(\mathcal{D}), \rho(\mathcal{D}') \subseteq \mathcal{D}'$,
- $\forall \mathcal{D}' \in \mathscr{P}(\mathcal{D}), \forall (x_1, \ldots, x_n) \in \mathcal{D}', c(x_1, \ldots, x_n) \implies (x_1, \ldots, x_n) \in \rho(\mathcal{D}')$

The first condition makes the propagators always decreasing for the $\subset$-order.[2] The second condition ensures that a propagator does not remove solutions for its

---

[2] Contrarily to the evolution of abstract elements during a static analysis in AI, constraint domains always decrease.

constraint. Constraint propagators are usually built to tighten the search space as much as possible. For instance, Hull-consistency propagation on boxes [3], which is similar to the bottom-up top-down algorithm in AI, reduces the domains by analyzing the expressions inside the constraints with interval arithmetics.

The propagation step in a solver applies the propagators for each constraint, until it reaches a given consistency. Consistencies are properties on the satisfiability of a problem. The application of a propagator makes it possible to establish such properties. For example, the HC4 propagator [3] establishes the Hull-Consistency property (*i.e.* it computes the smallest box containing all of the solutions of the problem). For example, given two real variables x and y defined respectively on the intervals $[0; 5]$ and $[0; 10]$, the smallest box that contains all of the solutions of the constraint $x^2 + y^2 \leq 4$ is the store that maps x to $[0; 2]$ and y to $[0; 2]$. Propagation is usually not sufficient to find solutions of the problems, for instance when the solution set cannot be exactly represented by a single abstract element (*e.g.*, Cartesian products cannot represent complex shapes). Thus, the solver alternates propagation steps and choice operations (split), as detailed below.

2.2 Abstract Domains for Constraint Solving

A key point in our work is the use and combination of abstract domains. In AI, they have been introduced to over-approximate program states [6]. For example with the Interval abstract domain, each variable of a program is mapped to an interval with floating point bounds, and a program state is a *box*. An abstract domain is a partially ordered set (a *poset*), where several operations can be made: transfer functions compute the result of an operation on an abstract element, the meet operator represent intersections of abstract elements, etc.

Abstract domains have already been extended to be used in a CP solver in [16]. We recall the main definitions and algorithms in this section. A classic CP solver alternates two main steps: propagation and search. The abstract-solving method is defined by lifting up these operations to abstract domains. An abstract CP domain must thus feature a propagation operation, a size function and a split operator. Propagation is quite specific in our work, and is defined in the next subsection.

Definition 3 (Abstract Domain for Constraints). *An abstract domain is given by:*

- *a poset $(E, \subseteq)$, with a computer representation for the elements of E,*
- *a propagator $\rho : E \to E$ for each constraint c,*
- *a splitting operator on E, $\oplus_E : E \to \mathscr{P}(E)$,*
- *a size function $\tau_E : E \to \mathbb{R}^+$.*

Here, the poset $(E, \subseteq)$ defines the sets of points that can be exactly represented (boxes, octagons, etc). The propagator must return an over-approximation, so that it does not lose solutions (as in Definition 2). The propagators may be designed specifically for an abstract domain, in particular when

---

Algorithm 1: Solving with abstract domains.

```
function solve(e, C)          // e: initial abstract element, C: constraints
    sols ← ∅                                       // abstract solutions
    toExplore ← ∅                       // abstract elements to explore
    append e in toExplore
    while toExplore ≠ ∅ do
        e ← pop(toExplore)
        e ← φ(e, C)                      // propagation of all constraints
        if e ≠ ⊥ then
            if τ_E(e) ≤ r or ∀c ∈ C, c(e) then
            └  sols ← sols ∪ e
            else
            └  ∀e_i ∈ ⊕_E(e), append e_i in toExplore          // splitting
```

---

the abstract domain is naturally defined with constraints: for example, Octagons are defined by a set of constraints of a given format ($\pm v_i \pm v_j \leq c$ for c a constant), and propagating these constraints correspond to the refined Floyd Warshall algorithm proposed in [13] to compute the normal form of an Octagon. But they may also be defined in a generic way to handle any type of constraints, as are most of the classical CP propagators on cartesian domains, such as the HC4 algorithm [3] described above. The size function gives a metric on the size of an abstract element. It is used for the termination condition and should be designed such that an abstract element $e \in E$ is considered as *too small to be split* if $\tau_E(e)$ is less than or equal to a parameter $r \in \mathbb{R}^+$. Moreover, if an element e is an atom of E, $\tau_E(e)$ should be equal to 0 as it is not possible to split e into smaller elements (*e.g.*, interval singletons).

We call split the action of dividing an abstract element into smaller ones w.r.t. $\subseteq$. The split operator $\oplus_E$ must respect some conditions and should be designed in accordance with τ_E.

Definition 4. *Let $(E, \subseteq)$ be a poset. A split operator $\oplus_E : E \to \mathscr{P}(E)$ is such that, for $e \in E$ an abstract element, we have:*

- $\cup \oplus_E (e) = e$ *(no solution must be lost, nor added),*
- $|\oplus_E(e)|$ *is finite (this ensures finite width of the search tree),*
- $\exists \epsilon > 0, \forall e, \forall e_i \in \oplus_E(e), \tau_E(e_i) \leq \tau_E(e) - \epsilon$, *(this ensures finite depth of the search tree, hence termination).*

If an abstract domain features all these operators, it can be used in the abstract solving method defined in [16], which solves CSPs by computing and refining covers of their solution space using abstract elements. Algorithm 1 gives its pseudo-code. It proceeds as follows: given an initial abstract element e, supposed to represent exactly the domains of definitions of the variables, and a set of constraints C, we maintain a list of abstract elements `toExplore`, containing

$$x^2 + 4y^2 \leq 4$$

$$2y^2 \leq x$$

(a) Constraint system

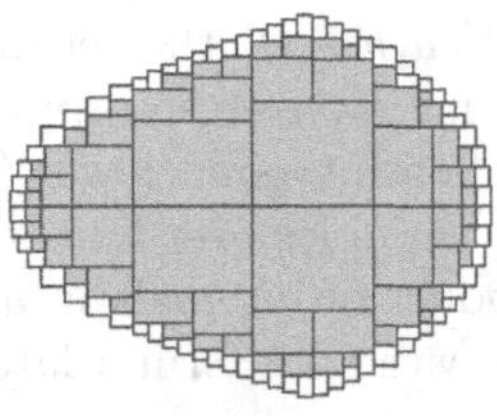

(b) Resolution with the interval domain

Fig. 1. Resolution of a continuous constraint problem using the interval abstract domain.

all the abstract elements which remain to be explored, and initialized with e. The main loop takes one element in toExplore, and performs the propagation of the constraints on e, where ϕ is the successive application of ρ for each constraint in C: $\phi(e, \{c_1, c_2, \ldots, c_n\}) = \rho(\ldots \rho(\rho(e, c_1), c_2) \ldots c_n)$. If e is empty, then it contains no solution and is discarded. Otherwise, if e either fully satisfies all the constraints, or is small enough, it is added to the solutions of the problem. And in the other case, the status of e remains undecided, thus e is split and the resulting new elements are added to toExplore. Any abstract domain can be used within this algorithm, given that the constraint propagators are defined.

Figure 1(b) shows the result of this solving method on an example from the Coconut benchmark. We can distinguish two kinds of elements in the resulting cover: the one that are proven to satisfy the CSP, and the one that were too small to be split. Considering only the former gives an under-approximation of the solution set and considering both kinds gives the same result as the continuous solving method in CP, that is a union of boxes over-approximating the solutions.

3   Boxes and Polyhedra as Constraint Abstract Domains

Abstract domains from AI can be adapted to be used in CP. We now introduce two of them, Boxes and Polyhedra, in their CP version. The Boxes abstract domain has been introduced in [16], and we recall the definitions here.

3.1   A Non-relational Abstract Domain: Continuous Boxes

In non-relational domains, variables are analyzed independently. In other words, each variable is assigned to a domain regardless of the domains of the other variables. We detail here the case of boxes, where a variable domain is a real interval with floating-point bounds.

Generally, CP solvers over continuous variables use as a representation intervals with floating-point bounds. This representation forms a lattice [2]. Consider $\mathbb{F}$ the set of (non special) floating point numbers according to the IEEE norm [9]. For $a, b \in \mathbb{F}$, let $[a, b] = \{x \in \mathbb{R}, a \leq x \leq b\}$ the real interval delimited by a

and b, and $\mathbb{I} = \{[a, b], a, b \in \mathbb{F}\}$ the set of all such intervals. For any interval I, we write $\underline{I}$ (resp. $\overline{I}$) its lower (resp. upper) bound. Similarly, for any real point x, $\underline{x}$ (resp. $\overline{x}$) is the floating-point lower (resp. upper) approximation of x.

Let $v_1, \ldots, v_n$ be variables over finite continuous domains $d_1, \ldots, d_n$. We call box a Cartesian product of intervals in $d_1 \times \cdots \times d_n$. Boxes built upon $\mathcal{D}$ (the initial domain of the variable) form a lattice:

$$\mathbb{B}(\mathcal{D}) = \left\{ \prod_i [a_i, b_i] \mid \forall i, [a_i, b_i] \subseteq d_i \right\}$$

The abstract domain is based on the lattice $\mathbb{B}$ ordered by inclusion. Its consistency is Hull-consistency [4]. The splitting operator first uses a variable selection strategy (e.g., the variable with the biggest range) and then splits the domain of the chosen variable in two. Let v_i be the variable chosen for the split and $d_i = [a_i, b_i] \in \mathbb{I}$ its domain. Let $h = \frac{a_i + b_i}{2}$. The split operator is:

$$\oplus_{\mathbb{B}}(d_1 \times \cdots \times d_n) = \{ d_1 \times \cdots \times [a_i, h] \times \cdots \times d_n,$$
$$d_1 \times \cdots \times [h, b_i] \times \cdots \times d_n\}$$

The size function corresponds to the Manhattan distance between two extremities of a diagonal of a box:

$$\tau_{\mathbb{B}}([a_1, b_1] \times \ldots \times [a_n, b_n]) = \sum_i (b_i - a_i)$$

Here, $\oplus_{\mathbb{B}}$ and $\tau_{\mathbb{B}}$ are designed in accordance with Definition 4, and we have $\forall e' \in \oplus_{\mathbb{B}}([a_1, b_1] \times \ldots \times [a_n, b_n]), \tau_{\mathbb{B}} e' = \tau_{\mathbb{B}}(e) - \frac{1}{2} \times \max_i (b_i - a_i)$. This respects our termination criteria as $\max_i (b_i - a_i) > 0$ (except if e is an atom, in which case we would not have split it).

Using this abstract domain with Algorithm 1, we retrieve the usual CP solving method on continuous variables. Results detailed in [17] show that this solver terminates and returns a cover over-approximating the solutions.

Relational abstract domains get their names from the fact that they can represent relations between variables. For instance, a linear relation $y \le x$ can be represented as a polyhedron, but not as an interval. This expressiveness comes at a price, the operators being costlier in relational than in non-relational abstract domains. We adapt here to CP a relational abstract domain, Polyhedra, and present a Reduced Product for CP where Polyhedra and Boxes coexist.

3.2 A Relational Abstract Domain: Polyhedra

The polyhedra domain $\mathbb{P}$ [8] abstracts sets as convex closed polyhedra.

Definition 5 (Polyhedron). *Given a set of linear constraints $\mathcal{P}$, the convex set of $\mathbb{R}^n$ points satisfying all the constraints in $\mathcal{P}$ is called a convex polyhedron.*

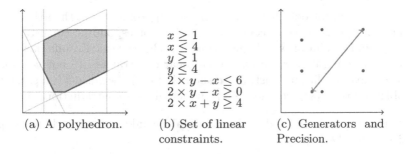

(a) A polyhedron.   (b) Set of linear   (c) Generators and
                          constraints.   Precision.

Fig. 2. Different representations for the polyhedra.

Modern implementations [11] generally follow the "double description app-roach" and maintain two dual representations for each polyhedron: a set of linear constraints and a set of generators. A generator is either a vertex or a ray of the polyhedron. However in practice, polyhedra are bounded in a constraint solver, hence they do not feature rays.

Figure 2 illustrates the different representations for a same polyhedron. The graphical representation Fig. 2(a), the set of linear constraints Fig. 2(b), and the generators and the maximal distance between two generators Fig. 2(c).

The double description is useful because classic polyhedra operators [11] are generally easier to define on one representation rather than the other. This also holds for the operators we introduce here for CP. We define the initialization and the consistency of a polyhedron on the set of linear constraints. The size function is defined on generators and the split operator relies on both representations.

Propagation is an important operator to effectively reduce the search space. In the following, we will consider a weak form of consistency for polyhedra: the non-linear constraints are ignored (not propagated), only the linear constraints are considered.

Definition 6 (Polyhedral consistency). *Let C_l be a set of linear constraints, C_{nl} a set of non-linear constraints, and $C = C_l \cup C_{nl}$. The consistent polyhedron for C is the smallest polyhedron including the solutions of C_l.*

With this weak definition, the consistent polyhedron given a set of constraints always exists and is unique. This simple consistency definition is sufficient when using the polyhedron in the Box-Polyhedra Reduced Product. Note that higher level consistencies could be defined to propagate non-linear constraints, using for instance quasi-linearization [15], linearization of polynomial constraints [12], cutting planes, or computing the hull box, to name a few. Our consistency can be directly computed by adding the constraints to the polyhedron representation.

Proposition 1 (Polyhedral consistency). *The polyhedral consistency returns an over-approximation of the solutions*

Proof. Assume that it does not return an over-approximation, then there exists a polyhedron $P \in \mathbb{P}$, a set of constraints $\mathcal{C}$, the corresponding consistent polyhedron $P_{\mathcal{C}}$, and a solution $s \in P$ such that $s \notin P_{\mathcal{C}}$. Necessarily, one has $c(s)$ for all non-linear constraints c, because non-linear constraints are not considered. Hence there exists a linear constraint c such that $c(s)$ (because s is a solution of the problem) and $\neg c(s)$ because $s \notin P_{\mathcal{C}}$, which gives a contradiction.

The size function is defined as the maximal Euclidean distance between pairs of vertices. Let $P \in \mathbb{P}$,

$$\tau_{\mathbb{P}}(P) = \max_{g_i, g_j \in P} \|g_i - g_j\|$$

Finally, the splitting operator for polyhedra can be defined in a similar way to that of boxes, *i.e.* by cutting the polyhedron into two parts according to a linear constraint. But we will not use this operator in the following, and omit here its definition.

4   Constraint-Oriented Reduced Products

We present here a generic way of defining Reduced Products for constraint abstract domains. The idea is to combine domains which are not equivalent in the product, and avoid duplicating constraint propagation in each domain. Thus, we introduce a hierarchy between the two components of the product. We make one of the component a specialized domain, dedicated to one type of constraints only, and the second one, a default domain which will apply to the other constraints. We will refer afterwards to these as the default and the specialized domains. This configuration avoids unnecessary computations on the constraints that are not precise or not cheap to represent on some domains (*e.g.*, $x = \cos(y)$ with the domain of polyhedra or $x = y$ with the domain of intervals). Nevertheless, we still keep the modular aspect of the reduced product: we can still add a new domain on top of a reduced product by defining a reduction operator with each existing component, and an attribution operator which specifies for a constraint c if the new specialized domain is able to handle it.

Definition 7. *Let $(A_d, \sqsubseteq_d), (A_s, \sqsubseteq_s)$ be two abstract domains. Let $\mathcal{C}$ a set of constraints, we define the product $A_d \times A_s$, ordered with $\sqsubseteq$ where A_s is the specialized domain and A_d the default one.*

- *The product $A_d \times A_s$ is an abstract domain ordered by component-wise comparison. Let x_d, y_d be two elements of A_d and x_s, y_s be two elements of A_s, then $(x_d, x_s) \sqsubseteq (y_d, y_s) \iff x_d \sqsubseteq_d y_d \wedge x_s \sqsubseteq_s y_s$.*
- *A reduction operator is a function $\theta : A_d \times A_s \to A_d \times A_s$ such that $\theta(x_d, x_s) = (y_d, y_s) \implies (y_d, y_s) \sqsubseteq (x_d, x_s)$.*
- *Let c be a constraint, an attribution operator κ is a predicate $\kappa : \mathcal{C} \to \{true, false\}$ such that $\kappa(c) = true$ if the domain A_s is well suited for the constraint c.*

Algorithm 2: Propagation in a reduced product

> **function** $\rho(e, c)$ `// e: abstract element, c: constraint`
>> $(e_s, e_d) \leftarrow e$
>> **if** $\kappa(c)$ **then**
>>> $e' \leftarrow (\rho_s(e_s, c), e_d)$
>>
>> **else**
>>> $e' \leftarrow (e_s, \rho_d(e, c))$
>>
>> **return** $\theta(e')$

Using the reduced product, the propagation loop given in Algorithm 2 slightly differs from the usual one in CP: for each constraint, either the specialized propagator (ρ_s) or the default one (ρ_d) is applied, according to the result of the attribution operator κ. When all of the constraints have been filtered, we then apply the reduction operator (θ) on the resulting abstract element.

Consider A_d, A_s two abstract domains ordered with inclusion, and $A = A_d \times A_s$ the product abstract domain with A_d the default domain and A_s the specialized one. The consistency in A is defined as follow:

Definition 8 (Product-consistency). *Let C be a set of constraints such that $C = C_d \cup C_s$ with $C_d = \{C \in C \mid \neg\kappa(C)\}$, the constraints for the default domain A_d, and $C_s = \{C \in C \mid \kappa(C)\}$, the constraints for the specialized domain A_s. The product-consistent element for C is the product of the smallest element of A_d including the solutions of C_d with the smallest element of A_s including the solutions of C_s.*

Proposition 2 (Product-consistency). *The Product-consistency returns an over-approximation of the solutions.*

Proof. Assume that it does not return an over-approximation, then there exists a product $P \in A$, a set of constraints C, the corresponding consistent product P_C, and a solution $s \in P$ of the problem which has been lost, *i.e.* $s \notin P_C$. Then, there exists a constraint c such that $c(s)$ (because s is a solution of the problem) and $\neg C(s)$ because $s \notin P_C$, which gives a contradiction.

4.1 The Box-Polyhedra Reduced Product

The Box-Polyhedra abstract domain $\mathbb{BP}$ is particularly useful when solving problems which involve both linear and non-linear constraints. Here, the Polyhedra domain is used as a specialized domain working only on the linear subset of the problem. We use the Box domain as the default domain to solve the non-linear part of the problem. More precisely, let C_l bet the set of linear constraints and V_l the set of variables appearing in C_l, and let C_{nl} be the set of non-linear constraints and V_{nl} the set of variables appearing in C_{nl}. We first build an exact representation of the space defined by C_l using the Polyhedra domain. By construction, this polyhedron is consistent with respect to C_l once it is created (conjunctions

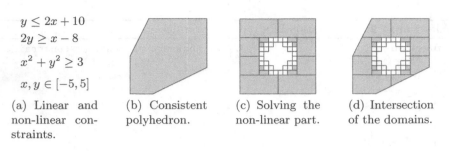

$$y \leq 2x + 10$$
$$2y \geq x - 8$$
$$x^2 + y^2 \geq 3$$
$$x, y \in [-5, 5]$$

(a) Linear and non-linear constraints.

(b) Consistent polyhedron.

(c) Solving the non-linear part.

(d) Intersection of the domains.

Fig. 3. Example of the reduced product of Box-Polyhedra.

of linear constraints can be expressed with a convex polyhedron with no loss of precision). In effect, the linear constraints are propagated once and for all at the initialization of the polyhedron. The variables V_{nl} appearing in at least one non-linear constraint are then represented with the box domain and the sub-problem containing only the constraints in C_{nl} is solved accordingly.

Figure 3 gives an example of the Box-Polyhedra abstract domain applied on a problem with both linear and non-linear constraints. Figure 3(a) gives the set of constraints, Fig. 3(b) the consistent polyhedron (for the linear constraints), Fig. 3(c) the union of boxes solving the non-linear constraints, and Fig. 3(d) the intersection of both domain elements obtained with the reduced product.

As, by construction, the initial polyhedron is consistent for all the linear constraints of the problem, the operators in the reduced abstract domain $\mathbb{BP}$ are defined only on the box part.

Definition 9 (Box-Polyhedra Consistency). *Let $C = C_l \cup C_{nl}$ with C_{nl} (resp. C_l) the set of non-linear (resp. linear) constraints. The box-polyhedra consistent element is the product of the smallest consistent box including the solutions of C_{nl} with the initial polyhedron.*

This definition being a particular case of the Product-consistency is thus a correct over-approximation of the solution set.

Let $X = X_b \times X_p \in \mathbb{BP}$ with X_b the box and X_p the polyhedron. The splitting operator splits on a variable in $V_{nl} = (v_1, \ldots, v_k)$ (in a dimension in X_b):

$$\oplus_{\mathbb{BP}}(X) = \{\oplus_{\mathbb{B}}(X_b) \times X_p\}$$

Finally, the size function is:

$$\tau_{\mathbb{BP}}(X) = \tau_{\mathbb{B}}(X_b)$$

Thus, we take advantage of both the precision of the polyhedra and the generic aspect of the boxes. Moreover, we bypass the disadvantages bound to the use of polyhedra. We do not need any kind of constraint linearization and we reduce the propagation/split phase to one step.

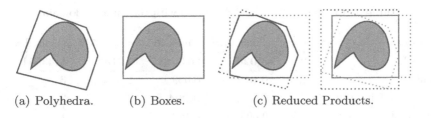

| (a) Polyhedra. | (b) Boxes. | (c) Reduced Products. |

Fig. 4. A reduced product for the Box-Polyhedra abstract domains. (Color figure online)

Proposition 3 (Completeness of solving with $\mathbb{BP}$). *The solving method in Algorithm 1 with the $\mathbb{BP}$ abstract domain returns a union of abstract element over-approximating the solution set.*

Proof. The Box-polyhedra consistency computes an over-approximation of the solutions; then, by Definition 10 in [16], the abstract solving method using the $\mathbb{BP}$ abstract domain returns a cover over-approximating the solutions.

5   Experiments

We have implemented the method presented above in the AbSolute constraint solver.[3] It implements the solving method presented in Algorithm 1 and in [16]. This solver is written in OCaml, and uses the APRON numerical abstract domain library [11]. Its current version features a generic implementation of the propagation loop with reduced products, the heuristic for the mixed box-polyhedra abstract domain, and a visualization tool.

Figure 4 shows the results of a Boxes-Polyhedra reduced product. The solution space (in green) is approximated using the polyhedra (resp. boxes), abstract domain on Fig. 4(a) (resp. Fig. 4(b)). The informations are then shared using the reduced product. The reduced product first transforms the polyhedron into a box by computing its bounding box (this operation is cheap using the generator representation), and then the box into a polyhedron (this step is straightforward as boxes are polyhedra). Finally, the reduction is performed for each abstract element: we propagate constraints from the box into the polyhedron (this step induces no loss of precision) and symmetrically from the polyhedron to the box which gives an over-approximation of their intersection Fig. 4(c). In this example, both abstract elements are reduced, but applying the reduced product does not necessarily change both or even either one of the abstract elements.

In our experiments, we compared our solver with the `defaultsolver` of Ibex 2.3.1 [5], on a computer equipped with an Intel Core i7-6820HQ CPU at 2.70 GHz 16 GB RAM running the GNU/Linux operating system.

We selected problems from the Coconut benchmark[4]. This benchmark is intended as a test set of continuous global optimization and satisfaction problems

---

[3] Available on GitHub https://github.com/mpelleau/AbSolute.

[4] Available at http://www.mat.univie.ac.at/~neum/glopt/coconut/.

Table 1. Comparing Ibex and AbSolute with the interval domain.

Problem	#var	#ctrs	Time, AbS	Time, Ibex	#sols AbS	#sols, Ibex
booth	2	2	**3.026**	26.36	**19183**	1143554
cubic	2	2	**0.007**	0.009	9	**3**
descartesfolium	2	2	0.011	**0.004**	3	**2**
parabola	2	2	0.008	**0.002**	1	1
precondk	2	2	0.009	**0.002**	1	1
exnewton	2	3	**0.158**	26.452	**14415**	1021152
supersim	2	3	0.7	**0.008**	1	1
zecevic	2	3	**16.137**	17.987	**4560**	688430
hs23	2	6	2.667	**2.608**	27268	74678
aljazzaf	3	2	**0.008**	0.02	42	43
bronstein	3	3	0.01	**0.004**	8	**4**
eqlin	3	3	0.07	**0.008**	1	1
kear12	3	3	0.043	**0.029**	12	12
powell	4	4	**0.007**	0.02	4	**1**
h72	4	0	**0.007**	0.012	1	1
vrahatis	9	9	0.084	**0.013**	2	2
dccircuit	9	11	0.118	**0.009**	1	1
i2	10	10	0.101	**0.010**	1	1
i5	10	10	0.099	**0.020**	1	1
combustion	10	10	**0.007**	0.012	1	1

and is described in detail in [22]. We have selected problems with only linear constraints, only non-linear constraints or both as this is the main focus of our work according to the constraint language recognized by the AbSolute solver. We have fixed the precision (the maximum size of the solutions, w.r.t. to the size metric of the employed domain) to 10^{-3} for all problems for both solvers.

Traditionally, constraint solvers are evaluated on their performances either on sets of benchmarks, or on new problems. Their performances are often measured as the time needed to find a solution, or as the quality of the solution in case of optimization problems. Here, we must define here the concept of solution for both solvers. Ibex and AbSolute try to entirely cover a space defined by a set of constraints with a set of elements. In Ibex, these elements are always boxes. In AbSolute, these are both polyhedra and boxes. Thus, the performance metric we adopt is, given a minimum size for the output elements, the number of elements required to cover the solution space.[5] Hence, the less elements we have, the faster

---

[5] Note that AbSolute discriminates the elements in two categories: the ones such that all of the points in them satisfy the constraints, and the one where it is not the case. We have not showed this information in the experiments as Ibex does not do any kind of discrimination on the resulting elements.

the computation will be. Furthermore, having fewer elements makes the reuse of the output easier.

The first three columns in Table 1 describe the problem: name, number of variables and number of constraints. The next columns indicate the time and number of solutions (*i.e.* abstract elements) obtained with AbSolute (col. 4 & 6) and Ibex (col. 5 & 7).

According to the metrics mentioned above, on most of these problems, AbSolute outperforms or at least competes with Ibex in terms of time and solution number. We justify the good results obtained by our method by two main facts: firstly, the linear constraints solving is almost immediate with our method. For example, the **booth** problem is composed of one linear constraint and one non-linear constraint. The linear constraint is directly representable with a polyhedron and thus, the solving process immediately finds the corresponding solution, while working only with boxes makes the search go through many splits before obtaining a set of boxes smaller than the required precision. Secondly, after each split operation, AbSolute checks for each resulting abstract elements whether it satisfies the set of constraints. If this is the case, the propagation/split phase stops for this element. This makes it possible to stop the computation as soon as possible. The **defaultsolver** of Ibex does not perform this verification and thereby goes much slower. This makes our implementation competitive on problems with only non-linear constraints. For the **exnewton** problem which only involves non-linear constraints (the resolution thus only uses boxes), we also obtain good performances, showing that the time overhead induced by the use of a specialized abstract domain is insignificant when this one is not used for a given problem. Note that disabling the satisfaction verification in AbSolute leads to results with the same number of solutions as for Ibex, but still with a gain in time. For instance, with this configuration, on **exnewton** without the satisfaction check, we obtain 1130212 elements in 9.032 s.

Finally, regarding the solving time, the two methods are similar. We can however notice that on bigger problems, using a polyhedron to represent the search space can be costly.

6   Conclusion

In this paper, we introduced a well-defined way of solving constraint problems with several abstract domains. Our idea is to use an expressive domain able to encode exactly a certain kind of constraints, and a low-cost domain to abstract the constraints that can not be exactly represented in the specialized domain. This allows us to get the best of both domains, while keeping the solver properties. We have detailed the case of the Polyedra-Boxes product, well suited for problems with linear and non-linear constraints.

The principle is generic enough to add as many specialized domain as one wishes. Integer domains need to be added to the framework, for instance, the Congruence domain, based on constraints of the form: $a \equiv b \pmod{n}$. We also plan to investigate abstract domains efficiently representing global constraints, as, for instance, Octagons and time precedence constraints. These domains could be combined with more basic domains handling any constraint. In general, the Reduced Product construction can be viewed as a way to combine different specific constraint solving mechanisms, within a formal framework to study their properties (soundness, completeness). Ultimately, each CP problem could be automatically solved in the abstract domains which best fits it, as in AI.

Note. The research described in this article has been partly funded by the Coverif ANR project 15-CE25-0002-03.

References

1. Apt, K.R.: The essence of constraint propagation. Theor. Comput. Sci. **221**, 179–210 (1999)
2. Benhamou, F.: Heterogeneous constraint solving. In: Hanus, M., Rodríguez-Artalejo, M. (eds.) ALP 1996. LNCS, vol. 1139, pp. 62–76. Springer, Heidelberg (1996). https://doi.org/10.1007/3-540-61735-3_4
3. Benhamou, F., Goualard, F., Granvilliers, L., Puget, J.-F.: Revisiting hull and box consistency. In: Proceedings of the 16th International Conference on Logic Programming, pp. 230–244 (1999)
4. Benhamou, F., Older, W.J.: Applying interval arithmetic to real, integer and boolean constraints. J. Logic Programm. **32**(1), 1–24 (1997)
5. Chabert, G., Jaulin, L.: Contractor programming. Artif. Intell. **173**, 1079–1100 (2009)
6. Cousot, P., Cousot, R.: Abstract interpretation: a unified lattice model for static analysis of programs by construction or approximation of fixpoints. In: Conference Record of the Fourth Annual ACM SIGPLAN-SIGACT Symposium on Principles of Programming Languages, pp. 238–252 (1977)
7. Cousot, P., Cousot, R., Mauborgne, L.: The reduced product of abstract domains and the combination of decision procedures. In: Hofmann, M. (ed.) FoSSaCS 2011. LNCS, vol. 6604, pp. 456–472. Springer, Heidelberg (2011). https://doi.org/10.1007/978-3-642-19805-2_31
8. Cousot, P., Halbwachs, N.: Automatic discovery of linear restraints among variables of a program. In: Proceedings of the 5th ACM SIGACT-SIGPLAN Symposium on Principles of Programming Languages, pp. 84–96 (1978)
9. Goldberg, D.: What every computer scientist should know about floating point arithmetic. ACM Comput. Surv. **23**(1), 5–48 (1991)
10. Goubault, E., Putot, S.: Static analysis of numerical algorithms. In: Yi, K. (ed.) SAS 2006. LNCS, vol. 4134, pp. 18–34. Springer, Heidelberg (2006). https://doi.org/10.1007/11823230_3
11. Jeannet, B., Miné, A.: APRON: a library of numerical abstract domains for static analysis. In: Bouajjani, A., Maler, O. (eds.) CAV 2009. LNCS, vol. 5643, pp. 661–667. Springer, Heidelberg (2009). https://doi.org/10.1007/978-3-642-02658-4_52
12. Maréchal, A., Fouilhé, A., King, T., Monniaux, D., Périn, M.: Polyhedral approximation of multivariate polynomials using Handelman's theorem. In: Jobstmann, B., Leino, K.R.M. (eds.) VMCAI 2016. LNCS, vol. 9583, pp. 166–184. Springer, Heidelberg (2016). https://doi.org/10.1007/978-3-662-49122-5_8

13. Miné, A.: A new numerical abstract domain based on difference-bound matrices. In: Danvy, O., Filinski, A. (eds.) PADO 2001. LNCS, vol. 2053, pp. 155–172. Springer, Heidelberg (2001). https://doi.org/10.1007/3-540-44978-7_10

14. Miné, A.: Domaines numériques abstraits faiblement relationnels. Ph.D thesis, École Normale Supérieure, December 2004

15. Miné, A.: Symbolic methods to enhance the precision of numerical abstract domains. In: 7th International Conference on Verification, Model Checking, and Abstract Interpretation (2006)

16. Pelleau, M., Miné, A., Truchet, C., Benhamou, F.: A constraint solver based on abstract domains. In: Giacobazzi, R., Berdine, J., Mastroeni, I. (eds.) VMCAI 2013. LNCS, vol. 7737, pp. 434–454. Springer, Heidelberg (2013). https://doi.org/10.1007/978-3-642-35873-9_26

17. Pelleau, M., Truchet, C., Benhamou, F.: The octagon abstract domain for continuous constraints. Constraints **19**(3), 309–337 (2014)

18. Puget, J.-F.: A fast algorithm for the bound consistency of alldiff constraints. In: Proceedings of the 15th National/10th Conference on Artificial Intelligence/Innovative Applications of Artificial Intelligence (AAAI 1998/IAAI 1998), pp. 359–366. American Association for Artificial Intelligence (1998)

19. Rival, X., Mauborgne, L.: The trace partitioning abstract domain. ACM Trans. Program. Lang. Syst. (TOPLAS) **29**(5), 1–44 (2007)

20. Schulte, C., Tack, G.: Weakly monotonic propagators. In: Gent, I.P. (ed.) CP 2009. LNCS, vol. 5732, pp. 723–730. Springer, Heidelberg (2009). https://doi.org/10.1007/978-3-642-04244-7_56

21. Scott, J.: Other things besides number: abstraction, constraint propagation, and string variables. Ph.D thesis, University of Uppsala (2016)

22. Shcherbina, O., Neumaier, A., Sam-Haroud, D., Vu, X.-H., Nguyen, T.-V.: Benchmarking global optimization and constraint satisfaction codes. In: Bliek, C., Jermann, C., Neumaier, A. (eds.) COCOS 2002. LNCS, vol. 2861, pp. 211–222. Springer, Heidelberg (2003). https://doi.org/10.1007/978-3-540-39901-8_16

23. van Hentenryck, P., Yip, J., Gervet, C., Dooms, G.: Bound consistency for binary length-lex set constraints. In: Proceedings of the 23rd National Conference on Artificial Intelligence (AAAI 2008), pp. 375–380. AAAI Press (2008)

An Abstract Domain for Objects in Dynamic Programming Languages

Vincenzo Arceri$^{(\boxtimes)}$, Michele Pasqua, and Isabella Mastroeni

Department of Computer Science, University of Verona, Verona, Italy
{vincenzo.arceri,michele.pasqua,isabella.mastroeni}@univr.it

Abstract. Dynamic languages, such as JavaScript, PHP, Python or Ruby, provide a memory model for objects data structures allowing programmers to dynamically create, manipulate, and delete objects' properties. Moreover, in dynamic languages it is possible to access and update properties by using strings: this represents a hard challenge for static analysis. In this paper, we exploit the finite state automata abstract domain, approximating strings, in order to define a novel abstract domain for objects. We design an abstract interpreter useful to analyze objects in a toy language, inspired by real-word dynamic programming languages. We then show, by means of minimal yet expressive examples, the precision of the proposed abstract domain.

1 Introduction

In the last years, dynamic languages such as JavaScript or PHP have gained a huge success in a very wide range of applications. This mainly happened due to the several features that such languages provide to developers, making the writing of programs easier and faster. One of this features is the way strings can be used to interact with programs' objects. Indeed, it is popular, especially in dynamic languages, to create, manipulate, and delete objects' properties at run-time, interacting with them using strings. If, on the one hand, this may help developers to simplify coding and to build applications faster, on the other hand, this may lead to misunderstandings and bugs in the produced code. Furthermore, because of these dynamic features, reasoning about dynamic programs by means of static analysis is quite hard, producing very often imprecise results.

For instance, let us consider the simple yet expressive example reported in Fig. 1, supposing that the value of the `if` guard is statically unknown. The value of `idx` is indeterminate after line 2 and it is updated at each iteration of the while loop (line 6). The `while` guard is also statically unknown and at each iteration we access `obj` with `idx`, incrementally saving the results in `n`. The goal is to statically retrieve the value of `idx` and `n` at the end of the program. It is worth noting that a crucial role here is played by the string abstraction used to approximate the value of `idx`, that is used to access `obj`. Indeed, adopting finite abstract domains, such as [13–15], will lead to infer that `idx` could be any possible string. Consequently, when `idx` is used to access `obj`, in order to

© Springer Nature Switzerland AG 2020
E. Sekerinski et al. (Eds.): FM 2019 Workshops, LNCS 12233, pp. 136–151, 2020.
https://doi.org/10.1007/978-3-030-54997-8_9

```
1   if (?) { idx = "a"; }
2   else { idx = "b"; };
3   n = 0; obj = new {a:1, aa:2, ab:3, ac:"world"};
4   while (?) {
5       n = n + obj[idx];
6       idx = concat(idx, "a");
7   }
8   obj[idx] = n; // value of idx and n ?
```

Fig. 1. Motivating example.

guarantee soundness, we need to access all properties of obj. For instance, we also have to consider the property ac, which is never used to access obj during the execution of the program. This ends up in an imprecise approximation of idx and, in turn, of n.

In this paper, we employ a more precise abstraction for string values. In particular, we abstract strings with the finite state automata abstract domain [2], able to derive precise results also when strings are modified in iterative constructs. Then, we define a novel abstract domain for objects, exploiting finite state automata. The idea is to abstract the objects' properties in the same domain used to abstract string values, namely the finite state automata abstract domain. We show that exploiting finite automata to abstract string values and objects properties produces precise results in abstract computations, in particular in objects' properties lookup and in objects' manipulation inside iterative constructs. We will formally present the objects abstract domain in Sect. 3.1.

Moreover, we use strings and objects abstract domains together with integers and booleans abstractions, presenting an abstract interpreter built upon the combination of these domains for a toy language, expressive enough to handle string operations, object declarations, objects' properties lookup and assignments.

2   Background

Notation. Given a finite set of symbols Σ, we denote by Σ^* the Kleene-closure of Σ, i.e., the set of all finite sequences of symbols in Σ. We denote an element of Σ^*, called *string*, by $s \in \Sigma^*$. If $s = s_0 s_1 \ldots s_n$, then the length of s is $|s| = n+1$ and the element in the i-th position is s_i. Given two strings s and s', ss' is their concatenation. We use the following notations: $\Sigma^i \triangleq \{s \in \Sigma^* \mid |s| = i\}$ and $\Sigma^{<i} \triangleq \bigcup_{0 \le j < i} \Sigma^j$, for $i \in \mathbb{N}$. We follow [12] for automata notation. A finite state automaton is a tuple $A = \langle Q, q_0, \Sigma, \delta, F \rangle$ where Q is a finite set of states, $q_0 \in Q$ is the initial state, Σ is the (finite) alphabet, $\delta \subseteq Q \times \Sigma \times Q$ is the transition relation and $F \subseteq Q$ is a set of final states. In particular, if $\delta \in Q \times \Sigma \to Q$ is a function, then A is called deterministic finite state automata (DFA). The class of languages recognized by finite state automata is the class of regular languages. Given an automaton A, we denote the language accepted by A as $\mathscr{L}(A)$. A language $\mathfrak{L}$ is regular iff there exists a finite state automaton A such that $\mathfrak{L} = \mathscr{L}(A)$. From the Myhill-Nerode theorem [9], we have that for each regular language there exists a unique minimum automaton, i.e., with the minimum number of states, recognizing the language. Given a regular language

$\mathfrak{L}$, we denote by $\mathsf{Min}(\mathfrak{L})$ the minimum DFA A such that $\mathfrak{L} = \mathscr{L}(\mathsf{A})$. For space limitations, in the following we will refer to finite state automata by using the corresponding regular expressions, which are isomorphic to regular languages and, in turn, to finite state automata. Given two regular expressions $\mathbf{r}_1$ and $\mathbf{r}_2$, we denote by $\mathbf{r}_1 \parallel \mathbf{r}_2$ the disjunction between $\mathbf{r}_1$ and $\mathbf{r}_2$, by $(\mathbf{r}_1)^*$ the Kleene-closure of $\mathbf{r}_1$, and by $(\mathbf{r}_1)^+$ the Kleene-closure of $\mathbf{r}_1$ with at least one repetition.

Given a partial function $f \in X \rightharpoonup Y$, we can define an equivalent total function $g \in X \rightarrow Y_\uparrow$, where $Y_\uparrow \triangleq Y \cup \{\uparrow\}$ and $\uparrow \notin Y$ denotes indefiniteness. The function g is defined as: $g(x) \triangleq f(x)$ when $f(x)$ is defined, and $g(x) \triangleq \uparrow$ otherwise. When we describe extensionally a function we omit the elements mapped to $\uparrow$, namely $g \in X \rightarrow Y_\uparrow$, described as $[x_1 \mapsto y_1 \ x_1 \mapsto y_1 \ \ldots \ x_n \mapsto y_n]$, is such that $g(x_i) = y_i$ for every $i \in \{1, 2, \ldots n\}$ and $g(x_i) = \uparrow$ otherwise.

Abstract Interpretation. The (concrete) semantic of a program is a representation of all its possible executions by means of a set of mathematical objects. This set is, in general, not computable. It is well known, due to Rice's theorem, that all non trivial properties of the concrete semantics of a program are undecidable. Abstract interpretation is born as a theory for soundly approximating the semantics of discrete dynamic systems. The approximation consists in the observation of the semantics at a specified level of abstraction, focusing only on some important aspects of computations. In this setting, abstract interpretation allows us to compute an abstract semantics of the program, depending on the properties of interest. The approximation is correct by design, in the sense that what holds in the abstract holds also in the concrete (no false negatives).

A theory of domains for abstract interpretation was defined in [7], based on the notion of *Galois insertion*. A Galois insertion (C, α, γ, A) consists of two partially ordered sets $\langle C, \leq_C \rangle$, $\langle A, \leq_A \rangle$ and two monotone functions $\alpha \in C \rightarrow A$, $\gamma \in A \rightarrow C$ such that for all c in C and a in A it holds: $\alpha(c) \leq_A a \Leftrightarrow c \leq_C \gamma(a)$ and $\alpha \circ \gamma = \mathsf{id}$ (the identity function $\lambda x \,.\, x$). C is the concrete domain, A is the abstract domain, α is the abstraction function and γ is the concretization function. Sometimes, abstract interpretations are given by means of Galois connections (instead of Galois insertions), relaxing the constraints $\alpha \circ \gamma = \mathsf{id}$. Let $f \in C \rightarrow C$ be a function on the concrete domain and $f^\sharp \in A \rightarrow A$ be a function on the abstract domain. $f^\sharp$ is a sound (or correct) approximation of f if $f \circ \gamma \leq_C \gamma \circ f^\sharp$ or, equivalently, if $\alpha \circ f \leq_A f^\sharp \circ \alpha$ [7].

Nevertheless, Galois insertions/connections represent the optimal case: sometimes we have to settle for weaker forms of abstract interpretation, as in the case of the Polyhedra abstract domain [8], where we have only the concretization function γ. In this setting, the soundness is expressed just as: $f \circ \gamma \leq_C \gamma \circ f^\sharp$.

Finite State Automata Abstract Domain. We report here the finite state automata abstract domain presented in [2], that over-approximates strings as regular languages, represented by the minimum deterministic finite state automata recognizing them [9]. The domain is $\langle \mathrm{DFA}_{/\equiv}, \sqsubseteq_{\mathrm{DFA}}, \sqcup_{\mathrm{DFA}}, \sqcap_{\mathrm{DFA}}, \mathsf{Min}(\varnothing), \mathsf{Min}(\Sigma^*) \rangle$, where

```
a ∈ AE ::= x  |  n  |  a + a  |  a - a  |  a * a  |  a / a
       |  length(s)  |  indexOf(s₁,s₂)
b ∈ BE ::= x  |  true  |  false  |  b && b  |  b || b  |  ! b  |  a < a
       |  a == a  |  s == s
s ∈ SE ::= x  |  "s"  |  substr(s,a₁,a₂)  |  charAt(s,a)  |  concat(s₁,s₂)
o ∈ OE ::= { }  |  { s₀ : e₀, s₁ : e₁, ..., sₙ : eₙ }
e ∈ E ::= a  |  b  |  s  |  x[s]
st ∈ STMT ::= st ; st  |  skip  |  x = e  |  x = new o  |  x[s] = e
        |  if b {st} else {st}  |  while b {st}

where x ∈ ID (identifiers), n ∈ Z and s, s₀, s₁, ..., sₙ ∈ Σ*
```

Fig. 2. μJS syntax.

$\mathrm{DFA}_{/\equiv}$ is the quotient set of DFA w.r.t. the equivalence relation induced by language equality, $\sqsubseteq_{\mathrm{DFA}}$ is the partial order induced by language inclusion, $\sqcup_{\mathrm{DFA}}$ and $\sqcap_{\mathrm{DFA}}$ are the least upper bound and the greatest lower bound, respectively. The minimum is $\mathrm{Min}(\varnothing)$, corresponding to the automaton recognizing the empty language and the maximum is $\mathrm{Min}(\Sigma^*)$, corresponding to the automaton recognizing any possible string over Σ. We abuse notation by representing equivalence classes in the domain $\mathrm{DFA}_{/\equiv}$ by one of its automaton (usually the minimum), i.e., when we write $A \in \mathrm{DFA}_{/\equiv}$ we mean $[A]_{\equiv}$. Since the domain $\mathrm{DFA}_{/\equiv}$ is infinite, and it is not ACC, i.e., it contains infinite ascending chains, it is equipped with the parametric widening ∇^n_{DFA}. The latter is defined in terms of a state equivalence relation merging states that recognize the same language, up to a fixed length $n \in \mathbb{N}$, a parameter used for tuning the widening precision [4,10]. For instance, let us consider the automata $A, A' \in \mathrm{DFA}_{/\equiv}$ recognizing the languages $\mathcal{L} = \{\epsilon, a\}$ and $\mathcal{L}' = \{\epsilon, a, aa\}$, respectively. The result of the application of the widening ∇^n_{DFA}, with $n = 1$, is $A \nabla^n_{\mathrm{DFA}} A' = A''$ such that $\mathscr{L}(A'') = \{a^n \mid n \in \mathbb{N}\}$.

The μJS Language. In this paper, we adopt as core language μJS [2], whose syntax is reported in Fig. 2. This simple toy language is able to express arithmetic (AE), boolean (BE) and string expressions (SE). There is not implicit type conversion, since the problem of analyzing programs with implicit conversions had been already addressed in [1,2]. Anyway, it is straightforward to merge our analysis with the ones proposed in [1,2]. In addition, we augment μJS with objects (OE), where an object can be empty, denoted {}, or a finite set of comma-separated property-expression associations, denoted { $s_0 : e_0, s_1 : e_1, ..., s_n : e_n$ }.

Concerning the language's semantics, the execution of a μJS program relies on the notion of state, which is composed by environments and heaps, namely states $\sigma \in$ STATE are pairs $\langle \xi, \rho \rangle \in$ ENV $\times$ HEAP. An environment is a map from identifiers to values, namely ENV $\triangleq$ ID $\rightarrow$ VAL, while a heap is a map from addresses to objects, namely HEAP $\triangleq$ ADDR $\rightarrow$ OBJ. Values v have domain VAL $\triangleq$ INT $\cup$ BOOL $\cup$ STR $\cup$ ADDR $\cup \{\uparrow\}$, where INT $\triangleq \mathbb{Z}$, BOOL $\triangleq \{\texttt{true}, \texttt{false}\}$, STR $\triangleq \Sigma^*$, ADDR $\triangleq \{\underline{n} \mid n \in \mathbb{N}\}$ and $\uparrow$ denotes indefiniteness. An object $o \in$ OBJ is represented as a map that associates strings to values, namely

$\text{OBJ} \triangleq \text{STR} \rightarrow \text{VAL}$. It is worth noting that there is no order relation between objects' properties, as it happens in standard programming languages. Environments update is defined as usual: $\xi[x \leftarrow v](y) \triangleq v$ when $x = y$, and $\xi[x \leftarrow v](y) \triangleq \xi(y)$ otherwise. The update for heaps and objects is analogous. The big-step semantics of a μJS program (i.e., a statement) is standard, following [1,2], and it is captured by the function $[\![\text{st}]\!] \in \text{STATE} \rightarrow \text{STATE}$. After showing the concrete semantics of object-related expressions, we will focus on the semantics of assignments, that slightly changes w.r.t. the standard one. As far as expression semantics is concerned, it is also standard [2]. We abuse notation denoting the semantics of an expression as $[\![\text{e}]\!] \in \text{STATE} \rightarrow \text{VAL}$. The evaluation of an object takes each association string-expression and it recursively evaluates the expressions. The result is a map containing the string-value associations.

$$[\![\{s_0 : e_0, s_1 : e_1, \ldots s_n : e_n\}]\!]\sigma \triangleq [s_n \mapsto [\![e_n]\!]\sigma] \bullet \ldots [s_1 \mapsto [\![e_1]\!]\sigma] \bullet [s_0 \mapsto [\![e_0]\!]\sigma]$$

where $f \bullet g(s) \triangleq g(s)$ if $g(s) \neq \uparrow \wedge f(s) = \uparrow$ and $f \bullet g(s) \triangleq f(s)$ otherwise

For example, the expression $\{\texttt{a:1, b:length("foo"), c:5+3}\}$ evaluates to the object $[\texttt{a} \mapsto 1 \ \texttt{b} \mapsto 3 \ \texttt{c} \mapsto 8]$. Following the JavaScript semantics, it is worth noting that, for instance, $\{\texttt{a:1, a:2}\}$ evaluates to $[\texttt{a} \mapsto 2]$, saving only the last association with the same property $\texttt{a}$. The semantics of objects' properties lookup checks whether the object contains a string-value association, where the string corresponds to the property. Hence, its definition is the following, supposing that $[\![\texttt{s}]\!]\langle\xi, \rho\rangle = s \in \text{STR}$:

$$[\![x[\texttt{s}]]\!]\langle\xi, \rho\rangle \triangleq \rho([\![x]\!]\langle\xi, \rho\rangle)(s) \text{ if } [\![x]\!]\langle\xi, \rho\rangle \in \text{ADDR} \quad \text{and} \quad [\![x[\texttt{s}]]\!]\langle\xi, \rho\rangle \triangleq \uparrow \text{ otherwise}$$

In our core language, we allow only to access already stored objects (condition $[\![x]\!]\langle\xi, \rho\rangle \in \text{ADDR}$). Moreover, it is worth noting that when we try to access a property s not present in the object pointed by x, then $\rho([\![x]\!]\langle\xi, \rho\rangle)(s)$ returns $\uparrow$.

The semantics of generic statements is standard, here we explain only the semantics for assignments, which is also used for objects allocation and update. We have three cases: $x = \texttt{e}$, where $\texttt{e}$ evaluates to a value; $x = \texttt{new o}$, where $\texttt{o}$ evaluates to an object; $x[\texttt{s}] = \texttt{e}$, where $\texttt{s}$ evaluates to a string and $\texttt{e}$ evaluates to a value. In the first case, we only update the environment, following the typical concrete semantics of assignments. In the second case, we need to allocate the object into a new address which x will point to. Then, both environment and heap are properly updated. In the third case, we update the object pointed by x in the heap. Formally, let $\underline{n} \in \text{ADDR}$ be a fresh, i.e., not-used, address:

$$[\![x = \texttt{e}]\!]\langle\xi, \rho\rangle \triangleq \langle\xi[x \leftarrow [\![\texttt{e}]\!]\langle\xi, \rho\rangle], \rho\rangle$$

$$[\![x = \texttt{new o}]\!]\langle\xi, \rho\rangle \triangleq \langle\xi[x \leftarrow \underline{n}], \rho[\underline{n} \leftarrow [\![\texttt{o}]\!]\langle\xi, \rho\rangle]\rangle$$

$$[\![x[\texttt{s}] = \texttt{e}]\!]\langle\xi, \rho\rangle \triangleq \langle\xi, \rho[\xi(x) \leftarrow \rho(\xi(x))[[\![\texttt{s}]\!]\langle\xi, \rho\rangle \leftarrow [\![\texttt{e}]\!]\langle\xi, \rho\rangle]]\rangle$$

As a final remark, we point out that in our extension of μJS we do not model features such as pointer arithmetic, objects comparisons and implicit type conversion (e.g., $\texttt{x = 1 ; y = true ; z = x == y}$ leads to an error).

3   Static Analysis of μJS

In order to reason about a μJS program we need to take into account all its possible executions, by means of the so called collecting semantics. Our concrete collecting semantics is a classic post-conditions semantics, computing state invariants at every statement. It is defined as the direct-image lift of the big-step semantics of μJS, hence it is a function from sets of states to sets of states. We denote by $(\!|\mathsf{st}|\!) \in \wp(\mathrm{STATE}) \to \wp(\mathrm{STATE})$ the concrete collecting semantics. For instance, the collecting semantics for assignments involving expressions, is defined as $(\!|x = \mathsf{e}|\!)X \triangleq \{[\![x = \mathsf{e}]\!]\sigma \mid \sigma \in X\}$. The semantics is similarly defined for the other constructs and for assignments involving objects. In particular, the collecting semantics for conditionals and loops is defined, as usual, as:

$$(\!|\text{if b }\{\,\mathsf{st}_1\,\}\text{ else }\{\,\mathsf{st}_2\,\}|\!)X \triangleq (\!|\mathsf{st}_1|\!)\mathsf{filter}_\mathsf{b}(X) \cup (\!|\mathsf{st}_2|\!)\mathsf{filter}_{!\mathsf{b}}(X)$$

$$(\!|\text{while b }\{\,\mathsf{st}\,\}|\!)X \triangleq \mathsf{filter}_{!\mathsf{b}}\big(\mathsf{lfp}\ \lambda T\,.\,X \cup (\!|\mathsf{st}|\!)\mathsf{filter}_\mathsf{b}(T)\big)$$

Here $\mathsf{filter}_\mathsf{b} \in \wp(\mathrm{STATE}) \to \wp(\mathrm{STATE})$ is a filtering function, namely it filters out the states that do not fulfill the boolean condition b. Unfortunately, we are not able to compute the concrete collecting semantics, since it is an infinite mathematical object. Hence, in order to perform static analysis, we approximate the collecting semantics, following the abstract interpretation framework. In order to make the computation, and in turn the analysis, feasible we need an abstract semantics $(\!|\mathsf{st}|\!)^\sharp$ computer-representable and ensuring termination of the analysis. Ideally, the abstract semantics computes on abstract states in $\mathrm{STATE}^\sharp$, approximations of the concrete ones. Precisely, $\mathrm{STATE}^\sharp$ is an approximation of $\wp(\mathrm{STATE})$, with a concretization $\gamma \in \mathrm{STATE}^\sharp \to \wp(\mathrm{STATE})$. The abstract semantics must be sound, meaning that what we prove in the abstract also holds for the concrete semantics. Put it in abstract interpretation terms, this means that for every $\sigma^\sharp \in \mathrm{STATE}^\sharp$ we have that $(\!|\mathsf{st}|\!)\gamma(\sigma^\sharp) \subseteq \gamma((\!|\mathsf{st}|\!)^\sharp\sigma^\sharp)$. Before defining the abstract semantics, we focus on the *objects abstract domain*, which is the core of our paper and it is used to represent, possibly infinite, sets of concrete objects.

3.1   Abstract Objects

As previously introduced, in order to make the analysis feasible, we need to finitely represent an infinite set of states. We start here with our representation of infinite sets of objects, namely we define an abstract domain approximating $\wp(\mathrm{OBJ})$. First, we have a non-relational abstraction between objects-properties and values, i.e., we abstract $\wp(\mathrm{OBJ})$ in $\wp(\mathrm{STR}) \to \wp(\mathrm{VAL})$.

Then we abstract $\wp(\mathrm{STR})$ with the automata domain, while for $\wp(\mathrm{VAL})$ we abstract separately each type of values in its abstract domain, obtaining the product domain $\mathrm{VAL}^\sharp \triangleq \mathrm{INT}^\sharp \times \mathrm{BOOL}^\sharp \times \mathrm{STR}^\sharp \times \wp(\mathrm{ADDR}^\sharp) \times \{\mathsf{def}, ?\}$. For numeric values we can use any non-relational domain, such as integer intervals. $\mathrm{BOOL}^\sharp \triangleq \{\bot, \mathsf{tt}, \mathsf{ff}, \top\}$ is isomorphic to $\wp(\mathrm{BOOL})$ and for sets of strings we use the automata domain, namely $\mathrm{STR}^\sharp \triangleq \mathrm{DFA}_{/\equiv}$. As we will see in the next subsection, we approximate heaps with an allocation-site abstraction of ADDR.

So, possibly infinite sets of addresses are abstracted into finite sets of allocation sites, namely $\text{ADDR}^{\sharp} \triangleq \text{LINES}$, where LINES is the finite set of lines of code of a given program. Here we abstract $\wp(\text{ADDR})$ in $\wp(\text{ADDR}^{\sharp})$, since an abstract object could have more than one allocation site. The domain $\{\text{def}, ?\}$ is isomorphic to $\wp(\{\uparrow\})$ and def represents the absence of indefiniteness while ? represents potential indefiniteness. An abstract value $v^{\sharp} = \langle i^{\sharp}, b^{\sharp}, s^{\sharp}, A, u^{\sharp} \rangle \in \text{VAL}^{\sharp}$ represents the union of the elements taken from every single-type abstraction:

$$\gamma_{\text{V}}(v^{\sharp}) = \gamma_{\text{I}}(i^{\sharp}) \cup \gamma_{\text{B}}(b^{\sharp}) \cup \gamma_{\text{S}}(s^{\sharp}) \cup \bigcup_{l \in A} \gamma_{\text{A}}(l) \cup \gamma_{\text{U}}(u^{\sharp})$$

where γ_{I} is the concretization defined in the numerical non-relational domain, $\gamma_{\text{B}}(\bot) \triangleq \varnothing$, $\gamma_{\text{B}}(\text{tt}) \triangleq \{\text{true}\}$, $\gamma_{\text{B}}(\text{ff}) \triangleq \{\text{false}\}$, $\gamma_{\text{B}}(\top) \triangleq \{\text{true}, \text{false}\}$, γ_{S} is the concretization for the automata domain (i.e., the language recognized by the given automaton) and $\gamma_{\text{U}}(\text{def}) = \varnothing$, $\gamma_{\text{U}}(?) = \{\uparrow\}$. The concretization for addresses γ_{A} will be introduced in Sect. 3.2, when we deal with abstract heaps. Briefly, the concretization of a given allocation site is the set of all possible addresses that can be allocated at that line of code. The abstract join $\sqcup_{\text{V}}^{\sharp}$ and the partial order $\sqsubseteq_{\text{V}}^{\sharp}$ for $\text{VAL}^{\sharp}$ are defined pointwise.

The partial order $\sqsubseteq_{\text{O}}^{\sharp}$ for $\text{OBJ}^{\sharp}$ is the pointwise ordering between functions, i.e., $o_1^{\sharp} \sqsubseteq_{\text{O}}^{\sharp} o_2^{\sharp} \triangleq (\forall \text{A} \in \text{DFA}_{/\equiv} . o_1^{\sharp}(\text{A}) \sqsubseteq_{\text{V}}^{\sharp} o_2^{\sharp}(\text{A}))$. This order is not optimal but it does not harm the analysis since, as we can see in Sect. 3.1, the order can be strengthen. Analogously, the join for $\text{OBJ}^{\sharp}$ is defined as $\bigsqcup_{\text{O}}^{\sharp} X \triangleq \lambda \text{A} . \bigsqcup_{\text{V}}^{\sharp} \{o^{\sharp}(\text{A}) \mid o^{\sharp} \in X\}$. It is straightforward to see that $\langle \text{OBJ}^{\sharp}, \sqsubseteq_{\text{O}}^{\sharp} \rangle$ is a lattice, with minimum mapping every automaton to the tuple composed by the minimum of each value-type domain, and maximum mapping every automaton to the tuple composed by the maximum of each value-type domain. The concretization $\gamma_{\text{O}} \in \text{OBJ}^{\sharp} \to \wp(\text{OBJ})$ is defined as:

$$\gamma_{\text{O}}(o^{\sharp}) \triangleq$$
$$\{o \in \text{OBJ} \mid \forall s \in \text{STR} \, \exists \text{A} \in \text{DFA}_{/\equiv} . (s \in \gamma_{\text{S}}(\text{A}) \wedge (o(s) \in \gamma_{\text{V}}(o^{\sharp}(\text{A})) \vee \text{\o}(s) = \uparrow))\}$$

In order to optimize the implementation of the abstract domain, we represent singleton sets of strings as they are, instead of converting them into automata. Indeed, it is worth noting that we can partition the finite state automata abstract domain as $\text{DFA}_{/\equiv} = \text{DFA}_{/\equiv}^{1} \cup \text{DFA}_{/\equiv}^{\omega}$, where $\text{DFA}_{/\equiv}^{1} \triangleq \{\text{A} \in \text{DFA}_{/\equiv} \mid |\mathscr{L}(\text{A})| = 1\}$, namely the set of finite state automata that recognize singleton languages, and $\text{DFA}_{/\equiv}^{\omega} \triangleq \text{DFA}_{/\equiv} \setminus \text{DFA}_{/\equiv}^{1}$, namely the set of finite state automata that recognizes languages of size 0 or size greater than 1 (possibly infinite). Clearly $\text{DFA}_{/\equiv}^{1}$ is isomorphic to STR, hence we can equivalently define abstract objects as maps in $\text{OBJ}^{\sharp} \triangleq (\text{STR} \cup \text{DFA}_{/\equiv}^{\omega}) \to \text{VAL}^{\sharp}$.

In order to show how our objects abstract domain works, we consider a simple yet expressive μJS example (Fig. 3, where we suppose that the boolean guards of while and if statements are statically unknown). The fragment declares the object o at line 1, and its abstract value at lines 1–7 is reported in Fig. 4a. Then, it indefinitely iterates over the string variable idx at lines 3–6 appending either the strings "x" or "y". Finally, idx is used to access the object o at line 7. Let us suppose to statically analyze the above program with the abstract

```
1   o = new {x:1, y:2, z:3};
2   idx = "x";
3   while (?) {
4       if (?) { idx = concat(idx, "x") }
5       else { idx = concat(idx, "y") }
6   };
7   o[idx] = 7;
```

Fig. 3. μJS program example.

$$
(a)\begin{bmatrix} x \mapsto [1,1] \\ y \mapsto [2,2] \\ z \mapsto [3,3] \\ \hline - \end{bmatrix}
\quad (b)\begin{bmatrix} x \mapsto [1,1] \\ y \mapsto [2,2] \\ z \mapsto [3,3] \\ \hline x(x \parallel y)^* \mapsto [7,7] \end{bmatrix}
\quad (c)\begin{bmatrix} x \mapsto [1,7] \\ y \mapsto [2,2] \\ z \mapsto [3,3] \\ \hline x(x \parallel y)^+ \mapsto [7,7] \end{bmatrix}
$$

Fig. 4. (a) Abstract value of o after line 1 of the fragment reported in Fig. 3 (b) Abstract value of o after line 6. (c) Normal form of o after line 6.

domain previously presented. Since the number of iterations of the while-loop is statically unknown, the computation of the value of idx, abstracted as a finite state automaton, may diverge. In order to enforce termination, the automata widening ∇_{DFA}^n is applied. Tuning ∇_{DFA}^n with $n = 3$, the abstract value of idx at line 7, after the while computation, corresponds to the automaton expressed by the regular expression $x(x \parallel y)^*$. Since idx does not represent just a single string, when we analyze o[idx] we may have to overwrite an object property (e.g., x) and add new properties to o (e.g., xyy). Since the abstract value of idx expresses an infinite number of object properties, we call this property *summary property*. The abstract value after line 6 is depicted in Fig. 4b, where the summary property $x(x \parallel y)^*$ is added to the object reported in Fig. 4a. Note that in the abstract object updated at line 7, the abstract properties x and $x(x \parallel y)^*$ share the common concrete property x. In particular, the value of o["x"] may be either 1 or 7. We aim at an objects' representation where every property does not share any property with the others, namely when objects are in normal form.

Normalization. We now formally define the notion of abstract object normal form. Given an abstract object $o^\sharp \in \text{OBJ}^\sharp$, we denote by $\text{props}(o^\sharp) \subseteq \text{STR}^\sharp$ the set of its abstract properties, namely the properties which are not undefined. We remind that $\text{STR}^\sharp$ is the optimized version of the automata domain, i.e., $\text{STR}^\sharp = \text{STR} \cup \text{DFA}^\omega_{/\equiv}$. Formally, $\text{props}(o^\sharp) \triangleq \{p \in \text{STR}^\sharp \mid o^\sharp(p) = \langle i^\sharp, b^\sharp, s^\sharp, A, u^\sharp \rangle \wedge u^\sharp = \text{def}\}$. Abstract properties represent sets of concrete properties. Hence, given $p \in \text{props}(o^\sharp)$, we abuse notation denoting by $\mathscr{L}(p)$ the language of the concrete properties captured by p. $\mathscr{L}(p)$ is the language recognized by the corresponding automaton, when $p \in \text{DFA}^\omega_{/\equiv}$ and it is the language $\{p\}$ when $p \in \text{STR}$.

Algorithm 1: Norm $\in$ OBJ$^\sharp$ $\rightarrow$ OBJ$^\sharp$ algorithm

Data: $o^\sharp \in$ OBJ$^\sharp$
Result: Norm($o^\sharp$)

1 **foreach** $p \in$ props($o^\sharp$) **do**
2      $v^\sharp \leftarrow o^\sharp(p)$;
3   **if** $|\mathscr{L}(p)| \notin \{1, \omega\}$ **then**
4   remove p from $o^\sharp$;
5   **foreach** $s \in \mathscr{L}(p)$ **do**
6              $o^\sharp \leftarrow o^\sharp \bullet^\sharp [s \mapsto v^\sharp]$;
7 **foreach** $p_1 \in$ props($o^\sharp$) **do**
8      $v_1^\sharp \leftarrow o^\sharp(p_1)$;   remove p_1 from $o^\sharp$;   normalized $\leftarrow$ **false**;
9   **foreach** $p_2 \in$ props($o^\sharp$) **do**
10          $v_2^\sharp \leftarrow o^\sharp(p_2)$;
11   **if** $p_1 \sqcap_s^\sharp p_2 \neq \mathsf{Min}(\varnothing) \wedge p_1 \neq p_2$ **then**
12   normalized $\leftarrow$ **true**;
13              $o^\sharp \leftarrow o^\sharp \bullet^\sharp [p_1 \sqcap_s^\sharp p_2 \mapsto o^\sharp(p_1 \sqcap_s^\sharp p_2) \sqcup_v^\sharp v_1^\sharp \sqcup_v^\sharp v_2^\sharp]$;
14              $o^\sharp \leftarrow o^\sharp \bullet^\sharp [p_1 \smallsetminus_s^\sharp p_2 \mapsto o^\sharp(p_1 \smallsetminus_s^\sharp p_2) \sqcup_v^\sharp v_1^\sharp]$;
15              $o^\sharp \leftarrow o^\sharp \bullet^\sharp [p_2 \smallsetminus_s^\sharp p_1 \mapsto o^\sharp(p_2 \smallsetminus_s^\sharp p_1) \sqcup_v^\sharp v_2^\sharp]$;
16   remove p_2 from $o^\sharp$;
17   **if** !normalized **then** $o^\sharp \leftarrow o^\sharp \bullet^\sharp [p_1 \mapsto v_1^\sharp]$
18 **return** $o^\sharp$;

Definition 1 (Abstract object normal form). *An abstract object $o^\sharp \in$ OBJ$^\sharp$ is in normal form when:*

$$\forall p \in \mathsf{props}(o^\sharp) \,.\, |\mathscr{L}(p)| \in \{1, \omega\} \wedge \forall p_1, p_2 \in \mathsf{props}(o^\sharp) \,.\, \mathscr{L}(p_1) \cap \mathscr{L}(p_2) = \varnothing$$

Informally, we say that an abstract object is in normal form when each property p represents only a single string (i.e., $|\mathscr{L}(p)| = 1$) or an infinite language (i.e., $|\mathscr{L}(p)| = \omega$) and it does not share any concrete property with other abstract properties. Hence, a normal form abstract object has two kind of properties: p is a *non-summary property*, if $|\mathscr{L}(p)| = 1$, and p is a *summary property*, if $|\mathscr{L}(p)| = \omega$. For instance, the abstract object in Fig. 4a is in normal form, since any abstract property expresses concrete properties that are not expressed by other abstract properties and it only contains non-summary properties. Instead, the abstract object in Fig. 4b is not in formal form, despite it has only summary and non-summary properties, since the string x is expressed by the non-summary property x and by the summary property x(x $\parallel$ y)*.

During abstract computations, it may happen that abstract objects are not in normal form, so we need to normalize them. We rely on the function Norm $\in$ OBJ$^\sharp$ $\rightarrow$ OBJ$^\sharp$ that normalizes an abstract object and its behaviour is captured by the algorithm reported by Algorithm 1, where $o_1^\sharp \bullet^\sharp o_2^\sharp$ is defined as:

let $\langle i_1^\sharp, b_1^\sharp, s_1^\sharp, A_1, u_1^\sharp \rangle = o_1^\sharp(p), \langle i_2^\sharp, b_2^\sharp, s_2^\sharp, A_2, u_2^\sharp \rangle = o_2^\sharp(p)$ in

$o_1^\sharp \bullet^\sharp o_2^\sharp(p) \triangleq o_2^\sharp(p)$ if $u_2^\sharp \neq ? \wedge u_1^\sharp = ?$ and $o_1^\sharp \bullet^\sharp o_2^\sharp(p) \triangleq o_1^\sharp(p)$ otherwise

In the algorithm, the operators $\sqcap_S^\sharp$ and $\searrow_S^\sharp$ are the operators $\sqcap_{\mathrm{DFA}}$ and $\searrow_{\mathrm{DFA}}$, respectively, of the automata domain adapted to its optimized versions $\mathrm{STR} \cup \mathrm{DFA}^\omega_{/\equiv}$. The first part of Algorithm 1, namely lines 1–6, checks if any property of $o^\sharp$ is summary or non-summary. If it finds a property p such that $|\mathscr{L}(p)| \notin \{1, \omega\}$ then the algorithm first remove that property from the object, and then looks at its language (that is finite) and adds any single property captured by p with its old corresponding value. All the automata operations reported above and the check $|\mathscr{L}(p)| \notin \{1, \omega\}$ can be performed with linear complexity w.r.t. the number of state of the automata. For example, let consider the object $[\mathsf{x} \parallel \mathsf{y} \mapsto [5, 5]]$, the algorithm returns as result the normal form abstract object $[\mathsf{x} \mapsto [5, 5], \mathsf{y} \mapsto [5, 5]]$. The idea of the second part of Algorithm 1 (lines 7–17) is to check, for any $p_1 \in \mathsf{props}(o^\sharp)$, if it shares at least a concrete property with any other $p_2 \in \mathsf{props}(o^\sharp)$ (lines 11–16). This boils down to check whether the intersection between p_1 and p_2 is not empty. If so, three new abstract properties are created in $o^\sharp$ (note that p_1 is removed at line 8 and p_2 will be removed at line 16). In particular:

- the property $p_1 \sqcap_S^\sharp p_2$ points to the join of the previous values of p_1 and p_2 and the previous value (if present) of $p_1 \sqcap_S^\sharp p_2$ in $o^\sharp$ (line 13);
- the property $p_1 \searrow_S^\sharp p_2$ points to the join of the previous value of p_1 and the previous value (if present) of $p_1 \searrow_S^\sharp p_2$ in $o^\sharp$ (line 14);
- the property $p_2 \searrow_S^\sharp p_1$ points to the join of the previous value of p_2 and the previous value (if present) of $p_2 \searrow_S^\sharp p_1$ in $o^\sharp$ (line 15);

Otherwise, if p_1 does not share any property with other abstract properties of $o^\sharp$, the association $\langle p_1, o^\sharp(p_1) \rangle$ is simply added to $o^\sharp$ (line 17). For example, let us consider again the abstract object reported in Fig. 4b. The result obtained by applying Algorithm 1 is the abstract object reported in Fig. 4c.

Proposition 1. *Given $o^\sharp \in \mathrm{OBJ}^\sharp$, the abstract object $\mathsf{Norm}(o^\sharp)$, computed by Algorithm 1, is in normal form (Definition 1). Moreover, we have that $\gamma_O(o^\sharp) = \gamma_O(\mathsf{Norm}(o^\sharp))$.*

As we have mentioned in Sect. 3, normalization strengthens the abstract order between objects. For example, the objects $[\mathsf{a} \mapsto [1, 1], \mathsf{b} \mapsto [1, 1]]$ and $[\mathsf{a} \parallel \mathsf{b} \mapsto [1, 2]]$ are not comparable, but, if we normalize the second object (i.e., in $[\mathsf{a} \mapsto [1, 2], \mathsf{b} \mapsto [1, 2]]$), then we have $[\mathsf{a} \mapsto [1, 1], \mathsf{b} \mapsto [1, 1]] \sqsubseteq_O^\sharp \mathsf{Norm}([\mathsf{a} \parallel \mathsf{b} \mapsto [1, 2]])$.

3.2 Abstract Semantics

Abstract states in $\mathrm{STATE}^\sharp$ are composed by abstract environments and abstract heaps, so we have an abstraction from $\wp(\mathrm{ENV} \times \mathrm{HEAP})$ to $\wp(\mathrm{ENV}) \times \wp(\mathrm{HEAP})$. As an abstract representation of the heap, we use a classic allocation-site abstraction of ADDR [16]. Possibly infinite sets of addresses are abstracted into finite sets of allocation sites, namely $\mathrm{ADDR}^\sharp \triangleq \mathrm{LINES}$, where LINES is the finite set of lines of code of a given program. Given a $\mu\mathsf{JS}$ program, we suppose to have a labeling assigning to each statement of the program a unique line of code (a natural number). Then, we define two functions, $\mathsf{line} \in \mathrm{STMT} \to \mathrm{LINES}$ and $\mathsf{code} \in \mathrm{LINES} \to \mathrm{STMT}$, returning the line of code of a given statement and the statement assigned to a given line of code, respectively. The concretization is

$$(\! | n | \!)_A^\sharp \triangleq \alpha_I(\{n\}) \quad (\! | x | \!)_A^\sharp \langle \xi^\sharp, \rho^\sharp \rangle \triangleq \xi^\sharp(x) \quad (\! | a_1 + a_2 | \!)_A^\sharp \sigma^\sharp \triangleq (\! | a_1 | \!)_A^\sharp \sigma^\sharp +^I (\! | a_2 | \!)_A^\sharp \sigma^\sharp$$

$$(\! | \mathsf{true} | \!)_B^\sharp \sigma^\sharp \triangleq \mathsf{tt} \quad (\! | x | \!)_B^\sharp \langle \xi^\sharp, \rho^\sharp \rangle \triangleq \xi^\sharp(x) \quad (\! | b_1 \,||\, b_2 | \!)_B^\sharp \sigma^\sharp \triangleq (\! | b_1 | \!)_B^\sharp \sigma^\sharp \sqcup_B^\sharp (\! | b_2 | \!)_B^\sharp \sigma^\sharp$$

$$(\! | \{\} | \!)_O^\sharp \sigma^\sharp \triangleq \lambda p \,.\, \langle \bot, \bot, \mathsf{Min}(\varnothing), \varnothing, ? \rangle$$

$$(\! | \{s_0 : e_0, s_1 : e_1, \ldots s_n : e_n\} | \!)_O^\sharp \sigma^\sharp \triangleq$$

$$[s_n \mapsto (\! | e_n | \!)_E^\sharp \sigma^\sharp] \bullet^\sharp \ldots [s_1 \mapsto (\! | e_1 | \!)_E^\sharp \sigma^\sharp] \bullet^\sharp [s_0 \mapsto (\! | e_0 | \!)_E^\sharp \sigma^\sharp]$$

$$(\! | x[\mathsf{s}] | \!)_E^\sharp \langle \xi^\sharp, \rho^\sharp \rangle \triangleq$$

$$\begin{cases} \bigsqcup_V^\sharp \{\rho^\sharp(l)(p) \mid l \in \xi^\sharp(x) \land \mathscr{L}(p) \cap \mathscr{L}((\! | \mathsf{s} | \!)_S^\sharp \langle \xi^\sharp, \rho^\sharp \rangle) \neq \varnothing\} & \text{if } \xi^\sharp(x) \in \mathrm{ADDR}^\sharp \\ \langle \bot, \bot, \mathsf{Min}(\varnothing), \varnothing, ? \rangle \end{cases}$$

$$\mathsf{filter}_{\mathsf{true}}^\sharp(\sigma^\sharp) \triangleq \sigma^\sharp \quad \mathsf{filter}_x^\sharp(\langle \xi^\sharp, \rho^\sharp \rangle) \triangleq \begin{cases} \langle \xi^\sharp, \rho^\sharp \rangle & \text{if } \xi^\sharp(x) \in \{\mathsf{tt}, \top\} \\ \sigma_\bot^\sharp & \text{otherwise} \end{cases}$$

$$\mathsf{filter}_{b_1||b_2}^\sharp(\sigma^\sharp) \triangleq \mathsf{filter}_{b_1}^\sharp(\sigma^\sharp) \sqcup^\sharp \mathsf{filter}_{b_2}^\sharp(\sigma^\sharp) \quad \mathsf{filter}_{\mathsf{false}}^\sharp(\sigma^\sharp) \triangleq \sigma_\bot^\sharp$$

Fig. 5. Abstract semantics for expressions and objects and the abstract filter

$$\gamma_A(l) \triangleq \left\{ \underline{n} \in \mathrm{ADDR} \,\middle|\, \exists \langle \xi, \rho \rangle \in \mathrm{STATE} \,.\, \begin{array}{l} [\![\mathsf{code}(l)]\!]\langle \xi, \rho \rangle = \langle \xi', \rho' \rangle \land \\ \rho(\underline{n}) = \lambda s \,.\, \uparrow \land \rho'(\underline{n}) \neq \lambda s \,.\, \uparrow \end{array} \right\}$$

meaning that the concretization of a given allocation site l is the set of all possible addresses that can be allocated at that line of code. An abstract heap is a map associating abstract addresses, i.e., lines of code, to abstract objects, namely $\mathrm{HEAP}^\sharp \triangleq \mathrm{ADDR}^\sharp \to \mathrm{OBJ}^\sharp$. As we have already seen, an abstract object is a map associating an automaton with an abstract value.

For what concerns environments, we consider a non-relational abstraction, approximating every identifier separately. This means that we abstract from $\wp(\mathrm{ID} \to \mathrm{VAL})$ to $\mathrm{ID} \to \wp(\mathrm{VAL})$. Abstract environments are maps from identifiers to abstract values, namely $\mathrm{ENV}^\sharp \triangleq \mathrm{ID} \to \mathrm{VAL}^\sharp$, exploiting the abstraction between $\wp(\mathrm{VAL})$ and $\mathrm{VAL}^\sharp$ we have introduced in the previous subsection. Finally, abstract states are, as in the concrete, pairs of abstract environments and abstract heaps, namely $\mathrm{STATE}^\sharp \triangleq \mathrm{ENV}^\sharp \times \mathrm{HEAP}^\sharp$. The definition of the abstract join $\sqcup^\sharp$ and the partial order $\sqsubseteq^\sharp$ for $\mathrm{STATE}^\sharp$ is straightforward.

The abstract semantics is then a function $(\! | \mathsf{st} | \!)^\sharp \in \mathrm{STATE}^\sharp \to \mathrm{STATE}^\sharp$, computing on abstract states. It relies on the abstract semantics for expressions $(\! | e | \!)_E^\sharp \in \mathrm{STATE}^\sharp \to \mathrm{VAL}^\sharp$, on the abstract semantics for objects $(\! | o | \!)_O^\sharp \in \mathrm{STATE}^\sharp \to \mathrm{OBJ}^\sharp$ and on the abstract filtering function $\mathsf{filter}_b^\sharp \in \mathrm{STATE}^\sharp \to \mathrm{STATE}^\sharp$[1]. All of them must be sound w.r.t. their concrete counterparts, namely $(\! | e | \!)\gamma(\sigma^\sharp) \subseteq \gamma_V((\! | e | \!)_E^\sharp \sigma^\sharp)$, $(\! | o | \!)\gamma(\sigma^\sharp) \subseteq \gamma_O((\! | o | \!)_O^\sharp \sigma^\sharp)$ and $\mathsf{filter}_b(\gamma(\sigma^\sharp)) \subseteq \gamma(\mathsf{filter}_b^\sharp(\sigma^\sharp))$, for every $\sigma^\sharp \in \mathrm{STATE}^\sharp$. In Fig. 5 we have a part of the definition of the abstract semantics for

---

[1] We assume that all negations ! have been removed using DeMorgan's laws and usual arithmetic laws: $!\,(b_1\,||\,b_2) \equiv !\,b_1\,\&\&\,!\,b_2$, $!\,(a_1 < a_2) \equiv (a_2 < a_1\,||\,a_2 == a_1)$, etc.

$$\text{(a)} \begin{bmatrix} \text{b} \mapsto [2,2] \\ \text{c} \mapsto [3,3] \\ \overline{\text{a(a)}^* \mapsto [4,4]} \end{bmatrix} \qquad \text{(b)} \begin{bmatrix} \text{a} \mapsto [1,1] \\ \text{b} \mapsto [2,2] \\ \underline{\text{c} \mapsto [3,3]} \\ \text{a}^* \mapsto [4,4] \end{bmatrix}$$

Fig. 6. Example of materialization.

expressions and objects and the abstract filter, where $\sigma_\perp^\sharp$ is the minimum of the lattice $\langle \text{STATE}^\sharp, \sqsubseteq^\sharp \rangle$. The abstract semantics for statements is quite standard:

$$(\!|\text{st}_1 \ ; \ \text{st}_2|\!)^\sharp \sigma^\sharp \triangleq (\!|\text{st}_2|\!)^\sharp (\!|\text{st}_1|\!)^\sharp \sigma^\sharp \qquad (\!|\text{skip}|\!)^\sharp \sigma^\sharp \triangleq \sigma^\sharp$$

$$(\!|\text{if b } \{\text{ st }\} \text{ else } \{\text{ st }\}|\!)^\sharp \sigma^\sharp \triangleq (\!|\text{st}_1|\!)^\sharp \text{filter}_b^\sharp(\sigma^\sharp) \sqcup^\sharp (\!|\text{st}_2|\!)^\sharp \text{filter}_{!b}^\sharp(\sigma^\sharp)$$

$$(\!|\text{while b } \{\text{ st }\}|\!)^\sharp \sigma^\sharp \triangleq \text{filter}_{!b}^\sharp \left(\text{lfp } \lambda \sigma_w^\sharp . \sigma^\sharp \sqcup^\sharp (\!|\text{st}|\!)^\sharp \text{filter}_b^\sharp(\sigma_w^\sharp) \right)$$

Concerning generic assignments, the abstract semantics follows the definition of the concrete one, so we have three cases: $x = e$, where e evaluates to a value; $x = o$, where o evaluates to an object; $x[s] = e$, where s evaluates to a string and e evaluates to a value. In the first, we have to modify the abstract environment, setting x to the (abstract) evaluation of e. In the second, we need to update the abstract address pointed by the identifier x, with the line of code of the assignment. Then we have to update the abstract object pointed, in the abstract heap, by the new line of code with the (abstract) evaluation of o. Formally:

$$(\!|x = e|\!)^\sharp \langle \xi^\sharp, \rho^\sharp \rangle \triangleq \langle \xi^\sharp[x \leftarrow (\!|e|\!)_E^\sharp \langle \xi^\sharp, \rho^\sharp \rangle], \rho^\sharp \rangle$$

$$(\!|x = \text{new o}|\!)^\sharp \langle \xi^\sharp, \rho^\sharp \rangle \triangleq \langle \xi^\sharp[x \leftarrow \{\text{line}(x = \text{new o})\}], \rho^\sharp[\text{line}(x = \text{new o}) \leftarrow (\!|o|\!)_O^\sharp \langle \xi^\sharp, \rho^\sharp \rangle] \rangle$$

As a third case, we have the abstract semantics of object-property update, namely $x[s] = e$, where *materialization* occurs. As we have already mentioned before, we allow to update only the objects that have been already stored into the heap. Suppose that $v^\sharp = (\!|e|\!)_E^\sharp \langle \xi^\sharp, \rho^\sharp \rangle$, $p = (\!|s|\!)_S^\sharp \langle \xi^\sharp, \rho^\sharp \rangle$ and $\{l_1, \ldots l_n\} = \xi^\sharp(x)$:

$$\text{let } o_i^\sharp = \text{Norm}(\rho^\sharp(l_i)[p \leftarrow v^\sharp \sqcup_{\text{VAL}^\sharp} \rho^\sharp(l_i)(p)]), \text{ with } i \in \{1, \ldots n\} \text{ in}$$

$$(\!|x[s] = e|\!)^\sharp \langle \xi^\sharp, \rho^\sharp \rangle \triangleq \langle \xi^\sharp, \rho^\sharp[l_1 \leftarrow o_1^\sharp, \ldots l_n \leftarrow o_n^\sharp] \rangle$$

The abstract semantics of $x[s] = e$ does not update the environment, since it only needs to update properties of abstract objects stored into the heap. For each location $l \in \text{ADDR}^\sharp$, associated to the identifier x (i.e., the ones contained in $\xi^\sharp(x)$), the abstract semantics updates $\rho^\sharp(l)$, at the property p, with the lub between $v^\sharp$ (i.e., the abstract evaluation of the expression e) and the previous value of $\rho^\sharp(l)(p)$. This corresponds to a *weak update* of the object contained in x [3]. Before storing the updated abstract object in $\rho^\sharp(l)$, the latter is normalized. In this paper, we only perform weak updates. We could improve the precision of the analysis performing a *must-may analysis* in order to differentiate between properties that certainly point to some value and properties that may point to others. This can be done improving the proposed analysis using standard techniques, such as the ones reported in [3, 16, 17].

(a)
```
1    o = new {a:1};
2    key = "a";
3    while (?) {
4        key = concat(key, "a");
5        o[key] = 1;
6    };
```

(b)
$$\left[\begin{array}{c} \mathtt{a} \mapsto [1,1] \\ \mathtt{aa} \mapsto [1,1] \\ \mathtt{aaa} \mapsto [1,1] \\ \hline \overline{\mathtt{aaaa(a)^*} \mapsto [1,1]} \end{array} \right]$$

Fig. 7. (a) μJS fragment, (b) Value of o after while-loop.

For example, let us suppose that $\rho^\sharp(l)$ is the object reported in Fig. 6(a) and we want to update the property a, with the interval $[1,1]$. Applying these values to the previously defined abstract semantics, we obtain, at the allocation site l, the abstract object reported in Fig. 6(b). We say that the property a has been *materialized*, since, before the update, it was part of a summary property, and after the update it is a non-summary property. We say that a (concrete) property is materialized when a string of an abstract object passes, during the update, from a summary property to a non-summary property. It is worth noting that normalization take care of materialization. The abstract semantics is sound w.r.t. the concrete collecting semantics, i.e., it computes an over-approximation of state invariants at every statement.

Theorem 1 (Soundness). *For every μJS program* st $\in$ STMT *we have that:*

$$\forall \sigma^\sharp \in \text{STATE}^\sharp . (\!|st|\!)\gamma(\sigma^\sharp) \subseteq \gamma((\!|st|\!)^\sharp \sigma^\sharp)$$

3.3   Widening

The domain $\langle \text{STATE}^\sharp, \sqsubseteq^\sharp \rangle$ is not ACC, i.e., it contains infinite ascending chains, because of the intervals abstract domain, the automata abstract domain and the novel objects abstract domain. Hence, fix-point computations in our abstract interpreter may diverge, if we do not introduce an extrapolation operator. In order to enforce termination, the abstract domain VAL$^\sharp$ is equipped with the widening operator $\nabla_\text{v} \in \text{VAL}^\sharp \times \text{VAL}^\sharp \to \text{VAL}^\sharp$ defined point-wisely. In particular, the intervals domain is equipped with its well-known widening defined in [7], the automata abstract domain is equipped with the widening ∇_{DFA}^n, reported in Sect. 2, while for addresses and booleans we can just use their least upper bound (they are finite). We can define the widening operator $\nabla_\varepsilon \in \text{ENV}^\sharp \times \text{ENV}^\sharp \to \text{ENV}^\sharp$ between environments upon ∇_v, applied point-wisely. For instance, suppose to use the widening ∇_{DFA}^n, with $n = 3$, for the finite state automata. We have that $[x \mapsto \langle [1,1], \bot, \text{Min(aaa)}, \varnothing, \text{def} \rangle] \nabla_\varepsilon [x \mapsto \langle [2,2], \bot, \text{Min(aaaa)}, \varnothing, \text{def} \rangle]$ is equal to the abstract environment $[x \mapsto \langle [1, +\infty], \bot, \text{Min(a}^*), \varnothing, \text{def} \rangle]$. Fix-point computations may also diverge on heaps, since also HEAP$^\sharp$ is not ACC, due to the objects abstract domain. In particular, this happens because we model objects' properties with the finite state automata domain, which is not ACC. Anyway, a slight extension of the join $\sqcup_o^\sharp$ is enough to guarantee termination of heap computations, exploiting the widening of the finite state automata domain. Informally speaking, abstract string values, in while-loop computations, always converge since finite state automata domain is equipped with a widening.

(a)
```
1  o = new {a:1};
2  while (?) {
3      o["a"] = o["a"] + 1;
4  };
```

$$(b) \begin{bmatrix} \text{a} \mapsto [1, +\infty] \\ \hline - \end{bmatrix}$$

Fig. 8. (a) μJS fragment, (b) Value of o after while-loop.

Let us consider the μJS fragment reported in Fig. 7a and suppose that the boolean guard value is statically unknown. At each iteration on the while-loop, the string "a" is concatenated to the string value of key and then it is used to add a new property to the object o. If the $\text{DFA}_{/\equiv}$ were not equipped with a widening, the computation of the value of key would diverge. Since convergence of string computations is enforced by the widening ∇_{DFA}^n (with $n = 3$), also the computations of objects' properties of o converge. Indeed, the while-loop converges and the abstract interpreter produces, for the variable o, the (normalized) object reported in Fig. 7b. Clearly, the simple object join is enough for objects' properties convergence but it is not for the associated value. For example, let consider the μJS fragment reported in Fig. 8a. In this case, the number of properties of the object o does not increase in the while-loop but the value of the property a increases at each iteration. The idea behind the widening for objects is to apply the widening of values point-wisely between the properties of the two objects. Hence, we define the widening on $\text{OBJ}^{\sharp}$ as: $o_1^{\sharp} \nabla_{\text{o}} o_2^{\sharp} \triangleq \lambda p \,.\, o_1^{\sharp}(p) \nabla_{\text{v}} o_2^{\sharp}(p)$. Coming back to the example, applying the widening defined above, the abstract value of o after the while-loop is reported in Fig. 8b. We then use this widening in order to define the widening for abstract heaps and, in turn, for abstract states.

Motivating Example. We now illustrate the so far defined analysis on the example reported in the introduction (Fig. 1). It is worth noting that, in this example, objects' widening does not occur. We have already commented it with the fragments reported in Fig. 7 and Fig. 8. The goal of the analysis is to reason about the value of idx (and, in turn, of n) at the end of the execution. At the beginning of the first iteration of the while loop, the value of n is $\langle [0,0], \bot, \text{Min}(\varnothing), \varnothing, \text{def} \rangle$ and the value of idx is $\langle \bot, \bot, (\text{a} \parallel \text{b}), \varnothing, \text{def} \rangle$. The latter is used during the first iteration to access obj and then the result is stored in n (line 5). Since the property b is not present in obj, only the property a is accessed by idx, and the value of n is $\langle [1,1], \bot, \text{Min}(\varnothing), \varnothing, \text{def} \rangle$. Before starting the next iteration, idx is updated at line 6 and its value becomes $\langle \bot, \bot, (\text{aa} \parallel \text{ba}), \varnothing, \text{def} \rangle$.

Widening is applied before starting new iterations. Supposing to apply the widening ∇_{DFA}^n, $n = 1$, and the widening for intervals, the values of the variables before the second iteration are: $n = \langle [0, +\infty], \bot, \text{Min}(\varnothing), \varnothing, \text{def} \rangle$, idx $= \langle \bot, \bot, (\text{a} \parallel \text{b} \parallel \text{aa} \parallel \text{ab}), \varnothing, \text{def} \rangle$ since, in this case, the widening for automata coincides with the automata join. In the second iteration idx accesses the properties a and aa, hence n gets the value $[1, +\infty] = [0, +\infty] + ([1,1] \sqcup [2,2])$. Similarly to the previous iteration, idx becomes $\langle \bot, \bot, (\text{aa} \parallel \text{ba} \parallel \text{aaa} \parallel \text{aba}), \varnothing, \text{def} \rangle$.

Before starting the new iteration we apply the widening, obtaining the values $\mathtt{n} = \langle [0, +\infty], \perp, \mathrm{Min}(\varnothing), \varnothing, \mathtt{def} \rangle$ and $\mathtt{idx} = \langle \perp, \perp, (\mathtt{a} \parallel \mathtt{b}) \mathtt{a}^\star, \varnothing, \mathtt{def} \rangle$. The third iteration does not change the values of $\mathtt{n}$ and $\mathtt{idx}$, hence the fixpoint is reached.

Finally, at line 8, the value of $\mathtt{n}$ is assigned to $\mathtt{obj[idx]}$, updating the abstract object $\mathtt{obj}$ as follows (we omit bottom values): $[\mathtt{a} \mapsto [0, +\infty], \mathtt{aa} \mapsto [0, +\infty], \mathtt{ab} \mapsto [3, 3], \mathtt{ac} \mapsto \mathrm{Min}(\{\texttt{"world"}\}), (\mathtt{a} \parallel \mathtt{b}) \mathtt{a}^* \smallsetminus \{\mathtt{a}, \mathtt{aa}\} \mapsto [0, +\infty]]$. The summary property $(\mathtt{a} \parallel \mathtt{b}) \mathtt{a}^* \smallsetminus \{\mathtt{a}, \mathtt{aa}\}$ is added and only the properties $\mathtt{a}$ and $\mathtt{aa}$ are modified. Properties already present in $\mathtt{obj}$ remain unaltered (e.g., $\mathtt{ab}$ and $\mathtt{ac}$).

4   Discussion and Conclusion

We have proposed an abstract domain suitable for the analysis of objects' properties in dynamic programming languages. The novelty consists in exploiting *finite state automata*, in order to approximate objects' properties. This leads to a better precision (less false positives), compared to state-of-the-art domains approximating strings (for instance, [5,6]). A key aspect of our abstract domain is the *normal form for objects* and, in the paper, we have presented a normalization algorithm: it transforms objects in their normal form. An object is in normal form if and only if it has only two kind of properties: *summary* and *non-summary*. The idea behind summarization, and hence materialization, is not new in static analysis, and comes from the well-known shape analysis [16]. For example, this idea has been adopted in [11], where the authors present a static analyzer for PHP that also involve heap analysis, where the heap, in their abstraction, is made of summary heap identifiers and non-summary heap identifiers. In particular, in [11], a summary heap identifier summarizes all the elements of the heap that could be updated by statically unknown assignments. We have adopted the same idea with the difference that we may have more summary properties, expressed by automata recognizing infinite languages, rather than a single summary property that merges together heap elements updated by statically unknown assignments. The idea of summarization has been also taken into account in [3], where the authors propose the recency abstraction, which consists in representing each abstract allocation site with two memory regions, namely the *most recently allocated block* and *the not most recently allocated blocks*. The latter is basically a summary memory region, since more than one block may be allocated. Recency abstraction has been implemented also in TAJS [13], an abstract interpretation-based static analyzer for JavaScript, showing that such abstraction outperforms other abstract allocation-based techniques. As future work, we aim to implement our objects' abstract domain upon TAJS. We believe that the combination of our abstract domain and the recency abstraction can produce good results, w.r.t. analysis precision, and it would be interesting to make a comparison with TAJS and other JavaScript static analyzers, such as SAFE [15] and JSAI [14].

References

1. Arceri, V., Maffeis, S.: Abstract domains for type juggling. Electr. Notes Theor. Comput. Sci. **331**, 41–55 (2017)
2. Arceri, V., Mastroeni, I.: Static program analysis for string manipulation languages. In: VPT 2019 (2019). https://doi.org/10.4204/EPTCS.299.5
3. Balakrishnan, G., Reps, T.: Recency-abstraction for heap-allocated storage. In: Yi, K. (ed.) SAS 2006. LNCS, vol. 4134, pp. 221–239. Springer, Heidelberg (2006). https://doi.org/10.1007/11823230_15
4. Bartzis, C., Bultan, T.: Widening arithmetic automata. In: Alur, R., Peled, D.A. (eds.) CAV 2004. LNCS, vol. 3114, pp. 321–333. Springer, Heidelberg (2004). https://doi.org/10.1007/978-3-540-27813-9_25
5. Cortesi, A., Olliaro, M.: M-string segmentation: a refined abstract domain for string analysis in C programs. In: TASE 2018 (2018)
6. Costantini, G., Ferrara, P., Cortesi, A.: A suite of abstract domains for static analysis of string values. Softw. Pract. Exp. **45**(2), 245–287 (2015)
7. Cousot, P., Cousot, R.: Abstract interpretation: a unified lattice model for static analysis of programs by construction or approximation of fixpoints. In: POPL 1977 (1977)
8. Cousot, P., Halbwachs, N.: Automatic discovery of linear restraints among variables of a program. In: POPL (1978)
9. Davis, M.D., Sigal, R., Weyuker, E.J.: Computability, Complexity, and Languages: Fundamentals of Theoretical Computer Science. Academic Press Professional, Inc., New York (1994)
10. D'Silva, V.: Widening for Automata. MsC Thesis, Inst. Fur Inform. - UZH (2006)
11. Hauzar, D., Kofron, J.: Framework for static analysis of PHP applications. In: ECOOP 2015 (2015). https://doi.org/10.4230/LIPIcs.ECOOP.2015.689
12. Hopcroft, J.E., Ullman, J.D.: Introduction to Automata Theory, Languages and Computation. Addison-Wesley, Reading (1979)
13. Jensen, S.H., Møller, A., Thiemann, P.: Type analysis for javascript. In: SAS 2009 (2009). https://doi.org/10.1007/978-3-642-03237-0_17
14. Kashyap, V., et al.: JSAI: a static analysis platform for javascript. In: FSE 2014 (2014)
15. Lee, H., Won, S., Jin, J., Cho, J., Ryu, S.: SAFE: formal specification and implementation of a scalable analysis framework for ECMAScript. In: FOOL (2012)
16. Nielson, F., Nielson, H.R., Hankin, C.: Principles of Program Analysis. Springer, Heidelberg (1999). https://doi.org/10.1007/978-3-662-03811-6
17. Wilhelm, R., Sagiv, M., Reps, T.: Shape analysis. In: Watt, D.A. (ed.) CC 2000. LNCS, vol. 1781, pp. 1–17. Springer, Heidelberg (2000). https://doi.org/10.1007/3-540-46423-9_1

OpenCERT 2019 - 9th International Workshop on Open Community Approaches to Education, Research and Technology

OpenCERT 2019 Organizers' Message

Open Community is a generalisation of the concept of Open Source to other collaborative efforts. It includes Open Content, that is, some form of non restrictive license, and Open Knowledge, that is, the freedom to use, reuse, and redistribute knowledge without legal, social or technological restriction.

The 9th International Workshop on Open Community approaches to Education, Research and Technology (OpenCERT 2019) expands the scope of the International Workshop on Foundations and Techniques for Open Source Software Certification, whose 8 editions run from 2007 to 2014. The new scope of the workshop aims at promoting the use of Open Community approaches in Education and Research while also exploiting them to achieve wide diffusion and proper assessment of new, innovative Technology.

The workshop received seven full paper submissions, which were reviewed for quality, correctness, originality and relevance. Each submission was posted on GitHub and reviewed by at least three Program Committee members. The review process was carried out as an interactive, open discussion between the authors and the reviewers. A final closed discussion among the PC members was carried out using EasyChair. Six contributions were accepted for presentation at the workshop and for publication in this volume. The workshop programme also featured a keynote talk titled "Open Community approaches to Education Publishing and Research — a look into the recent past" by Andreas Meiszner.

We would like to thank the Program Committee members for their enthusiasm and effort in actively participating in the open review process. We are also grateful to the General Chair, José Nuno Oliveira, the Finance Chair, José Creissac Campos, and the Workshop and Tutorial Chairs, Emil Sekerinski and Nelma Moreira. Finally, we would like to thank all workshop attendees for their active participation in discussions and for the feedback they provided to the authors.

December 2019

Antonio Cerone
Luís Barbosa

Organization

Program Committee Chairs

Luís Barbosa   University of Minho, Portugal,
           and UNU-EGOV, UN
Antonio Cerone   Nazarbayev University, Kazakhstan

Steering Committee

Lus Barbosa   University of Minho, Portugal,
           and UNU-EGOV, UN
Peter T. Breuer   Hecusys LLC, USA
Antonio Cerone   Nazarbayev University, Kazakhstan

Program Committee

Roberto Bagnara	University of Parma and BUGSENG, Italy
Lus Barbosa (Co-chair)	University of Minho, Portugal, and UNU-EGOV, UN
Marco C. Barbosa	Universidade Tecnológica Federal do Paraná, Brazil
Leonor Barroca	The Open University, UK
Soumaya Ben Dhaou	UNU-EGOV, UN
Peter T. Breuer	Hecusys LLC, USA
Daniel Burgos	Universidad Internacional de La Rioja (UNIR), Spain
F. Heron Carvalho Júnior	Universidade Federal do Ceará, Brazil
Antonio Cerone (Co-chair)	Nazarbayev University, Kazakhstan
Stefano De Paoli	Abertay University, UK
Yannis Dimitriadis	University of Valladolid, Spain
Elsa Estevez	Universidad Nacional del Sur, Argentina
Michela Fazzolari	Institute for Informatics and Telematics (CNR-IIT), Italy
João F. Ferreira	INESC-ID and University of Lisbon, Portugal
Roberta Gori	University of Pisa, Italy
Paddy Krishnan	Oracle, Australia
Maria Helena Martinho	University of Minho, Portugal
Andreas Meiszner	Scio, Portugal, and University of Liverpool, UK
Paolo Milazzo	University di Pisa, Italy
Renato Neves	University of Minho, Portugal

John Noll	University of East London, UK, and Lero, Ireland
Donatella Persico	Institute for Educational Technologies (CNR-ITD), Italy
Alexander K. Petrenko	Russian Academy of Sciences (ISP RAS), Russia, Russia
Marinella Petrocchi	Institute for Informatics and Telematics (CNR-IIT), Italy
Lucia Rapanotti	The Open University, UK
Steve Reeves	University of Waikato, New Zealand
Mona Rizvi	Nazarbayev Univeresity, Kazakhstan
Markus Roggenbach	Swansea University, UK
Sulayman K. Sowe	Carl von Ossietzky University of Oldenburg, Germany
Marcus Specht	Open University of The Netherlands, The Netherlands
Ioannis Stamelos	Aristotle University of Thessaloniki, Greece
Anthony Wasserman	Carnegie Mellon University Silicon Valley, USA

A Survey of Learning Methods in Open Source Software

Aidarbek Suleimenov, Assiya Khuzyakhmetova, and Antonio Cerone[✉]

Department of Computer Science, Nazarbayev University, Nur-Sultan, Kazakhstan
{aidarbek.suleimenov,assiya.khuzyakhmetova,antonio.cerone}@nu.edu.kz

Abstract. Open source software (OSS) is usually developed by heterogeneous groups of people, each with their own interests, motivations and
abilities. Therefore, it is important to establish the best software development and contributing practices early in the life-time of the project.
Such practices should foster the contributors' involvement in the OSS
project as quickly as possible. The sustainability of an OSS project is
heavily based on the underlying community of contributors and on the
knowledge and skills they bring to the project and they acquire and
develop through their participation in the project and interaction with
the project community. Therefore, identifying and investigating contributors' learning processes is an important research area in OSS.

This survey paper presents an overview of open source learning methods in order to explore how community interaction impacts the development and application of OSS learning processes in other areas, especially
in education. It is argued that collaboration with peers and consistent
code contributions result in learning progress in OSS. Typical research
in this area is based on case by case analysis, whereas this survey tries
to highlight and combine the outcomes of several research contributions
from the literature.

Keywords: Open source software · Learning processes · Learning
methods · Education

1 Introduction

Free/libre/open source software (FLOSS), or simply open source software (OSS),
is software that is released together with the source code under a license that
protects the right to study, change and distribute such source code. OSS is usually developed in a collaborative manner within a distributed OSS community.
Members of such a community are called contributors and their contributions
consist of pieces of code or documentation to the project, support provided to
the software users, etc [21]. OSS is widely used today in many households, small
businesses and enterprises, agricultural conglomerates, etc. It is estimated that
OSS saved dozens of billions of dollars for companies [26]. Furthermore, the field
is still expanding.

© Springer Nature Switzerland AG 2020
E. Sekerinski et al. (Eds.): FM 2019 Workshops, LNCS 12233, pp. 157–166, 2020.
https://doi.org/10.1007/978-3-030-54997-8_10

Important challenges in OSS development include how one can learn skills in the OSS environment. Skills can refer to technical and social skills which are required for contributing to OSS. Technical skills are those that help to make contributions in terms of code while social skills are those that help to interact with the community [5]. The open source environment requires individuals to gain skills through the process of using resources such as mailing lists, bug trackers, IRC chats, version control systems, etc.

It is important to understand learning processes in OSS projects as this helps maintain further development of the project and its support. As people learn more about OSS projects, there is empirical evidence that they become more active and efficient contributors to the community [4]. Ye and Kishida suggest that the main motivation for people to participate in OSS software development is primarily to acquire skills and learn [34], an extrinsic motivation that is normally associated with and complemented by a number of intrinsic motivations, including enjoyment, sense of creativity and accomplishment, and intellectual stimulation [3, 21]. Therefore, it is also important to investigate how one can gain skills in OSS projects in order to fulfill individual motivations, which is a significant factor of OSS development.

In this paper, we present an overview of learning processes in OSS communities and discuss the literature with a particular emphasis on formal and informal methods of learning. Section 2 clarifies the distinction between informal and formal learning both in general terms and in the specific OSS context. Section 3 reviews the literature on the analysis of OSS learning methods with reference to community interaction, code contribution, internet technologies and communication tools. Section 4 discusses how OSS skills acquisition frameworks could possibly be applied to learning in external activities in software development and higher education. Finally, Sect. 5 summarizes the contributions and limitations of the paper and envisages the future work in terms of both practical teaching and research.

2   Formal and Informal Methods of Learning

Formal learning refers to a structured form of learning that leads to certification by an official education organization [20]. Such a form of learning is normally highly teacher-centered as it requires some authority to conduct class sessions, provide feedback, give grades, etc. Examples of formal learning include higher education and professional certifications.

Informal learning [15, 17, 23], instead, occurs outside education organizations and has neither any set objective in terms of learning outcomes nor any specific structure. In general, informal learning is never intentional from the learner's standpoint and does not necessarily lead to certification. However, it should not be confused with non-formal learning, which often refers to organized learning outside the formal education system, such as in a short-term format and/or on a voluntary basis. There are several perspectives in defining informal learning that differ in terms of intentionality and awareness at the time of the learning experience [20]. In the context of OSS environments informal learning specifically refers to learning-by-doing or project-based collaboration. This also includes community interactions, code contributions, source code reading, technology usages, etc.

In order to make contributions to OSS, it is essential to have required technical and social skills [1]. In our survey we focus on contributions that identify how these skills can be acquired. Due to the distributed nature of OSS development and its project based approach, it could be hypothesized that OSS skills are acquired through informal learning [5]. Therefore, it is necessary to identify the specific informal learning methods that help individuals to acquire such skills.

One of the biggest challenges of this task is the fact that it is not trivial to assess the learning dynamics within an OSS environment. There are no assignments or exams to check whether contributors gained any skills or learned some concepts. Thus it is challenging to gather empirical evidences. One of the main research approaches in this area is to perform data mining analysis on OSS artifacts, such as mailing lists or code history changes [13,22,28]. In addition, surveys are also used [9]. In the next sections some informal methods of learning will be considered and their effects on learning will be discussed.

3   Learning Methods in OSS

Learning methods in OSS not only refer to an informal learning context but are also heavily based on practice rather on acquiring notions. Moreover, practice not only occurs at individual level but it is fostered and mediated by the participation in the OSS community and the communication and development infrastructure built around the OSS project.

3.1   Open Source Community Interaction

Community growth around some projects could actually decrease the complexity of the system over time when compared to projects with only one individual maintainer [11], thus making community an essential part of any big OSS project. Moreover, open source communities play a vital role in contributors' skill acquisition. A specific OSS community grows around a particular project. This makes each community different from each other, thus making it hard to generalize and create comprehensive guidelines for newcomers.

The distributed nature of software development in these communities and the constant increase in software complexity make it inevitable for contributors to communicate with other peers within the community during the process of skill acquisition [5]. However, the question arises on whether or not the interaction with the community is actually beneficial for acquiring skills.

Singh et al. [28], collected data from 251 developers contributing to 25 OSS projects hosted on SourceForge over a period of six years. In their study a developer is a person that contributed at least 10 times in the period including both contributions to emails and to CVS. Then a Hidden Markov Model was built out of such data and it was discovered that learning from peers is one of the most important sources of learning in OSS. According to Wen [32] such a form of learning can also facilitate knowledge-sharing for some domain-specific skills, for example in the area of security.

Moreover, Kuk [14] found out that active interaction with the community not only increases the individual's skills but, combined with code and content contributions, also moves contributors "to the center of OSS development". Furthermore, personal experience within the community and interactions with the community have a long term dynamic impact rather than a short term static impact on a developer's code contribution behavior [28].

The "center of OSS development" refers to the core members of the OSS community, who do make the majority of contributions [29] and decisions [21]. In the study by Kuk [14], 1500 messages from two OSS development mailing lists were analyzed and it was found out that contributors with high degree of interaction with others are more likely to become core members of OSS projects. Kuk stresses that such interactions also accelerate releases of individual knowledge resources and exchange of information within the community [14].

Finally, Sowe and Stamelos [29] divide the learning process of individual actors in four phases through which knowledge evolves: socialization, in which knowledge is implicitly shared, externalization, in which tacit knowledge is made explicit to the community, combination, in which community explicit knowledge is combined and organized as abstract knowledge, and internalization, in which abstract knowledge is absorbed and further combined with individual knowledge and experiences to produce new tacit knowledge. Building on this conceptual learning model, Cerone and Sowe [7] describe OSS projects as learning and development environments in which heterogeneous communities get together to exchange knowledge through discussion and put it into practice through actual contributions to software development, revision and testing. This leads to the view of OSS communities as open participatory ecosystems in which actors create not only source code but a large variety of resources that include the implicit and explicit definitions of learning processes and the establishment and maintenance of communication and support systems [6].

3.2   Code Contributions

Code contributions play a vital part in OSS learning due to the project-based nature of OSS development. Code contributions can also show the level of expertise of the contributor. On the one hand, level of complexity of the code, frequency of code contributions, domain the code was written for and number of bugs that appeared after the new code was introduced could possibly show the learning progress of the individual contributor. On the other hand, the level of expertise increases the reputation of the contributor, thus serving as a major source of motivation for developers to participate in a community [27].

There are empirical evidences that confirm the importance of code contributions and bug fixes in the learning process. For example, Kim and Jiang [13] analyzed the history of code changes of five OSS projects with overall 100 contributors. According to their study, the number of bugs resolved increases the chances for individuals to learn and reduces the chances to produce bugs in the future. This is particularly important, since it was also found out that experienced developers are as prone to introduce bugs as inexperienced developers [13].

In addition, Krogh *et al.* [30] found that it is expected for newcomers to specialize only in one area of expertise. Their study was based on the analysis of Freenet OSS project contributors' behavior. After interviewing contributors, it appeared that they made contributions on the basis of prior knowledge. There are several reasons for this. One reason is the fact that contributing code to OSS projects can be hard [12] and therefore requires extensive experience. It might be more beneficial and easier to focus on one area in order to make significant contributions. A second reason is that expertise in some particular area could be highly beneficial for the community as a whole, once such expertise undergo the process of knowledge sharing. Thus, these benefits can make the community more than willing to accept newcomers in exchange for their experience [32].

Learning through code contributions and learning from community interactions are not necessarily mutually exclusive. Interaction between newcomers and experienced project members is essential for newcomers to make code contributions. Newcomers need to be allowed to make contributions that are equivalent to their abilities and experienced members could potentially help them in identifying such kinds of contributions via collaborative efforts [8].

Finally, we can say that code production not only fosters learning through practice in the code contributor, but also drives learning in those community members who study and test that code. A similar role is played by other artifacts of the OSS production process, such as documentations, guidelines and even licenses.

3.3   Internet Technologies and Communication Tools

OSS is usually developed by a heterogeneous group of people distributed all over the world [21], each having own role in the development of the final product. Every software engineering project depends on collaboration, and collaboration is essential in OSS. Since synchronized actions are significant for the completion of complex tasks, effective communication and collaboration play an important role in the production process [33]. Thus, developers are required to use some sort of internet technologies in order to interact with each other. In OSS communities this role is usually performed by mailing lists, internet relay chats (IRC), remote version control systems, discussion forums, bug trackers, project management tools, documentation web pages and many other tools depending on the projects' needs.

All these tools serve as a way for knowledge manifestation, which makes it unnecessary for face to face contact or for newcomers to use the bandwidth of their experienced peers in order to answer already answered questions. All these conclusions were made from an observation of K Desktop Environment (KDE) OSS project community [10]. Other kind of tools that can facilitate learning in OSS environments are Question & Answer internet communities such as Stack

Exchange. Users can post questions on a wide variety of topics and answer questions of other people. Since participants are not paid for their efforts in giving answers, anyone can freely benefit from interacting with this community in a similar way to participating in OSS project communities [25].

We can conclude that the use of internet technologies and communication tools may lead to more efficient development and faster learning processes.

4   Application of OSS Learning Methods

There are several ways of transferring informal OSS learning methods to formal education: opening course materials and making them free to access, making students generate content for the course and contribute to its processes and usage of technologies. Weller and Meizsner [31] report on some of these ways, and analyze their effectiveness and benefits when applied to formal education.

However, the main strength of OSS learning methods is the process of collaboration and how it results in learning-by-doing. In fact, after recognizing the importance of OSS learning-by-doing in building big projects in a collaborative manner, we now consider how to apply such methods to other areas, especially to education. One of the main aspects of education in an OSS environment is the fact that both expert (teacher) and learner (student) participate in content creation and knowledge sharing [19]. Another fundamental aspect is that traditional learning techniques are limited in terms of applications of knowledge, whereas in OSS there is a clear visibility of results of skills acquisition in terms of code submitted or questions replied. This means that there is a big opportunity for transferring novel learning techniques from OSS communities to traditional learning environments [18].

One of the most obvious applications of the OSS learning approach is to use it as a part of a specific teaching module on OSS. Although learning project details normally does not require classroom participation or any other formal learning methods, it could be investigated if one could learn how to contribute to OSS within the limits of the class. Some studies provide evidence of success of such experience. One example is the Master courses in Open Source and Distributed Development Models at the University of Skövde, Sweden [16]. A group of 12 students were introduced to the OSS community aspects and required to put effort in making contributions with increasing complexity gradually overtime. As a result, the students managed to make contributions to OSS projects in terms of documentation, bug reports and desktop themes [16]. On the other hand, there are evidences that contributing to OSS can be difficult and time-consuming [12]. Therefore, it is required to keep balance between students' abilities and course requirements. Students should be evaluated in terms of their efforts or progress rather than based on the number of their code submissions or bugs fixes. This approach is adopted in the 3rd and 4th year course on Open Source Software at Nazarbayev University, Kazakhstan.

A more general exploitation of the OSS learning approach is as part of a core subject in the area of software engineering. Undergraduate students at the

Aristotle University Thessaloniki, Greece, participate as project team members in real-life OSS projects as part of a course assignment on Software Engineering [24]. Students are allowed to select an OSS project and assume a number of possible contributor roles, thus getting to understand through real participation how different professionals are involved in the software development process.

At the University of Minho, Fernandes *et al.* [9] carried out a pilot project in teaching software engineering to students in the last year of a MSc course whose completion entitles the students to teach Informatics at secondary school level. Students spontaneously got together in small groups (up to 3 elements) and chose an OSS project to get involved in. Data collection by the instructors was carried out during the pilot project using direct observation and unstructured interviews aiming at designing a learning-by-doing e-Learning framework for teaching software engineering topics.

Finally, a recent approach that may contribute to the understanding of the dynamics of learning processes is process mining [2], that is, the use of event data to extract process-related information. With the aim of understanding the learning dynamics of OSS communities, Mukala *et al.* [22] used process mining to extract learning processes from mailing archives of OSS projects. Their results provide insights on the possible discrepancies that are observed between an initial theoretical representations of learning processes and the real behavior observed from the data. Moreover, such a comparison helps foster the understanding on how learning actually takes place in OSS environments.

5   Conclusion

We have seen that OSS represents an important approach to software development and is a field that is expected to grow within the next few years. It is essential to enable newcomers to easily join OSS projects in order for the projects to be sustainable. For this reason understanding and fostering learning processes is crucial in OSS.

We discussed that learning in OSS projects can be beneficial not only to newcomers but also to core members. Newcomers can learn and acquire new skills by contributing, while core members can receive help through newcomers' contributions and possibly from their domain expertise.

We have surveyed a number of research works in the area of OSS in order to summarize how learning occurs in OSS environment. We have found that informal and project based learning methods are the most common in OSS communities. Such methods include active interaction with a community and code contributions.

We noted that the learning processes associated with such methods were identified by empirical evidences and are an essential part of the individual contributor's learning process. Finally, we discussed how such methods have been applied and can be effectively applied to education.

This paper does not pretend to provide an exhaustive review of learning methods in OSS. It essentially shows the approaches that have been investigated or have been used in the development of the course on Open Source Software at Nazarbayev University, Kazakhstan.

Part of our future work is to analyze the effectiveness of this course and its impact on the students' post-graduation involvement in OSS activities and, more in general, on their careers. Furthermore, the analysis of OSS learning carried out in previous work [9,22] will be further developed, especially aiming to the integration of data collection through direct observation and unstructured interviews [9] and process mining techniques [22].

References

1. Ghosh, R.A., Glott, R., Krieger, B., Robles, G.: Free/Libre and Open Source Software: Survey and Study, January 2002
2. van der Aalst, W.: Process Mining. Data Science in Action, 2nd edn. Springer, Heidelberg (2016)
3. Androutsellis-Theotokis, S., Spinellis, D., Kechagia, M., Gousios, G.: Open source software: a survey from 10,000 feet. Found. Trends Technol. Inf. Oper. Manage. 4(3–4), 187–347 (2010)
4. Au, Y.A., Carpenter, D., Chen, X., Clark, J.G.: Virtual Organizational Learning in Open Source Software Development Projects (0013), May 2007. https://ideas. repec.org/p/tsa/wpaper/0041is.html
5. Barcomb, A., Grottke, M., Stauffert, J.-P., Riehle, D., Jahn, S.: How developers acquire FLOSS skills. In: Damiani, E., Frati, F., Riehle, D., Wasserman, A.I. (eds.) OSS 2015. IAICT, vol. 451, pp. 23–32. Springer, Cham (2015). https://doi.org/10. 1007/978-3-319-17837-0_3
6. Cerone, A.: Learning and activity patterns in OSS communities and their impact on software quality. In: Proceedings of OpenCert 2011, Electronic Communications of the EASST, vol. 48 (2012)
7. Cerone, A., Sowe, S.K.: Using free/libre open source software projects as e-learning tools. In: Proceedings of OpenCert 2010, Electronic Communications of the EASST, vol. 33 (2010)
8. Edwards, K.: Epistemic communities, situated learning and open source software development. In: Proceedings from the conference on Epistemic Cultures and the Practice of Interdisciplinarity (2001)
9. Fernandes, S., Martinho, M.H., Cerone, A., Barbosa, L.S.: Integrating formal and informal learning through a FLOSS-based innovative approach. In: Antunes, P., Gerosa, M.A., Sylvester, A., Vassileva, J., de Vreede, G.-J. (eds.) CRIWG 2013. LNCS, vol. 8224, pp. 208–214. Springer, Heidelberg (2013). https://doi.org/10. 1007/978-3-642-41347-6_15
10. Hemetsberger, A., Reinhardt, C.: Learning and knowledge-building in open-source communities: a social-experiential approach. Manage. Learn. 37(2), 187–214 (2006). https://doi.org/10.1177/1350507606063442
11. Huntley, C.L.: Organizational learning in open-source software projects: an analysis of debugging data. IEEE Trans. Eng. Manage. 50(4), 485–493 (2003)
12. Jaccheri, L., Osterlie, T.: Open source software: a source of possibilities for software engineering education and empirical software engineering. In: First International Workshop on Emerging Trends in FLOSS Research and Development (FLOSS 2007: ICSE Workshops 2007), p. 5, May 2007. https://doi.org/10.1109/FLOSS. 2007.12

13. Kim, Y., Jiang, L.: The learning curves in open-source software (OSS) development network. In: Proceedings of the Sixteenth International Conference on Electronic Commerce (ICEC 2014), pp. 41–48. ACM (2014). https://doi.org/10.1145/2617848.2617857

14. Kuk, G.: Strategic interaction and knowledge sharing in the KDE developer mailing list. Manage. Sci. **52**(7), 1031–1042 (2006). https://doi.org/10.1287/mnsc.1060.0551

15. Livingstone, D.W.: Informal learning: conceptual distinctions and preliminary findings. Counterpoints **249**, 203–227 (2006)

16. Lundell, B., Persson, A., Lings, B.: Learning through practical involvement in the OSS ecosystem: experiences from a masters assignment. In: Feller, J., Fitzgerald, B., Scacchi, W., Sillitti, A. (eds.) OSS 2007. ITIFIP, vol. 234, pp. 289–294. Springer, Boston, MA (2007). https://doi.org/10.1007/978-0-387-72486-7_30

17. Marsick, V.J., Watkins, K.E.: Informal and incidental learning. New Dir. Adult Continuing Educ. **89**, 25–34 (2001)

18. Meiszner, A., Glott, R., Sowe, S.K.: Free/libre open source software (FLOSS) communities as an example of successful open participatory learning ecosystems. UPGRADE Eur. J. Inform. Profess. **9**(3), 62–68 (2008). http://oro.open.ac.uk/16852/

19. Meiszner, A., Glott, R., Sowe, S.K.: Preparing the Ne(x)t Generation: Lessons Learnt from Free/libre Open Source Software Why Free and Open are Preconditions and Not Options for Higher Education (2008)

20. Merriam, S.B., Cafarella, R.S., Baumgartner, L.M.: Learning in Adulthood : A Comprehensive Guide, 3rd edn. Jossey-Bass, San Francisco (2007)

21. Muffatto, M.: Open Source: A Multidisciplinary Approach (Series on Technology Management). Imperial College Press, London (2006)

22. Mukala, P., Cerone, A., Turini, F.: An empirical verification of a-priori learning models on mailing archives in the context of online learning activities of participants in free/libre open source software (floss) communities. Educ. Inf. Technol. **22**(6), 3207–3229 (2017)

23. Overwien, B.: Informal learning and the role of social movements. Int. Rev. Educ. **46**(6), 621–640 (2000)

24. Papadopoulos, P.M., Stamelos, I.G., Meiszner, A.: Enhancing software engineering education through open source projects: four years of students' perspectives. Educ. Inf. Technol. **18**(2), 381–397 (2013)

25. Posnett, D., Warburg, E., Devanbu, P., Filkov, V.: Mining stack exchange: expertise is evident from initial contributions. In: 2012 International Conference on Social Informatics, pp. 199–204, December 2012. https://doi.org/10.1109/SocialInformatics.2012.67

26. Riehle, D.: The economic motivation of open source software: stakeholder perspectives. Computer **40**, 25–32 (2007). https://doi.org/10.1109/MC.2007.147

27. Roberts, J., Hann, I., Slaughter, S.: Understanding the motivations, participation, and performance of open source software developers: a longitudinal study of the apache projects. Manage. Sci. **52**(7), 984–999 (2006)

28. Singh, P.V., Youn, N., Tan, Y.: Developer Learning Dynamics in Open Source Software Projects : A Hidden Markov Model Analysis (2006)

29. Sowe, S.K., Stamelos, I.: Reflection on knowledge sharing in F/OSS projects. In: Russo, B., Damiani, E., Hissam, S., Lundell, B., Succi, G. (eds.) OSS 2008. ITIFIP, vol. 275, pp. 351–358. Springer, Boston, MA (2008). https://doi.org/10.1007/978-0-387-09684-1_32

30. Vonkrogh, G., Spaeth, S., Lakhani, K.: Community, joining and specialization in open source software innovation: a case study, July 2003. https://www.alexandria.unisg.ch/30623/
31. Weller, M., Meiszner, A.: Flosscom phase 2: Report on the effectiveness of a floss-like learning community in formal educational settings. FLOSSCom Project (2008)
32. Wen, S.F.: An empirical study on security knowledge sharing and learning in open source software communities. Computers $7(4)$ (2018). http://www.mdpi.com/2073-431X/7/4/49
33. Xuan, Q., Filkov, V.: Building it together: synchronous development in OSS. In: Proceedings of the 36th International Conference on Software Engineering (ICSE 2014), pp. 222–233. ACM (2014). https://doi.org/10.1145/2568225.2568238
34. Ye, Y., Kishida, K.: Toward an Understanding of the Motivation of Open Source Software Developers, pp. 419–429, June 2003. https://doi.org/10.1109/ICSE.2003.1201220

A Calculus of Chaos in Stochastic Compilation
Engineering in the Cause of Mathematics

Peter T. Breuer[1(✉)] and Simon J. Pickin[2]

[1] Hecusys LLC, Atlanta, GA, USA
ptb@hecusys.com
[2] Universidad Complutense de Madrid, Madrid, Spain
simon.pickin@fdi.ucm.es

Abstract. An unexpected outcome from an open project to develop a 'chaotic' compiler for ANSI C is described here: a trace information entropy calculus for stochastically compiled programs. A stochastic compiler produces randomly different object codes every time it is applied to the same source code. This calculus quantifies the entropy introduced into run-time program traces by a compiler that aims for the maximal possible entropy, furnishing a definition and proof of security for encrypted computing (Turing-complete computation in which data remains in encrypted form throughout), where the status was formerly unknown.

Keywords: Computer security · Encrypted computing · Program logic

1 Introduction

This article describes a program calculus that quantifies the entropy introduced into a run-time trace by a stochastic compiler, developed as part of an open source project (http://sf.net/p/obfusc) to develop a secure computing infrastructure. Open source projects may embrace changes of direction because the goals are defined by community appetites, and that is what has happened here. To be clear from the outset, the stochastic element occurs not in the execution of a program but in the compilation. The software part of the project aims to develop a complete tool-chain (compiler, assembler, linker, loader) for *encrypted computing* [1] platforms [3,5,8,11,18,23]. Those are general purpose processors in which data remains in encrypted form throughout processing. Obviously computing encrypted is not less 'secure' than no encryption at all, but how secure has little formal backing. A danger point is marked in [7] with a program for an encrypted computing platform that decrypts ciphertexts back to plaintext in real time and, intuitively, the constants in it 'ought' to be as hard to guess as the encryption is to crack, but that needs proof. It turns out that key to a security proof is a stochastic compiler and that story is set out here.

© Springer Nature Switzerland AG 2020
E. Sekerinski et al. (Eds.): FM 2019 Workshops, LNCS 12233, pp. 167–184, 2020.
https://doi.org/10.1007/978-3-030-54997-8_11

Also introduced in [7] are properties of a machine code instruction set architecture (ISA) necessary for a secure runtime environment. Important is *malleability*: the constants in each machine code instruction may be varied to offset independently by any amount its inputs and outputs. That allows the data beneath the encryption in a program trace to be varied arbitrarily by the compiler while the program black-box semantics remains the same, the code remains the same apart from the varied constants, and the same sequence of instructions appears in the trace [2,4,6]. Intuitively that means an attacker cannot be sure they have 'cracked the encryption', as their solution is one of many. How many?

This paper will touch on security but focus on that pure computer science problem of getting the maximum number of possible variations into run-time traces via stochastic compilation, and how to state if it is so with assurance. Introducing maximum variation will be called **chaotic compilation**. It was not known if it were possible but this paper quantifies the notion and shows how to guarantee a compiler gets it right via a formal logic. Then that is used to formalise and answer the question 'is secure computing possible'. As the subtitle to this paper puts it, it is a case of engineering in the cause of mathematics.

The nearest existing applicable security concept is classic 'Holy Grail' *cryptographic semantic security* [14] for encryptions, best known via the game theory version of it [15]: there is no method of attack M of polynomial time complexity in the encryption block size n that infinitely often does non-negligibly better than chance (i.e., probability $1/2 + B$ for $B > 0$) at guessing the value of a given bit of data beneath the encryption, as $n \rightarrow \infty$. In the encrypted computing context, the encryption block size n is the same as the hardware word size n, the size of the processor's registers. The plaintext word beneath the encryption is constant size, typically 32 bits, but the hardware word may be 128, 256 bits or more. IBM's work on (non-Turing complete) computation over fully homomorphic encryptions (FHEs; encryptions $\mathcal{E}$ that respect addition and multiplication, with $\mathcal{E}[a + b] = \mathcal{E}[a] + \mathcal{E}[b]$ and $\mathcal{E}[a * b] = \mathcal{E}[a] * \mathcal{E}[b]$) [10,12] uses custom vector machines with word sizes in the millions of bits and atomic operations that take on the order of one second [13]. But the word size n cannot vary arbitrarily, because hardware cannot change, so the concept must be tested mathematically.

The similar security concept this project has created for encrypted computing is *relative semantic security*: there is no successful method of attack M that (i) has polynomial-time complexity in the number of bits n in the hardware word on the encrypted computing platform, and (ii) reveals the run-time data beneath the encryption, given (iii) there is no such method that is successful against the encryption. 'Success' means the method has probability of guessing right on each bit it reports that beats chance by a margin that does not tend to 0 as $n \rightarrow \infty$. Formally, if T_n is the trace of the program on an encrypted computing platform with an n-bit word and b is the targeted bit beneath the encryption, and (i) the worst case running time of M is $\mathbf{O}n^k$ for some k, then (ii) prob$[M(T_n)=b]>1/2+B$ for some $B > 0$ infinitely often as $n \rightarrow \infty$ is impossible, *provided* (iii) there is no such method M' against the encryption alone (classic cryptographic semantic security). Put $1/2^m+B$ in (ii) if guessing m bits at a time.

The argument for that is sketched out further in Sect. 6. It proceeds via a quantification of the entropy induced in a program trace by a chaotic compiler. The formal method involved is a program logic expressing the trace entropy. Extant program logics with stochastic aspects [16,20] all, as far the authors know, deal with run-time randomness and we have not been able to discover any that deal with compile-time randomness. Program logics are abstractions of program semantics and in this case the aspect of interest is how much the program trace varies when the same program is compiled to make it vary 'as much as possible' from recompilation to recompilation. If the compiler works successfully as required, its variations statistically swamp the programmed information content in the trace, meaning that any attack is effectively against statistically independent random data, which reduces it to an attack against the encryption alone.

This paper is organised as follows. Section 2 gives an informal introduction to the 'trick' of stochastic compilation and the so-called maximum ($\widetilde{h}$) and minimum ($\underline{h}$) entropy principles. Section 3 gives a slightly formal view-from-the-top of stochastic compilation and introduces a modified OpenRISC (http://openrisc. io) machine code instruction set as concrete target for chaotically stochastic compilation. Compilation is described in Sect. 4 in 4.1 and 4.2. A pre-/post-condition Hoare program logic [17] for the calculus of differences that tracks a compiler's code variations is introduced in Sects. 4.3, and in Sect. 4.4 it is modified to an information entropy ('chaos') calculus for run-time traces. Section 5 gives examples and Sect. 6 sketches the chaotic compilation security argument.

2   Overview of the Technical Foundation

The source language is ANSI C [19] here but the approach is generic. Chaotic compilation is guided by the *maximal entropy principle*:

> *Every machine code arithmetic instruction that writes should introduce maximal possible entropy into the run-time trace.*   ($\widetilde{h}$)

The restriction to arithmetic instructions is because copy and goto must work normally. The mechanism (introduced in [6]) is as follows: the object-code differs from the nominal semantics beneath the encryption by a planned and different randomly generated 'delta' at every register and memory location before and after every instruction. That is a *difference scheme*:

Definition 1. *A difference scheme is a set of vectors of deltas from nominal for the data per memory and register location, one vector per point in the control graph of the machine code, i.e., before and after each machine code instruction.*

The scheme is generated by the compiler and is shared with the user/owner of the code, so they may validate or verify the run-time trace and create inputs for the running program and read outputs from it.

A thought experiment illustrates the trick of this mechanism. Consider the following pseudo-code loop:

$$\text{while } x < y + z + 1 \text{ do } \{x \leftarrow x + 2; x \leftarrow x + 3; \}$$

Imagine new program variables X, Y, Z, shifted by different deltas from the program variables x, y, z at different points in the code as shown below:

$$\text{while } \underbrace{X+4}_{x} < \underbrace{Y+5}_{y} + \underbrace{Z+6}_{z} +1 \text{ do } \{\underbrace{X+7}_{x} \leftarrow \underbrace{X+4}_{x} +2; \underbrace{X+4}_{x} \leftarrow \underbrace{X+7}_{x} +3; \}$$

The relation $x = X + 4$ has to be the same at the end of the loop as at the beginning, but otherwise the choice of 4, 5, 6, 7 is free. Simplifying, that is:[1]

$$\text{while } X < Y + Z + 8 \text{ do } \{X \leftarrow X - 1; X \leftarrow X + 6;\}$$

An observer can watch the first while loop execute and understand it as the second loop. Conversely, a user intending the second while loop can execute the first, with the translations above in mind.

A stochastic compiler systematically does the above, but at the object code level. It introduces different deltas like 4, 5, 6, 7 above at every register and every memory location, per machine code instruction. A summary is that the object codes generated from the same source code

(a) all have the same structure, differing only in the constant parameters embedded in the individual machine code instructions; also
(b) run-time traces have the same instructions (modulo (a)) in the same order reading and writing the same registers and memory locations; but
(c) data varies from nominal by planned but randomly chosen and arbitrary deltas, different at every point in the run-time trace and registers/memory.

The catch is, as with the $x = X + 4$ above, a *minimal entropy principle* applies:

deltas must be equal across copy or skip, and wherever control paths meet.   ($\underset{\sim}{h}$)

That is necessary in order for computation to work properly.

Compilation must be systematic, or it will produce neither the intended semantics nor properties. So this paper first (Sect. 4) describes 'correct by construction' compilation along the lines of the thought experiment above, introducing the 'deltas' of a difference scheme as compile-time parameters.

The question is if those can be chosen without restriction as ($\underset{\sim}{h}$) demands. The induced variation in the run-time program traces is measurable as (information-theoretic) entropy.[2] What ($\widetilde{h}$) expresses is that at every instruction in the run-time trace where, say, a 32-bit value is written beneath the encryption, the

---

[1] Signed 2s complement comparison is translation-invariant. I.e., $x<y$ iff $x+k<y+k$.
[2] Entropy is formally the stochastic expectation $H = -E[\log_2 p_i]$ of the probability p_i of the possible observations i, thus $H = -\sum_i p_i \log_2 p_i$ with $0 \leq p_i \leq 1$ and $H \geq 0$.

chaotic compiler should introduce a delta with 32 bits of entropy in the choice available. Shannon's theorem [21] holds that adding one signal to another in fixed length arithmetic does not decrease entropy. Here, one input is the compiler's, the other is the programmer's. When the compiler's has maximal entropy (32 bits) then the combined signal also has maximal entropy and the information from the programmer has been statistically swamped and an observer cannot infer any deterministic relation or statistical tendency from the programmer's input. The two inputs are (i) not separately visible to a run-time observer, having been combined at compile time (and in encrypted computing the unencrypted form of the data is itself not visible), and (ii) the programmed data can be recovered afterwards by the intended user with the help of the difference scheme.

Box 1: A stochastic (expression) compiler for encrypted computing.

The compiler $\mathbb{C}[-]$ translates an expression e of type Expr that should end up in register r at run-time to machine code mc of type MC and plans a 32-bit integer delta Δr (type Off) for it in r:

$$\mathbb{C}[\text{-}]^r :: \text{Expr} \rightarrow (\text{MC}, \text{Off})$$
$$\mathbb{C}[e]^r = (mc, \Delta r) \tag{1}$$

Let s_r be the value in register (or memory location) r in state s of the processor at run-time. The state is comprised by the values in registers and memory. Let $\ulcorner e \urcorner s$ be a nominal evaluation of expression e in state s.[a] Running the code mc changes the state s after several steps to state s' that holds a value in r whose value differs by Δr from the nominal value of the expression. That is:

$$s \overset{mc}{\rightsquigarrow} s' \text{ where } s'_r = \mathcal{E}[\mathcal{D}[\ulcorner e \urcorner s] + \Delta r] \tag{2}$$

where $\mathcal{E}$ is encryption (it may be trivial), $\mathcal{D}$ is decryption.

---

[a] If source code variable x is in register r with delta Δr, then the nominal value $\ulcorner x \urcorner s = \mathcal{E}[\mathcal{D}[s_r] - \Delta r]$, $\ulcorner e_1 + e_2 \urcorner s = \mathcal{E}[\mathcal{D}[\ulcorner e_1 \urcorner s] + \mathcal{D}[\ulcorner e_2 \urcorner s]]$, etc.

But ($\natural$) acts to constrain entropy. Section 4 will show that, in a chaotically compiled program, at any m points in the trace *not* related as in ($\natural$), variations with $32m$ bits of entropy are produced among the traces, on a 32-bit machine. For each pair of points related as in ($\natural$), entropy reduces by 32 bits. That analysis leads to the argument (Sect. 6) that there is no successful[3] method of attack on the run-time data with polynomial-time complexity in the number of bits n in a processor word on an encrypted computing platform, given there is no such method that succeeds against the encryption in use (it has an n-bit block-size).

---

[3] 'Success' is stochastic: the method has probability of being right on each bit that beats chance by a ('non-negligible') margin B that does not tend to 0 as $n \rightarrow \infty$.

3   Overview of Stochastic Compilation

The action of a stochastic compiler (Box 2) parallels (a-c) of Sect. 1: (A) the constants embedded in the machine code instructions are varied so (B) all feasible trace variations are exercised (C) *equiprobably*, because an equiprobable distribution over the full range of values (uniquely) has maximal entropy.

An implementation generates a new difference scheme at each recompilation, as set out in Box 1 for compilation of pure expressions. The Δr is the entry in the difference scheme for register r at the given point in the program.

Box 2: A stochastically 'chaotic' compiler implements the following strategy:

(A) *change only program constants, generating an arrangement of planned* deltas *from nominal for instruction inputs and outputs* (a difference scheme);

(B) *leave run-time traces unchanged, apart from differences in the program constants* (A) *and run-time data;*

(C) *equiprobably generate all possible difference schemes satisfying* (A), (B).

Table 1. RISC 'FxA' machine code instruction set.

op. fields	mnem.	semantics		
add $r_0 r_1 r_2 \mathcal{E}k$	add	$r_0 \leftarrow \mathcal{E}[\mathcal{D}r_1 + \mathcal{D}r_2 + k]$		
sub $r_0 r_1 r_2 \mathcal{E}k$	subtract	$r_0 \leftarrow \mathcal{E}[\mathcal{D}r_1 - \mathcal{D}r_2 + k]$		
mul $r_0 r_1 r_2 \mathcal{E}k_0 \mathcal{E}k_1 \mathcal{E}k_2$	multiply	$r_0 \leftarrow \mathcal{E}[(\mathcal{D}r_1 - k_1) * (\mathcal{D}r_2 - k_2) + k_0]$		
div $r_0 r_1 r_2 k_0 k_1 k_2$	divide	$r_0 \leftarrow \mathcal{E}[(\mathcal{D}r_1 - k_1) \div (\mathcal{D}r_2 - k_2) + k_0]$		
...				
mov $r_0 r_1$	move	$r_0 \leftarrow r_1$		
beq $i\ r_1 r_2 \mathcal{E}k$	branch	if b then $pc \leftarrow pc+i$, $b \Leftrightarrow \mathcal{D}r_1 = \mathcal{D}r_2 + k$		
bne $i\ r_1 r_2 \mathcal{E}k$	branch	if b then $pc \leftarrow pc+i$, $b \Leftrightarrow \mathcal{D}r_1 \neq \mathcal{D}r_2 + k$		
blt $i\ r_1 r_2 \mathcal{E}k$	branch	if b then $pc \leftarrow pc+i$, $b \Leftrightarrow \mathcal{D}r_1 < \mathcal{D}r_2 + k$		
bgt $i\ r_1 r_2 \mathcal{E}k$	branch	if b then $pc \leftarrow pc+i$, $b \Leftrightarrow \mathcal{D}r_1 > \mathcal{D}r_2 + k$	LEGEND	
ble $i\ r_1 r_2 \mathcal{E}k$	branch	if b then $pc \leftarrow pc+i$, $b \Leftrightarrow \mathcal{D}r_1 \leq \mathcal{D}r_2 + k$	r	– register index
bge $i\ r_1 r_2 \mathcal{E}k$	branch	if b then $pc \leftarrow pc+i$, $b \Leftrightarrow \mathcal{D}r_1 \geq \mathcal{D}r_2 + k$	k	– 32-bit integer
...			pc	– prog. count reg.
b i	branch	$pc \leftarrow pc + i$	j	– prog. count
sw $(\mathcal{E}k_0)r_0\ r_1$	store	mem$[\![\mathcal{E}[\mathcal{D}r_0 + k_0]]\!] \leftarrow r_1$	'$\leftarrow$'	– assignment
lw $r_0\ (\mathcal{E}k_1)r_1$	load	$r_0 \leftarrow$ mem$[\![\mathcal{E}[\mathcal{D}r_1 + k_1]]\!]$	ra	– return addr. reg.
jr r	jump	$pc \leftarrow r$	i	– prog. incr.
jal j	jump	$ra \leftarrow pc + 4$; $pc \leftarrow j$	r	– register content
j j	jump	$pc \leftarrow j$	$\mathcal{E}$	– encryption
nop	no-op		$\mathcal{D}$	– decryption

A reduced instruction set (RISC) machine code with 'fused anything and add' (FxA) [6] -style ISA will be the compilation target here, adapted originally from OpenRISC v1.1 (http://openrisc.io/or1k.html), The portion needed for this paper is shown in Table 1. The general pattern of the ISA is that instructions access up to three 32 general purpose registers (GPRs), and one of those may instead be a ('immediate') constant embedded in the instruction. The salient feature here is that every arithmetic instruction embeds encrypted constants that may displace the instruction's inputs and outputs independently ('malleability').

Add and branch would suffice for Turing completeness (c.f. Fractran [9]).

4 Chaotic Compilation

The compiler works with *difference scheme sections* $D : \mathrm{Loc} \to \mathrm{Off}$ with integer entries Δl (type Off), indexed per register or memory location l (type Loc). A difference scheme $\{D_p \,|\, p \in P\}$ has one section per point p in the object code program P's control graph, i.e., before and after every machine code instruction. The delta Δl is how much the run-time data is to differ from nominal in l at point p.

A database $L : \mathrm{Var} \to \mathrm{Loc}$ that maps source code variables to registers and memory will be assumed. Then the expression compiler $\mathbb{C}[e]^r$ described in Box 1 that puts a result in register r is more exactly $\mathbb{C}^L[D : e]^r$ of type:

$$\mathbb{C}^L[\_ : \_]^r : \mathrm{Dsect} \times \mathrm{Expr} \to \mathrm{MC} \times \mathrm{Off} \tag{3}$$

where Dsect is the type of D, MC is the type of machine code, a sequence of (FxA) instructions mc. The compiler aims to vary the deltas Δl equiprobably over the full range across recompilations. The following paragraphs explain how.

4.1 Pure Expressions

How source code is translated has to be shown in some detail in order to confirm or deny ($\tilde{\mathrm{h}}$), because every time an 'instruction that writes' is emitted, it must be checked if it can be varied by the compiler to the maximum extent possible. Compilers work compositionally, so structural induction suffices for that. For pure expressions, every operation in it requires that the operands be in registers and a single machine code instruction then acts on them arithmetically and writes the result into another register. That instruction must be varied.

Translating $\mathsf{x+y}$ where x, y are signed 32-bit integer source code variables, the compiler emits machine code mc_1 as in (4a) that at run-time puts the value of x in register $r_1 = L\mathsf{x}$ with offset delta Δr_1 (a pair $(D, \_)$ is written $D : \_$ here):

$$(mc_1, \Delta \mathsf{x}) = \mathbb{C}^L[D : \mathsf{x}]^{r_1} \tag{4a}$$

By inductive hypothesis, that is the nominal value plus the target register' delta:

$$s_0 \overset{mc_1}{\leadsto} s_1 \ : \ s_1\, r_1 = \mathcal{E}[\mathcal{D}[\ulcorner \mathsf{x} \urcorner s_0] + \Delta r_1] \tag{4b}$$

The small step semantics is from Table 1, with $s_r = s\, r$ for the value in register r in state s of the processor. The nominal value $\ulcorner \mathsf{x} \urcorner s$ of variable x, as defined in footnote a of Box 1, is preserved as the state s changes from s_0 to s_1 via mc_1:

$$\ulcorner \mathsf{x} \urcorner s_1 = \mathcal{E}[\mathcal{D}[s_0\, L\mathsf{x}] - D\, L\mathsf{x}] = \mathcal{E}[\mathcal{D}[s_0\, r_1] - \Delta r_1] = \ulcorner \mathsf{x} \urcorner s_0 \tag{4c}$$

By induction too, machine code mc_2 for y is emitted preserving its nominal value:

$$(mc_2, \Delta y) = \mathbb{C}^L[D : y]^{r_2} \tag{5a}$$

$$s_1 \overset{mc_2}{\rightsquigarrow} s_2 \ : \ s_2\, r_2 = \mathcal{E}[\mathcal{D}[\ulcorner y \urcorner s_1] + \Delta r_2] \tag{5b}$$

$$\ulcorner y \urcorner s_2 = \ldots = \ulcorner y \urcorner s_1 \tag{5c}$$

The compiler then emits the extra **add** instruction that at run-time sums r_1 and r_2 into r_0 with an increment k, a constant embedded in the instruction:

$$\mathbb{C}^L[D : x + y]^{r_0} = (mc_0, \Delta e) \tag{6a}$$

$$mc_0 = \ulcorner mc_1; mc_2; \textbf{add } r_0 \ r_1 \ r_2 \ k \urcorner$$

Choosing $k = \Delta r_0 - \Delta r_1 - \Delta r_2$, the following value goes in r_0 at run-time:

$$s_0 \overset{mc_0}{\rightsquigarrow} s_2 \ : \ s_2\, r_0 = \mathcal{E}[\mathcal{D}[\ulcorner x \urcorner s_0] + \mathcal{D}[\ulcorner y \urcorner s_1] + \Delta r_0] \tag{6b}$$

$$= \mathcal{E}[\mathcal{D}[\ulcorner x + y \urcorner s_2] + \Delta r_0] \tag{6c}$$

The nominal value plus a delta ends up in register r_0 and the delta Δr_0 is independently and arbitrarily chosen by the compiler via its choice of k. The induction shows $(\widetilde{h})$ is satisfied for pure expressions.

4.2   Statements

Let Stat be the type of statements, then compiling a statement changes the deltas and produces a new difference scheme section, as well as machine code:

$$\mathbb{C}^L[\_ : \_] : \text{Dsect} \times \text{Stat} \to \text{Dsect} \times \text{MC} \tag{7}$$

Consider an assignment z=x + y of expression x + y to a source code variable z, which the location database L binds in register $r_z = Lz$. Let x+y be called e here. The compiler emits code mc_0 that evaluates expression e in register **t0** with (randomly chosen) offset Δr_0 as described in (6a) with **t0** $= r_0$. A short-form **add** instruction with semantics $r_z \leftarrow \textbf{t0} + k$ is emitted to move that to r_z:

$$\mathbb{C}^L[D_0 : z = e] = D_1 : \ulcorner mc_0; \textbf{add } r_z \ \textbf{t0} \ k \urcorner \tag{8a}$$

The compiler sets $k = \Delta r_z - \Delta r_0$ to choose delta Δr_z arbitrarily:

$$s_0 \overset{mc_0}{\rightsquigarrow} s_2 \overset{\text{add}}{\rightsquigarrow} s_3 \ : \ s_3\, r_z = \mathcal{E}[\mathcal{D}[\ulcorner x + y \urcorner s_2] + \Delta r_z] \tag{8b}$$

The difference scheme section is updated at r_z from $D_0 r_z$ to $D_1 r_z = \Delta r_z$, so:

$$\ulcorner z \urcorner s_3 = \ulcorner x + y \urcorner s_2 \tag{8c}$$

The final delta $\Delta r_z = D_1 Lz$ may be freely and independently chosen by setting the instruction constant k appropriately. This is the induction step for the assignment statement, with the inductive result for pure expressions as hypothesis, and it implies side-effecting expressions are compiled both to preserve the intended 'nominal value' per (8c) and to preserve principle $(\widetilde{h})$.

4.3   Difference Calculus

A Hoare-style deterministic pre-/post-condition calculus [17] is a natural stepping stone to a stochastic calculus. The Hoare-style calculus expresses the evolution of the current difference scheme section during a compiler pass. The operational semantics of the code is not at issue, freedom of choice is.

Assignment. Generalise the x+y with intermediates in r_1, r_2 of Sect. 4.1 to e with intermediates in $\rho = \{r_0, \ldots, r_n\}$. The result z is stored in r_0. The delta offsets have value Δr_i in r_i before and value $\Delta' r_i$ after the assignment. That is:

$$\begin{gathered} \{\Delta r_0,\ \Delta r_1,\ \ldots,\ \Delta r_n\} \\ \text{z} = e \\ \{\Delta' r_0,\ \Delta' r_1,\ \ldots,\ \Delta' r_n\} \end{gathered} \tag{9}$$

By (6b, 8b), $\Delta' r, \Delta r$ can be independently chosen. Reading the Δ as a vector:

$$\{\Delta\}\ \text{z} = e\ \{\Delta'\} \tag{9a}$$

$$\Delta \supseteq \Delta'|_{\bar{\rho}} \tag{9b}$$

That is, Δ extends $\Delta'|_{\bar{\rho}}$, Δ (possibly) differs from Δ' on ρ and is unaltered from it on the *complement* $\bar{\rho}$ of ρ. The Δ are indexed by the full range of registers and memory locations but in practice only a small subset need be considered.

When pointers (memory addresses calculated dynamically) are available to programmers, the type system of the source language must be augmented so each pointer is declared as pointing into a named global array as workspace:

int A[100]; ... ; **restrict** A int $*$ ptr;

That limits the possible memory locations (indices of Δ) for ptr to A. An unrestricted pointer may gain any address at runtime, which results in the compiler producing impossibly large/slow code, so the programmer wants to use **restrict**.

Conditionals. An if then else is compiled to machine code using branch instructions, but which branch is for true and which for false is varied by the compiler. It randomly chooses to generate code for b or for $\neg b$ at each level of boolean subexpression. The compile procedure is detailed in [6], but it has been described here already: the result b of each boolean subexpression is modified by a randomly chosen 1-bit delta δ to $b + \delta$ mod 2 just as for arithmetic expressions except that the arithmetic is 1-bit (i.e., mod 2), not 32-bit (mod 2^{32}).

The same technique is used in classic 'garbled circuits' [24] technology for obfuscating hardware logic circuit design – an arbitrarily selected exclusive-or (i.e., addition mod 2) mask is applied to inputs and outputs of every gate in the circuit in order to recover the designer's intended logic.

The compiler ensures that whichever branch is taken at runtime, the same difference scheme avails for the instruction after the conditional. It appends **add**

instructions at the end of each branch as necessary for that. The upshot is the
logic is nondeterministic choice. Let ρ be the registers written in e. The rule is:

$$\frac{\{\Delta_1\}\ s_1\ \{\Delta'\}\quad \{\Delta_2\}\ s_2\ \{\Delta'\}}{\{\Delta\}\ \text{if}\ (e)\ s_1\ \text{else}\ s_2\ \{\Delta'\}} \tag{10a}$$

$$\Delta \supseteq \Delta_1|_{\bar{\rho}} \cup \Delta_2|_{\bar{\rho}} \tag{10b}$$

and Δ_1, Δ_2 are equal on $\bar{\rho}$ after e, independently chosen on ρ by the compiler,
and deltas Δ' are set up by it to be equal at the end of both branches, per (♭).

Loops. The compiler implements do while loops as code for the body followed
by a conditional branch back to the start. Let ρ be the registers written in e
and put $\Delta_1|_{\bar{\rho}}=\Delta_2|_{\bar{\rho}}=\Delta'|_{\bar{\rho}}$ in (10a), (10b) to get the following rule for compiled
code:

$$\frac{\{\Delta\}\ s\ \{\Delta'\}}{\{\Delta\}\ \text{do}\ s\ \text{while}\ e\ \{\Delta'\}} \tag{11a}$$

$$\Delta \supseteq \Delta'|_{\bar{\rho}} \tag{11b}$$

The compiler sets deltas $\Delta|_{\rho}$, $\Delta'|_{\rho}$ independently. Per (♭), the deltas are arranged
to be the same values $\Delta'|_{\bar{\rho}}$ at beginning and end of the loop.

4.4   Calculus of Chaos

Let f_r be the probability distribution of offset Δr from nominal value v in
register r, as the compilation varies stochastically. That is $\text{prob}[s_r = v+d] = \text{prob}[\Delta r{=}d] = f_r(d)$, where s is the processor state. A stochastic analogue (12)
of (9) is obtained by regarding each Δr, $\Delta' r$ as a random variable. Let variable
x be stored in location $r_x = Lx$, y in $r_y = Ly$, z in $r_z = Lz$. Then:

$$\begin{array}{c} \{\Delta r_x,\ \Delta r_y,\ \Delta r_z\} \\ z = x + y \\ \{\Delta' r_x,\ \Delta' r_y,\ \Delta' r_z\} \end{array} \tag{12}$$

That asserts possibly different probability distributions before and after the
assignment. Now let T be the run-time trace of a program. That is a sequence
consisting of instructions executed and the values each read and wrote.

The entropy $H(T)$ of the random variable T distributed as f_T is the expectation $\mathbb{E}[-\log_2 f_T]$. The increase in entropy from T to longer T' (it cannot
decrease) is interpretable as the number of bits of unpredictable information
introduced. These two facts from information theory will be needed:

Fact 1. *The flat distribution $f_X{=}1/k$ constant is the unique one with maximal
entropy $H(X){=}\log_2 k$, on a signal X that can take k values.*

Fact 2. *Adding a maximal entropy signal to any random variable on a n-bit space (i.e., with 2^n values) gives another maximal entropy, flat, distribution.*

Fact 1 identifies maximal entropy as n on n-bit space, achieved when each of the 2^n possible values is equiprobable. That is a disordered, i.e., 'chaotic', signal. Fact 2 uses the result (Shannon [21]) that the entropy of the sum of two n-bit signals is no less than that of either. The inference is that the characteristics of any distribution on a finite point space are obscured completely, not partially, by adding a 'chaotic' signal to it, i.e., one with flat, uniform distribution.

Below, logic is given for this stochastic view of compilation for the three source code constructs treated in Sect. 4.3, supposing the compiler implements ($\widetilde{\mathbb{h}}$).

Assignment. As in (9a), for pre-/post-condition:

$$\{\Delta\}\ z = e\ \{\Delta'\} \tag{13a}$$

but the Δ, Δ' are vectors of random variables Δr, $\Delta'r$. Let $\rho=\{r_0,\ldots,r_n\}$ be the registers written in e or in writing to z. For $r\notin\rho$, $\Delta'r=\Delta r$, as those r are unchanged, by (9b), so the same condition $\Delta|_{\bar\rho}=\Delta'|_{\bar\rho}$ holds here. I.e.:

$$\Delta \supseteq \Delta'|_{\bar\rho} \tag{13b}$$

We suppose the compiler follows ($\widetilde{\mathbb{h}}$), and that means each new random variable is independent with maximal entropy and each represents the compiler's free choice of embedded constant, like k of (6a, 8a), in 'an arithmetic instruction that writes'. Then the machine code instruction that writes r_z does so with a delta that is a uniformly distributed independent random variable U and that increases the trace entropy to $H(T')=H(T)+H(U)$. The delta is 32-bit on a 32-bit platform, chosen with flat distribution by the compiler, per ($\widetilde{\mathbb{h}}$), so $H(U)=32$. There are $n+1$ registers $r_0,\ldots,r_n$ written independently, including that for z, so trace entropy increases by $32(n+1)$ bits. For any predicate $p(x)$, e.g., $h = x$:

$$\{p(H(T)+32(n+1))\}\ z =\cdot e\ \{p(H(T'))\} \tag{13c}$$

If the machine code instruction that writes has appeared earlier in the trace, the delta is already known, and the increment in trace entropy is zero second time:

$$\{p(H(T))\}\ z = e\ \{p(H(T'))\} \tag{13c0}$$

Conditionals. As in (9b), (10b) but with random variables for the deltas:

$$\frac{\{\Delta_1\}\ s_1\ \{\Delta'\}\quad \{\Delta_2\}\ s_2\ \{\Delta'\}}{\{\Delta\}\ \text{if}\ (b)\ s_1\ \text{else}\ s_2\ \{\Delta'\}} \tag{14a}$$

$$\Delta \supseteq \Delta_1|_{\bar\rho} \cup \Delta_2|_{\bar\rho} \tag{14b}$$

The deltas $\Delta r = \Delta_1 r = \Delta_2 r$ are all the same for $r \notin \rho$ by (10b). The entropy added to the trace T is from the trace of b, say $32n$ bits of entropy from n writes to n registers, plus the entropy from the trace through branch s_1 or s_2:

$$\frac{\{p(\mathrm{H}(T'))\}\, s_1\, \{q\} \quad \{p(\mathrm{H}(T'))\}\, s_2\, \{q\}}{\{p(\mathrm{H}(T)+32n)\}\ \text{if}\ (b)\ s_1\ \text{else}\ s_2\ \{q\}} \tag{14c}$$

The compiler inserts extra 'arithmetic instructions that write' (**add**s) so the entropy increase is the same in both branches. It can because, even for loops, the entropy increase is finite and bounded (see below).

If the conditional appears in the trace a second time and branches the same way again then that contributes zero entropy as the deltas are already known:

$$\{p(\mathrm{H}(T))\}\ \text{if}\ (b)\ s_1\ \text{else}\ s_2\ \{p(\mathrm{H}(T'))\} \tag{14c0}$$

If it branches differently from the first time, the branch (but not the test) contributes entropy, as the deltas in that branch are yet unknown. But the, say m, instructions that align final deltas are constrained in (10b) to agree with the deltas in the other branch, which are already known. So those m do not count:

$$\frac{\{p(\mathrm{H}(T'))\}\, s_1\, \{q\} \quad \{p(\mathrm{H}(T'))\}\, s_2\, \{q\}}{\{p(\mathrm{H}(T)+32m)\}\ \text{if}\ (b)\ s_1\ \text{else}\ s_2\ \{q\}} \tag{14c1}$$

Those m instructions that 'align final deltas' with the other branch have a name:

Definition 2. *An instruction emitted by the compiler to adjust a final delta to agree with that in a joining control path is called a* trailer *instruction.*

Loops. Let $\rho = \{r_1, \ldots, r_n\}$ be the registers written during b. Then, per (11a), (11b), but with random variables as deltas, the following rule holds:

$$\frac{\{\Delta\}\ s\ \{\Delta'\}}{\{\Delta\}\ \text{do}\ s\ \text{while}\ (b)\ \{\Delta'\}} \tag{15a}$$

$$\Delta \supseteq \Delta'|_{\bar{\rho}} \tag{15b}$$

That means $\Delta r = \Delta' r$ for $r \notin \rho$. Those distributions are equal because the values are equal, by (13b), and trailer instructions reestablish Δ on the loop back-path.

A trace over the loop is always the same length between recompiled codes, because the compiler varies data values, not the semantics at a deeper level (see conserved nominal values in Sect. 4.1). Say the loop repeats $N \geq 1$ times for a

particular set of input values. Then it could be unrolled to N instances of the
loop body s and N instances of the loop test b. The variation in the trace is
only that of (a) s repeated once, because the same m deltas appear second time
too, and (b) b repeated once, for the same reason, with n deltas. The entropy
calculation is (a) plus (b), no matter what $N \geq 1$ is (a do while loop repeats at
least once):

$$\frac{\{p(\mathrm{H}(T){+}32m)\} \; s \; \{p(\mathrm{H}(T'))\}}{\{p(\mathrm{H}(T){+}32(n{+}m))\} \;\; \text{do} \; s \, \text{while} \; b \; \{p(\mathrm{H}(T'))\}} \tag{15c}$$

So **do while** lengthens the trace like a loop but adds entropy to it like a conditional. Note that second time through the loop, zero entropy is added, because
the same deltas are repeated:

$$\{p(\mathrm{H}(T))\} \;\; \text{do} \; s \; \text{while} \; b \; \{p(\mathrm{H}(T'))\} \tag{15c0}$$

Equations (13c), (13c0), (14c), (14c0), (14c1), (15c), (15c0) are an information
entropy calculus for runtime traces when compilation follows ($\widetilde{\mathbb{h}}$). Counting up:

Lemma 1. *The entropy of a trace is $32(n{+}i)$ bits where n is the number in it
of distinct arithmetic instructions that write (a pair of trailer instructions that
regulate the same delta count as one and a trailer instruction that reestablishes
an earlier delta does not count) and i is the number of inputs.*

'Inputs' are those instructions that read a location that has not been written.
(*Remark*) The logic holds for incomplete and/or non-contiguous sub-traces too.
    The following characterises the compiler strategy that produces the maxi-
mum run-time trace entropy:

Proposition 1. *The entropy in the run-time traces induced by a compiler fol-
lowing the principle ($\widetilde{\mathbb{h}}$) as modified by ($\mathbb{h}$) is maximal among compositional
compilation strategies.*

Proof. The issue is over whether a compiler could put more entropy into the
run-time trace. The final deltas for data that is not read by following code do
not have to be in agreement along both branches of a conditional, for example,
so not following ($\mathbb{h}$) for them does no harm. But a compiler that works compositionally does not know the eventual context in which the code will be used so
it must suppose that data that is written will later be read, and so must arrange
for agreement between all final offset deltas in both branches of conditionals,
enforcing ($\mathbb{h}$) in that case, indeed in all cases.
    The other way to put more entropy into the trace is to vary instructions
more, but that is impossible if the compiler already implements ($\mathbb{h}$).   ∎

That characterisation decides details of chaotic compilation. For example,
to the question of whether an array should have (a) one delta common to the
whole array or (b) one per entry, the answer is (b) one per entry. One per array
would mean each write to an entry must be followed by a 'write storm' to all

other entries too, to realign their deltas to the newly written entry's (which is changed because the write instruction must add entropy to the trace). But the write storm's write instructions import no entropy as their deltas are all the same as the first, contradicting the characterisation.

The Proposition implies that, on a 32-bit platform, 32 bits of entropy per datum are provided by a chaotic compiler, a (weak) form of semantic security:

Corollary 1. *The probability across different compilations that any particular 32-bit value x beneath the encryption is in a given register or memory location at any given point in the trace at run-time is uniformly $1/2^{32}$.*

The general interest is with multiple data values observed at different points in the trace. The result depends on how they are connected computationally:

Definition 3. *Two data values in the trace are (entropy) dependent if they are from the same register or memory location at the same point, are input and output of a copy instruction, or are from the same register or location at a join of two control paths after the last write to it in each and before the next write.*

If data is taken at m independent points, the variation obtained by a chaotic compiler is maximal, i.e., $32m$ bits, because the data is not constrained by (♭):

Theorem 1. *The probability across different compilations that any m particular 32-bit values beneath the encryption in the trace are precisely x_i, provided they are pairwise independent, is $1/2^{32m}$.*

(*Remark*) Each dependent pair reduces the entropy by 32 bits.

5   Implementation

Our prototype 'chaotic' compiler http://sf.net/p/obfusc is for ANSI C [19], where pointers and arrays present particular difficulties. Currently, the compiler has near total coverage of ANSI C and GNU C extensions, including statements-as-expressions and expressions-as-statements, gotos, arrays, pointers, structs, unions, floating point, double integer and floating point data. Pointers are obligatorily declared via ANSI **restrict** to point into arrays. It is missing **longjmp** and efficient strings (**char** and **short** are same as **int**). The largest C source compiled (correctly) so far is 22,000 lines for the IEEE floating point test suite at http://jhauser.us/arithmetic/TestFloat.html. A trace[4] of the Ackermann function[5] [22] is shown in Table 2, with null encryption for better visibility. The instruction constants and values written to registers are encrypted on an encrypted computing platform, with, e.g., $\mathcal{E}[-86921031]$ in place of -86921031.

---

[4] For readability here, the final delta in register **v0** is set to zero.
[5] C code: **int** A(**int** m, **int** n) { if(m=0)return n+1; if(n=0)return A(m−1, 1); return A(m−1, A(m, n−1)); }.

Table 2. Trace for Ackermann(3,1), result 13.

PC	instruction				trace update
...					
35	add	t0	a0	zer	−86921031	t0 = −86921028
36	add	t1	zer	zer	−327157853	t1 = −327157853
37	beq	t0	t1	2	240236822	
38	add	t0	zer	zer	−1242455113	t0 = −1242455113
39	b 1					
41	add	t1	zer	zer	−1902505258	t1 = −1902505258
42	xor	t0	t0	t1	−1734761313 1242455113 1902505258	
						t0 = −17347613130
43	beq	t0	zer	9	−1734761313	
53	add	sp	sp	zer	800875856	sp = 1687471183
54	add	t0	a1	zer	−915514235	t0 = −915514234
55	add	t1	zer	zer	−1175411995	t1 = −1175411995
56	beq	t0	t1	2	259897760	
57	add	t0	zer	zer	11161509	t0 = 11161509
...						
143	add	v0	t0	zer	42611675	v0 = 13
...						
147	jr	ra				# (return 13 in **v0**)

Legend (registers)

a0	=	function argument
sp	=	stack pointer
t0, t1	=	temporaries
v0	=	return value
zer	=	null reference

6   (Informal) Security Argument

Here is a sketch proof that a chaotic compiler makes programs 'safe from polynomial-time discovery' of what the data in the runtime-trace is intended to mean, in the context of encrypted computing. The claim is that there is no polynomial time method M that can estimate the value of a designated bit b in the trace of a program P, if there is none that succeeds against the encryption alone. Success means with a probability that exceeds 1/2 by some margin $B > 0$ infinitely often as the word size n tends to infinity, but the precise notion may be varied for the proof: for example, being correct about b with probability $p > 1/2 + 1/n$.

Proof: [Sketch] Let the compiler unroll source code loops to depth $N=2^n$ and inline function calls to depth N and push code after conditional blocks into both branches to depth N, leaving no branches, loops or function calls for N steps. By Theorem 1 a chaotic compiler generates object code for P with maximal entropy in at least the first N instruction cycles of the run-time traces, measured from one recompilation to the next, following ($\widetilde{\mathbb{h}}$). The constraint ($\underline{\mathbb{h}}$) does not apply.

By Theorem 1, there is no algebraic or any other relation M can rely on among the $m \leq p(n) \leq N$ trace-points it has time to access, for polynomial p of order k, and M must depend on its capability against the encryption alone, which it is hypothesised to be not successful against. ∎

The same argument works for any number of bits.

7   Conclusion

In summary, this paper discusses stochastic compilation and defines chaotic compilation as stochastic compilation with maximum entropy. The compiler works with a difference scheme describing the variation from nominal of the value in each register and memory location, differing per instruction in the machine code program. A program logic of differences extends to an information entropy calculus for run-time traces that quantifies chaotic compilation. That feeds an argument for security against polynomial-time complexity methods of attack against encrypted computing. The unusual aspect here is software engineering in the cause of mathematics. Definition and proof of security for encrypted computing has been the goal, and the idea of a chaotic compiler is to allow mathematical reasoning for the stochastic properties to be replaced by engineering for them.

The chaotic C compiler ('havoc') is available from the open source project at http://sf.net/p/obfusc and covers all of ANSI C except longjmp/setjmp. Array access is $\mathbf{O}n$ but otherwise the compiled code is not slower than normal.

Acknowledgments. Simon Pickin's work has been supported by the Spanish MINECO-FEDER (grant numbers DArDOS, TIN2015-65845-C3-1-R and FAME, RTI2018-093608-B-C31). Peter Breuer thanks Hecusys LLC for continued support in encrypted computing research.

References

1. Breuer, P.T., Bowen, J.P.: A fully homomorphic crypto-processor design: correctness of a secret computer. In: Jürjens, J., Livshits, B., Scandariato, R. (eds.) ESSoS 2013. LNCS, vol. 7781, pp. 123–138. Springer, Heidelberg (2013). https://doi.org/10.1007/978-3-642-36563-8_9

2. Breuer, P., Bowen, J.: Chaotic compilation: a (statistical) cloak for a secret computer. In: Proceedings of 1st Annual International Workshop SW/HW Interaction Faults (SHIFT 2019), IEEE International Symposium on SW Reliability Engineering Workshops (ISSREW 2019), CA, USA, pp. 428–433. IEEE, October 2019. https://doi.org/10.1109/ISSREW.2019.00106

3. Breuer, P., Bowen, J.: A fully encrypted high-speed microprocessor architecture: the secret computer in simulation. Int. J. Crit. Comput.-Based Sys. **9**(1/2), 26–55 (2019). https://doi.org/10.1504/IJCCBS.2019.10020015

4. Breuer, P., Bowen, J.: (Un)encrypted computing and indistinguishability obfuscation, January 2019. http://arxiv.org/abs/1811.12365v1. Principles of Secure Compilation (PriSC 2019) at 46th ACM Symposium on Principles of Programming Languages (POPL 2019)

5. Breuer, P., Bowen, J., Palomar, E., Liu, Z.: A practical encrypted microprocessor. In: Callegari, C., et al. (eds.) Proceedings of 13th International Conference on Security and Cryptography (SECRYPT 2016), Port, vol. 4, pp. 239–250. SCITEPRESS, July 2016. https://doi.org/10.5220/0005955902390250

6. Breuer, P., Bowen, J., Palomar, E., Liu, Z.: On obfuscating compilation for encrypted computing. In: Samarati, P., et al. (eds.) Proceedings of 14th International Conference on Security and Cryptography (SECRYPT 2017), Port, pp. 247–254. SCITEPRESS, July 2017. https://doi.org/10.5220/0006394002470254

7. Breuer, P.T., Bowen, J.P., Palomar, E., Liu, Z.: On security in encrypted computing. In: Naccache, D., et al. (eds.) ICICS 2018. LNCS, vol. 11149, pp. 192–211. Springer, Cham (2018). https://doi.org/10.1007/978-3-030-01950-1_12

8. Breuer, P., Bowen, J., Palomar, E., Liu, Z.: Superscalar encrypted RISC: the measure of a secret computer. In: Proceedings of 17th International Conference on Trust, Security and Privacy in Computing and Communications (TrustCom 2018), pp. 1336–1341. IEEE Computer Society (2018). https://doi.org/10.1109/TrustCom/BigDataSE.2018.00184

9. Conway, J.H.: FRACTRAN: a simple universal programming language for arithmetic. In: Cover, T.M., Gopinath, B. (eds.) Open Problems in Communication and Computation, pp. 4–26. Springer, Heidelberg (1987). https://doi.org/10.1007/978-1-4612-4808-8_2

10. van Dijk, M., Gentry, C., Halevi, S., Vaikuntanathan, V.: Fully homomorphic encryption over the integers. In: Gilbert, H. (ed.) EUROCRYPT 2010. LNCS, vol. 6110, pp. 24–43. Springer, Heidelberg (2010). https://doi.org/10.1007/978-3-642-13190-5_2

11. Fletcher, C.W., van Dijk, M., Devadas, S.: A secure processor architecture for encrypted computation on untrusted programs. In: Proceedings of 7th ACM Workshop on Scalable Trusted Computing (STC 2012), pp. 3–8. ACM, New York (2012). https://doi.org/10.1145/2382536.2382540

12. Gentry, C.: Fully homomorphic encryption using ideal lattices. In: Proceedings of 41st Annual ACM Symposium on Theory of Computing (STOC 2009), NY, USA, pp. 169–178 (2009). https://doi.org/10.1145/1536414.1536440

13. Gentry, C., Halevi, S.: Implementing gentry's fully-homomorphic encryption scheme. In: Paterson, K.G. (ed.) EUROCRYPT 2011. LNCS, vol. 6632, pp. 129–148. Springer, Heidelberg (2011). https://doi.org/10.1007/978-3-642-20465-4_9

14. Goldwasser, S., Micali, S.: Probabilistic encryption & how to play mental poker keeping secret all partial information. In: Proceedings of Annual ACM Symposium on Theory of Computing (STOC 1982), pp. 365–377. ACM (1982). https://doi.org/10.1145/800070.802212

15. Goldwasser, S., Micali, S.: Probabilistic encryption. J. Comput. Syst. Sci. **28**, 270–299 (1984)

16. den Hartog, J.I.: Verifying probabilistic programs using a hoare like logic. In: Thiagarajan, P.S., Yap, R. (eds.) ASIAN 1999. LNCS, vol. 1742, pp. 113–125. Springer, Heidelberg (1999). https://doi.org/10.1007/3-540-46674-6_11

17. Hoare, C.A.R.: An axiomatic basis for computer programming. Commun. ACM **12**(10), 576–580 (1969). https://doi.org/10.1145/363235.363259

18. Irena, F., Murphy, D., Parameswaran, S.: CryptoBlaze: a partially homomorphic processor with multiple instructions and non-deterministic encryption support. In: Proceedings of 23rd Asia and South Pacific Design Automation Conference (ASP-DAC 2018), pp. 702–708. IEEE (2018)

19. ISO/IEC: Programming languages - C. 9899:201x Technical report, n1570, International Organization for Standardization, August 2011. JTC 1, SC 22, WG 14

20. Morgan, C., McIver, A., Seidel, K.: Probabilistic predicate transformers. ACM Trans. Prog. Lang. Syst. (TOPLAS) **18**(3), 325–353 (1996). https://doi.org/10.1145/229542.229547
21. Shannon, C.E.: A mathematical theory of communication. Bell Syst. Tech. J. **27**(3), 379–423 (1948). https://doi.org/10.1002/j.1538-7305.1948.tb01338.x
22. Sundblad, Y.: The Ackermann function: a theoretical, computational, and formula manipulative study. BIT Numer. Math. **11**(1), 107–119 (1971)
23. Tsoutsos, N.G., Maniatakos, M.: The HEROIC framework: encrypted computation without shared keys. IEEE TCAD IC Syst. **34**(6), 875–888 (2015)
24. Yao, A.C.C.: How to generate and exchange secrets. In: 27th Annual Symposium on Foundations of Computer Science, pp. 162–167. IEEE (1986). https://doi.org/10.1109/SFCS.1986.25

Runtime Verification of Linux Kernel Security Module

Denis Efremov$^{(\boxtimes)}$ and Ilya Shchepetkov

ISP RAS, Moscow, Russia
{efremov,shchepetkov}@ispras.ru

Abstract. The Linux kernel is one of the most important Free/Libre
Open Source Software (FLOSS) projects. It is installed on billions of
devices all over the world, which process various sensitive, confidential or
simply private data. It is crucial to establish and prove its security properties. This work-in-progress paper presents a method to verify the Linux
kernel for conformance with an abstract security policy model written in
the Event-B specification language. The method is based on system call
tracing and aims at checking that the results of system call execution do
not lead to accesses that violate security policy requirements. As a basis
for it, we use an additional Event-B specification of the Linux system
call interface that is formally proved to satisfy all the requirements of
the security policy model. In order to perform the conformance checks
we use it to reproduce intercepted system calls and verify accesses.

Keywords: Runtime verification · Operating system kernel · Security
policy model · Event-B · Linux security modules

1 Introduction

Access control mechanisms in operating systems are usually implemented based
on a security policy model, which contains description of the security properties
to be enforced by these mechanisms. A security policy model may be a simple
text document, but for a certain level of assurance it should be formalized and
verified, as stated by the Common Criteria standard [17,18]. An additional level
of assurance may be achieved by demonstrating that the implementation of an
access control mechanism indeed conforms to its formal specification.

Access control mechanisms in Linux are implemented in the kernel. We propose to intercept system calls to the kernel while performing various actions like
creating, reading, writing, deleting files, spawning processes, etc., and check that
the results of their execution do not lead to accesses that are forbidden by the
security policy model. It is difficult to check directly because of the abstraction gap. Security policy models are often too high-level comparing to concrete

This work has received funding from the Ministry of Education and Science of Russia
under grant agreement RFMEFI60719X0295.

data structures and functions of the Linux kernel. To overcome the difference between the specification and the implementation we develop an Event-B [1] specification of the Linux system call interface, formally prove that it satisfies all requirements of the security policy model (which is also formalized in Event-B), and then translate it to an executable form which is more suitable for checking correctness of intercepted system calls.

The following section briefly describes the security policy model in use. Section 3 depicts the Event-B language in which the model was formalized and verified. Section 4 briefly describes the formal specification of the security model. Section 5 provides a description of an additional Event-B specification required to perform a conformance verification. Section 6 describes the Linux security modules framework, which is used to implement security policy models inside the kernel. Section 7 presents the runtime verification method itself. Related work is observed in Sect. 8. The final section concludes the paper and considers future work.

2   Security Policy Model

A security policy is a high-level specification of the security properties that a given system should possess, and of security mechanisms that enforce those properties. Security policies are described in the form of security policy models as *state transition systems*, where each possible state transition from a *secure* state must preserve security properties and produce another secure state. The state is declared secure if all current accesses and permissions are in accordance with a security policy.

Operating system (OS) security policy models define the rules for controlling accesses of subjects (users and programs running on their behalf) to various objects (files, directories, devices) and other subjects. They define state transitions as transition functions that model usual OS actions, like creating and deleting files, processes, requesting accesses, etc. Examples of such models would be the classic Bell-LaPadula [4,5] and Biba [7] models, which were first to describe semantics and security properties of multilevel security and mandatory integrity control respectively.

In this paper we use a Hierarchical Integrated Model of Access Control and information Flows (the HIMACF model, previously known as the MROSL DP-model [8,9]). It describes means to enforce the separation of information based on confidentiality and integrity requirements. It combines several security mechanisms:

- Role Based Access Control (RBAC). In RBAC, permissions to perform various actions are grouped intro roles and are assigned to a user by an administrator or obtained through special administrative roles. RBAC is often used as a replacement for more simple discretionary access control;
- Mandatory Integrity Control (MIC). In MIC, an integrity level is assigned to all users, processes and files. That level represents their level of trustworthiness, so the higher the level—the more trusted and important a user, a

process or a file. MIC controls accesses of subjects to objects according to their integrity levels. MIC is implemented in Windows and macOS to protect system files from modification by users or malicious software;
- Multilevel Security based on Mandatory Access Control (MLS, MAC). It was designed to deal with classified documents in military computer systems. MLS controls accesses according to the user's clearance and the file's classification.

These mechanisms are integrated into a linear hierarchy, where each next level is based on the previous ones. Also since the sequence of perfectly normal and secure accesses may lead to insecure information flows, there is an additional level that contains proofs of their absence (see Fig. 1).

The HIMACF model is implemented in the certified distribution Astra Linux Special Edition [24] using the Linux Security Modules framework [23]. The model is written in plain text with extensive use of math and consists of approximately 300 pages. We have formalized and verified [10] it using the Event-B specification language. It took us 4 years, and during this process we have found and fixed a number of issues and inconsistencies in the HIMACF model.

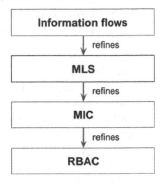

Fig. 1. The hierarchy of levels in the HIMACF model.

3 Event-B

Event-B is a formal method based on set theory and predicate logic. It has a simple notation and comes with a tool support in the form of the Rodin Platform [2]. It is mainly used for developing models of various control systems, but it is also particularly well suited for security policy modeling.

An Event-B specification is a *discrete transition system* and consists of *contexts* and *machines*. Contexts contain the static, or unchanged parts of the specification: definitions of *carrier sets*, *constants*, *axioms*. Machines contain the dynamic or behavioral parts of the specification: *variables*, *invariants* and *events*.

Event-B is a state-based method, so values of variables form the current state of the specification. Events represent the way the state changes over time—the transition. Events may contain *parameters*, *guard conditions* that are necessary for the event to be enabled (or preconditions), and *actions*, that change variables' values. Invariants describe important properties of the system and are supposed to hold whenever variable values change, so such changes need to be explicitly proven to be correct. For each case that requires a proof the Rodin platform generates a corresponding *proof obligation*, that can be discharged automatically using various provers and solvers or interactively. Interactive proofs are also automatically checked for soundness.

4   Event-B Specification of the HIMACF Model

The HIMACF model uses set theory and predicate logic for defining the state and the properties that the state must satisfy, and it also contains several atomic state transition rules which describe events taking place in the operating system. It makes its structure very similar to the structure of a typical Event-B specification, so its formalization in Event-B was quite straightforward[1].

The state variables of the Event-B specification are expressed as sets and functions (set of ordered pairs with additional restrictions):

- Sets:
  - user accounts;
  - entities (objects and containers);
  - subjects;
  - roles (administrative, ordinary, negative).
- Functions:
  - integrity and security levels (in the form of lattice);
  - current accesses and access rights (or permissions) to entities and roles;
  - hierarchies of roles, entities and subjects;
  - some additional relations between elements of the specification;
  - various flags.

These variables describe the usual operating system elements like user accounts, subjects (which are processes), entities (files, directories, sockets, etc.), and roles. Each of these elements have integrity and security labels that are mapped to them by a number of corresponding functions. Some additional things are also modelled as functions, like current accesses, permissions, hierarchies, and so on.

In total the specification contains 65 state variables. There are also 80 events that describe possible state transitions typical for an OS:

- Create or delete entities, user accounts, subjects, roles;
  - create or delete hard links for entities and roles;
  - rename entities or roles;
- Get or delete accesses, access rights to roles, entities;
- Change security, integrity labels, various flags;
- Additional events for analysis of information flows;
  - example: if an entity x have write access to a subject y, which have write access to a subject z, then there can be an information flow from x to z.

Finally, the specification contains 260 invariants divided into three groups. First one are type invariants: they describe types of all state variables. For example, the type of the variable that contains accesses of subjects to entities is expressed in Event-B like this: $SubjectAccesses \in Subjects \rightarrow (Entities \leftrightarrow Accesses)$. Another group is consistency invariants: they impose correctness constraints on the system state. For instance, if we have a variable that describes

---

[1] Publicly available part of the specification: https://github.com/17451k/base-model.

filesystem (hierarchy of files and folders), then it must not contain cycles, i.e., a folder cannot contain itself, even indirectly.

The last group of invariants is the most important one: it contains all security properties of corresponding security mechanisms. For example, there is the following security property: if a subject has write access to an entity, then its integrity label must be greater or equal than the integrity label of this entity. It is expressed in Event-B like this: $\forall s, e \cdot s \in Subjects \land e \mapsto WriteA \in SubjectAccesses(s) \implies EntityInt(e) \leqslant SubjectInt(s)$.

5   Event-B Specification of the System Call Interface

The HIMACF model and its Event-B specification, however, are quite abstract and different from the concrete data structures and functions of the Linux kernel, which contain the security policy implementation as the Linux Security Module. To prove their conformance it is necessary to reduce this gap. Event-B supports *the refinement technique* [3] to represent systems at different abstraction levels that can be used to resolve this issue.

We have used refinement to develop an additional Event-B specification of the Linux kernel system call interface. Using Rodin we have formally proved that the additional specification correctly refines the Event-B specification of the HIMACF model and thus satisfies its properties. Hence, if we will show the conformance between the additional specification of the system call interface and the Linux kernel, then the desired conformance between the Linux kernel and the security policy model will be derived automatically.

The additional specification, however, has quite an unusual structure. The difference lies in the nature of system calls: the exact sequence of actions that will be performed as the result of the system call depends on the current state of the OS and on the arguments of the call. Because of this variability it is impossible to model them as single atomic events. Instead, we used a different approach.

To overcome this issue we have decided to represent each system call as a *graph of events* connected together with the special state variable called *Next*. *Next* is used to specify the order in which normally independent events should occur. This is achieved as follows: each event in the graph of events have a guard condition specifying that it can only occur if the current value of the *Next* variable is the name of this event. Depending on other guards the event also changes the value of the *Next* variable with the name of the event that should follow next.

Each graph of events representing a system call have a single entry node (the "initial" event), a single exit node (the "final" event) and a large amount of paths in between. Each path is a series of events and the next event in the path is specified by the current value of the *Next* state variable. The path (concrete series of events representing a particular execution of the system call) is defined by the parameters of the "initial" event and the current state of the specification in a way that for each event in the path there is no more than one possible next event.

Let's consider the open() system call to open or create a file. This system call has the following declaration[2]: int open(const char *pathname, int flags). The open() call has two arguments: pathname specifies the file to open, and flags determines its access mode: read-only, write-only, or read/write. These access modes are expressed by corresponding flags O_RDONLY, O_WRONLY and O_RDWR. flags may also contain additional file creation and status flags. The return value of open() is a file descriptor, which can be later used in subsequent system calls (read(), write(), etc.).

Now let's consider a specific case of open() system call in which the file from the pathname argument does not exist, and the flags argument contains O_WRONLY (open file to write) and O_CREAT (create file if it does not exist) flags. If the process which calls open() has all necessary permissions, then open() performs the following sequence of actions:

- parse and validate values of it arguments;
- check that the process has all necessary permissions. In this case the check is successful;
- get the process write access to the directory where the file will be created;
- create the file;
- get the process permission to write to the created file;
- get the process write access to the created file;
- return file descriptor of created and opened to write file.

This case can be formalized in the Event-B specification of the system call interface as the sequence of 8 events: open_start, open_check_p, open_write_p, open_create, open_grant, open_check, open_write, open_finish, where:

- open_start contains preconditions (guards) that analyze arguments of the (open) call and decide which event should occur next. In the given case, the file being opened does not exist, so the next event is open_check_p. If the file existed, the next event would be open_check, and the sequence of events would be different;
- open_check_p checks that the process has all necessary permissions. In this case the check is successful, so the next event is open_write_p;
- open_write_p is a refinement of the access_write_entity event of the Event-B specification of the HIMACF model. This event grants the process write access to the directory where the file will be created;
- open_create is a refinement of the create_object event of the Event-B specification of the HIMACF model. This event creates the file;
- open_grant is a refinement of the grant_rights event of the Event-B specification of the HIMACF model. This event grants the process permission to write to the created file;

---

[2] According to the Linux manual page
http://man7.org/linux/man-pages/man2/open.2.html.

- **open_check** checks that the process has necessary permissions to obtain access to the created file and decides which event should occur next. In this case the process opens file to write, so the next event is **open_write**;
- **open_write** is a refinement of the **access_write_entity** event of the Event-B specification of the HIMACF model. This event grants the process write access to created file;
- **open_finish** returns the requested file descriptor.

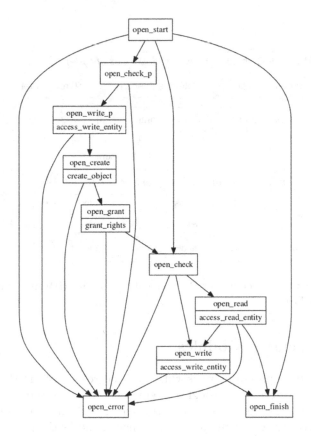

Fig. 2. Graph of events corresponding to several special cases of open() system call.

This sequence of events corresponds to one specific case of open() system call. To demonstrate our approach we have formalized a few more cases[3] (see Fig. 2). You can see that the graph consists mostly from the same events, but there are more possible paths between them.

If we formalize all the remaining cases, the resulting graph will be a formal specification of the behavior of the open() system call. Due to the use of refinement, this specification will be correct by construction and fully conform to the

---

[3] Code can be found here: https://github.com/17451k/base-model/tree/open.

rules and events of the HIMACF model. In turn, this will mean that for any combination of parameters and the state of the system, executing the `open()` system call will hold all the security properties of the HIMACF model.

All system calls can be formalized in a similar way, resulting in the specification of the system call interface that is proved to be consistent and complete. But such specification can turn out to be extremely large (several times more than the Event-B specification of the HIMACF model) and difficult to write and prove, mainly from the complicated refinement relation between them (see Fig. 3).

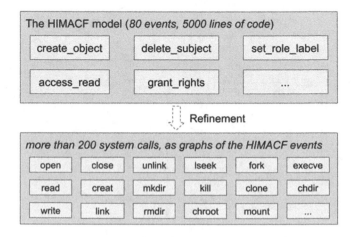

Fig. 3. Refinement between Event-B specifications of the HIMACF model and the system call interface.

6   Linux Security Modules

In Linux, userspace programs work with external resources via the kernel, and make requests for accesses through system calls. When a program executes a system call to, for example, open a file, the kernel performs a number of checks. It verifies the correctness of the passed arguments, checks the possibility of their allocation, and also checks that the program has the permission to obtain the requested resource by the discretionary access control. If more advanced access control mechanisms are used, then the kernel also checks that the access request satisfies their security policy. Such mechanisms are called security modules and based on the Linux Security Modules (LSM) framework. LSM adds a call to a security module after the discretionary access checks in a control flow of a system call handling. These calls are placed across the kernel and called LSM hooks (see Fig. 4).

There are several potential cases when the kernel manages permissions and accesses incorrectly. First, it is possible that the control flow does not reach a security module [6,12,27]. The LSM interface may not be complete enough, so

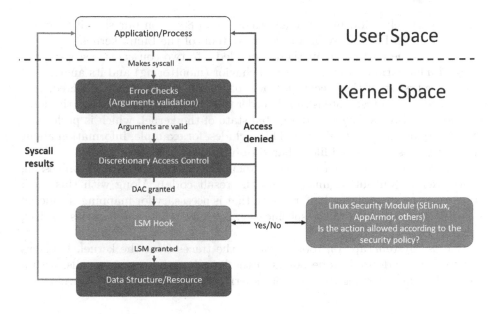

Fig. 4. Linux Security Modules (LSM) hooks.

it may lack hooks to check certain situations [14,20]. A security module can also be implemented incorrectly and grant accesses that should not be granted, or deny accesses that should be granted. There is always place for errors due to the abstraction gap and specifics of kernel—module interactions. Thus, we want to verify that the kernel of Astra Linux distribution with the security module indeed conforms the Event-B specification of the HIMACF model and this includes all enumerated errors.

It is worth to note that the Event-B specification of the system call interface does not model such things as the availability of resources (number of processes, virtual memory), and does not contain description of the discretionary access control mechanism. So, for example, the kernel could deny an access due to the lack of physical resources of the machine, but at the same time the specification grants it assuming that the resources are unlimited. Thus the divergence between the specified behavior and the real one should be treated as an error only in case the security policy model denies the access, but the security module grants it.

7   Runtime Verification Method

We propose to demonstrate the absence of such divergences by means of runtime verification, which require a test suite. The test suite should cover various patterns of access requests. In this paper we do not consider the issue of constructing tests and instead use special tests for our model and whole system tests such as Spruce [25], ltp [22] fuzzing with syzkaller [26]. These test suites allow us to achieve relatively good line coverage (more than 80%) on our security module and to cover all LSM hooks in target subsystems of the Linux kernel.

The runtime part of the method is divided into two consecutive steps: gathering of information about the kernel behavior (monitoring) and its analysis.

At the first step, the execution traces of the Linux kernel are collected. It is performed while a test suite is run. In order to reproduce such traces on the specification we also need to record a global state of the kernel, which is performed at the very beginning of this step. This includes, for example, information about running processes, opened files, shared resources, etc.

Traces contain arguments of the system call and the result of its processing by the kernel (output arguments and the result code). Along with this, each trace contains an additional information that is necessary for mapping the global kernel state to the state of the specification, such as inodes and dentries for files, user ids, etc.

We use SystemTap [19] tool to gather the traces from the kernel. It allows one to describe desired probe points in the kernel, such as system calls, with a special language and log the state of in-kernel data structures to a journal.

Algorithm 1. Replay of single system call on the Event-B specification

---

1: **procedure** REPLAY_SYSCALL(spec, syscall)
2:     $syscall\_graph := spec[syscall[name]]$
3:     $params := syscall[args]$
4:     $event := syscall\_graph[initial]$
5:     **while** $event \neq syscall\_graph[final]$ **do**
6:         **if** $guards\_hold(spec[state], event, params)$ **then**
7:             $spec[state] \leftarrow event(spec[state], params)$ ▷ update
8:         **else**
9:             **return** $Denied$
10:        **end if**
11:        $event := next(spec[state], event, params)$
12:    **end while**
13:    **return** $Granted$
14: **end procedure**

At the second step, we initialize the state of the Event-B specification with the state of the kernel and replay system calls from the trace on the Event-B specification.

The replay algorithm consists of the following steps (see Algorithm 1):

1. Pass the arguments of the system call as parameters to the "initial" event of its specification;
2. Check that all guards of the current event are satisfied. If they are not satisfied, then report that the access is denied according to the security policy rules (lines 6, 9);

3. If current event is not "final", then compute the "next" event, apply event to the current state to change it (line 7), mark the "next" event as current and return to step 2;
4. If current event is "final", then apply it to the current state and report that the access is granted according to the security policy rules;

Algorithm 2. Replay of kernel traces on the spec

1: **procedure** REPLAY_TRACE(trace, spec, journal)
2:     $spec[state] \leftarrow trace[init\_state]$ ▷ initial state of the specification
3:     **while** $syscall := shift(trace[syscalls])$ **do**
4:         $real\_result := syscall[result]$
5:         $spec\_result := Replay\_Syscall(spec, syscall)$
6:         **switch** $(spec\_result, real\_result)$ **of**
7:             **case** $(Denied, Granted)$:
8:                 $journal \leftarrow (CRIT, syscall)$ ▷ An error with its level
9:                 **return**$(Failure, journal)$
10:             **case** $(Granted, Denied)$:
11:                 $journal \leftarrow Check\_ErrCode(syscall)$
12:                 $spec[state] \leftarrow revert(spec[state], syscall)$ ▷ rollback update
13:         **end switch**
14:     **end while**
15:     $journal \leftarrow compare\_states(trace[final\_state], spec[state])$
16:     **return** $(Success, journal)$
17: **end procedure**

We need to check that the result of the replaying conforms the result of the real system trace execution (see Algorithm 2):

1. If access is granted or denied on both the specification and the real system, then we should proceed to the next system call (lines 3, 14);
2. If access is granted on the real system, but it is denied on the Event-B specification (line 7), this clearly signals about an error in the kernel or in the security module. It is not possible to proceed further after this kind of error, the analysis is stopped;
3. If access is denied on the real system, but it is granted on the Event-B specification (line 10), the return code of the system call is investigated (see Algorithm 3). For example, if the return code signals about[4]:
   - not enough memory in the system, then no additional actions are taken;
   - invalid values in the system call's arguments, then with high probability this means that the specification is not complete. This divergence is recorded to the anomaly journal;
   - not enough permissions. That means there is an error in the kernel or in the security module. This kind of divergence is recorded to the journal.

---

[4] The listed error codes are taken from the Linux kernel file
`include/uapi/asm-generic/errno-base.h`.

After this we restore the previous state of the specification (line 12) and proceed to the next system call from the trace.

4. If the replay reaches the end of the trace the global states of the kernel and the specification are compared. The divergences are logged to the anomaly journal.

Algorithm 3. Investigation of the error code of a system call

---

```
 1: procedure CHECK_ERRCODE(syscall)
 2:     err_code := syscall[result][err_code]
 3:     switch err_code of
 4:         case ENOMEM :                                  ▷ Out of memory
 5:             return ∅
 6:         case EINVAL :                                  ▷ Invalid argument
 7:             return (WARN, syscall)
 8:         case EACCES :                                  ▷ Permission denied
 9:             return (CRIT, syscall)
10:         case ... :
11:             ...
12:     end switch
13: end procedure
```

The replay analysis outputs the journal of the divergences between the behavior of the real system and the modelled behavior of the Event-B specification. The journal records need to be analyzed manually to reveal flaws in the specification or the implementation. However, if no divergences were found then with a certain level of certainty based on obtained sources and specification coverage, we can claim that we successfully demonstrated conformance between the implementation and its specification.

We measure the coverage by lines of code of the security module and the number of covered LSM hooks across the kernel. The specification allows more behaviors (states) than it is possible to observe on the real system, thus the specification coverage consists of covered global invariants and different conjuncts of guards conditions. To evaluate the proposed algorithms we have manually translated a part of the Event-B specification of the HIMACF model to an executable program and tested it on the system call traces gathered with SystemTap.

8   Related Work

In [28] Zanin and Mancini present a formal model for analyzing an arbitrary security policy configuration for SELinux. At the end of the paper the authors propose an algorithm based on their model for verifying whether, given an arbitrary security policy configuration, a given subject can access a given object in a given mode. However, they don't go down to the SELinux implementation.

Guttman et al. [15] present a formalization of the access control mechanism of the SELinux security server together with a labeled transition system representing an SELinux configuration. Linear temporal logic is used to describe the desired security objectives. The authors use model checking to determine whether security goals hold in a given system.

There are other examples of using formal methods such as B and TLA+ to formalize and prove correctness of various access control mechanisms or security policy models [16,21], but they also do not consider the implementation.

In [11] the correctness of LSM hooks placement in the Linux kernel is analyzed. The proposed runtime verification method leverages the fact that most of the LSM hooks are correctly placed to find the misplaced ones.

The authors of [13] analyze the information flows in the LSM framework. They verify that for any execution path in the kernel starting with a system call and leading to an information flow, there is at least one LSM hook before the flow is performed. The analysis statically checks the control flow graphs of kernel functions, which are obtained by a compiler plugin during the kernel build, for existence of feasible paths without mediation of the LSM framework.

9   Conclusion and Future Work

We have outlined a method for verification of the access control mechanisms implemented as a module inside the Linux kernel for conformance with its abstract specification. The method consists of several steps. First, one needs to formalize the specification of the access control mechanisms in the Event-B language and prove its correctness. Then, since the resulting Event-B specification is high-level and too different from the concrete data structures and functions of the Linux kernel, we propose to develop an additional specification of the Linux system call interface and prove that it conforms to the Event-B specification of access control mechanisms. Next, we trace system calls to the kernel while performing a series of typical user actions and tests. Finally, we replay them on the Event-B specification of the system call interface to check the obtained accesses satisfy the security policy model.

We have evaluated the proposed method on the HIMACF model, which integrates several advanced access control mechanisms, and its implementation inside Astra Linux distribution. We have developed and proved both Event-B specifications, which are required by the method. We have found that the specification of the system call interface, which is required by the method, turns out to be much larger and more complex than the specification of the security policy model. A part of the specification was manually translated to an executable form to obtain the proof of concept and test the replay algorithm of the proposed method. For this we have gathered system call traces with the SystemTap tool. The future work involves development of a translator from Event-B to an effective executable form and research the possibility of simultaneous OS execution and in-kernel verification of accesses.

References

1. Abrial, J.R.: Modeling in Event-B: System and Software Engineering, 1st edn. Cambridge University Press, New York (2010)
2. Abrial, J.R., et al.: Rodin: an open toolset for modelling and reasoning in event-B. Int. J. Softw. Tools Technol. Transf. **12**(6), 447–466 (2010). https://doi.org/10. 1007/s10009-010-0145-y
3. Abrial, J.R., Hallerstede, S.: Refinement, decomposition, and instantiation of discrete models: application to event-B. Fundamenta Informaticae **77**, 1–28 (2007)
4. Bell, D.E., La Padula, L.J.: Secure Computer System: Unified Exposition and MULTICS Interpretation. ESD-TR-75-306, Electronic Systems DivisiUon, AFSC, Hanscom AFB, 1976 (1976)
5. Bell, D.E., LaPadula, L.J.: Secure Computer Systems: Mathematical Foundations. ESD-TR-73-278 v. 1, Electronic Systems Division, AFSC, Hanscom AFB (1973)
6. Belousov, K., Viro, A.: Linux kernel LSM file permission hook restriction bypass (2006). https://vulners.com/osvdb/OSVDB:25747
7. Biba, K.: Integrity considerations for secure computer systems. Technical report MTR-3153, The MITRE Corporation (1977)
8. Devyanin, P.N.: The models of security of computer systems: access control and information flows. Goryachaya Liniya-Telecom, Moscow, Russia (2013). (in Russian)
9. Devyanin, P., Khoroshilov, A., Kuliamin, V., Petrenko, A., Shchepetkov, I.: Formal verification of OS security model with alloy and event-B. In: Ait Ameur, Y., Schewe, K.D. (eds.) ABZ 2014. LNCS, vol. 8477, pp. 309–313. Springer, Heidelberg (2014). https://doi.org/10.1007/978-3-662-43652-3_30
10. Devyanin, P.N., Khoroshilov, A.V., Kuliamin, V.V., Petrenko, A.K., Shchepetkov, I.V.: Using refinement in formal development of OS security model. In: Mazzara, M., Voronkov, A. (eds.) PSI 2015. LNCS, vol. 9609, pp. 107–115. Springer, Cham (2016). https://doi.org/10.1007/978-3-319-41579-6_9
11. Edwards, A., Jaeger, T., Zhang, X.: Runtime verification of authorization hook placement for the Linux security modules framework. In: Proceedings of the 9th ACM Conference on Computer and Communications Security, pp. 225–234. CCS 2002. ACM, New York (2002). https://doi.org/10.1145/586110.586141, http://doi. acm.org/10.1145/586110.586141
12. Georget, L.: Add missing LSM hooks in MQ timed send, receive and splice (2016). http://thread.gmane.org/gmane.linux.kernel.lsm/28737
13. Georget, L., Jaume, M., Tronel, F., Piolle, G., Tong, V.V.T.: Verifying the reliability of operating system-level information flow control systems in Linux. In: 2017 IEEE/ACM 5th International FME Workshop on Formal Methods in Software Engineering (FormaliSE), pp. 10–16, May 2017. https://doi.org/10.1109/ FormaliSE.2017.1
14. Goyal, V.: Overlayfs SELinux support (2016). https://lwn.net/Articles/693663/
15. Guttman, J.D., Herzog, A.L., Ramsdell, J.D., Skorupka, C.W.: Verifying information flow goals in security-enhanced linux. J. Comput. Secur. **13**(1), 115–134 (2005)
16. Huynh, N., Frappier, M., Mammar, A., Laleau, R., Desharnais, J.: Validating the RBAC ANSI 2012 standard using B. In: Ait Ameur, Y., Schewe, K.D. (eds.) ABZ 2014. LNCS, vol. 8477, pp. 255–270. Springer, Heidelberg (2014). https://doi.org/ 10.1007/978-3-662-43652-3_22
17. ISO/IEC 15408–1:2009. Information technology - Security techniques - Evaluation criteria for IT security - Part 1: Introduction and general model. ISO (2009)

18. ISO/IEC 15408–2:2008. Information technology - Security techniques - Evaluation criteria for IT security - Part 2: Security functional components. ISO (2008)
19. Jacob, B., Larson, P., Leitao, B., Da Silva, S.: SystemTap: instrumenting the Linux kernel for analyzing performance and functional problems. In: IBM Redbook, vol. 116 (2008)
20. Jurgens, D.: SELinux support for Infiniband RDMA (2016). https://lwn.net/Articles/684431/
21. Kozachok, A.: TLA+ based access control model specification. In: Proceedings of the Institute for System Programming of the RAS, vol. 30, pp. 147–162, January 2018. https://doi.org/10.15514/ISPRAS-2018-30(5)-9
22. Larson, P.: Testing Linux with the Linux test project. In: Ottawa Linux Symposium, p. 265 (2002)
23. Morris, J., Smalley, S., Kroah-Hartman, G.: Linux security modules: general security support for the Linux kernel. In: USENIX Security Symposium, pp. 17–31. ACM Berkeley, CA (2002)
24. RusBITech: Astra Linux® Special Edition. https://astralinux.ru/products/astra-linux-special-edition/
25. Tsirunyan, K., Martirosyan, V., Tsyvarev, A.: The Spruce System: quality verification of Linux file systems drivers. In: Proceedings of the Spring/Summer Young Researchers Colloquium on Software Engineering. ISP RAS (2012)
26. Vykov, D.: Syzkaller (2015). https://github.com/google/syzkaller
27. Write, C.: LSM update, another missing hook (2005). https://lwn.net/Articles/155496/
28. Zanin, G., Mancini, L.V.: Towards a formal model for security policies specification and validation in the SELinux system. In: Proceedings of the Ninth ACM Symposium on Access Control Models and Technologies, pp. 136–145. ACM (2004)

Open and Interactive Learning Resources
for Algorithmic Problem Solving

João F. Ferreira[1]($\boxtimes$) and Alexandra Mendes[2,3]

[1] INESC-ID & Instituto Superior Técnico, University of Lisbon, Lisbon, Portugal
joao@joaoff.com
[2] Department of Informatics, Universidade da Beira Interior, Covilhã, Portugal
alexandra@archimendes.com
[3] HASLab, INESC TEC, Porto, Portugal

Abstract. *Algorithmic problem solving* is a way of approaching and solving problems by using the advances that have been made in the principles of correct-by-construction algorithm design. The approach has been taught at first-year undergraduate level since September 2003 and, since then, a substantial amount of learning materials have been developed. However, the existing materials are distributed in a conventional and static way (e.g. as a textbook and as several documents in PDF format available online), not leveraging the capabilities provided by modern collaborative and open-source platforms.

In this paper, we propose the creation of an online, *open-source* repository of *interactive* learning materials on algorithmic problem solving. We show how the existing framework Mathigon can be used to support such a repository. By being open and hosted on a platform such as GitHub, the repository enables collaboration and anyone can create and submit new material. Furthermore, by making the material interactive, we hope to encourage engagement with and a better understanding of the materials.

Keywords: Algorithmic problem solving · Formal methods · Interactive learning materials

1 Introduction

Algorithmic problem solving is about the formulation and solution of problems where the solution involves, possibly implicitly, the principles and techniques that have been developed to assist in the construction of correct algorithms. Algorithms have been studied and developed since the beginning of civilisation, but, over the last few decades, the unprecedented scale of programming problems and the consequent demands on the reliability of computer software led to massive improvements in our algorithmic-problem-solving skills. The improvements are centred on goal-directed, calculational construction of algorithms as opposed to the traditional guess-and-verify methodology.

Algorithmic problem solving has been taught at first-year undergraduate level since September 2003 and, since then, its adoption became easier due to

E. Sekerinski et al. (Eds.): FM 2019 Workshops, LNCS 12233, pp. 200–208, 2020.
https://doi.org/10.1007/978-3-030-54997-8_13

the publication of a textbook [1] and to the development of a substantial amount of learning materials (in particular, a collection of teaching scenarios is available for educators to use [8]). Recreational problems are often used to teach APS concepts, since they can make serious concepts more palatable to students and encourage interactivity in the classroom [10–12]. However, the materials available to support the teaching of APS are distributed in a conventional and static way (e.g. as several documents in PDF format available online), not leveraging the capabilities provided by modern collaborative and open-source platforms. In this paper, we present the first steps towards changing this current state of affairs.

We propose the creation of an online, *open-source* repository of *interactive* learning materials on algorithmic problem solving. We show how the existing framework Mathigon[1] can be used to support such a repository. By being open and hosted on a platform such as GitHub, the repository enables collaboration and anyone can create and submit new material allowing the material to evolve over time as a collaborative effort by the community. Furthermore, by making the material interactive, we hope to reach a wider audience and encourage engagement with and a better understanding of APS.

Outline. To illustrate the type of recreational problems that we use when teaching APS, we show in Sect. 2 an example of a river-crossing problem, which we use as a running example. We use it to introduce concepts such as state and state-transition diagram, and to illustrate principles such as the importance of avoiding unnecessary naming. In Sect. 3 we present an example of how APS material can be made more interactive. We conclude in Sect. 5, where we also present some ideas for the next steps.

2   Example: River-Crossing Puzzles

River crossing puzzles are about carrying items from one river bank to another, usually in the fewest trips possible and typically with restrictions that make a solution non-obvious. According to Wikipedia[2], the earliest known river-crossing problems occur in the manuscript *Propositiones ad Acuendos Juvenes* (English: Problems to sharpen the young), traditionally said to be written by Alcuin. The earliest copies of this manuscript date from the 9th century.

We use river-crossing problems to illustrate and introduce concepts and principles such as state-transition diagrams, symmetry, and the importance of avoiding unnecessary naming. Consider, for example, the following puzzle:

Goat, Cabbage and Wolf
A farmer wishes to ferry a goat, a cabbage and a wolf across a river. However, his boat is only large enough to take one of them at a time, making several trips across the river necessary. Also, the goat should not

---

[1] Mathigon's website: https://mathigon.org (accessed 18 July 2019).
[2] Wikipedia link: https://en.wikipedia.org/wiki/River_crossing_puzzle (accessed 18 July 2019).

be left alone with the cabbage (otherwise, the goat would eat the cabbage), and the wolf should not be left alone with the goat (otherwise, the wolf would eat the goat).
How can the farmer achieve the task?

We typically structure the discussion of this puzzle as follows.

On Algorithmic Problems. The first discussion we have with the students is divided into two parts. First, we ensure that the problem statement is clear and that students understand the goal of the puzzle. For example, implicit in the problem statement is that initially all the four elements are at the same river bank and that the farmer has to accompany each of the other elements when crossing the river. Also, we adopt what E. W. Dijkstra called the rule of *no cancellation*, i.e. we reject any schedule in which a subsequence of successive moves results in no change [6].

Second, we discuss why this puzzle can be considered an algorithmic puzzle. We reach the conclusion that this is clearly an algorithmic problem, because the solution consists of a *sequence of instructions* (i.e. an algorithm) indicating who or what should cross. A typical instruction would be: "the farmer crosses with the wolf" or "the farmer returns alone".

On States and State-Transition Diagrams. We proceed our discussion by noting that to solve this problem, it is useful to introduce a notation that identifies the position of each element. We name the two river banks as left and right and we introduce a simple notation that denotes whether each element is on the left or on the right bank. For example, we write LLRR to denote that the farmer is on the left bank, the goat is on the left bank, the cabbage is on the right bank, and the wolf is on the right bank (exactly by that order). We thus introduce the notion of *state*, representing the initial and final states of this problem as:

This discussion leads to a very natural question: *how many states exist in this problem?* Given that there are 4 elements, and each element can be in either one of two river banks, we quickly conclude that there is a total of 2^4 (i.e. 16) states. We also take the opportunity to explore how many states we would have if the number of elements were different. After only a few examples, students see that the number of states grows very quickly.

We also observe that not all of the 16 states are valid. For example, the following states are invalid:

At this point, most students already have a solution to the puzzle. After enquiring some of them about the methodology that they followed to find their solutions, we notice that they have tried multiple steps until reaching a satisfactory solution. We use this to introduce the notion of *brute-force search*.

We describe the technique and introduce the concept of *state-transition diagram*. Together with the class, we build the following state-transition diagram and we observe that there are indeed two solutions to this problem:

We also take the opportunity to observe that river-crossing problems have a property that reduces the amount of effort required to solve them: they are symmetric. In other words, suppose that we have a solution that takes the elements from the left bank to the right bank; if we reverse that solution, we immediately have a solution that takes the elements from the right bank to the left bank. The state-transition diagram is an excellent device to observe this property.

On Unnecessary Naming. It is impossible to solve problems without introducing names. However, if we name unnecessary elements or if we make unnecessary distinctions, we add unnecessary detail and complexity to the solution.

This puzzle is a good example to illustrate that the avoidance of unnecessary naming leads to more effective and simple solutions. Recall that the problem is about taking across four individuals without violating the two conditions:

1. the goat should not be left alone with the cabbage;
2. the wolf should not be left alone with the goat.

These two conditions expose a similarity between the wolf and the cabbage: the goat cannot be left with either the wolf or the cabbage. Moreover, there are no restrictions on leaving the wolf alone with the cabbage. This clearly suggests that *both the cabbage and the wolf are playing the same role*. Why, then, are the "wolf" and the "cabbage" distinguished by giving them different names?

We restate the problem[3], this time with a naming convention that omits the unnecessary distinction between the wolf and the cabbage. In the restated problem, we call the goat an "alpha" and the cabbage and the wolf "betas":

> *A farmer wishes to ferry an alpha and two betas across a river. However, his boat is only large enough to take one of them at a time, making several trips across the river necessary. Also, an alpha should not be left alone with a beta.*
> *How can the farmer achieve the task?*

Now the problem becomes much easier to solve and most students find a solution immediately. Indeed, there is only one solution: take the alpha across, and then one beta across, returning with the alpha; then take the second beta across, followed by the alpha. Because there is only one solution, it is easy to discover

---

[3] The restatement of the problem and the subsequent two paragraphs are extracted from [1].

(note that in the problem with the four individuals, we have two solutions, since we have two different choices when choosing the first beta to take across).

When elements of a problem are given individual names, it distinguishes them from other elements of the problem, and adds to the size of the state space. The process of omitting unnecessary detail, and reducing a problem to its essentials is called *abstraction*. Poor solutions to problems are ones that fail to "abstract" adequately, making the problem more complicated than it really is.

3   Interactive Learning Materials

The material presented in the previous section is taught during lectures in an interactive manner, with students being encouraged to participate actively in solving the problem individually and as a whole-class effort. For deep learning to be achieved, students need to think about what they are learning and engage with the material, rather than sit and listen—we believe that the nature of our lectures helps to achieve that. As Tyler (1949) points out (cited by Biggs and Tang [4]),

> *Learning takes place through the active behavior of the student: it is what he does that he learns, not what the teacher does.*

However, when it comes to revising the material and to further study, the interactivity disappears and students are left with only books and slides to assist them, which are static. We thus propose the creation of online, open-source, interactive material that gives students a further opportunity to take on a more active role in learning APS, even when they are alone. By making it widely available via a website, APS can potentially reach a larger audience than it would if it continued limited to lectures and static supporting material (even if available online); by being open-source, anyone can contribute with new material and improvements.

Initial Prototype. To implement and experiment with some of our initial ideas, we wrote parts of the material presented in Sect. 2 for Mathigon, a groundbreaking new education open-source platform that enables interactive learning.

Mathigon makes it possible to present the material in a way that encourages the learner to become a participant by e.g. answering multiple choice questions, by solving interactive puzzles, and by exploring further reading (e.g. biographies and further context) presented to them via non-intrusive popups. As the learner navigates through the content and interacts with it, further information is provided to complement their learning.

For example, Fig. 1 shows how multiple choice answers can be integrated in the material. The sentence that starts with *"Indeed, since we have 4 elements"* is only displayed after the student selects the correct answer. Moreover, the box with arrows is a *variable slider*, which allows inline variables to be manipulated by the student. In this example, the student is able to interactively see how the

How many states are there?

The *state space* of a problem (or system) is the set of all possible states (i.e. configurations) that the problem (or system) can have. This information is important because it can give us a better idea of the complexity of the problem.

In this case, since we only have 4 elements (the farmer, the goat, the cabbage, and the wolf), we conclude that there is a total of [???] states. Indeed, since we have 4 elements and each element can be in one of two possible [10] er *L* or *R*), the total number of states is $2 \cdot 2 \cdot 2 \cdot 2$ (i.e. $2^4 = 16$).

The number of states grows [64] means that it grows very quickly! The total number of states is 2^n, where *n* is the num [16] ents. To see how quickly it grows, note that for [◄ 4 ►] elements the total number of states is **16** (change the number of elements by sliding over it).

Note that not all states are valid, in the sense that some violate the constraints of the problem. For example, the state *LRLR* is invalid because [???].

Fig. 1. Multiple choice and variable slider.

Introduction

Before we proceed, it is important that we understand clearly the problem statement. Usually, with puzzles, there is a substantial amount of implicit information in the problem statement that needs to be made explicit. For example, initially, all the four elements are at the same river bank. Also, [× goat] has to accompany each of the other elements when crossing the river.

Note that we adopt what E. W. Dijkstra called the rule of *no cancellation*, i.e. we reject any schedule in which a subsequence

> **Edsger W. Dijkstra**
> (1930 – 2002) was a
> Dutch systems
> scientist,
> programmer, software
> engineer, science
> essayist, and pioneer
> in computing science.
> One of the most
> influential figures of computing science's

This is an algorithmic pr[o]   solution to this puzzle consists of a sequence of instruct[ions]   mer crosses with the wolf" or "the farmer returns alon[e]   le?

Fig. 2. Incorrect answers are clearly marked. Biographies are shown as popups.

total number of states grows (e.g. if the value of the variable increases from 4 to 5, the number 16 is automatically updated to 32).

Figure 2 illustrates a correct choice (*"all the four elements are at the same river bank"*) and an incorrect choice, clearly marked with a cross (*"goat"*). It also shows an example of a biographical popup.

Given that the material is offered as a web application, we can easily incorporate interactive artefacts that are programmed in, for example, Javascript. Figure 3 shows the integration of an external Javascript implementation of the puzzle[4]. Our work-in-progress is available on GitHub[5]; everyone is welcome to contribute.

Fig. 3. External artefacts can be incorporated (e.g. Javascript code)

4   Effectiveness and Students' Feedback

This paper describes a new open community project that is at a very early stage of development and that has not yet been thoroughly evaluated. The problems, puzzles, techniques, and approach have been evaluated to some extent, but the online Mathigon-based interactive material has not.

We argue that the approach is effective given that the techniques and methods taught have been used to find new solutions to non-trivial problems (e.g. new results in number theory [2,3,7] and in solitaire games [1]). However, measuring whether the approach helps students become better problem solvers is more difficult and requires further work. So far, we performed a small-scale experiment to try to determine if a cohort of students became better problem solvers [9]. The focus was the calculational method and, generally, they adopted what was taught in the module for solving problems, but their use of the calculational style was not effective. We also tested some APS material with pre-university

---

[4] The implementation of the puzzle that we used was created by Victor Ribeiro (https://github.com/victorqribeiro/bridge).

[5] See the repository **textbooks** (folder **content/river-crossing**) in https://github.com/ algprobsolving.

students [12]: after being exposed to the material, students were able to apply techniques like invariants by themselves.

Our experience is that students appreciate the approach. This is confirmed by feedback about a session that we delivered on analysing an algorithmic card trick [10]. This is further confirmed by feedback about a session delivered to pre-university students [12], which also shows that the material (or, at least, parts of the material) can even be taught at pre-university level. During some teaching sessions, we have also collected feedback from our students. In general, they appreciate the use of recreational problems and the interactivity that arises from solving those problems.

Thousands of students have been exposed to the APS material throughout the years. The material was taught for about 10 years at the University of Nottingham (it started in 2003). It was taught at Teesside University from 2011 to 2018. Backhouse's book on APS [1] is used in the course CS2104 at Virginia Tech. We believe that creating an interactive APS book will help to increase the adoption of this approach to teach APS.

5 Conclusion

The famous quote *"Learning is not a spectator sport"*[5] could not be more true for a subject like APS. We believe that the idea proposed in this paper supports this quote, by encouraging learners to become *participants*. Moreover, it is our view that Mathigon offers a sound and extensible base for the creation of interactive APS material that supports active learning. With this initiative, and by making all the artefacts open-source and available on Github, we hope to encourage the community to make a joint effort to create and use these materials.

Future Work. As an immediate next step, we intend to create further interactive material to support APS. We will also explore how to create interactive material to support teaching programming methodology following an approach such as that proposed in [13]. To facilitate collaboration, we will also create documentation on how to contribute to the project. In order to incorporate in the web application all the APS material that we have been teaching in the last few years, we envisage that Mathigon will have to be extended with a few technical features. For example:

- To support the formats used in the calculational method (e.g. proof format), we might have to write extensions to AsciiMath (Mathigon is currently able to parse AsciiMath and convert it to MathML). This is important, because the calculational method is central to our approach [9,11].
- To enable support for handwritten calculational mathematics and build on previous work [14,15], we will explore frameworks such as MyScript[6].
- To encode some of our case studies (e.g. [10]), we might have to write specialised Javascript libraries that allow richer interactions.

---

[6] MyScript webpage: https://www.myscript.com.

Acknowledgments. This work is partially financed by National Funds through the Portuguese funding agency, FCT - Fundação para a Ciência e a Tecnologia through the project: UID/EEA/50014/2019.

References

1. Backhouse, R.: Algorithmic Problem Solving. Wiley, New York (2011)
2. Backhouse, R., Ferreira, J.F.: On Euclid's algorithm and elementary number theory. Sci. Comput. Programm. **76**(3), 160–180 (2011). https://doi.org/10.1016/j.scico.2010.05.006
3. Backhouse, R., Ferreira, J.F.: Recounting the rationals: twice!. In: Audebaud, P., Paulin-Mohring, C. (eds.) MPC 2008. LNCS, vol. 5133, pp. 79–91. Springer, Heidelberg (2008). https://doi.org/10.1007/978-3-540-70594-9_6
4. Biggs, J., Tang, C.: Teaching for Quality Learning at University: What the Student does (Society for Research Into Higher Education), 4th edn. Open Univ. Press, Buckingham (2011)
5. Chickering, A.W., Gamson, Z.F.: Seven principles for good practice in undergraduate education. AAHE Bull. **3**, 7 (1987)
6. Dijkstra, E.W.: Pruning the search tree, January 1997. http://www.cs.utexas.edu/users/EWD/ewd12xx/EWD1255.PDF
7. Ferreira, J.F.: Designing an algorithmic proof of the two-squares theorem. In: Bolduc, C., Desharnais, J., Ktari, B. (eds.) MPC 2010. LNCS, vol. 6120, pp. 140–156. Springer, Heidelberg (2010). https://doi.org/10.1007/978-3-642-13321-3_10
8. Ferreira, J.F.: Principles and applications of algorithmic problem solving. Ph.D. thesis, School of Computer Science, University of Nottingham (2010)
9. Ferreira, J.F., Mendes, A.: Students' feedback on teaching mathematics through the calculational method. In: 2009 39th IEEE Frontiers in Education Conference, pp. 1–6. IEEE (2009)
10. Ferreira, J.F., Mendes, A.: The magic of algorithm design and analysis: teaching algorithmic skills using magic card tricks. In: ACM ITiCSE (2014)
11. Ferreira, J.F., Mendes, A., Backhouse, R., Barbosa, L.S.: Which mathematics for the information society? In: Gibbons, J., Oliveira, J.N. (eds.) TFM 2009. LNCS, vol. 5846, pp. 39–56. Springer, Heidelberg (2009). https://doi.org/10.1007/978-3-642-04912-5_4
12. Ferreira, J., et al.: Logic training through algorithmic problem solving. In: Blackburn, P., van Ditmarsch, H., Manzano, M., Soler-Toscano, F. (eds.) TICTTL 2011. LNCS (LNAI), vol. 6680, pp. 62–69. Springer, Heidelberg (2011). https://doi.org/10.1007/978-3-642-21350-2_8
13. Hoare, T., Mendes, A., Ferreira, J.F.: Logic, algebra, and geometry at the foundation of computer science. In: Dongol, B., Petre, L., Smith, G. (eds.) FMTea 2019. LNCS, vol. 11758, pp. 3–20. Springer, Cham (2019). https://doi.org/10.1007/978-3-030-32441-4_1
14. Mendes, A.: Structured editing of handwritten mathematics. Ph.D. thesis, School of Computer Science, University of Nottingham, UK (2012)
15. Mendes, A., Backhouse, R., Ferreira, J.F.: Structure editing of handwritten mathematics: improving the computer support for the calculational method. In: ACM ITS (2014). http://doi.acm.org/10.1145/2669485.2669495

Challenges Faced by Students in an Open Source Software Undergraduate Course

Dias Issa(✉) iD

Computer Science Department, Nazarbayev University,
Nur-Sultan 010000, Republic of Kazakhstan
dias.issa@nu.edu.kz

Abstract. The Open Source Software (OSS) development is gaining popularity from year to year, however, entering the OSS community still remains a challenging task. In this work, we describe challenges faced by a beginner OSS code-developer during the first contribution. Additionally, we analyze our experience and offer hints for potential newcomers. Whole work was done as the project of the Open Source Software undergraduate course at the Computer Department of Nazarbayev University.

Keywords: Open Source Software · Code developer · OSS challenges

1 Introduction

The paper reports the student's experience in contributing to the open-source software project from GitHub gained during studying at the undergraduate Open Source Software course. We included a number of failed attempts to contribute to different projects alongside the successful one. Each project's background information and each contribution attempt were analyzed, while the acquired experience was digested into some useful advises for a newcomer. Finally, we drew several conclusions and noted about our future plans.

Our background includes experience in developing software systems and applications, and Machine Learning models for different platforms including mobile devices, personal computers, and sensor devices. Therefore, we decided to take the Open Source Software (OSS) course in the final semester in order to have a broader view of the field of Software Engineering. In detail, our motivations in taking OSS class were both intrinsic and extrinsic [1,13]. We love coding and solving problems, so working on OSS project was a new experience for us. Additionally, we wanted to enhance our coding skills and learn novel things. Last but not least was that contribution to the project could improve the "experience" section of our resume.

Furthermore, our expectations from the course were both in theoretical and practical areas. We wanted to identify the main features of open source software development together with the reasons for its emergence and successful existence. At the same time, we wanted to get a practical experience of contribution to one

© Springer Nature Switzerland AG 2020
E. Sekerinski et al. (Eds.): FM 2019 Workshops, LNCS 12233, pp. 209–223, 2020.
https://doi.org/10.1007/978-3-030-54997-8_14

of OSS projects. Finally, the internal structure of the OSS community was an aspect which we were curious to know.

The Open Source Software course has perfectly met our expectations due to its twofold structure. The first part was comprised of regular lectures about the history of OSS development, its features and tools. This material was taught using *Open Source: A Multidisciplinary Approach* authored by M. Mufatto [13] and *Open Source Software: A Survey from* 10,000 ft authored by Androutsellis-Theotokis et al. [1]. The material was checked during examinations.

The second part was about contributing to OSS project and it was totally independent work. A student was responsible for searching an open source software project and for becoming its active contributor. This part was examined utilizing the milestone reports and presentations. The next sections describe some of these milestones and outcomes of the work.

The paper is structured in the following order: the project selection section with specifications for each option and their comparison, the contribution section, the learned lessons, and conclusion.

2   Project Selection

Despite the enthusiasm at the beginning of the course, the process of finding an appropriate project for further contribution was not an easy task. During the class, we changed the chosen projects two times due to different reasons that are described below. Therefore, project selection state is one of the most important steps during the open source software contribution process. Right decision at the beginning would help young contributor a lot in decreasing the amount of resistance during the development. By "resistance" we mean the generalized term for various factors hindering the process of contribution. In the next subsections, we describe our project selections, motivations for such selections as well as expectations, and reasons for withdrawal.

2.1   First Project: AVA

The first project was chosen after a long time spent on project search in GitHub. The variety of interesting projects there combined with our knowledge of several programming languages made this decision last so long.

General Project Description. AVA [21] is the testing library on Node.js [18], so the main language of the project is JavaScript. The library allows executing tests in parallel, therefore, much faster. The community was medium active. According to AVA's statistics by February 4, the project had over 1.4k commits, with the last commit done on 18th of January 2019. During the previous month, there were done 15 pull requests, 9 issues were closed and 5 issues were opened. AVA was released 50 times and had 200 contributors. The project has very decent documentation translated to 8 other languages including English. There were 141 open issues, with 73 issues good for the first contribution by February

2019. AVA is under MIT license and has support on Twitter, Stack Overflow and Spectrum [21].

Justification of the Decision. This project seemed for us as an appropriate option for OSS class due to its detailed documentation, friendly community, and a variety of issues for beginners. Additionally, parallel programming was a new and interesting field for involvement. Subsequently, we tended to consider that the code developing for this project could lead to learning a great variety of new concepts. Finally, we consider AVA as a good project to enhance our skills in JavaScript.

Detailed Role Description and Provisional Activity Plan. As a developer for this project, we planned to work on issues tagged as "enhancement" and "bug". It was also desirable that these issues were tagged as "good for beginner". As the first stage of contribution, we chose to get familiar with the code of the project and its documentation for contributors. Then, depending on the understanding of the code, we were going to solve bugs or perform enhancements.

Activities and Reasons for Withdrawal. After a more detailed analysis of the project, it was found out that most of the "good for beginner" issues were outdated and were not solved for a long period of time. Moreover, most of them were in the field of documentation, while we wanted to solve developer issues [21]. Additionally, there almost did not appear new propositions with "good for beginner" tag, while other issues required skill and knowledge which, in our opinion, we could not provide. Figure 1 clearly demonstrates all these drawbacks. As a result, after several unsuccessful attempts to solve issues, we were compelled to search for a new project to contribute.

2.2   Second Project: Coala

The second project was chosen also after a long time spent on project search in GitHub. The first failure and aspiration for successful contribution forced us to treat this process carefully. Therefore, the project is analyzed and described in details in following subsections: the general description of the project, the reasons for selection, the role description and provisional activity plan, the governance structure of the project, its community structure, its architecture, and the justification for withdrawal of the project.

General Project Description. The project is aimed to help programmers during revising their codes for bugs. Coala [5,7] is a software designed for linting and fixing codes in a very broad range of languages. It is highly customizable, so the user could utilize Coala from his favorite coding environment (editor) and add extra Coala plugins whenever he needs. The main language of the source code of the project is Python.

Fig. 1. Issues tagged as "good for beginner". AVA.

Justification of the Selection. We had several reasons for choosing Coala for OSS class. Firstly, automatic code linting was an undiscovered and intriguing area for us. Secondly, the community is open for new members and helps them to make their first contributions. Thirdly, the project has good structured and well-written guide dedicated to newcomers. Fourthly, a wide range of issues with difficulty levels suitable for beginners. Finally, we liked their motto, the words of John F. Woods: "Always code as if the guy who ends up maintaining your code will be a violent psychopath who knows where you live." [5].

Detailed Role Description and Provisional Activity Plan. For this project, we planned to work on coding issues rather than documentation issues due to the reasons listed in the introduction of this paper. In the beginning, besides studying contributors guide of the project and its code, we decided to solve bugs because this procedure seemed to us less complex than developing new features. After that, when we would gain experience, we were going to perform enhancements of the code or to develop new functionality. According to the plan, the first issues with which we wanted to start would have had tags "difficulty/newcomer" or "difficulty/low", because it is the part of the requirements of Coala community for new developers [6].

Governance Structure. We could not properly identify the governance structure of the project, however, we tend to think that it is monarchical.

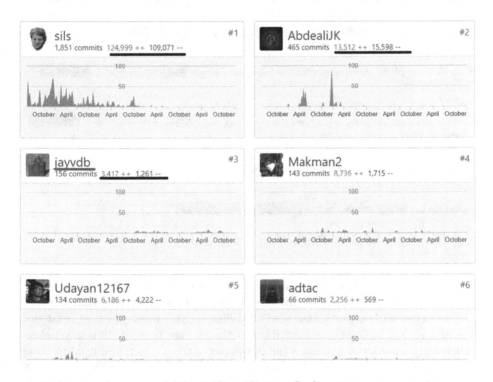

Fig. 2. Contributors. Coala.

The reasons for this claim are the following: from the Fig. 2 one could clearly see that the owner of the project, sils [15], is the most valuable contributor with almost 7 times and 50 times larger contribution than the second and third valuable contributors. Also, according to the forum posts depicted on the Fig. 3, he delegated some of his responsibilities to other players in his team, for example, he delegated to javdb [19] the work with the community. However, with the owner's much better knowledge of the project and his amount of contribution, we assert that the project owner's voice is the most valuable.

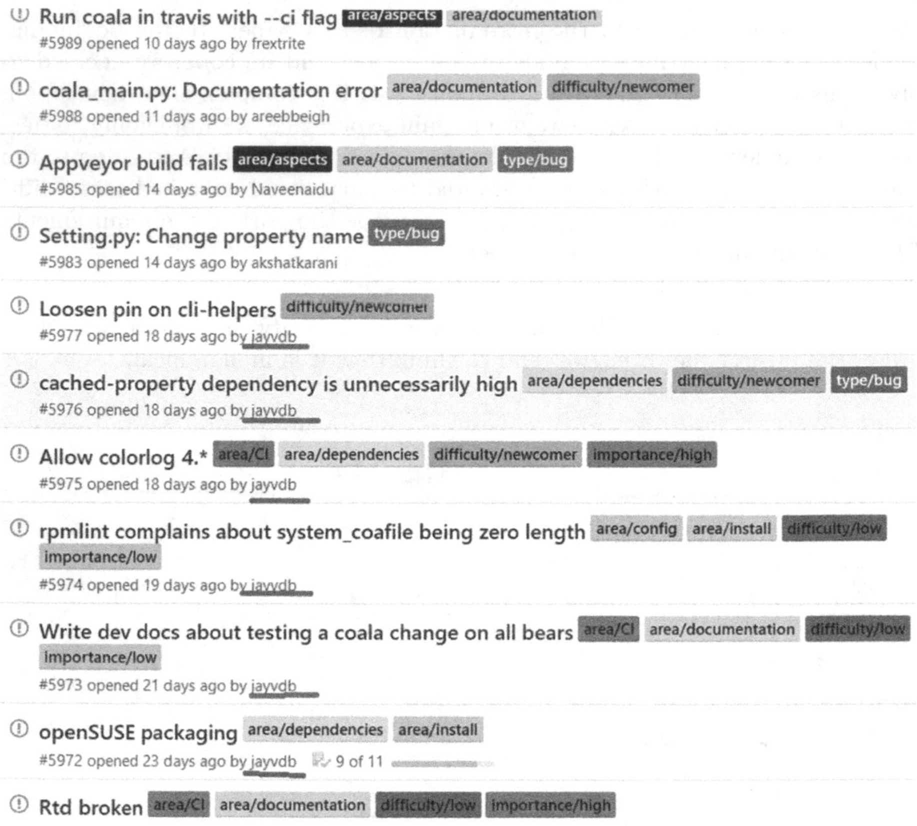

Fig. 3. Issue forum. Coala.

Community Structure. The community structure of Coala is hierarchical. This could be seen from their contribution guide [6], which states that in order to solve issues with a particular level of difficulty, you need to fix at least one issue and review at least one contribution that is one level of difficulty below. Additionally, in order to become a full developer of the project, you need to make a promotion request. Though Coala has such a strict structure that is typical for more proprietary software development, it resides under the strongest copyleft license: GNU Affero General Public License v3.0 [5]. This license obligates potential users to open the source code of possible derivatives of the project.

It could be said that such structure of Coala project is beneficial for the role of new developer of the project because a newbie has a clear understanding of which issues he or she should work and what to do next. At the same time, more experienced developers will not take out the potential issues that the new developer could solve due to the strict division of difficulty levels.

Architecture. The general architecture of the project is modular. Basically, Coala consists of different modules each dedicated to a particular programming language. Most of the popular languages are supported right now. The project has working builds on Linux and MacOS, and it is planned to develop a working build for Windows because currently, it is failing [7]. Most of the issues of the project reside in the area of documentation and dependencies, some of the issues are bugs [5]. Also, due to such variety in supported programming languages, there are lots of issues connected with a particular language. Additionally, the project does not have a nice user interface and the work is performed using a command line [6]. This is acceptable for the current auditorium, however, better UI could attract more people who are not professionals (students, newbies in programming, etc.)

Activities and Interaction. We started to search for an issue at the issue forum of Coala on GitHub [5]. There was a strong deficit of "newcomer" issues, so it was decided to monitor the forum for the appearance of new issues in this category. At the time when a new issue appeared, we were too hesitant in taking it. Therefore, because of this several minute long hesitancy, another contributor was assigned to the issue. After that, the sudden freeze of the project occurred, so we decided to communicate with the owner of the project in order to get any issues to work on. The owner of Coala, sils [15], stated that he is no longer engaged in the project and cannot help us much. Sils suggested us to check out "newcomer" issues on the GitHub forum. We also wrote an email to another active community member, jayvdb [19]. However, he did not answer the letter.

Reasons for Withdrawal. Coala was an ideal potential project for OSS class, the only drawback was that there were a large number of new contributors, so the number of issues was not enough for everyone. Nevertheless, the main reason for withdrawal was in project freeze, which occurred suddenly. Eventually, we were forced to search a new OSS project, because we needed to contribute as soon as possible due to deadlines of the OSS class schedule.

2.3 Third Project: Jarvis

The third and final project was chosen in a short amount of time, mostly spent on traversing GitHub. Jarvis [17] was listed as the third and the second project for potential contribution during two previous searches. Therefore, after two unsuccessful attempts, it was Jarvis' time to come on stage.

General Project Description. Jarvis is an open source personal assistant for Linux and MacOS platforms, which works using command line interface. Additionally, it supports voice response. The assistant has such features as telling the weather, finding nearby places for having meal, etc. [17] The community is medium active. Jarvis has the following statistics by March 26: the project has over 800 commits, with the last commit done on the 26th of March. During the last month, there were done 11 pull requests, 7 issues were closed and 5 issues were opened. Jarvis has 74 contributors. The project is young and ambitious. Jarvis is under MIT license and has support on Gitter [17].

Justification of the Selection. We state that this project was a good option for the OSS course due to its young age, which gives an opportunity to find bugs and design new functionality. Additionally, personal assistance was a very interesting field to study and develop, especially for us, because we could apply our knowledge in Machine Learning in order to design new features for Jarvis. Also, we assert that we learned Python better during solving the issues because all code of the project is written in this language.

Detailed Role Description and Provisional Activity Plan. As a developer for this project, we planned to work on issues tagged as "bug". We also wanted to design new features for Jarvis, several of them we published at the forum [8,9].

Governance Structure. We again could not properly identify the governance structure of the project due to the absence of a document with the rules of Jarvis' community [17]. Nevertheless, we tend to think that the governance structure is federal. The reason for this claim is the following: the owner of the project is only the 6th most valuable contributor of the project (Fig. 4).

Moreover, according to Fig. 4, appi147 [4], the core member of Jarvis, has the largest amount of code contributed. Additionally, the owner allowed to the other major contributors to work with the master branch [10]. Also, according to the forum posts, the new functionality could be confirmed by the core team of the project, not only by the owner [8]. Therefore, we state that the major contributors have the most valuable vote, which corresponds to the meritocracy that is the base of the federal model.

Community Structure. The community structure of Jarvis is not clear, because of its small size and anarchistic way of contributions. Subsequently, we assume that the community structure of this project is based on a fluid community organization model. The reasons for such assertion are the following: every member of the community, even newbies with no contribution, could offer new features and implement them, which was proved by our contribution [8]. This, in turn, leads to the second point, that membership in the community and its roles are fluid, so a developer could be an idea creator or a tester. Finally, according to the issue forum, the project evolution depends on the innovations offered by the members of the community [17].

Architecture. The architecture of Jarvis is highly modular. Basically, Jarvis operates using a variety of plugins, which are independent of each other and

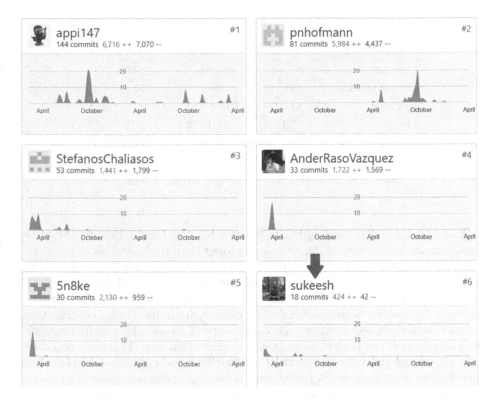

Fig. 4. Contributors and the highlighted owner of the project. Jarvis.

are responsible for different features of the personal assistant. The project has working builds only on MacOS and Linux platforms, while Windows is not supported at all and is not planned to be supported in the near future. Most of the issues of the project are located in the area of enhancements of the current functionality and in the area of implementation of new features. Jarvis has no GUI and operates through the command line and voice commands, which are not supported well [17]. Therefore, we claim that in order to increase the popularity of the project, Jarvis needs GUI.

2.4   Comparison of the Projects

Table 1 shows the comparison of the three projects described in this section. The "starting complexity" entry of the table was assessed by the following criteria: the effort spent for understanding the code of the project, the amount of knowledge of the project needed to perform a contribution, time spent on learning the documentation to become familiar with the project and its order of contribution, and the effort spent for getting assigned for an issue. From the table, we can see that both Coala [7] and AVA [21] were founded in 2014, while Jarvis [17] is relatively young. Also, according to the number of contributors,

Table 1. General comparison

	AVA [21]	Coala [5]	Jarvis [17]
Commits number	>1.4k	>4.4k	>800
Contributors	200	439	74
Releases	50	17	0
License	MIT	AGPL-3.0	MIT
Documentation	Very decent	Decent	Poor
Time of 1st commit	Nov. 2014	Jul. 2014	Mar. 2017
Starting complexity	Hard	Medium Hard	Easy

AVA and Coala projects are significantly more popular than Jarvis. At the same time, starting complexity at Jarvis is much lower than in the two older projects. Therefore, using the given data, it could be said that as a project gets older and more popular, the "resistance" for making the first contribution increases, such that even well-written documentation does not facilitate this procedure to the right degree. By "resistance" here we mean such hindrances for contribution as individual skills requirement, the complexity of issues, the requirements on the knowledge of the project to make the contribution, etc. This issue could be addressed using the following method utilized by some OSS projects [12]: new contributors start their development via pair coding sessions organized by other experienced members of the project, which in turn helps newbies to adapt, popularizes the project and leaves a good impression that motivates them to join its community.

To conclude, entering the OSS community for a new member is a complex procedure that is mostly dependent on the user's individual skills, project's age and its attitude towards new contributors.

3　Contribution

As said before, Jarvis was the most appropriate project for us to contribute. We contributed to the project in four different ways: fixed the bug, offered the new features, implemented the new features, and found the bug in the code of the project [8–10]. The subsections below describe each of the contributions.

3.1　Bug Fix

We decided to start our first contribution to Jarvis with the simple task of fixing a bug. Fortunately, the project owner had found an "easy to fix" bug and offered it to community members [10]. We took into the account the last experience with the issue assignment in Coala project, and answered immediately, without any idea of solving the bug. Fortunately, we were assigned this bug and started working on it. Though the bug was easy and eventually was solved by us, we spent a very large amount of time fixing it. This happened mostly because of the absence of experience in contribution to OSS projects using GIT framework. Additionally, the time was also spent on multiple corrections of the submitted code due to our limited knowledge of such OSS code writing rules as no empty lines with spaces, or space after comment sign, etc. Finally, we had done our pull request and it was merged with the master branch of the project [10].

3.2   New Feature Offers

Furthermore, we offered two new features for Jarvis. First of them was about adding the functionality of searching images using their description [9]. We even implemented the basic functionality using deep neural networks, however, the core team did not give an answer for this request. We assume that this happened due to the large complexity of implementation and usage of the offered feature.

Additionally, we offered a console game "Bulls and Cows", which was immediately accepted with strong enthusiasm [8]. We suppose that this occurred due to the simplicity of the idea and implementation process. Also, there could be other reasons for this. The nature of OSS encourages community members for voluntary contributions. The silence of the core members of Jarvis to our previous feature offer could made them feel uncomfortable due to possible "misconduct" on the subconscious level. Thus, unconscious desire to improve could affected the level of their enthusiasm.

Finally, we have a lot of ideas of new features that could be added to Jarvis, and which we could offer to the community.

3.3   New Feature Implementation

We implemented our first feature before it was offered, however, the feature was not accepted by the core team of Jarvis [9]. Therefore, we moved to create a plugin for our next offered feature - the game [8]. The programming part of the game was easy, so we wrote the code considerably faster than in bug fix case. However, the way of plugin creation and its insertion to Jarvis was not so clear, so most of the time was spent on these two tasks. Finally, after some attempts, we were able to submit our pull request, which passed all tests. The plugin was tested by the core members of Jarvis, and the pull request was merged with the master branch [8].

3.4   Bug Investigation

Finally, we detected bugs occasionally while submitting our pull request. It was found out that some of the tests on Python 2.7 were not passing on the remote code checking server. However, according to the error report, the problem was not in the game plugin but in another plugin, which was part of the project, and, subsequently, was downloaded during cloning Jarvis. After the post on the forum, one member of the core team answered that he had merged his contribution with the master branch without checking it with lower Python version. Finally, he fixed the bug himself, which allowed us to finish our pull request [8].

4   Lessons Learned

The project contribution procedure is not an easy process. Additionally, the right decision at the beginning could substantially affect the future performance of a contributor. This could be clearly seen from the evidence given in Sect. 2.

From Sects. 2.1 and 2.2 we learned several lessons. Firstly, the contribution to OSS project requires some amount of courage. One should not stand in awe of potential failures because failure always could happen even with the most experienced programmers as clearly illustrates "bug investigation" section [8]. A newbie should be worried more about not contributing. It is better to try and fail rather than stay in silence. In the end, the only important thing in OSS contribution is an experience both technical and behavioral.

Secondly, it is better to search for projects, which have a considerable amount of issues dedicated to beginners. Also, these issues should be fresh enough, not problems that are not solved for months. The issue of finding a task to start was emphasized in works of Von Krogh et al. [20], Ben et al. [2] and Capiluppi and Michlmayr [3].

Finally, communicate with core community members in advance, do not wait for an appropriate moment. Core members could be busy and answer after a significant amount of time. In cases when no answer is received, it could be a sign for a newbie to immediately withdraw from a potential project. This situation was described in the work of Jensen et al. [11], where they note that the posts of newcomers which were replied, especially within 48 h, had a positive correlation with their future project activity.

These lessons were learned by us at the time when we approached our third project selection - Jarvis [17]. Another lesson was learned from Jarvis's section: do not hesitate to offer something new. Even if one's offer is rejected, it gives him an experience, which could be used in the next attempt. Additionally, people do not like to reject, especially in the OSS community, where volunteering is encouraged. Therefore, one should propose his offer because even rejections eventually will lead to acceptance.

Furthermore, governance and community structures substantially affected the challenges we had to face. According to our own experience, the strict hierarchical structure could be beneficial for newbies due to its clear guidance offered by a project. This assertion is indirectly supported by the works of Park and Jensen [14], and Von Krogh et al. [20], where they claim that the community delegates the process of picking up the task for contribution to a newcomer [20], while the newcomer is not aware how to perform it [14]. However, on the other hand, the severe hierarchy limits the potential of a new contributor, it confines him in particular boundaries restricting from different possible ways of contribution. We encountered this phenomenon during interaction with Coala project's community [6], eventually ending with the contribution to Jarvis [17], which has fluid community structure.

Additionally, younger projects could be a better source of contribution than mature ones. The reasons are that younger projects are less complex and have more space for new ideas and creativity. At the same time, they offer a decent opportunity of finding new bugs and designing new features. Studies of Capiluppi and Michlmayr [3] support this point by stating that new members of a project "tend to work more easily on new modules than on older ones". Moreover, they claim that new developers should be encouraged to create new ideas for a project. At the same time, mature projects are more stable, therefore, have fewer bugs. They tend to enhance existing features rather than creating new ones. Mature projects could be a good option for experienced developers, while young projects are better suited for beginners.

To sum up, we faced a number of challenges connected with the lack of knowledge, hesitancy to contribute, difficulty in getting feedback from the community, convincing its members, issues connected with the code design and its readability, etc. We discussed these issues with other members of the OSS course, a large amount of them faced similar problems. From one of them, we have discovered the excellent OSS project Gatsby [12], which has a very active and friendly community. This motivated us to not give up after failures and keep trying. Therefore, the last lesson learned and which could be suggested to a new OSS contributor: share the unsuccessful experience with the community, as well as, successful. In the first case, someone could help you to overcome challenges. At the same time, your failure would prevent others to make the same mistake. While in the second case, your success could encourage other community members and it could be a source for important lessons.

Finally, the only suggestion for instructors is in organizing classroom practice sessions for the first project contribution. It would substantially enhance the overall students' experience during course connected with open-source software. At the same time, these sessions could be also beneficial for different projects which have easy-to-solve questions but lack of people who would work on them.

According to the categorization offered by Steinmacher et al. [16] the challenges described above cover 4 out of 5 barrier classes:

- Social Interaction
- Technical Hurdles
- Finding a Way to Start
- Newcomers' Previous Knowledge

This clearly indicates that the challenges described by Steinmacher et al. [16] still remain prevalent in the field of OSS. Despite the growth of open source movement, the quality of its organization stays the same, so that contributors face the same issues again and again. This leads to the idea that the organization of OSS should be enhanced in order to overcome the barriers. For example, by creating some common organizational criteria which are mandatory in order to a project be part of the OSS community, for instance, pair programming sessions as in case of Gatsby [12].

5   Conclusion

To conclude, in the paper we described our experience, as a new open source software programmer, about the entrance to the world of OSS development.

According to the evidence given above, it could be said that contributing to OSS, especially for the first time, is a tricky procedure. However, it could be clearly seen, that a successful contribution motivates the contributor to contribute more. Therefore, the first experience is very significant during the development of open source software. The experience with Jarvis motivated us to continue contributing to OSS projects in the future. We plan to enter Gatsby's community suggested by one of the members of the OSS course.

Acknowledgement. Thanks to Professor Antonio Cerone from the Department of Computer Science in Nazarbayev University for valuable discussions.

References

1. Androutsellis-Theotokis, S., Spinellis, D., Kechagia, M., Gousios, G., et al.: Open source software: a survey from 10,000 feet. Found. Trends® Technol. Inf. Oper. Manag. **4**(3–4), 187–347 (2011)
2. Ben, X., Beijun, S., Weicheng, Y.: Mining developer contribution in open source software using visualization techniques. In: 2013 Third International Conference on Intelligent System Design and Engineering Applications, pp. 934–937. IEEE (2013)
3. Capiluppi, A., Michlmayr, M.: From the Cathedral to the Bazaar: an empirical study of the lifecycle of volunteer community projects. In: Feller, J., Fitzgerald, B., Scacchi, W., Sillitti, A. (eds.) OSS 2007. ITIFIP, vol. 234, pp. 31–44. Springer, Boston, MA (2007). https://doi.org/10.1007/978-0-387-72486-7_3
4. Choudhary, A.: appi147 - overview, April 2019. https://github.com/appi147
5. Developers, T.C.: Coala github, April 2019. https://github.com/coala/coala
6. Developers, T.C.: Coala newcomers' guide, April 2019. https://api.coala.io/en/latest/Developers/Newcomers_Guide.html
7. Developers, T.C.: Coala website, April 2019. https://coala.io/
8. Issa, D.: New feature - game. https://github.com/sukeesh/Jarvis/issues/448
9. Issa, D.: New feature - image search using captions. https://github.com/sukeesh/Jarvis/issues/438
10. Issa, D.: Solution for two broken methods in movie.py. https://github.com/sukeesh/Jarvis/pull/447
11. Jensen, C., King, S., Kuechler, V.: Joining free/open source software communities: an analysis of newbies' first interactions on project mailing lists. In: 2011 44th Hawaii International Conference on System Sciences, pp. 1–10. IEEE (2011)
12. Mathews, K., Mathews, S.: gatsbyjs/gatsby, April 2019. https://github.com/gatsbyjs/gatsby
13. Moreno, M.: Open Source: A Multidisciplinary Approach, vol. 10. World Scientific, Singapore (2006)
14. Park, Y., Jensen, C.: Beyond pretty pictures: examining the benefits of code visualization for open source newcomers. In: 2009 5th IEEE International Workshop on Visualizing Software for Understanding and Analysis, pp. 3–10. IEEE (2009)
15. Schuirmann, L.: SILS - overview, April 2019. https://github.com/sils
16. Steinmacher, I., Silva, M.A.G., Gerosa, M.A., Redmiles, D.F.: A systematic literature review on the barriers faced by newcomers to open source software projects. Inf. Softw. Technol. **59**, 67–85 (2015)

17. Sukeesh: sukeesh/jarvis, April 2019. https://github.com/sukeesh/Jarvis
18. Tilkov, S., Vinoski, S.: Node.js: Using javascript to build high-performance network programs. IEEE Internet Comput. **14**(6), 80–83 (2010)
19. Vandenberg, J.: jayvdb - overview, April 2019. https://github.com/jayvdb
20. Von Krogh, G., Spaeth, S., Lakhani, K.R.: Community, joining, and specialization in open source software innovation: a case study. Res. Policy **32**(7), 1217–1241 (2003)
21. Wubben, M., Sorhus, S., Demedes, V.: Avajs/ava, April 2019. https://github.com/avajs/ava

Open Source Software as a Learning Tool for Computer Science Students

Assiya Khuzyakhmetova$^{(\boxtimes)}$ and Aidarbek Suleimenov$^{(\boxtimes)}$

Nazarbayev University, Astana, Kazakhstan
{assiya.khuzyakhmetova,aidarbek.suleimenov}@nu.edu.kz

Abstract. In this paper authors' experience of contributing to Open Source Software (OSS) is described. Contributions were done as a part of the OSS course taken at Nazarbayev University during the Spring 2019 term. Two junior bachelors degree students described their experience, motivations to contribute to OSS, selected projects, course structure and the lists of activities they performed. Assessment of this experience by other community members and the course instructor are also reported in this publication. This paper also studies how the course structure can affect people's ability to make contributions in general.

Keywords: Open source software · Student experience · Distributed development · Computer science learning

1 Introduction

This paper describes the authors' experience in contribution to Open Source Software (OSS). Although there are differences in terms of background, motivations, and expectations, both of junior bachelors degree students took OSS course in Nazarbayev University during the Spring 2019 term. The structure of the course allowed flexibility in terms of project selection and types of contributions with the only requirement of being fluent with the programming language of the project. Students were allowed to freely choose any OSS project in any language they are proficient with. Therefore, this paper tries to evaluate if freedom of choice in terms of OSS project and technology affects students' ability to contribute. One example of a similar approach took place in University of Skövde [1]. This study shows that masters students successfully made contributions to OSS projects as a part of the course. However, the question if the same approach could be applied to bachelors degree students remains open. This paper aims to investigate this issue and proof or disproof if freedom of choice in OSS course affects the outcome. This is done by evaluating two chosen students' experience in contributing to OSS projects. The individual experience of each student is described and they are referred to as Student A and Student B respectively next in this paper. Generalized conclusion of both students' work and a piece of advice for future contributors are presented in the paper.

© Springer Nature Switzerland AG 2020
E. Sekerinski et al. (Eds.): FM 2019 Workshops, LNCS 12233, pp. 224–232, 2020.
https://doi.org/10.1007/978-3-030-54997-8_15

1.1   Course Structure and Study Participants

One part of the OSS course included information about the types of communities, governance structures, licenses, and other theoretical topics about OSS. Another part included project selection, interaction with the community supporting the chosen project, work on the project, and presentations of students' contributions to the class and professor. Speaking about the flexibility of roles, students could choose between roles of OSS contributor, OSS observer, and OSS consultant, and each of the roles had their assessment criteria. Both of these students have chosen OSS contributor roles, specifically being Code Developers. Although both of them were junior Computer Science students they had different programming background that was influenced by previous experience in Competitive Programming, having different courses in university and different prior work experience. This resulted in different challenges that they faced during the course, i.e. Student A had challenges in learning new technologies, while Student B had mostly challenges related to interaction with the community.

1.2   Students' Motivations

Both of the students also had the motivation to learn new technologies and things during the period of the course through contributions to OSS. Student A wanted to learn more about Machine Learning, whereas Student B wanted to learn how to use different databases. Moreover, Student B also wanted to improve his career prospects through OSS contributions. Speaking about their intrinsic motivation, they are interested in Open Source and they wanted to feel like a part of a big team of Open Source Developers doing something useful for the society. This resulted in Student A choosing "Mozilla BugBug" project and Student B choosing "Redash" project. Descriptions of these projects will be described in this paper. Moreover, the following paper will combine their experience of contributing to these OSS projects and will describe their motivations, contributions, and challenges that they faced more closely.

2   Contributed OSS Projects Description

2.1   Mozilla BugBug

Mozilla BugBug project is a Platform for Bugzilla Machine Learning projects. Bugzilla is server software designed to help manage software development [4]. The project aims to apply Machine Learning models to Bugzilla Dataset with bugs to learn it to automatically detect such thing as types of bugs, to identify whether a bug needs quality assurance, or to automatically assign a person to the bug, etc. This project, like any other Machine Learning project, heavily relies on data collection, and for this purpose, there is a Bugzilla Data Collector project written in JavaScript as a Firefox Web Extension. Since Student A wanted to learn Machine Learning, BugBug project was chosen because of its technical aspects.

Technical Aspects of the Project. Mozilla BugBug project is written in Python and XGBoost optimized distributed gradient boosting library is used as a classifier but any other classifier can be applied. The project contains data processing pipelines that use several Mozilla APIs to feed the data to the classifier. Training is performed with the neural-network library. Simple JSON database implemented for data storage. Taskcluster with Docker is used for building and testing of the project. Dependency updates are done by PyUp bot [10]. Firefox Web Extension[3] is used primarily for data extraction. It is written in JavaScript with NodeJS framework and HTML. Collected data is saved as CSV file. Open issues that are available for contributors are under the issues tab of the projects. There are currently 104 issues in BugBug [6] and 4 in Bugzilla Data Collector [7].

General Aspects of the Project and Community. This particular project belongs to the Mozilla Foundation. While Mozilla can be considered to have Federal Leadership model, BugBug has Monarchical Leadership model since the main decisions are made by one person. The tasks allocation process is voluntary. Specifically, tasks are freely selected by participants. Issues are not assigned to any of the contributors until there is a Pull Request referring to this issue. Code owner is the same person as a Leader of the Community. The license that this project has is MPL (Mozilla Public License).

2.2   Redash Project

As today's world is becoming more and more data-driven, it is important for companies and governments to analyze data that they have and to easily extract some valuable insights from them. There are many solutions to this problem, but most of them are proprietary and expensive (like Tableau). On the contrary, Redash [11] is an open-source solution, which helps to democratize the data analysis and visualization and makes it available for all. For this reason, Student B found the project's mission quite appealing.

Technical Aspects of the Project. The project itself is a single repository on Github hosting provider [11]. Currently, the repository consists of 2 server applications: one is the API written in Python programming language with Flask framework and another one is a server dedicated to distributing code for front end application written in Angular/ReactJS. Project data is stored in the PostgreSQL database and project uses Docker image for simplifying hosting and testing. There are currently more than 300 different issues raised in the areas of the front end, back end, UI, UX, etc. 2 big improvements are being made to the project. First is complete migration from Angular to a ReactJS and second one is to redo of the permission system.

General Aspects of the Project. The leader of the project is the CEO of the company with the same name, which was established on top of the open-source software. In theory, all critical decisions regarding the project could be made by company employees. However, the number of employees is so small that governance structure can be considered as monarchical, which essentially means that all decisions are made by the CEO. Most of the big decisions are proposed by him, but anyone can make some suggestions or raise issues. Several people are the core members of the project, but not all of them work in the Redash company. Some of the core members are working at Mozilla or the biggest Russian sports website, while others still studying at university. The typical contribution path is going from looking for issues on the GitHub page, forking the project, committing changes and opening a pull request. The Open Source software is distributed under the BSD-2 license.

3 Contribution

3.1 Contributions to Mozilla BugBug Project

Project Selection Process. Motivation is a significant factor to consider when speaking about the project selection process. Student A motivation could have been divided into 4 main kinds: personal intrinsic, social intrinsic, technical extrinsic and economic extrinsic [12]. Technical extrinsic motivation had the most important impact on her choice since she wanted to gain experience in Machine Learning and improve existing skills in Python, and Mozilla BugBug project was the best candidate for this. During Spring term Student A accomplished 2 tutorials on Machine Learning and learned how to add a feature, what does labeling of data means and how accuracy can be changed from the addition of wrong features. This also made her interested in Machine Learning and she started Coursera Stanford course on Machine Learning upon completion of Spring term. She has also learned how to work with web extensions for the Firefox browser and how to collect data using them.

Role in the Selected Project. Student A has chosen a Contributor role, specifically, a Code Developer. The project can be considered active since it has many closed Pull Requests in the last month and the average response time is less than 1 day during the workweek. Also, due to the number of commits to the repository of BugBug (4 commits), on the end date of Spring term (April 14) Student A was the 7th contributor in the project out of 24.

Interaction with the Community. Student A started an interaction with the community on January 22 by adding an issue related to a bug that she found in Bugzilla Data Collector. After fixing that issue, Student A started communication with BugBug project and her contributions described in the next section (Fig. 1).

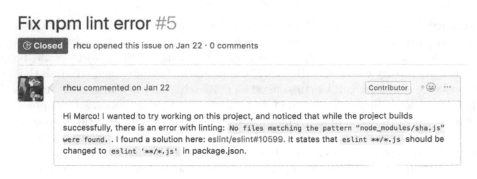

Fig. 1. Initial interaction with the community [5].

Activities and Challenges. Student A's contributions to the project could be divided into 3 parts: code commits, code reviews, and creation of issues or feature requests. Statistics on contributions in terms of issues or feature requests, code reviews, pull requests, commits and number of lines of code changed can be found in Fig. 2 below. Speaking about the challenges that were faced, it was challenging to contribute to the project that used technologies that were not used before.

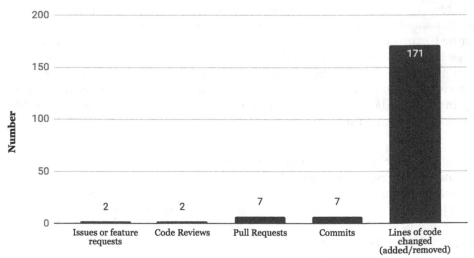

Fig. 2. Statistics on Student A activity during the Spring Term.

3.2 Contributions to Redash Project

Project Selection Process. The main motivation of Student B for choosing the project was to acquire new skills, learn new technologies and to improve his employment opportunities. On the other hand, the project should have used programming languages that he already knew, since otherwise, his contributions wouldn't be valuable enough. Therefore, there always should be a good balance between what he already knew and what he would like to learn. Firstly, Student B was looking for projects in **Go** programming language, since he wanted to learn more about it. However, he couldn't find an appropriate project with this programming language, because he was too novice in using it. That's why Student B decided to find a project in **Python** programming language with which he was more familiar. Regarding improving his employment opportunities, Student B wanted the project to be popular enough, but not too popular since it's hard to make contributions with many community members. Redash has more than 13 000 "stars" on the Github page and widely used in different organizations [11]. For that reason, Student B had chosen Redash as the selected project.

Role in the Selected Project. Student B chose the Redash project and decided to be a contributor there. More specifically, he decided to be Code Contributor. Firstly, Student B planned to look at the issues of the project from the Github page and search for the ones he can solve. The project is very popular with more than 300 issues open [8], which makes it easy enough to find different types of problems. He planned to solve as many simple issues as possible so that Student B could become more comfortable in solving harder ones.

Interaction with the Community. Student B's community interaction was done asynchronously and took place during discussions of certain issues on the Github issues page [8]. Mainly it was asking for clarifications regarding the issues. There were also some discussions in the comments to the Pull Requests page as well [9].

Activities and Challenges. During the course, Student B made 3 pull requests accepted to the main project's repository and 2 were waiting to be accepted. Moreover, he also made one contribution once the course was finished. Almost all of these were made using Python programming language and one was made using Bash. Scope of his code heavily varied: adding HTTP headers to the response, MongoDB type error fixes, Clickhouse and Presto settings configuration changes, creation of Celery tasks and Bash script writing. The main reason for choosing such a different type of tasks was to learn how to use new technologies. It was also a challenging thing to do, as each issue turned out to be related to a different technology. Apart from technologies, the scope of work also differed completely. Some issues took only a couple of hours to solve with more than a hundred lines of code, while others required to spend up to one week for them resulting

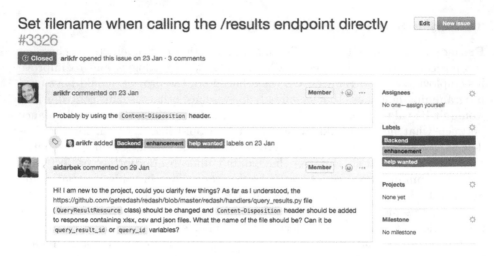

Fig. 3. Example of student B' clarifications to the issue

Fig. 4. List of student B's Pull Requests (closed and open)

only in three lines of code. The community itself was very helpful in solving different issues as well as providing feedback to solutions. As a result of Student B's interaction and contributions, he was invited to become maintainer in the Redash community. The role of the maintainer is rather symbolic but has some additional privileges like labeling certain issues, assigning people to review and accepting other Pull Requests. Apart from Redash, Student B also contributed to Beats [2] project after the course finished. The project and contributions were written in **Go** programming language, which he was eager to learn at the beginning of the course. His experience with the Redash project helped to increase confidence and try more challenging tasks and also learn a new language (Figs. 3 and 4).

4   Conclusion and Future Work

4.1   Students' Conclusion

Contribution to Open Source projects can be considered as a powerful learning tool for students that allows to learn and practice technical skills [13]. Both students indicated that the experience of contributing to Open Source Software was very helpful for the professional development and helped to understand how big projects are done, how to interact with OSS communities, create contributions and overcome technical obstacles. Both students were happy with the choice of projects they made and the results of the work done during the course. As was noted by Student B, the things that were learned during contribution, according to his experience, then were easily transferred when contributing to completely different OSS projects. Speaking about differences in experiences, there were delays in communication with the community from the side of Student B, while it was not the case at Student A. The reason for that is that Mozilla's community has instant messaging communication IRC channel IRC in Mozilla IRC Cloud in contrast to Redash, where communication was mostly done on GitHub. For that reason, Student B needed to ask for a response of community core members several times. The possible reason for this is the high volume of work taken by the main creator of the Student B's project. This created some inconveniences that are usually absent at the regular software engineering job.

As for advice from both students to newbie contributors, it is significant to find a middle between the desire to learn new technologies relevant to the project and being able to be useful in the project with your current knowledge. This could prevent many difficulties in contributing to Open Source Software. One more thing is not to be afraid of asking questions and making mistakes. Usually, a contributor can simply ask for help in the comments under issues or Pull Requests and to get help in a short period.

4.2   Study Conclusion

Introduction of the course of Open Source Software to the curriculum of universities and colleges could benefit many students in both short-term and long-term perspectives boosting their CVs, technical and social skills. Furthermore, the freedom of choice in terms of projects to contribute and technologies to use has proven to result in successful OSS contributions, which supports current studies [1]. The success of contributions is assessed by OSS communities' members as each piece of code passed a rigorous assessment by several people. Speaking about assessment from the course side, both students received the highest possible mark by the course instructor.

4.3   Future Work

The future work in this research could include analysis of the experience of a higher number of students in OSS. Moreover, feedback and survey of the core members of the OSS community could be included.

References

1. Lundell, B., Persson, A., Lings, B.: Learning through practical involvement in the OSS ecosystem: experiences from a masters assignment. In: Feller, J., Fitzgerald, B., Scacchi, W., Sillitti, A. (eds.) OSS 2007. ITIFIP, vol. 234, pp. 289–294. Springer, Boston, MA (2007). https://doi.org/10.1007/978-0-387-72486-7_30
2. Beats Repository. https://github.com/elastic/beats
3. Bugzilla Data Collector Repository. https://github.com/marco-c/bugzilla-data-collector
4. Bugzilla Official Site. https://www.bugzilla.org/
5. GitHub Issue 5 in Bugzilla Data Collector. https://github.com/marco-c/bugzilla-data-collector/issues/5. Accessed 6 July 2019
6. List of Issues in BugBug project. https://github.com/mozilla/bugbug/issues. Accessed 6 July 2019
7. List of Issues in Bugzilla Data Collector project. https://github.com/marco-c/bugzilla-data-collector/issues. Accessed 7 July 2019
8. List of Issues in Redash project. https://github.com/getredash/redash/issues. Accessed 7 July 2019
9. List of Pull Requests in Redash project. https://github.com/getredash/redash/pulls. Accessed 7 July 2019
10. PyUp Bot Repository. https://github.com/pyup-bot
11. Redash Repository. https://github.com/getredash/redash
12. Androutsellis-Theotokis, S., Spinellis, D., Kechagia, M., Gousios, G.: Open Source Software: A Survey from 10,000 Feet (2010)
13. Kuk, G.: Strategic Interaction and Knowledge Sharing in the KDE Developer Mailing List (2006). https://doi.org/10.1287/mnsc.1060.0551

Overture 2019 - 17th Overture Workshop

Overture 2019 Organizers' Message

The 17th Overture Workshop was held on 07 October 2019 in association with the 3rd World Congress on Formal Methods (FM2019).

The 17th Overture Workshop was the latest in a series of workshops around the Vienna Development Method (VDM), the open-source project Overture, and related tools and formalisms. VDM is one of the best established formal methods for systems development. A lively community of researchers and practitioners in academia and industry has grown around the modelling languages (VDM-SL, VDM++, VDM-RT, CML) and tools (VDMTools, Overture, Crescendo, Symphony, and the INTO-CPS chain). Together, these provide a platform for work on modelling and analysis technology that includes static and dynamic analysis, test generation, execution support, and model checking.

The workshop received 8 submissions. Every submission was reviewed by 3 members of the program committee. Of these 8 submissions, 6 were accepted and presented at the workshop. The workshop also featured a keynote presentation by Ana Paiva, entitled *Teaching VDM*.

Of the 6 papers presented at the workshop, 4 have been revised and included in these post-proceedings. Each revised paper was reviewed by two members of the program committee.

The accepted papers reflect the diversity of the Overture community and the flexibility of the VDM family of languages. This year those submissions demonstrate both the use of VDM for the formal analysis of specifications and configurations of simulations, through to the use of VDM to model human behaviour and the development of a simulation environment that supports the co-simulation of VDM alongside other formalisms.

December 2019

Luís Diogo Couto
Carl Camble

Organization

Program Committee Chairs

Luís Diogo Couto   Forcepoint, Ireland
Carl Gamble   Newcastle University, UK

Program Committee

Nick Battle   Newcastle University, UK
Leo Freitas   Newcastle University, UK

John Fitzgerald	Newcastle University, UK
Fuyuki. Ishikawa	NII, Japan
Peter Gorm Larsen	Aarhus University, Denmark
Paolo Masci	National Institute of Aerospace (NIA), USA
Ken Pierce	Newcastle University, UK
Peter W. V. Tran-Jørgensen	Aarhus University, Denmark

Exploring Human Behaviour in Cyber-Physical Systems with Multi-modelling and Co-simulation

Ken Pierce[1]([✉]), Carl Gamble[1], David Golightly[2], and Roberto Palacín[2]

[1] School of Computing, Newcastle University, Newcastle upon Tyne, UK
{kenneth.pierce,carl.gamble}@newcastle.ac.uk
[2] School of Engineering, Newcastle University, Newcastle upon Tyne, UK
{david.golightly,roberto.palacin}@newcastle.ac.uk

Abstract. Definitions of cyber-physical systems often include humans within the system boundary, however design techniques often focus on the technical aspects and ignore this important part of the system. Multi-modelling and co-simulation offer a way to bring together models from different disciplines to capture better the behaviours of the overall system. In this paper we present some initial results of incorporating ergonomic models of human behaviours within a cyber-physical multi-model. We present three case studies, from the autonomous aircraft and railway sectors, including initial experiments, and discuss future directions.

Keywords: Cyber-physical systems · Ergonomics · Human behaviour · Multi-modelling

1 Introduction

Cyber-Physical Systems (CPSs) are systems constructed of interacting hardware and software elements, with components networked together and distributed geographically [25]. Importantly, humans are a key component of CPS design, for example, Rajkumar et al. call for "systematic analysis of the interactions between engineering structures, information processing, humans and the physical world" [36, p.734]. Humans may act as operators, acting with or in addition to software controllers; or as users, interpreting data from or actions of the CPS.

Model-based design techniques offer opportunities to achieve this systematic analysis. When considering the diverse nature of disciplines however, and therefore diverse modelling techniques and even vocabulary, creating models that sufficiently capture all aspects of a CPS presents a challenge. Multi-modelling techniques present one solution, where models from appropriate disciplines are combined into a multi-model and are analysed, for example, through co-simulation [16,21]. Multi-modelling has demonstrated its utility in a range of scenarios (for example, building automation [9], smart agriculture [12] and manufacturing [30]).

An open challenge in CPS design is how to accurately reflect human capabilities and behaviours. Without considering such an important part of a CPS, observed performance in an operation context may differ from that predicted by models [10,17].

© Springer Nature Switzerland AG 2020
E. Sekerinski et al. (Eds.): FM 2019 Workshops, LNCS 12233, pp. 237–253, 2020.
https://doi.org/10.1007/978-3-030-54997-8_16

For example, train systems not achieving optimal performance due to drivers not following eco-driving advice [35], or optimal performance requiring unrealistic demands on operators (e.g. challenging peaks or reduced wellbeing) [28].

There is a body of work in modelling human behaviours within the field of ergonomics—the study of people's efficiency in their working environment—which is discussed in Sect. 2. Multi-modelling would seem to offer an ideal way for these existing models to be incorporated into system-level models of CPSs. This paper reports on three initial studies where ergonomics models were incorporated into multi-models with cyber and physical components. The first looks at operator loading in drone inspection of infrastructure, and the second at the effect of driving style on energy use within an urban rail system. The third extends the urban rail model by importing the UAV operator model and using that as a signaller model. The studies focus on the use of VDM and Overture as a vehicle for initial experimentation, with references provided to papers on the ergonomic implications published within that domain.

In the remainder of the paper, Sect. 2 presents technical background on multi-modelling and brief survey of ergonomic modelling techniques, including related work describing their limited use in multi-modelling scenarios. Sections 3, 4 and 5 describe three case studies in which ergonomic models were employed within a multi-modelling context, including simulation results. Finally, Sect. 6 concludes the paper and describes avenues for future work in this area.

2   Background

This section provides background material necessary to understand the case studies presented in the later sections. It begins by describing the technologies used: the INTO-CPS technologies for multi-modelling, based on FMI (the Functional Mock-up Interface); VDM-RT for discrete-event modelling using the Overture tool; and the 20-sim for modelling physical phenomena. It then outlines a range of models from the ergonomics domain that could help in analysis of CPSs, and highlights some related work where ergonomic models have been used within a multi-modelling context.

2.1   Multi-modelling Technologies

The FMI standard is an emerging standard for co-simulation of multi-models, where individual models are packaged as Functional Mockup Units (FMUs). FMI defines an open standard that any tool can implement, and currently more than 30 tools can produce FMUs, with the number expected to surpass 100 soon, taking into account partial or upcoming support[1]. INTO-CPS is a tool chain based on FMI for the modelling and analysis of CPSs [21]. At the core of the tool chain is Maestro [38], an open-source and fully FMI-compliant co-simulation engine supporting variable- and fixed-step size Master algorithms across multiple platforms. Maestro includes advanced features for simulation stabilisation and hardware-in-the-loop simulation. INTO-CPS also provides a graphical front end for defining and executing co-simulations.

---

[1] http://fmi-standard.org/tools/.

The Vienna Development Method (VDM) [22] is a family of formal languages based on the original VDM-SL language for systematic analysis of system specifications. The VDM-RT language allows for the specification of real-time and distributed controllers [39], including an internal computational time model. VDM-RT is an extension of the VDM++ object-oriented dialect of the family, which itself extends the base VDM-SL language. VDM is a state-based discrete-event (DE) language, suited to modelling system components where the key abstractions are state, and modifications of that state through events or decisions. Overture[2] is an open-source tool for the definition and analysis of VDM models, which supports FMU export of VDM-RT models.

The 20-sim tool[3] supports modelling and simulation of physical formula based on differential equations. 20-sim can represent phenomena from the mechanical, electrical and even hydraulic domains, using graphs of connected blocks. Blocks may contain further graphs, code or differential equations. The connections represent channels by which phenomena interact; these may represent signals (one-way) or bonds (two-way). Bonds offer a powerful, compositional and domain-independent way to model physical phenomena, as they carry both effort and flow, which map to pairs of familiar physical concepts, e.g. voltage and current. 20-sim is a continuous-time (CT) tool which solves differential equations numerically to produce high-fidelity simulations of physical components.

2.2 Ergonomics Modelling

There are a variety of modelling techniques which attempt to predict human behaviour and performance that could be used to enhance the analysis of CPS designs through inclusion in multi-models. The examples presented below highlight the potential of this area and are not intended to be an exhaustive list.

Some models suggest algebraic relationships from which predictions can be made. For example, Fitts' Law predicts that the time taken for a human to reach a target is a ratio of the distance to and size of the target [27], while models of response time processing can predict the impact of operator delay on a real-time system [37]. Models of operator attention can predict choice of tasks and likelihood of completion [41], while combinations of workload, fatigue and task complexity can make predictions for optimum configurations of control [19].

The Yerkes-Dodson arousal model suggests that poorer performance occurs as both the lowest and highest levels of demand [6], implying that humans can be both underloaded (potentially leading to distraction effects and vigilance decrements) and overloaded (where high workload either slows action due to multi-tasking or impedes decision making). This model has been applied to performance under varying levels of demand [6] and predicts an inverted U-shaped curve of performance, with poorer performance at both lower and upper bounds of demand. Empirical evidence suggests these bounds to be around 30% and 70% of occupancy [7,32].

A range of bespoke modelling tools incorporate these types of models computationally. These include discrete-event simulation of train operator availability under given

---

[2] http://overturetool.org/.
[3] http://www.20sim.com/.

schedules [32], Monte Carlo simulations of human behaviour in Microsaint [23], and cognitive architectures such as ACT-R [2] and Soar [31] that include cognition, perception and movement performance models. Tools such as Jack [4] can also analyse complex physical models of individual human performance, while Legion supports agent-based modelling of groups of individuals in social situations such as evacuations [34].

There are limited examples of ergonomics within multi-modelling, despite the promise of bringing together work in the CPS and human factors domains. Examples include making models of human thermal comfort [1,29] and user interactions [8] FMI compliant, and integrating agent-based models with building energy models using FMI [5,26]. Other examples of FMI use in ergonomic studies primarily focus on bringing the human into the loop to study nuclear reactors [40], urban mobility [3], medical devices [33], and demands on telecommunications networks [24].

While performance modelling is a mature field, a significant gap remains between the CPS and ergonomics domains. These applications suggest a clear opportunity to improve CPS design by bringing ergonomics modelling into the CPS domain. The next sections provide three case studies which show the potential of multi-modelling as one way to achieve this.

3   Case Study 1: Operator Loading in Drone Searching

The first case study incorporating ergonomic models within a multi-model is in the area of Unmanned Aerial Vehicle (UAV) control. The low price and capabilities of multi-rotor UAVs make them an enticing option for inspection and searching tasks [20]. UAVs fitted with high-resolution cameras are routinely used for visual inspection of infrastructure such as railway lines [11], where physically sending inspection workers carries risk of injury and fatality.

While we can envision highly-autonomous UAV systems using software flight control and image recognition to perform inspections, the current state of practice includes humans in the loop, in particular to intervene and inspect images of assets as they are relayed from UAVs. This human element means that there is an effect on system performance based on the relationship between tasks and operator availability. An existing multi-model of UAV searching [42] was enhanced with a model of operator availability to demonstrate the potential of understanding human performance within CPS design[4].

3.1   Scenario

The baseline multi-model [42] had UAVs systematically searching a wide area in a zigzag pattern, able to travel at approximately six metres per second. In this new scenario, four UAVs are tasked with visiting waypoints along a railway line, setting off from a central launch site, to perform a visual inspection by relaying images back to an operator. Each UAV has three distinct waypoints to visit with maximum distance of 1500 m and mission time of approximately six minutes, as shown in Fig. 1.

---

[4] See also Golightly et al. [13] which is aimed at an ergonomics audience.

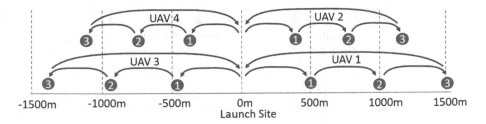

Fig. 1. Waypoints visited by each of the four UAVs

At each waypoint, the UAV must wait until the inspector has checked the image before moving to the next waypoint. The model represents human performance in three ways:

Task activity The operator must realise that UAV requires attention (duration = T_{SA}), check the images (duration = T_{dec}), and interact with the UAV (duration = T_{int}). The total time (duration = T) suggested by ergonomics models is 28 s [13].

Operator occupancy The operator is not available to attend a UAV while occupied with another. Given the operator's capacity, a rolling window of operator occupancy was calculated over the previous 100 simulated seconds.

Task switching The operator must decide which of the waiting UAVs to attend. This was achieved by always attending to the UAV that has been waiting longest.

Dynamic performance In addition to the above (static) calculations, a real-time model allows for feedback to affect the performance model based on the evolving conditions in the simulation. In this case, the Yerkes-Dodson-like underload/overload model was used, with time penalties (increase in T_{SA}) added for an underloaded operator losing track of UAV status (under 30%), and an overloaded worker dealing with high task demands (above 70%).

There are three scenarios presented in the results section: the baseline static scenario including task activity, occupancy, and task switching); a dynamic scenario including dynamic performance; and a dynamic scenario including wind in the physical model, representing external perturbations of the system by the environment.

3.2 Multi-model

The multi-model comprises three FMUs, as shown in Fig. 2. The **UAV** is realised as a continuous-time model in 20-sim. It contains a model of a quadcopter, which accepts inputs to control flight in three dimensions (throttle, pitch, roll, and yaw) and reports its position. An optional 3D visualisation FMU is not shown, which connects to these outputs to show the UAVs in a 3D environment. The **Controller** is realised as a VDM model. It contains both a low-level loop controller, which moves the UAV within 3D space, and a high-level waypoint controller, which visits a sequence of waypoints using the loop controller. A single **UAV** instance is paired with a single **Controller** instance, and these pairs are replicated to realise multiple UAVs. This part of the multi-model is an updated version after Zervakis et al. [42].

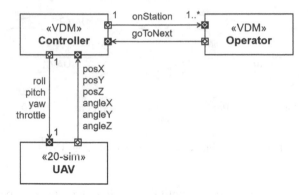

Fig. 2. The FMUs in the UAV control multi-model and their relationships

To this baseline model, an **Operator** model was added to consider human performance element of the inspection system. Again, VDM was used as this is the most appropriate modelling language from which FMUs can be readily produced. The **Operator** is aware of each **Controller** instance and receives a signal when the UAV is "on station" (read for the image to be inspected). Once the inspection is complete, a return signal is sent to allow the UAV to continue to the next waypoint. The **Operator** encodes the Yerkes-Dodson-like model of occupancy described above by selecting a waiting UAV, then simulating processing of the data by occupying time before releasing the UAV to the next waypoint. When dynamic performance is switched on, the baseline time to process input is increased if the workload is below the underload threshold (under 70%) or above the overloaded threshold (over 70%) as seen in the listing for the `updateErgonomicTimings()` operation:

```
updateErgonomicTimings() == (
  if inspector_workload < work_load_n_curve_lower then (
    sa_time := sa_time_normal + workload_uload_sa_modifier;
  ) else (
    sa_time := sa_time_normal;
  );

  if inspector_workload > work_load_n_curve_upper then (
    d_time := d_time_normal + workload_oload_sa_modifier;
  ) else (
    d_time := d_time_normal;
  )
)
```

3.3 Results

Figure 3 shows output from the three scenarios for two metrics. The scenarios are as described above: static occupancy calculation without wind (blue, dot-dashed line),

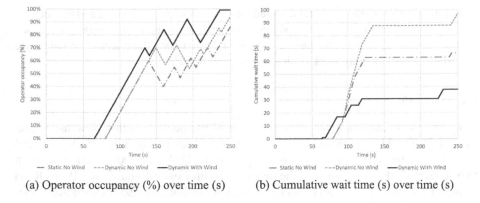

(a) Operator occupancy (%) over time (s)   (b) Cumulative wait time (s) over time (s)

Fig. 3. Operator occupancy and cumulative UAV waiting time during three scenarios (Colour figure online)

dynamic occupancy calculation without wind (orange, dashed line), and finally dynamic occupancy calculation with wind (black, solid line). The first graph, Fig. 3a, shows operator occupancy as a percentage during the three scenarios. The peaks and troughs show the operator receiving and clearing inspection tasks. It can be seen that the more realistic dynamic occupancy model indicates that the operator is close to saturation by the end of the simulation. When wind is included, the altered arrival times happen to push the operator to saturation, indicating a likely reduction in wellbeing and performance.

The second graph, Fig. 3b, shows the cumulative wait time of the UAVs during the simulation. This is clearly a monotonically increasing value, so it is the rate of accumulation that is indicative of system performance. Again, it can be seen that the more-realistic dynamic occupancy model shows a significantly increased wait time for the UAVs, which will impact on battery life and performance. Interestingly, when wind is introduced, the cumulative wait time is significantly reduced, indicating a more favourable arrival time due to some UAVs getting a speed boost with a tailwind, while others are slowed down with a headwind. Although this indicates a favourable scenario for battery performance, it is clear that operator wellbeing is impacted. This shows the potential of multi-models to reveal hidden interactions between human, cyber and physical aspects of CPSs which otherwise might not be discovered until deployment.

4   Case Study 2: Driver Behaviour in Urban Rail

The second case study demonstrating inclusion of ergonomics models within multi-models is in the area of de-carbonisation in urban rail. De-carbonisation can be achieved principally through reducing overall energy usage, and reducing energy wastage through recovering energy from braking. While some urban rail lines are autonomous, most are still driven by human operators. Driving style has a significant effect on energy usage [35], because electrical current has a squared relationship to power, therefore accelerating and braking aggressively uses more energy. Drivers who follow defensive techniques—accelerating and braking gradually—should use less power and reduce carbon footprint, though this driving style must be traded-off against potentially increased journey times. A multi-model was developed to demonstrate the effect of driving style and more efficient rolling stock (trains) on energy usage[5].

4.1 Scenario

This study was based upon the Tyne and Wear Metro network within Newcastle upon Tyne, UK. The Metro cars weigh 40 metric tons and are powered by 1.5 kV overhead lines throughout. The chosen scenario, illustrated in Fig. 4 is an 800 m section between two stations on the busiest part of the network, South Gosforth station and Ilford Road station. Peak throughput is 30 trains per hour. This section has also been studied previously [35], which provides baseline data to validate the co-simulation against.

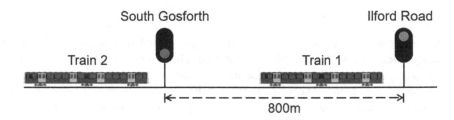

Fig. 4. The trains, stations and signals in the train control scenario (Colour figure online)

Each station is within a track section, and each section must only contain a single train at any one time. A "movement authority" controls access to each section using stop-go (two-aspect) signals. Drivers must stop when the signal is red, and may go when the signal is green. The movement authority changes the signals when trains enter and leave sections.

In the simulated scenario, there are two trains. One train begins at Ilford Road station (Train 1), and the other at South Gosforth station (Train 2). Train 2 cannot leave South Gosforth until Train 1 departs from Ilford Road, therefore the signal for Train 2 is red. The signal for Train 1 is green, so it may leave as soon as the simulation begins. Once it has left, the signal for Train 2 goes green, so it may accelerate to leave its station, drive, then brake to stop at the next station. This gives a full accelerate, drive and brake cycle to study driver behaviour.

There are two types of drivers: aggressive drivers who use full throttle and full brake, and defensive drivers who use half throttle and half brake. There are also two types of rolling stock, the baseline Metro cars as they exist today, and a hypothetical lighter rolling stock with 30% energy recovery from regenerative braking. This gives four scenarios: aggressive drivers with existing rolling stock, aggressive drivers with lightweight rolling stock, defensive drivers with existing rolling stock, and defensive drivers with lightweight rolling stock.

---

[5] See also Golightly et al. [14] which is aimed at an urban rail audience.

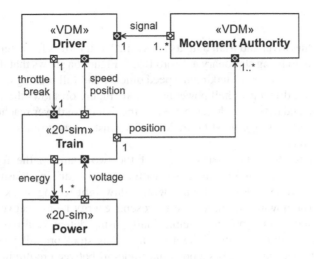

Fig. 5. The FMUs in the train control multi-model and their relationships

4.2 Multi-model

The multi-model comprises four FMUs, as shown in Fig. 5. The **Train** is realised as a continuous-time model in 20-sim. It accepts a throttle and brake signal and computes the position, speed and energy usage of the train. Two different FMUs were produced for the baseline and lightweight rolling stock, which were swapped between scenarios. A **Power** model was also realised in 20-sim, which provides a voltage to each train and receives back the energy consumed, calculating the overall power usage of the scenario. In this experiment the model is ideal and does not include voltage drop or line losses.

The **Movement Authority** is informed of the positions of all trains and updates the state of the stop-go signals as trains enter and leave track sections. These enter and leave events mean that VDM was the most appropriate modelling language for this component. Each Train instance is paired with a **Driver** instance, which observes the speed and position of their train and the state of the next signal ahead on the track. The throttle and brake in Metro cars are notched, and can only take three values (off, half, and full), therefore VDM is again an appropriate choice. The aggressive and defensive styles of driving are given as a parameter to the Driver model, with the listing below showing what happens when throttle() operation is applied:

```
private throttle: () ==> ()
throttle() == (
    if mode = <AGGRESSIVE> then (
        throttleActuator.setValue(AGGRESSIVE_THROTTLE);
    ) elseif mode = <DEFENSIVE> then (
        throttleActuator.setValue(DEFENSIVE_THROTTLE);
    );
    brakeActuator.setValue(0)
)
```

4.3   Results

Figure 6 shows the driver and train outputs for Train 2 as it moves from being stationary at South Gosforth to being stationary at Ilford Road. Figure 6a shows that the aggressive driver uses full power to reach maximum speed quickly and full braking to stop quickly, while the defensive driver uses half power and brake. Figure 6b shows the speed profiles of the aggressive and defensive driver. Note that the defensive driver reaches the station later, so lower energy usage must be traded-off against journey times and timetables updated accordingly.

Figure 7 shows the total energy usage of the two trains in the four scenarios described above. The existing rolling stock with aggressive driving (dashed line) uses the most energy, while defensive driving with lightweight rolling stock (dotted line) uses the least. The downward curve here represents energy being recovered from the brakes and returning to the power system. Finally, using defensive driving with existing rolling stock or simply acquiring lightweight rolling stock provide a similar reduction in energy usage. This suggests a potential trade-off between retraining drivers and enforcing defensive driving versus investing in new stock and accepting current driver performance.

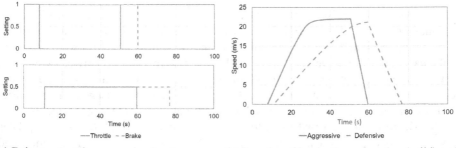

(a) Driver output for aggressive (top) and defensive (bottom) driving

(b) Speed profiles for for aggressive (solid) and defensive (dashed) driving

Fig. 6. Driver outputs and corresponding speed profiles for aggressive and defensive driving

5   Case Study 3: Signaller Modelling Within Urban Rail

The third case study extends the urban metro model to include a human signaller. The signaller (also known as a dispatcher or controller) is the operator who controls the signals that provide movement authority to trains. Historically, this involved manual input on the part of the signaller to set signals and points. Increasingly, this has moved to a monitoring role where signals are set automatically, while the human signaller oversees the process and intervenes where appropriate. Signallers may still need to control signals directly in the event of disruption or system failures.

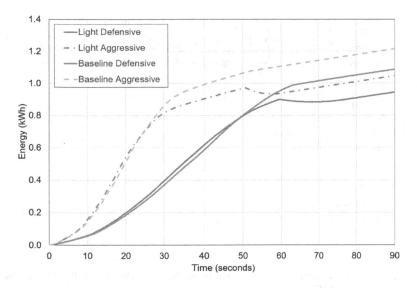

Fig. 7. Total energy usage for combinations of driving style and rolling stock

Like the hypothetical UAV controller in Case Study 1, signallers maintain situation awareness of overall system state, and the state of specific vehicles (trains rather than UAVs) [15]. Signallers act to monitor and potentially set signals. Also, the signaller task is one where workload can be a critical concern: as underload in highly automated, low-traffic situations; as high workload in very high demand, high-traffic situations; and in times of disruption and significant deviation from the timetable.

This workload model may potentially follow the 30%/70% relationship seen in UAV control [18]. Drawing on the capabilities of FMI, the Operator FMU from Case Study 1 can be plugged into the MovementAuthority FMU in the urban control multi-model of Case Study 2. This is a first-pass proof of concept about the flexibility of FMI allowing deployment of ergonomics models to a variety of different domains.

5.1 Scenario

The scenario is essentially the same as the scenario in Case Study 2, with two trains moving through the South Gosforth to Ilford Road section of the Tyne and Wear Metro. The scenario is adapted to accommodate a model of a human signaller, where part of the signalling system is under manual control. Green signals are set to red automatically by an interlock, but the human signaller needed to change red signals to green. Specifically, the signaller needs to set the red signal in front of Train 2 at South Gosforth to green once Train 1 has passed Ilford Road station and reached the next section of track.

5.2 Multi-model

Figure 8 shows the updated multi-model for the train control multi-modeller. The Movement Authority FMU was updated to send a request to a **Signaller** FMU for

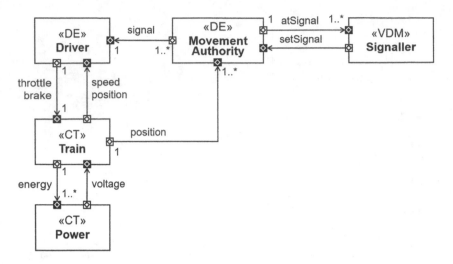

Fig. 8. The FMUs in the train control multi-model with an additional signaller FMU, which is based on the operator FMU from the UAV case study

a signal could be turned green (once the track section was clear). This model then processes the request and informs the movement authority to change the signal to green. Changing of green signals to red once a train passes still occurs automatically, representing a hardware interlock.

The Signaller FMU is essentially the Operator FMU taken from Case Study 1. The timing parameters of the signaller model were altered to reflect the simpler task of setting a signal. The time attending to a new request, T_{SA}, deciding what to do, T_{dec}, and interacting to perform the task, T_{int}, were all set to two seconds. This gives an overall time of six seconds. In addition to updating the timings, the input and output ports were renamed, and an override was included to set the initial workload of the signaller model to a preset level. Apart from these small updates, the two FMUs are materially the same. This suggests the potential to produce a generic, customisable FMU to encode processing of tasks by humans in a range of CPSs.

It was necessary to include an initial workload parameter in order to observe that signaller overload could cause delays in the system, because the scenario only includes a single task for the signaller to process which is insufficient to cause overload unless the signaller is already highly loaded. It should be borne in mind that whereas the Operator FMU in the UAV system is monitoring the whole system, the track section covered in the metro simulation is only a small part of the overall system. The Tyne and Wear Metro system contains 60 stations over 78 km, including significantly more track sections and signals, so a simulation that incorporated more of the Metro operator's area of control could easily demonstrate realistic instances of signaller overload effects.

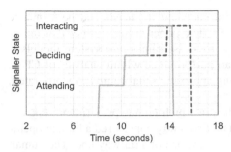
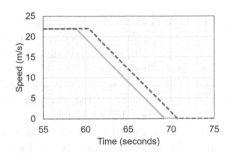

(a) Processing time for moderate occupancy (solid) and high occupancy (dotted) signaller

(b) Train arrival time for moderate occupancy (solid) and high occupancy (dotted) signaller

Fig. 9. Signaller processing and train arrival times for an signaller at 50% capacity and a signaller at 85% capacity. The signaller experiencing high task occupancy and workload shows increased decision time. (Colour figure online)

5.3 Results

Figure 9 shows outputs from two co-simulations. In order to explore effects under different conditions, the first co-simulation was run with the signaller at an initial occupancy of 50% (representing a moderate workload), while the second co-simulation was run with an initial occupancy of 85% (representing a very high workload), a situation that might be experienced during disruption. Figure 9a shows the state of the signaller model near the beginning of the co-simulation. In both scenarios, Train 1 passes the green signal at eight seconds. The interlock changes this signal to red and a request is sent to the signaller to change the signal in front of Train 2 to green.

The scenarios are shown for both moderate load (solid green line) and high load (dotted red line), with the request being received at 8 s. The height of the line indicates when the operator is attending to (T_{SA}), deciding on (T_{dec}), or interacting with (T_{int}) a request. The dotted red line shows the increased decision time in the second scenario due to the operator being over the 75% workload threshold. This delays the changing of the signal by two seconds. Figure 9b shows the speed of Train 2 later in the co-simulation as it arrives at Ilford Road and comes to a halt. Train 2 arrives two seconds late at the station in the overloaded signaller simulation due to the corresponding delay of the change of signal.

The overall goal of such a study would be to assess the effect of signaller overload on system-wide performance. Although the delay observed in this single scenario is small, scaled up to multiple trains over a network of 60 stations over 78 km, the knock-on effects can be significant. In addition, this current demonstration does not account for drivers becoming frustrated at being held at signals, which might cause aggressive driving in previously defensive drivers.

6   Conclusions and Future Work

This paper argued that CPSs necessarily include humans within the system boundary, as operators or users of parts of the system. Until such time as we achieve full autonomy within these systems, it is necessary to take into account the needs and performance characteristics of humans when designing CPSs. The paper argues further that multi-modelling—combining domain models from across disciplines into system models—offers a promising avenue for exploring human performance within analysis of CPSs, supported by a brief survey of existing modelling approaches that could be incorporated, and promising related work in a similar vein.

The paper then described three initial studies in which human performance characteristics were included within multi-models. The first study considered a human operator responding to data from UAVs performing inspections of a railway line. The human performance aspects included the time taken for operators to process images and switch tasks, and included performance penalties for underloading and overloading. The second study considered the effect of driver behaviour on energy usage in an urban rail system. The human performance aspects here considered aggressive drivers using maximum throttle and brake versus defensive drivers using half throttle and break. In both case studies, inclusion of human performance in the multi-model enabled trade-offs between human aspects (e.g. workload, wellbeing) and physical aspects (e.g. energy usage, system performance). The third study combined the first two by incorporating the human operator FMU from the UAV case study as signaller within the urban rail system. This demonstrated the flexibility of FMI to combine existing models within new scenarios, and suggests the possibility to create a generic human performance model as an FMU that could be incorporated into a wide variety of CPS and other multi-models.

Not only has the inclusion of ergonomic models shown potential for increasing the validity of the CPS multi-models, this process has benefits for the ergonomist by forcing a clearer definition of terms and values. For example, in the UAV operator model, occupancy is a function of task load over a time period. Implementing this performance characteristic into the model forces the ergonomist to reflect on considerations such as whether the impact of occupancy is linear or more complex, and what the preceding time period over which an experience of occupancy occurs or dissipates is. There are therefore not only benefits for CPS engineers of the inclusion of ergonomics in multi-models, but there are also benefits for the ergonomist.

In terms of concrete next steps, all three studies can be expanded to validate the results against observed data from experiments and improve the human performance models to incorporate state-of-the-art ergonomics models. All human models were built using VDM-RT and generated as FMUs using Overture, based on appropriate performance calculations from ergonomics literature. While this was an appropriate choice for experimentation, a clear avenue for future work is to add FMI functionality to specific ergonomics modelling tools. Alternatively, dedicated FMUs could be produced to allow others to incorporate human performance factors without being ergonomics experts.

Applying the techniques to other domains should also yield interesting insights. We envision incorporating physiological models (such as Jack) to multi-models of smart manufacturing [30] to account for physical effort and movement time while interacting with an assembly line, for example. Finally, incorporating human-in-the-loop simulation, potentially using virtual reality, will allow us to refine the parameters used in the multi-models and potentially serve as training tools for operators.

Acknowledgements. The work reported here is supported in part by the Rail Safety and Standard Board (RSSB) project "Digital Environment for Collaborative Intelligent De-carbonisation" (DECIDe, reference number COF-IPS-06). The authors wish to thank the anonymous reviewers of both the workshop and extended version of this paper for their efforts.

References

1. Alfredson, J., Johansson, B., Gonzaga Trabasso, L., Schminder, J., Granlund, R., Gårdhagen, R.: Design of a distributed human factors laboratory for future airsystems. In: Proceedings of the ICAS Congress. International Council of the Aeronautical Sciences (2018)
2. Anderson, J., Bothell, D., Byrne, M., Douglass, S., Lebiere, C., Qin, Y.: An integrated theory of the mind. Psychol. Rev. **111**(4), 1036–1060 (2004)
3. Beckmann-Dobrev, B., Kind, S., Stark, R.: Hybrid simulators for product service-systems: innovation potential demonstrated on urban bike mobility. Procedia CIRP **36**, 78–82 (2015). 25th CIRP Design Conference on Innovative Product Creation
4. Blanchonette, P.: Jack human modelling tool: a review. Technical report DSTO-TR-2364, Defence Science and Technology Organisation (Australia) Air Operations Division (2010)
5. Chapman, J., Siebers, P.O., Robinson, D.: On the multi-agent stochastic simulation of occupants in buildings. J. Build. Perform. Simul. **11**(5), 604–621 (2018)
6. Cummings, M., Nehme, E.C.: Modeling the impact of workload in network centric supervisory control settings. In: Steinberg, R., Kornguth, S., Matthews, M.D. (eds.) Neurocognitive and Physiological Factors During High-Tempo Operations, chap. 3, pp. 23–40. Taylor & Francis, Abingdon (2010)
7. Cummings, M., Guerlain, S.: Developing operator capacity estimates for supervisory control of autonomous vehicles. Hum. Factors **49**(1), 1–15 (2007)
8. Filippi, S., Barattin, D.: In-depth analysis of non-deterministic aspects of human-machine interaction and update of dedicated functional mock-ups. In: Marcus, A. (ed.) DUXU 2014. LNCS, vol. 8517, pp. 185–196. Springer, Cham (2014). https://doi.org/10.1007/978-3-319-07668-3_19
9. Fitzgerald, J., Gamble, C., Payne, R., Larsen, P.G., Basagiannis, S., Mady, A.E.D.: Collaborative Model-based Systems Engineering for Cyber-Physical Systems - a Case Study in Building Automation. In: Proceedings of INCOSE International Symposium on Systems Engineering. Edinburgh, Scotland (July 2016)
10. Flach, J.M.: Complexity: learning to muddle through. Cogn. Technol. Work **14**(3), 187–197 (2012)
11. Flammini, F., Pragliola, C., Smarra, G.: Railway infrastructure monitoring by drones. In: 2016 International Conference on Electrical Systems for Aircraft, Railway, Ship Propulsion and Road Vehicles International Transportation Electrification Conference (ESARS-ITEC), pp. 1–6 (2016)
12. Foldager, F.F., Larsen, P.G., Green, O.: Development of a driverless lawn mower using co-simulation. In: Cerone, A., Roveri, M. (eds.) SEFM 2017. LNCS, vol. 10729, pp. 330–344. Springer, Cham (2018). https://doi.org/10.1007/978-3-319-74781-1_23
13. Golightly, D., Gamble, C., Palacín, R., Pierce, K.: Applying ergonomics within the multi-modelling paradigm with an example from multiple UAV control. Ergonomics (2019, to appear)
14. Golightly, D., Gamble, C., Palacín, R., Pierce, K.: Multi-modelling for decarbonisation in urban rail systems. Urban Rail Transit (2019, submitted)
15. Golightly, D., Wilson, J.R., Lowe, E., Sharples, S.: The role of situation awareness for understanding signalling and control in rail operations. Theor. Issues Ergon. Sci. **11**(1–2), 84–98 (2010)

16. Gomes, C., Thule, C., Broman, D., Larsen, P.G., Vangheluwe, H.: Co-simulation: a survey. ACM Comput. Surv. **51**(3), 49:1–49:33 (2018)
17. Hollnagel, E., Woods, D.D.: Joint Cognitive Systems: Foundations of Cognitive Systems Engineering, 1st edn. CRC Press, Boca Raton (2005)
18. Huang, L., Cummings, M.L., Nneji, V.C.: Preliminary analysis and simulation of railroad dispatcher workload. Proc. Hum. Factors Ergon. Soc. Annu. Meet. **62**(1), 691–695 (2018)
19. Humann, J., Spero, E.: Modeling and simulation of multi-UAV, multi-operator surveillance systems. In: Annual IEEE International Systems Conference (SysCon 2018), pp. 1–8 (2018)
20. Kingston, D., Rasmussen, S., Humphrey, L.: Automated UAV tasks for search and surveillance. In: 2016 IEEE Conference on Control Applications (CCA), pp. 1–8 (2016)
21. Larsen, P.G., Fitzgerald, J., Woodcock, J., Gamble, C., Payne, R., Pierce, K.: Features of integrated model-based co-modelling and co-simulation technology. In: Cerone, A., Roveri, M. (eds.) SEFM 2017. LNCS, vol. 10729, pp. 377–390. Springer, Cham (2018). https://doi. org/10.1007/978-3-319-74781-1_26
22. Larsen, P.G., et al.: VDM-10 language manual. Technical report TR-001, The Overture Initiative, April 2013. www.overturetool.org
23. Laughery Jr., K.R., Lebiere, C., Archer, S.: Modeling human performance in complex systems, chap. 36, pp. 965–996. Wiley (2006)
24. Leclerc, T., Siebert, J., Chevrier, V., Ciarletta, L., Festor, O.: Multi-modeling and co-simulation-based mobile ubiquitous protocols and services development and assessment. In: Sénac, P., Ott, M., Seneviratne, A. (eds.) MobiQuitous 2010. LNICST, vol. 73, pp. 273–284. Springer, Heidelberg (2012). https://doi.org/10.1007/978-3-642-29154-8_23
25. Lee, E.A.: Cyber physical systems: design challenges. Technical report UCB/EECS-2008-8, EECS Department, University of California, Berkeley, January 2008. http://www.eecs. berkeley.edu/Pubs/TechRpts/2008/EECS-2008-8.html
26. Li, C., Mahadevan, S., Ling, Y., Choze, S., Wang, L.: Dynamic Bayesian network for aircraft wing halth monitoring digital twin. AIAA J. **55**(3), 930–941 (2017)
27. MacKenzie, I.S.: Fitts' law as a research and design tool in human-computer interaction. Hum. Comput. Interact. **7**(1), 91–139 (1992)
28. de Mattos, D.L., Neto, R.A., Merino, E.A.D., Forcellini, F.A.: Simulating the influence of physical overload on assembly line performance: a case study in an automotive electrical component plant. Appl. Ergon. **79**, 107–121 (2019)
29. Metzmacher, H., Wölki, D., Schmidt, C., Frisch, J., van Treeck, C.A.: Real-time assessment of human thermal comfort using image recognition in conjunction with a detailed numerical human model. In: 15th International Building Simulation Conference, pp. 691–700 (2017)
30. Neghina, M., Zamrescu, C.B., Larsen, P.G., Lausdahl, K., Pierce, K.: Multi-paradigm discrete-event modelling and co-simulation of cyber-physical systems. Stud. Inf. Control **27**(1), 33–42 (2018)
31. Newell, A.: Unified Theories of Cognition. Harvard University Press, Cambridge (1990)
32. Nneji, V.C., Cummings, M.L., Stimpson, A.J.: Predicting locomotive crew performance in rail operations with human and automation assistance. IEEE Tran. Hum. Mach. Syst. **49**(3), 250–258 (2019)
33. Palmieri, M., Bernardeschi, C., Masci, P.: A flexible framework for FMI-based co-simulation of human-centred cyber-physical systems. In: Mazzara, M., Ober, I., Salaün, G. (eds.) STAF 2018. LNCS, vol. 11176, pp. 21–33. Springer, Cham (2018). https://doi.org/10.1007/978-3-030-04771-9_2
34. Pelechano, N., Malkawi, A.: Evacuation simulation models: challenges in modeling high rise building evacuation with cellular automata approaches. Autom. Constr. **17**(4), 377–385 (2008)
35. Powell, J., Palacín, R.: A comparison of modelled and real-life driving profiles for the simulation of railway vehicle operation. Transp. Plan. Technol. **38**(1), 78–93 (2015)

36. Rajkumar, R., Lee, I., Sha, L., Stankovic, J.: Cyber-physical systems: the next computing revolution. In: 2010 47th ACM/IEEE Design Automation Conference (DAC), pp. 731–736 (2010)
37. Teal, S.L., Rudnicky, A.I.: A performance model of system delay and user strategy selection. In: SIGCHI Conference on Human Factors in Computing Systems, pp. 295–305. ACM (1992)
38. Thule, C., Lausdahl, K., Gomes, C., Meisl, G., Larsen, P.G.: Maestro: The INTO-CPS CO-simulation framework. Simul. Model. Pract. Theory **92**, 45–61 (2019). http://www.sciencedirect.com/science/article/pii/S1569190X1830193X
39. Verhoef, M., Larsen, P.G.: Enhancing VDM++ for modeling distributed embedded real-time systems. Technical report, Radboud University Nijmegen, March 2006. A preliminary version of this report is available on-line at http://www.cs.ru.nl/~marcelv/vdm/
40. Vilim, R., Thomas, K.: Operator support technologies for fault tolerance and resilience. In: Advanced Sensors and Instrumentation Newsletter, pp. 1–4. U.S. Department for Energy (2016)
41. Wickens, C.D., Gutzwiller, R.S., Vieane, A., Clegg, B.A., Sebok, A., Janes, J.: Time sharing between robotics and process control: validating a model of attention switching. Hum. Factors **58**(2), 322–343 (2016)
42. Zervakis, G., Pierce, K., Gamble, C.: Multi-modelling of Cooperative Swarms. In: Pierce, K., Verhoef, M. (eds.) The 16th Overture Workshop, pp. 57–70. Newcastle University, School of Computing, Oxford, July 2018. TR-1524

Migrating the INTO-CPS
Application to the Cloud

Hugo Daniel Macedo$^{(\boxtimes)}$, Mikkel Bayard Rasmussen, Casper Thule,
and Peter Gorm Larsen

DIGIT, Department of Engineering, Aarhus University, Aarhus, Denmark
{hdm,casper.thule,pgl}@eng.au.dk,
mbrbayard@live.dk

Abstract. The INTO-CPS Application is a common interface used to
access and manipulate different model-based artefacts produced by the
INTO-CPS tool chain during the development of a cyber-physical system. The application was developed during the INTO-CPS project. It
uses web-technologies on top of the Electron platform, and it requires
local installation and configuration on each user local machine. In this
paper, we present a cloud-based version of the INTO-CPS Application
which was developed while researching the potential of cloud technologies to support the INTO-CPS tool chain environment. The proposed
application has the advantage that no configuration or installation on a
local machine is needed. It makes full usage of the cloud resource management, and its architecture allows for a local machine version, keeping
the current local approach option open.

1 Introduction

In Cyber-Physical Systems (CPSs), computing and physical processes interact
closely. Their effective design, therefore, requires methods and tools that bring
together the products of diverse engineering disciplines. Without such tools, it
would be difficult to gain confidence in the system-level consequences of design
decisions made in any one domain, and it would be challenging to manage trade-
offs between them.

The INTO-CPS project created a tool chain supporting different disciplines
such as software, mechatronics, and control engineering. All have notations and
theories that are tailored to their needs, and it is undesirable to suppress this
diversity by enforcing uniform general-purpose models [4,5,10,12,13]. The goal is
to achieve a practical integration of diverse formalisms at the semantic level (performing co-simulation of different models) and to realise the benefits in integrated
tool chains. In order to demonstrate that the technology works industrially, it
has been applied in very different application domains (e.g., [3,6,8,12,17,18]).

Practice shows that the integration of the diverse tools in the INTO-CPS
tool chain forces users to install several software packages and to configure their
desktops to satisfy the multiple dependencies required by the different tools.

E. Sekerinski et al. (Eds.): FM 2019 Workshops, LNCS 12233, pp. 254–271, 2020.
https://doi.org/10.1007/978-3-030-54997-8_17

To guide users, the INTO-CPS Application was developed. It includes a download manager with links to specific versions of the tools, alongside other interfacing features allowing users to explore the tool chain.

The INTO-CPS Application is a cross-platform desktop app developed using web-technologies enabled by the Electron framework[1]. Although it is built on top of a modern framework and provides a good fit for its purpose, the solution has several drawbacks. For instance, when unzipped, the current version[2] occupies 268 MB in size and comprises 11080 items. For an interface, those are overwhelming numbers, which then cause the Microsoft Windows Malicious Software Removal Tool to consume 50% of CPU time during a lengthy unzipping operation. Moreover, as desktop specifications differ, variations in performance are often observed, thus frustrating the user experience.

To deploy a lightweight web-based interface, alleviate the installation burden, and to obtain a unified and improved performance, it is possible to migrate the application to the cloud providing a lean, pre-configured and elastic resources solution. As the current usage of the tool is seasonal, a cloud solution can launch several co-simulation servers during the short periods of intensive usage and provide a green approach (shutting down the co-simulation servers) during the currently characteristic lengthy periods of downtime.

Another advantage is that the cloud is capable of redistributing its resources on-demand, resulting in dynamic upscaling and downscaling, while resources are only paid for when needed. All can be handled from the cloud provider's interface and allows for cloud users to measure their usage of cloud resources. In summary, the cloud enables the INTO-CPS Application to be offered as a service.

This paper reports on work in progress towards the migration of the INTO-CPS Application to the cloud, which originated in the work of [19]. The current results consist of a prototype of a cloud solution consisting of several packages, which was experimentally tested as a local service and as an Amazon Web Services EC2 service. The test results indicate that a cloud solution for co-simulation is feasible, yet whether it is possible to migrate the full set of features of the previous desktop is still an open question.

In the remainder of this paper, we provide background information in Sect. 2, the cloud solution overview in Sect. 3, and experimental results in Sect. 4. Finally, Sect. 5 contains concluding remarks and envisaged future work.

2 Background

This section briefly introduces the tool chain features and typical usage. In it, we also provide details about the application software architecture to migrate.

2.1 The INTO-CPS Tool Chain

The INTO-CPS Application combines the capabilities of several tools that a user interacts with to design components and to perform co-simulations of the

---

[1] https://electronjs.org/.

[2] into-cps-app-3.4.9-win32-x64.zip.

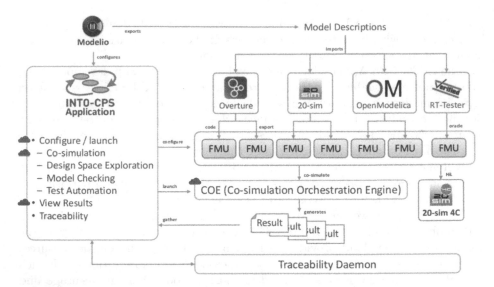

Fig. 1. Illustrates an overview of the INTO-CPS tool chain (taken from [11]). The cloud icon labels the features that were migrated during our research work.

combined behaviour. The chain of tools is illustrated in Fig. 1, where the components that have been migrated are labelled with a small cloud symbol.

At the core is the INTO-CPS Application itself, which provides a User Interface (UI) to the tool chain, where the user is able to configure and launch co-simulations and visualise the results, perform Design Space Exploration (DSE), among other tasks.

Co-simulations are performed by the Co-simulation Orchestration Engine (COE) called Maestro, which is used by the INTO-CPS Application [20,21]. The INTO-CPS Application is capable of optimising a CPS design using DSE to carry out multiple co-simulations to search for optimal designs [9].

Modelio is a tool within the toolchain that supports the Systems Modelling Language (SysML) and is capable of creating a range of different diagrams describing the connectivity between the Functional Mock-up Units (FMUs). The tool generates a configuration file (.mm) known as the Multi-Model describing the local instances and connections between the FMUs variables, along with values for parameters of the FMUs. This can be read by the INTO-CPS Application to generate a co-simulation configuration file (.coe) that offers a configuration of the co-simulation, specifying how it should be performed by the COE. This file can be modified using the INTO-CPS Application, for instance specifying changes to co-simulation parameters defaults (e.g. logging, live streaming, step size). An experimental alternative to the SysML graphical overview of the connection between FMUs directly inside the INTO-CPS Application is also underway [14].

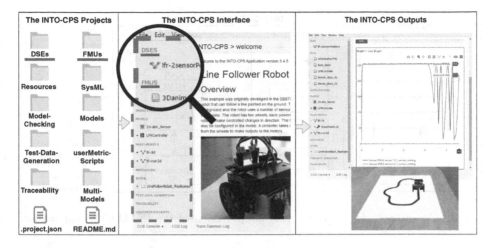

Fig. 2. Illustrates an INTO-CPS project structure and the INTO-CPS Application's representation of a project. Additionally, it illustrates the outputs that the INTO-CPS Application and the COE, are capable of producing.

Modelio also produces a description of a model that can be imported by the other tools within the INTO-CPS tool chain[3]. Overture, 20-sim, OpenModelica, and RT-Tester import the model description to produce, for instance, a skeleton of the FMU definitions to be completed by the user, enabling them to interconnect using the Functional Mock-up Interface (FMI) standard to generate compatible co-simulation FMUs [2] to be used by the INTO-CPS Application[4].

2.2   The INTO-CPS Application

The application provides a UI to individual projects developed using the INTO-CPS tool chain. To read project contents, the application uses a specific folder structure, which is illustrated to the left in Fig. 2. A project has two essential folders: the FMU folder and the Multi-models (MM) folder. The FMU folder contains the project developed FMU's files (.fmu), and the MM folder includes the (.mm) and (.coe) files mentioned in Subsect. 2.1. The cloud migration of the UI and project structure posed no major difficulty.

The project files are presented in the application left menu, as illustrated within the dotted lines in the middle of Fig. 2. Using the left menu, users can navigate to different files within an INTO-CPS project, and, for instance, by clicking on a model, which is made using one of the tools of the INTO-CPS tool chain, the application launches the corresponding tool with the corresponding

---

[3] https://www.modelio.org/about-modelio/features.html.

[4] Note that currently none of the modelling and simulation tools have been migrated, but it is envisaged the HUBCAP project (see http://hubcap.au.dk) will establish a collaboration platform in the cloud where this could be possible.

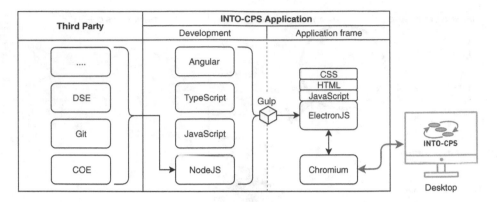

Fig. 3. The technologies used in the desktop-version of the INTO-CPS Application and their interactions.

model loaded. Although in a cloud application the first is easy to implement, the latter is not straightforward.

Additionally, the INTO-CPS Application includes a download manager which supports fetching the tools of the INTO-CPS tool chain, including the COE and the DSE scripts, which must be downloaded to carry out simulations and DSEs. In a cloud version, a COE and DSE scripts would be expected to be available by default, and download links may be provided as well.

The INTO-CPS Application, in combination with the COE, generates a set of simulation results stored in the MM folder. These results can be presented to a user in multiple ways, as they are based on raw data files that describe the FMUs interactions over time. A typical use case is to present live streaming of the simulation using 2D plots or 3D animations. Both outputs are illustrated to the right in Fig. 2, depending on the use of 20-sim, which in this case provides the 3D capability. The 20-sim requirement posed an additional challenge during the cloud migration research, and our work focused on 2D plots only.

Technologies of the INTO-CPS Application. The INTO-CPS Application is a complex web app, making usage of several technologies. Figure 3 provides an overview of the different technologies that power the INTO-CPS Application (in the application frame), the software development environment, and the third-party applications used.

Architecture of the Desktop Version of the INTO-CPS Application. The Type-Script class architecture of the pre-existing desktop version of the INTO-CPS Application caters for all INTO-CPS project features, thus we chose to reverse engineer the architecture, which we generated from the codebase, as a top-down architecture for the INTO-CPS GUI. This is still work in progress, and our research focuses on a subset (project management plus launch and visualisation of co-simulation) of the desktop version features. Figure 4 is generated from the

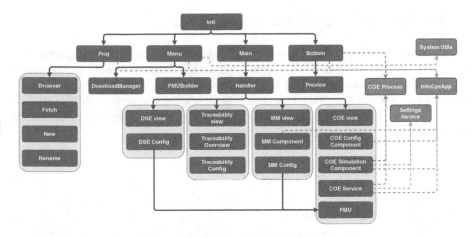

Fig. 4. Illustrates an extract of an architecture diagram of the INTO-CPS Application codebase. Note that the dotted lines illustrate relations with classes that are shared across the entire application, the coloured lines are only for distinguishing between lines and carry no meaning.

code base and illustrates its monolithic approach. The diagram also shows the nested relationship found within a part of the INTO-CPS Application.

Allowing multiple users to commonly access and use the desktop application poses a problem, due to the usage of global classes and variables. Users could configure settings on the cloud, potentially affecting other users' experience, thus a cloud version requires an architectural redesign.

Fig. 5. Illustrates a comparison between the new and the old user interface, with the desktop version illustrated on the left and the cloud version illustrated on the right.

3   The INTO-CPS Cloud Application

A cloud solution allows users to interact with the application from a wider range of devices because it delegates the computationally intensive tasks to the cloud devices. Therefore, it made sense to explore visual re-designs during the migration process reported in [19]. The result is a new user interface, illustrated in Fig. 5, and the cloud application presents a modern visual design with increased colour contrast.

3.1   Use-Cases of the Cloud Prototype

In the cloud version, users are able to create accounts, to add projects, to configure co-simulations by modifying the MM (.mm) configurations and the corresponding co-simulation configuration (.coe) files, and to run and visualise a co-simulation. The explored use cases are illustrated in Fig. 6.

Users must sign up to access projects, which can be either uploaded to the cloud or an existing project can be selected and configured. The two types of configuration can be carried out and saved, and lastly, a co-simulation can be started and the results viewed while a co-simulation is executing.

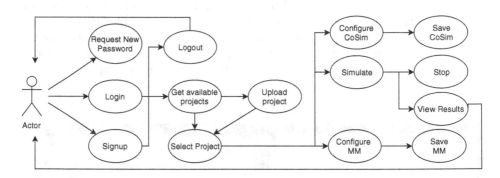

Fig. 6. Illustrates the use-case diagram of the users interacting with the cloud-based version of the INTO-CPS Application.

The desktop version of the INTO-CPS Application does not include authentication and user registration, nor does it provide the ability to upload and store files or projects in a cloud server for long term use. These functionalities were added and allow users to be recognised by their unique ID and map the users to their uploaded files.

Furthermore, the addition enabled the management of COE servers, letting a user reserve a COE for the time it takes to carry out a co-simulation. Additionally, it enables keeping track of the users and provides each with an encapsulated experience, a trusted platform that safely handles confidential data.

3.2 Architecture of the Cloud Version of the INTO-CPS Application

The software architecture of the developed prototype follows the micro-services approach. The application is structured as a collection of four web services, four distributed processes hosted in potentially different nodes connected using the popular TCP/IP protocol suite, namely:

- a frontend server providing the user interface (dynamic web application),
- a backend server providing a public Application Programming Interface (API) to be called by the frontend when core functionality is to be executed (authentication, storage, co-simulation service management),
- a COE server to be scaled up and down on demand to provide an encapsulated simulation server to each user, and
- a web server functioning as a reverse proxy channelling traffic directly to the front-end.

The joint behaviour of the application as a unit, as experienced by the user, is, in fact, an illusion emerging from the result of intrinsic communication coordination mediated through the reverse proxy web server. The communication involves an amalgam of HyperText Transfer Protocol (HTTP), Representational State Transfer (REST) API, and ad hoc protocol connections.

The joint behaviour experience starts when a user points its browser to the web server proxy, which itself redirects the client to the frontend. Further interaction with the user interface leads to further communication via the proxy with the backend service, which itself communicates with the other services, for instance, with the servers in the pool of COEs via an ad hoc JavaScript Object Notation (JSON) over HTTP protocol defined API.

3.3 Technologies of the Cloud-Based INTO-CPS Application

To run the four micro-service architecture described in Sect. 3.2 in the cloud, the cloud solution uses Docker[5] to easily package the different application components in the form of containers, which also eases the burden of executing the application in a suitable environment (with libraries...).

Figure 7 provides an overview of the different technologies that take part in the cloud-based INTO-CPS Application and may be compared with Fig. 3, where the desktop version technologies are depicted.

The cloud solution consists of four Docker containers, one for each micro-service: the frontend, the backend, the COE, and the reverse proxy:

- The frontend uses the Angular framework[6] to provide the web application with the visual elements of the INTO-CPS Application, and it connects to the backend to handle more extensive tasks.

---

[5] https://docs.docker.com/get-started.
[6] See https://angular.io/.

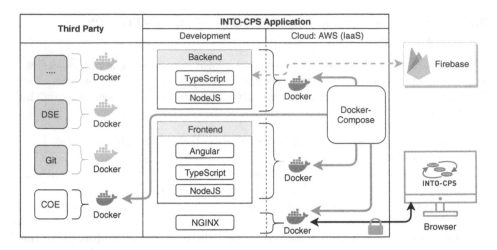

Fig. 7. Illustrates the technologies used in the cloud-based INTO-CPS Application and their interaction. Artefacts marked in grey mark technologies that did not migrate during the first migration iteration, but are expected to be easily executed using Docker.

- The backend is a server developed using NodeJS, providing a REST API offering the functions and operations made available to users via the frontend.
- The COE container deploys a pool of COE instances.
- The reverse proxy is provided via an NGINX[7] web server to securely interface the micro-services with the internet. Users access the cloud application using a browser to connect to the NGINX instance, which, by default, redirects the user to the frontend.

The different Docker containers are managed and started by the docker-compose tool[8], which orchestrates the build and launch of the Docker containers.

To authenticate users, the backend uses an API provided by Firebase, which offers a database and a preconfigured authentication module, that allows users to register for the platform and login. Firebase, therefore, stores the user credentials, and handles the user registration and access, providing each user with a unique identifier, which is used by the INTO-CPS Application to distinguish between users.

In our research experiments, all the Docker components were hosted on an IaaS offered by Amazon Web Services' EC2 instance[9] to scale resources to the necessary amount on demand. The EC2 service offers a virtual Linux server running Docker.

---

[7] https://www.nginx.com/resources/glossary/nginx.

[8] https://docs.docker.com/compose/.

[9] https://docs.aws.amazon.com/AWSEC2/latest/UserGuide/concepts.html.

3.4 Micro-services Details

This section describes the details of the architectural structure of the two micro-services and the COE container that were developed for the cloud solution. The micro-services are based on the monolithic architecture, that was illustrated in Fig. 4 and we embedded the desktop COE into a container.

Micro-service: Frontend. The frontend of the cloud-based INTO-CPS Application must provide the different views found in the desktop version of the INTO-CPS Application. Angular is used for some of the visuals elements found on the desktop version of the INTO-CPS Application. It was therefore chosen as the frontend framework of the cloud-based solution. The Angular framework is component-based development, and the frontend components are illustrated in Fig. 8.

The components and services included in the frontend are combined within the *frontend server* found at the top of Fig. 8, which acts as a starting point for the micro-service. The different components carry out different tasks:

- The *management component* contains the logic associated with user management (signup, login...), thereby offering an authentication unit.
- The *menu component* contains the components that allow a user to select between uploaded projects and present their content.
- The *context component* allows the configuration files to be presented as GUI offering users a useful configuration method. Additionally, it allows users to start a co-simulation and visualise the results.
- The *communication component* allows the frontend to interact with the backend, as a service. It offers a connection to the REST API offered by the backend, and bridges the components depicted in Fig. 8 and Fig. 9.

Micro-service: Backend. The backend of the cloud-based INTO-CPS Application contains different handlers each connected to the server element that offers the REST API for the frontend. Figure 9 illustrates the components implemented, including the handlers, and the desktop version components yet to be migrated in grey.

The backend contains three handlers: the *COE handler*, *storage handler*, and the *authentication handler*:

- The *authentication handler* manages user access, resourcing to Firebase, which is a service provided by Google, which stores the user credentials securely, and allows for an easy authentication integration.
- The *storage handler* manages the files that are uploaded by the individual users. It prevents users from accessing unauthorised files and enables the user to upload files and entire projects to the cloud.

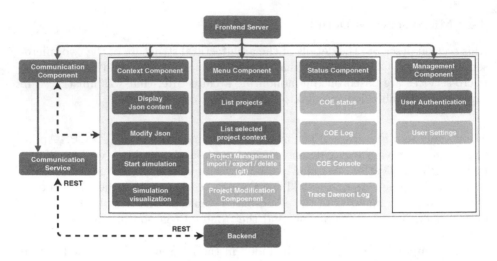

Fig. 8. Illustrates the architecture diagram of the frontend of the cloud solution, the grey boxes were excluded during the first migration iteration.

– The *COE handler* manages the reservation of the COEs and provides the communication with each COE. The handler registers users and checks if a COE is available. If a COE is available, it adds the user and virtual IP of that COE to a ledger indicating that the COE is occupied. The handler takes care of the simulation status and data and provides the necessary information back to the frontend. Once the backend receives a notification from the COE asserting that a simulation has ended, it removes the user and the COE from the ledger freeing the COE for other users.

Cloud Challenges to the *COE Handler*. If all COEs are busy, users are required to wait, as the co-simulation only starts if a COE is available. Our solution is not ideal, yet the cloud allows several solutions to this challenge. A cloud approach is to offer subscription-based dedicated COEs while keeping the free COEs for new users that want to try the INTO-CPS application.

If a user's COE breaks during a co-simulation, the COE remains reserved, preventing the user to reserve another one. This issue can be addressed using the feedback that the backend receives from the COE to remove the user from the ledger.

COEs Container and Pooling. The COE container wraps the COE in a suitable java runtime, and a shell script is used to launch a pool of COEs. The pool launching is carried out using the features offered by the local network creation features of docker-compose, which provides each COE with a unique virtual IP, rather than a fixed IP with a different port number, allowing better encapsulation and security management.

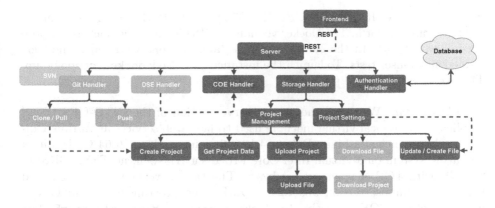

Fig. 9. Illustrates the components that exist on the backend of the cloud solution, the grey boxes were excluded in the first migration iteration.

During the launch of the container, docker-compose defines a folder on the cloud environment that the backend and the pool of COEs share. This folder is used to provide a direct sharing of co-simulation required files.

4   Implementation, Experiments, and Results

We implemented the migration during the project reported in [19]. The software development was carried out over 80 days including the migration of existing components (project management UI plus co-simulation launching and visualization UI) and the complete development of the many cloud-specific components (authentication, encrypted web connection, shared COEs pool. . .) absent in the desktop version.

Our experiments confirm that the migration deals with the complexity of local tool configuration problems for the INTO-CPS Application, COE, and their dependencies (e.g.: Java runtime). Given the elasticity of the cloud resources, the uniform user experience in terms of performance was also achieved with the migration. Nevertheless, the solutions to those problems come at the cost of operating the app in the cloud beyond our experiments.

Our research results also included a study on cloud deployment options [19]. We considered at least two possibilities to migrate a desktop application to the cloud: a private hosting (local machine installed with cloud-like services) or a cloud hosting (provided by any of one of the major vendors). In the following, we present the details about two experiments one for each of the options.

Cloud Hosting. We tested the cloud option of the INTO-CPS Cloud Application by deploying the services into an AWS machine running in its EU (Frankfurt) region. We used the AWS console to launch a Canonical, Ubuntu, 18.04 LTS, amd64 bionic image running on a single Amazon EC2 Instance Type t2.micro providing an Intel(R) Xeon(R) CPU E5-2676 v3 @ 2.40 GHz with 1 GB of memory hardware platform. The Docker version was 18.09.7 and the docker-compose version was 1.23.1. In the cloud setup, we launched one COE only and performed single-user tests. To launch the instances, we used: `docker-compose up`. The average cost was 6$ per month.

Private Hosting. We tested the private server option of the INTO-CPS Cloud Application in a local virtual machine used to host web services at Aarhus University. We launched a Linux Debian 4.19.0-6-cloud-amd64 x86_64 GNU/Linux operating system on a virtual Intel Core Processor (Haswell, no TSX, IBRS) @ 2.4 GHz with 4 GB of memory) hardware. The Docker version was 19.03.2 and the docker-compose version was 1.24.1. During the experiment, we launched 5 instances of the COE resourcing to: `docker-compose up --scale coe=5`. The 5 COEs version allowed multiple user access and to test the COE Pool management functionality defined in the backend. Costs are not computable as the hosting cost is shared with other services.

Performance Results. We observed no difference in performance between the *Private* and the *Cloud* hosting in terms of timings regarding page loading and co-simulation performance. During our experiments, when loading the landing page, there were around 15 requests performed by the browser, which total in 14.10 MB to be downloaded by the client and take an average of 2.5 s. Compared to the huge size app size and the lengthy process of unzipping of the Desktop version, the cloud version seems more attractive. Nevertheless, the two apps are not comparable as one provides more and different features than the other.

Regarding the memory resources usage, the results between the *Private* and the *Cloud* deployments diverged because there was a time gap between each, and the Docker configurations were optimized for memory reduction in the posterior *Private* deployment. In Table 1 we display the memory usage results. For each of the options, we show the memory occupation for the Docker images (roughly corresponding to the folder containing the desktop app) and the sizes of the containers, which are created while launching the cloud app using docker-compose.

The deployment in the *Private* hosting totals 570 MB in memory occupation. In that total, the COE occupies 318 MB. Therefore, for a fair comparison with the Desktop application (COE jar not included), we obtain a total of 252 MB occupied to serve the application. This number is slightly better, yet there are several missing features in the cloud version. In addition, each image contains a full snapshot of an operating system root and running environment beyond the application code. Thus, the numbers are not comparable, but it is fair to claim that it is possible to store the cloud version with roughly the same amount of space spent by a single user of the desktop app. If the cloud app reaches the maturity to serve thousands of users, the gains are compelling.

The deployment in the *Cloud* hosting environment is more expensive in terms of memory consumption due to the deployment of larger Docker images containing unnecessary resources that were later discarded in the second and optimized *Private* hosting experiment.

Table 1. Application size for the Cloud hosting experiment with a single COE and for the Private hosting experiment with 5 COEs. The results are according to the output of `docker system df -v` and express the size of the images and of the containers themselves.

Experiment	Type		Total	Active	Size (MB)
Cloud	Images	Proxy	1	1	20
		Frontend	1	1	53
		Backend	1	1	344
		COE	1	1	892
		Total	4	4	1246
	Containers	Total	4	4	3.3
Private	Images	Proxy	1	1	15
		Frontend	1	1	49
		Backend	1	1	188
		COE	1	1	318
		Total	4	4	570
	Containers	Total	8	8	41

5   Concluding Remarks and Future Work

The INTO-CPS Application was migrated from a locally installed desktop application to a cloud-based application that users can access and interact with using a web browser. As it is discussed in Sect. 4, the cloud solution mitigates the problems related to the local installation and configuration requirement of the Desktop app. The results indicate the cloud solution improves storage efficiency, running time, and provides a uniform experience to its users.

Although the cloud-based INTO-CPS Application is still missing some of the functionality available in the desktop version, as detailed in Sect. 2.1, we claim that the result is a reasonable proof-of-concept and that our research clarified the feasibility boundaries of the migration.

The cloud-based INTO-CPS Application is the first and only tool of the INTO-CPS tool chain to migrate to the cloud. The result illustrates that such a migration is possible, even though only a fraction of the application was migrated. An additional outcome is that it also offers users a configuration free experience, and directs the developers to focus on a single OS, rather than multiple OSs.

An alternative approach to offering the previously existing desktop version of the application as a cloud application would be to provide a cloud running a virtual machine and with remote desktop access to users. This approach requires additional resources due to the overhead of the virtualised OS, as each user would require an isolated OS without a connection to other users' files for both operational and data security reasons. This becomes a challenge in terms of resources needs and costs.

5.1 Future Work

The cloud solution misses fundamental additional functionalities to be made available for users. The intent is also to use the co-simulation technology described here in a digital-twin setting with live streaming of data [7]. The application developed in [19] is a prototype. As it is usual in the outcomes of the research projects of this kind, there are several improvements that need to be in place before the prototype reaches a fully functional state. The immediate needs are to improve the test coverage (unit tests are sparse and end-to-end testing is minimal). Also, current users are accustomed to high-availability and fault-tolerant web services, therefore the need to perform a fault analysis and develop a fault-tolerant architecture (for instance adapting the one in [15] where the several services are monitored and new Docker instances are launched in case of failures).

The INTO-CPS Application proposes a new architecture, which allows the application to offer a frontend that can be expanded allowing new functionalities. We expect to see improvements in visualisation capabilities with the opening of new research projects on new alternatives for co-simulation configuration inside the INTO-CPS Application, like the one in [14].

A cloud solution poses substantial security risks. There is a need to develop a secure platform that encrypts data and guarantees allows authorised users to decrypt it, as co-simulations often involve sensitive data. Also, the shift from the desktop running environment to a cloud co-simulation environment opens the possibility for cyber-attacks and malware deployment embedded in the libraries to be launched by the COE. A continuation of the work in [16] to cover FMUs is a possibility.

As the cloud is billed depending on the used resources, resource measurement and a payment wall must be implemented (or contracted to a cloud provider) to ensure extensive users pay the associated costs.

Another possible extension is the inclusion of FMU static checkers as the one proposed in [1], to prevent running co-simulations, and thus usage and billing of resources, that are known in advance to be bound to non-compliant FMUs.

Another advantage of the new architecture is that the cloud application was developed with the possibility for deployment both in the cloud and in a desktop. Such work is to be taken in the future, as it requires overhead for developers, but it can be handled using a builder tool such as Gulp. The previous desktop-based approach is most useful when using the app in environments where cloud access is restricted.

In the near future, we expect to port more features from the desktop version into the cloud, for instance porting the grey boxes in Fig. 7, Fig. 8, and Fig. 9. In the following, we provide a priority list of features to be added to the application.

- Logging: The COE produces two logs, a status of the simulation and a status of the COE. Furthermore, the Traceability Daemon also produces a log. The logs must be presented for the users when connected to either of the technologies.

- Download Manager: Allowing the users to download the tools found within the INTO-CPS toolchain. This requires changes to offer the files for download using the user's browser.
- Single File Upload: Users are currently only capable of uploading entire projects. Uploading individual files must be handled to allow users to append an FMU or other files to an existing project.
- DSE, Traceability, and Test Case Generation: Those features introduce new technologies, which must be developed. Additionally, this would require further development on the backend and frontend and their Docker containers to get the technologies to work.
- git: Used to manage project folders as git repositories using the supporting tooling. Handling multiple users and their git credentials is a sensitive issue in a cloud setup, thus requiring in-depth analysis and development.

Acknowledgements. We would like to thank all stakeholders that have been involved in the development of the INTO-CPS Application. We acknowledge the EU for funding the INTO-CPS project (grant agreement number 644047) which was the original source of funding for the INTO-CPS Application. We are also grateful to the Poul Due Jensen Foundation, which has supported the establishment of a new Centre for Digital Twin Technology at Aarhus University, which will take forward the principles, tools and applications of the engineering of digital twins. Finally, we would like to thank Nick Battle and the anonymous reviewers for valuable feedback on earlier versions of this paper.

References

1. Battle, N., Thule, C., Gomes, C., Macedo, H.D., Larsen, P.G.: Towards static check of FMUs in VDM-SL. In: Gamble, C., Couto, L.D. (eds.) The 17th Overture Workshop: New Capabilities and Applications for Model-based Systems Engineering. Newcastle University Technical Report Series CS-TR-1530, Porto, Portugal, pp. 17–31, October 2019
2. Brosse, E., Quadri, I.: SysML and FMI in INTO-CPS: Integrated Tool chain for model-based design of Cyber Physical Systems, p. 37, December 2017
3. Couto, L.D., Basagiannis, S., Ridouane, E.H., Mady, A.E.-D., Hasanagic, M., Larsen, P.G.: Injecting formal verification in FMI-based co-simulations of cyber-physical systems. In: Cerone, A., Roveri, M. (eds.) SEFM 2017. LNCS, vol. 10729, pp. 284–299. Springer, Cham (2018). https://doi.org/10.1007/978-3-319-74781-1_20
4. Fitzgerald, J., Gamble, C., Larsen, P.G., Pierce, K., Woodcock, J.: Cyber-physical systems design: formal foundations, methods and integrated tool chains. In: FormaliSE: FME Workshop on Formal Methods in Software Engineering, ICSE 2015, Florence, Italy, May 2015
5. Fitzgerald, J., Gamble, C., Payne, R., Larsen, P.G., Basagiannis, S., Mady, A.E.D.: Collaborative model-based systems engineering for cyber-physical systems – a case study in building automation. In: Proceedings of INCOSE International Symposium on Systems Engineering, Edinburgh, Scotland, July 2016

6. Fitzgerald, J., Gamble, C., Payne, R., Larsen, P.G., Basagiannis, S., Mady, A.E.D.: Collaborative model-based systems engineering for cyber-physical systems, with a building automation case study. In: INCOSE International Symposium, vol. 26, no. 1, pp. 817–832 (2016)

7. Fitzgerald, J., Larsen, P.G., Pierce, K.: Multi-modelling and co-simulation in the engineering of cyber-physical systems: towards the digital twin. In: ter Beek, M.H., Fantechi, A., Semini, L. (eds.) From Software Engineering to Formal Methods and Tools, and Back. LNCS, vol. 11865, pp. 40–55. Springer, Cham (2019). https://doi.org/10.1007/978-3-030-30985-5_4

8. Foldager, F., Larsen, P.G., Green, O.: Development of a driverless lawn mower using co-simulation. In: 1st Workshop on Formal Co-Simulation of Cyber-Physical Systems, Trento, Italy, September 2017

9. Gamble, C.: Design Space Exploration in the INTO-CPS Platform: Integrated Tool chain for model-based design of Cyber Physical Systems. Aarhus University, October 2016

10. Larsen, P.G., et al.: Integrated tool chain for model-based design of cyber-physical systems: the INTO-CPS Project. In: CPS Data Workshop, Vienna, Austria, April 2016

11. Larsen, P.G., Fitzgerald, J., Woodcock, J., Gamble, C., Payne, R., Pierce, K.: Features of integrated model-based co-modelling and co-simulation technology. In: Cerone, A., Roveri, M. (eds.) SEFM 2017. LNCS, vol. 10729, pp. 377–390. Springer, Cham (2018). https://doi.org/10.1007/978-3-319-74781-1_26

12. Larsen, P.G., Fitzgerald, J., Woodcock, J., Lecomte, T.: Trustworthy Cyber-Physical Systems Engineering, Chapter 8: collaborative modelling and simulation for cyber-physical systems. Chapman and Hall/CRC, September 2016. ISBN 9781498742450

13. Larsen, P.G., Fitzgerald, J., Woodcock, J., Nilsson, R., Gamble, C., Foster, S.: Towards semantically integrated models and tools for cyber-physical systems design. In: Margaria, T., Steffen, B. (eds.) ISoLA 2016. LNCS, vol. 9953, pp. 171–186. Springer, Cham (2016). https://doi.org/10.1007/978-3-319-47169-3_13

14. Legaard, C.M., Thule, C., Larsen, P.G.: Towards Graphical Configuration in the INTO-CPS Application. In: Gamble, C., Couto, L.D. (eds.) The 17th Overture Workshop. Newcastle University TR CS-TR-1530, Porto, Portugal, pp. 1–16, October 2019

15. Macedo, H., Nilsson, R., Larsen, P.: The harvest coach architecture: embedding deviation-tolerance in a harvest logistic solution. Computers **8**(2), 31 (2019)

16. Macedo, H.D., Touili, T.: Mining malware specifications through static reachability analysis. In: Crampton, J., Jajodia, S., Mayes, K. (eds.) ESORICS 2013. LNCS, vol. 8134, pp. 517–535. Springer, Heidelberg (2013). https://doi.org/10.1007/978-3-642-40203-6_29

17. Neghina, M., Zamrescu, C.B., Larsen, P.G., Lausdahl, K., Pierce, K.: A discrete event-first approach to collaborative modelling of cyber-physical systems. In: Fitzgerald, T.O. (ed.) The 15th Overture Workshop: New Capabilities and Applications for Model-based Systems Engineering. Newcastle University, Computing Science. Technical Report Series. CS-TR- 1513, Newcastle, UK, pp. 116–129, September 2017

18. Pedersen, N., Lausdahl, K., Sanchez, E.V., Larsen, P.G., Madsen, J.: Distributed co-simulation of embedded control software with exhaust gas recirculation water handling system using INTO-CPS. In: Proceedings of the 7th International Conference on Simulation and Modeling Methodologies, Technologies and Applications (SIMUL-TECH 2017), Madrid, Spain, pp. 73–82, July 2017. ISBN 978-989-758-265-3
19. Rasmussen, M.B.: A process for migrating desktop applications to the cloud. Master's thesis, Aarhus University, Department of Engineering, June 2019
20. Thule, C., Lausdahl, K., Gomes, C., Meisl, G., Larsen, P.G.: Maestro: The INTO-CPS co-simulation framework. Simul. Modell. Pract. Theory **92**, 45–61 (2019). http://www.sciencedirect.com/science/article/pii/S1569190X1830193X
21. Thule, C., et al.: Towards reuse of synchronization algorithms in co-simulation frameworks. In: Co-Sim-19 workshop, September 2019

Towards a Static Check of FMUs in VDM-SL

Nick Battle[1]([⊠]), Casper Thule[1], Cláudio Gomes[2], Hugo Daniel Macedo[1], and Peter Gorm Larsen[1]

[1] DIGIT, Department of Engineering, Aarhus University, Aarhus, Denmark
{casper.thule,hdm,pgl}@eng.au.dk
[2] University of Antwerpen, Antwerp, Belgium
claudio.gomes@uantwerp.be

Abstract. In order to ensure that the co-simulation of Cyber-Physical Systems (CPSs) is possible with as wide a variety of tools as possible, a standard called the Functional Mockup Interface (FMI) has been defined. The FMI provides the means to compute the overall behaviour of a coupled system by the coordination and communication of simulators, each responsible for a part of the system. The contribution presented in this paper is an initial formal model of the FMI standard using the VDM Specification Language. Early results suggest that the FMI standard defines a number of FMU static constraints that are not enforced by many of the tools that are able to export such FMUs.

1 Introduction

In Cyber-Physical Systems (CPSs), computing and physical processes interact closely. Their effective design therefore requires methods and tools that bring together the products of diverse engineering disciplines [19,20]. This has been the motivation for establishing common co-simulation technologies to enable full system evaluation through the interconnection of individual simulators [10]. One of the most widely adopted simulation interfaces is the Functional Mock-up Interface (FMI) standard [2,3,7].

In the context of the FMI standard, the simulators are encapsulated with their corresponding models in an executable format. These are denoted as Functional Mock-up Units (FMUs). The FMI interface establishes which operations, and parameters, can be used to communicate with the FMUs.

While the FMI allows for the integration of many simulation tools, it underspecifies the interaction protocol with the simulators. That is, the same pair of simulators can synchronise data in different ways, each leading to a potentially different result. This is a feature and not a limitation: the FMI steering committee recognised that, in order to produce reliable results, different sets of simulators (and the corresponding models) may require different synchronisation algorithms. In fact, finding the best algorithm for a particular co-simulation is one of the main research challenges in this field [1,8,9].

N. Battle—Independent

© Springer Nature Switzerland AG 2020
E. Sekerinski et al. (Eds.): FM 2019 Workshops, LNCS 12233, pp. 272–288, 2020.
https://doi.org/10.1007/978-3-030-54997-8_18

However, as recognised in a recent empirical survey [16], "The most acknowledged challenge is related to practical aspects. These include: faulty/incomplete implementations of the FMI standard, ambiguities/omissions in the specification and documentation of the FMUs, ...". We argue that one of the contributing factors is the fact that the FMI specification is semi-formal, and that the ambiguities lead to different implementations of FMUs. This is a challenge for the orchestration of a collection of FMUs in a semantically sound fashion [17].

Contribution. We propose to formalise what the FMI standard actually states, and this paper is an attempt at moving towards a common agreement about the static constraints for FMUs used for co-simulation in such a formal specification. This work has been released as an open source tool that is able to rigorously test the static validity of FMUs. We present early empirical results regarding the application of this tool to the FMI Cross Check repository, the repository used to evaluate whether tools successfully support the standard. We hope to be able to later extend this with the different allowed dynamic semantics interpretations of the actual co-simulation engines.

The rest of this paper starts with background information for the reader in Sect. 2. This is followed by Sect. 3 which provides an overview of the VDM-SL formalisation and Sect. 4 which summarises the results discovered by using the model to analyse FMUs. Finally, Sect. 5 provides a few concluding remarks and comments on the future directions expected for this work.

2   Background

2.1   The Functional Mockup Interface

The FMI standard is purely concerned with specifying the packaging of, API interface to, and common configuration of individual FMUs. It does not define what particular FMUs model, or the different ways of coordinating the simulation of a collection of FMUs.

By offering a common standard for simulated components, the FMI standard promotes interoperability between a wide variety of tools for exploring the creation of systems that are composed of multiple interacting components. Today[1] there are around 50 independent tools that conform to version 2.0 of the co-simulation part of the FMI standard. This includes the INTO-CPS tool chain which integrates several tools that are able to deal with FMUs [4,5,13–15].

The FMI standard has both static and dynamic semantics, though both are defined informally. The static semantics are concerned with the configuration of FMUs according to the rules defined in the standard. The dynamic semantics are concerned with the behavioural constraints placed on FMUs when a sequence of API calls are made to them, as defined in the standard. The current work is only concerned with the formal definition of the static semantics.

---

[1] From https://fmi-standard.org/tools/, as of August 2019.

2.2 VDM Modelling

VDM is a long established formalism for the specification and analysis of discrete systems [6,12]. A VDM specification comprises a set of data types, constant values, functions, state information and operations that describe the functional behaviour of a system. A specification relies heavily on constraints to define the correct behaviour of the model, for example via data type invariants, function preconditions and postconditions, state data invariants and so on.

A VDM function is an expression over its arguments which returns a result; if the same arguments are passed, the same result is returned. A type invariant is a total function over the possible values of the type, returning "true" for all valid values.

A VDM annotation is a comment in the source of the model which allows user-written plugins to observe values on the fly (but not change them) and affect the behaviour of analyses (e.g., suppressing or generating warnings). By annotating subclauses of a complex expression, a VDM function can be traced or report multiple problems without affecting the behaviour or meaning of the specification.

3   The VDM Model of the FMI Standard

The VDM model presented here is based on version 2.0.1 of the FMI standard, dated October 2nd 2019. A later version 3.0 of the standard is being worked on, but that has not yet been released. Most tools work with the 2.0 standard, so this is the most useful version to formalise initially. Release 2.0.1 of the standard added clarification and corrected minor errors, rather than adding functionality to 2.0.

The FMI standard defines how to configure individual FMUs and it also defines a common API for interacting with all FMUs. The VDM model currently only defines the constraints on the static configuration, though a formal specification of the API semantics is a natural extension of this work. The current work builds on earlier work [11] that defined the static semantics of part of the FMI standard.

3.1 The FMI V2.0 XSD Schema

The FMI standard defines an XML configuration file format for FMUs. The structure of the file is defined using an XSD schema with annotations, combined with an informal description of the meaning and constraints on the various fields in the document text. The XSD defines basic constraints, such as the xs:types of fields, and the minOccurs and maxOccurs attributes for repeating or optional elements and attributes. An example XML extract is shown in Listing 1.1.

Listing 1.1. Extract of an FMU configuration XML file.

```
<ScalarVariable
   name="h"
   valueReference="0"
   causality="output"
   variability="continuous"
   initial="exact">
     <Real
        start="1"
        declaredType="Position"/>
</ScalarVariable>
```

A tool has been developed in this work to parse FMU configuration XML files and convert them to the equivalent in VDM, so that specific FMU configurations may be checked automatically using VDM constraint checking tools. The FMI standard deliberately defines an XSD schema that is very simple, and this makes the VDM translation straightforward. The authors are not aware of any XML constraint checking technology that has the power and flexibility of a VDM model, especially as the VDM formalism has the potential to define both the static and the dynamic semantics, which is future work presented in Sect. 5.

3.2 The VDM-SL Modelling Approach

The VDM model is currently written in the VDM-SL dialect. This is the simplest dialect, without support for object orientation or concurrency, but it is compatible with more sophisticated dialects if their capabilities become essential. The authors hope that the simplicity of the VDM-SL dialect makes the formal FMI specification more readily accessible to domain experts who are not familiar with the VDM notation.

Since it currently only formalises the XSD schema, the VDM model is comprised entirely of type definitions with supporting invariant functions. The type definitions correspond to the XSD element definitions (and have the same names); the invariants correspond to the constraints that are added by the XSD, its informal annotations and descriptions in the main text. The value of the VDM specification is therefore almost entirely contained in the invariant functions, with their ability to unambiguously specify the rules concerning the construction of each XML element.

The most common way to construct a VDM model of a static system is to define types with invariants as an explicit property of each type. This means that it is not possible to construct a value of the type which does not meet the invariant constraints. Unfortunately, when using such a model to *test* real FMU XML configurations, the VDM tools stop when they encounter the first invariant violation (for example, a variable `start` attribute which is not between its `min` and `max` values). Although this is reasonable behaviour (the `start` attribute is definitely wrong), there may well be other errors in the XML that the VDM tools do not report until the first problem is resolved and the specification re-tested.

So to make the VDM model more useful, it defines types without explicit invariants, and provides a number of (nested) isValid... functions that do the invariant checks and report all of the errors that they encounter. This is a similar approach to that taken in [11]. To report all of the errors, the normal boolean pattern of check1 and check2 and check3 and ... is converted to a style that uses a set of boolean results, {check1, check2, check3, ...} = {true}. This causes the evaluation to perform every check in the set, and only fail at the end, if at least one of the checks fails.

3.3   VDM Annotations

The invariant checking functions described above need to be able to capture which sub-clauses are in error, and then carry on with the evaluation. To enable this, a new annotation was developed as part of this work, called @OnFail. The annotation has to be applied to a bracketed boolean sub-clause. If (and only if) the sub-clause returns false then a string with embedded arguments is printed to the console (the arguments work like printf, with "%s" placeholders being substituted for the arguments that follow). The evaluation of the function overall is not affected by this. For example:

```
checkMinMax: int * int * int +> bool
checkMinMax(min, max, start) ==
{
    -- @OnFail("2.2.7 min (%s) must be <= max (%s)", min, max)
    ( min <= max ),
    -- @OnFail("2.2.7 start (%s) must be >= min (%s) and <= max (%s)", start, min, max)
    ( start >= min and start <= max )
}
= {true};
```

That produces the following result, when the function is evaluated from the console:

```
> print checkMinMax(1, 10, 5)
= true

> print checkMinMax(1, 10, 123)
2.2.7 start (123) must be >= min (1) and <= max (10)
= false

> print checkMinMax(10, 1, 123)
2.2.7 min (10) must be <= max (1)
2.2.7 start (123) must be >= min (10) and <= max (1)
= false
```

Note the set-comparison pattern. This will always perform both checks in the set. If either fail, the corresponding message(s) will be written to the console, but @OnFail cannot affect the overall result (which will be false). If the tests in the set pass, the @OnFail annotation will not be triggered.

The number at the start of the messages is (by convention) a link to the FMI standard section number where the corresponding rule is defined. This linkage could be strengthened in future.

3.4   The Top Level Structure - FMIModelDescription

The top level XML element in the configuration of an FMU is called FMIModelDescription. The equivalent structure in VDM-SL is as follows:

```
-- XSD definition in section 2.2.1
FMIModelDescription ::
    -- The common model attributes
    attributes          : ModelAttributes        -- XSD 2.2.1
    -- ModelExchange settings
    modelExchange       : [ModelExchange]         -- XSD 3.3.1
    -- CoSimulation settings
    coSimulation        : [CoSimulation]          -- XSD 4.3.1
    -- Unit Definitions that are utilised in "ModelVariables"
    unitDefinitions     : [seq1 of Unit]          -- XSD 2.2.2
    -- A global list of type definitions that are utilised in "ModelVariables"
    typeDefinitions     : [set1 of SimpleType]    -- XSD 2.2.3
    -- Log categories for debugging
    logCategories       : [seq1 of Category]      -- XSD 2.2.4
    -- Default experiment settings
    defaultExperiment   : [DefaultExperiment]     -- XSD 2.2.5
    -- Vendor annotations
    vendorAnnotations   : [seq1 of Tool]          -- XSD 2.2.6
    -- Variables that are visible/accessible via the FMU API functions.
    modelVariables      : seq1 of ScalarVariable  -- XSD 2.2.7
    -- Defines the structure of the model. Especially, the ordered lists of
    -- outputs, continuous-time states and initial unknowns.
    modelStructure      : ModelStructure;         -- XSD 2.2.8
```

The commented XSD section references refer to the section in the FMI standard where the corresponding XML element types are defined. The names of the VDM-SL types are the same as the XSD types. Note that most fields are optional types (that is, the type is shown in [brackets] and may have the value nil, indicating "no value", which is the same as the absence of an element in XML).

In addition to this type definition, a validation function is defined, which applies all of the checking rules recursively to each of the fields of an FMIModelDescription. The function (truncated for brevity) is as follows:

```
/**
 * Invariant definition for FMIModelDescription
 */
isValidModelFMIDescription: FMIModelDescription +> bool
isValidModelFMIDescription(md) ==
    -- First fill in effective values for model variables' missing attributes
    let eModelVariables =
        [ effectiveScalarVariable(sv) | sv in seq md.modelVariables ]
    in
    {
        -- @OnFail("2.2.1 ModelAttributes invalid")
        ( isValidModelAttributes(md.attributes) ),

        -- @OnFail("2.2.1 ModelExchange invalid")
        ( isValidModelExchange(md.modelExchange) ),

        -- @OnFail("2.2.1 CoSimulation invalid")
        ( isValidCoSimulation(md.coSimulation) ),

        -- @OnFail("2.2.1 UnitDefinitions invalid")
        ( isValidUnitDefinitions(md.unitDefinitions) ),

        -- etc... for all fields, then inter-field checks...

        (
            let outputIndexes = { svi | svi in set inds eModelVariables &
                eModelVariables(svi).causality = <output> }
            in
                if outputIndexes <> {}
                then
                    -- @OnFail("2.2.1 ModelStructure.Outputs should be %s", outputIndexes)
                    ( md.modelStructure.outputs <> nil
                        and { u.index | u in seq md.modelStructure.outputs } = outputIndexes )
                else
                    -- @OnFail("2.2.1 ModelStructure.Outputs should be omitted")
                    ( md.modelStructure.outputs = nil )
        ),

        -- etc...
} = {true};
```

The first part of the validation function produces a modified version of the ModelVariables. This is because variable definitions can omit fields, which then default to an *effective* value according to rules defined in the FMI standard (i.e. p. 50 of the FMI standard). Subsequent checks that depend on the modelVariables then use these effective values.

The main body of the validation function is a set of boolean checks, as discussed in Sect. 3.2. All of the validation functions are named isValid<type>, and they are defined for each type in the schema. So the first field of the FMI-ModelDescription structure is of type ModelAttributes (corresponding to the XML attributes of the FMIModelDescription element) and its validity function is isValidModelAttributes. That function may have @OnFail annotations, but if the attributes are not valid, this outer level will raise its own @OnFail to say that the attributes have problem(s).

Checks at this level also verify that values are consistent *between* fields, for example that all of the output variables in the ModelStructure exist in the ModelVariables and are of type output, as shown.

3.5   Model Variables - ScalarVariable

The ModelVariables section of an FMIModelDescription is a sequence of at least one ScalarVariable definition. This section has to be modelled as a sequence (rather than a set) because the order of the variable declarations is used to identify them elsewhere in the configuration. These indexes start at 1, which is the same convention as VDM. The equivalent types in VDM-SL are as follows:

```
Real ::           -- XSD 2.2.7
    declaredType     : [NormalizedString1]
    quantity         : [NormalizedString1]
    unit             : [NormalizedString1]
    displayUnit      : [NormalizedString1]
    relativeQuantity : [bool]
    min              : [real]
    max              : [real]
    nominal          : [real]
    unbounded        : [bool]
    start            : [real]
    derivative       : [nat1]
    reinit           : [bool];

-- ... also Integer, Boolean, String and Enumeration defined similarly

Variable = Real | Integer | Boolean | String | Enumeration;

VarName = NormalizedString1;    -- Has a syntax defined in section 2.2.9

ScalarVariable ::                     -- XSD 2.2.7
    -- attributes
    name                              : VarName
    valueReference                    : nat
    description                       : [AnyString]
    causality                         : [Causality]
    variability                       : [Variability]
    initial                           : [Initial]
    canHandleMultipleSetPerTimeInstant : [bool]

    -- elements
    variable         : Variable
    annotations      : [seq1 of Tool];
```

The isValidScalarVariable function checks the validity of the fields, which involves checking the min/max/start values of the variables, and checking that the causality, variability, initial and variable start field values, are a valid combination according to the rules in the standard. The (truncated) function is as follows:

```
/**
 * Verify a sequence of ScalarVariables.
 */
isValidScalarVariables: seq1 of ScalarVariable +> bool
isValidScalarVariables(svs) ==
    {
        -- @OnFail("2.2.7 ScalarVariables.causality defines more than one independent variable")
        ( card { sv | sv in seq svs & sv.causality = <independent> } <= 1 ),
        -- @OnFail("2.2.7 ScalarVariable names are not unique")
        ( card { sv.name | sv in seq svs } = len svs ),
        -- @OnFail("2.2.7 Invalid ScalarVariable aliasing")
        ( -- ... check aliasing of variables with same valueReference )
    }
  union
    {
        -- @OnFail("2.2.7 ScalarVariables[%s] invalid", sv.name)
        ( isValidScalarVariable(sv) )
        | sv in seq svs
    } = {true};

/**
 * ScalarVariable invariant. Rules defined in the table on p49.
 */
isValidScalarVariable: ScalarVariable +> bool
isValidScalarVariable(sv) ==
  let eCausality   = effectiveCausality(sv.causality),
      eVariability = effectiveVariability(sv.variability),
      eInitial     = effectiveInitial(sv.initial, eCausality, eVariability)
  in
  {
      -- @OnFail("2.2.7 Causality/variability/initial/start %s/%s/%s/%s invalid",
      --            eCausality, eVariability, eInitial, sv.variable.start)
      (
          cases eCausality:
              <parameter> ->
                  eVariability in set {<fixed>, <tunable>}
                  and eInitial = <exact>,
              ...
      ),
      -- @OnFail("2.2.7 Variability/causality %s/%s invalid", eVariability, eCausality)
      (
          cases eVariability:
              <constant> ->
                  eCausality in set {<output>, <local>},
              ...
      ),
      -- @OnFail("2.2.7 Initial/causality %s/%s invalid", sv.initial, eCausality)
      (
          sv.initial <> nil =>
              (eCausality not in set {<input>, <independent>})
      ),
      -- @OnFail("2.2.7 Initial/variability/start %s/%s/%s invalid",
      --            eInitial, eVariability, sv.variable.start)
      (
          cases eInitial:
              <exact> ->
                  sv.variable.start <> nil,
              ...
      ),
      -- @OnFail("2.2.7 Variable min/max/start invalid")
      (
          cases sv.variable:
              mk_Real(-, min, max, -, -, start, -) ->
                  isInRange[real](min, max, start),
              ...
      ),
      -- @OnFail("2.2.7 VendorAnnotations invalid")
      (isValidVendorAnnotations(sv.annotations))
  } = {true};
```

The main validation function checks that the whole sequence of variables passed defines unique names, at most one of **independent** causality and that the aliased variables follow the rules. Then it calls a second function to check each **ScalarVariable** in isolation. The second function checks that for each of causality, variability and initial, the other two values are valid. For example,

if the effective causality is `parameter`, then the effective variability must be
`fixed` or `tunable` and the initial value must be `exact`; and later, if the effective
initial value is `exact`, then the variable must have a `start` value defined.

3.6   The Model Structure - ModelStructure

The ModelStructure section of an FMIModelDescription lists the outputs,
derivatives and initial unknown values for the FMU. This is represented in VDM-
SL as follows:

```
-- XSD 2.2.8
DependencyKind = <dependent> | <constant> | <fixed> | <tunable> | <discrete>;

Unknown ::
    index              : nat1
    dependencies       : [seq of nat1]
    dependenciesKind   : [seq of DependencyKind];

ModelStructure ::
    outputs            : [seql of Unknown]
    derivatives        : [seql of Unknown]
    initialUnknowns    : [seql of Unknown];
```

The `isValidModelStructure` function is small enough to list here in full:

```
/**
 * Validate an Unknown structure in isolation.
 */
isValidUnknown: Unknown +> bool
isValidUnknown(u) ==
    -- @OnFail("2.2.8 Unknown %s has invalid dependencies/kinds", u.index)
    (
        if u.dependencies <> nil
        then u.dependenciesKind <> nil =>
        {
            -- @OnFail("2.2.8 Dependencies does not match dependenciesKind")
            (len u.dependencies = len u.dependenciesKind),
            -- @OnFail("2.2.8 Dependencies has duplicates")
            (len u.dependencies = card elems u.dependencies),
            -- @OnFail("2.2.8 Unknown cannot depend on itself")
            (u.index not in set elems u.dependencies)
        } = {true}
        else
            u.dependenciesKind = nil
    );

/**
 * Validation of a ModelStructure.
 */
isValidModelStructure: ModelStructure +> bool
isValidModelStructure(ms) ==
{
    -- @OnFail("2.2.8 ModelStructure has invalid unknowns")
    (
        {list <> nil =>
            { isValidUnknown(u) | u in seq list } = {true}
        | list in set {ms.outputs, ms.derivatives, ms.initialUnknowns}
        } = {true}
    ),

    -- @OnFail("2.2.8 ModelStructure.InitialUnknowns are not of kind dependent or constant")
    (
        ms.initialUnknowns <> nil =>
            forall iu in seq ms.initialUnknowns &
            iu.dependenciesKind <> nil =>
                forall dk in seq iu.dependenciesKind &
                    dk in set { <dependent>, <constant>, nil }
    )
} = {true};
```

The validation of the `Unknown` type checks that the dependencies and `dependenciesKind` are consistent: if `dependencies` is defined, then `dependenciesKind` need not be, but if it is then it has the same number of elements as dependencies; `dependencies` must not have duplicate entries; if there are no dependencies, then there must be no `dependenciesKind`.

The validation of the overall `ModelStructure` of `Unknowns` checks that each Unknown is valid, and that any dependencyKinds defined for the initial unknowns can only be `dependent` or `constant`.

3.7   Other Types

There are other types defined at the top level of FMIModelDescription, but their definitions and validation functions are not as complex as those covered in previous sections. The remaining `@OnFail` messages are listed below for completeness:

```
"2.2.1 DefaultExperiment invalid"
"2.2.1 Effective ScalarVariables invalid"
"2.2.1 LogCategories invalid"
"2.2.1 ModelAttribute fmiVersion should be 2.0"
"2.2.1 ModelStructure invalid"
"2.2.1 Neither ModelExchange nor CoSimulation specified"
"2.2.1 ScalarVariables invalid"
"2.2.1 ScalarVariables typecheck against TypeDefinitions failed"
"2.2.1 TypeDefinitions invalid"
"2.2.1 UnitDefinitions invalid"
"2.2.1 VendorAnnotations invalid"
"2.2.2 UnitDefinitions names are not unique: %s"
"2.2.3 SimpleType %s, EnumerationType item name/values do not form a bijection"
"2.2.3 SimpleType %s, Integer max %s not >= min %s"
"2.2.3 SimpleType %s, Real max %s not >= min %s"
"2.2.3 SimpleType %s, Real unit must be defined for displayUnit %s"
"2.2.3 SimpleType %s, Real unit %s not defined in UnitDefinitions"
"2.2.3 TypeDefinition and ScalarVariable names overlap: %s"
"2.2.3 TypeDefinition %s invalid"
"2.2.3 TypeDefinitions names are not unique: %s"
"2.2.3 Typedefs have multiple matching names: %s"
"2.2.4 LogCategory names are not unique: %s"
"2.2.5 DefaultExperiment stepSize must be less than start-stop interval"
"2.2.5 DefaultExperiment stop time must be later than start time"
"2.2.6 VendorAnnotations tool names are not unique: %s"
"2.2.7 Aliases of reference %s/%s are settable and independent: %s"
"2.2.7 Aliases of reference %s/%s must all be constant or variable"
"2.2.7 Aliases of reference %s/%s must all have same unit/baseUnits"
"2.2.7 Constant aliases of reference %s/%s have different start values"
"2.2.7 Continuous variable must be Real"
"2.2.7 Independent variable must be Real"
"2.2.7 Invalid ScalarVariable aliasing"
"2.2.7 min %s is not <= max %s"
"2.2.7 Multiple aliases of reference %s/%s are settable: %s"
"2.2.7 Real nominal must be >0.0"
"2.2.7 ScalarVariable names are not unique: %s"
"2.2.7 ScalarVariable %s, BooleanType not referenced by Boolean variable %s"
"2.2.7 ScalarVariable %s, canHandleMultipleSetPerTimeInstant invalid"
"2.2.7 ScalarVariables define more than one independent variable: %s"
"2.2.7 ScalarVariable %s, EnumerationType not referenced by Enumeration variable %s"
```

```
"2.2.7 ScalarVariable %s, IntegerType not referenced by Integer variable %s"
"2.2.7 ScalarVariable %s invalid"
"2.2.7 ScalarVariable %s min/max exceeds IntegerType %s"
"2.2.7 ScalarVariable %s min/max exceeds RealType %s"
"2.2.7 ScalarVariable %s, Real reinit for model exchange continuous time only"
"2.2.7 ScalarVariable %s, RealType not referenced by Real variable %s"
"2.2.7 ScalarVariable %s, Real unit must be defined for displayUnit %s"
"2.2.7 ScalarVariable %s, Real unit %s not defined in UnitDefinitions"
"2.2.7 ScalarVariable %s, StringType not referenced by String variable %s"
"2.2.7 start %s is not within min %s/max %s"
"2.2.7 Too many aliases of reference %s/%s have start set"
"2.2.7 Variable %s causality/variability/initial/start %s/%s/%s/%s invalid"
"2.2.7 Variable %s initial/causality %s/%s invalid at %s"
"2.2.7 Variable %s initial/variability/start %s/%s/%s invalid"
"2.2.7 Variable %s min/max/start/nominal invalid"
"2.2.7 Variable %s variability/causality %s/%s invalid"
"2.2.7 VendorAnnotations invalid"
"2.2.7 Warning: aliases of reference %s/%s must all be %s"
"2.2.7 Warning: aliases of reference %s/%s must all be %s, because of %s"
"2.2.7 Warning: implicit start of 0 is not within min %s/max %s"
"2.2.8 Dependencies list does not match dependenciesKind"
"2.2.8 Derivatives declared, but no Real/derivative variables"
"2.2.8 Derivatives indexes out of range"
"2.2.8 Derivatives section does not match Real/derivative variables"
"2.2.8 InitialUnknowns are not of kind dependent or constant"
"2.2.8 InitialUnknowns are not sorted: %s"
"2.2.8 InitialUnknowns must include: %s"
"2.2.8 InitialUnknowns must include: %s"
"2.2.8 Output indexes out of range"
"2.2.8 Outputs section does not match output variables"
"2.2.8 Outputs should be omitted"
"2.2.8 Output variables but no outputs declared"
"2.2.8 Real/derivative variables but no Derivatives declared"
"2.2.8 Unknown has duplicate indexes %s"
"2.2.9 Name %s is not Real"
"2.2.9 Structured name %s invalid"
"3.3.1 ModelExchange source file names are not unique: %s"
"4.3.1 CoSimulation source file names are not unique: %s"
```

3.8   Automated FMU Checking in VDM

A VDM model is useful in itself, because it encodes a more precise and unambiguous description of the constraints in the FMI standard than either the XSD or informal documentation alone. But to be actively useful, the model and supporting VDM tools need to be able to analyse an FMU file directly.

To do this, the FMU package file first has to be unpacked to access the "modelDescription.xml" file within it. That XML then has to be converted into VDM-SL such that the result can be put together with the VDM-SL representation of the XSD types, and the top level isValidFMIModelDescription function can be called to check it.

This process can be completely automated. Unpacking an FMU package is a simple matter as the package is a ZIP format. The extracted XML file can be converted to VDM-SL with a fairly simple SAX parser (using standard Java libraries). Combining the main VDM model files with the generated file and then calling isValidFMIModelDescription is simple because the command line VDM tools accept input from multiple files, and a function to evaluate can be passed.

The whole process is combined into a bash shell script called `VDMCheck.sh`, which either prints the result of `isValidFMIModelDescription` as `true` or lists the `@OnFail`'s that were raised and prints `false`. For example:

```
$ VDMCheck.sh
Usage: VDMCheck.sh [-v <VDM outfile>] <FMU or modelDescription.xml file>

$ VDMCheck.sh WaterTank_Control.fmu
true

$ VDMCheck.sh MixtureGases.fmu
2.2.7 start -1 is not within min 1/max 10000
2.2.7 Variable min/max/start/nominal invalid at line 1143
2.2.7 ScalarVariables["Medium2.fluidConstants[6].normalBoilingPoint"] invalid at
line 1143
2.2.1 ScalarVariables invalid
2.2.8 Derivatives declared, but no Real/derivative variables at line 3130
2.2.8 InitialUnknowns must include: {353, 354}
false
```

Note that several messages relate to the same area: the first two messages relate to the fields of the `normalBoilingPoint` variable identified in the third message, and the last two messages say that there are ModelStructure Derivatives but no derivative variables declared, and that the InitialUnknowns are missing two index entries.

The locations given are line numbers within the XML file. Each `@OnFail` message starts with a section reference in the FMI standard where the corresponding rule is defined. An alpha release of VDMCheck is available[2].

3.9   Online FMU Checking

A command line tool such as VDMCheck is useful, but it can be difficult to package the tool in such a way that it will run easily in multiple user environments (Windows, Linux, Mac and so on). To try to simplify this, the VDM model can be used to verify an FMU via an online website, where an FMU binary is uploaded and checked, and a report of any problems given.

The site is currently being developed, but a very early preview is available here: https://sweng.au.dk/fmiutils/fmichecker.

4   Empirical Evaluation of Static Conformance

The VDMCheck.sh tool[3] described in Sect. 3.8 has been executed on all of the FMUs within the version 2.0 branch of the Modellica FMI Cross Check repository[4]. The preliminary results are as follows, though these "faults" have to be investigated to determine whether the VDM model is being too strict:

---

[2] https://github.com/INTO-CPS-Association/FMI2-VDM-Model/releases.

[3] Version 0.0.2 build 191107.

[4] https://github.com/modelica/fmi-cross-check/tree/master/fmus/2.0/.

- There are 692 FMUs in this branch the repository (many are duplicated for different architectures and tools)
- 294 (42%) of them pass without any @OnFail messages (ie. isValidFMIModelDescription returns true)
- 175 of them have aliases that do not have compatible settings
- 123 of them have malformed structured variable names
- 118 of them have invalid InitialUnknowns
- 112 of them have ModelStructure Derivatives indexes that do no match Real/derivative variables
- 65 of them have ScalarVariable attribute inconsistencies
- 56 of them have aliased variables that do not all have the same units
- 24 have the reinit flag set for co-simulation models
- 14 have Real units that are not declared in UnitDefinitions
- 13 of them have ModelStructure Outputs that do not match the "output" variables
- 4 of them have InitialUnknowns that are not sorted in ascending order

We wish to emphasise that these results are preliminary and may be a reflection of faults in the VDM model rather than faults with the FMUs concerned. The same FMUs produce the following results with the current FMU Compliance Checker[5] (version 2.0.4):

- The same 692 FMUs were tested
- 488 (65%)of them pass without any error or warnings messages
- 123 of them have malformed structured variable names
- 27 of them have Derivatives that do not refer to a derivative variable
- 12 of them have inconsistent ScalarVariable causality/variability/initial/start settings

The most frequent discrepancy between the checking tools is regarding the variability of sets of aliased variables. The rules for this were clarified in FMI 2.0.1 (Sect. 2.2.8, p53), but 25% of the models in the repository do not follow these rules.

The second most frequent discrepancy is regarding the population of the InitialUnknowns field of the Model Structure. The rules for this seem fairly clear (Sect. 2.2.8, p60), but 17% of the models in the repository do not follow these rules.

Similarly, the rules for the remaining discrepancies are stated in the FMI Standard, and yet many models do not follow them.

Note that the problem of malformed structured names is reported *identically* in both tools: the same 123 files are reported, and within them the same errors are identified. Given the degree of discrepancy otherwise found between the tools, this may be surprising. But it is because the section of the FMI standard that defines the rules uses a formal notation (EBNF in Sect. 2.2.9). This means that FMUChecker and VDMCheck can agree exactly on what the rules are.

---

[5] https://github.com/modelica-tools/FMUComplianceChecker/releases.

4.1   Tailored XML Test Results

A set of 24 modelDescription.xml files have been produced in order to test each one of the @OnFail messages in the VDM model. The same set of XML files can be packaged into minimal FMU ZIP files and processed with the FMUChecker for comparison. The FMUChecker currently reports that only 10 of the files contain errors, so here again FMUChecker is identifying far fewer problems than the VDM model. We have yet to determine whether this is the VDM model being too strict.

5   Concluding Remarks and Future Work

This paper has demonstrated that producing a formal specification of the semi-formal FMI standard highlights a number of issues that are not sufficiently clearly described in the standard, nor checked by the FMUChecker tool. Most commonly this leads to misconfigured aliased variables, InitialUnknowns and inconsistent Derivatives declarations. Significantly, the only area where the FMUChecker tool agrees precisely with the formal VDM model is with structured variable names, which are defined in the FMI standard using a formal grammar (EBNF). This is added evidence that formal specifications reduce ambiguity and lead to more consistent implementations.

The work to try to determine the correct semantics, based on the FMUs in the Cross-Check repository and the behaviour of the FMUChecker tool, is ongoing. We hope that the FMI community at large will welcome the kinds of verification we are able to perform in this manner.

The current work can naturally be migrated to cover subsequent versions of the FMI standard, and the process of migrating the model may identify weaknesses in the supporting standard documentation. We also plan to extend the scope of the work to cover the dynamic semantics of the orchestration of the co-simulation of a collection of FMUs that is defined in the FMI standard. This would then allow the behaviour of different orchestration algorithms to be explored, from a formal footing (e.g., as done in [8]), and enable verification of the modular version of the Maestro co-simulation engine [18].

Acknowledgements. We are grateful to the Poul Due Jensen Foundation, which has supported the establishment of a new Centre for Digital Twin Technology at Aarhus University, which will take forward the principles, tools and applications of the engineering of digital twins. We also acknowledge EU for funding the INTO-CPS project (grant agreement number 644047) which was the original source of funding for the INTO-CPS Application, and the Research Foundation - Flanders (Grant File Number 1S06316N). Finally, we thank the reviewers for their throughout feedback.

References

1. Bastian, J., Clauß, C., Wolf, S., Schneider, P.: Master for co-simulation using FMI. In: 8th International Modelica Conference, pp. 115–120. Linköping University Electronic Press, Linköpings universitet, Dresden, Germany, June 2011

2. Blochwitz, T., et al.: The functional mockup interface for tool independent exchange of simulation models. In: 8th International Modelica Conference, pp. 105–114. Linköping University Electronic Press, Linköpings universitet, Dresden, Germany, June 2011

3. Blockwitz, T., et al.: Functional mockup interface 2.0: the standard for tool independent exchange of simulation models. In: 9th International Modelica Conference, pp. 173–184. Linköping University Electronic Press, Munich, Germany, November 2012

4. Fitzgerald, J., Gamble, C., Larsen, P.G., Pierce, K., Woodcock, J.: Cyber-physical systems design: formal foundations, methods and integrated tool chains. In: FormaliSE: FME Workshop on Formal Methods in Software Engineering. ICSE 2015, Florence, Italy, May 2015

5. Fitzgerald, J., et al.: Collaborative model-based systems engineering for cyber-physical systems - a case study in building automation. In: Proceedings of INCOSE International Symposium on Systems Engineering. Edinburgh, Scotland, July 2016

6. Fitzgerald, J., Larsen, P.G.: Modelling Systems - Practical Tools and Techniques in Software Development, 2nd edn. Cambridge University Press, Cambridge (2009). ISBN 0-521-62348-0

7. FMI: Functional Mock-up Interface for Model Exchange and Co-Simulation. Technical report, FMI development group (2014)

8. Gomes, C., et al.: Semantic adaptation for FMI co-simulation with hierarchical simulators. SIMULATION **95**(3), 1–29 (2018)

9. Gomes, C., et al.: HintCO - hint-based configuration of co-simulations. In: International Conference on Simulation and Modeling Methodologies, Technologies and Applications, Prague, Czech Republic, pp. 57–68 (2019). https://doi.org/10.5220/0007830000570068

10. Gomes, C., Thule, C., Broman, D., Larsen, P.G., Vangheluwe, H.: Co-simulation: a Survey. ACM Comput. Surv. **51**(3), 49:1–49:33 (2018). Article 49

11. Hasanagić, M., Tran-Jørgensen, P.W.V., Lausdahl, K., Larsen, P.G.: Formalising and validating the interface description in the FMI standard. In: Fitzgerald, J., Heitmeyer, C., Gnesi, S., Philippou, A. (eds.) FM 2016. LNCS, vol. 9995, pp. 344–351. Springer, Cham (2016). https://doi.org/10.1007/978-3-319-48989-6_21

12. Jones, C.B.: Systematic Software Development Using VDM, 2nd edn. Prentice-Hall International, Englewood Cliffs (1990). ISBN 0-13-880733-7

13. Larsen, P.G., et al.: Integrated tool chain for model-based design of cyber-physical systems: the INTO-CPS project. In: CPS Data Workshop. Vienna, Austria, April 2016

14. Larsen, P.G., Fitzgerald, J., Woodcock, J., Lecomte, T.: Trustworthy Cyber-Physical Systems Engineering. Chapter 8: Collaborative Modelling and Simulation for Cyber-Physical Systems. Chapman and Hall/CRC, Boca Raton (2016). ISBN 9781498742450

15. Larsen, P.G., Fitzgerald, J., Woodcock, J., Nilsson, R., Gamble, C., Foster, S.: Towards semantically integrated models and tools for cyber-physical systems design. In: Margaria, T., Steffen, B. (eds.) ISoLA 2016. LNCS, vol. 9953, pp. 171–186. Springer, Cham (2016). https://doi.org/10.1007/978-3-319-47169-3_13

16. Schweiger, G., et al.: An empirical survey on co-simulation: promising standards, challenges and research needs. Simul. Model. Pract. Theor. **95**, 148–163 (2019)

17. Thule, C., Lausdahl, K., Gomes, C., Meisl, G., Larsen, P.G.: Maestro: the INTO-CPS co-simulation framework. Simul. Model. Pract. Theor **92**, 45–61 (2019). http://www.sciencedirect.com/science/article/pii/S1569190X1830193X

18. Thule, C., et al.: Towards reuse of synchronization algorithms in co-simulation frameworks. In: Accepted for Publication at the Co-Sim-19 Workshop, September 2019
19. Tomiyama, T., D'Amelio, V., Urbanic, J., ElMaraghy, W.: Complexity of multidisciplinary design. CIRP Ann. Manuf. Technol. **56**(1), 185–188 (2007)
20. Van der Auweraer, H., Anthonis, J., De Bruyne, S., Leuridan, J.: Virtual engineering at work: the challenges for designing mechatronic products. Eng. Comput. **29**(3), 389–408 (2013)

ViennaDoc: An Animatable and Testable Specification Documentation Tool

Tomohiro Oda[1]([✉]), Keijiro Araki[2], Yasuhiro Yamamoto[3], Kumiyo Nakakoji[1,3], Hiroshi Sako[4], Han-Myung Chang[5], and Peter Gorm Larsen[6]

[1] Software Research Associates, Inc., Tokyo, Japan
tomohiro@sra.co.jp, kumiyo@acm.org
[2] National Institute of Technology, Kumamoto College, Kumamoto, Japan
araki@kyudai.jp
[3] Future University Hakodate, Hakodate, Japan
yxy@acm.org
[4] Designer's Den, Tokyo, Japan
sakoh@ba2.so-net.ne.jp
[5] Nanzan University, Nagoya, Japan
chang@nanzan-u.ac.jp
[6] DIGIT, Department of Engineering, Aarhus University, Aarhus, Denmark
pgl@eng.au.dk

Abstract. An obstacle to applying formal specification techniques to industrial projects is that stakeholders with little engineering background may experience difficulty comprehending the specification. Forming a common understanding of a specification is indeed essential in software development because a specification is consulted by many kinds of stakeholders, including those who do not necessarily have an engineering background.

This paper introduces ViennaDoc, a specification documentation tool that interleaves animation of a formal specification into informal texts written using natural language. ViennaDoc helps readers to understand the behaviour of the specified system by providing opportunities to verify their understanding by executing the specification in the context of the informal explanation. ViennaDoc also helps maintainers of the specification by enabling unit testing that asserts equality between values embedded in the informal specification and formal expressions.

1 Introduction

A development team needs a common understanding of the system to be developed. Ambiguity, looseness and inconsistency in a specification may result in disagreement in understanding among the development stakeholders. Misunderstandings of a specification between stakeholders may lead the development to produce a useless system.

VDM-SL [5] is a formal specification language with rigorous syntax and semantics, and therefore gives an unambiguous meaning to the specification. However, the mathematical meaning of a formal specification is not enough to avoid disagreement of understanding because the specification of a software system should also be situated in the context of the real world as well. In industrial projects, informal documents in a natural language are created along with formal specifications. Such informal documents typically explain the operational usage of the formal specification to stakeholders

© Springer Nature Switzerland AG 2020
E. Sekerinski et al. (Eds.): FM 2019 Workshops, LNCS 12233, pp. 289–302, 2020.
https://doi.org/10.1007/978-3-030-54997-8_19

unfamiliar with formal notations, and illustrate the concrete situations that the formally specified system is expected to be used inside. In this paper, we call such informal descriptions *specification documents* to distinguish them from formal specifications.

Specification documents are literature to explain the meaning of the specification. Conventional IDEs for VDM, such as VDMTools [3] and the Overture tool [4], support the VDM-SL's literate format that embed VDM-SL modules in a LATEX document. Although LATEX is a practical tool to print documents such as books, its main target is to print on paper and to produce PDF files with static contents, and it does not afford dynamic representations that are suitable for explaining dynamic behaviour of the system in particular scenarios.

Specification animation is a technique to simulate behaviour of the system to be realised [6,8]. Animation has been used mainly by formal engineers in practice. Integrated Development Environments (IDEs) for VDM provide animation mechanisms including interpreters and transpilers so that the specification engineers can confirm the formal specification *means* what was intended. Those IDEs also provide unit testing mechanisms to automatically test whether or not the operational meaning of the formal specifications is kept as intended.

The authors have been developing a formal specification environment called ViennaTalk that supports stakeholders with little engineering skills to understand the specified system in contexts of specific domains [9]. One of the major objectives of ViennaTalk is to enable more features for animation techniques for a wider range of stakeholders. A stakeholder, in general, uses animation to check whether the stakeholder's understanding is correct or not. The stakeholder typically has a particular situation in mind, and reproduces it in the animation. If the animation provides the expected behaviour, the stakeholder gains confidence on the validity of the formal specification and also the correctness of the stakeholder's understanding. Animation techniques can thus be used in the context of comprehension support.

It is, however, often hard for stakeholders without sufficient training in formal specifications to articulate an expression to evaluate. Some of the difficulties are of the VDM-SL language features such as its formal syntax and semantics. ViennaTalk addresses the language difficulty by collaborative approaches. Lively Walk-Through is a User Interface (UI) prototyping environment provided in ViennaTalk to develop shared understanding of the formal specification between formal engineers and UI designers. Other stakeholders, such as product owners and end user representatives, can also use Lively Walk-Through to experience the specified system. Those systems support stakeholders to understand formal specifications without knowledge of VDM-SL.

This paper introduces ViennaDoc, a web publishing tool for VDM-SL specification documents with live animation and testing features. In ViennaDoc, formal expressions expressed using VDM-SL are placed along with use scenarios of the system. Stakeholders with little formal background can understand the scenario exemplified with predefined animations without writing any formal expressions. ViennaDoc can also help maintenance of the specification document by unit testing. ViennaDoc is developed as a part of ViennaTalk and its source code is available under the MIT license[1].

---

[1] https://github.com/tomooda/ViennaTalk/.

In Sect. 2, overall design objectives of ViennaDoc will be presented. In Sect. 3, implementation and features of ViennaDoc are explained and discussed. Section 4 will introduce related work, and Sect. 5 will conclude the discussion and describes possible future work.

2   Informal Documents Augmented with Formal Specifications

Formal specification often complements informal specification documents for many purposes. A specification document is not only for stakeholders with little engineering background, but also for formal engineers to understand how the specified system will be used in the real world. Situating the formal specification is a critical role of its documentation for stakeholders to share a common understanding of the system to be developed. Formal engineers can use interpreters to confirm the specified system exhibits the intended behaviour in particular situations. However, the use of animation was mainly limited to formal engineers due to difficulty of articulating appropriate formal expressions.

Inconsistency between a formal specification and its documentation may become one of the barriers for stakeholders to have a shared understanding. For example, a piece of formal specification that appears in a specification document should be the right version. The effects of an action are often explained informally in a specification document. Such an explanation must naturally agree with the behaviour of the formal specification. Nevertheless, it is not a trivial task to maintain a documentation consistent with the formal specification. A specification document needs to be revised for many reasons, such as a change of the formal specification, a change of the expected uses of the system, and inaccurate discourse of the explanation. Animation has been used to test formal specifications in practice, and case studies report that those tests were effective [2]. However, the use of animation in testing was limited to the formal specification.

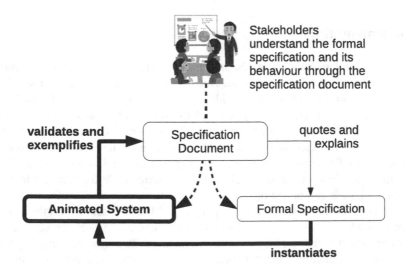

Fig. 1. Formal specification, specification document and animation

This paper proposes to apply specification animation techniques to informal specification documents. Figure 1 describes the relationship among a formal specification, its documentation and the animated system. This paper discusses roles of animation mechanisms in the documentation environment, drawn in the thick box and the thick arrows. ViennaDoc is a simple animation tool for HTML documents on a VDM-SL specification. ViennaDoc provides the following three features to support documentation:

- Source expansion to include a VDM-SL source;
- animation to illustrate the system's behaviour; and
- assertion to validate values in the document.

The source expansion feature helps the author of a specification document to keep the embedded source up to date. It is a simple and effective way to maintain a document without spoiling the agility of the specification phase.

The animation feature is meant to explain the system's behaviour in a particular scenario. When a user scenario is explained in natural language, the user can see how the system will behave in the scenario by executing an operation with the given contextual state of the system. The user can even explore different series of actions by performing animation in an arbitrary order. Animation can be used for exercises to check whether the reader's understanding is correct. This flexibility cannot be provided by a static PDF file.

The assertion is a declaration of a certain property of the system or a part of it, and software testing is one of its major applications. The assertion in ViennaDoc is to test the specification document whether or not a VDM-SL value displayed in a document is equal to the result of evaluating the given expression in the given state of the system. If they are not equal, the document is inconsistent with the formal specification.

Section 3 will describe how ViennaDoc is implemented and how it works inside a web browser.

3   Implementation

ViennaDoc is implemented in JavaScript enabling HTML documents to animate a VDM-SL specification. Figure 2 illustrates the overview of ViennaDoc and related components. The `ViennaDoc` object provided by the `ViennaDoc.js` script has two responsibilities: 1) to perform animation and assertion and 2) to scan the Document Object Model (DOM) to insert the formal specification sources, animation mechanisms and assertions into the ViennaDoc specific DOM elements. The HTML file also loads a specification specific script (`Counter.js` in Fig. 2) generated by ViennaTalk [9]. The specification specific script defines a dictionary of source code for each module, type, value, function, state and operation.

The `ViennaDoc.js` script uses the public VDMPad [9] server[2] via the functions provided by the `ViennaClient.js` script. The `ViennaClient.js` script extends the `String` object with the `vienna_eval()` method. To animate a formal specification, the source specification, the state before evaluation, the expression to evaluate and

---

[2] https://vdmpad.viennatalk.org/.

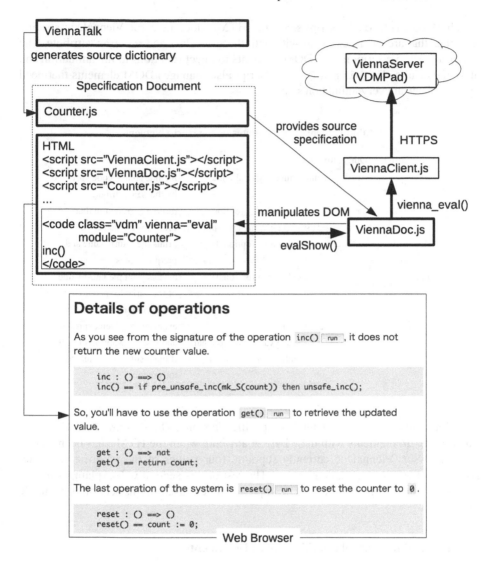

Fig. 2. Overview configuration of a typical ViennaDoc document

the namespace (module) must be specified. The `vienna_eval()` method uses the receiver string as the VDM-SL source specification. The expression to evaluate is given as the first argument. The state before evaluation and the module are optionally given as the second and the third arguments in order. The return value of the `vienna_eval()` method is triple of the return value, the post-state, and the error message.

The `ViennaDoc.evalShow()` method is called by an event on a DOM element, such as a clicked event on a `code` element. The `ViennaDoc.evalShow()` method manipulates the requesting DOM element to show the animation result. The `String.vienna_eval()` method is used to get the animation result.

The `ViennaDoc.js` script scans the HTML document for ViennaDoc specific elements, that are `code` elements with both the `vdm` class and `vienna` attribute. The `ViennaDoc.js` script inserts DOM elements to inject functions to run animation and show the results. The `ViennaDoc.js` script also manages DOM elements that need active updates at every animation step.

Table 1. ViennaDoc attributes on the `code` element

`vienna` attribute	Other attributes	Description
`"source"`	`src` = module name or global name	include source code specified by the `src` attribute
`"eval"`	`prestates` = variable list (optional) `poststates` = state variables (optional) `module` = module name (optional)	insert a `run` button that evaluates the content and prints the return value and pre/post states
`"watch"`	`module` = module name (optional)	always print the latest value of the variable specified in the content
`"assert"`	`eval` = expression `prestates` = state variables (optional) `module` = module name (optional)	evaluate the given expression and insert a warning message if the result is not equal to the content

Table 1 summarises the ViennaDoc specific elements. The `ViennaDoc.js` script scans for `code` elements with the `vienna` attribute when the HTML has been loaded to the browser. ViennaDoc currently supports four values of the `vienna` attribute; `source`, `eval`, `watch` and `assert`. The rest of this section will explain each kind of `code` elements one by one. The example document used in this section is available online[3].

3.1 Embedding Formal Specification in Documents

ViennaDoc provides access to source listings of modules and definitions. Figure 3 illustrates how a `code` element for source listing is specified in ViennaDoc and how it appears inside a browser.

A `code` element with the `vienna="source"` attribute fills the element with the corresponding source specified by the `src` attribute. In Fig. 3, the `Counter` module is specified by the `src` attribute. Using the source embedding feature of ViennaDoc, the source listings shown in the document are kept identical to the ones used for the animation.

---

[3] https://viennatalk.org/ViennaDoc/counter.html.

```
<code class="vdm" vienna="source" src="Counter"></code>
```

⇓ rendered on a browser

Here is the full specification of the counter system.

```
module Counter
exports
    operations
        inc : () ==> ();
        get : () ==> nat;
        reset : () ==> ();
definitions
state S of
    count : nat
inv mk_S(c) == c < 10
init s == s = mk_S(0)
end

operations
    inc : () ==> ()
    inc() == if pre_unsafe_inc(mk_S(count)) then unsafe_inc();

    unsafe_inc : () ==> ()
    unsafe_inc() == count := count + 1
    pre  count < 9;

    get : () ==> nat
    get() == return count;

    reset : () ==> ()
    reset() == count := 0;

end Counter
```

The objective of the system is to help the user to count the number of a certain event. We

Fig. 3. Screenshot of a ViennaDoc page that includes a module source

```
<code class="vdm" vienna="source" src="Counter`inc"></code>
```

⇓ rendered on a browser

counter value.

```
inc : () ==> ()
inc() == if pre_unsafe_inc(mk_S(count)) then unsafe_inc();
```

So, you'll have to use the operation get() to retrieve the updated value.

Fig. 4. Screenshot of a ViennaDoc page that includes an operation's source

The value of the `src` attribute is either a module name or a global name. In Fig. 4, the `Counter`unsafe_inc` operation is specified by the `src` attribute. Please note that a global name should be specified to include a source listing of an operation, function or any other definition. A global name should be in the form of ⟨*module name*⟩ `⟨*identifier*⟩, and the source is stored at `ViennaDoc.sources[⟨*global name*⟩]`. ViennaDoc needs the source listings from an external source for source embedding as well as animation and assertions. ViennaTalk's VDM browser generates JavaScript source code to supply the source listings.

VennaDoc automatically enclose the `code` element with a `pre` element so that newline and indentations are preserved when rendered on the browser. Although ViennaDoc does not have any feature to decorate source code, the HTML file can use an external engine to highlight the source specifications inserted by ViennaDoc. For example, the source listings in Fig. 3 and Fig. 4 are highlighted by the `highlight.js`[4] package.

3.2 Animated Specification Documents

VennaDoc employs animation to exhibit concrete behaviour of the specified system. VennaDoc provides user interfaces for animation in a controlled manner comparing to those in IDEs. For example, VDMPad enables the user to evaluate an arbitrary expression in an arbitrary state by providing entry fields for state variables and the expression to evaluate. VDMPad allows the user as much freedom as possible so that the user can explore a wider range of use scenarios. On the other hand, VennaDoc does not allow the user to change the expression to evaluate. The objective of the animation capability inside VennaDoc is to help the user's comprehension of the specification document in a natural language by showing simulated behaviour of the system. Agreement between the explanation in natural language and animation in a formal language is crucial and therefore the expression to evaluate is hardcoded.

VennaDoc provides two kinds of user interfaces for animation. One is a push button. `ViennaDoc.js` inserts a push button after a `code` element with the `vienna="eval"` attribute. Figure 5 shows how a push button is placed in a VennaDoc document and how it can present the animation result. The `code` element shown in the upper box is rendered on a web browser while the middle box shows the rendered element. A push button labeled `run` is placed after the `code` node (`inc()` in a grey background). When the user clicks on the `run` button, a brief text in the gray background is appended after the `run` button as shown in the lower box. The appended text is in the form of {*bindings before evaluation*}*expr* ☞ *ret value*{*bindings after evaluation*}.

The animation state is managed by the `ViennaDoc.states` variable. At every animation, ViennaDoc first reads the state from the `ViennaDoc.states`, evaluates the given expression, and updates the `ViennaDoc.states`. If the `prestates` attribute has bindings indicated by =, the value will be used instead of the corresponding value in the `ViennaDoc.states`. In Fig. 6, the value of the state variable `count` is set to 5 before evaluating `inc()`.

---

[4] See https://highlightjs.org/.

```
<code class="vdm" vienna="eval"
  prestates="count"
  poststates="count"
  module="Counter">
inc()
</code>
, it does not return the new counter value.
```

⇓ rendered on a browser

inc() run , it does not return the new

⇓ the push button clicked

inc() run {count=0} inc() ☞ () {count=1}

Fig. 5. Animation of a ViennaDoc page with a run button

```
<code class="vdm" vienna="eval"
  prestates="count=5"
  poststates="count"
  module="Counter">
inc()
</code>
```

Fig. 6. An HTML source for animation with a prestate value specified

Another user interface for animation is a watch variable. `ViennaDoc.js` inserts a brief text after a `code` element with the `vienna="watch"` attribute. Figure 7 shows how a watch variable is shown in a ViennaDoc. The `code` element shown in the upper box is rendered on a web browser as shown in the middle box. The text ☞ 0 in a grey background is placed after the `code` node (`count` also in the grey background) to indicate that the value of the state variable `count` is now set to 0. Whenever the user clicks on any of the `run` buttons in the document, the value after the `hand` symbol is updated with the new value of the variable `count`.

In Fig. 7, the module `Counter` is specified in the `code` element and its content is in a short name of the variable inside that module. A global name in form of *module name`state variable name* can be specified in the content without the `module` attribute.

The state variables are managed as a JavaScript object on the page. If the user reloads the page, the state will be initialised by the formal specification. The state will

```
<code class="vdm" vienna="watch"
  module="Counter">
count
</code>
```

⇓ rendered on a browser

count ☞ 0

⇓ any push button clicked

count ☞ 1

Fig. 7. Animation of a ViennaDoc page with a watch variable

also be initialised when the web page transitions by hyperlinks. ViennaDoc has been designed to employ the volatile state that a ViennaDoc page always opens with a fresh initial state.

3.3 Testable Specification Documents

Software testing is a widely used technique to find a deviation from the expected behaviour. ViennaDoc provides testing feature on an HTML document to find such deviations from the actual behaviour of the formal specification. ViennaDoc performs a test on a code element with the vienna=assert attribute.

```
<code class="vdm" vienna="assert"
  module="Counter"
  prestates="count=5"
  eval="mk_(reset(),_count).#2">
0
</code>
```

⇓ rendered on a browser

0.

Fig. 8. A successful assertion and its appearance on a browser

Figure 8 shows a successful case of the assertion. ViennaDoc evaluates the given expression mk_(reset(), count).#2 with count=5, which returns the value of the `count` variable after the `reset()` operation call. ViennaDoc will get 0 as the result which is identical to the value in the content of the `code` element. The assertion is successful and the web browser shows the `code` element without modification.

```
<code class="vdm" vienna="assert"
  module="Counter"
  prestates="count=5"
  eval="mk_(inc(),_count).#2">
0
</code>
```

⇓ rendered on a browser

0 [invalid: {count=5} mk_(inc(), count).#2 ☞ 6].

Fig. 9. An assertion failure and its appearance on a browser

On the other hand, Fig. 9 shows a failure case. ViennaDoc evaluates the given expression `mk_(inc(), count).#2` with `count=5`, which returns the value of the `count` variable after the `inc()` operation call instead of the `reset()` operation call. ViennaDoc will get 6 as the result which is different from 0 in the content of the `code` element. The assertion fails and the web browser warns that the value in the document does not agree with the actual result.

Assertion failures may happen due to various causes. One possible cause of failure is that the document is not updated after a change of the VDM-SL specification. Another possible cause is that the author misunderstands the formal specification. ViennaDoc's assertion enables specification documents tested its consistency with the formal specification on the readers' web browsers just in time.

4 Related Work

This section introduces four software tools and explains their differences from this work.

4.1 Lively Walk-Through

Lively Walk-Through [9] is a UI prototyping tool to support formal methods engineers and UI designers to share a common understanding of the specified system. Lively Walk-Through can be also used as a prototyping tool for stakeholders with little engineering background to experience the expected use of the system in the specific domain. ViennaDoc and Lively Walk-Through share the same objective to provide a dynamic medium for stakeholders without formal engineering skills to understand what the formal specification means through animation.

A major difference between ViennaDoc and Lively Walk-Through is flexibility of animation. ViennaDoc provides a restrictive UI for animation while Lively Walk-Through provides full flexibility to evaluate arbitrary expressions. ViennaDoc is a documentation tool and therefore takes a more instructive approach to explain the formal specification. Lively Walk-Through does not provide textual explanations in natural languages, and thus expects emergent understanding in action.

4.2 PVSio-web

PVSio-web [7] is a prototyping environment that combines formal specification in PVS and human interface. One major application field of PVSio-web is embedded systems such as medical devices. With PVSio-web, the user can virtually manipulate the target device with feedback by animated specification.

A major difference between ViennaDoc and PVSio-web is the way the presentation is made. While PVSio-web is a simulator with photo realistic visual interface of the target device, ViennaDoc is documentation tool with textual descriptions.

4.3 Pillar

Pillar [1] is a documentation tool built on top of the Pharo Smalltalk system. Pillar has its own lightweight markup language with many dynamic features such as importing the source code from a live Smalltalk system, programmatically taking a snapshot image of the GUI, evaluating Smalltalk expressions, and testing assertions attached with Smalltalk expressions. Pillar can publish a document in various formats including LATEX, PDF, HTML and Smalltalk's Text objects. Pillar has already been used for publishing numerous books and online documents shared among the Pharo community. *Agile Visualization*[5] is a book authored with Pillar and published in paperback, eBook and HTML.

The conceptual design of ViennaDoc was highly inspired by Pillar. Both ViennaDoc and Pillar can incorporate source code into the document. Pillar also checks consistency between a book content and the actual behaviour of the system using assertion mechanisms in a way similar to that of ViennaDoc.

The major difference is that Pillar processes dynamic elements in a document source within Pillar itself. For example, a document is generated after assertions in the document source have been all checked. The readers of the book do not see its validation process. ViennaDoc, on the other hand, provides dynamic features such as the `run` button and watch variables on the browser. Animations performed on those elements are commenced by the reader, and the animation results are exposed to the reader. Assertions are also checked on the reader's browser, and the results are rendered inline on the browser.

---

[5] http://agilevisualization.com/.

4.4 Jupyter Notebook

Jupyter Notebook is a web-based interpreter interface initially for Python. Jupyter Notebook basically provides a REPL (Read, Eval, Print Loop) interface in a form of a webpage, and the server runs the Python interpreter to execute the commands given by the user. Code fragments given by the user and the resulting output of the Python interpreter are recorded on the webpage. The user can review those command lines and outputs to summarise the exploratory process and store it for later reference. The resulting page can be seen as a documentation of the exploration process.

Jupyter Notebook is also used for documenting software systems. Some development hosting services, such as github, provide functionality to view Jupyter Notebook files.

Both Jupyter Notebook and ViennaDoc provide an execution engine on the web and help the user understand code fragments. Although they have common technical elements such as dynamic web content, evaluation engine on the server side, and mixed use of natural languages and computational language, their objectives and supposed users are different.

Jupyter Notebook is primarily a tool for exploration among diverse usage in practice. The user types a fragment of code, and the system runs it to display the result. Each code fragment and its result are recorded so that the user can review the whole exploration process and other users can check whether or not the same results can be reproduced. As a documentation tool, Jupyter Notebook generates HTML pages on the server side. Styles and dynamic features of documents depends on the Jupyter Notebook server.

ViennaDoc is, on the other hand, a tool for explanation. The author of a ViennaDoc page already have a formal specification at hand, and writes explanation quoting a fragment of specification. A reader of the ViennaDoc page does not necessarily write a formal expression, but follows the explanation with help of animation. Because ViennaDoc manipulates only specific elements in HTML files, VIennaDoc can be used along with other documenting tools and formats. It is possible to use markdown to author a document with ViennaDoc specific elements while Jupyter Notebook controls the whole document.

5 Concluding Remarks

Lightweight formal methods inherently need to work with informal notations and methods. ViennaDoc is an attempt to utilise the specification animation techniques in informal documents. Although we have been focused on specification documents, we believe this approach could be applied to many other formal specification tools.

One possible future work direction is using this inside VDM-SL tutorials. Many online tutorials for programming language learners provide functionality to evaluate a piece of code. ViennaDoc's animation feature can provide such a playground for VDM. Tutorials also need to be maintained along with growth of the languages and libraries. ViennaDoc's assertion mechanism could help authors of tutorials to keep them conformant to the latest version of the language and libraries.

Another possible application is for other open source communities. There are many emerging open source efforts associated with VDM. ViennaDoc is an HTML-based technology and thus could be an affordable medium for open source communities. The authors expect ViennaDoc could support more use of VDM in open source projects.

Acknowledgments. The authors gratefully acknowledge Stèphane Ducasse for his inspiring comments on the initial idea of this research. We would also thank anonymous reviewers for their thoughtful and constructive feedback. A part of this research was supported by JSPS KAKENHI Grant Number JP 18K18033.

References

1. Arloing, T., Dubois, Y., Ducasse, S., Cassou, D.: Pillar: a versatile and extensible lightweight markup language. In: Proceedings of the 11th Edition of the International Workshop on Smalltalk Technologies, p. 25. ACM (2016)
2. Kurita, T., Chiba, M., Nakatsugawa, Y.: Application of a formal specification language in the development of the "Mobile FeliCa" IC chip firmware for embedding in mobile phone. In: Cuellar, J., Maibaum, T., Sere, K. (eds.) FM 2008. LNCS, vol. 5014, pp. 425–429. Springer, Heidelberg (2008). https://doi.org/10.1007/978-3-540-68237-0_31
3. Larsen, P.G.: Ten years of historical development: "Bootstrapping" VDMTools. J. Univ. Comput. Sci. **7**(8), 692–709 (2001)
4. Larsen, P.G., Battle, N., Ferreira, M., Fitzgerald, J., Lausdahl, K., Verhoef, M.: The overture initiative - integrating tools for VDM. SIGSOFT Softw. Eng. Notes **35**(1), 1–6 (2010). https://doi.org/10.1145/1668862.1668864
5. Larsen, P.G., et al.: VDM-10 language manual. Technical report, TR-001, The Overture Initiative, April 2013. www.overturetool.org
6. Lausdahl, K., Larsen, P.G., Battle, N.: A deterministic interpreter simulating a distributed real time system using VDM. In: Qin, S., Qiu, Z. (eds.) ICFEM 2011. LNCS, vol. 6991, pp. 179–194. Springer, Heidelberg (2011). https://doi.org/10.1007/978-3-642-24559-6_14. http://dl.acm.org/citation.cfm?id=2075089.2075107. ISBN 978-3-642-24558-9
7. Masci, P., Couto, L.D., Larsen, P.G., Curzon, P.: Integrating the PVSio-web modelling and prototyping environment with Overture. In: Ishikawa, F., Larsen, P.G. (eds.) Proceedings of the 13th Overture Workshop, pp. 33–47. Center for Global Research in Advanced Software Science and Engineering, National Institute of Informatics, 2-1-2 Hitotsubashi, Chiyoda-Ku, Tokyo, Japan, June 2015. http://grace-center.jp/wp-content/uploads/2012/05/13thOverture-Proceedings.pdf. gRACE-TR-2015-06
8. Nielsen, C.B., Lausdahl, K., Larsen, P.G.: Combining VDM with executable code. In: Derrick, J., et al. (eds.) ABZ 2012. LNCS, vol. 7316, pp. 266–279. Springer, Heidelberg (2012). https://doi.org/10.1007/978-3-642-30885-7_19
9. Oda, T., Araki, K.: ViennaTalk: an integrated specification environment focused on the early stage of the formal specification phase. Comput. Softw. **34**(4), 4_129–4_143 (2017). https://www.jstage.jst.go.jp/article/jssst/34/4/34_4_129/_article/-char/ja/

Refine 2019 - 19th Refinement Workshop

Refine 2019 Organizers' Message

This volume contains the papers presented at Refine 2019: Refinement Workshop 2019 held on October 7, 2019 in Porto, co-located with FM 2019.

This 19th workshop continued a 20+ year tradition in refinement workshops run under the auspices of the British Computer Society (BCS) FACS special interest group. After the first seven editions had been held in the UK, in 1998 it was combined with the Australasian Refinement Workshop to form the International Refinement Workshop, hosted at The Australian National University. More editions have followed in a variety of locations, all with electronic published proceedings and associated journal special issues.

Like previous editions, the 19th edition was co-located with a major formal methods conference. This year we were delighted to be co-located with the FM international conference, which again proved to be a very productive pairing of events. Each submission was reviewed by 3, program committee members. The committee decided to accept 6 full papers. The program also included 1 invited talk. The papers cover a wide range of topics in the theory and application of refinement.

The organisers would like to thank everyone: the invited speakers, the authors, BCS-FACS, and the organisers of FM 2019 for their help in organising this workshop, the participants of the workshop, and the reviewers involved in selecting the papers.

October 2019

John Derrick
Brijesh Dongol
Steve Reeves

Organization

Program Committee Chairs

John Derrick	University of Sheffield, UK
Brijesh Dongol	University of Surrey, UK
Steve Reeves	University of Waikato, New Zealand

Program Committee

Bernhard Aichernig	TU Graz, Austria
Richard Banach	The University of Manchester, UK
Luis Barbosa	University of Minho, Portugal
Eerke Boiten	De Montfort University, Leicester, UK
Ana Cavalcanti	University of York, UK
John Derrick	Unversity of Sheffield, UK

Brijesh Dongol	University of Surrey, UK
Lindsay Groves	Victoria University of Wellington, New Zealand
Rob Hierons	The University of Sheffield, UK
Larissa Meinicke	The University of Queensland, Australia
Marcel Oliveira	Universidade Federal do Rio Grande do Norte, Brazil
Steve Reeves	University of Waikato, New Zealand
Gerhard Schellhorn	Universitaet Augsburg, Germany
Steve Schneider	University of Surrey, UK
Emil Sekerinski	McMaster University, Canada
Graeme Smith	The University of Queensland, Australia
Heike Wehrheim	University of Paderborn, Germany

A Map of Asynchronous Communication Models

Florent Chevrou[1], Aurélie Hurault[1], Shin Nakajima[2],
and Philippe Quéinnec[1(✉)]

[1] Université de Toulouse – IRIT, Toulouse, France
{florent.chevrou,aurelie.hurault,philippe.queinnec}@irit.fr
[2] National Institute of Informatics, Tokyo, Japan
nkjm@nii.ac.jp

Abstract. Asynchronous communication encompasses a variety of features besides the decoupling of send and receive events. Those include message-ordering policies which are often crucial to the correctness of a distributed algorithm. This paper establishes a map of communication models that exhibits the relations between them along two axes of comparison: the strength of the ordering property and the level of abstraction of the specification. This brings knowledge about which model can be substituted by another without breaking any safety property. Furthermore, it brings flexibility and ready-to-use modules when developing correct-by-construction distributed systems where model decomposition exposes the communication component. Both criteria of comparison are covered by refinement. We consider seven ordering policies and we model in Event-B these communication models at three levels of abstraction. The proofs of refinement between all of these are mechanized in Rodin.

Keywords: Asynchronous communication · Formal verification · Refinements of communication models · Event-B

1 Introduction

A classic way to develop distributed algorithms is to start with a global goal, such as mutual exclusion or global agreement. A distributed version of the algorithm is then derived, either directly or by progressive transformation of the specification, e.g. by refinement. This approach dates back to early work by Dijkstra [11], Chandy-Misra with UNITY [7], Back and Kurki-Suonio with action systems [5], or Lamport with TLA+ [19]. It is still bustling in the correct-by-construction community and Event-B [1] is a framework which embodies this methodology. At one point in the development process, communication is explicitly introduced, to express the flow of information from one site to another, and it eventually takes the form of message exchanges. When the development is conducted with formal verification, the properties of the communication are shown to be sufficient for the correctness of the algorithm. However, it is often unclear what are the specific

© Springer Nature Switzerland AG 2020
E. Sekerinski et al. (Eds.): FM 2019 Workshops, LNCS 12233, pp. 307–322, 2020.
https://doi.org/10.1007/978-3-030-54997-8_20

properties of this communication that are necessary to ensure the correctness of the algorithm. Especially, it may be difficult to replace one communication model with another without doing again the complete proof.

The present work aims at alleviating these difficulties for asynchronous point-to-point communication with message ordering policies. These policies control message deliveries based on past events or involved peers, and their relative strength forms a hierarchy of communication models. To this end, we use simulation: if a model M_1 simulates another model M_2, M_2 has less non-determinism, hence fewer behaviors. Thus a safety property proved under M_1 in a given system will hold if M_1 is substituted by M_2 (there is no guarantee of preservation for liveness properties). A distributed application is refined up to the point where communication is introduced. Then, model decomposition isolates the communication part and the hierarchy is used to choose an adequate ordering policy.

There exist several approaches to decomposition in Event-B [14]: shared-variable [3], shared-event [6] and modularization [16]. Our map is well suited for shared-event decomposition, where variables are partitioned and a set of events are synchronized and shared by sub-models. During the refinement of a system, asynchronous communication appears via two events: send and receive. These events are isolated in a sub-model to be refined using the results of this paper.

Nevertheless, the proposed one-dimensional scale is not sufficient as several communication models may realize the same ordering policy. They often have little in common: some directly map the ordering property on high level data structures such as distributed executions while others will make use of ad-hoc concrete approaches (e.g. counters on messages) from which the property arises. Mapping the communication models depending on their level of abstraction completes the approach. Therefore, we draw a bidimensional map of communication models and use refinement as a common ground for the two orthogonal comparison criteria: refinement for simulation, and data refinement for concretization. Our results, summed up in the map in Fig. 1, are proved and mechanized in Event-B. Regarding decomposition, this means once an ordering policy has been chosen across the simulation direction, the model can be refined across the concretization direction as part of a correct-by-construction development.

The outline of this paper is the following. Section 2 recalls basic definitions of the theory of asynchronous distributed systems and their modeling in Event-B. Section 3 presents seven communication models and proves the hierarchy of their ordering policies, based on simulation, using refinement. Section 4 presents variants of the models based on message histories, and proves that the hierarchy still holds. Section 5 refines them one step further towards practical concrete models. Section 6 discusses proof effort and localization. Section 7 provides related work.

The page http://hurault.perso.enseeiht.fr/MenagerieOfRefinements contains all the models discussed in this paper and gives indications to replay the proofs.

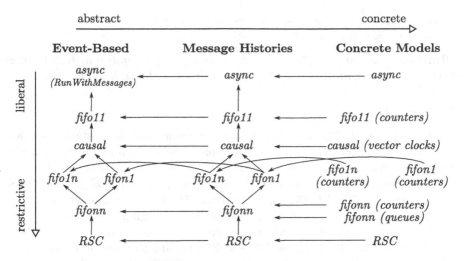

Fig. 1. Map of the asynchronous communication models. A black arrow means "refines". The two axis of refinement are the level of abstraction (data refinement) and the strength of the ordering policy (reduction of non-determinism).

2 Distributed Systems

2.1 Distributed Executions

An asynchronous message-passing distributed system is composed of a set of peers that exchange messages. This paper considers point-to-point communication where a message has exactly one sender and at most one receiver. A distributed execution is a partially ordered set of events, where events are communication events: message send events and message receive events; internal events are ignored. The partial order is named the causal order [18,23], and it abstracts independent events. Events occur on peers: a labeling function states where the event e has occurred. Assuming interleaving of independent events and no true concurrency, a run is a linear extension of a distributed execution.

Let PEER be the set of peers, MESSAGE an enumerable set of messages identifiers, and COM $\triangleq \{Send, Receive\}$ the communication labels.

Definition 1. *A distributed execution* $(E, \prec_c, com, mes, peer)$ *is a partially ordered set with labeling functions, where E is an enumerable set, $\prec_c$ is a partial order on E, and com, mes and peer are labeling functions from E to COM, MESSAGE and PEER. An event e that occurs on peer(e) is either the sending or the reception (com(e)) of message mes(e). $(E, \prec_c, com, mes, peer)$ satisfies:*

- *no message is sent or received more than once:*
  $\forall e, e' \in E : (com(e) = com(e') \land mes(e) = mes(e')) \Rightarrow e = e'$
- *a receive event is preceded by a send event:*
  $\forall e \in E : com(e) = Receive$
  $\Rightarrow \exists e' \in E : (com(e') = Send \land mes(e') = mes(e) \land e' \prec_c e)$

– *events occurring on the same peer are totally ordered:*
$$\forall e, e' \in E : peer(e) = peer(e') \Rightarrow e \prec_c e' \vee e' \prec_c e$$

Definition 2. *A run $\sigma = (E, \prec_c, <_\sigma, com, mes, peer)$ extends a distributed execution $(E, \prec_c, com, mes, peer)$: $(E, <_\sigma)$ is a linear extension of $(E, \prec_c)$.*

2.2   Event-B

A model in Event-B [1] is an abstract state machine containing state variables, invariants, and events (the word "event" refers either to an element of a distributed execution or a part of an Event-B machine – a transition predicate –; the context hopefully makes it clear which is which). An event E parameterized by x has the form EVENT E ANY x WHERE $G(v, x)$ THEN $A(v, x)$ END, where $G(v, x)$ is the guard of the event and $A(v, x)$ an action changing the values of v. In this paper, actions are deterministic assignments of the form $v := expr$ where v is a state variable. INITIALISATION specifies the initial state of a machine. A machine can be related to an Event-B context (SEES) that specifies sets, constants, axioms and theorems.

The main concept of the Event-B method is the refinement (REFINES) of machines. It consists of a refinement of the events: the guards may be weakened and the behavior must conform to the abstract event. New events refine the special event called "skip". The Rodin tool [2] generates proof obligations for the refinements and the preservation of the invariants by the events.

In Event-B, $x_1 \mapsto x_2$ denotes a pair (x_1, x_2). Relations are sets of pairs. $dom(r)$ and $ran(r)$ denote the domain and range of a relation r. $E \leftrightarrow F$ denotes the set of relations between E and F, $E \leftrightarrow\!\!\!\!\rightarrow F$ the set of total surjective relations, and $E \rightarrow F$ total functions from E to F. The relation $r_1; r_2$ denotes the forward composition of relations r_1 and r_2. "$\lhd$" is the domain restriction operator such that given a relation r and a set E, $E \lhd r \triangleq \{x \mapsto y \mid x \mapsto y \in r \wedge x \in E\}$. "$\lhd\!\!\!-$" is the domain subtraction operator such that given a relation r and a set E', $E' \lhd\!\!\!- r \triangleq \{x \mapsto y \mid x \mapsto y \in r \wedge x \notin E'\}$. "$\lhd\!\!+$" is the overriding operator such that given relations r_1 and r_2, $r_1 \lhd\!\!+ r_2 \triangleq r_2 \cup (dom(r_2) \lhd\!\!\!- r_1)$. $\mathbb{P}(E)$ denotes the powerset of E.

2.3   Event-B Distributed Executions

First, we introduce each feature of asynchronous communication through a series of initial refinements: concept of "events", "happening", and "past", then the pairing of two events (communication), localization of the events (distribution) and causality (distributed executions), linearization of the executions (totally ordered runs), and eventually messages which label the exchanges. This paper skips these preliminary refinements. The resulting machine called RunWithMessages, presented in Fig. 2, is a boilerplate for any asynchronous point-to-point communication model. It conforms to the distributed executions and runs of Definitions 1 and 2. By playing with the guards, other communication paradigms can be specified (e.g. synchronous communication, multicast, join).

```
MACHINE E_RunWithMessages
SEES E_Messages
VARIABLES past peerOf prec run mesOf comOf
INVARIANTS // (excerpt)
   TmesOf: mesOf ∈ past →MESSAGE                                                    //
   TpeerOf: peerOf ∈ past →PEER          TcomOf: comOf ∈ past →COM   // Type invariants
   Tprec:    prec ∈ past ↔ past           Trun:    run ∈ past ↔ past     //

   // prec is  reflexive ,  transitive ,  and anti−symmetric. So is run (omitted).
   inv1: (past ◁ id) ⊆ prec          inv2: prec ; prec ⊆ prec          inv3: prec ∩ prec⁻¹ ⊆ id
   // Events occurring on the same peer are  totally  ordered
   inv4: ∀ e1, e2 · e1∈ past ∧e2∈ past ∧peerOf(e1) = peerOf(e2) ⇒e1 ↦ e2 ∈ prec ∨e2 ↦ e1 ∈ prec
   inv5:  prec ⊆ run  // run extends prec.
   inv6: ∀ e1, e2 · e1 ∈ past ∧ e2 ∈ past ⇒ e1 ↦ e2 ∈ run ∨e2 ↦ e1 ∈ run // run is total .
   // No message is sent or  received  more than once.
   inv7: ∀ e1,e2 · e1∈ past ∧e2∈ past ∧comOf(e1)=comOf(e2) ∧mesOf(e1)=mesOf(e2) ⇒e1 = e2
   inv8: ∀ e · e ∈ past ∧  comOf(e) = Receive // A receive event is  preceded by a send event.
                  ⇒ (∃ es · es ∈ past ∧  comOf(es) = Send ∧mesOf(e) = mesOf(es) ∧es ↦ e ∈ prec)

EVENT send ANY e p m // New event, Peer where the event occurs, Sent message
WHERE
   grd1: e ∈ EVENT \ past ∧ p ∈ PEER ∧ m ∈ MESSAGE
   grd3: m ∈ MESSAGE \ ran(mesOf) // m has not already been sent
THEN
   act1:  past := past ∪ {e}
   act2:  peerOf := peerOf ∪{e ↦ p}
   act3:  prec := prec ∪ {e ↦ e} ∪ {ep · ep ∈ past ∧ (∃ ep2 · ep2 ∈ past ∧ peerOf(ep2) = p ∧ep ↦
   ep2 ∈ prec) | ep ↦ e}
   act4:  run := run ∪{e ↦ e} ∪ {ep · ep ∈ past | ep ↦ e}
   act5:  mesOf := mesOf ∪{e ↦ m}                act6:  comOf := comOf ∪{e ↦ Send}

EVENT receive ANY e p m // new event; receiver; received  message
WHERE
   grd1: e ∈ EVENT \ past ∧ p ∈ PEER ∧ m ∈ MESSAGE
   grd6: ∀ ep · ep ∈ past ∧ comOf(ep) = Receive ⇒mesOf(ep) ≠ m // m has not already been received
   grd7: ∃ es · es ∈ past ∧ comOf(es) = Send ∧mesOf(es) = m    // m has been sent
THEN // Same as send except
   act4:              // The new event is causally  after all  the events that  causally precede
      prec := prec   // an event from the same peer (penultimate  line ) and after all  the events
         ∪ {e ↦ e}    // that causally precede the send event ( last  line ).
         ∪ {ep · ep ∈ past ∧ (∃ ep2 · ep2 ∈ past ∧ peerOf(ep2) = p ∧ep ↦ ep2 ∈ prec) | ep ↦ e}
         ∪ {ep · ep ∈ past
             ∧ (∃ es · es ∈ past ∧ comOf(es) = Send ∧mesOf(es) = m ∧ep ↦ es ∈ prec) | ep ↦ e}
   act6:  comOf := comOf ∪{e ↦ Receive}
```

Fig. 2. Event-B machine for asynchronous point-to-point communication

The machine relies on sets defined in the contexts: EVENT the set of event identifiers labeled by elements of PEER, MESSAGES, and COM (Send or Receive). Events are labeled by variables peerOf, mesOf, and comOf once they are introduced in the machine (e.g. $e \mapsto Send \in comOf$). New communication events are introduced by the actions of the two Event-B events send and receive. They are stored in the past variable and the labeling functions evolve according to the parameters of send and receive: the peer it has occurred on and the exchanged message. Additionally, variables prec (partial causal order $\prec_c$) and run (total order $<_\sigma$) log the dependencies between the events which serves to specify the communication properties (including ordering policies in future machines).

3   Abstract Communication Models

The communication model specifies when a communication action (send or receive) is possible in order to ensure specific properties on the communication. We focus on message ordering properties (e.g. global ordering: all messages are received in their emission order). In this section, each abstract communication model is a machine based on `RunWithMessages` that is characterized by an ordering invariant on distributed executions or runs. We use this invariant to filter out the distributed executions and runs that do not abide to the ordering policy and keep all those that do.

The communication models constitute steps between fully asynchronous distributed communication (*async*) where sending and receiving a message is always possible, partially ordered communication (*fifo11*, *causal*, *fifo1n*, *fifon1*), totally ordered communication (*fifonn*), and almost synchronous communication (*RSC*) where a message must be received immediately after it has been sent. We use simulation to define a hierarchy based on the strength of the delivery order. Stronger models have less non-determinism on the receptions. Machine `RunWithMessages` models asynchronous communication and corresponds to the *async* model. The other models impose more and more determinism on reception (and, for RSC, on send). The first column of Fig. 1 accounts for the hierarchy of these models. Refinement is used to prove the simulation relations between the models. Note that these are *not* concretization refinements: no model can be called more (or less) concrete or realizable. Concretization of the communication models follow a specific path for each model and is described later.

3.1   Informal Specifications

In this paper, we study seven asynchronous point-to-point communication models. A detailed description with figures of each model is given in [10].

RSC. Realizable with Synchronous Communication [8,17]. The send event of a message is immediately followed by the receive event of this message (viewed atomically, it corresponds to synchronous communication).

fifo n-n. Messages are globally ordered and are delivered in their send order.

fifo 1-n. Messages from the same peer are delivered in their send order.

fifo n-1. On a given peer, messages are received in their send order.

fifo 1-1. Messages between a couple of peers are delivered in their send order. Messages from/to different peers are independently delivered.

causal. Messages are delivered according to the causality of their emission [18]. If a message m_1 is causally sent before a message m_2 (i.e. there exists a causal path from the first emission to the second one), then a peer cannot get m_2 before m_1.

async. Fully Asynchronous. No order on message delivery is imposed. The machine `RunWithMessages` is this model.

3.2   Event-B Specifications

We consider the specifications of the communication models with events. Each communication model is characterized by an invariant that describes the ordering properties it ensures on the communication. The invariants of the models all introduce es_1 and es_2, the send events of two distinct messages, as well as er_1 and er_2, the corresponding receive events. The model-specific part imposes an order on the receive events (er_1 and er_2) based on the causal or run order of the send events (es_1 and es_2) and whether or not the sending or receiving peers are the same (same sending peer and same receiving peer for *fifo 1-1*, same sending peer for *fifo 1-n*, same receiving peer for *fifo n-1* and *causal*). For instance, the ordering invariant in the machine `CausalEvent` is:

```
// Given two transmissions of messages and the four corresponding events: es1 er1 and es2 er2
∀ es1, er1, es2, er2 · es1 ∈ past ∧ er1 ∈ past ∧ es2 ∈ past ∧ er2 ∈ past
    ∧ comOf(es1) = Send ∧comOf(es2) = Send ∧comOf(er1) = Receive ∧comOf(er2) = Receive
    ∧ mesOf(es1) = mesOf(er1) ∧ mesOf(es2) = mesOf(er2)
// Model−specific part:
    ∧ es1 ↦ es2 ∈ prec        // If es1 CAUSALLY precedes es2
    ∧ peerOf(er1) = peerOf(er2) // and the corresponding RECEPTIONS occur on the SAME PEER
    ⇒ er1 ↦ er2 ∈ run         // then they must occur in the emission order.
```

Our next goal is to compare the communication models, by proving that some have less transitions than others (i.e. are more deterministic). Later in Sects. 4 and 5, we derive more concrete specifications of these models. However, at this point, having machines that are as liberal as the ordering allows is important. Thus, the weakest preconditions of the ordering invariants are stipulated for the guards of the send and receive events. As the actions are assignments of the form $var := var \cup \{\cdots\}$, the computation of the weakest preconditions is trivial [12]. As an example, Fig. 3 presents the resulting structure of the `CausalEvent` machine with a close up on the ordering guard of the receive event.

3.3   Proofs and Invariants

The difference between the models is an invariant directly related to the order of delivery and the associated weakest precondition used as a guard on the communication events. A proof of refinement consists in proving the logical implications between these invariants. Most of the time these proofs require little manual intervention thanks to auto-provers, post-tactics, and SMT solvers.

The refinements of *causal* in *fifo-n1* and *fifo-1n* need manual intervention with a specific invariant that states that two causally related events on different peers are necessary linked by (at least) one message. Informally, it means that causality between events on distinct peers only exists due to message exchanges.

```
∀ e1, e2 · e1 ↦ e2 ∈ prec ∧peerOf(e1) ≠ peerOf(e2) ⇒
(∃ es,er · e1 ↦ es ∈ prec ∧ es ↦ er ∈ prec ∧ er ↦ e2 ∈ prec ∧peerOf(e1) = peerOf(es)
         ∧ comOf(es) = Send ∧comOf(er) = Receive ∧mesOf(es) = mesOf(er))
```

```
MACHINE E_ CausalEvent
REFINES E_fifo11 // (which refines E_RunWithMessages)
SEES E_ Messages
VARIABLES past peerOf prec run mesOf comOf

INVARIANTS
     ... // Invariants from E_RunWithMessages
     ordering : // causal ordering invariant : see 3.2

EVENT send REFINES send ... // from E_RunWithMessage with additional invariant

EVENT receive REFINES receive // receive event with a
ANY e p m
WHERE
 grd1: e ∈ EVENT \ past
 grd2: p ∈ PEER
 grd3: m ∈ MESSAGE \ ran(mesOf)
 ... // guards from E_RunWithMessage
 // weakest precondition of the causal ordering invariant
 ordering : ∀ es1, er1, es2, er2 ·
          es1 ∈ past ∪ {e} ∧ er1 ∈ past ∪ {e}
       ∧ es2 ∈ past ∪ {e} ∧ er2 ∈ past ∪ {e}
       ∧ (comOf ∪ {e ↦ Send})(es1) = Send
       ∧ (comOf ∪ {e ↦ Send})(es2) = Send
       ∧ (comOf ∪ {e ↦ Send})(er1) = Receive
       ∧ (comOf ∪ {e ↦ Send})(er2) = Receive
       ∧ (mesOf ∪ {e ↦ m})(es1) = (mesOf ∪ {e ↦ m})(er1)
       ∧ (mesOf ∪ {e ↦ m})(es2) = (mesOf ∪ {e ↦ m})(er2)
       ∧ (peerOf ∪ {e ↦ p})(er1) = (peerOf ∪ {e ↦ p})(er2)
       ∧ es1 ↦ es2 ∈ run ∪ {e ↦ e} ∪ {ep · ep ∈ past | ep ↦ e}
       ⇒ er1 ↦ er2 ∈ run ∪ {e ↦ e} ∪ {ep · ep ∈ past | ep ↦ e}
 THEN // same actions as E_RunWithMessage
     act1: past := past ∪ {e}
     act2: peerOf := peerOf ∪{e ↦ p}
     act3: prec := prec ∪ ...
     act4: run := run ∪ ...
     act5: mesOf := mesOf ∪{e ↦ m}
     act6: comOf := comOf ∪{e ↦ Receive}
```

Fig. 3. Structure of the causal communication model described with events. The machine corresponds to E_RunWithMessages with an additional ordering invariant and the associated guards.

4 History-Based Models

In this section, we take one step forwards in the direction of concretization. These new specifications share a common framework in which the ordering properties rely upon keeping track of dependent messages in histories. This makes it easier to compare them much like in the previous section. Yet, the specifications are now operational and realistic enough to be implemented and used as such.

There are two directions involved in the mapping of these communication models. First, each history-based model relates to its execution-based counterpart: it is a concretization of the latter, which means the underlying ordering properties still hold, and we use refinement to prove it in Sect. 4.2. For example, Fifo11History is a concretization of Fifo11Event. Second, it is expected that the history-based communication models, which model the same ordering policies, preserve the hierarchy of these ordering policies. Once again, the simulation relations (i.e. the reduction of the non-determinism of the communication events send and receive) are made explicit and proved by refinement. For instance `CausalEvent` is stronger than (refines) `FifollEvent` and `CausalHistory` is stronger than (refines) `FifollHistory`.

4.1 Specifications with Histories

We consider specifications of the asynchronous point-to-point interaction models where communication occurs according to two parameterized events: $send(p, m, d)$ (peer p sends message m to an explicit peer d) and $receive(p, m)$ (peer p receives message m).

The models rely on a state variable **net** that contains messages in transit. Sent messages are labeled to carry information about the communication: the origin peer, the destination peer, and the history of the message. The history of a message is the set of messages on which it depends, i.e. the set of messages which precede it. As two notions of precedence exist (causal/execution), two kinds of message histories are defined: namely causal and global.

Definition 3. *(Message Histories) For a run $\sigma = (E, \prec_c, <_\sigma, com, mes, peer)$, and a message m:*

$$
hcOf(m) \triangleq \left\{
\begin{array}{l}
m' \in MESSAGE : \exists e, e' \in E : \\
\quad com(e) = Send \land com(e') = Send \\
\land\ mes(e) = m \land mes(e') = m' \\
\land\ e' \prec_c e
\end{array}
\right\}
$$

$$
hgOf(m) \triangleq \left\{
\begin{array}{l}
m' \in MESSAGE : \exists e, e' \in E : \\
\quad com(e) = Send \land com(e') = Send \\
\land\ mes(e) = m \land mes(e') = m' \\
\land\ e' <_\sigma e
\end{array}
\right\}
$$

In the Event-B models, the message histories are built upon state variables `hg` $\subseteq$ `MESSAGE`, the global history, and `hc` $\in$ `PEER` $\rightarrow$ $\mathbb{P}(\text{MESSAGE})$, the causal histories of each peer. When peer p sends a message m, the global history (`hgOf`) and the causal history (`hcOf`) of m are the current values of `hg` and of `hc(p)`. The new message is also added to the history state variables (`hg` and `hc(p)`). The causal history `hc(p)` of peer p is updated when a message m is received to account for the causal relation induced by the transmission of the message from one peer to another: m and its causal history `hcOf(m)` are added to `hc(p)`. The validity of these constructions with regard to the above definitions is stated as two invariants. The ordering properties of a model are determined by guards on the **send** and **receive** events that depend on the message histories, origin, and destination of a message.

4.2 Concretization

For each communication model, the refinement of the event-based model by the history-based model is split in two steps to facilitate the proofs. First, add new variables to hold histories and message destination (net, hg, hc, hgOf, hcOf, destOf), and replace the guards about events by guards about histories. Then, remove the now useless variables related to events (past, prec, run, ...).

As an example, Fig. 4 is the resulting machine for the *causal* model. Its ordering invariant states that if m_1 and m_2 have the same destination, and m_1 was sent causally before m_2 (thus m_1 is in the causal history of m_2), then m_1 cannot be in transit when m_2 is not. This means that m_1 must be received before m_2. Accordingly, the ordering guard for receive allows to deliver a message m if there does not exist another message m_2 in transit, with same destination, and which is in the history of m.

```
MACHINE G2_CausalHistory
REFINES F2_CausalHistory
// (which refines E_CausalEvent)
SEES E_Messages
VARIABLES
    net           // Network
    hg            // Global history
    hc            // Causal history per peer
    origOf        // sender of message
    destOf        // destination of message
    hgOf          // global history of message
    hcOf          // causal history of message
INVARIANTS
    Tnet:      net      ∈ ℙ (hg)
    Thg:       hg       ∈ ℙ (MESSAGE)
    Thc:       hc       ∈ PEER →ℙ (hg)
    TorigOf:   origOf ∈ hg   →PEER
    TdestOf:   destOf ∈ hg   →PEER
    ThgOf:     hgOf   ∈ hg   →ℙ (hg)
    ThcOf:     hcOf   ∈ hg   →ℙ (hg)
    ordering :
      ∀ m1, m2 · m1 ∈ hg ∧m2 ∈ hg ∧m1 ≠ m2
            ∧ destOf(m1) = destOf(m2)
            ∧ m1 ∈ hcOf(m2)
            ⇒ ¬ (m1 ∈ net ∧m2 ∉ net)
```

```
EVENT send REFINES send
    ANY p m d
    WHERE
      Tpd: p ∈ PEER ∧d ∈ PEER
      Tm: m ∈ MESSAGE \ hg // new message id
    THEN
      a1: net    := net   ∪ {m}
      a2: hg     := hg    ∪ {m}
      a4: hc(p)  := hc(p) ∪ {m}
      a5: origOf := origOf ∪ {m↦ p}
      a6: destOf := destOf ∪ {m↦ d}
      a7: hgOf   := hgOf  ∪ {m↦ hg}
      a8: hcOf   := hcOf  ∪ {m↦ hc(p)}

EVENT receive REFINES receive
    ANY p m
    WHERE
      intransit : m ∈ net
      destination : p ∈ PEER ∧ destOf(m) = p
      ordering : ¬ (∃ m2 · m2 ∈ net
                      ∧ destOf(m2) = p
                      ∧ m2 ∈ hcOf(m))
    THEN
      a1: net    := net \ {m}
      a2: hc(p) := hc(p) ∪ hcOf(m) ∪ {m}
```

Fig. 4. History-based Event-B model for causal communication

Data refinement consist in proving that the model-specific guards on the communication events guarantee the ordering properties on the distributed executions. The proofs rely on the ordering invariant, and wisely formulated gluing and consistency invariants. The gluing invariants relate the state variables of the abstract (events, executions) and concrete machines (network, histories). For instance, a message m_1 is in the causal history of m_2 if the send event of m_1 is causally anterior to the send event of message m_2. The consistency invariants clarify links between the state variable of the concrete machine (e.g. if a message m_1 is in the causal history of m_2, it is also in its global history). Besides, significant manual interventions have to be carried out to supervise the proof process as the number of state variables and invariants misdirect the automatic provers. Finding the optimal formulation (e.g. proposition vs. contraposition), through trial and error, is a large portion of the proof effort.

5   Concrete Models

In the first approach, the models based on events directly translate the ordering policies of the communication models. The second approach using message histories is more concrete: the locality and transmission of data is taken into account with messages that carry their history. However, keeping trace of all the previously sent messages is still unrealistic in practice. Therefore we refine the models that use histories with concrete structures such as counters of messages or queues of messages.

5.1   Logical Clocks

Regarding the causal communication model as described in Fig. 5, the causality relation can be explicit, using pruned causal histories [17] (in the worst case, this is as costly as our version with histories), or derived from logical vector clocks of size n or matrix clocks of size $n \times n$ [23].

Every peer p has a vector clock $vcOf(p)$. For peers p and pp, $vcOf(p)(pp)$ holds the number of send events on pp that are in the current past of peer p. When a peer sends a message, it increments its own count $(vcOf(p)(p))$ and piggybacks its vector with the message. At reception, a peer updates every component of its vector with the max of its current value and of the component of the received vector. Thus, $vcOf(p)(pp)$ holds the number of messages sent by pp and known by p. A message m is in the causal history of m' iff every vector component of m is lower or equal than the one of m' (and at least one is strictly lower: distinct messages have different vectors). To ensure causal reception, a message can be delivered to a peer iff no other message exists for this peer with a lower vector.

The refinement of CausalHistory replaces the history variables with vector clocks. The events are refined to update these variables and, in the receive event, the guard built on histories is replaced with a property on the vectors. The refinement proof requires gluing invariants on causal histories and vector clocks.

5.2   Other Concretizations

As shown in Fig. 1, other concrete models have been defined. The various *fifo** models are easily described with counters. If n denotes the number of peers, 2 counters (*fifonn*), $2 \times n$ counters (*fifon1* and *fifo1n*), or $2 \times n^2$ counters (*fifo11*) are used to account for the ordinal rank of the last sent and last received messages in the system (*fifonn*), a peer (*fifon1* and *fifo1n*), or a couple of peers (*fifo11*). The ranks of the last received messages determine the rank of the messages that can be received. Alternatively, message queues can be used: if n denotes the number of peers, we need a global queue (*fifonn*), n inbox queues (*fifon1*), n outbox queues (*fifo1n*), or n^2 queues (*fifo11*).

```
MACHINE H3_CausalVector          │ EVENT receive REFINES receive
REFINES G3_CausalHistory         │   ANY p m WHERE
SEES E_Messages                  │     Tm:  m ∈ net
VARIABLES net hg origOf destOf   │     Tp:  p ∈ PEER
  rankOf // message →vector clock │     dest: destOf(m) = p
  vcOf // peer →vector clock      │     order: ¬(∃m2 ·
EVENT send REFINES send          │              m2 ∈ net \ {m}
  ANY p m d WHERE                 │              ∧ destOf(m2) = p
    Tm: m ∈ MESSAGE \hg           │              ∧ (∀ pp · pp ∈ PEER
    Tpd: p ∈ PEER ∧d ∈ PEER       │                 ⇒ rankOf(m2)(pp) ≤ rankOf(m)(pp)))
  THEN                           │   THEN
    ...                          │     ...
  act5: vcOf(p) := vcOf(p)       │     act2: vcOf(p) := { pp ·pp ∈ PEER |
        ⩤ {p ↦ vcOf(p)(p) + 1}   │                       pp ↦ max({ vcOf(p)(pp),
    act6: rankOf(m) := vcOf(p)   │                                   rankOf(m)(pp) })}
        ⩤ {p ↦ vcOf(p)(p) + 1}   │     act3: rankOf := {m} ⩤rankOf
```

```
INVARIANTS
  TrankOf: rankOf ∈ net →(PEER →ℕ)
  TvcOf:   vcOf ∈ PEER →(PEER →ℕ)
  inv1: ∀ m1, m2 ·m1 ∈ net ∧m2 ∈ net ∧m1 ≠ m2
        ⇒ (m1 ∈ hcOf(m2) ⇒(∀ p ·p ∈ PEER ⇒rankOf(m1)(p) ≤ rankOf(m2)(p)))
  inv2: ∀ m1, m2 ·m1 ∈ net ∧m2 ∈ net ∧m1 ∈ hcOf(m2)
        ⇒ rankOf(m1)(origOf(m2)) < rankOf(m2)(origOf(m2))
  inv3: ∀ m, p · m ∈ net ∧p ∈ PEER ∧m ∈ hc(p)
        ⇒ (∀ pp · pp ∈ PEER ⇒rankOf(m)(pp) ≤ vcOf(p)(pp))
```

Fig. 5. Concrete model for causal communication using vector clocks

6 Additional Remarks

6.1 Proof Effort

The full menagerie holds 42 machines, 41 refinements, 329 invariants, and more than 1400 proof obligations. Once the necessary invariants are stated, the large majority of these proof obligations are automatically proved by Rodin with SMT solvers (49 manual proofs, 3.5% of the proof obligations). The main difficulties are described below.

To make the proofs automatic, the trick is to find additional invariants. For instance, to prove that RscHistory refines RscEvent, the invariant

```
∀ e1, e2 · e1 ↦ e2 ∈ run ∧ comOf(e1) = Send ∧ e1 ≠ e2 ⇒ mesOf(e1) ∉ net
```

has to be made explicit (it says that if there exists at least one event after a send event e_1, then the message sent at e_1 is no longer in transit). As expected, the discovery of the necessary invariants is the hardest part in the proofs, and the largest part of our proof effort was devoted to this point. Our methodology consists in running the automatic provers and analyzing the failure (if any). After some case analysis of the disjunctions, a contradiction often appears in the hypotheses. This contradiction leads us to a relevant new invariant. Once stated and proved, this new invariant may, with good luck, suppress the unsuccessful branch and advance towards the fully automatic proof.

The refinements involving *causal* are never easy. One essential invariant is:

$$
\begin{aligned}
&\forall\ \mathsf{e1,\ e2 \cdot e1 \mapsto e2 \in prec \wedge peerOf(e1) \neq peerOf(e2) \Rightarrow (\exists\ es,er \cdot e1 \mapsto es \in prec \wedge es \mapsto er \in}\\
&\mathsf{prec \wedge er \mapsto e2 \in prec \wedge peerOf(e1) = peerOf(es) \wedge comOf(es) = Send \wedge comOf(er) = Receive}\\
&\mathsf{\wedge\ mesOf(es) = mesOf(er))}
\end{aligned}
$$

It states that two causally related events on different peers are necessarily linked by (at least) one message, or conversely, that causality between peers only arises from message exchanges. This invariant had to be manually instantiated.

Lastly, concrete models need ad-hoc reasoning. For instance, Sect. 5.1 presents the specific invariants that are required to prove that `CausalVector` refines `CausalHistory`. These invariants are expected as they state that vector clocks encode causality. Nevertheless, the refinement proofs require to manually recall and instantiate these invariants.

6.2 Localization

The last point concerns the distributed nature of the communication models. The first abstract models, based on properties of the executions, are purely logical and offer a global point of view of the communication models. The second models, based on histories, are actually directly implementable even if costly. The third concrete models offer realistic implementations. By looking at their definitions, one can distinguish two classes of communication models. The models *async, fifo11, causal* and *fifo1n* only need meta information piggybacked with the message and local knowledge available on the peer. On the other hand, *fifon1,* *fifonn* and *rsc* require global shared variables, and their implementation in a distributed system requires a central coordinator or totally ordered multicast.

7 Related Work

Asynchronous communication models in distributed systems are studied and compared in [17] (notion of ordering paradigm), [8] (notion of distributed computation classes), and [13] (for message sequence charts). Implementations of the basic communication models (*causal, fifo11*) using histories or clocks are explained in classic textbooks [17,23]. In our previous work, we have unified and extended these results in [10]. The goal was to develop a framework to mechanically verify algorithms [9], and to give a unified description of the models. However only the communication models with message histories were specified in TLA+. All the Event-B models presented here are new, as well as the refinement relations leading to the distributed executions (Sect. 2), between the abstract communication models (Sect. 3), and between the concretizations (abstract model to history-based model to ad-hoc model, Sects. 4.2 and 5).

Formal verification of distributed algorithms have been conducted with success. However the hypotheses on the communication are often fuzzy or unclear and one has to dive deep into the proofs to identify them. For instance, [22] studies the topology maintenance in structured peer-to-peer networks. Different algorithms are studied, some assume FIFO channels and some do not. It is unclear why it is required, and if it is required for all channels.

Refinement has been used to verify distributed algorithms. [20] describes the addition of Byzantine resilience to standard Paxos. The proof is conducted by refinement of the distributed non-Byzantine algorithm and has been mechanically checked with the TLA$^+$ Proof System. Another approach is presented in [21]. Three versions of Paxos (the classic one, disk Paxos and Byzantine Paxos) are derived from an abstract, non-distributed algorithm.

The Event-B book [1] presents several examples of refinements of distributed algorithms. The *simple file transfer protocol* decomposes the atomic sending of a file in a sequence of send events, and uses counters to coordinate the progression. This protocol is later extended to handle loss and re-transmission with an alternating bit protocol. In this example, asynchronous communication appears implicitly during refinement, and properties of the communication are directly embedded in the resulting machine. A logical clock is used in the *routing algorithm for a mobile agent* to order the messages sent by a mobile agent while it moves. This example can be seen as the development of an ordered communication model down to a concrete localizable model. Lastly, the *leader election on a connected graph network* deals with the difficulties of splitting an atomic action (in a shared-memory model) into several actions (in a message-passing model). This creates deadlocked states (a situation called *contention* in the algorithm) where two nodes are each waiting for the other to progress. This development is more concerned with providing a algorithmic solution in presence of non-atomic actions, than with the development of non-atomicity (i.e. messages).

[4] presents the development by refinement of snapshot algorithms. It starts with the specification of the snapshot problem, which is by essence a global property. A generic architecture with asynchronous communication is presented, which allows the derivation of several algorithms. At one point, the set of messages (which models fully asynchronous communication) is refined by FIFO queues (which models ordered communication). This leads to a simpler snapshot algorithm, which ends being the well-known Chandy-Lamport algorithm.

[15] describes the formal derivation of an algorithm for leader election in Event-B. The abstract model is centralized, and refinement introduces distribution. The behavioral part of the communication model first comprises two events, *send* and *receive* which directly access the state variable of the other peers. Then, a new refinement introduces new variables to decouple the peers and to get a "one-to-one asynchronous communication channel".

8   Conclusion

This paper provides a guide for the design of the communication component in the development of distributed systems and algorithms. It considers a wide range of asynchronous communication models that enforce message-ordering properties on the system and positions each one of them on a map of refinement relations. The map, shown in Fig. 1, has two dimensions: it compares the models according to the strength of the underlying ordering properties and their level of abstraction. All these models are specified and the refinements proved in Event-B which paves the way for reusing part of the mechanization in a correct-by-construction development of a distributed system thanks to shared-event model decomposition. Our machines are indeed pluggable to any system where communication occurs according to two events send and receive with usual parameters (message, destination). A classic development process consists in introducing asynchronous communication which corresponds to our RunWithMessages machine, the root of our map, and make use of the rest of the map to strengthen the ordering policy depending on the needs, pursue the development towards the concrete practical specifications models (with counters or queues), or even substitute models afterwards knowing the safety properties are preserved. Besides, each one of the three sets of communication models we provide has its assets: the concrete models are close to practical implementations, the event-based models clearly translate the ordering policies which ease theoretical reasoning on the properties themselves, and the history-based models offer a compromise with operational descriptions that are implementable and yet remain uniform to ease formal reasoning.

References

1. Abrial, J.R.: Modeling in Event-B - System and Software Engineering. Cambridge University Press, Cambridge (2010)
2. Abrial, J., Butler, M.J., Hallerstede, S., Hoang, T.S., Mehta, F., Voisin, L.: Rodin: an open toolset for modelling and reasoning in Event-B. STTT 12(6), 447–466 (2010). https://doi.org/10.1007/s10009-010-0145-y
3. Abrial, J., Hallerstede, S.: Refinement, decomposition, and instantiation of discrete models: application to Event-B. Fundam. Inform. 77(1–2), 1–28 (2007)
4. Andriamiarina, M.B., Méry, D., Singh, N.K.: Revisiting snapshot algorithms by refinement-based techniques. Comput. Sci. Inf. Syst. 11(1), 251–270 (2014)
5. Back, R., Kurki-Suonio, R.: Distributed cooperation with action systems. ACM Trans. Program. Lang. Syst. 10(4), 513–554 (1988)
6. Butler, M.J.: Decomposition structures for Event-B. In: Leuschel, M., Wehrheim, H. (eds.) IFM 2009. LNCS, vol. 5423, pp. 20–38. Springer, Heidelberg (2009). https://doi.org/10.1007/978-3-642-00255-7_2
7. Chandy, K.M., Misra, J.: Parallel Program Design: A Foundation. Addison-Wesley, Boston (1988)
8. Charron-Bost, B., Mattern, F., Tel, G.: Synchronous, asynchronous, and causally ordered communication. Distrib. Comput. 9(4), 173–191 (1996)
9. Chevrou, F., Hurault, A., Quéinnec, P.: Automated verification of asynchronous communicating systems with TLA$^+$. In: Electronic Communications of the EASST (PostProceedings of AVoCS 2015), vol. 72 (2015)
10. Chevrou, F., Hurault, A., Quéinnec, P.: On the diversity of asynchronous communication. Formal Aspects Comput. 28(5), 847–879 (2016). https://doi.org/10.1007/s00165-016-0379-x
11. Dijkstra, E.W.: EWD851b - reducing control traffic in a distributed implementation of mutual exclusion (1983)
12. Dijkstra, E.W., Scholten, C.S.: Predicate Calculus and Program Semantics. Springer, New York (1990). https://doi.org/10.1007/978-1-4612-3228-5
13. Engels, A., Mauw, S., Reniers, M.A.: A hierarchy of communication models for message sequence charts. Sci. Comput. Program. 44(3), 253–292 (2002)

14. Hoang, T.S., Iliasov, A., Silva, R., Wei, W.: A survey on Event-B decomposition. ECEASST **46**, 1–15 (2011)
15. Iliasov, A., Laibinis, L., Troubitsyna, E., Romanovsky, A.: Formal derivation of a distributed program in Event B. In: Qin, S., Qiu, Z. (eds.) ICFEM 2011. LNCS, vol. 6991, pp. 420–436. Springer, Heidelberg (2011). https://doi.org/10.1007/978-3-642-24559-6_29
16. Iliasov, A., et al.: Supporting reuse in Event B development: modularisation approach. In: Frappier, M., Glässer, U., Khurshid, S., Laleau, R., Reeves, S. (eds.) ABZ 2010. LNCS, vol. 5977, pp. 174–188. Springer, Heidelberg (2010). https://doi.org/10.1007/978-3-642-11811-1_14
17. Kshemkalyani, A.D., Singhal, M.: Distributed Computing: Principles, Algorithms, and Systems. Cambridge University Press, Cambridge (2011)
18. Lamport, L.: Time, clocks and the ordering of events in a distributed system. Commun. ACM **21**(7), 558–565 (1978)
19. Lamport, L.: Specifying Systems. Addison Wesley, Boston (2002)
20. Lamport, L.: Byzantizing paxos by refinement. In: Peleg, D. (ed.) DISC 2011. LNCS, vol. 6950, pp. 211–224. Springer, Heidelberg (2011). https://doi.org/10.1007/978-3-642-24100-0_22
21. Lampson, B.W.: The ABCD's of Paxos. In: Symposium on Principles of Distributed Computing, PODC 2001, p. 13. ACM (2001)
22. Li, X., Misra, J., Plaxton, C.G.: Active and concurrent topology maintenance. In: Guerraoui, R. (ed.) DISC 2004. LNCS, vol. 3274, pp. 320–334. Springer, Heidelberg (2004). https://doi.org/10.1007/978-3-540-30186-8_23
23. Raynal, M.: Distributed Algorithms for Message-Passing Systems. Springer, Heidelberg (2013). https://doi.org/10.1007/978-3-642-38123-2

An Abstract Semantics of Speculative Execution for Reasoning About Security Vulnerabilities

Robert J. Colvin[1,2(✉)] and Kirsten Winter[1,2]

[1] Defence Science and Technology Group, Brisbane, Australia
[2] School of Information Technology and Electrical Engineering,
University of Queensland, Brisbane, Australia
r.colvin@uq.edu.au

Abstract. Reasoning about correctness and security of software is increasingly difficult due to the complexity of modern microarchitectural features such as out-of-order execution. A class of security vulnerabilities termed Spectre that exploits side effects of speculative, out-of-order execution was announced in 2018 and has since drawn much attention. In this paper we formalise speculative execution and its side effects as an extension of a framework for reasoning about out-of-order execution in weak memory models. Our goal is to allow speculation to be reasoned about abstractly at the software level. To this end we encode speculative execution explicitly using a novel language construct and modify the definition of conditional statements correspondingly. Underlying this extension is a model that has sufficient detail to enable specification of the relevant microarchitectural features. We add an abstract cache to the global state of the system, and derive some general refinement rules that expose cache side effects due to speculative loads. The rules are encoded in a simulation tool, which we use to analyse an abstract specification of a Spectre attack and vulnerable code fragments.

1 Introduction

Modern multicore architectures exhibit several features to speed up execution: commands may appear to occur out of order, allowing computation to proceed past some bottleneck (e.g., loading a value from memory), several levels of faster intermediate memory (caches) to speed up repeated accesses, and in particular, *speculative execution*, where a branch is optimistically executed, even though local computation may not yet have determined if it is the correct branch. Such features are difficult to reason about, though there has been significant work in understanding weak memory models [1,2,15,23,35,36] and also detailed formal microarchitectural models (e.g., [4]).

Recently several significant security vulnerabilities have been found related to out-of-order execution, e.g., Meltdown [27], Foreshadow [5], and Spoiler [22]. In this paper we focus on the recently published Spectre class of attacks [24,25]. Spectre differs in that the attack may target the victim's code to retrieve private

© Springer Nature Switzerland AG 2020
E. Sekerinski et al. (Eds.): FM 2019 Workshops, LNCS 12233, pp. 323–341, 2020.
https://doi.org/10.1007/978-3-030-54997-8_21

information, while other attacks exploit processor features only. While complex to exploit, Spectre is a vulnerability present in almost all modern architectures. It allows malicious code to access the memory of a victim process, potentially reading private data, without sharing the virtual memory space. The attack works by detecting footprints in the cache left by speculative execution; for instance, a branch that includes a bounds check on an index i into an array A may speculatively load the element at $A[i]$, before it knows for certain that i is within the bounds of A. Though the speculative computations leading up to the point where the mis-speculation is detected are discarded, depending on the subsequent access patterns there may still be an effect on the cache, which is not discarded, and which can be used to infer the value in memory at out-of-bounds address $A[i]$.

In earlier work we have proposed a semantic framework to support reasoning about weak memory models [12] which is implemented in a simulation/model checking tool based on Maude [8]. In this paper we extend this framework with a model of cache behaviour and speculative execution. Although Spectre may occur in memory models that provide sequential consistency, a weak memory model framework is a natural fit for speculative execution as speculated instructions may begin out of order, i.e., before the relevant branch is reached. This enables not only a close inspection of Spectre-like attacks but also the analysis of other related potential vulnerabilities that may arise in modern hardware architectures. Our intention for the semantics is to allow analysis of vulnerability to Spectre-like attacks to be integrated within a more general, software-level reasoning framework; we do not aim to precisely model the implementation of speculative execution or caches for a particular architecture.

Speculative execution presents several challenges. Firstly, it requires a model of the cache which, for our concerns, needs to be modelled at a level that presents enough details to realistically capture the effects of speculative execution, but is abstract enough to not over-complicate reasoning. Secondly, speculative execution should allow side effects to take effect before the relevant branch is reached. Thirdly, speculation can be nested, and the target of future branches may depend on speculatively executed computations, necessitating the creation of *transient* state that can be discarded if speculation is found to be incorrectly chosen. Finally, we want to be able to model and explore possible mitigations, e.g., memory barriers to halt speculation, such as Intel's **LFENCE** instruction [21, Sect. 11.4.4.3].

The paper is structured as follows: in Sect. 2 we summarise a wide-spectrum language and its semantics for reasoning about weak memory models. In Sect. 3 we extend this with new constructs for reasoning about speculative execution, and give its semantics. We formalise some attacker and victim patterns, in particular those of Spectre, in Sect. 4. Related work is discussed in Sect. 5.

2   Background: IMP-ro

A wide-spectrum language for reasoning about weak memory models, **IMP-ro**, is introduced in [11,12]. It is essentially an imperative language with assignments, conditionals and loops, with the difference that instead of sequential composition (c_1 ; c_2 for c_i a command) it has prefixing, α ; c, where α is an instruction (as in process algebras such as CSP [20] and CCS [30]). The semantics of prefixing is defined so that either α may be executed, or some instruction β from within c may be executed, provided that β can be *reordered* before α according to the rules of the memory model. To instantiate IMP-ro for a particular memory model a "reordering relation" $\overset{R}{\Leftarrow}$ on instructions is defined, stating when instructions can occur out of order; in addition, different models may also have different instruction types, for instance, memory barriers for enforcing order.

We recap IMP-ro below, before extending it to include speculative execution in later sections. We ground our work in a weak memory framework because speculation can occur before preceding instructions are executed, even when speculative execution is implemented on architectures which enforce sequential consistency. In addition, it appears that increasingly security vulnerabilities will be found due to instruction reordering on modern architectures, e.g., [22]. However, the particular reordering relation is not important for the analysis in this paper, and to avoid distraction we mostly assume sequential consistency.

The elements of IMP-ro are actions (instructions) α, commands (programs) c, processes (local state and a command) p, and the top level system s, encompassing a shared state and all processes. We assume a set of variables *Var*, divided into locals (registers) and globals. By convention we use r, r_1, r_2, etc., to name local variables, and unless otherwise stated, x, y, z for global variables. A state σ is a mapping from *Var* to values, with the notation $\sigma_{[x := v]}$ representing an update of σ to map x to v. Below x is a variable (shared or local) and e an expression.

$$\alpha ::= x := e \quad | \quad [e]$$
$$c ::= \mathbf{nil} \quad | \quad \alpha \; ; \; c \quad | \quad \alpha \bullet c \quad | \quad c_1 \sqcap c_2 \quad | \quad \mathbf{while} \; b \; \mathbf{do} \; c$$
$$p ::= (\mathbf{local} \; \sigma \bullet c)$$
$$s ::= (\mathbf{global} \; \sigma \bullet p_1 \parallel p_2 \parallel \ldots)$$

An action may be an update $x := e$ or a guard $[e]$. For weak memory models the set of actions may also include fences (memory barriers); we introduce an abstract barrier in later sections. Commands include the terminated command **nil**, prefixing, choice, and iteration. We also include the abstract command type for "true prefixing", $\alpha \bullet c$, where reordering is forbidden, i.e., $\bullet$ is prefixing in the usual CSP [20] and CCS [30] sense. For brevity, for a command α ; β ; **nil** we omit the trailing **nil** and just write α ; β. A process encapsulates a command within a local state σ (total on local variables), representing registers. A system is structured as the parallel composition of processes sharing a global state, each with their own values for local variables.

A relevant subset of the operational rules are given in Fig. 1. Transitions are labelled with the syntax of the transition, i.e., assignments and guards, with the addition of the *silent* label τ, modelling an internal step of a process with no effect on the context. For brevity and ease of explanation we tend to focus on rules involving guards of a particular form, $[x = v]$, which represents a load of x

Rule 1 (Prefix)

$$(\alpha \,;\, c) \xrightarrow{\alpha} c \quad (a) \qquad \frac{c \xrightarrow{\beta} c' \quad \alpha \overset{R}{\Leftarrow} \beta_{\langle\alpha\rangle}}{(\alpha \,;\, c) \xrightarrow{\beta_{\langle\alpha\rangle}} (\alpha \,;\, c')} \quad (b)$$

Rule 2 (Choice)

$$c \sqcap d \xrightarrow{\tau} c$$

$$c \sqcap d \xrightarrow{\tau} d$$

Rule 3 (While)

while b do $c \xrightarrow{\tau}$ if b then $(c \,;\, $ while b do $c)$ else nil

Rule 4 (Locals)

$$\frac{c \xrightarrow{r := v} c'}{(\text{local } \sigma \bullet c) \xrightarrow{\tau} (\text{local } \sigma_{[r := v]} \bullet c')}$$

Rule 5 (Locals/store)

$$\frac{c \xrightarrow{x := r} c' \quad \sigma(r) = v}{(\text{local } \sigma \bullet c) \xrightarrow{x := v} (\text{local } \sigma \bullet c')}$$

Rule 6 (Locals/load)

$$\frac{c \xrightarrow{r := x} c'}{(\text{local } \sigma \bullet c) \xrightarrow{[x = v]} (\text{local } \sigma_{[r := v]} \bullet c')}$$

Rule 7 (Locals/guard)

$$\frac{c \xrightarrow{[e]} c'}{(\text{local } \sigma \bullet c) \xrightarrow{[e_\sigma]} (\text{local } \sigma \bullet c')}$$

Rule 8 (Parallel)

$$\frac{p_1 \xrightarrow{\alpha} p_1'}{p_1 \parallel p_2 \xrightarrow{\alpha} p_1' \parallel p_2} \qquad \frac{p_2 \xrightarrow{\alpha} p_2'}{p_1 \parallel p_2 \xrightarrow{\alpha} p_1 \parallel p_2'}$$

Rule 9 (Globals/store)

$$\frac{p \xrightarrow{x := e} p'}{(\text{global } \sigma \bullet p) \xrightarrow{\tau} (\text{global } \sigma_{[x := e_\sigma]} \bullet p')}$$

Rule 10 (Globals/load)

$$\frac{p \xrightarrow{[x = v]} p' \quad \sigma(x) = v}{(\text{global } \sigma \bullet p) \xrightarrow{\tau} (\text{global } \sigma \bullet p')}$$

Fig. 1. Semantics of the language

when $x = v$. The more general rules are given in [12]. We omit some rules, such as terminating rules like $(\text{local } \sigma \bullet \text{nil}) \xrightarrow{\tau} \text{nil}$.

Rule 1 is the key rule that allows later instructions to happen earlier, according to an architecture-specific reordering relation $\overset{R}{\Leftarrow}$. For instance, for TSO, the main part of the reordering relation is that loads can come before stores, i.e., $x := 1 \overset{R}{\Leftarrow} r := y$, while $\alpha \overset{R}{\nLeftarrow} \beta$ for all other instruction types. Relations for TSO, ARM and POWER are given in [12]. To avoid distraction in this paper we assume sequential consistency, i.e., $\alpha \overset{R}{\nLeftarrow} \beta$ for the basic instruction types, with the exception that τ steps can be reordered (allowing future local calculations to be executed ahead of time). In Rule 1 the notation $\beta_{\langle\alpha\rangle}$ accounts for *forwarding*, where in a case such as $x := 1 \,;\, r := x$ the instruction $r := x$ can take effect before $x := 1$ provided the value 1 is forwarded to r, meaning that $r := 1$ is executed (rather than $r := x$, which it would not be sensible to execute before

$x := 1$ from a sequential semantics perspective). Forwarding is defined straight-forwardly in [12], and we do not repeat it here. The semantics for true prefixing, $\alpha . c$, is given by an equivalent version of Rule 1(a).

Rule 2 is straightforward for nondeterministic choice. In Rule 3 we unfold a loop into a conditional; the definition of conditional in a speculative context is crucial and is deferred until Sect. 3.2. Rule 4 covers the case of some change to the local registers. This is an internal step of the process and is a silent τ step at the global level. Rule 5 applies when a store $x := r$ is executed by a process: the local value v for r is substituted so that the label $x := v$ is promoted to the global state (this rule can be generalised to cover any assignment of the form $x := e$ [10]). Rule 6 states that when a load $r := x$ instruction is executed internally it becomes a load of x, i.e., a guard $[x = v]$, for any value v. Although there is a transition $[x = v]$ for every possible v, only the guard with the correct value for x will be possible at the system level (via Rule 10). The loaded value becomes the new value for r in the local state. Rule 7 states that a guard is evaluated with respect to the registers, and is promoted for evaluation with respect to the global state. Rule 8 gives the usual interleaving model of concurrency. Rules 9 and 10 straightforwardly update and access the global store via promoted stores (Rule 5) and loads (Rule 6).[1]

Refinement ($\sqsubseteq$) is defined so that $c \sqsubseteq d$ iff all terminating traces of d are also traces of c, ignoring subsequences of internal (τ) steps. Terminating traces are those retrieved from the operational semantics where eventually **nil** is reached. (For simplicity we ignore non-terminating behaviours, that is, for this paper we consider only partial correctness, which is sufficient for detecting Spectre-like attacks.) Note that if a behaviour is blocked (no rules are applicable, e.g., a false guard) it is not considered terminating. This eliminates behaviours where the wrong branch is incorrectly taken (as opposed to incorrectly speculated), as discussed in more detail in [12].

We lift reasoning from the operational to refinement level via Law 11, which allows us to straightforwardly derive Law 13. More specific laws may also be straightforwardly derived, such as resolving nondeterminism via Law 12, and Law 14 that hides local effects, exposing a process's global effect; this helps later to abstract from the details of transient speculative contexts.

$$c \xrightarrow{\alpha} c' \Rightarrow c \sqsubseteq \alpha . c' \quad (11) \qquad\qquad \alpha ; c \sqsubseteq \alpha . c \quad (13)$$

$$c_1 \sqcap c_2 \sqsubseteq c_1 \quad (12) \qquad (\textbf{local } \{r \mapsto 1\} \bullet x := r) \sqsubseteq x := 1 \quad (14)$$

3   Caches in Weak Memory Models: IMP-ro-spec

From the perspective of functional correctness, speculative execution may be ignored: in the case where a process speculates along the branch that is eventually taken (after the conditional is evaluated) implementations ensure that speculated

---

[1] In this paper we assume a multicopy atomic storage system; for memory models which lack this (e.g., POWER) the storage system described in [12] may be used.

instructions are committed in a consistent order; and when speculation was down the incorrect branch any speculative computation is discarded. However, as revealed by Spectre and other vulnerabilities, incorrect speculation can have side effects, and in this section we extend IMP-ro to expose them.

For convenience we call the extended language IMP-ro-spec, which defines conditionals to expose (incorrect) speculative execution, and records operations on the cache in a global variable. Speculation occurs within a *transient context*, which is discarded if speculation is found to be incorrect.

3.1 Syntax of IMP-ro-spec

Speculative Execution. We introduce three new commands to capture speculative execution in IMP-ro.

$$\alpha ::= \dots \ \mid \ \text{SPECFENCE} \tag{15}$$

$$c ::= \dots \ \mid \ \mathbf{spec}(c) \ \mid \ c_1 \bigtriangleup c_2 \ \mid \ (\mathbf{buf}\ \sigma \bullet c) \tag{16}$$

$$\widetilde{c} \mathrel{\widehat{=}} (\mathbf{buf}\ \varnothing \bullet (\mathbf{local}\ \sigma \bullet c)) \tag{17}$$

$$\text{if } b \text{ then } c_1 \text{ else } c_2 \mathrel{\widehat{=}} \mathbf{spec}(\widetilde{c_2}) \bigtriangleup ([b]\ ;\ c_1) \ \sqcap \ \mathbf{spec}(\widetilde{c_1}) \bigtriangleup ([\neg b]\ ;\ c_2) \tag{18}$$

The instruction type SPECFENCE blocks load speculation; this is an abstract command type that may correspond to, for instance, the LFENCE command of Intel architectures [21]. We include it to demonstrate the relevance of reordering relations and how mitigation techniques can be considered in our framework. A *speculation command* $\mathbf{spec}(c)$ gives the effect of executing command c speculatively, that is, no effects on the global or local state can be seen, however, there can be cache side effects based on the steps of c. A *partial pre-execution command* $c_1 \bigtriangleup c_2$ partially executes c_1 before c_2 begins. The initial command c_1 may not execute at all, execute to completion, or partially execute. It is the well-known CSP "interrupt" operator, but we rename it in this context to avoid confusion with hardware interrupts. The *transient buffer command* $(\mathbf{buf}\ \sigma \bullet c)$ is used to keep track of modifications to globals executed speculatively.

We also introduce the abbreviation $\widetilde{c}$ which creates the *transient context* for a speculative execution of c, that is, a (temporary) mapping of (all) registers, and an initially empty transient buffer (17). The values for the speculative copy of registers σ created here is left unconstrained and may differ to the actual local state in the outer context; this accounts for different strategies that different architectures may take. Because the specifics of the local state are not relevant for reasoning about Spectre we do not model a specific strategy, which could be given by adding an explicit transition that sets up the local state according to the current context. A speculative execution of code c is of the form $\mathbf{spec}(\mathbf{buf}\ \sigma_b \bullet (\mathbf{local}\ \sigma_l \bullet c))$, where a copy of the locals is encapsulated in σ_l, stores to globals are encapsulated in σ_b, and the outer speculative command generates the cache side effects. An example of how they interact is given in Sect. 3.3.

Speculation is evident at branch points, and hence we model conditionals differently. Whereas in [12] a conditional if b then c_1 else c_2 was defined in the standard way as $([b] \; ; \; c_1) \sqcap ([\neg b] \; ; \; c_2)$ here we extend the definition to potentially pre-execute speculation down the alternative branches as given in (18). This says there are two possibilities: speculatively execute the second branch (ignoring the guard) up until the point where the first branch is chosen, or speculatively execute the first branch until the point the second branch is chosen. These two possibilities cover all behaviours relevant in the context of Spectre; as far as is known speculation down the eventually correct branch has no impact on the security of the system that is not already visible through other analysis techniques, e.g., information flow [32]. However, speculation down the correct branch is straightforward to capture, as discussed in Appendix A.

To explain the relevance of the transient context (initialised in (17)) consider the execution of $\mathbf{spec}(x := 1; \; r := x; \; \dots)$. The effect of $x := 1$ must not be seen globally (as it is difficult to unwind), however during speculation r must use the value 1. If instead r was to use a value of x loaded from main memory this would violate local consistency (see [1]). This detail is especially important if r is used in later (speculated) calculations, including future branches. In our approach it emerges from the semantics that x is not loaded nor drawn into the cache during speculation of the above code. A purely syntactic approach to determining the effect of speculative execution might conclude that x is added to the cache, and hence could be overly pessimistic from a security analysis perspective.

Nested speculation, which may arise from nested conditionals or a speculated loop, is straightforward in our framework; a new, nested, transient context is created, and if an inner speculation attempts to load a global which the outer speculation has buffered then the cache effect is removed (see Rule 24(e)).

The Cache. The cache is modelled as a single global variable CACHE, kept in the shared state, which holds a set of type *Addr*, representing addresses (for this work we do not care what values are in the cache; however it is straightforward to modify the type of CACHE). We assume an uninterpreted function $\&: Var \to Addr$ such that $\&x$ returns the address of the (global) variable x. We introduce three operations on CACHE to model cache side channels abstractly: cache fetching (adding something to the cache), cache clearing (clearing the (entire) cache), and cache querying (checking if an address is in the cache). Other explicit cache operations could be added, but these are sufficient for modelling the attack patterns utilised to instrument Spectre attacks [24].

$$\text{CACHE} += x \; \hat{=} \; \text{CACHE} := \text{CACHE} \cup \{\&x\} \tag{19}$$

$$\text{CCLEAR} \; \hat{=} \; \text{CACHE} := \varnothing \tag{20}$$

$$x \in \text{CACHE} \Leftrightarrow \&x \in \text{CACHE} \tag{21}$$

As these are abbreviations for updates to and guards on a global variable they fit in with the framework introduced in Sect. 2. A cache fetch represents the side effect of a speculated load. The instruction CCLEAR captures abstractly flushing as well as eviction of particular cache lines as it ensures that a certain address is not present in the cache any more.

The variable CACHE is kept in the global state and hence is shared between all processes. An alternative would be to explicitly model it as a separate construct, e.g., (**cch** $C \bullet c$) where C is a set of addresses. This approach would allow more fine-grained control over cache levels, e.g., each process could have its own L1 cache, with some subset sharing an L2 cache, with the L3 cache at the top level.

$$(\textbf{cch } L3 \bullet (\textbf{cch } L2_a \bullet (\textbf{cch } L1_1 \bullet p_1) \parallel (\textbf{cch } L1_2 \bullet p_2)) \parallel (\textbf{cch } L2_b \bullet \ldots))$$

We are interested in the worst case behaviour of the cache, where it leaks private information, and are not concerned with the specifics of how that may happen. However details of the cache, such as its update policy, may also be captured with extra machinery. In that sense our model of the cache is an abstraction of the underlying microarchitecture implementation, which could be verified using data and action refinement techniques [3,19,31].

3.2   Semantics of IMP-ro-spec

Partial Pre-execution. The semantics of a partial pre-execution process is based on that of the interrupt operator from CSP [20].

Rule 22 (Partial pre-execution)

$$\frac{c_1 \xrightarrow{\alpha} c_1'}{c_1 \triangle c_2 \xrightarrow{\alpha} c_1' \triangle c_2} \ (a) \qquad\qquad \frac{c_2 \xrightarrow{\alpha} c_2'}{c_1 \triangle c_2 \xrightarrow{\alpha} c_2'} \ (b)$$

For commands of the form **spec**$(c)\triangle d$ the speculation of c occurs for some period of time (Rule 22(a)) before discarding the computation and starting down the d branch (Rule 22(b)). The arbitrariness of when c_2 starts captures the unknown time at which speculation may be found to be incorrect. We make use of the following law that covers the interruption occurring after a single action.

$$(\alpha \bullet c_1) \triangle c_2 \sqsubseteq \alpha \bullet c_2 \tag{23}$$

Transient Buffers. Transient buffers catch stores and record them in a state; recorded values may be used for speculative computations.

Rule 24 (Buffer)

$$\frac{c \xrightarrow{x := v} c'}{(\textbf{buf } \sigma \bullet c) \xrightarrow{\tau} (\textbf{buf } \sigma_{[x := v]} \bullet c')} \ (a)$$

$$\frac{c \xrightarrow{[x = v]} c' \quad (x \mapsto v) \in \sigma}{(\textbf{buf } \sigma \bullet c) \xrightarrow{\tau} (\textbf{buf } \sigma \bullet c')} \ (b) \qquad \frac{c \xrightarrow{[x = v]} c' \quad x \notin \text{dom}(\sigma)}{(\textbf{buf } \sigma \bullet c) \xrightarrow{[x = v]} (\textbf{buf } \sigma \bullet c')} \ (c)$$

$$\frac{c \xrightarrow{\text{CACHE} += x} c' \quad x \in \text{dom}(\sigma)}{(\textbf{buf } \sigma \bullet c) \xrightarrow{\tau} (\textbf{buf } \sigma \bullet c')} \ (d) \qquad \frac{c \xrightarrow{\text{CACHE} += x} c' \quad x \notin \text{dom}(\sigma)}{(\textbf{buf } \sigma \bullet c) \xrightarrow{\text{CACHE} += x} (\textbf{buf } \sigma \bullet c')} \ (e)$$

Rule 24(a) states that (speculated) stores are recorded in the transient buffer; Rule 24(b) states that (speculated) loads are serviced by the buffer (similar to *forwarding* [12]) if a value is available; Rule 24(c) states that otherwise the load is promoted (to be handled by the global state via Rule 10). In cases where nested speculation has resulted in a cache fetch, Rule 24(d), similarly to Rule 24(b), hides a fetch of x if a store of x is in the buffer already; Rule 24(e) states that otherwise the cache fetch is promoted. In addition a transient buffer command promotes other instruction types not covered above (e.g., τ, SPECFENCE), and the rules do not need to cover registers since the transient buffer encloses a local state (17).

Speculation (Down an Incorrect Path). Speculation should have no observable effect on registers or globals (the "CPU state"), however in reality it may leave a footprint in the cache. The main concept is to make explicit a cache fetch with each speculated load.

Rule 25 (Speculative context)

$$\frac{c \xrightarrow{[x=v]} c'}{\mathbf{spec}(c) \xrightarrow{\text{CACHE} \mathrel{+}= x} ([x = v] \,;\, \mathbf{spec}(c'))} \quad (a) \qquad \frac{c \xrightarrow{\tau} c'}{\mathbf{spec}(c) \xrightarrow{\tau} \mathbf{spec}(c')} \quad (b)$$

$$\frac{c \xrightarrow{\text{CACHE} \mathrel{+}= x} c'}{\mathbf{spec}(c) \xrightarrow{\text{CACHE} \mathrel{+}= x} \mathbf{spec}(c')} \quad (c) \qquad \mathbf{spec}(\mathbf{nil}) \xrightarrow{\tau} \mathbf{nil} \ (d)$$

Rule 25(a) states that speculated loads of global variables have an initial side effect on the cache. The load is delayed until after the cache fetch. Rule 25(b) states that speculative execution can perform local computation. Rule 25(c) states that cache fetches are promoted (from nested speculation). Rule 25(d) states that speculation may silently complete. By omission, i.e., since there is no corresponding rule, speculation is blocked if c executes a SPECFENCE command. We do not need to consider further action types, since speculation always encompasses a transient context out of which only loads and cache fetches are exposed.

Reordering of Cache Instructions. The semantics of IMP-ro is instantiated for a particular memory model by defining the relation $\overset{\text{R}}{\Leftarrow}$, as used in Rule 1(b). We must therefore define the cases under which the new (cache-based) instruction types can be reordered. The concept of speculative execution is that loads can be initiated ahead of time, though they must still (appear to) conform to the particular memory model. However the cache fetches are not so constrained. We therefore allow cache fetch instructions to be reordered before the majority of instruction types.

$$y := e \overset{\text{R}}{\Leftarrow} \text{CACHE} \mathrel{+}= x \quad \text{iff } x, y \text{ distinct} \tag{26}$$

$$\text{SPECFENCE} \overset{\text{R}}{\not\Leftarrow} r := x \qquad \text{SPECFENCE} \overset{\text{R}}{\not\Leftarrow} \text{CACHE} \mathrel{+}= x \tag{27}$$

Equation (26) states that a cache fetch of x may occur earlier than loads, and stores of other variables (note that $x := 1 \not\stackrel{R}{\Leftarrow} \text{CACHE} += x$ as the assignment will service the corresponding load, rather than memory). Equation (27) states that SPECFENCE instructions block loads and cache fetches. A potential mitigation for the Spectre vulnerability (short of turning off speculation entirely) is to insert (concrete) SPECFENCE instructions at the start of each potentially affected branch. However, this would have too great an impact on processor speed to be seriously considered as a blanket fix [29].

As an example of out-of-order execution with cache side effects consider a command of the following form, where l_i are loads and s_i are store instructions to distinct locations.

$$l_1 \,;\;\; l_2 \,;\;\; (\textbf{if } b \textbf{ then } l_3 \,;\;\; s_1 \textbf{ else } s_2 \,;\;\; l_4)$$

Speculation allows cache fetches to come earlier (out-of-order), although whether the loads themselves can come earlier than preceding loads depends on the architecture; ARM and POWER allow loads to be reordered, whereas TSO doesn't [1,36]. Let c_3 be the cache fetch corresponding to load l_3. One possible behaviour, where the *true* branch is speculated before the *false* branch is executed, is given by the following sequence, which exposes the cache fetch for l_3.

$$c_3 \,\bullet\, l_1 \,\bullet\, l_2 \,\bullet\, l_3 \,\bullet\, [\neg b] \,\bullet\, s_2 \,\bullet\, l_4$$

The cache fetch for l_3 occurs before the earlier loads, which, for some execution- and architecture-specific reason, have taken longer to resolve. Note l_3 itself occurs in an order consistent with the memory model.

For simplicity we enforce ordering on cache operations, though the framework is flexible (for instance, on Intel architectures cache flush instructions do not necessarily prevent *pre-fetching* [21]).

$$\alpha \not\stackrel{R}{\Leftarrow} \text{CCLEAR} \qquad \text{CCLEAR} \not\stackrel{R}{\Leftarrow} \alpha \qquad x \in \text{CACHE} \not\stackrel{R}{\Leftarrow} \alpha \qquad \alpha \not\stackrel{R}{\Leftarrow} x \in \text{CACHE}$$

We do not intend for these to be definitive, but rather develop a framework that is flexible enough to cope with different models.

3.3   Example of Cache Side Effects Due to Speculation

In this section we show the particular behaviour of a conditional statement, where the *true* branch is (partly) speculated before the *false* branch begins. We construct the *true* branch, branch$_T$, so that it modifies some global x and a register r_1, before loading z into register r_2 and proceeding as branch$'_T$. A (partial) behaviour of branch$_T$ is given by (28).

$$\text{branch}_T \;\widehat{=}\; x := 1 \,;\;\; r_1 := 2 \,;\;\; r_2 := z \,;\;\; \text{branch}'_T$$

$$\text{branch}_T \xrightarrow{\;\; x := 1 \quad r_1 := 2 \quad r_2 := z \;\;} \text{branch}'_T \tag{28}$$

The trace ends with a load of z. We will take the case where globally z has the value 42. Now consider speculating branch$_T$.

$\qquad \mathbf{spec}(\widetilde{\mathsf{branch}_\mathsf{T}})$

$= \quad$ Set up new transient context $(17)^2$

$\qquad \mathbf{spec}(\mathbf{buf}\ \varnothing \bullet (\mathbf{local}\ \sigma \bullet \mathsf{branch}_\mathsf{T}))$

$\xrightarrow{\ \tau\ }{}^{*}$ From (28), locally update x by Rule 24(a) and r_1 by Rule 4

$\qquad \mathbf{spec}(\mathbf{buf}\ \{x \mapsto 1\} \bullet (\mathbf{local}\ \sigma_{[r_1\,:=\,2]} \bullet r_2 := z\,;\ \mathsf{branch}'_\mathsf{T}))$

$\xrightarrow{\ \text{CACHE}\ +=\ z\ }$ Fetch z (Rule 25(a)); arbitrarily assume z is 42

$\qquad [z = 42]\,;\ \mathbf{spec}(\mathbf{buf}\ \{x \mapsto 1\} \bullet (\mathbf{local}\ \sigma_{[r_1\,:=\,2][r_2\,:=\,42]} \bullet \mathsf{branch}'_\mathsf{T}))$

The cache fetch has been exposed in the trace (the corresponding load $[z = 42]$ is pending). We abbreviate the remaining code as $\mathsf{branch}''_\mathsf{T}$, and may derive (29) by the above calculation and Law 11.

$$\mathsf{branch}''_\mathsf{T} \mathrel{\widehat{=}} [z = 42]\,;\ \mathbf{spec}(\mathbf{buf}\ \{x \mapsto 1\} \bullet (\mathbf{local}\ \sigma_{[r_1\,:=\,2][r_2\,:=\,42]} \bullet \mathsf{branch}'_\mathsf{T}))$$

$$\mathbf{spec}(\widetilde{\mathsf{branch}_\mathsf{T}}) \sqsubseteq \text{CACHE} += z\ \centerdot\ \mathsf{branch}''_\mathsf{T} \tag{29}$$

Now we show how the cache fetch in the *true* branch may be seen in behaviours where the *false* branch is taken.

$\qquad \mathbf{if}\ b\ \mathbf{then}\ \mathsf{branch}_\mathsf{T}\ \mathbf{else}\ \mathsf{branch}_\mathsf{F}$

$\mathrel{\widehat{=}} \quad$ Definition 18

$\qquad \mathbf{spec}(\widetilde{\mathsf{branch}_\mathsf{F}}) \mathbin{\triangle} ([b]\,;\ \mathsf{branch}_\mathsf{T}) \sqcap \mathbf{spec}(\widetilde{\mathsf{branch}_\mathsf{T}}) \mathbin{\triangle} ([\neg b]\,;\ \mathsf{branch}_\mathsf{F})$

$\sqsubseteq \quad$ Arbitrarily choose *false* branch by Law 12

$\qquad \mathbf{spec}(\widetilde{\mathsf{branch}_\mathsf{T}}) \mathbin{\triangle} ([\neg b]\,;\ \mathsf{branch}_\mathsf{F})$

$\sqsubseteq \quad$ by (29)

$\qquad (\text{CACHE} += z\ \centerdot\ \mathsf{branch}''_\mathsf{T}) \mathbin{\triangle} ([\neg b]\,;\ \mathsf{branch}_\mathsf{F})$

$\sqsubseteq \quad$ by Law 23

$\qquad \text{CACHE} += z\ \centerdot\ ([\neg b]\,;\ \mathsf{branch}_\mathsf{F})$

From the system's perspective the speculation has had no effect: the assignment to x was caught in the transient buffer, and then discarded, and the computations involving registers r_1 and r_2 became silent steps that did not affect the outer state. However, the cache has (potentially) been modified.

At the system level this gives the following behaviour, assuming global state σ_g satisfies $\sigma_g(z) = 42$ and assuming $\sigma_g(\text{CACHE}) = C$ (the value for x is irrelevant), and σ_l is the local state (mapping r_1 and r_2).

$\qquad (\mathbf{global}\ \sigma_g \bullet (\mathbf{local}\ \sigma_l \bullet \mathbf{if}\ b\ \mathbf{then}\ \mathsf{branch}_\mathsf{T}\ \mathbf{else}\ \mathsf{branch}_\mathsf{F})\ \|\ \ldots)$

$\sqsubseteq \quad$ By the above derivation (note that neither σ_g nor σ_l are affected)

$\qquad (\mathbf{global}\ \sigma_g \bullet (\mathbf{local}\ \sigma_l \bullet \text{CACHE} += z\ \centerdot\ ([\neg b]\,;\ \mathsf{branch}_\mathsf{F}))\ \|\ \ldots)$

$\sqsubseteq \quad$ Execute instruction (Rule 1(a)), (19), Rule 9

$\qquad (\mathbf{global}\ \sigma_{g[\text{CACHE}\,:=\,C \cup \{\&z\}]} \bullet (\mathbf{local}\ \sigma_l \bullet [\neg b]\,;\ \mathsf{branch}_\mathsf{F})\ \|\ \ldots)$

The processes in '$\ldots$' could include a malicious attacker that may be able to exploit the existence of z in the cache. We give an example of this in the next section.

---

^{2} Note that $\mathsf{branch}_\mathsf{T}$ does not depend on any of the values it buffers/loads, and hence we may choose an arbitrary local σ; for other cases the choice of σ may be important.

The derivations above cover the situation where a single speculated load is promoted to a cache fetch. The variant of the Spectre attack we consider in the next section contains two speculated loads; using similar reasoning to the above we can straightforwardly show the following.

$$\mathbf{spec}(r_1 := \widetilde{x} \; ; \; \widetilde{r_2} := y)$$
$$\sqsubseteq \text{CACHE} += x \bullet [x = v_1] \; ; \; \mathbf{spec}(\widetilde{r_2 := y})$$
$$\sqsubseteq \text{CACHE} += x \bullet \text{CACHE} += y \bullet [x = v_1] \; ; \; [y = v_2] \; ; \; \mathbf{spec}(\widetilde{\mathbf{nil}})$$

And hence by generalising Law 23 we may deduce the following.

$$\mathbf{spec}(r_1 := \widetilde{x} \; ; \; \widetilde{r_2} := y) \triangle c \sqsubseteq \text{CACHE} += x \bullet \text{CACHE} += y \bullet c \qquad (30)$$
$$\mathbf{if} \; b \; \mathbf{then} \; r_1 := x \; ; \; r_2 := y \; \mathbf{else} \; c \sqsubseteq \text{CACHE} += x \bullet \text{CACHE} += y \bullet [\neg b] \; ; \; c \qquad (31)$$

4   Security Vulnerabilities

4.1   Attack Patterns

Cache-based timing attacks often utilise certain attack strategies to set up the cache as a covert or side channel to expose secret information. Generally, an attacker that shares a cache with a victim can observe through the variation in access time whether a particular memory address resides in the cache (a cache hit) and hence has been accessed previously, or not (a cache miss). To reduce noise on this covert channel, the attacker first "clears" the cache to make sure the memory address in question does not reside in the cache. This can be achieved by either flushing the cache line in question (some Intel architectures offer an instruction clflush), or by filling the cache with other content (by accessing physically congruent addresses in a large array [17]), so that due to the contention the memory addresses in question (if present) will be evicted. Both these options are captured in our model through the instruction CCLEAR (as emptying the cache and filling the cache with other content amounts to the same desired effect).

For example consider the following code that iterates over the elements of an array B to determine which of $B[i]$ is in the cache.

$$Atk \; \widehat{=} \; i := 0 \; ; \; (\mathbf{while} \; i < 256 \; \mathbf{do} \; (\mathbf{if} \; B[i] \in \text{CACHE} \; \mathbf{then} \; r := i) \; ; \; i \mathrel{+}= 1) \qquad (32)$$

If the attacker is trying to determine the value of some byte of data D, then under the assumption $B[\text{D}] \in \text{CACHE}$ and for all $i \neq \text{D}$ we have $B[i] \notin \text{CACHE}$ then we have $r = \text{D}$.

The guard $B[i] \in \text{CACHE}$ is an abstraction of a timing attack that loads $B[i]$ and checks the amount of time against an architecture-specific threshold. For our level of analysis we do not need to explicitly model such detail, we care only that it is possible.

FLUSH+RELOAD [45] and also EVICT+RELOAD [17], two examples that follow the above pattern, can be used to target the last level cache (LLC), which is shared between cores, and hence works on any cross-core as well as cross-VM settings [26]. In cases where a flush instruction is not available eviction is used to "clear" the cache. The following fundamental concepts of micro-architectures are exploited in these attack patterns [17]: 1) the LLC is shared amongst all CPUs; 2) the LLC is inclusive (i.e., contains all data that is stored in the L1 and L2 caches, hence modifications on the LLC influence caches on all other cores); 3) single cache lines are shared amongst processes on the same core; and 4) programs can map any other program binary/library into their address space.

4.2 The Spectre Attack

Spectre attacks typically use an attack pattern based on those described above. Additionally to setting up the cache as a channel, the attacker (mis)trains the branch predictor to speculate down the desired branch. Depending on the processor-specific branch prediction mechanism used, the training can occur by repeatedly running the code with "correct" input. When unexpectedly supplied with an "incorrect" input, the processor will (incorrectly) speculate the desired branch, in which secret information is loaded from memory (e.g., execute a memory access at an address that is chosen by the attacker), or in other variants the attacker may leverage its own code to access the secret from the same process, for instance, a webpage script run from within a browser process. In a third phase of the attack the timing difference between a cache hit and a cache miss is observed by the attacker, as in (32), allowing it to deduce the secret value.

An example of victim's code that is susceptible to a Spectre attack is given below (following [25]). Assume that the attacker wishes to know the value of some data D, held at some address in the private space of the victim process V and which can be retrieved via variable K, i.e., D is at address &K. The attacker knows/calculates the address of K relative to the victim array A, which we will call χ, loading the value into r_2 via an out-of-bounds index into A. That is, $A[\chi] = $ D. This private data is then used as an index into *another* array B.

$$V \mathrel{\widehat{=}} r_1 := \chi \,;\; n := \#A;\; \textbf{if } r_1 < n \textbf{ then } (r_2 := A[r_1]\,;\; r_3 := B[r_2])$$

We apply Law 31 to observe the potential effects of speculation.

$$V \sqsubseteq r_1 := \chi\,;\; n := \#A\,;\; \text{CACHE} \mathrel{+=} A[\chi] \bullet \text{CACHE} \mathrel{+=} B[\text{D}] \bullet [r_1 \not< n]$$

(We let $\&A[i]$ return a unique address for the array A at index i.) Let σ_l be the local state for V ($A, n, r_1, r_2, r_3 \in \text{dom}(\sigma_l)$), and σ_g the global state ($B \in \text{dom}(\sigma_g), \sigma_g(\text{CACHE}) = C$); then we can derive the following refinement.

$$\begin{aligned}
&(\textbf{global } \sigma_g \bullet (\textbf{local } \sigma_l \bullet V) \parallel p) \sqsubseteq \\
&\qquad (\textbf{global } \sigma_{g[\text{CACHE} := C \cup \{\&\text{K}, \&B[\text{D}]\}]} \bullet (\textbf{local } \sigma_l' \bullet \textbf{nil}) \parallel p)
\end{aligned}$$

The data D does not appear explicitly in the shared state, but indirectly through a cache fetch. Note that the values of the variables whose addresses are in the cache are not accessible.

To infer D the attacker may perform an attack as given by Atk in (32). For simplicity here we assume Atk and V share B, for instance if B is a read-only array of data shared by processes in a system; alternatively Atk does not need to share B, but rather know where B maps to in a shared cache, and map an array B_{Atk} of its own so that the addresses in the cache line up. At this level of abstraction we do not distinguish these alternatives. To establish the precondition that all elements of B are not in the cache the attacker sets up the context to ensure that it executes a CCLEAR before the victim's code is run. For instance, if the vulnerable code is in a function call provided by the server V, with the initial value of r_1 passed as an argument,

$$(\textbf{global } \{\text{CACHE} \mapsto \_, \ldots\} \bullet \text{CCLEAR} ; \ V(\chi) ; Atk)$$

This pattern can be repeated; in fact χ need not be a specific address, as data from V's private space can be read consecutively byte-by-byte by incrementing χ on each attack.

Model Checking. We validated the semantics by encoding the refinement laws as an extension to the simulation tool described in [12], which is written in the Maude rewriting engine [8, 41]. The refinement laws and auxiliary definitions (such as $\overset{R}{\Leftarrow}$ for cache fetches) were encoded straightforwardly. We then encoded the Spectre attacker and victim processes, extending the array A so that its contents went beyond its stated length to model an out-of-bounds index into private memory; the simulation runs showed that $r = D$ is established in the attacker (32) in the cases where speculation is not interrupted in the victim until after the two cache fetches.

5   Related Work

Cache side channels have been studied in the past decade (see [16, 46] for an overview), and a number of tools have been developed to support the detection of vulnerabilities (e.g., [6, 14, 38, 43]). However, these developments predate the publication of the Spectre vulnerability [24, 25] and hence do not consider the effects of speculative execution. Since the effects of speculation do not affect the functional correctness of an implementation (the results of incorrect speculation are thrown away), they could be safely ignored in earlier work on the semantics of weak memory models (e.g., [12]). Detailed formal models of microarchitecture describe the interaction of the cache with processors [4], but are not readily integrated with language-level analysis techniques.

A model of speculative execution to study vulnerabilities and support the evaluation of software mitigations is presented in [29]. That work assumes a uniprocessor system and is not integrated with a weak memory model, and is designed to give a precise description of the behaviour of the microarchitecture. The work of [13] gives a model of execution that highlights speculative behaviours by explicitly modelling executions down false branches within a partially-ordered multiset graph-based model. In contrast to our framework, they don't consider nested speculation, nor reorder speculated instructions.

A number of tools have been developed for detecting Spectre-vulnerable code and injecting fences to mitigate the danger [25,42,44] as well as information flow approaches to ensuring security in the presence of speculative execution [7,18]. The operational semantics underlying these approaches is less abstract than that presented in this paper, and the analysis is performed at the semantic level. The key difference of our work is that we encode speculative execution at the command level, and hence our framework supports algebraic, or refinement-based reasoning.

The CheckMate tool [39] integrates a model of speculative execution into a weak memory model framework [28]. Since the work aims at the verification of microarchitectures, their model is set at that level and does not provide high-level properties such as Law 31 to support reasoning on the program level. Their tool is used to synthesise Spectre-style attacks and generate assembler test programs that can be used to determine if a particular processor is susceptible. We can potentially use these test programs to investigate the security implications within our more abstract framework. We have focused on cache effects from speculative loads, however two variants of Meltdown and Spectre discovered by the CheckMate tool [39,40] work from speculative stores. On architectures where speculatively executed stores affect the cache we can adapt our semantics such that Rule 24(a) emits the appropriate cache-modifying action (rather than being a purely internal step).

6 Conclusion

We have captured the side effects of speculative execution down the wrong path with a relatively small extension to an existing framework for reasoning about weak memory models (out-of-order execution). To calculate speculated computations (beyond loads) we introduced a transient context, which is discarded in the case of incorrect speculation. In our semantic framework, in contrast to Plotkin-style semantics where states appear in the configuration of the operational rules [34], we expose the effect of a transition in its label. This simplifies semantic issues concerning redeclaration of variables (see [9,10] for a further discussion); operations on variables in the inner (transient) scope become silent τ steps that do not effect the variables in the outer scope, despite sharing the same names. Allowing early execution of speculated instructions was straightforward to specify in the reordering relation of IMP-ro [12].

Our intention is to allow abstract functional analysis techniques to be used alongside security analysis techniques, reusing existing tools. In particular, the information flow analysis framework in [32,33] has been extended to weak memory models [37] based on the reordering semantics of IMP-ro [12]. We envisage a further extension of that work based on IMP-ro-spec to find information leaks resulting from speculative execution. We have aimed to provide just enough detail so that cache effects can be modelled, but not so much that the ability to derive generic algebraic laws (such as Law 31) is lost.

Acknowledgements. We thank Samuel Chenoweth, Patrick Meiring, Mark Beaumont, Harrison Cusack and the anonymous reviewers for helping us improve the paper.

A   Speculation Down the Correct Branch; Parallel Speculation

As far as is currently known correct speculation has no security implications, and therefore we do not model such behaviours explicitly. However if needed we can capture this in several ways. For instance, a cache fetch can be associated with every load, whether inside or outside a speculation, similarly to Rule 25(a). Such semantics can be given by annotating each load that may exhibit this side effect.

$$(r := x)_{\text{CACHE}} \xrightarrow{\text{CACHE} \, += \, x} r := x$$

Alternatively we could add the possibility of speculation down the eventually chosen branch as a choice.

$$\mathbf{spec}(c_2 \sqcap c_1) \,\triangle\, ([b] \,;\, c_1) \,\sqcap\, \mathbf{spec}(c_1 \sqcap c_2) \,\triangle\, ([\neg b] \,;\, c_2)$$

A more precise model that commits the transient context when correct speculation is found is possible, though significantly more complicated.

The concept of speculation down either branch can be extended straightforwardly to parallel speculation down multiple branches, for instance,

$$(\mathbf{spec}(c_1) \,\|\, \mathbf{spec}(c_2)) \,\triangle\, ([b] \,;\, c_1)$$

References

1. Alglave, J., Maranget, L., Tautschnig, M.: Herding cats: Modelling, simulation, testing, and data mining for weak memory. ACM Trans. Program. Lang. Syst. **36**(2), 7:1–7:74 (2014)
2. Alglave, J., Maranget, L., Sarkar, S., Sewell, P.: Litmus: running tests against hardware. In: Abdulla, P.A., Leino, K.R.M. (eds.) TACAS 2011. LNCS, vol. 6605, pp. 41–44. Springer, Heidelberg (2011). https://doi.org/10.1007/978-3-642-19835-9_5
3. Back, R.J.R., von Wright, J.: Trace refinement of action systems. In: Jonsson, B., Parrow, J. (eds.) CONCUR 1994. LNCS, vol. 836, pp. 367–384. Springer, Heidelberg (1994). https://doi.org/10.1007/978-3-540-48654-1_28
4. Bijo, S., Johnsen, E.B., Pun, K.I., Lizeth Tapia Tarifa, S.: An operational semantics of cache coherent multicore architectures. In: Proceedings of the 31st Annual ACM Symposium on Applied Computing, SAC 2016, pp. 1219–1224. ACM, New York (2016)
5. Van Bulck, J., et al.: Foreshadow: extracting the keys to the intel SGX kingdom with transient out-of-order execution. In: USENIX Security Symposium (2018)
6. Chattopadhyay, S., Roychoudhury, A.: Symbolic verification of cache side-channel freedom. CoRR, abs/1801.01203 (2018)

7. Cheang, K., Rasmussen, C., Seshia, S., Subramanyan, P.: A formal approach to secure speculation. Cryptology ePrint Archive, Report 2019/310 (2019). https://eprint.iacr.org/2019/310

8. Clavel, M., et al.: Maude: specification and programming in rewriting logic. Theor. Comput. Sci. **285**(2), 187–243 (2002)

9. Colvin, R., Hayes, I.J.: CSP with hierarchical state. In: Leuschel, M., Wehrheim, H. (eds.) IFM 2009. LNCS, vol. 5423, pp. 118–135. Springer, Heidelberg (2009). https://doi.org/10.1007/978-3-642-00255-7_9

10. Colvin, R.J., Hayes, I.J.: Structural operational semantics through context-dependent behaviour. J. Logic Algebraic Programm. **80**(7), 392–426 (2011)

11. Colvin, R.J., Smith, G.: A high-level operational semantics for hardware weak memory models. CoRR, abs/1812.00996 (2018)

12. Colvin, R.J., Smith, G.: A wide-spectrum language for verification of programs on weak memory models. In: Havelund, K., Peleska, J., Roscoe, B., de Vink, E. (eds.) FM 2018. LNCS, vol. 10951, pp. 240–257. Springer, Cham (2018). https://doi.org/10.1007/978-3-319-95582-7_14

13. Disselkoen, C., Jagadeesan, R., Jeffrey, A., Riely, J.: Code that never ran: modeling attacks on speculative evaluation. In: Proceedings of IEEE Symposium on Security and Privacy (S&P) (2019)

14. Doychev, G., Köpf, B., Mauborgne, L., Reineke, J.: CacheAudit: a tool for the static analysis of cache side channels. ACM Trans. Inf. Syst. Secur. **18**(1), 4:1–4:32 (2015)

15. Flur, S., et al.: Modelling the ARMv8 architecture, operationally: concurrency and ISA. In: Proceedings of the 43rd Annual ACM SIGPLAN-SIGACT Symposium on Principles of Programming Languages, POPL 2016, pp. 608–621. ACM, New York (2016)

16. Ge, Q., Yarom, Y., Cock, D., Heiser, G.: A survey of microarchitectural timing attacks and countermeasures on contemporary hardware. J. Cryptographic Eng. **8**(1), 1–27 (2016). https://doi.org/10.1007/s13389-016-0141-6

17. Gruss, D., Spreitzer, R., Mangard, S.: Cache template attacks: automating attacks on inclusive last-level caches. In: 24th USENIX Security Symposium (USENIX Security 15), pp. 897–912. USENIX Association (2015)

18. Guarnieri, M., Köpf, B., Morales, J.F., Reineke, J., Sánchez, A.: SPECTEC-TOR: principled detection of speculative information flows. CoRR, abs/1812.08639 (2018)

19. He, J., Hoare, C.A.R., Sanders, J.W.: Data refinement refined resume. In: Robinet, B., Wilhelm, R. (eds.) ESOP 1986. LNCS, vol. 213, pp. 187–196. Springer, Heidelberg (1986). https://doi.org/10.1007/3-540-16442-1_14

20. Hoare, C.A.R.: Communicating Sequential Processes. Prentice-Hall Inc, Upper Saddle River (1985)

21. Intel. Intel 64 and IA-32 Architectures Software Developers Manual, January 2019

22. Islam, S., et al.: SPOILER: Speculative Load Hazards Boost Rowhammer And Cache Attacks (2019)

23. Kang, J., Hur, C.-K., Lahav, O., Vafeiadis, V., Dreyer, D.: A promising semantics for relaxed-memory concurrency. In Proceedings of the 44th ACM SIGPLAN Symposium on Principles of Programming Languages, POPL 2017, pp. 175–189. ACM, New York (2017)

24. Kocher, P., et al.: Spectre attacks: exploiting speculative execution. In 40th IEEE Symposium on Security and Privacy (S&P 2019) (2019)

25. Li, P., Zhao, L., Hou, R., Zhang, L., Meng, D.: Conditional speculation: an effective approach to safeguard out-of-order execution against Spectre attacks. In: 2019 IEEE International Symposium on High Performance Computer Architecture (HPCA), pp. 264–276, February 2019

26. Lipp, M., Gruss, D., Spreitzer, R., Maurice, C., Mangard, S.: Armageddon: cache attacks on mobile devices. In: 25th USENIX Security Symposium (USENIX Security 2016), pp. 549–564. USENIX Association (2016)

27. Lipp, M., et al.: Meltdown: reading kernel memory from user space. In USENIX Security Symposium (2018)

28. Lustig, D., Pellauer, M., Martonosi, M.: PipeCheck: specifying and verifying microarchitectural enforcement of memory consistency models. In: Proceedings of the 47th Annual IEEE/ACM International Symposium on Microarchitecture, MICRO-47, pp. 635–646, Washington, DC, USA. IEEE Computer Society (2014)

29. Mcilroy, R., Sevcik, J., Tebbi, T., Titzer, B.L., Verwaest, B.L.: Spectre is here to stay: an analysis of side-channels and speculative execution. CoRR, abs/1902.05178 (2019)

30. Milner, R.: A Calculus of Communicating Systems. LNCS, vol. 92. Springer, Heidelberg (1980). https://doi.org/10.1007/3-540-10235-3

31. Morgan, C., Gardiner, P.: Data refinement by calculation. Acta Informatica **27**, 481–503 (1990)

32. Murray, T.C., Sison, R., Engelhardt, K.: COVERN: a logic for compositional verification of information flow control. In: 2018 IEEE European Symposium on Security and Privacy, EuroS&P 2018, pp. 16–30. IEEE (2018)

33. Murray, T.C., Sison, R., Pierzchalski, E., Rizkallah, C.: Compositional verification and refinement of concurrent value-dependent noninterference. In: IEEE 29th Computer Security Foundations Symposium, CSF 2016, pp. 417–431. IEEE Computer Society (2016)

34. Plotkin, G.D.: A structural approach to operational semantics. J. Logic Algebraic Program. **60–61**, 17–139 (2004)

35. Sarkar, S., Sewell, P., Alglave, J., Maranget, L., Williams, D.: Understanding POWER multiprocessors. SIGPLAN Not. **46**(6), 175–186 (2011)

36. Sewell, P., Sarkar, S., Owens, S., Nardelli, F.Z., Myreen, M.O.: X86-TSO: a rigorous and usable programmer's model for x86 multiprocessors. Commun. ACM **53**(7), 89–97 (2010)

37. Smith, G., Coughlin, N., Murray, T.: Value-dependent information-flow security on weak memory models. In: ter Beek, M.H., McIver, A., Oliveira, J.N. (eds.) FM 2019. LNCS, vol. 11800, pp. 539–555. Springer, Cham (2019). https://doi.org/10.1007/978-3-030-30942-8_32

38. Touzeau, V., Maïza, C., Monniaux, D., Reineke, J.: Fast and exact analysis for LRU caches. Proc. ACM Program. Lang. **3**(POPL), 54:1–54:29 (2019)

39. Trippel, C., Lustig, D., Martonosi, M.: Checkmate: automated synthesis of hardware exploits and security litmus tests. In: 2018 51st Annual IEEE/ACM International Symposium on Microarchitecture (MICRO), pp. 947–960 (2018)

40. Trippel, C., Lustig, D., Martonosi, M.: MeltdownPrime and SpectrePrime: automatically-synthesized attacks exploiting invalidation-based coherence protocols. CoRR, abs/1802.03802 (2018)

41. Verdejo, A., Mart-Oliet, N.: Executable structural operational semantics in Maude. J. Logic Algebraic Programm. **67**(1–2), 226–293 (2006)

42. Wang, G., Chattopadhyay, S., Gotovchits, I., Mitra, T., Roychoudhury, A.: oo7: low-overhead defense against spectre attacks via binary analysis. CoRR, abs/1807.05843 (2018)

43. Wang, S., Wang, P., Liu, X., Zhang, D., Wu, D.: CacheD: identifying cache-based timing channels in production software. In: 26th USENIX Security Symposium (USENIX Security 2017), pp. 235–252. USENIX Association (2017)
44. Wu, M., Wang, C.: Abstract interpretation under speculative execution. In: Proceedings of the 40th ACM SIGPLAN Conference on Programming Language Design and Implementation, PLDI 2019, pp. 802–815. ACM, New York (2019)
45. Yarom, Y., Falkner, K.: FLUSH+RELOAD: a high resolution, low noise, L3 cache side-channel attack. In: USENIX Security Symposium (USENIX Security 2014), pp. 719–732. USENIX Association (2014)
46. Zhang, Y.: Cache side channels: state of the art and research opportunities. In: Proceedings of the 2017 ACM SIGSAC Conference on Computer and Communications Security, CCS 2017, pp. 2617–2619. ACM (2017)

Weakening Correctness and Linearizability for Concurrent Objects on Multicore Processors

Graeme Smith[1]([✉]) and Lindsay Groves[2]

[1] School of Information Technology and Electrical Engineering,
The University of Queensland, Brisbane, Australia
smith@itee.uq.edu.au
[2] School of Engineering and Computer Science, Victoria University of Wellington,
Wellington, New Zealand

Abstract. In this paper, we argue that there are two fundamental ways of defining correctness of concurrent objects on the weak memory models of multicore processors: we can abstract from concurrent interleaving and weak memory effects at the specification level, or we can abstract from concurrent interleaving only, leaving weak memory effects at the specification level. The first allows us to employ standard linearizability as the correctness criterion; a result proved in earlier work. The second requires a weakening of linearizability. We provide such a weakening and prove it sound and complete with respect to this notion of correctness.

1 Introduction

Libraries of efficient concurrent objects are central to developing concurrent programs. High-level concurrent algorithms utilise concurrent objects for sharing data between threads, e.g., concurrent queues and stacks, and for inter-thread synchronisation, e.g., locks [15]. Correctness of such objects is usually defined with respect to a sequential specification. For example, a concurrent queue being accessed concurrently by multiple threads should still behave essentially like a queue. The standard criterion for relating concurrent implementations of objects to their sequential specifications is *linearizability* [16]. In recent years, however, the question has arisen as to whether linearizability is the appropriate correctness criterion in the presence of weak memory models.[1] This has led to several proposals for weaker versions of linearizability which either change the sequential specification to allow weak memory effects [4,14], or change the definition of linearizability itself [8,9,11,25], as well as new approaches to verifying correctness unrelated to linearizability [21].

On sequentially consistent (SC) memory models, *observational refinement* [12] and *contextual refinement* [10] have been proposed as reference points with

---

[1] In this paper, we refer solely to *hardware* weak memory models of multicore processors, e.g., x86-TSO [19], ARM [13,20] and IBM POWER [22], and not *software* weak memory models that allow for compiler optimisations, e.g., C11 [3].

© Springer Nature Switzerland AG 2020
E. Sekerinski et al. (Eds.): FM 2019 Workshops, LNCS 12233, pp. 342–357, 2020.
https://doi.org/10.1007/978-3-030-54997-8_22

which to judge such correctness criteria. These take the view that an object implementation is correct if and only if a client program calling the object's operations cannot distinguish the object from one that behaves according to the specification. Filipović et al. [12] prove that under certain assumptions observational refinement is equivalent to linearizability.

A similar reference point for judging correctness criteria on weak memory models, called *object refinement*, was recently proposed by Smith et al. [23]. In follow-on work, they prove the (somewhat surprising) result that the standard definition of linearizability for SC is also equivalent to object refinement [24]. Their proof holds for all current memory models, including SC, and without the assumptions required by Filipović et al. For SC, this suggests that object refinement captures exactly what was intended by linearizability.

The result for weak memory models, however, is quite strong. A number of efficient implementations of concurrent objects are incorrect under standard linearizability. This is due to the fact that under weak memory models the effect of an operation on one thread may be delayed from the perspective of other threads. In this paper, we suggest a relaxation of object refinement that allows more implementation flexibility, and discuss the consequences in terms of the verification and use of concurrent objects. In particular, we present a definition of *weak linearizability* that is sound and complete with respect to our relaxed notion of object refinement, and argue why both weak linearizability and standard linearizability are required in practice.

2   Correctness

The operations of a concurrent object may be called by multiple threads simultaneously. This results in an interleaving of their code in which interference must be handled using locks or, when efficiency is important, non-blocking techniques [18]. The behaviour of such interleaved code is difficult to reason about, and specifications usually abstract from interleaving by having operations which are atomic. For example, operations may be specified with a precondition/postcondition pair. An implementation C of a concurrent object is considered correct in this setting when any program P which calls C's operations behaves in a way consistent with calling the atomic operations of A:

$$\forall P \bullet P[A] \sqsubseteq P[C] \tag{1}$$

where $P[A]$ and $P[C]$ denote the program P calling the atomic operations of A, and the potentially interleaving operations of C, respectively, and $\sqsubseteq$ denotes trace refinement [1,2] where observations are of changes to *program variables*, i.e., variables declared as part of P.

2.1   Linearizability

The standard notion of correctness on SC is linearizability [16]. The semantics $[\![C]\!]$ of a concurrent object C is expressed as a prefix-closed set of *histories*, where each history is a sequence of events corresponding to *invocations* and *responses* of operations calls. The semantics $[\![A]\!]$ of an object specification A can similarly be expressed as a prefix-closed set of histories. Since operations are regarded as atomic (i) operation calls cannot overlap, i.e., an invocation is immediately followed by its matching response, and (ii) prefixes are restricted to *complete* histories in which the final event cannot be an invocation.

Linearizability relates histories of an object implementation, which may have *pending* invocations, i.e., invocations for which there is no response, to histories of an object specification which do not. To do this, it needs to *complete* the implementation histories. This can be done by adding a response when a pending invocation is deemed to have taken effect, and removing the invocation when it has not [16].

Let $ext(h)$ be the set of extensions of a history h formed by adding a sequence of responses for an arbitrary subset of the pending invocations, and $comp(h)$ complete h by removing all pending invocations. A concurrent object C is said to *linearize* with an object specification A when the following holds.

$$C \ lin \ A \ \hat{=} \ \forall h : [\![C]\!] \bullet \exists h' : [\![A]\!] \bullet \exists h^+ : ext(h) \bullet comp(h^+) \sim h' \wedge \prec_{comp(h^+)} \subseteq \prec_{h'}$$

where $h \sim h'$ denotes that h and h' are *thread equivalent*, i.e., when restricted to the events of any one thread they have the same sequence of invocations and responses, and $\prec_h$ captures the order of operations in a trace, where one operation comes before another if its response is before the other's invocation.

The intuition behind the definition is that operations which are overlapping in $comp(h^+)$ are not ordered by $\prec_{comp(h^+)}$ and, with $\prec_{h'}$ being a superset of $\prec_{comp(h^+)}$, can occur in any order in h'. The implementation history h is said to linearize to h'.

Linearizability is *compositional*, allowing us to prove the correctness of a system of interacting objects by showing each component object is linearizable with respect to its specification [16].

3   Weak Memory Models

Weak memory models optimise performance by allowing the hardware to control accesses to shared memory. As a consequence, the effect of operations on one thread may be delayed from the perspective of another. On TSO, for example, writes to shared variables are placed in a FIFO store buffer, and only take effect in memory at a later time determined by the hardware, or when a fence is reached in the code [19]. Such fences may be added liberally by the programmer, but can negate the optimisations that the memory model offers.

POWER and ARM are weaker than TSO, allowing delayed writes to take effect out of FIFO order unless a specific dependency exists between them [13,22]. They additionally support *non-multi-copy atomicity*.[2] This allows writes by one thread to be seen by other threads at different times, again determined by the

---

[2] This is no longer true for the latest version of ARMv8 [20].

hardware. This can be captured semantically by a *write list* [6] which orders all writes which have occurred in a program execution along with which threads have seen those writes.

3.1 Modelling Weak Memory Behaviour

Following [23], we model additional behaviours under weak memory models by adding an *effect* event for each program step and each operation call. An effect event indicates when the program step or operation takes place from the global perspective of all threads in the program. For a program step, this will be after the program step occurs, and for an operation after its invocation. The exact position of the effect event is determined by the memory model semantics.

For program steps and operations which write to shared variables, the effect will be when all threads have seen all of the writes. For example, on TSO the effect will be when the last write associated with the program step or operation takes place in the global memory. On non-multi-copy atomic processors, the effect will be when, for each updated variable, all threads have seen the write, or have seen a later write to the same variable.

Given a memory model M, we let $[\![C]\!]_M$ denote the set of histories of an implementation C under M, and $[\![A]\!]_M$ the set of histories of a specification A under M. These histories will include effects, as well as invocations and responses.

Returning to correctness as defined in (1), while the behaviour of $P[C]$ under M can be determined from $[\![C]\!]_M$, a choice needs to be made about the meaning of $P[A]$. On SC, the behaviour of $P[A]$ abstracts from interleaving of operations, as A's operations are regarded as atomic. On weak memory models, there are two fundamental possibilities:

1. $P[A]$ abstracts from the interleaving of operations (as on SC) *and* weak memory model effects.
2. $P[A]$ abstracts from the interleaving of operations but includes weak memory effects.

In [23], the first option was taken, resulting in correctness being equivalent to linearizability for *all* memory models [24]. As discussed in [24], a consequence of this choice is that any operation whose effect can influence the output of a later operation needs to be fenced to be correct on a weak memory model. This is quite strict as it disallows many implementations where fences are avoided to improve efficiency. In the remainder of this paper we consider the second option above by allowing weak memory effects in $P[A]$.

4 Weakening Correctness

Program behaviour under a weak memory model is modelled in terms of *traces*, which are sequences of (program) step, invocation, response and effect events:

$$Event \mathrel{\widehat=} step(PS) \mid \mathit{eff}(PS) \mid inv(Op,\ Val) \mid res(Op,\ Val) \mid \mathit{eff}(Op,\ Val)$$

where PS is a program step by a particular thread, Op an operation call by a particular thread, and Val a set of values for inputs and outputs, including $\perp$ meaning no input or output.

Each event in a trace is unique (calls to the same operation, for example, being distinguished by annotating the operation name with its order of occurrence):

$$Trace \triangleq \{t : \text{seq } Event \mid (\forall\, i, j \leq \#t \bullet i \neq j \Rightarrow t_i \neq t_j) \wedge wf(t)\}$$

where wf, the well-formedness condition on traces, states that an invocation of an operation always occurs before the associated response and effect, a program step always occurs before its effect, and the output value of an operation's effect is the same as that of the corresponding response event.

$$
\begin{aligned}
wf(t) \triangleq\ & (\forall\, a : Op;\ out : Val \bullet \forall\, j \leq \#t \bullet t_j \in \{res(a, out), \mathit{eff}(a, out)\} \Rightarrow \\
& \qquad\qquad\qquad\qquad \exists\, in : Val;\ i < j \bullet t_i = inv(a, in)) \wedge \\
& (\forall\, p : PS \bullet \forall\, j \leq \#t \bullet t_j = \mathit{eff}(p) \Rightarrow \exists\, i < j \bullet t_i = step(p)) \wedge \\
& (\forall\, a : Op \bullet \exists\, out : Val \bullet \\
& \qquad \forall\, i \leq \#t;\ o : Val \bullet t(i) = res(a, o) \vee t(i) = \mathit{eff}(a, o) \Rightarrow o = out)
\end{aligned}
$$

A *sequential trace* is one where operations are atomic, i.e., all invocations have a matching response, and no events apart from effects may occur between the invocation and response of an operation.

$$
\begin{aligned}
SeqTrace \triangleq\ & \{t : Trace \mid (\forall\, a : Op;\ in : Val;\ i \leq \#t \bullet t_i = inv(a, in) \Rightarrow \\
& \qquad\qquad\qquad \exists\, out : Val;\ j \leq \#t \bullet t_j = res(a, out)) \wedge \\
& (\forall\, a : Op;\ in, out : Val;\ i < j < k \leq \#t \bullet \\
& \qquad t_i = inv(a, in) \wedge t_k = res(a, out) \Rightarrow \\
& \qquad\qquad \exists\, b : Op;\ out_b : Val \bullet t_j = \mathit{eff}(b, out_b))\}
\end{aligned}
$$

The events of a trace t determine a set, $events(t)$, and the (total) order in which these events occur is denoted by a relation, $<_t$:

$$
\begin{aligned}
events(t) &\triangleq \{a : Event \mid \exists\, i \leq \#t \bullet t_i = a\} \\
<_t &\triangleq \{(a, b) : Event \times Event \mid \exists\, i, j \leq \#t \bullet i < j \wedge t_i = a \wedge t_j = b\}
\end{aligned}
$$

A program P has a set of events, $events(P)$, which it can undergo (according to the program text) and, for each memory model M, a partial order, $<_{P_M}$, which captures when an event can occur only after another under M (see [24] for further details). The traces of P are defined as follows:

$$[\![P]\!]_M \triangleq \{t : Trace \mid events(t) \subseteq events(P) \wedge <_{P_M} \Subset <_t\}$$

where $<_{P_M} \Subset <_t$ specifies whether an order is *allowed* by P on M, formally defined as:

$$<_{P_M} \Subset <_t \triangleq \forall (a, b) : <_{P_M} \bullet b \in events(t) \Rightarrow (a, b) \in <_t$$

That is, for any event b that occurs in trace t, if this event is constrained to come after another event a by $<_{PM}$, then event a must also occur in t before event b.

The semantics of $P[C]$ under M are those traces t of $[\![P]\!]_M$ whose restriction to *object events* (invocation, responses and operation effects), denoted $t_{|o}$, is in $[\![C]\!]_M$.

$$[\![P[C]]\!]_M \,\hat{=}\, \{t : [\![P]\!]_M \mid t_{|o} \in [\![C]\!]_M\}$$

The semantics of $P[A]$ is given similarly:

$$[\![P[A]]\!]_M \,\hat{=}\, \{t : [\![P]\!]_M \mid t_{|o} \in [\![A]\!]_M\}$$

To motivate our definition of $[\![A]\!]_M$, consider an object with two operations: W, which writes to an object variable x, whose value is initially 0, and R, which reads x. One possible behaviour under a weak memory model such as TSO is:

$$\langle inv(n.W, 1), res(n.W, \bot), inv(m.R, \bot), \mathit{eff}(m.R, 0), res(m.R, 0), \mathit{eff}(n.W, \bot)\rangle$$

where the read by thread m returns 0 since the effect of the write by thread n has not yet taken effect. The operations do not overlap (the invocation of $m.R$ occurs after the response of $n.W$), modelling that the operations are atomic. However, weak memory effects are included, due to the effect of $n.W$ being delayed.

The above trace corresponds to a history of A, the specification of the object, where $m.R$ occurs before $n.W$. In general, a history h of A_M will be thread equivalent to a history h' of A such that the operations of h are ordered consistently with placing them between the corresponding invocations and effects of h. This can be defined in terms of the notation $h \sim h'$ and $\prec_h$ introduced to define linearizability in Sect. 2:

$$[\![A]\!]_M \,\hat{=}\, \{h : SeqTrace \mid h_{|o} = h \wedge \exists h' : [\![A]\!] \bullet h \sim h' \wedge \prec_{trans(h)} \subseteq \prec_{h'}\}$$

where $trans(h)$ replaces the effect of each operation in h by its response:

$$
\begin{array}{lcl}
trans(\langle\rangle) & = & \langle\rangle \\
trans(\langle inv(a, in)\rangle \frown h') & = & \langle inv(a, in)\rangle \frown trans(h') \\
trans(\langle res(a, out)\rangle \frown h') & = & trans(h') \\
trans(\langle \mathit{eff}(a, out)\rangle \frown h') & = & \langle res(a, out)\rangle \frown trans(h')
\end{array}
$$

Object refinement, our notion of correctness, is then defined as:

$$P[A] \sqsubseteq_M P[C] \,\hat{=}\, \forall t : [\![P[C]]\!]_M \bullet \exists t' : [\![P[A]]\!]_M \bullet t'_{|global} = t_{|global}$$

where $t_{|global}$ is the restriction of t to *observable* program steps, i.e., those which change global variables.

5   Weak Linearizability

We now present a notion of weak linearizability, and prove it sound and complete with respect to our notion of object refinement defined in Sect. 4. This notion has been previously suggested for concurrent objects on TSO [8,25]. It involves allowing an operation to linearize anywhere between its invocation and effect (i.e., when the operation's final write takes place in global memory on TSO). Here we show it corresponds to our notion of correctness not just for TSO, but for any weak memory model.

Let *ext* return the set of traces which extend a given trace with a sequence of responses such that the result is still a trace, i.e., responses are only added for pending invocations:

$$ext(t) \cong \{t \frown tr : Trace \mid \forall i \leq \#tr \bullet \exists a : Op;\ out : Val \bullet tr_i = res(a, out)\}$$

and let *comp* return the trace obtained by removing all invocations from a given trace which have neither an effect nor a response:

$$
\begin{aligned}
comp(\langle \rangle) &= \langle \rangle \\
comp(\langle inv(a, in) \rangle \frown t') &= comp(t'), \text{ if } NoResp(a, t') \\
comp(\langle e \rangle \frown t') &= \langle e \rangle \frown comp(t'), \text{ otherwise}
\end{aligned}
$$

where $NoResp(a, t) \cong \nexists\, i \leq \#t;\ out : Val \bullet t_i \in \{res(a, out), eff(a, out)\}$.

Weak linearizability, lin_M, is defined for any weak memory model M. By weak memory model, we mean a memory model where effects of program steps and operations may be delayed—this definition is not intended to be used with SC.

$$C\ lin_M\ A \cong \forall h : \llbracket C \rrbracket_M \bullet \exists h' : \llbracket A \rrbracket \bullet \\
\exists h^+ : ext(h) \bullet comp(h^+) \sim h' \wedge \prec_{trans(comp(h+))} \subseteq \prec_{h'}$$

Note that we linearize with respect to the original specification A which is independent of the memory model M.

Weak linearizability is proved to be compositional in [7]. The proofs of soundness and completeness below rely on the following lemmas proved in [24].

Lemma 1. *If the events of a trace t are events of a program P, then so are the events of any completion of t.*

$$\forall P \bullet \forall t : Trace \bullet \forall t^+ : ext(t) \bullet \\
events(t) \subseteq events(P) \Rightarrow events(comp(t^+)) \subseteq events(P)$$

Lemma 2. *If a trace t is allowed by a program P on memory model M, then so is any completion of t that only adds responses for operations whose effects have occurred.*

$$\forall P, M \bullet \forall t : Trace \bullet \forall t \frown tr : ext(t);\ a : Op;\ out : Val \bullet \\
(\forall i \leq \#tr \bullet tr_i = res(a, out) \Rightarrow \exists j \leq \#t \bullet t_j = eff(a, out)) \wedge <_{P_M} \in <_t \Rightarrow \\
<_{P_M} \in <_{comp(t \frown tr)}$$

Our proofs also use the notion of a *matching trace*, which is formed from a trace t as follows. Firstly, t is extended with responses for exactly those pending invocations for which there is an effect, and the remaining pending invocations are removed. Secondly, each response is moved to immediately after any contiguous sequence of effects following its invocation.

5.1 Soundness

We now show that our notion of weak linearizability is sound with respect to our definition of object refinement.

Theorem 1. *If an object implementation C linearizes with an object specification A on memory model M, then C is an object refinement of A on M.*

$$C \; lin_M \; A \; \Rightarrow \; \forall P \bullet P[A] \sqsubseteq_M P[C]$$

Proof. Assume that $C \; lin_M \; A$ holds, and consider an arbitrary program P with $[\![P[C]]\!]_M \neq \varnothing$ (when $[\![P[C]]\!]_M = \varnothing$ the consequent is trivially true). We must show that for any trace, t, of $P[C]$ under weak memory model M, there is a corresponding trace, t', of $P[A]$ under M.

Since $t \in [\![P[C]]\!]_M$, there is an $h \in [\![C]\!]_M$ such that $t_{|o} = h$, and since $C \; lin_M \; A$, there is also an $h' \in [\![A]\!]$ and $h^+ \in ext(h)$ such that:

$$comp(h^+) \sim h' \;\wedge\; \prec_{trans(comp(h+))} \subseteq \prec_{h'} \tag{S1}$$

There may be several possible choices for h^+. We choose h^+ so that a response is added for each pending invocation whose effect occurs in t. This is always possible since we know that there exists at least one extension and related abstract history. Call them h_0^+ and h_0', respectively. h_0^+ cannot have less than the required responses. If it did, $comp(h^+)$ would be left with a pending invocation (with an effect) but no response. Hence, $comp(h^+) \sim h'$ would not hold. If h_0^+ has more than the required responses, since $[\![A]\!]$ is prefixed-closed, we can find an h' which is a subsequence of h_0' which does not have the additional operations corresponding to the extra responses.[3] This h' will satisfy (S1) for our chosen $h+$.

Let t' be the matching trace of t. Since a matching trace maintains the order of program steps and their effects we have:

$$t'_{|global} = t_{|global} \tag{S2}$$

To complete the proof, it remains to show that $t' \in [\![P[A]]\!]_M$.

Since there are no overlapping operations on a given thread, the order of invocations and responses on a given thread in $comp(h^+)$ will be maintained in t'. Hence from (S1) we have:

$$t'_{|o} \sim h' \tag{S3}$$

Since the relative order of invocations and effects in $comp(h^+)$ will be maintained in t', we have that $trans(t'_{|o}) = trans(comp(h^+))$. Hence from (S1) we have:

$$\prec_{trans(t'_{|o})} \subseteq \prec_{h'} \tag{S4}$$

---

[3] Since there is at most one pending invocation per thread, such an h' will be in the prefix-closed set $[\![A]\!]$.

Since invocations and responses are only separated by effects in t', provided that it satisfies the well-formedness property of traces and is in *Trace*, it will be in *SeqTrace*:

$$t' \in Trace \Rightarrow t' \in SeqTrace \tag{S5}$$

Therefore, from (S3), (S4) and (S5) and the definition of $[\![A]\!]_M$, we have:

$$t' \in Trace \Rightarrow t'_{|_o} \in [\![A]\!]_M \tag{S6}$$

Given the definition of $[\![P[A]]\!]_M$ and (S6), to prove that $t' \in [\![P[A]]\!]_M$ we need to show that $t' \in Trace$, and that $t' \in [\![P]\!]_M$, i.e., $events(t') \subseteq events(P)$ and $<_{P_M} \, \subseteq \, <_{t'}$. We prove each of these below, where t^+ is the trace t extended with the sequence of responses added to h to form h^+.

(i) $t' \in Trace$:
Since $t \in [\![P[C]]\!]_M$, it follows from Lemmas 1 and 2 that $comp(t^+) \in [\![P]\!]_M$ and hence is a *Trace*. Since t' has the same events as $comp(t^+)$, its events are unique. Also, since the construction of t' does not alter the relative order of program steps with their effects, nor invocations with their responses and effects, *wf* holds. Hence, $t' \in Trace$.

(ii) $events(t') \subseteq events(P)$:
Since $comp(t^+) \in [\![P]\!]_M$, it follows that $events(comp(t^+)) \subseteq events(P)$ from the definition of $[\![P]\!]_M$. Since t' has the same events as $comp(t^+)$, it follows that $events(t') \subseteq events(P)$.

(iii) $<_{P_M} \, \subseteq \, <_{t'}$:
To prove this property we show that $\forall (a, b) : \, <_{P_M} \bullet \, b \in events(t') \Rightarrow (a, b) \in \, <_{t'}$. We consider four cases, according to whether a and b are program events or object events.

(a) The order between two *program events* (i.e., program steps or their effects) that is enforced by $<_{P_M}$ is maintained in t'.
This holds as the relative order of program events of t is unchanged in t'.

(b) If $<_{P_M}$ enforces that a program event has to occur before an *object event* (i.e., an invocation, response or effect of an operation) then this order is maintained by t'.
The relative order of program events with invocations and effects of t is unchanged in t'. Since an object's state is only accessed via its operations, there can be no synchronisation between a program event and the object's state while the operation is executing. Hence, if a program step must come before an operation's response, it must come before its invocation too. Since the response of an operation is not moved before its invocation, it is not moved before any program events which must come before it.

(c) If $<_{P_M}$ enforces that an object event has to occur before a program event then this order is maintained by t'.
The relative order of program events with invocations and effects of t is unchanged in t'. Since responses are only moved earlier in the trace, all program events after a response remain after the response.

(d) The order between two object events that is enforced by $<_{P_M}$ is maintained in t'.

The response of an operation op is not moved before its invocation, and its effect (on a weak memory model) cannot be constrained by P to occur before the response (since this would require the operation to either not write to shared variables or have a fence, and the operation's implementation is outside of P's control).

Also, since the implementation of object operations is outside P's control, synchronisation between operations cannot be enforced by P. Hence, if a response of an operation op must occur after another operation event e, other than op's invocation, then op's invocation must also occur after e. Hence, op's response is not moved before e. □

5.2 Completeness

We now show that our notion of weak linearizability is complete with respect to our definition of object refinement. The completeness proof uses a notion of a *recording program*, which records each program step and operation call in a global variable g. For each program step PS on thread n we have:

$$PS; \ g := \text{``}n.PS\text{''}$$

and for each call on an operation Op on thread n we have:

$$l := in; \ x := Op(in); \ g := \text{``}n.Op(in, out)\text{''}$$

where l is a local variable used to hold the value of the input until after the operation. Since the changes to g will appear in the observable part of any trace of the recording program, when $t_{|global} = t'_{|global}$ for any traces t and t', we know that these traces have undergone the same program steps, operation calls and outputs of operation calls up until the last recording on each thread. These events may occur in a different order, however, since the recordings made by different threads can be interleaved.

The completeness proof uses the following lemma.

Lemma 3. *If P is a recording program and C is an object refinement of A, then for a given implementation trace $t \in [\![P[C]]\!]_M$ either the matching trace t' is in $[\![P[A]]\!]_M$, or there is a trace t'' in $[\![P[A]]\!]_M$ which is formed by moving one or more effects in t' earlier than in t.*

Proof. Following the reasoning for matching traces in the proof of Theorem 1, t' will be in $[\![P]\!]_M$. Hence, the relative order of program steps and invocations in t' will be allowed by $P[A]$ on memory model M.

Since P is a recording program, if any effect allowed in t is not allowed by A, C will have a trace which is observably different to any of A. This contradicts the assumption that C is an object refinement of A. Hence, all effects in t are allowed by A. It remains for us to show that the effects may occur in the order of t' or some t'' formed from t' by moving one or more effects earlier.

We proceed using a proof by contradiction. Suppose that $[\![P[A]]\!]_M$ does not contain t' or any trace t'' formed from t' by moving one or more effects earlier. For C to be an object refinement of A, there must be a trace s in $[\![P[A]]\!]_M$ with the same events as t but with one or more effects occurring later than in t.

Let $\bar{t}$ denote the trace t with all responses removed, and u and v be non-empty sequences of events, and w be a possibly empty sequence of events. Let $\bar{t} = u ^\frown \langle eff_a \rangle ^\frown v ^\frown w$ and $\bar{s} = u ^\frown v ^\frown \langle eff_a \rangle ^\frown w$, i.e., where a single effect eff_a, of an event a, occurs later in s than in t. This implies that the occurrence of the last event of v, or when that event is an invocation the required output of its associated operation, requires that the effect of a has not occurred. From this we can deduce that:

(i) the last event of v is not a program step. If it were a program step then this program step would need to refer directly to a change made by a to a program variable (otherwise eff_a could occur before it). Since the program step is identical in the implementation (both use P), the implementation traces would also require eff_a to occur after v.

(ii) the last event of v is not an invocation. Let the last event of v be b. If b were an invocation then the associated operation's outputs in A would rely on a's effect not having occurred. On the other hand, the operation in C can produce the outputs in t after a has taken effect.

If a depends on earlier events of the same thread in t then there will be a dependency between those events that will prevent the effect of a occurring before the effects of the earlier events [6]. Hence, C allows the operation associated with b to produce the outputs in t when all such earlier events of a's thread have taken effect.

Therefore, it is possible to construct a recording program P' similar to P which forces a to take effect before b, e.g., eliding the recording events, P' could be:

$$...;\ a;\ fence;\ z = 1;\ ...\ ||\ ...;\ await(z = 1);\ b;\ ...\ ||\ ...$$

where the fence forces a (and all earlier events in a's thread) to take effect, and the await instruction ensures that b does not occur until this has happened.

There will be a trace in $[\![P'[C]]\!]_M$ in which the operation invoked by b has the same output as in t. However, there will not be such a trace in $[\![P'[A]]\!]_M$. The operation invoked by b will behave differently due to the effect of a. This will result in a different recording, and hence implies C is not an object refinement of A.

(iii) the last event of v is not an effect. The specification and implementation execute on the same memory model. Hence, any constraint on the ordering of effects in $P[A]$ will also hold in $P[C]$ [23].

Hence, the last step of v is neither a program step, invocation nor effect and we have a contradiction. The proof can be generalised to more than one effect event occurring later in s. $\square$

We can now state and prove the completeness theorem.

Theorem 2. *If an object implementation C is an object refinement of a specification A on memory model M then C linearizes to A on M.*

$$(\forall P \bullet P[A] \sqsubseteq_M P[C]) \;\Rightarrow\; C \; lin_M \; A$$

Proof. Assume the antecedent is true and that $[\![C]\!]_M \neq \varnothing$. Let h be a history in $[\![C]\!]_M$, and let P be a recording program which can generate a trace t corresponding to h, i.e., $t_{|o} = h$. Let $t^+ \in ext(t)$ be an extension of t which adds a response for exactly those pending invocations for which there is an effect in t.

Let t' be the matching trace of t. From Lemma 3 we know that there exists a trace s in $[\![P[A]]\!]_M$ such that $s = t'$ or s is formed from t' by moving one or more effects earlier. Therefore, from the definition of $[\![P[A]]\!]_M$, there exists an $h' \in [\![A]\!]$ such that:

$$s_{|o} \sim h' \;\wedge\; \prec_{trans(s_{|o})} \subseteq \prec_{h'} \tag{C1}$$

Since there are no overlapping operations on a given thread, the order of invocations and responses on a given thread in $comp(t^+)$ and s are the same.

$$comp(t^+)_{|o} \sim s_{|o} \tag{C2}$$

The relative ordering of invocations and effects in t' is the same as that in t. Hence, $\prec_{trans(comp(t^+)_{|o})} = \prec_{trans(t'_{|o})}$. Any trace formed from t' by moving effects earlier, will have less overlapping operations when $trans$ is applied to it than t' when trans is applied to it. Therefore, we have:

$$\prec_{trans(comp(t^+)_{|o})} \subseteq \prec_{trans(s_{|o})} \tag{C3}$$

Hence, from (C1), (C2) and (C3), we have:

$$comp(t^+)_{|o} \sim h' \;\wedge\; \prec_{trans(comp(t^+)_{|o})} \subseteq \prec_{h'} \qquad\qquad \square$$

6   Chase-Lev Deque

In this section we consider the consequences of using our weakened definition of correctness with respect to a typical concurrent object: a version of the Chase-Lev work-stealing deque (double-ended queue) [5] developed specifically for ARM [17]. The code in Fig. 1 corresponds to a version used in [6] which for simplicity eliminates returns from within a branch, and assumes the elements of the deque are integers. It also uses the fixes suggested in [6] for errors regarding the placement of control fences[4] present in [17].

---

[4] A control fence (`ctrl_isync` in ARM and denoted cfence in Fig. 1) ensures that all branch instructions occurring before it take effect before any *loads*, i.e., reads of global variables, occurring after it.

```
put(v)                 take                          steal
    int t;                 int h,t,task;                 int h,t,task;
    t=tail;                t=tail-1;                     h=head;
    tasks[t mod L]=v;      tail=t;                       fence;
    fence;                 fence;                        t=tail;
    tail=t+1;              h=head;                       if (h < t)
    return;                if (h <= t)                       cfence;
                               task=tasks[t mod L];          task=tasks[h mod L];
                               if (h=t)                      if !CAS(head, h, h+1)
                                   if !CAS(head, h, h + 1) then      task=fail;
                                       task=empty;        else
                                   tail=tail+1;               task=empty;
                           else                          return task;
                               task=empty;
                               tail=tail+1;
                           return task;
```

Fig. 1. A version of Lê et al.'s work-stealing deque algorithm for ARM [17]

The deque is implemented as a circular array of size L with a head and tail pointer. Elements may be *put* on or *taken* from the tail by a worker thread, and additionally, other (thief) threads may *steal* an element from the head of the deque (in order to balance system workload). Since the put and take operations are executed by a single thread, there is no interference between these two operations.

The full details of the implementation can be found in [6,17]. What is interesting for us is that the put operation has as assignment to tail which is unfenced, and hence may be delayed from the point of view of the thief threads.

A possible history of the implementation on ARM is:

$$\langle inv(\mathsf{n.put}, \mathsf{v}), res(\mathsf{n.put}, \perp), inv((\mathsf{m.steal}), \perp), res((\mathsf{m.steal}), \mathsf{empty}) \rangle$$

This occurs when the effect of the put operation is delayed until after the steal operation has occurred. Specifically, tail is not updated until after the steal operation and hence h < t in steal is false.

This behaviour would not be available in a specification of the work-stealing deque. Hence, the implementation is not linearizable. To make it linearizable we would need to add a fence to the put operation, reducing efficiency. The behaviour is, however, weakly linearizable. Therefore, whether the implementation is considered correct depends on which of the two notions of correctness we assume.

There is an obvious trade-off. Abstracting from weak memory effects at the specification level simplifies high-level reasoning: a steal operation following a put may not return empty. If weak memory effects are included at the specification level, any reasoning involves understanding the details of the processor implementation: in this case, understanding that the steal may return empty.

While this is not too much of a burden for this example, it may become so for more complex code.

However, abstracting from weak memory effects at the specification level disallows certain efficient implementations such as that in Fig. 1, as fences are required for many operations.

Ultimately, the choice will reside with the developer of the program; specifically how confident they are with interpreting the behaviour of their program using the concurrent object under the weak memory models they wish it to run on. We envisage a library with a range of implementations for particular concurrent objects: one for the programmer who has limited knowledge of weak memory models, and other, more optimised, implementations aimed at programmers with a deeper understanding of particular weak memory models.

7 Conclusion

In this paper we have introduced a notion of object correctness which allows weak memory model effects at the specification level, and provided a weakening of linearizability which is sound and complete with respect to it. We have compared this correctness notion with a perhaps more standard one which abstracts from weak memory model effects at the specification level. While abstracting from weak memory model effects simplifies high-level reasoning, it also limits what is allowed in implementations regarded as being correct. In particular, it can disallow many implementations which limit the use of fences to obtain efficiency.

As not all programmers will be confident with interpreting the use of concurrent objects in the presence of weak memory models, it seems reasonable to expect libraries to have implementations satisfying both correctness notions for a given object specification.

Acknowledgement. Thanks to Kirsten Winter for fruitful discussions on this topic. This work was supported by Australian Research Council Discovery Grant DP160102457.

References

1. Back, R.-J.R.: Refinement calculus, part II: Parallel and reactive programs. In: de Bakker, J.W., de Roever, W.-P., Rozenberg, G. (eds.) REX 1989. LNCS, vol. 430, pp. 67–93. Springer, Heidelberg (1990). https://doi.org/10.1007/3-540-52559-9_61
2. Back, R.-J.R., von Wright, J.: Trace refinement of action systems. In: Jonsson, B., Parrow, J. (eds.) CONCUR 1994. LNCS, vol. 836, pp. 367–384. Springer, Heidelberg (1994). https://doi.org/10.1007/978-3-540-48654-1_28
3. Batty, M., Owens, S., Sarkar, S., Sewell, P., Weber, T.: Mathematizing C++ concurrency. In: POPL, pp. 55–66. ACM (2011)
4. Burckhardt, S., Gotsman, A., Musuvathi, M., Yang, H.: Concurrent library correctness on the TSO memory model. In: Seidl, H. (ed.) ESOP 2012. LNCS, vol. 7211, pp. 87–107. Springer, Heidelberg (2012). https://doi.org/10.1007/978-3-642-28869-2_5

5. Chase, D., Lev, Y.: Dynamic circular work-stealing deque. In: SPAA 2005, pp. 21–28. ACM Press (2005)
6. Colvin, R.J., Smith, G.: A wide-spectrum language for verification of programs on weak memory models. In: Havelund, K., Peleska, J., Roscoe, B., de Vink, E. (eds.) FM 2018. LNCS, vol. 10951, pp. 240–257. Springer, Cham (2018). https://doi.org/10.1007/978-3-319-95582-7_14
7. Derrick, J., Smith, G.: A framework for correctness criteria on weak memory models. In: Bjørner, N., de Boer, F. (eds.) FM 2015. LNCS, vol. 9109, pp. 178–194. Springer, Cham (2015). https://doi.org/10.1007/978-3-319-19249-9_12
8. Derrick, J., Smith, G., Dongol, B.: Verifying linearizability on TSO architectures. In: Albert, E., Sekerinski, E. (eds.) IFM 2014. LNCS, vol. 8739, pp. 341–356. Springer, Cham (2014). https://doi.org/10.1007/978-3-319-10181-1_21
9. Doherty, S., Derrick, J.: Linearizability and causality. In: De Nicola, R., Kühn, E. (eds.) SEFM 2016. LNCS, vol. 9763, pp. 45–60. Springer, Cham (2016). https://doi.org/10.1007/978-3-319-41591-8_4
10. Dongol, B., Groves, L.: Contextual trace refinement for concurrent objects: safety and progress. In: Ogata, K., Lawford, M., Liu, S. (eds.) ICFEM 2016. LNCS, vol. 10009, pp. 261–278. Springer, Cham (2016). https://doi.org/10.1007/978-3-319-47846-3_17
11. Dongol, B., Jagadeesan, R., Riely, J., Armstrong, A.: On abstraction and compositionality for weak-memory linearisability. VMCAI 2018. LNCS, vol. 10747, pp. 183–204. Springer, Cham (2018). https://doi.org/10.1007/978-3-319-73721-8_9
12. Filipović, I., O'Hearn, P.W., Rinetzky, N., Yang, H.: Abstraction for concurrent objects. Theor. Comput. Sci. 411(51–52), 4379–4398 (2010)
13. Flur, S., et al.: Modelling the ARMv8 architecture, operationally: concurrency and ISA. In: Bodik, R., Majumdar, R. (eds.) POPL 2016, pp. 608–621. ACM (2016)
14. Gotsman, A., Musuvathi, M., Yang, H.: Show no weakness: sequentially consistent specifications of TSO libraries. In: Aguilera, M.K. (ed.) DISC 2012. LNCS, vol. 7611, pp. 31–45. Springer, Heidelberg (2012). https://doi.org/10.1007/978-3-642-33651-5_3
15. Herlihy, M., Shavit, N.: The Art of Multiprocessor Programming. Morgan Kaufmann, San Francisco (2008)
16. Herlihy, M., Wing, J.M.: Linearizability: a correctness condition for concurrent objects. ACM Trans. Program. Lang. Syst. 12(3), 463–492 (1990)
17. Lê, N.M., Pop, A., Cohen, A., Zappa Nardelli, F.: Correct and efficient work-stealing for weak memory models. In: PPoPP 2013, pp. 69–80. ACM (2013)
18. Moir, M., Shavit, N.: Concurrent Data Structures. Handbook of Data Structures and Applications, pp. 47:1–47:30 (2004)
19. Owens, S., Sarkar, S., Sewell, P.: A better x86 memory model: x86-TSO. In: Berghofer, S., Nipkow, T., Urban, C., Wenzel, M. (eds.) TPHOLs 2009. LNCS, vol. 5674, pp. 391–407. Springer, Heidelberg (2009). https://doi.org/10.1007/978-3-642-03359-9_27
20. Pulte, C., Flur, S., Deacon, W., French, J., Sarkar, S., Sewell, P.: Simplifying ARM concurrency: multicopy-atomic axiomatic and operational models for ARMv8. Proc. ACM Program. Lang. 2(POPL), 19:1–19:29 (2018)
21. Raad, A., Doko, M., Rožić, L., Lahav, O., Vafeiadis, V.: On library correctness under weak memory consistency: specifying and verifying concurrent libraries under declarative consistency models. Proc. ACM Program. Lang. 3(POPL), 68:1–68:31 (2019)
22. Sarkar, S., Sewell, P., Alglave, J., Maranget, L., Williams, D.: Understanding POWER multiprocessors. SIGPLAN Not. 46(6), 175–186 (2011)

23. Smith, G., Winter, K., Colvin, R.J.: Correctness of concurrent objects under weak memory models. In: Derrick, J., Dongol, B., Reeves, S. (eds.) Refine 2018, EPTCS, vol. 282, pp. 53–67. Open Publishing Association (2018)
24. Smith, G., Winter, K., Colvin, R.J.: A sound and complete definition of linearizability on weak memory models. CoRR, abs/1802.04954v2 (2019)
25. Travkin, O., Mütze, A., Wehrheim, H.: SPIN as a linearizability checker under weak memory models. In: Bertacco, V., Legay, A. (eds.) HVC 2013. LNCS, vol. 8244, pp. 311–326. Springer, Cham (2013). https://doi.org/10.1007/978-3-319-03077-7_21

Towards a Method for the Decomposition by Refinement in Event-B

Kenza Kraibi[1]([⊠]), Rahma Ben Ayed[1], Joris Rehm[2], Simon Collart-Dutilleul[3,1],
Philippe Bon[3,1], and Dorian Petit[4,1]

[1] Institut de Recherche Technologique Railenium, 59300 Famars, France
{kenza.kraibi,rahma.ben-ayed}@railenium.eu
[2] CLEARSY, Strasbourg, France
joris.rehm@clearsy.com
[3] Univ Lille Nord de France, University Gustave Eiffel, COSYS, ESTAS,
59650 Villeneuve d'Ascq, France
philippe.bon@ifsttar.fr
[4] Université Polytechnique Hauts-de-France, LAMIH UMR CNRS 8201,
59313 Valenciennes, France
dorian.petit@uphf.fr

Abstract. Refinement consists of detailing the specification in order to get a more concrete model. However, this technique leads to large models. Hence, model decomposition is used to reduce model complexity. In this paper, we present the main methods of decomposition and their limitations. Then, we define the decomposition by refinement method that deals with these limitations. Thereafter, we proceed with the rules to follow in order to get a correct decomposed model.

Keywords: Event-B · Refinement · Decomposition · System behavior

1 Introduction

In Event-B [5], there are different techniques to facilitate systems modeling such as refinement and decomposition. Refinement [6] consists of adding more details to the system and concreting the model. Then, at each stage of refinement, one should ensure that the transitions of a machine preserve the invariant as the first main proof activity in B called *consistency checking*. The second main proof activity is *refinement checking*, which is used to show that one machine is a valid refinement of another [16]. In other words, a refinement relationship ensures consistency between two levels of modeling and is carried out in an incremental way up to a certain level. However, after many steps of refinements the model can become complex and difficult to prove. So, decomposition comes to deal with this issue by partitioning the model. Several methods of decomposition exist, among others we find shared variables [3] and shared events [10] decompositions, the most cited and used methods in the literature as presented in Sect. 2. The first one allows to partition the system functionality and the second

© Springer Nature Switzerland AG 2020
E. Sekerinski et al. (Eds.): FM 2019 Workshops, LNCS 12233, pp. 358–370, 2020.
https://doi.org/10.1007/978-3-030-54997-8_23

one decomposes the behavior of the system. Nevertheless, these two methods have some limitations as the loss of invariants containing shared variables, the difficulty of decomposing complex predicates and the need of several intermediate steps of refinement to decompose [4,15]. As a consequence, we propose a new method of decomposition in Sect. 4 called the Decomposition by Refinement method as well as the rules to follow.

2   Event-B Syntactic Definition

In this section, we give the necessary syntactic definitions of an Event-B model which are used in this paper. An Event-B model is composed of two types of components: machine and context. A machine contains the dynamic part of a model whereas a context contains the static part of a model. Figure 1 illustrates a general structure of an Event-B model. A context C_0 defines sets s, constants c and axioms $A(s,c)$. This context can be extended by another context C_1. C_1 defines the sets d, the constants t and the axioms $A(d,t)$. A machine M_0 $SEES$ the context C_0. M_0 defines variables v called *state variables*, invariants $I(s,c,v)$ that describe the system properties to preserve, and abstract events ae. Events ae define guards $G(s,c,v)$ and substitutions $v : |R(s,c,v,v')$ where v' is the new state of v and R is the before/after predicate. M_0 can be refined by another machine M_1 with variables w. w are the variables refining v or/and the new variables. M_1 defines also gluing invariants $J(d,t,v,w)$ that describe the new variables properties and relations between the abstract variables and the refining variables. Events re are refining abstract events ae. re define guards $H(d,t,w)$ and substitutions $w : |Q(d,t,w,w')$.

3   Event-B Refinement and Decomposition Background

Event-B refinement involves modeling the system incrementally from an abstract model on the basis of the system specification. At each stage of refinement, details of the system are gradually added in a concrete model that must preserve the functionality and the properties of the refined model. Two Event-B refinement techniques exist: horizontal refinement and vertical refinement [1,9]. The latter contains the *data refinement* and the *events refinement*. In fact, a large model can be partitioned or decomposed into smaller components after several steps of refinement. This step of partitioning can be a result of a model complexity or simply an architectural decision [19]. Among others, we find the shared event decomposition and the shared variable decomposition which are the most cited and used in the literature.

3.1   Refinement

Horizontal Refinement: consists in adding the specification details in order to define progressively new functionalities of the system in the refinement such

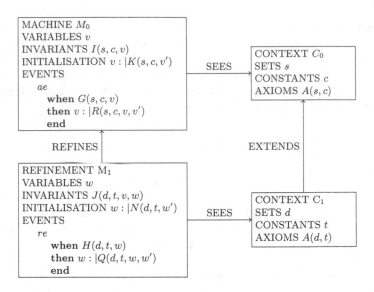

Fig. 1. Event-B model structure

as introducing new variables and new events evolving these new variables. New events refine a particular event of an abstract model which is the empty event with *skip* substitution.

Vertical Refinement: has as a goal the concretization of the abstract model by adding variables through a *data refinement* [8] and of the behavior by detailing abstract events or adding new events by *events refinement*, also called *algorithmic refinement* [1]. These two types of refinement, *data refinement* and *algorithmic refinement*, are not exclusive: they can be operated in the same stage of refinement. It is obvious that any refinement of data leads to an algorithmic refinement. Vertical refinement can be achieved by one or many of the following methods:

- *Data refinement*: consists in defining concrete variables w in the refinement machine in order to replace abstract variables v. Since substitutions are no longer evolving the same abstract variable v space, they must be rewritten (refined) with respect to the new variable w space. In this case, a predicate $J(v, w)$, called a *gluing invariant*, must be specified. This invariant makes it possible to establish the link between the variables v and w. The gluing invariant $J(v, w)$ is specified in the INVARIANT clause of the refining component. Proof obligations are generated at each refinement stage to ensure the refinement correctness. In B method, refinement is based on this technique to bring the model closer to the implementation.
- *Events refinement*: aims to refine one abstract event by one or many events in the refinement machine in order to make the event more concrete. It is the transformation of an abstract substitution evolving v into a less abstract substitution evolving w. A graphical approach of events refinement has been

presented in [10–12]. Its main goal is to represent explicitly the events refinement and the behavior sequencing [13].

3.2 Decomposition

An Event-B machine can have so many events and state variables that an additional refinement can become difficult to manage. Model decomposition tackles this difficulty by providing a mechanism to divide a large model into several sub-models. Models decomposition is another technique that completes refinement. It is based on decomposing models in order to reduce their voluminosity. In the following we present tho most known approaches of decomposition:

Decomposition by Shared Event: Butler proposes in [10] the decomposition by shared events. This method allows the distribution of variables on several sub-machines and events can be split into multiple sub-machines [10].

Decomposition by Shared Variable: In [6], Abrial proposes the decomposition by shared variables. It consists in distributing the events of a machine on the selected sub-machines. It allows the introduction of shared variables and external events.

Other decomposing methods exist such as modularization [14], instantiation [6], fragmentation and distribution [18]... The detailed description and analysis of these approaches have been presented in [15].

3.3 Synthesis

Refinement allows to add more details to the initial specification but the models become huge and complex. So we follow the Principle of divide-to-concur in order to resolve this issue by using the decomposition technique. Another reason behind the decomposition is the management of the different elements and requirements that can be provided by the engineers from different entities (academic and/or industrial). After the analysis of the existing approaches of decomposition we find that shared variables decomposition requires several steps of refinement in order to simplify the model decomposition. In addition, the shared variables should be replicated in the sub-machine and cannot be refined. The invariants involving a shared variable together with other variables is not copied. Concerning the shared events decomposition, the distribution of the variables is not always possible: complex predicates (invariants and guards) or complex actions involving distributed variables over different sub-machines. This requires the separation of these variables by several steps of refinement with mathematical proofs. We present the details and the analysis of these limitations in [15].

As a consequence we propose an approach called the **Decomposition by refinement** that we consider also as a **multiple refinement** method. Contrary to the linear refinement, this approach aims for the decomposition of the model with respect to the refinement principles. Its goal, on the one hand, is to preserve the modeled behavior in the abstraction and, on the other hand, to reduce the model voluminosity [15]. The approach that we propose includes both the refinement and the decomposition. Figure 2 shows the relations between the different types of refinements, the models decomposition and the proposed approach.

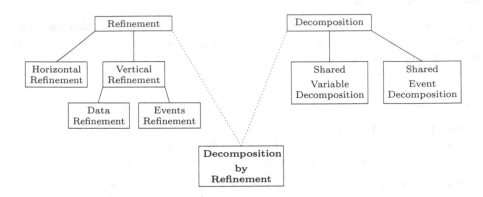

Fig. 2. Different refinement and decomposition techniques

4   Decomposition by Refinement

Our goal is to define a new method of decomposition in order to:

- Decompose at any level of refinement without proceeding with the preparation steps of refinement;
- Keep the formal link *REFINES* between the decomposed machine and the sub-machines;
- Refine shared variables by one or many sub-machines;
- Define a new link between the resulting sub-machines to have a visibility on the private variables of the other sub-machines.

As a consequence, we propose the multiple refinement method called the decomposition by refinement method [15] (cf. Fig. 3). At a certain level $(n-1)$ of refinement, one can proceed with the decomposition by refinement method. This method decomposes a machine M_{n-1} into two or m machines. These machines are refining the decomposed machine M_{n-1}. *REFSEES* is a new clause that we intend to define in order to get a visibility on the private variables of the other sub-machines by transitivity.

As we described in a previous work [15], our decomposition by refinement approach defines a new semantic link between sub-machines: *REFSEES*. This link allows the visibility of variables, invariants, constants, sets and properties of a sub-machine by the other sub-machines. *REFSEES* clause is a combination of *REFINEMENT* and *SEES* which means that one sub-machine can see or rather make reference to another sub-machine, taking into account the refinement link between the decomposing sub-machine and the abstract decomposed machine. This link is different from the *SEES* clause in *classical-B* since it allows a machine to *see* a refinement machine and there is a possibility of circular dependency between sub-machines.

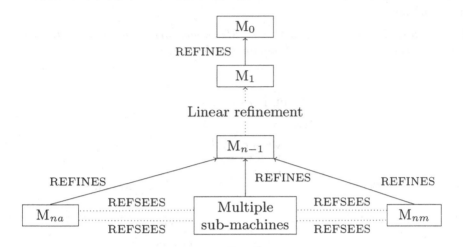

Fig. 3. Structure of the proposed approach

Let us consider the case of two sub-machines, as presented in Fig. 2:

- Machine M, with state variables $v \in S$ and relation transition ae over S such as $ae = \{v \mapsto v' | I(s,c,v) \wedge G(s,c,v) \wedge R(s,c,v,v')\}$;
- Sub-machine M_a, with state variables $w_a \in T_a$ and relation transition re_a over T_a such as $re_a = \{w_a \mapsto w_a' | (\exists v.I(s,c,v) \wedge J_a(d_a,t_a,v,w_a)) \wedge H_a(d_a,t_a,w_a,w_b) \wedge Q_a(d_a,t_a,w_a,w_b,w_a')\}$;
- Sub-machine M_b, with state variables $w_b \in T_b$ and relation transition re_b over T_b such as $re_b = \{w_b \mapsto w_b' | (\exists v.I(s,c,v) \wedge J_b(d_b,t_b,v,w_b)) \wedge H_b(d_b,t_b,w_a,w_b) \wedge Q_b(d_b,t_b,w_a,w_b,w_b')\}$.

Note that the sub-machines M_a and M_b can see different contexts C_{1a} and C_{1b}, for example, where C_{1a} (resp. C_{1b}) defines sets d_a, constants t_a and axioms $A(d_a,t_a)$ (resp. sets d_b, constants t_b and axioms $A(d_b,t_b)$).

In order to formalize this approach, we define some rules **Ri** to follow. These rules allow a correct decomposition by refinement:

R1: *the state variables v of the decomposed machine M should all be present at least in M_a or M_b. Some state variables can only be in one of the sub-machines.* We believe this still constitutes a refinement of M by M_a (and respectively M_b). In the semantics of Event-B [3], there is a notion of external-set which allows to ignore some "internal" variables in the refinement. We believe we can use this concept to justify this new usage of the refinement.

R2: *the main difference with normal refinement, is the fact that the sub-machine M_a (resp. M_b) can refer (in their events guards) to variables that can be only present in M_b (resp. M_a).*

This might be possible because we did already prove the M is correct. But we must prove that this refinement is correct regarding the theoretical definition of the B method [2].

R3: *the resulting sub-machines M_a and M_b should correspond to a one transition system that corresponds to the behavior of M_0 (Fig. 4).*

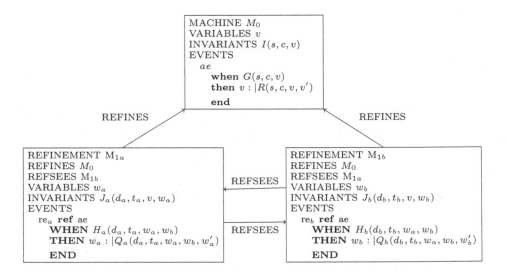

Fig. 4. Decomposition by refinement approach

R4: *M_a and M_b transitions are interlaced and then they are not synchronized contrary to the decomposition by shared events.*

This is done by the definition of the (theoretical) re-composition of the sub-machines. Consequently, we can demonstrate that this way of re-composition is a refinement of the machine M, following what has been presented in [4].

R5: *in addition to the partial correctness, which consists on proving that the system is safe i.e. preserving the safety invariants, we should ensure the complete correctness. This later consists on ensuring the vivacity properties such as those of the variant and the deadlock freedom. A transition should not be triggered indefinitely. So, a variant proof obligation rule should be defined. Concerning the deadlock freedom, it allows to prove that the system is conform to the specification need. There are two types of deadlock freedom rules: the weak one and the stronger one. The first one means that at least one of the events is triggered. Whereas the stronger rule requires that each event is at least triggered one time.*

In case of adding new events in the sub-machines, the deadlock freedom rules and the variant rules should also be defined.

5   Correctness of the Proposed Approach

A linear refinement is the classical refinement in Event-B when one machine can refine another higher-level machine. In the following, for reasons of simplification, sets and constants of the contexts are not taken into consideration since they are static. Let consider, as shown in Fig. 5, a set S of state variables v of the abstract machine M_0. v preserve the invariant $I(v)$ such as:

$$S = \{v | I(v)\}$$

Let T be a set of state variables w of the refinement machine M_1. w preserve the gluing invariant $J(v, w)$. T is defined as:

$$T = \{w | \exists v.(I(v) \wedge J(v, w))\}$$

The state changes of the abstract variables v are done by the transition ae such as v is preserving the invariant $I(v)$. v' is the variable describing the new state of v after the transition ae:

$$ae = \{v \mapsto v' | I(v) \wedge G(v) \wedge R(v, v')\}$$

Similarly for the refining machine M_1, the transition re describes the state changes of the refining variable w such as preserving the gluing invariant $J(v, w)$ and satisfying the guard $H_i(w)$:

$$re = \{w \mapsto w' | (\exists v.I(v) \wedge J(v, w)) \wedge H(w) \wedge Q(w, w')\}$$

r defines the refinement relation between abstract state variables v and the refining state variables w:

$$r = \{w \mapsto v | I(v) \wedge J(v, w)\}$$

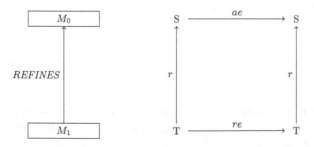

Fig. 5. Relations between the abstract machine and its refinement

In [5], some sets and functions are defined, as shown in Fig. 6. On the basis of observable variables definition, the set S is considered as able to be projected on an external set E. This latter defines what can be observed in a model. Similarly, the refined state variables w are together moving within a certain set T, which is considered also able to be projected on an external set F. So f and g denote the functions projecting the sets S and T on the sets E and F respectively. In order to link E and F sets, a total function h is defined.

The Abrial's demonstration is based on f, h and g functions using the expression (1) and the definition of the relation r in (2).

$$\forall x.y.(y \mapsto x : r \Rightarrow f(x) = h(g(y))) \tag{1}$$

$$r : T \leftrightarrow S \tag{2}$$

Predicates (1) and (2) lead to the conclusion:

$$r^{-1}; re \subseteq ae; r^{-1}$$

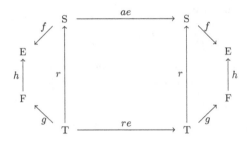

Fig. 6. Relations between state variables and observable variables [5]

In order to justify the correctness of the refinement in our approach, let consider the expression defined in [5] where observable variables are used for the demonstration. The proof obligation rules of the linear refinement imply the semantics definition of refinement:

- $r_a^{-1}; re_a \subseteq ae; r_a^{-1}$ where $r_a = \{w_a \mapsto v | I(v) \wedge J_a(v, w_a)\}$, I the invariant of M, J_a the invariant of M_a;
- $r_b^{-1}; re_b \subseteq ae; r_b^{-1}$ where $r_b = \{w_b \mapsto v | I(v) \wedge J_b(v, w_b)\}$, I the invariant of M, J_b the invariant of M_b.

In [3,4], after proceeding with the decomposition, the re-composition should be proved without explicitly composing. Our goal is to follow this concept and to define a relation between $r_a^{-1}; re_a \subseteq ae; r_a^{-1}$ and $r_b^{-1}; re_b \subseteq ae; r_b^{-1}$ in order to prove the correctness of the proposed approach.

We note that shared event decomposition considers only the syntactic decomposition of the abstract machine by sharing the same event in the independent sub-machines so as to model mainly the architecture communication between different components, based on transitions synchronization [17]. However, the

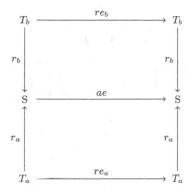

Fig. 7. Relations between the abstract machine and its refining sub-machines

shared variable decomposition considers the syntactic/semantic coherence of the decomposition later when it verifies the correctness of the sub-machines composition vs. the initial abstract machine which requires additional rules on the observable variables [7]. This decomposition shares a same variable by independent sub-machines so as to model mainly complexity division inside the same component, based on states synchronization [17]. For example, as shown in the left of Fig. 8, a machine M can be decomposed into sub-machines N and P. The machine N (resp. P) can be refined by several steps till the refinement NR (resp. PR). Then, the semantic re-composition MR of the resulting refinements NR and PR should be a refinement of M.

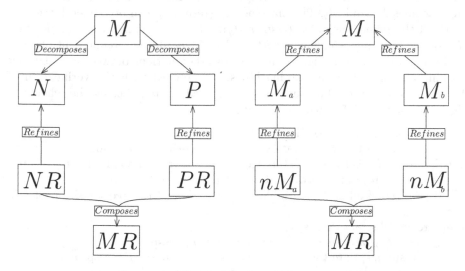

Fig. 8. Difference between the decomposition by shared variable and the decomposition by refinement

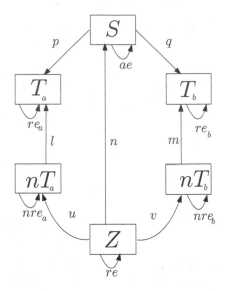

Fig. 9. Demonstration of the decomposition by refinement

In our approach, by refining the abstract machine when decomposing, the resulting sub-machines keep the syntactic/semantic coherence as described in the previous section on the basis of the states synchronization so as to ensure the preservation of the invariants implicitly from the beginning and to make the possibility to share events and variables according to the industrial context needs. For instance, in the right of Fig. 8) a machine M can be *refined* by two sub-machines M_a and M_b. The machine M_a (resp. M_b) can be refined by several steps till the refinement nM_a (resp. nM_b). Then, the semantic re-composition MR of the resulting refinements nM_a and nM_b should be a refinement of M.

Then, on the basis of Fig. 7 that describes the relations between the abstract machine and the resulting sub-machines, we proceed with the verification of the correctness of the refinement in the proposed approach using the schema in Fig. 9. We define the following sets and functions:

- S is the set of state variables v in the abstract machine M;
- T_a (resp. T_b) is the set of state variables w_a (resp. w_b) refining v;
- nT_a (resp. nT_b) is the set of state variables nw_a (resp. nw_b) refining $(n-1)w_a$ (resp. $(n-1)w_b$) at a certain level n of refinement;
- Z is the set of all states variables resulting from the re-composition of nT_a and nT_b;
- ae are the abstract events;
- re_a (resp. re_b) are the events refining ae in T_a (resp. T_b);
- nre_a (resp. nre_b) are the refining events of machines nT_a (resp. nT_b);
- re are the resulting events from the re-composition of nre_a and nre_b;

Then we define the relation between each of the machines. For example, p (resp. q) is the refinement relation between M and M_a (resp. M_b). l (resp. m) is the refinement relation between M_a and nM_a (resp. nM_b). u and v are the relation between the resulting re-composition and the re-composed sub-machines. Then, we define n the relation between the initial decomposed machine and the re-composition of the resulting refinements. The demonstration and the resulting proof obligation rules will be detailed in a future work.

6   Conclusion

In the literature, refinement and decomposition are defined in such a way that they can coexist in the formal modeling process in order to manage the system complexity through multiple levels of abstraction. None of the existing approaches of decomposition rely on the refinement correctness to define the decomposition and preserve the syntactic/semantic coherence from the beginning to the lower-level of modeling. Therefore, we propose an Event-B decomposition approach based on the multiple refinement. In the context of the *PRESCOM* project, we are working on a specific industrial context: railway systems modeling. This application domain of safety-critical systems recognizes the relevance of the decomposition in the railway systems modeling. It identifies some needs to separate the key features of the abstract specification system in a number of lower-level sub-machines. This separation is realized according to the intended purpose of the system modeling to get more readable and manageable specifications. In a future work, we will define the followed steps for the correctness of the approach and the resulting proof obligations rules and then we will apply the decomposition by refinement approach in a railway case study.

References

1. Abrial, J.-R., Lee, M.K.O., Neilson, D.S., Scharbach, P.N., Sørensen, I.H.: The B-method. In: Prehn, S., Toetenel, H. (eds.) VDM 1991. LNCS, vol. 552, pp. 398–405. Springer, Heidelberg (1991). https://doi.org/10.1007/BFb0020001
2. Abrial, J.R.: The B-Book: Assigning Programs to Meanings. Cambridge University Press, New York (1996)
3. Abrial, J.R.: Discrete system models. Internal notes (www-lsr.imag.fr/B) (2002)
4. Abrial, J.R.: Event model decomposition. Technical report, ETH, Department of Computer Science 626 (2009)
5. Abrial, J.R.: Modeling in Event-B: System and Software Engineering. Cambridge University Press, Cambridge (2010)
6. Abrial, J.R., Hallerstede, S.: Refinement, decomposition, and instantiation of discrete models: application to Event-B. Fundamenta Informaticae **77**(1–2), 1–28 (2007)
7. Abrial, J.R., Metayer, C., Voisin, L.: Rodin deliverable 3.2. Event-B language. Technical report, School of Computing Science, Newcastle University (2005)
8. Back, R.J.R.: Refinement calculus, part II: parallel and reactive programs. In: de Bakker, J.W., de Roever, W.-P., Rozenberg, G. (eds.) REX 1989. LNCS, vol. 430, pp. 67–93. Springer, Heidelberg (1990). https://doi.org/10.1007/3-540-52559-9_61

9. Bolusset, T., Oquendo, F.: Formal refinement of software architectures based on rewriting logic. In: ZB2002 International Workshop on Refinement of Critical Systems: Methods, Tools and Experience, Grenoble, vol. 29, pp. 1–20 (2002)

10. Butler, M.: Decomposition structures for Event-B. In: Leuschel, M., Wehrheim, H. (eds.) IFM 2009. LNCS, vol. 5423, pp. 20–38. Springer, Heidelberg (2009). https://doi.org/10.1007/978-3-642-00255-7_2

11. Dghaym, D., Butler, M., Fathabadi, A.S.: Extending ERS for modelling dynamic workflows in Event-B. In: 2017 22nd International Conference on Engineering of Complex Computer Systems (ICECCS), pp. 20–29. IEEE (2017)

12. Dghaym, D., Trindade, M.G., Butler, M., Fathabadi, A.S.: A graphical tool for event refinement structures in Event-B. In: Butler, M., Schewe, K.-D., Mashkoor, A., Biro, M. (eds.) ABZ 2016. LNCS, vol. 9675, pp. 269–274. Springer, Cham (2016). https://doi.org/10.1007/978-3-319-33600-8_20

13. Fathabadi, A.S., Rezazadeh, A., Butler, M.: Applying atomicity and model decomposition to a space craft system in Event-B. In: Bobaru, M., Havelund, K., Holzmann, G.J., Joshi, R. (eds.) NFM 2011. LNCS, vol. 6617, pp. 328–342. Springer, Heidelberg (2011). https://doi.org/10.1007/978-3-642-20398-5_24

14. Hoang, T.S., Iliasov, A., Silva, R.A., Wei, W.: A survey on Event-B decomposition. Electron. Commun. EASST **46** (2011)

15. Kraibi., K., Ben Ayed., R., Rehm., J., Collart-Dutilleul., S., Bon., P., Petit., D.: Event-B decomposition analysis for systems behavior modeling. In: Proceedings of the 14th International Conference on Software Technologies-Volume 1: ICSOFT, pp. 278–286. INSTICC, SciTePress (2019).https://doi.org/10.5220/0007929602780286

16. Leuschel, M., Butler, M.: ProB: a model checker for B. In: Araki, K., Gnesi, S., Mandrioli, D. (eds.) FME 2003. LNCS, vol. 2805, pp. 855–874. Springer, Heidelberg (2003). https://doi.org/10.1007/978-3-540-45236-2_46

17. Romanovsky, A., Thomas, M.: Industrial Deployment of System Engineering Methods. Springer, Heidelberg (2013). https://doi.org/10.1007/978-3-642-33170-1

18. Siala, B., Tahar Bhiri, M., Bodeveix, J.P., Filali, M.: Un processus de Développement Event-B pour des Applications Distribuées. Université de Franche-Comté (2016)

19. Silva, R., Butler, M.: Shared event composition/decomposition in Event-B. In: Aichernig, B.K., de Boer, F.S., Bonsangue, M.M. (eds.) FMCO 2010. LNCS, vol. 6957, pp. 122–141. Springer, Heidelberg (2011). https://doi.org/10.1007/978-3-642-25271-6_7

Transformations for Generating Type Refinements

Douglas R. Smith[✉] and Stephen J. Westfold

Kestrel Institute, 3260, Hillview Avenue, Palo Alto, CA 94304, USA
{smith,westfold}@kestrel.edu

Abstract. We present transformations for incrementally defining both inductive sum/variant types and coinductive product/record types in a formal refinement setting. Inductive types are built by incrementally accumulating constructors. Coinductive types are built by incrementally accumulating observers. In each case, when the developer decides that the constructor (resp. observer) set is complete, a transformation is applied that generates a canonical definition for the type. It also generates definitions for functions that have been characterized in terms of patterns over the constructors (resp. copatterns over the observers). Functions that input a possibly-recursive sum/variant type are defined inductively via patterns on the input data. Dually, functions that output a possibly-recursive record type are defined coinductively via copatterns on the function's output. The transformations have been implemented in the Specware system [4] and have been used extensively in the automated synthesis of concurrent garbage collection algorithms [9,12] and families of protocol-processing codes for distributed vehicle control [5].

1 Introduction

We address the problem of incrementally defining types and their operators. Rather than work in the context of a programming language, where expressions are intended to have a single precise meaning, we work in a specification and refinement setting, where a specification denotes a set of possible models or implementations that satisfy a set of constraints. Incremental development by refinement can allow a more natural staged introduction of design commitments in a formal derivation. For example, program families are naturally expressed as a refinement tree where each branch defines a distinct subfamily of programs. A natural way to express such family trees is via the incremental accumulation of constraints on the types, functions, procedures, components, and other system structure. A type may have alternative elaborations in the various branches of the family tree. A similar pattern is seen in product lines of systems and the class hierarchies of object-oriented languages.

This work has been sponsored in part by DARPA under agreements FA8750-10-C-0241 and FA8750-12-C-0257.

E. Sekerinski et al. (Eds.): FM 2019 Workshops, LNCS 12233, pp. 371–387, 2020.
https://doi.org/10.1007/978-3-030-54997-8_24

The development of correct-by-construction code via a formal refinement process has the abstract derivation form $S_0 \longrightarrow S_1 \longrightarrow \ldots \longrightarrow S_n \rightsquigarrow Code$. A derivation process starts with a specification S_0 of the requirements on a desired software artifact. Each S_i, $i = 0, 1, \ldots, n$ represents a structured specification and the arrows $\rightarrow$ are refinements. The refinement from S_i to S_{i+1} embodies a design decision which narrows down the number of possible implementations. In our approach, most refinement steps are generated (semi)automatically by specification transformations. The final step translates the lowest-level specification S_n to code in a suitable programming language. Semantically the effect is to narrow down the set of possible implementations of S_0 to just one, so specification refinement can be viewed as a constructive process for proving the existence of an implementation of specification S_0; i.e. proving its consistency.

We are interested in specification transformations that generate refinements together with machine-checkable proofs [11]. If a formal derivation is generated by a sequence of such refinement+proof-generating transformations, then we can chain the resulting proofs together to get a proof that the final generated specification is a correct refinement of the initial requirement-level specification. Here, we introduce transformations for incrementally defining both (1) inductive sum/variant-types and functions inductively defined on them, and (2) coinductive product/record-types and functions that are coinductively defined to produce them.

Inductive types are characterized by their constructors. In a refinement setting, we can introduce a type symbol, say T, for an intended inductive type in a specification, with some of its constructors, and without a definition. A function f that takes a T input can be characterized by axioms that specify how f acts on the existing constructors. A *pattern-based* or *constructor-based* characterization of function $f : T \rightarrow A$ with respect to constructor c is an axiom that essentially has the form $f \circ c = e$ for some well-defined expression e (e.g. see Fig. 1). In subsequent refinements, we add other constructors, and add pattern-based axioms for f. At each stage in the derivation (i.e. at an intermediate specification), the models of T include a set for T defined by just the current set of constructors, as well as models that allow other constructors, and even models that are not inductive. At some point in the derivation, the developer decides that the constructor set is complete by applying a transformation, called COM-PLETESUMTYPE, that gives a canonical definition of T as a sum/named-variant type with just the current set of constructors. It also generates inductive definitions for functions that have been characterized by pattern-based axioms.

Dually, *coinductive types* are characterized by their observers – all that can be known about an element of the type is given by various observations of it. In a refinement setting, we can introduce a type symbol T for an intended coinductive type (cotype) in a specification, along with some of its observers. A function f that produces a T value can be characterized by axioms that specify observations of its output. A *copattern-based* or *observer-based* characterization of function $f : A \rightarrow T$ with respect to observer p is an axiom that essentially has the form $p \circ f = e$ for some well-defined expression e (e.g. see Fig. 6).

In subsequent refinements, we add other observers, and add appropriate copattern-based axioms that specify the output of f. At each stage in the derivation, the models of T include a set for T with just the current set of observers, as well as models that allow other observers, and even models that are not coinductive. At some point in the derivation, we declare that the observer set is complete by applying a transformation, called COMPLETEPRODUCTTYPE, that gives a canonical definition of T as a product/record type with just the current set of observers as projections/fields. It also generates coinductive definitions for functions that have been characterized by copattern-based axioms.

A variety of examples illustrate these transformations. Although our techniques are applied in a purely logical/functional setting, we show how to use the transformations to develop mutable global states and heap-allocated mutable types for targeting imperative and object-oriented programming languages.

2   Basic Concepts

We present basic concepts of the formal specification-and-refinement approach used in our Specware system [4,13]. A *specification* defines a language and constrains its possible meanings via axioms. A specification is given by a finite collection of type symbols (optionally including a definition), function symbols and their signature (optionally including a definition), and axioms over the type and function symbols. We treat predicates as Boolean-valued functions. For purposes of this paper, we focus on first-order specifications (i.e. functions do not take functions as arguments), although Specware allows higher-order specifications. The deductive closure of the axioms is a theory, so a specification is a finite presentation of a theory. Let *Spec* denote the type of specifications.

A refinement can be expressed formally via a *specification morphism* which translates the language of one specification into the language of another specification in a way that preserves theorems. Formally, a *signature morphism* from specification $S0$ to specification $S1$ is a type-consistent map from the vocabulary of $S0$ (i.e. its type and function symbols) to the vocabulary of $S1$. A *specification morphism* from $S0$ to $S1$ is a signature morphism that preserves theorems; i.e. that translates each theorem of $S0$ to a theorem of $S1$. To establish a specification morphism, it is sufficient to prove that each axiom of $S0$ translates to a theorem of $S1$. Let *Morphism* denote the type of specification morphisms (or simply morphisms).

Specification $S1$ is an *extension* of specification $S0$ if there is an specification morphism $S0 \rightarrow S1$ whose underlying signature morphism is injective. We use importation (with possible renaming) to express extension, allowing the construction of complex specifications. More generally, specifications and their morphisms constitute a category that has colimits, which provide a general means for constructing complex specifications. A *pushout* is a special case of a colimit that we will use frequently. The pushout of two morphisms with a common domain specification $B \xleftarrow{\ i\ } A \xrightarrow{\ j\ } C$ is another pair of morphisms with a common codomain, $B \xrightarrow{j'} D \xleftarrow{i'} C$, called a *cocone*, where D is the pushout specification. Intuitively, D is the simplest specification that combines B and C modulo the common structure of A [13].

As models of specification S, we admit any structure of sets and functions that interprets at least each type and function symbol in S and that satisfies the function signatures and the axioms. This loose semantics allows structures for extensions of S to be models of S. The denotation of a specification morphism m is a map from models of the codomain of m into models of the domain – every model of $S1$ is mapped to some model of $S0$.

Specification $S0$ *refines to* $S1$ if there is a specification morphism m : $S0 \to S1$. We refer to m as a refinement and a morphism, and in context, $S1$ as a refinement of $S0$. In this paper we are interested in transformations that (semi)automatically generate refinements. A *specification transformation* is a partial function on specifications that generates a refinement: $t : Spec \to Morphism$. That is, if $t(S) = m$, then $m : S \to codomain(m)$ is a refinement of S.

An extension $e : S0 \to S1$ is *conservative* if every theorem of $S1$ that is expressed over the language of $S0$, is also a theorem of $S0$. A specification morphism is *consistent* if it preserves consistency – whenever the source specification is consistent (has a nonempty set of models), then the target specification is also consistent.

The following "modularization" theorem provides general conditions for the generation of consistent refinements [10, 15].

Theorem 1. *Let P, P', and S be first-order specifications, where $c : P \to S$ is a conservative extension and $r : P \to P'$ is a consistent refinement. If S' is the pushout with cocone morphisms $c' : P' \to S'$ and $r' : S \to S'$, then c' is a conservative extension and r' is a consistent refinement.*

Theorem 1 is typically applied when the goal is to refine a given specification S. A generic specification transformation based on the theorem performs the following steps (we present several instances below):

SpecTransformation(S:Spec):Morphism
    1. analyze S
    2. generate the refinement morphism $r : P \to P'$
    3. generate a classification morphism $c : P \to S$ which shows how r applies to S
    4. compute the pushout of $P' \xleftarrow{c} P \xrightarrow{r} S$ yielding cocone $P' \xrightarrow{c'} S' \xleftarrow{r'} S$
    5. return r'.

The generated morphism $r' : S \to S'$ is the desired consistent refinement of S. The refinement r represents the core design decision and each transformation embodies its own class of design knowledge. The pushout extends its application to the whole specification. Theorem 1 provides the most general conditions known to us under which the generated refinement r' is consistent. A proof that r' is a consistent morphism from S and that it embodies an instance of the design knowledge codified by the transformation can be generated automatically at refinement-generation time [11].

3 Incrementally Constructing Sum/Variant/Inductive Types

A constructor for a type T is a function of type $c : A[T] \to T$ where $A[T]$ is a (possibly empty) product of auxiliary types and zero or more positive occurrences of T. A *base constructor* has a signature $c : A \to T$ with no occurrence of T in its domain. A constructor set is *well-founded* if it contains at least one base constructor. An inductive type is defined by a well-founded set of constructors (aka injections).

For example, the specification to the left in Fig. 1 contains a well-founded set of constructors for the type of leaf-labeled binary trees, where Empty constructs the empty BinTree, Leaf constructs leaves labeled with natural numbers, and Fork builds a BinTree from a pair of (unlabeled) subtrees. There are many possible models of spec BinTree (including some with even more constructors), but if we refine BinTree to BinTree1 where type BinTree is now defined as recursive variant type (i.e. named sum-type), then there is only one model (up to isomorphism); i.e. the type BinTree has been refined. Spec BinTree1 also defines a function on BinTrees by means of pattern-based axioms that specify how BinTreeDepth behaves on each constructor. Overall, Fig. 1 exemplifies the kind of refinement that we generate. This definition can be proved complete, consistent, and terminating using the induction rule for BinTree. The construction gives rise to an induction rule which reflects that, by construction, every element of the type is the valuation of a unique term built out of constructors, and conversely, that each term built out of constructors evaluates to a unique element of the type. Under various conditions it is possible to allow axioms that,

```
Bintree = spec
  type BinTree
  op Empty: BinTree
  op Leaf: Nat -> BinTree
  op Fork: BinTree*BinTree -> BinTree
  op BinTreeDepth: BinTree -> Nat
  ax BinTreeDepth Empty = 0
  ax BinTreeDepth Leaf n = 1
  ax BinTreeDepth Fork(bt1,bt2)
      = max(BinTreeDepth(bt1),
            BinTreeDepth(bt2))
end-spec
```

$$\xrightarrow{\ n\ }$$

```
Bintree1 = spec
  type BinTree = | Empty | Leaf Nat
                 | Fork BinTree*BinTree
  op BinTreeDepth(bt:BinTree):Nat =
    case bt of
    | Empty  ->  0
    | Leaf n ->  1
    | Fork(bt1,bt2) -> max(BinTreeDepth(bt1),
                           BinTreeDepth(bt2))
end-spec
```

Fig. 1. Refinement to inductive Bintree specification

for example, identify two distinct terms over the constructors (e.g. to admit a commutative constructor). Our examples will not require this capability.

3.1 Incremental Accumulation of Constructors

```
Tspec = spec
  type T
  op c0:T
  op c1:Nat*T-> T
  op f:T->B
  ax f(c0) = b0
  ax f(c1(n,a1)) = b1
end-spec

Tspec1 = spec
  import Tspec
  op c2:T*T->T
  ax f(c2(a1,a2)) = b2
end-spec
```

The idea of incrementally defining an inductive type is simple. During a derivation, we introduce a new undefined type symbol and incrementally add constructors. We also introduce function symbols and incrementally add pattern-based axioms that specify how the function behaves on each constructor. In the end, the developer declares the constructor set complete and applies a transformation that defines the type as a sum/variant type and provides inductive definitions for the function symbols.

As an abstract example, Tspec introduces T as an undefined type that has two constructors c0 and c1. Tspec also introduces f as an undefined function that is constrained by its type and by axioms that characterize its functionality by specifying how it behaves on the two constructors. Tspec1 refines Tspec by (1) extending it with a new constructor c2, and (2) extending the characterization of f by showing how it behaves on the new constructor. Tspec1 can be further extended in a similar manner.

3.2 COMPLETESUMTYPE Transformation

At some point in a derivation, the developers decide that no more constructors are needed. The COMPLETESUMTYPE transformation is then applied to generate a refinement in which T and its functions are given definitions. This is a strong refinement in the sense that it narrows down the possible interpretations of T and its functions from a possibly infinite set to a singleton – they are given canonical definitions (up to isomorphism) as sum types.

We present the COMPLETESUMTYPE transformation as an instance of the SpecTransformation transformation pattern in Sect. 2. We factor the transformation into two steps. The first, exemplified in Fig. 2, analyzes an arbitrary given specification S to abstract out a subspecification Scons that contains just the constructors over a given undefined type T. If the constructor set is well-founded, then it generates a refinement/morphism r:Scons → Scons', where Scons' introduces a sum-type definition for T in place of the constructor signatures. It then generates a refinement of S by taking the pushout of r and the conservative extension c:Scons → S. It is straightforward to show that r is a consistent refinement, since it picks out the one model of T that is the least fixpoint of the well-founded constructor set. By Theorem 1, if c is conservative and S' is the pushout of r and c, then the generated refinement r':S→ S' is consistent.

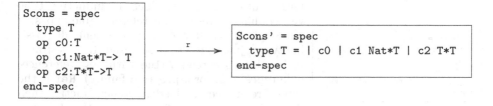

```
Scons = spec
  type T
  op c0:T
  op c1:Nat*T-> T
  op c2:T*T->T
end-spec
```
```
Scons' = spec
  type T = | c0 | c1 Nat*T | c2 T*T
end-spec
```

Fig. 2. Abstract refinement morphism

The second step analyzes S' to abstract out a subspecification Sfuns that contains just the function symbols that have pattern-based axioms over the constructors in Scons. It then generates a refinement n:Sfuns → Sfuns' where Sfuns' introduces case-based definitions for each function in place of the inductive axioms, as exemplified in Fig. 3. It then generates a refinement of S' by taking the pushout of r and the conservative extension c:Sfuns → S'. It is straightforward to show that r is a consistent refinement, using the induction rule that goes with the definition of a recursive sum-type. By Theorem 1, if c is conservative and S'' is the pushout of r and c, then the generated refinement r':S→ S'' is consistent. Note that specification S may have constraints on f beyond the pattern-based axioms, but the conservativeness of c requires that they imply no additional theorems.

```
Sfuns = spec
  type T = | c0 | c1 Nat*T | c2 T*T
  op f:T->B
  ax f(c0)        = b0
  ax f(c1(n,a1))  = b1
  ax f(c2(a1,a2)) = b2
end-spec
```
```
Sfuns' = spec
  type T = | c0 | c1 Nat*T | c2 T*T
  op f(a:T):B =
    case a of
      | c0          -> b0
      | c1(n,a1)   -> b1
      | c2(a1,a2)  -> b2
end-spec
```

Fig. 3. Generated refinement morphism

3.3   Example: Specifying Reference Types

The need to specify and design programs that use references in Specware was a motivation for developing COMPLETESUMTYPE. A key challenge is knowing the type of a reference. A polymorphic definition of a reference type does not allow retrieval of the underlying type. One solution is to maintain a ghost record of the current types at all memory locations, where the allowed types are those supported by the underlying architecture [6,14], sometimes implemented by fat pointers. However, in a refinement setting, it is necessary to reference user-introduced types that may not yet have a definition, so a more general mechanism is needed.

Our solution is to introduce an inductive type `Value` that represents all referenceable types in our application. It need not represent all possible types, just those that are used. It is desirable to be able to extend `Value` with new referenceable types (e.g. for a program family). `Ref` is the type of references, and a dereference function then determines in a given `State`, what the `Value` is of a given `Ref`.

```
RefTypes = spec
  type State
  type Value
  type Ref
  op deref: State -> Ref -> Value
end-spec
```

During the refinement process, for each referenceable type `T` that is introduced, we introduce a new constructor for `T`. We also introduce testors (to decide if a `Value` represents a `T` element) and coercion/destructor functions (to invert a constructor).

```
Nat32Ref = spec
  import RefTypes
  type Nat32
  op c_Nat32: Nat32 -> Value
  op Nat32?(val:Value):Bool =
    (ex(n:Nat32) val = c_Nat32 n)
  op coerce_Nat32(val:Value | Nat32? val):
            {n:Nat32 | val=c_Nat32 n}
end-spec

PacketRef = spec
  import RefTypes, Nat32Ref
  type Packet
  op c_Packet: Packet -> Value
  op pkt?(val:Value):Bool =
    (ex(pkt:Packet) val = c_Packet pkt)
  op coerce_Packet(val:Value | pkt? val):
            {pkt:Packet | val=c_Packet pkt}
  op data: Packet -> Nat32
  op get_data(st:State, pktRef:Ref
            | pkt?(deref st pktRef)):Int32 =
    data(coerce_Packet(deref st pktRef))
end-spec
```

For example, specification `PacketRef`, introduces constructors for `Nat32` (eventually refining to unsigned 32-bit integers) and `Packet` (a user-defined type for use in communication software). The predicate `Nat32?` tests whether a `Value` represents a `Nat32`, using an existential quantification. The function `coerce_Nat32` coerces a `Value` back to a `Nat32` assuming that it represents a `Nat32`. Its input and output types are expressed as dependent types. `coerce_Nat32` would be implemented as a type cast in many programming languages. Analogous functions are introduced for the user-defined `Packet` type.

As a simple example, the function `get_data` takes in a reference to a `Packet` and returns the data value of the packet. In Sect. 4.3, we extend this development by allowing referenceable types that are also mutable.

3.4   Subtyping

One might want a family tree of sum-types and an appropriate notion of sum-type subtyping. The example in Fig. 4 introduces `T` as an intended inductive type, and then introduces `T1` as an intended supertype `T1:>T`, and `T2` as another intended supertype `T2:>T`. We can then import `S1` and `S2` and transform as shown in Fig. 5. In specification `S3'`, the function `f1` may be passed a `T` or `T1` element, and `f2` may be passed a `T` or `T2` element.

```
S = spec                          S1 = spec                    S2 = spec
  type T  % intended sum-type       import S                     import S
  op c1: D1 -> T                    type T1 :> T                 type T2 :> T
  op c2: D2 -> T                    op c3: D3 -> T1              op c4: D4 -> T2
  op f(a:T):A =                     op f1(a:T1):A1 =             op f2(a:T2):A2 =
  ... pattern-based axioms          ... pattern-based axioms     ... pattern-based axioms
  over c1 and c2 ...                over c1, c2, and c3 ...      over c1, c2, and c4 ...
end-spec                          end-spec                     end-spec
```

Fig. 4. Sum subtype development

```
                                               S3' = spec
                                                 type T  = |c1:D1 | c2:D2
S3 = spec        COMPLETESUMTYPE(S3,T)           type T1 = |c1:D1 | c2:D2 | c3:D3 :> T
  import S1,S2   ──────────────────────▶         type T2 = |c1:D1 | c2:D2 | c4:D4 :> T
  ...            COMPLETESUMTYPE(S3,T1)           op f(a:T)   :A  = ... inductive def on T  ...
end-spec         COMPLETESUMTYPE(S3,T2)           op f1(a:T1):A1 = ... inductive def on T1 ...
                                                  op f2(a:T2):A2 = ... inductive def on T2 ...
                                                  ...
                                               end-spec
```

Fig. 5. Sum refinement

4   Incrementally Constructing Product/Record Types

Suppose that our requirement modeling or design direction requires a type T but a priori we don't know its content. It may be natural to introduce constraints on T as needed during the derivation process in the form of additional observations of T. An *observer* of type T is a function $p : T \to A[T]$ where $A[T]$ is a (possibly empty) product of auxiliary types and zero or more positive occurrences of T. An observer extracts information of type $A[T]$ from a T object.

For example, in a vehicle context, we might introduce a State type together with observations about the current time, and position of the vehicle, and a drive function that changes state; see specification Vehicle in Fig. 6. Later we might add an observation of the vehicle's velocity; see specification Vehicle1 in Fig. 6. There are many possible models of State, but if we refine Vehicle1 to Vehicle2 where State is now defined as record type (i.e. named product), then there is only one model (up to isomorphism). The refinement in Fig. 6 also defines a function that changes State by means of copattern-based axioms that specify drive in terms of observations of its output. This definition can be proved complete, consistent, and terminating using the coinduction rule that can be generated for State. Overall, Fig. 6 exemplifies the kind of refinement that our COMPLETEPRODUCTTYPE transformation generates.

A possibly-recursive record (named product) is defined in the form

$$\text{type T = \{p1 : A1[T], ..., pn: An[T]\}}$$

where `pi:T-> Ai[T]` for `1<=i<=n` is the complete set of observers of T (aka projections and fields). An element of `st:State` is written as a constant in the form

$$st = \{time=0, \ position=-1, \ velocity=2\}$$

and a functional update to a record is written

$$st << \{time = 1, position = 1\}$$

to denote a new record that differs from `st` only in the fields `time` and `position`:

$$\{time = 1, position = 1, velocity = 2\}.$$

Streams provide a prototypical example of a recursive record type:

$$\text{type Stream Nat} = \{hd : Nat, tl : Stream \ Nat\}$$

Possibly-recursive record types and especially the infinite objects in coinductive types are best understood in terms of their observers [3].

Deciding that the observers of `State` are complete, we can define `State` as a record of current observations, and then give a definition to `drive` by simply updating the input state to satisfy its copattern-based axioms. Completeness and consistency can be proved trivially by coinduction. The resulting specification can be readily translated to monadic or imperative form, when the occurrences of T are single-threaded. The construction of T gives rise to a coinduction rule which reflects that, by construction, every element of the type is uniquely identified by its observed values. Intuitively, if we cannot distinguish two elements of T through any sequence of observations, then the elements are equal. It is possible to allow axioms that, for example, require a relationship between observers (e.g. that $p_1(t) \leq p_2(t)$ for all $t \in$ T). Our examples will not require this capability.

```
Vehicle = spec
  type State
  op time      : State -> Nat
  op position : State -> Integer
  op drive:Integer->State->State
  ax time (drive newVel st) = time st + 1
  ax position (drive newVel st)
      = position st + newVel
end-spec

Vehicle1 = spec
  import Vehicle
  op velocity : State -> Integer
  ax velocity (drive newVel st) = newVel
end-spec
```

```
Vehicle2 = spec
  type State = {time    : Nat,
               position: Integer,
               velocity: Integer}

  op drive(newVel:Integer)(st:State):State
      = st << {    time = st.time + 1,
                 position = st.position + newVel,
                 velocity = newVel}
  end-spec
```

$\xrightarrow{n}$

Fig. 6. Refinement to record-based coinductive vehicle specification

4.1 COMPLETEPRODUCTTYPE **Transformation**

The idea of incrementally defining a coinductive type T is simple. During a derivation, we introduce a new type symbol and incrementally add observers. We also introduce function symbols and incrementally add copattern-based axioms on them. At some point in the derivation, the developers decide that no more observers are needed on type T. The COMPLETEPRODUCTTYPE transformation is then applied to generate a refinement in which T and its functions are given definitions. This is a strong refinement in the sense that it narrows down the possible interpretations of T and its functions from a possibly infinite set to a singleton – they are given canonical definitions (up to isomorphism) as record types.

We present the COMPLETEPRODUCTTYPE transformation as an instance of the SpecTransformation transformation pattern in Sect. 2. As before, we factor the transformation into two steps. The first, shown in Fig. 7, analyzes the given specification S to abstract out a subspecification Sobservers that contains just the observers over a given undefined type T. It then generates a refinement/morphism r:Sobservers → Sobservers' where Sobservers' introduces a record-type definition for T, as exemplified in Fig. 7. It then generates a refinement of S by taking the pushout of r and the extension c:Sobservers → S. It is straightforward to show that r is a consistent refinement, since it picks out the one model of T that is the greatest fixpoint of the recursive record type. By Theorem 1, if c is conservative and S' is the pushout of r and c, then the generated refinement r':S→ S' is consistent.

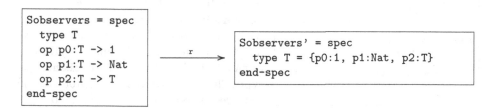

Fig. 7. Abstract refinement morphism on type T

The second step analyzes S' to abstract out a subspecification Sfuns that contains just the function symbols that have copattern-based axioms over the observers in Sobservers. It then generates a refinement r:Sfuns → Sfuns' where Sfuns' introduces record update definitions for each function, as exemplified in Fig. 8. Since the function definition is co-recursive, and producing a recursive record-type may not terminate, its translation to a programming language must be handled with care. The transformation then generates a refinement of S' by taking the pushout of r and the extension c:Sfuns → S'. It is straightforward to show that r is a consistent refinement, using the coinduction rule that goes with the definition of a recursive record type. By Theorem 1, if c is conservative and S' denotes the pushout of r and c, then the generated refinement n':S→ S' is consistent.

```
Sfuns = spec
   type T = {p0:1, p1:Nat, p2:T}
   ax p0(f(a)) = e0(a)
   ax p1(f(a)) = e1(a)
   ax p2(f(a)) = e2(a)
end-spec
```
r →
```
Sfuns' = spec
   type T = {p0:1, p1:Nat, p2:T}
   op f(a:A):T = {p0 = e0(a), p1 = e1(a), p2 = e2(a)}
end-spec
```

Fig. 8. Abstract refinement morphism for a coinductively defined function

4.2 Example: Packets

Communication streams provide a source of examples for incremental construction, which we illustrate by developing network-layer and transport-layer packet structures.

```
BasicPacket = spec
   type Data
   type Packet
   op data: Packet -> Data
end-spec
```

BasicPacket introduces a Packet type and one observer data of the content of a Packet which has some unspecified type Data.

```
TransportPacket = spec
   import BasicPacket
   type Port = Nat16
   op srcPort,dstPort: Packet -> Port
   op SeqNum : Packet -> Nat32
end-spec
```

TransportPacket extends BasicPacket with observers of a packet's source port srcPort, its destination port dstPort, and a sequence number SeqNum.

NetworkPacket extends BasicPacket with observers of a packet's source address srcAddr, its destination address dstAddr, and packet length pktLen. The types Nat16 and Nat32 are subtypes of Nat restricted to $[0..2^{16})$ and $[0..2^{32})$ respectively.

```
NetworkPacket = spec
   import BasicPacket
   type NetAddr = Nat32
   op srcAddr,dstAddr: Packet -> NetAddr
   op pktLen : Packet -> Nat16
end-spec
```

```
FlatNetTransPacket = spec
   import NetworkPacket,
          TransportPacket
end-spec
```
FCT →
```
FlatNetTransPacket1 = spec
   import BasicPacket
   type Port
   type NetAddr = Nat32
   type Packet =
        {srcAddr, dstAddr: NetAddr,
         pktLen : Nat16,
         srcPort, dstPort: Port,
         SeqNum : Nat32, data: Data}
end-spec
```

FlatNetworkTransportPacket incorporates the observers of BasicPacket, NetworkPacket, and TransportPacket. The refinement m generated by COM-PLETEPRODUCTTYPE creates the record-type definition for Packet.

A variation on the above formulation of `Packet` would distinguish header information (i.e. metadata) from payload content (i.e. data).

```
BasicPacket = spec
   type Data
   type Packet
   op data: Packet -> Data
   type Metadata
   op metadata: Packet -> Metadata
end-spec
```

Extending this specification with various observers of `Metadata` would give rise to the familiar header structures of the TCP/IP stack, by applying COMPLETEPRODUCTTYPE to both `Packet` and `Metadata`.

4.3   Example: Mutable Types

Suppose that we wish to treat `Packet`s as dynamically allocated mutable objects. This example combines the development of both inductive types (references from Sect. 3.3) and coinductive types (`Packet` from Sect. 4.2). Continuing the example from Sect. 4.2, specification `MutableBasicPacket` introduces a coinductive type `Packet` together with its `data` observer. Continuing the example in Sect. 3.3, we treat `Packet` as a referenceable type by introducing a constructor `c_Packet` of inductive type `Value`. We also introduce a defined observer `get_data` of `State` which observes the `data` of the `Packet` referenced by the argument `pktref`. We also specify a `State` transformer `set_data` that has the effect of changing the `data` observation of the `Packet` referenced by the argument `pktref`. Finally, we introduce a constructor of `Packet` that returns a reference. Effectively, `MutablePackets` provides a class-like specification, with a constructor, observers for getter methods, and transformers serving as setters and other methods. Translation to a suitable object-oriented language such as Java would be straightforward.

```
MutableBasicPacket = spec
  import RefTypes, BasicPacket
  op c_Packet: Packet -> Value
  op pkt?(val:Value):Bool = (ex(pkt:Packet) val = c_Packet pkt)
  op coerce_Packet(val:Value | pkt? val): {pkt:Packet | val=c_Packet pkt}

  op get_data(st:State)(pktref:Ref | pkt?(deref st pktref)): Data
             = data(coerce_Packet(deref st pktref))
  op set_data(st:State)(pktref:Ref | pkt? (deref st pktref))(d:Data):
          {(pktRef,st'):Ref*State | get_data st' pktRef = d }
  op new_Packet(d:Data)(st:State): {(pktRef,st'):Ref*State | pkt? (deref st' pktRef)
                          && get_data st' pktRef = d}
end-spec
```

Fig. 9. MutableBasicPacket

As in the previous section, we can extend `Packet` structure with Network structure by adding observers `srcAddr`, `dstAddr`,and `pktLen`, and their corresponding getters and setters. We also define a constructor for `MutableNetworkPacket`, which effectively becomes a subclass of `MutableBasicPacket`. See Fig. 10.

4.4   Example: Mutable Heaps for a Garbage Collector

One motivation for the development of the CompleteProduct transformation was the derivation of a family tree of garbage collectors [9,12] that we carried out using the Specware system [4].

cotype Graph	
Observers	**Functions**
nodes	add/delete node
nodeValue	set node value
arcs	add/delete arc
source (of an arc)	
target (of an arc)	setTarget (ptr swing)

In this context a model of memory starts with a directed graph type with observers for the nodes and arcs and associated observers of the content or value of a node and the source and target of each arc. Various functions for adding/deleting nodes and arcs, setting the value of a node, and setting the target of an arc are characterized using copattern-based axioms.

cotype Heap (extending Graph)	
Observers	**Functions**
roots	add/delete root
supply	add/delete supply node
	allocate node

The Graph specification is general-purpose and reusable, but a collector also needs to extend it to model the runtime heap, with additional observer for roots to specify the registers and stack sources of pointers, and the supply of nodes that can be dynamically allocated.

```
MutableNetworkPacket = spec
  import MutableBasicPacket
  type NetAddr = Nat32
  op srcAddr, dstAddr: Packet -> NetAddr
  op pktLen : Packet -> Nat16
  op get_srcAddr(st:State)(pktref:Ref | pkt?(deref st pktref)):Nat16
          = srcAddr (coerce_Packet (deref st pktref))
  op set_srcAddr(st:State)(pktref:Ref | pkt?(deref st pktref))(saddr:Nat16):
                        {(pktRef,st'):Ref*State | get_data st' pktRef = get_data st pktRef
                        && get_srcAddr st' pktRef = saddr }
  ... similar definitions for get/set_dstAddr ...
  op get_pktLen(st:State)(pktref:Ref | pkt? (deref st pktref)):Nat16
          = pktLen (coerce_Packet (deref st pktref))
  op set_pktLen(st:State)(pktref:Ref | pkt? (deref st pktref))( len:Nat16):
                        {(pktRef,st'):Ref*State | get_data st' pktRef = get_data st pktRef
                        && get_pktLen st' pktRef = len}
  op new_NetworkPacket(st:State)(d:Data)(saddr:NetAddr)(daddr:NetAddr)(pktlen:Nat16):
                  {(pktRef,st'):Ref*State | pkt? (deref st' pktRef)
                        && get_data st' pktRef = d
                        && get_srcAddr st' pktRef = saddr
                        && get_dstAddr st' pktRef = daddr
                        && get_pktLen  st' pktRef = pktlen}
end-spec
```

Fig. 10. MutableNetworkPacket

```
S = spec
  type T
  op p1: T -> D1
  op p2: T -> D2
  op g(a:A):T =
  ... copattern-based axioms
  over p1 and p2 ...
end-spec
```

```
S1 = spec
  import S
  type T1 <: T
  op p3: T1 -> D3
  op g1(a:A1):T1 =
  ... copattern-based axioms
  over p1, p2, and p3 ...
end-spec
```

```
S2 = spec
  import S
  type T2 <: T
  op p4: T2 -> D4
  op g2(a:A2):T2 =
  ... copattern-based axioms
  over p1, p2, and p4 ...
end-spec
```

Fig. 11. Record subtype development

CollectionHeap (extending Heap)	
Observers	**Functions**
black	insert/delete black
	mark, sweep

Finally, we add observers that are needed by the particular collection algorithm. For example, a mark-and-sweep algorithm requires an observer of the mark bit (called black by tradition dating to Dijkstra) per node, and associated functions.

4.5 Subtyping

One might want a family tree of record-types and an appropriate notion of record-type subtyping, as illustrated in Fig. 11. We can import S1 and S2 and transform as shown in Fig. 12. In specification S3', the function g may be passed a T, T1, or T2 element, but g1 may only be passed a T1 element and g2 may only be passed a T2 element. This transformation naturally leads to the development of object class hierarchies in an object-oriented language.

```
S3 = spec
  import S1,S2
  ...
end-spec
```

COMPLETEPRODUCTTYPE(S3,T)
————————————————→
COMPLETEPRODUCTTYPE(S3,T1)
COMPLETEPRODUCTTYPE(S3,T2)

```
S3' = spec
  type T  = {p1:D1, p2:D2}
  type T1 = {p1:D1, p2:D2, p3:D3} <: T
  type T2 = {p1:D1, p2:D2, o4:D4} <: T
  op g(a:A)   :T  = ... coinductive def over T  ...
  op g1(a:A1):T1 = ... coinductive def over T1 ...
  op g2(a:A2):T2 = ... coinductive def over T2 ...
  ...
end-spec
```

Fig. 12. Subtype record refinement

5   Implementation

An implementation of COMPLETEPRODUCTTYPE must gather the observers on a given type symbol T. Observers are functions of a particular type $T \rightarrow A$ for some A that is not T. Of these, there are three subclasses of observers that can arise in a derivation: (1) undefined observers, (2) defined observers that are eagerly maintained (e.g. by a Finite Differencing transformation [7,8]), (3) defined observers that are computed when needed. Only the observers in classes 1 and 2 are gathered for inclusion in the state definition. Class 3 is excluded for efficiency reasons only, under the presumption that they are called infrequently. If it is called frequently, then it may be more efficient to maintain a state variable for its value under all transformers (in which case it falls under class 2).

The transformations have been implemented in the Specware system [4] and have been used extensively in the automated synthesis of families of protocol-processing codes for distributed vehicle control [5], and concurrent garbage collection algorithms [9,12] as summarized in Sect. 4.4.

6   Related Work

These transformations can be seen as addressing the *expression problem* which arises from the desire to define a type and its functions incrementally by cases while preserving static type checking and avoiding recompilation [2,16]. It was observed that (1) in functional languages it is easy to add new functions but not to add cases to a type, and (2) in object-oriented languages it is easy to add cases to a type, but not to add new functions. The refinement setting provides a simple, natural approach for developers (1) to incrementally add cases/constructors to an inductive type, and (2) to extend functions that are defined inductively over the constructors, and to add new functions. Dually, developers can incrementally add new observers to a coinductive type, and extend functions/transformers that are defined coinductively with respect to the observers.

The literature on (co)algebra has long noted the duality of defining functions that input an inductive type by patterns versus defining functions that produce a coinductive type by copatterns [3]. Recent work by Abel et al. [1] laid the foundation for integrating this duality into Haskell and other programming languages by formalizing patterns and copatterns, and supporting pattern-based definitions for inductive functions, and copattern-based definitions for functions returning a coinductive type.

7   Concluding Remarks

We hope that the view expressed herein offers a richer understanding of programs and program development in general. Algebraic/inductive datatypes and functions are useful for specifying immutable finite data structures. They naturally support a functional programming style. Coalgebraic/coinductive datatypes and functions are useful for specifying mutable data structures, non-well-founded data structures, as well as dynamical systems that are possibly nonterminating and concurrent. They naturally support imperative, object-oriented, and multi-threaded programming styles. Together they provide a natural foundation for a mixed use of functional, imperative, object-oriented and concurrent programming. Embedding these dual concepts in a refinement setting provides flexibility in the face of pressures to vary software, either to produce the products of a product line (via alternative product requirements), or to respond to evolutionary changes to requirements.

Acknowledgements. Thanks to Christoph Kreitz, Peter Pepper, Florian Rabe, and the reviewers for helpful discussions and comments on the text.

References

1. Abel, A., Pientka, B., Thibodeau, D., and Setzer, A. Copatterns: programming infinite structures by observations. In: Proceedings of the 40th Annual ACM SIGPLAN-SIGACT Symposium on Principles of Programming Languages, POPL 2013, pp. 27–38 (2013)
2. Cook, W.R.: Object-oriented programming versus abstract data types. In: de Bakker, J.W., de Roever, W.P., Rozenberg, G. (eds.) REX 1990. LNCS, vol. 489, pp. 151–178. Springer, Heidelberg (1991). https://doi.org/10.1007/BFb0019443
3. Jacobs, B., Rutten, J.: A tutorial on (co)algebras and (co)induction. Bull. EATCS **62**, 222–259 (1996)
4. Kestrel Institute: Specware System and documentation (2003). http://www.specware.org/
5. Kreitz, C., Smith, D.R.: Synthesis of network protocols: final report. Technical report, Kestrel Institute (2016). http://www.kestrel.edu/home/people/smith/pub/HACMS-Final-Report.pdf
6. Leroy, X., Blazy, S.: Formal verification of a C-like memory model and its uses for verifying program transformations. J. Autom. Reason. **41**(1), 1–31 (2008)
7. Liu, Y.: Systematic Program Design: From Clarity to Efficiency. Cambridge University Press, Cambridge (2013)
8. Paige, R., Koenig, S.: Finite differencing of computable expressions. ACM Trans. Program. Lang. Syst. **4**(3), 402–454 (1982)
9. Pavlovic, D., Pepper, P., Smith, D.R.: Formal derivation of concurrent garbage collectors. In: Bolduc, C., Desharnais, J., Ktari, B. (eds.) MPC 2010. LNCS, vol. 6120, pp. 353–376. Springer, Heidelberg (2010). https://doi.org/10.1007/978-3-642-13321-3_20. Extended version in http://arxiv.org/abs/1006.4342
10. Smith, D.R.: Another proof of the modularization theorem. Technical report, Kestrel Institute, February 1993. http://www.kestrel.edu/home/people/smith/pub/modularization.pdf
11. Smith, D.R.: Generating programs plus proofs by refinement. In: Meyer, B., Woodcock, J. (eds.) VSTTE 2005. LNCS, vol. 4171, pp. 182–188. Springer, Heidelberg (2008). https://doi.org/10.1007/978-3-540-69149-5_20
12. Smith, D.R., Westbrook, E., Westfold, S.J.: Deriving concurrent garbage collectors: final report. Technical report, Kestrel Institute (2015). http://www.kestrel.edu/home/people/smith/pub/CRASH-Final-Report.pdf
13. Srinivas, Y.V., Jüllig, R.: Specware: formal support for composing software. In: Möller, B. (ed.) MPC 1995. LNCS, vol. 947, pp. 399–422. Springer, Heidelberg (1995). https://doi.org/10.1007/3-540-60117-1_22
14. Tuch, H.: Formal verification of C systems code: structured types, separation logic and theorem proving. J. Autom. Reason. **42**(2), 125–187 (2009)
15. Veloso, P.A., Maibaum, T.: On the modularization theorem for logical specification. Inf. Process. Lett. **53**(5), 287–293 (1995)
16. Wadler, P.: The expression problem. Technical report, Bell Labs, Murray Hill, NJ (1998). http://homepages.inf.ed.ac.uk/wadler/papers/expression/expression.txt

Comparing Correctness-by-Construction with Post-Hoc Verification—A Qualitative User Study

Tobias Runge[1]([⊠]), Thomas Thüm[2]([⊠]), Loek Cleophas[3,4]([⊠]), Ina Schaefer[1]([⊠]), and Bruce W. Watson[4,5]([⊠])

[1] TU Braunschweig, Braunschweig, Germany
{tobias.runge,i.schaefer}@tu-bs.de
[2] University of Ulm, Ulm, Germany
thomas.thuem@uni-ulm.de
[3] TU Eindhoven, Eindhoven, The Netherlands
loek@fastar.org
[4] Stellenbosch University, Stellenbosch, South Africa
bruce@fastar.org
[5] Centre for Artificial Intelligence Research, Stellenbosch, South Africa

Abstract. Correctness-by-construction (CbC) is a refinement-based methodology to incrementally create formally correct programs. Programs are constructed using refinement rules which guarantee that the resulting implementation is correct with respect to a pre-/postcondition specification. In contrast, with post-hoc verification (PhV) a specification and a program are created, and afterwards verified that the program satisfies the specification. In the literature, both methods are discussed with specific advantages and disadvantages. By letting participants construct and verify programs using CbC and PhV in a controlled experiment, we analyzed the claims in the literature. We evaluated defects in intermediate code snapshots and discovered a trial-and-error construction process to alter code and specification. The participants appreciated the good feedback of CbC and state that CbC is better than PhV in helping to find defects. Nevertheless, some defects in the constructed programs with CbC indicate that the participants need more time to adapt the CbC process.

1 Introduction

Correctness-by-construction (CbC) [17,19,25,30] as proposed by Dijsktra is a method for the construction of formally correct programs. The programmer refines an abstract statement with pre-/postcondition specification to a concrete implementation, guided by the specification and refinement rules. It is claimed that programmers construct programs with low defect rates with CbC [20]. There are three reasons for this that need to be evaluated. First, the structured reasoning discipline which is enforced by the refinement rules reduces the possibility to introduce

E. Sekerinski et al. (Eds.): FM 2019 Workshops, LNCS 12233, pp. 388–405, 2020.
https://doi.org/10.1007/978-3-030-54997-8_25

defects. Second, defects in the code can be traced to their source through the refinement structure. Third, programmers and users gain trust in the program because a formal methodology was used to create the program [25]. We implemented the correctness-by-construction approach in a graphical IDE called CorC,[1] which support users during the construction and verification of programs.

With deductive post-hoc verification (PhV), we refer to techniques as used in the KeY community [4], which verify a program after its creation. A verifier checks whether the program satisfies its pre-/postcondition specification. PhV does not provide a strict guideline on how to construct the program; the programmer can freely implement the program. This can decrease the time taken to create a first (potentially faulty) version of a program, but can increase the program verification time because it is more likely that defects occur in the code [36]. In order to evaluate this claim, we consider the post-hoc verifier KeY [4] as an instance. KeY can verify Java programs annotated with pre-/postcondition specifications in the Java Modeling Language (JML).

As the title suggests, we compare correctness-by-construction with post-hoc verification. In a qualitative user study, participants use CorC and KeY to implement and verify an algorithm with each tool. By analyzing 347 intermediate code snapshots, we get better insights in the process used by participants to construct and verify algorithms. With a user experience questionnaire, we compare which advantages and disadvantages of the verification techniques and the tools have been experienced. Our contributions in this paper are the following.

- We give an overview of advantages and disadvantages of CbC and PhV.
- We designed and performed a user study to compare both approaches. We analyze the defects in code and specification of each intermediate snapshot for both tools.
- We discuss our insights and compare CbC with PhV based on our user study.

2   Verification Techniques

In our user study, we evaluate the techniques PhV and CbC. Therefore, we first present and compare the foundations of both techniques. We also survey claims about their advantages and disadvantages as discussed in the research literature.

2.1   Post-hoc Verification

With post-hoc verification, we refer to a method which is used to verify whether a program satisfies a given specification. A programmer develops a program and a pre-/postcondition specification. Besides the pre-/postcondition specification, loop invariants can be defined to specify the behavior of loops in the code. The correctness of the program can be verified by using a deductive verification tool, such as KeY [4]. It translates the program and the specification to a dynamic logic formula (i.e., proof obligations). The program is executed symbolically, and

---

[1] see https://github.com/TUBS-ISF/CorC and [34] for explanation of the editor.

the formula is updated according to the new symbolic state. After the program is completely executed, it no longer appears in the formula, and the remaining first-order proof goal can be evaluated by theorem proving. The verification can be performed (semi-)automatically or interactively. We use automatic verification in this paper in order to be able to focus the user study on the construction of programs and specification. Most users in industry do not have a theoretical background to verify programs interactively.

2.2   Correctness-by-Construction

Correctness-by-construction in the classical Dijkstra-style [17,25] is a programming method which starts with a Hoare triple specification. This Hoare triple contains a precondition, an abstract statement (i.e., a statement that is a placeholder for concrete code), and a postcondition. The triple asserts total correctness. If the program is in a state where the precondition holds, its execution will terminate in a state where the postcondition holds. An abstract statement in a Hoare triple can be refined to a concrete program using refinement rules. The rules introduce new statements, such as loops or assignments. By refining the program, the pre-/postcondition specification is propagated through the constructed program, so that the refined statements are also surrounded by a pre- and a postcondition, forming more Hoare triples [17,25]. These refinement rules introduce proof obligations which have to be discharged to establish the correct application of the refinements rules. E.g., it has to be verified that by executing an assignment the corresponding postcondition is implied, or that a loop invariant holds after each iteration. The correctness of these proof obligations can be checked using verification tools [1,34]. We implemented tool support for the construction of programs following CbC [34]. The graphical editor CorC visualizes program refinements in a tree-like structure.

2.3   Contrasting Correctness-by-Construction and Post-hoc Verification

CbC and PhV are two different methods to create verified software. Nevertheless, they share commonalities. Both start with a pre-/postcondition specification and result in a program that satisfies this specification. The procedure to construct the program, however, is different. With CbC, the program is constructed stepwise by applying checkable refinement rules. With PhV, the program is constructed without a strict guideline (i.e., the programmer can freely develop the program and intermediate steps are not proven). Afterwards, the final program can be verified.

It is claimed that CbC can lead to well-structured code that can be verified more easily [25,36]. The additional time needed to construct the code is said to be amortized with a significantly reduced time to prove the code. When applying CbC, every refined statement leads to a provable side condition, where a theorem prover can check whether this condition is satisfied. If the check fails, the programmer can alter the refined statement to establish the proof. This is a potential advantage compared to PhV because problems in the verification process can be pinned to small parts of the program. In contrast, with PhV additional expertise or sophisticated tool support is necessary to infer the defect from open goals in the proof [33].

Programmers who use the CbC approach are bound to the stepwise refinement using rules. Therefore, after each refinement the program with all conditions can be reviewed by the programmers. They can continuously check the surrounding specification of every statement. This can raise awareness of defects in the program, resulting in fewer defects in comparison to PhV programming. The number of required iterations to get to a correct program with CbC may also be reduced because defects are detected early, even before a prover is used [36].

An open question is whether the experience of developers is crucial for the development of correct code. Using PhV, programmers can implement algorithms as they normally do and verify whether the program is correct afterwards. Using CbC, the programmer needs an understanding of the refinement rules to construct programs. Whether this barrier noticeably increases the time of the construction process, or whether the CbC method does not have a negative influence needs to be evaluated.

These claims are established in the literature but need to be evaluated in a user study. We analyze defects in intermediate and final programs and interpret the answers of a questionnaire to provide evidence for the claims.

3   Design of a User Study

To qualitatively evaluate CbC and PhV, we performed a user study with the two tools, CorC and KeY. We decided explicitly for a controlled experiment to monitor all participants in parallel during the tasks and to collect all programming results. We selected CorC because it is a new tool that supports the CbC method in a graphical user interface and which has been taught to the participants. KeY, which is a major tool for the automatic verification of Java programs, is used to get good comparability as CorC uses KeY as back-end for the verification. Therefore, we have a comparable expressiveness with both tools.

We provide the participants a pre-/postcondition specification for an algorithm, and they developed code to satisfy this specification. The algorithms can be implemented in under ten lines of code. We decided explicitly for this size, so the whole experiment could be done in 90 min because it is complicated to motivate people to do longer experiments. We also excluded the process of writing an adequate pre-/postcondition specification because this has to be done for both techniques and highly influences what needs to be implemented and verified. The same starting point reduces the divergence, so that we can analyze the results on the same basis. We want to qualitatively analyze how the participants develop and verify code. Therefore, we took intermediate snapshots of the code every time the code was verified and analyzed the defects created during the development process. We checked a total of 347 versions of programs, something which is not feasible with larger programs and more participants. The user experience with the tools was measured qualitatively by a questionnaire in order to find improvement potentials. The material of the user study is published on GitHub.[2]

Objective. We surveyed in Sect. 2.3 whether CbC can have a positive impact on programming and verifying code. Hence, we want to evaluate whether a positive impact can be detected (i.e, programmers appreciate that defects could be more easily detected with CbC). We consider three research questions to evaluate the methodologies (RQ1–2) and the tools (RQ3) qualitatively.

RQ1: What errors do participants make with CbC or PhV?
RQ2: What is the process of participants to create programs with CbC or PhV?
RQ3: Do participants prefer CorC or KeY?

Participants. Our participants were students of a software quality course at TU Braunschweig, Germany. We decided for these students because they were taught the fundamentals of software verification, and they got an introduction to both tools. They have experience in verifying methods with both tools although the specific algorithms of this experiment were new to them. We had ten participants which were divided into two groups randomly. The programming experience that was measured with an initial questionnaire [18] was 2.189 for group A and 1.791 for group B.[3] The experience of individuals ranged between 1.609 and 2.777. With a Mann-Whitney test, we calculated no significant difference between both groups (p-value = 0.1514). Most of the students have several years of programming experience in industry, and therefore, can be compared to junior developers. Six participants had three to seven years experience as programmer in industry, two were new programmers in larger projects, and only two never programmed in larger projects.

The participants voluntarily attended in the experiment. They knew that they took part in an experiment and that this experiment did not affect the grade of the course. Every participant was paid € 10 to create an incentive for them. Participants who solved one or both exercises also had the chance to win € 50 (i.e., one of them was randomly selected). This lottery should increase the motivation to solve the exercises by creating a realistic pressure to succeed.

Material. In our experiment, the participants had to implement and verify two algorithms. For every participant, we prepared a computer with an Eclipse installation that supports CorC and KeY, and contained a workspace with the two exercises. We also provided a cheat sheet containing the syntax of KeY and CorC to help the participants. In order for us to properly analyze the experiment, participants took the programming experience questionnaire before the exercises

---

[2] https://github.com/Runge93/UserstudyCbCPhV.
[3] The calculation is explained in the work by Feigenspan et al. [18]. They derived with stepwise regression testing that the experience in comparison to classmates with factor 0.441 summed up with the logical programming experience with factor 0.286 is the best indicator for programming experience.

and a user experience questionnaire afterwards. The user experience questionnaire is a combination of open questions (OQ 1–4) and the User Experience Questionnaire[4] (UEQ).

OQ1: What was better in CorC/KeY?
OQ2: How did you proceed with the task in CorC/KeY?
OQ3: Which tool would you use for verification, and why?
OQ4: Which tool better supports avoiding or fixing defects, and why?

UEQ is an established questionnaire which measures six properties of a product (e.g., attractiveness) by asking the user to rate the product with 26 items. Each item describes the product positively and negatively, and the user must evaluate which and to what extent one of the descriptions fits. Additionally, the workspaces were saved to analyze the created code and specifications.

Tasks. We used the Latin square design to arrange the participants. Group A used CorC for a `maximum element` algorithm, and KeY for `modulo`. Group B did the exercises in the same order, but each one with the other tool. We switched the order of the tools to address learning and ordering effects. We believe that an order between tools is worse than an order between exercises because we want to get insights in the usability of the tools. Additionally, the order between exercises was not varied because a split into four groups was not manageable. For each exercise, we provided a pre-/postcondition, and a task description in which we explained the purpose of the algorithm, so that the partcipants understood what the implementation should achieve.

The algorithm `maximum element` finds the index of the maximum element in an array. The array is assumed to be non-empty to simplify the algorithm, so that an index of the array should always be returned. The algorithm `modulo` gets two integers a and b as input and computes the two values factor and remainder for the equation $factor * b + remainder = a$. For the construction of the algorithm, the division and modulo operations are prohibited. Both algorithms are similar in size and cyclomatic complexity.

The tasks were designed such that a small, manageable subset of Java is sufficient to implement the algorithms. `Assignments`, `If-Then-Else`, and `While` were the only necessary statements. We excluded method calls because they complicate the verification for these two algorithms unnecessarily.

Variables. In our experiment, the tool is an independent variable, with the two treatments CorC and KeY. To check the correctness of the code in KeY, we reran the proof for the solution of every participant. In CorC, we checked that all nodes in the refinement hierarchy are proven. If a solution was not proven, we checked whether the code is correct with KeY and, if necessary, adjusted the specification, such as a loop invariant, to close the proof. If the code was also incorrect, we checked how many defects were in the code by adjusting the code. To evaluate the programming and verification process, we analyzed the intermediate snapshots. Here, the changes and defects were also counted in

---

[4] https://www.ueq-online.org/.

Table 1. Defects in code and specification of the final programs of participants

#Defects	KeY		CorC	
	Code	Specification	Code	Specification
Verified	2		3	
No defects	8	2	4	3
Minor defects	1	4	3	2
Major defects	1	3	1	2
Incomplete	0	1	2	3

terms of changed lines. For example, if an incorrect assignment was fixed by a participant, we count one change in the program and reduce the number of defects by one. The time needed for every exercise was measured manually. If a participant solved a task, the time was noted. After 30 min, we interrupted the participants when they were not finished.

Deviations. The participants assigned themselves randomly to a group by selecting one computer. We missed that the participants per groups were unequal. Group A had six participants, and group B had only four. This unequal distribution changed which exercise was done with which tool. Since we used the Latin square design, the influence should not be significant because we still had ten results for each treatment.

4   Results and Discussion

In this section, we present the results of our evaluation. We analyzed the data of the created programs and the answers of the questionnaire. The comparably small number of participants reduces the generalizability of the results, but allows us to evaluate the process of the participants in detail by analyzing all 347 intermediate code snapshots. This gives us anecdotal evidence to qualitatively discuss advantages and disadvantages of CbC and PhV.

4.1   Defects in Implementation

To answer the first research question, RQ1, what errors do participants make with CbC or PhV, we analyze defects in the program and the specification.

There are ten implementations with each tool. The defects in the code are shown in Table 1 in column two and four, numbered left-to-right from one. With KeY, eight programs were correct and two of them were verified. In one case, only a loop guard was slightly incorrect (e.g., two variables were compared with less than, but less than or equal was correct). Only one program contained major defects. We classified a program to have major defects, if we could not correct

Table 2. Initial and final defects in the programs of participants

Row	Initial defects	Final defects	KeY	CorC
1	0	0	6	1
2	1	0	1	1
3	2	0	1	0
4	3	0	0	1
5	4	0	0	1
6	1	1	1	0
7	2	1	0	2
8	3	1	0	1
9	>5	>5	1	1
10	Incomplete		0	2

the program with at most five changes. With CorC, four programs were correct and three of them could be verified. In three programs, a minor defect occurred, one program had numerous mistakes, but also two programs were incomplete.

In the case of intermediate specifications which needed to be provided, for both tools the results were worse. In Table 1, the defects in intermediate and loop invariant specifications are shown in column three and five. Only in two cases for KeY and three cases for CorC no defects occurred. In KeY, four specifications contained minor defects, such as a missing boundary for a control variable or an incorrect comparison of two variables. Three programs had major defects in the specification. For example, it was not properly specified which elements of the array were already examined in the `maximum element` algorithm. One participant did not create an invariant. In the case of CorC, two minor and two major defects occurred, but also three algorithms had incomplete specifications. Two of these three incomplete specifications could be explained as incomplete programs. In the third case, the algorithm was created but not specified.

To analyze the defects in more detail, we counted the defects during the programming task. In Table 2, the defects in the initial (i.e., programs at the first verification attempt) and final programs are shown. One difference between programming in KeY and CorC is that the participants in KeY started the first verification after the program was completely constructed. In CorC, some users started earlier, with incomplete programs because they could verify Hoare triples for parts of the programs that were already completely concretized. With KeY, six participants created a program without any defects (Row 1). In two cases (rows 2 and 3), one or two defects were found. One participant started with one defect, but could not find the defect (Row 6). The participant also had three defects in an intermediate result, but never found the incorrect loop guard condition. One program had more than five defects in the beginning and the end (Row 9). With CorC, only one program had no defects in the beginning (Row 1). Three participants started with one to four defects and fixed the defects (rows 2, 4, and 5). One participant who started with two defects and ended with one (Row 7), had a correct intermediate result, but inserted one defect in the final version. One participant had a result which could not be fixed easily (Row 9).

Two programs were incomplete in CorC (Row 10). Their developers started with the first refinements, but could not finalize the program in the CorC editor.

The construction of algorithms with KeY was mostly the same. The participants created a correct or nearly correct algorithm. Afterwards, a loop invariant was constructed and the program was verified. Astonishingly, no participant could verify the program on the first try even though the program was correct because the loop invariants were incorrect or too weak (e.g., for modulo the special case that the input parameters could be equal was not handled). The approach of the participants to get the program to a verifiable state was different. Some participants mostly changed the invariant and verified the program again. Others changed the loop and the invariant. A correct program was changed up to ten times to another correct solution, but no sufficient invariant for KeY to verify the program was found. Some participants also changed whether the loop variable was increased or decreased several times.

With CorC, the most common approach was to create the program with all refinements and specify the intermediate conditions or loop invariants in parallel. Often the program was completely refined before the first verifier call. If the verification was not possible, missing parts such as the initialization of control variables were added, assignment or conditions were changed. In three cases, the initial defects were found, but in one case, a correct intermediate program was changed to an incorrect program. The participant with the incorrect result started with a program where he forgot to decrease the control variable in the loop. Afterwards, the participant decreased the variable correctly, but the loop invariant was wrong, so the statements could not be verified. So, the program was changed again to decrease the control variable at another place in the program. In the process, the participant introduced an incorrect execution path where the variable is not decreased. Two other participants started with a loop, but forgot the initialization of necessary variables. This mistake was recognized during the exercise.

In summary, both tools in some cases lead to correct and verified programs. Small defects occurred with both tools, but in CorC, we observed incomplete programs. If the program could not be verified, participants mostly changed the loop guards, the loop body, or loop invariants. The changes in the code are fewer with CorC than with KeY. If a program could not be verified, the problem was in most cases an insufficient loop invariant or a wrong loop guard. With PhV, most participants created correct code in the first place. As shown in Table 2, only three defects were found in the process in total. With CbC, the users started mostly with a defective program and found twelve defects in total. This higher number of found defects may be explained with better tool support in CorC, but also with the higher number of existing defects. With PhV, only four defects existed by excluding the completely wrong program. Thus 75% of the defects were found. For CbC, there are 15 defects in total, so 80% have been found.

RQ1. Comparing the defects in code, participants made similar errors with both techniques (e.g., incorrect loop guard), but they made fewer and mostly minor errors with PhV. This could be explained with the familiar environment of standard Java with JML. The two incomplete programs in CorC can be explained by problems interacting with the tool. Thus in total, more correct programs were created with PhV than with CbC. That more programs were verified with CbC anyway is interesting. One explanation could be that programs with CbC were less changed. The participants might have thought more about the program instead of changing the program by trial-and-error. Due to the similar correction rates of defects for both tools, we cannot confirm a negative influence of CbC in the programming process, but we should further investigate why more defect programs with CbC exist.

4.2   Analysis of Programming Procedure

From the intermediate snapshots, we can evaluate the programming procedure by analyzing the changes and defects in code and intermediate specification, and missing program or specification parts. We analyzed 20 solutions containing between 9 and 39 snapshots. We excluded the incomplete and entirely incorrect cases because we could not count wrong or missing parts with the same scale as for the other cases. In the following, three typical results are shown.

In Fig. 1, we show the graph of a participant solving the `maximum element` task in CorC. The participant started the verification process with two missing lines of code and two missing intermediate specification lines. The participant also had two defects in the intermediate specification. Overall, 25 steps were taken by the participant to achieve the correct solution. In the first 13 steps, the program and the specification were changed, but no defects were fixed. In Step 14, the invariant of the program was corrected. The special case that there can be more than one maximum element in the array was included in the invariant. The next steps were used to verify the program, until the participant realized that the initialization of variables was missing. After this fix in Step 21, the program was verified.

In Fig. 2, the process to construct the `maximum element` algorithm in KeY is shown. The participant started with a correct program where the invariant was missing. After introducing the invariant with a defect, the participant changed the code and the invariant during the whole task without finding a sufficient invariant. The program was changed to iterate the array from forward to backward and vice versa several times. The main reason that the program could not be verified was that the invariant did not specify which elements of the array were already visited. There were similar cases with KeY where also only the invariant was wrong. The code and intermediate specifications were changed by most participants during their development process. There were two participants who mostly changed the invariant instead of the code.

In Fig. 3, we show a graph of a user developing the `modulo` algorithm in CorC. The participant started with one defect in the code, an incorrect loop guard, and two missing specification parts, the invariant and an intermediate condition. In the first steps, the participant tried to verify the whole program without changing it. Then, the missing specifications were added, but both were wrong. In the invariant, the comparison operator was the wrong way around, and the intermediate condition was too weak (i.e., it was not specified that the correct factor was found). The specification was changed until step twelve, then the participant tried to verify the program again. As this did not lead to a

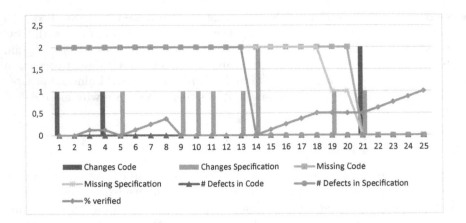

Fig. 1. Process to construct `maximum element` algorithm in CorC

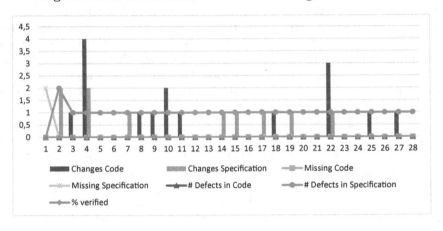

Fig. 2. Process to construct `maximum element` algorithm in KeY

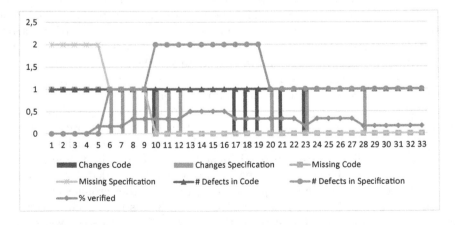

Fig. 3. Process to construct `modulo` algorithm in CorC

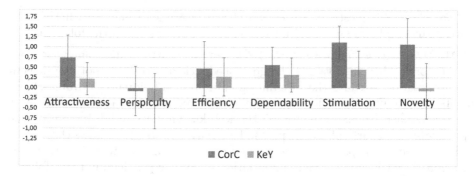

Fig. 4. Results of the user experience questionnaire

solution, the code and specification were changed again. The wrong comparison in the invariant was found, but the other two problems remained until the end.

RQ2. With the detailed analysis of all 347 program snapshots, we can discuss the programming process of the participants. We saw that correct programs were changed several times if they could not be verified, and surprisingly remained correct. The participants did not realize that only the intermediate specification was insufficient. They need better tool support to pinpoint the defects in code or specification. We also noticed a non-monotonic construction process for both techniques. By monotonic, we mean that a program is specified, constructed, and then verified to be correct. An example for the non-monotonic construction process with CbC and PhV are the trial-and-error changes in specification and code. For example with PhV, the users changed to iterate the array from forward to backward in several cases. With CbC, the users verified a correct part of the program, but changed it if they could not verify the complete program. In comparison to PhV, participants using the CbC approach changed the code less. Furthermore, a correct specification may favor the finding of mistakes in the program. Often defects were found after a correct loop invariant was introduced. In our evaluation, all programs with correct specifications had no defects.

4.3 User Experience

The results of the UEQ are presented in Fig. 4. The answers of the participants were evaluated according to the six measurements: attractiveness, perspicuity, efficiency, dependability, stimulation, and novelty. The scale is between +3 and −3 for each item. Overall, the average answers of the participants are higher for CorC. For perspicuity both tools got a negative mean value. KeY also has a negative result for novelty. We measured a significant difference with the T-test.[5] Stimulation ($p = 0.0457$) and novelty ($p = 0.0274$) are significantly different.

---

[5] Statistical hypothesis test to compare two independent samples which are normally distributed.

For the open questions, we clustered the answers to analyze whether the participants had similar experiences. The results are shown in the following.

OQ1. *What was better in CorC/KeY?* Five to six participants valued the clarity of CorC. They also valued the good feedback of CorC to spot the defects in the program because the program is split into individually provable statements. On the negative side, the unfamiliar syntax and the handling of the tool were mentioned. In the case of KeY, the well-known Java and JML syntax was appreciated by nearly all participants. Two participants also valued the clarity of KeY. One participant disliked the bad error messages of KeY. Another one mentioned that KeY gives more information about the problem, but this follows from the design of the experiment. CorC uses KeY as back-end for verification, but we suppressed the KeY editor on purpose in CorC because the verification problems for the implemented algorithms should be small enough to be verified automatically [34]. In the normal configuration, CorC can deliver the same information by opening the proof in KeY. In summary, the known syntax in KeY was an advantage, but the participants appreciated the better potential in CorC to find the defects because the program was decomposed into provable statements.

OQ2. *How did you proceed with the task in CorC/KeY?* In KeY, all participants created the code first, then they created the loop invariant and verified the program. One participant emphasized that the program was inferred from the postcondition. In CorC, the common case was to construct the code stepwise. Two participants explicitly mentioned that they created the program in CorC first, then specified the program. Two others started with the specification in CorC. In contrast to KeY, the participants wrote specifications only in CorC before or during the construction of the code.

OQ3. *Which tool (CorC/KeY) would you use for verification, and why?* Five participants decided to use CorC for verification. They appreciated the clarity. Two participants mentioned the support to verify and debug individual statements. One participant highlighted the reflective coding process that is encouraged by CorC. Four participants decided to use KeY. They liked the familiar environment and syntax. As in the first question, one participant mentioned that KeY gives more information. There is no clear trend towards one tool.

OQ4. *Which tool (CorC/KeY) better supports avoiding or fixing defects, and why?* Most participants decided for CorC to avoid or fix defects. They appreciated that defects are assigned to individual statements, therefore, it was easier to understand the problem. One participant mentioned that the stepwise construction helped to create correct programs. For both tools, some participants indicated that defects were detected and only correct code could be verified. Although nearly the same number of participants would use KeY or CorC for verification, most participants wanted to use CorC to find or fix defects in the coding process. That defects were associated to specific statements was well received by the participants.

RQ3. The third research question, whether participants prefer CorC or KeY, can be answered with the results of the questionnaire. The participants preferred

KeY because of the familiar syntax, and CorC for the better feedback if there were defects in the code. This leads to a balanced vote on which tool the participants would use for verification. Interestingly, the participants voted in favor of CorC when it comes to finding and fixing defects. This should be further investigated; what keeps participants from using CorC even though they mention that it helped better to find defects. With the answers of the participants and the analysis of the snapshots, we can also confirm how the participants worked on the tasks. In KeY, the program was developed, and afterwards the specification was constructed. So, the code was mostly correct in the first place. In CorC, they had different approaches. They interleaved coding and specification or started with the specification. This results in starting the verification earlier with incomplete or incorrect programs. Surprisingly, nobody complained about the additional specification effort in CorC.

4.4 Threats to Validity

In our experiment, we had only 10 participants. This reduces the generalizability of the results, but allowed us to analyze all 347 versions of program snapshots in detail. The participants were all students of a software quality course. We could ensure that all students had the required theoretical and practical precognition. They are no experts in verifying software, but smaller tasks, such as those of our experiment, were solved before by the participants in class. Most students also have part-time jobs in companies, so the results are generalizable to junior developers. The motivation of the students is doubtful, but the lottery gave an incentive to accomplish the tasks. Another limitation for the experiment was the limited time. Most participants have accomplished to write correct code, but only five out of twenty algorithms were also verified. With more time it is possible that more algorithms would have been verified. We only used two small size exercises in our experiment, and therefore, cannot generalize the results to bigger problems. The results of the experiment also depend on our introduction of the tools—though we tried to introduce both tools equally without bias to the students.

5 Related Work

In the literature, tool support for verification was previously evaluated, but PhV was not compared with CbC.

Spec# is an extension of the programming language C# to annotate code with pre-/postconditions and verify the code using the theorem prover Boogie [10,11]. Barnett et al. [11] explained their lessons learned of constructing this verification framework. In contrast, we focus on how users solve programming and specification tasks. Petiot et al. [33] examined how programmers could be supported when a proof is not closed. They implemented tool support that categorizes the failure and gives counter examples to improve the user feedback. This idea is complementary to the CbC method by pinpointing the failure to a small Hoare triple, which was appreciated by the participants in this study. Johnson et al. [23] interviewed developers about the use of static analysis tools. They came to the same result as we did that good error reporting is crucial for developers. Hentschel et al. [21] studied the influence of formal methods to improve code reviews. They detected a positive impact of using the symbolic execution debugger (SED) to locate errors in already existing programs. This setup is different to our evaluation where the participants had to program actively. The KeY tool [12,13] was already evaluated to get insight into how participants use the tool interactively. In contrast, we wanted to evaluate the automatic part of KeY because we think that most users do not have a theoretical background to verify a program interactively.

Besides CorC and KeY, there are other programming languages and tools using specification for program verification. For example Eiffel [28,29] with the verifier AutoProof [24,35], SPARK [9], Whiley [32], OpenJML [15], Frama-C [16], VCC [14], Dafny [26,27], VeriFast [22], and VerCors [5]. These languages and verification tools can be used to compare CbC with post-hoc verification. As we only used a subset of the Java language in our experiment (comparable to a simple while language), the difference to other programming languages is minimal, and we expect similar results for those tools as with KeY.

A related CbC approach is the Event-B framework [1]. Here, automata-based systems are specified, and can be refined to concrete implementations. The Rodin platform [3] implements the Event-B method. For the predecessor of Event-B, namely the B method, Atelier B [2] is used to prove correctness. The main difference to CorC is the different abstraction level. CorC uses source code with specification rather than automata-based systems. The CbC approaches of Back [8] and Morgan [30] are related to CbC by Dijkstra, and it would be interesting to evaluate these approaches in comparison to our CbC tool in a future study. For example, ArcAngel [31] could be used as an implementation of Morgan's refinement calculus. Back et al. [6,7] build the invariant based programming tool SOCOS. They start explicitly with the specification of not only pre-/postconditions but also invariants before the coding process. In their experiment, they discovered that good tool support is needed and that invariants are found iteratively by refining an incomplete and partly wrong invariant; an insight which we can confirm.

6   Conclusion and Future Work

We compared correctness-by-construction and post-hoc verification by using the tools CorC and KeY. Participants could create and verify programs, but the majority failed to create invariants that were strong enough. When a program could not be verified, trial-and-error was the most popular strategy to fix the program. Regarding user experience, KeY and CorC were both considered useful to verify software, but the good feedback of CorC was explicitly highlighted. Nevertheless, the defects in the programs with CorC indicate that the participants need more time to get used to CorC.

We evaluated the user study qualitatively to get insights in how users create verified programs. For future work, we could repeat the experiment with more participants to get quantitative data about defects in the programs. Furthermore, our insights about the trial-and-error programming process could be used to improve the usability of both tools.

Acknowledgment. We would like to thank Alexander Knüppel and Domenik Eichhorn for their help with the user study. The hints and suggestions of Alexander helped to construct the final version of the study. Thanks to Domenik for setting up the tools.

References

1. Abrial, J.: Modeling in Event-B: System and Software Engineering. Cambridge University Press, Cambridge (2010)
2. Abrial, J.R., Abrial, J.R.: The B-Book: Assigning Programs to Meanings. Cambridge University Press, Cambridge (2005)
3. Abrial, J.R., Butler, M., Hallerstede, S., Hoang, T.S., Mehta, F., Voisin, L.: Rodin: an open toolset for modelling and reasoning in event-B. Int. J. Softw. Tools Technol. Transf. **12**(6), 447–466 (2010)
4. Ahrendt, W., Beckert, B., Bubel, R., Hähnle, R., Schmitt, P.H., Ulbrich, M.: Deductive Software Verification-The KeY Book: From Theory to Practice, vol. 10001. Springer, Heidelberg (2016). https://doi.org/10.1007/978-3-319-49812-6
5. Amighi, A., Blom, S., Darabi, S., Huisman, M., Mostowski, W., Zaharieva-Stojanovski, M.: Verification of concurrent systems with VerCors. In: Bernardo, M., Damiani, F., Hähnle, R., Johnsen, E.B., Schaefer, I. (eds.) SFM 2014. LNCS, vol. 8483, pp. 172–216. Springer, Cham (2014). https://doi.org/10.1007/978-3-319-07317-0_5
6. Back, R.-J.: Invariant based programming: basic approach and teaching experiences. Formal Aspects Comput. **21**(3), 227–244 (2009)
7. Back, R.-J., Eriksson, J., Myreen, M.: Testing and verifying invariant based programs in the SOCOS environment. In: Gurevich, Y., Meyer, B. (eds.) TAP 2007. LNCS, vol. 4454, pp. 61–78. Springer, Heidelberg (2007). https://doi.org/10.1007/978-3-540-73770-4_4
8. Back, R.-J., Wright, J.: Refinement Calculus: A Systematic Introduction. Springer, Heidelberg (2012)
9. Barnes, J.G.P.: High Integrity Software: The Spark Approach to Safety and Security. Pearson Education, London (2003)
10. Barnett, M., Fähndrich, M., Leino, K.R.M., Müller, P., Schulte, W., Venter, H.: Specification and verification: the Spec# experience. Commun. ACM **54**(6), 81–91 (2011)
11. Barnett, M., Leino, K.R.M., Schulte, W.: The Spec# programming system: an overview. In: Barthe, G., Burdy, L., Huisman, M., Lanet, J.-L., Muntean, T. (eds.) CASSIS 2004. LNCS, vol. 3362, pp. 49–69. Springer, Heidelberg (2005). https://doi.org/10.1007/978-3-540-30569-9_3
12. Beckert, B., Grebing, S., Böhl, F.: A usability evaluation of interactive theorem provers using focus groups. In: Canal, C., Idani, A. (eds.) SEFM 2014. LNCS, vol. 8938, pp. 3–19. Springer, Cham (2015). https://doi.org/10.1007/978-3-319-15201-1_1

13. Beckert, B., Grebing, S., Böhl, F.: How to put usability into focus: using focus groups to evaluate the usability of interactive theorem provers. Electron. Proc. Theor. Comput. Sci. **167**, 4–13 (2014)
14. Cohen, E., et al.: VCC: a practical system for verifying concurrent C. In: Berghofer, S., Nipkow, T., Urban, C., Wenzel, M. (eds.) TPHOLs 2009. LNCS, vol. 5674, pp. 23–42. Springer, Heidelberg (2009). https://doi.org/10.1007/978-3-642-03359-9_2
15. Cok, D.R.: OpenJML: JML for Java 7 by extending OpenJDK. In: Bobaru, M., Havelund, K., Holzmann, G.J., Joshi, R. (eds.) NFM 2011. LNCS, vol. 6617, pp. 472–479. Springer, Heidelberg (2011). https://doi.org/10.1007/978-3-642-20398-5_35
16. Cuoq, P., Kirchner, F., Kosmatov, N., Prevosto, V., Signoles, J., Yakobowski, B.: Frama-C. In: Eleftherakis, G., Hinchey, M., Holcombe, M. (eds.) SEFM 2012. LNCS, vol. 7504, pp. 233–247. Springer, Heidelberg (2012). https://doi.org/10.1007/978-3-642-33826-7_16
17. Dijkstra, E.W.: A Discipline of Programming. Prentice Hall, Upper Saddle River (1976)
18. Feigenspan, J., Kästner, C., Liebig, J., Apel, S., Hanenberg, S.: Measuring programming experience. In: 2012 IEEE 20th International Conference on Program Comprehension (ICPC), pp. 73–82. IEEE (2012)
19. Gries, D.: The Science of Programming. Springer, Heidelberg (1987)
20. Hall, A., Chapman, R.: Correctness by construction: developing a commercial secure system. IEEE Softw. **19**(1), 18–25 (2002)
21. Hentschel, M., Hähnle, R., Bubel, R.: Can formal methods improve the efficiency of code reviews? In: Ábrahám, E., Huisman, M. (eds.) IFM 2016. LNCS, vol. 9681, pp. 3–19. Springer, Cham (2016). https://doi.org/10.1007/978-3-319-33693-0_1
22. Jacobs, B., Smans, J., Piessens, F.: A quick tour of the VeriFast program verifier. In: Ueda, K. (ed.) APLAS 2010. LNCS, vol. 6461, pp. 304–311. Springer, Heidelberg (2010). https://doi.org/10.1007/978-3-642-17164-2_21
23. Johnson, B., Song, Y., Murphy-Hill, E., Bowdidge, R.: Why don't software developers use static analysis tools to find bugs? In: Proceedings of the 2013 International Conference on Software Engineering, pp. 672–681. IEEE Press (2013)
24. Khazeev, M., Rivera, V., Mazzara, M., Johard, L.: Initial steps towards assessing the usability of a verification tool. In: Ciancarini, P., Litvinov, S., Messina, A., Sillitti, A., Succi, G. (eds.) SEDA 2016. AISC, vol. 717, pp. 31–40. Springer, Cham (2018). https://doi.org/10.1007/978-3-319-70578-1_4
25. Kourie, D.G., Watson, B.W.: The Correctness-by-Construction Approach to Programming. Springer, Heidelberg (2012). https://doi.org/10.1007/978-3-642-27919-5
26. Leino, K.R.M.: Specification and verification of object-oriented software. Eng. Methods Tools Softw. Saf. Secur. **22**, 231–266 (2009)
27. Leino, K.R.M.: Dafny: an automatic program verifier for functional correctness. In: Clarke, E.M., Voronkov, A. (eds.) LPAR 2010. LNCS (LNAI), vol. 6355, pp. 348–370. Springer, Heidelberg (2010). https://doi.org/10.1007/978-3-642-17511-4_20
28. Meyer, B.: Eiffel*: a language and environment for software engineering. J. Syst. Softw. **8**(3), 199–246 (1988)
29. Meyer, B.: Applying "design by contract". Computer **25**(10), 40–51 (1992)
30. Morgan, C.: Programming from Specifications, 2nd edn. Prentice Hall, Upper Saddle River (1994)
31. Oliveira, M.V.M., Cavalcanti, A., Woodcock, J.: ArcAngel: a tactic language for refinement. Formal Aspects Comput. **15**(1), 28–47 (2003)

32. Pearce, D.J., Groves, L.: Whiley: a platform for research in software verification. In: Erwig, M., Paige, R.F., Van Wyk, E. (eds.) SLE 2013. LNCS, vol. 8225, pp. 238–248. Springer, Cham (2013). https://doi.org/10.1007/978-3-319-02654-1_13

33. Petiot, G., Kosmatov, N., Botella, B., Giorgetti, A., Julliand, J.: Your proof fails? Testing helps to find the reason. In: Aichernig, B.K.K., Furia, C.A.A. (eds.) TAP 2016. LNCS, vol. 9762, pp. 130–150. Springer, Cham (2016). https://doi.org/10.1007/978-3-319-41135-4_8

34. Runge, T., Schaefer, I., Cleophas, L., Thüm, T., Kourie, D., Watson, B.W.: Tool support for correctness-by-construction. In: Hähnle, R., van der Aalst, W. (eds.) FASE 2019. LNCS, vol. 11424, pp. 25–42. Springer, Cham (2019). https://doi.org/10.1007/978-3-030-16722-6_2

35. Tschannen, J., Furia, C.A., Nordio, M., Polikarpova, N.: AutoProof: auto-active functional verification of object-oriented programs. In: Baier, C., Tinelli, C. (eds.) TACAS 2015. LNCS, vol. 9035, pp. 566–580. Springer, Heidelberg (2015). https://doi.org/10.1007/978-3-662-46681-0_53

36. Watson, B.W., Kourie, D.G., Schaefer, I., Cleophas, L.: Correctness-by-construction and post-hoc verification: a marriage of convenience? In: Margaria, T., Steffen, B. (eds.) ISoLA 2016. LNCS, vol. 9952, pp. 730–748. Springer, Cham (2016). https://doi.org/10.1007/978-3-319-47166-2_52

RPLA 2019 - Workshop on Reversibility in Programming, Languages, and Automata

RPLA 2019 Organizers' Message

The International Workshop on Reversibility in Programming, Languages, and Automata (RPLA 2019) was organized by the Institut für Informatik of the Universität Giessen as a one-day event at October 9, 2019 to the 3rd World Congress of Formal Methods (FM 2019). The workshop took place in Porto, Portugal. Reversibility has attracted increasing interest in recent years. Many reversible computation models are natural objects of theoretical computer science. They are studied from different points of view in various areas with strong relations to both theoretical concepts and as formal models for applications. The aim of this workshop is to bring together researchers working on different aspects of reversibility in programming, languages, and automata in order to exchange and develop novel ideas. A deeper and interdisciplinary coverage of this particular area may gain new insights and substantial progress.

This chapter contains an extended abstract of the invited contribution and the papers accepted and presented at RPLA. We warmly thank the invited speaker Robert Glück (University of Copenhagen, Denmark) for accepting the invitation and presenting us several diverse perspectives on reversible programming. Altogether, there were six further presentations at RPLA 2019 presented by a total of 9 authors from 8 different countries. Three of this papers have been submitted and could be accepted as full papers. The submission and refereeing process was supported by the EasyChair conference management system. Each submission was single-blind reviewed by at least three referees and discussed by the Program Committee. We would like to thank all members of the Program Committee and the external reviewers for their excellent work. We also thank all authors and speakers for their contributions and work without which this event would not have been possible. All these efforts were the basis for the success of the workshop. We like to thank in particular Nelma Moreira from the University of Porto for her help and support for the workshop.

Finally, we are indebted to all participants for attending the workshop. We hope that this conference will be a successful and fruitful meeting, will bear new ideas for investigations, and will bring together people for new scientific collaborations.

December 2019

Markus Holzer
Martin Kutrib

Organization

Program Committee Chairs

Markus Holzer   Universität Giessen, Germany
Martin Kutrib   Universität Giessen, Germany

Program Committee

Markus Holzer   Universität Giessen, Germany
Jarkko Kari   University of Turku, Finland
Martin Kutrib   Universität Giessen, Germany
Kenichi Morita   Hiroshima University, Japan
Giovanni Pighizzini   University of Milan, Italy
Rogério Reis   University of Porto, Portugal
Sylvain Lombardy   Bordeaux INP – Institut Polytechnique de
                                    Bordeaux, France
Iain Phillips   Imperial College London, UK
Irek Ulidowski   University of Leicester, UK
Robin Kaarsgaard   University of Copenhagen, Denmark
Tetsuo Yokoyama   Nanzan University, Japan

Sponsoring Institutions

Centro de Matemática   Universidade do Porto, Portugal
Institut für Informatik   Universität Giessen, Germany

Reversible Computing from a Programming Language Perspective (Extended Abstract)

Robert Glück

DIKU, Department of Computer Science, University of Copenhagen,
Copenhagen, Denmark
glueck@acm.org

Software plays a central role in all aspects of reversible computing systems and a variety of reversible programming languages has been developed. This presentation highlights the principles and main ideas of reversible computing viewed from a programming language perspective with a focus on clean reversible languages. What I present is the "Copenhagen interpretation" of reversible computing.

Mainstream programming languages, such as C++ and Java, are deterministic in the forward direction of computation and nondeterministic in the backward direction. That is, at each state during the computation of a program, the next state is always uniquely determined, but not always the previous state. For instance, it is clear which branch of a conditional to choose, but after the conditional, in general, we cannot say which of the branches was chosen. Because their computation is forward deterministic (D) and backward nondeterministic (N), we categorize many of today's mainstream languages as (D, N).

Reversible programming languages are deterministic in both directions. At each state during a computation, both the next *and* the previous states are uniquely determined. We categorize reversible languages as (D, D). Exploring this domain fills a blank spot on the map of computing and is interesting in its own right. Sometimes it is a necessity, as in the case of quantum-inspired computing models and to overcome Landauer's physical limit [6]. Reversible computing complements, but does not replace, conventional (irreversible) computing.

Our hypothesis is that reversible computing principles manifest themselves in different guises on all levels of reversible computing systems, ranging from reversible hardware to reversible software, and across all language abstractions from low-level machine code to high-level languages. Our investigation into computing principles across the entire computation stack in a 100% clean reversible setting and independent of a particular language proved to be very fruitful, following the observation that it is easier to dilute than to distil essences.

Computationally speaking, mainstream languages are Turing-complete, *i.e.* they are as powerful as classical Turing machines. Reversible languages on the other hand are *r-Turing-complete*, *i.e.* they are as powerful as *reversible Turing machines* [3]. Given unbounded resources, they can realize any *injective* computable functions, which are only a subset of the computable functions. This may seem a severe limitation, but any computable function can be embedded in an injective computable function. For reversible programming, this means that either the functional specification of a program needs to be *injectivized* before writing the reversible program or an irreversible program needs to be *reversibilized* into a reversible program, *e.g.*, by recording the computation history. Injectivization of functions and reversibilization of programs are always possible, but at the expense of semantic modifications and operational overhead.

Reversible programs operate on the same data structures as irreversible programs (*e.g.*, stacks, arrays, lists), but they cannot overwrite any data, and can only perform *reversible updates* [2]. This makes reversible languages fundamentally different from their irreversible counterparts, which can perform destructive updates. Control-flow operators must be made backward deterministic in order to become reversible. Typically, each join point in the control flow is equipped in one way or another with a predicate that asserts from where control came. Reversible conditionals, reversible iterations, and reversible recursions are all available for programming. As a bare minimum, an r-Turing-complete reversible programming language consists of a reversible assignment, a reversible while-loop, and data built from a single constructor and a single symbol [4].

Because of their backward determinism, reversible languages can provide unconventional features that invoke the *inverse computation* of a program unit (*e.g.*, by allowing one to uncall a procedure, while standard computation of a procedure is invoked as usual by a call.) This enables code sharing and improved program reliability. Instead of writing two separate implementations of a procedure, *e.g.*, a lossless encoder and decoder [5], it is sufficient to write and verify one of them and to obtain the effect of the other by an uncall. However, reversible programming demands certain sacrifices because data cannot be overwritten and join points in the control flow require explicit assertions.

There are two and only two ways to implement a language, namely by an interpreter or a translator. The corresponding methods exist for implementing the inverse semantics of a language, namely by an *inverse interpreter* or a *program inverter* [1]. Like a translator, a program inverter takes a program as input but, instead of performing an equivalence transformation, transforms the program into its inverse. An inverse interpreter performs inverse computation. It should be stressed that both tools exist for *any* language, including irreversible ones (in all probability, the first inverse interpreter was for irreversible Turing machines [7]). In the special case of a reversible language, both methods are efficient and straightforward [8]. As usual, in practice various combinations exist, such as inverters in translators and interpreters on inverse interpreters.

As with conventional languages, there is no 'best' reversible language, but a variety of possibilities. There are structured and unstructured reversible flowcharts, low-level reversible assembler languages and high-level languages with imperative, functional and object-oriented features supported by dynamic memory management on reversible hardware, as well as domain-specific languages, such as reversible hardware description languages, and theoretically-oriented languages for abstract models such as reversible pushdown automata. Moreover, hybrid languages may combine irreversible and reversible features in novel ways.

In short, reversible computation is an emerging field of computer science that comprises all aspects of computing (theoretical, practical, technical and applied) and complements many of the traditional fields. It is here to stay.

References

1. Abramov, S.M., Glück, R.: The universal resolving algorithm and its correctness: inverse computation in a functional language. Sci. Comput. Program. **43**(2–3), 193–229 (2002)
2. Axelsen, H.B., Glück, R., Yokoyama, T.: Reversible machine code and its abstract processor architecture. In: Diekert, V., et al. (eds.) Computer Science – Theory and Applications, LNCS 4649, 56–69. Springer (2007)
3. Bennett, C.H.: Logical reversibility of computation. IBM J. Res. Dev. **17**(6), 525–532 (1973)
4. Glück, R., Yokoyama, T.: A minimalist's reversible while language. IEICE Trans. Inf. Syst. E100-D(5), 1026–1034 (2017)
5. Glück, R., Yokoyama, T.: Constructing a binary tree from its traversals by reversible recursion and iteration. Inf. Process. Lett. 147, 32–37 (2019)
6. Landauer, R.: Irreversibility and heat generation in the computing process. IBM J. Res. Dev. **5** (3), 183–191 (1961)
7. McCarthy, J.: The inversion of functions defined by Turing machines. In: Shannon, C.E., McCarthy, J., (eds.) Automata Studies, 177–181. Princeton Univ. Press (1956)
8. Yokoyama, T., Glück, R.: A reversible programming language and its invertible self-interpreter. In: Partial Evaluation and Program Manipulation, pp. 144–153. ACM (2007)

Reversible Programs Have Reversible Semantics

Robert Glück[1(✉)], Robin Kaarsgaard[1], and Tetsuo Yokoyama[2]

[1] DIKU, Department of Computer Science, University of Copenhagen,
Copenhagen, Denmark
`glueck@acm.org`, `robin@di.ku.dk`
[2] Department of Software Engineering, Nanzan University, Nagoya, Japan
`tyokoyama@acm.org`

Abstract. During the past decade, reversible programming languages have been formalized using various established semantic frameworks. However, these semantics fail to effectively specify the distinct properties of reversible languages at the metalevel, and even neglect the central question of whether the defined language is reversible. In this paper, we build on a metalanguage foundation for reversible languages based on the category of sets and partial injective functions. We exemplify our approach through step-by-step development of the full semantics of an r-Turing complete reversible while-language with recursive procedures. This yields a formalization of the semantics in which the reversibility of the language and its inverse semantics are immediate, as well as the inversion of programs written in the language. We further discuss applications and future research directions for reversible semantics.

1 Introduction

Over the past years, reversible programming languages ranging from imperative to functional and object-oriented languages have been formalized using established semantic frameworks, such as state transition functions, structural operational semantics and, recently, denotational semantics (*e.g.* [7,8,21,22]). These frameworks, which have been used to provide meaning to advanced language features and computation models, such as nondeterminism and parallelism, have turned out to be ineffective at specifying the distinct semantic properties of reversible languages. Immediate answers to questions regarding the uniqueness of the inverse semantics, the inversion of programs and, in particular, the central question of whether a language is reversible, are unavailable.

In this paper, we build on a metalanguage foundation for reversible languages based on the category **PInj** of sets and partial injective functions. The rationale behind this approach is straightforward: Interpretations of syntax are composed in ways that preserve their injectivity. More specifically, interpretations of syntax are composed of sequential composition, cartesian product, disjoint union, function inversion, iteration, and recursion. To achieve this, we make use of the categorical foundation developed elsewhere (*e.g.* [5,13]). Our approach exploits

© Springer Nature Switzerland AG 2020
E. Sekerinski et al. (Eds.): FM 2019 Workshops, LNCS 12233, pp. 413–427, 2020.
https://doi.org/10.1007/978-3-030-54997-8_26

the fact that reversible programs have reversible semantics: We regard a program as (compositionally) reversible iff each of its meaningful subprograms are partially invertible. This allows us to provide a clean reversible semantics to a reversible language.

We demonstrate the aforementioned idea through step-by-step development of a full formal semantics for the reversible procedural language R-WHILE, which includes iteration and recursion. This leads to a formal semantics in which the reversibility of the language and its inverse semantics are immediate, along with program inversion. The reversibility of the language follows immediately from the formalization. It is apparent from the signatures of semantic functions that the language is clean and without any hidden tracing. Note that this approach is independent of the specific details of the language and can be extended to other ways of composing semantic functions, provided their injectivity is preserved.

R-WHILE with procedures is a reversible while-language with structured control-flow operators and dynamic data structures [7,8].[1] This language is reversibly universal (r-Turing complete), which means that it is computationally as powerful as any reversible programming language can be. It has features representative of reversible imperative and functional languages, including reversible assignments, pattern matching, and inverse invocation of recursive procedures.

The metalanguage used here has a distinct property familiar from reversible programming: It is not possible to define an irreversible (non-injective) language semantics. To ensure reversibility, conventional metalanguages require discipline in the formalization, e.g., a standard denotational semantics. In the case of operational semantics, it is quite unclear how to restrict an inference system to a purely reversible one. One possible future direction is an investigation of metalanguage extensions to capture other composition forms and language features, which may include object-oriented features, combinators, and machine languages.

Overview: Sect. 2 introduces the elements of the formal semantics and Sect. 3 describes the reversible language R-WHILE with procedures. In Sect. 4, the formal semantics of the language is developed in a step-by-step manner. Sections 5 and 6 present related work, concluding remarks, and directions for future work. We assume the reader is familiar with the basic concepts of reversible languages (*e.g.*, [21]) and formal semantics (*e.g.*, [19]).

2   Elements of the Formal Semantics

This section is concerned with some of the details of sets and partial injective functions as they will be used in the following sections (compare, *e.g.*, [2,4, 17]). While the constructions mentioned in this section are extracted from the study of the category **PInj** of sets and partial injective functions, no categorical background is assumed (though a basic understanding of sets, partial functions, and domain theory is).

---

[1] An online interpreter for R-WHILE with procedures and the example program considered in this paper are available at http://tetsuo.jp/ref/RPLA2019.

2.1 Composition and Inversion

Partial functions are ordinary functions, save for the fact that they may be undefined on parts of their domain. To indicate that a partial function $X \xrightarrow{f} Y$ is undefined on some $x_0 \in X$ (*e.g.*, in the definition of a piecewise function), we use symbol ↑. A partial function is *injective* iff, whenever $f(x)$ and $f(y)$ are both defined and $f(x) = f(y)$, it is also the case that $x = y$. Injectivity is preserved by *composition* (*i.e.*, if $X \xrightarrow{f} Y$ and $Y \xrightarrow{g} Z$ are both partial injective functions so is $X \xrightarrow{g \circ f} Z$), and each identity function $X \xrightarrow{\text{id}} X$ is trivially injective.

Partial injective functions can be *inverted* in a unique way: for every partial injective function $X \xrightarrow{f} Y$, there exists a unique partial injective function $Y \xrightarrow{f^\dagger} X$, which undoes whatever f does (how rude!), in the sense that $f \circ f^\dagger \circ f = f$, and, vice versa, $f^\dagger \circ f \circ f^\dagger = f^\dagger$.

Aside from sequential composition, partial injective functions can also be composed in parallel in two ways. The first method utilizes the *cartesian product of sets* X and Y, which we denote $X \otimes Y$. If $X \xrightarrow{f} X'$ and $Y \xrightarrow{g} Y'$ are partial injective functions, we can form a new partial injective function on the cartesian product, $X \otimes Y \xrightarrow{f \otimes g} X' \otimes Y'$, by $(f \otimes g)(x, y) = (f(x), g(y))$. Note, however, that projections (such as $X \otimes Y \xrightarrow{\pi_1} Y$ given by $\pi_1(x, y) = x$) are *unavailable*, as these are never injective. We denote the unit, up to bijective correspondence, of the cartesian product (any distinguished singleton set is acceptable) by 1.

The second method of parallel composition is given on the *disjoint union of sets* X and Y, which we denote $X \oplus Y$. We think of elements of $X \oplus Y$ as being tagged with either left (inl ·) or right (inr ·) depending on their set of origin; for example, if $x \in X$ then inl $x \in X \oplus Y$, and if $y \in Y$ then inr $y \in X \oplus Y$. Up to bijective correspondence, the unit of disjoint union is the empty set $\emptyset$, which we will also denote as 0. The tagged union of partial injective functions $X \xrightarrow{f} X'$ and $Y \xrightarrow{g} Y'$ is then a partial injective function of tagged unions, $X \oplus X' \xrightarrow{f \oplus g} Y \oplus Y'$, which performs a case analysis of the inputs and tags the outputs with their origins:

$$(f \oplus g)(x) = \begin{cases} \text{inl } f(x') & \text{if } x = \text{inl } x' \\ \text{inr } g(x') & \text{if } x = \text{inr } x' \end{cases}$$

The cartesian product loses its projections in the setting of partial injective functions. However, the disjoint union retains its usual *injections*: $X \xrightarrow{\kappa_1} X \oplus Y$ and $Y \xrightarrow{\kappa_2} X \oplus Y$ given by $\kappa_1(x) = \text{inl } x$ and $\kappa_2(y) = \text{inr } y$, respectively. Note in particular that since we consider *partial* injective functions, these injections have partial inverses $\kappa_i^\dagger$ (sometimes called *quasiprojections*), which remove the tag but are only defined for elements from the i'th part of the union. For example, $X \oplus Y \xrightarrow{\kappa_1^\dagger} X$ is given by $\kappa_1^\dagger(\text{inl } x) = x$ and $\kappa_1^\dagger(\text{inr } y) = \uparrow$.

2.2   Fixed Points and Iteration

Both sets and partial injective functions are well-behaved as regards recursive definitions. For sets, any recursive definition of a set involving only disjoint unions, cartesian products, and already defined sets (including 0 and 1) has a unique least and greatest solution. As is usual in domain theory, we use $\mu X \ldots$ for the least solution (the least fixed point) and $\nu X \ldots$ for the greatest solution (the greatest fixed point), respectively. For example, the set of flat lists with entries taken from a set A is given by the least fixed point $\mu X.1 \oplus (A \otimes X)$.

A useful property of partial functions, as opposed to total functions, is that the set of all partial functions with a specified domain and target forms a directed complete partial order. This has useful consequences for the recursive description of partial injective functions. In particular, any continuous function $\mathbf{PInj}(X,Y) \to \mathbf{PInj}(X,Y)$ (where $\mathbf{PInj}(X,Y)$ denotes the set of partial injective functions between sets X and Y) has a least fixed point, which, by its definition, must be a partial injective function $X \to Y$ (*i.e.*, an element of $\mathbf{PInj}(X,Y)$). For the continuity requirement, we note that all previously presented operations on partial injective functions are continuous (*i.e.*, sequential composition, partial inversion, parallel composition using cartesian products and disjoint unions). Thus, any function involving only these operations is guaranteed to be continuous.

Finally, partial injective functions can also be tail-recursively described using the *trace* operator. Intuitively, the trace of a partial injective function $X \oplus U \xrightarrow{f} Y \oplus U$ is a function $X \xrightarrow{\mathrm{Tr}(f)} Y$, which is given as follows: if $f(\mathsf{inl}\ x) = \mathsf{inl}\ y$ for some y, this y is returned directly. Otherwise, if f is defined at $\mathsf{inl}\ x$, it must be the case that $f(\mathsf{inl}\ x) = \mathsf{inr}\ u$ for some u. If that case, this $\mathsf{inr}\ u$ is fed back into f, and the feedback loop continues until it either terminates to some $\mathsf{inl}\ y$, which is then returned, or fails to do so. In the latter case, the trace is undefined at x.

This trace operator may be described as a function $\mathbf{PInj}(X \oplus U, Y \oplus U) \xrightarrow{\mathrm{Tr}} \mathbf{PInj}(X,Y)$. It is most easily defined using a tail-recursively described pretrace $\mathbf{PInj}(X \oplus U, Y \oplus U) \xrightarrow{\mathsf{pretrace}} \mathbf{PInj}(X \oplus U, Y)$, which is defined as follows:

$$\mathsf{pretrace}(f)(x) = \begin{cases} y & \text{if } f(x) = \mathsf{inl}\ y \\ \mathsf{pretrace}(f)(\mathsf{inr}\ y) & \text{if } f(x) = \mathsf{inr}\ y \end{cases}$$

Hence, it is defined simply as $\mathrm{Tr}(f)(x) = \mathsf{pretrace}(f)(\mathsf{inl}\ x)$. The data flow of $\mathrm{Tr}(f)$ is illustrated in Fig. 1, in which the flow is from left to right and the feedback loop represents the repeated application of f to elements of U.

While less general than the fixed point (which can be used to describe arbitrary recursion), this tail recursion operator is very well behaved with respect to inversion, as it satisfies

Fig. 1. Data flow of trace $\mathrm{Tr}(f)$ with feedback loop.

$$\mathrm{Tr}(f^{\dagger}) = \mathrm{Tr}(f)^{\dagger}$$

for all partial injective functions $X \oplus U \xrightarrow{f} Y \oplus U$. (Formally, the trace operator can also be defined as a fixed point using the *trace formula*, see [9].)

$$e ::= x \mid \overline{s} \mid (e.e) \mid \mathsf{hd}(e) \mid \mathsf{tl}(e) \mid =?\ e\ e$$

$$q ::= x \mid \overline{s} \mid (q.q) \mid \mathsf{call}\ f(q) \mid \mathsf{uncall}\ f(q)$$

$$c ::= x \mathrel{\hat{=}} e \mid q \Leftarrow q \mid c; c \mid \mathsf{if}\ e\ \mathsf{then}\ c\ \mathsf{else}\ c\ \mathsf{fi}\ e \mid \mathsf{from}\ e\ \mathsf{do}\ c\ \mathsf{loop}\ c\ \mathsf{until}\ e$$

$$p ::= \mathsf{proc}\ f(q)\ c; \mathsf{return}\ q;$$

$$m ::= p \cdots p$$

Fig. 2. Syntax of the reversible language R-WHILE with procedures.

2.3 Summary of the Metalanguage

Collecting the injective constructs for the formal semantics introduced above, we can specify a clean reversible metalanguage $\mathcal{L}$ to describe objects of **PInj**:

$$f ::= a \mid \kappa_i \mid \mathsf{id} \mid \mu\phi.f \mid f \oplus f \mid f \otimes f \mid f \circ f \mid \mathrm{Tr}(f) \mid f^\dagger \mid \phi.$$

An atomic function a can be any auxiliary partial injective function, such as "swap" for cartesian products: $swap_\otimes(x, y) = (y, x)$. For any expression in $\mathcal{L}$, the least fixed point exists. The formal argument of the least fixed point ϕ expects a *program context*, i.e., a disjoint union of partial injective functions. $\mathcal{L}$ is closed under inversion, and the inverse semantics of each expression is unique and immediate. Any language described by the metalanguage is (compositionally) reversible. $\mathcal{L}$ is sufficiently expressive for full formalization of the semantics of reversibly-universal languages. This is demonstrated below for R-WHILE.

3   R-WHILE with Reversible Recursion and Iteration

We informally describe the semantics of the reversible language R-WHILE with procedures, and illustrate it with a recursive program that translates infix expressions to Polish notation; this is a classic translation that is reversible. The data domain of the language is tree-structured data (lists known from Lisp and many modern languages). Readers familiar with reversible programming can skip to Example 1 below and return to the informal description later.

The syntax of the language [8] is shown in Fig. 2. A *program* m is a sequence of procedures $p \cdots p$, where the topmost procedure is the main procedure. A *procedure* p has a name f, an argument pattern q, a command c as its body, and a return pattern q. The input to and output from a procedure is through the argument and return patterns, respectively. All procedures have arity and coarity one. Thus, it is convenient to compose and decompose input and output values via patterns.

A *command* c is a *reversible assignment* $x \mathrel{\hat{=}} e$, a *reversible replacement* $q \Leftarrow q$, a *reversible conditional* if...fi, or a *reversible loop* from...until. The latter are two control structures familiar from reversible flowchart languages (*e.g.*, [21]). The variable x in a reversible assignment $x \mathrel{\hat{=}} e$ must not occur in expression e, which calculates a value (*e.g.*, $x \mathrel{\hat{=}} x$ is not well formed). It is important

```
 1: proc infix2pre(t)            (* infix exp to Polish notation *)
 2:   y ⇐ call pre((t.nil));     (* call preorder traversal       *)
 3:   return y;
 4:
 5: proc pre2infix(y)            (* Polish notation to infix exp *)
 6:   (t.nil) ⇐ uncall pre(y);   (* uncall preorder traversal     *)
 7:   return t;
 8:
 9: proc pre((t.y))             (* recursive preorder traversal *)
10:   if =? t 0̄ then            (* tree t is a leaf?            *)
11:     y ⇐ (t.y)              (* add leaf to list y           *)
12:   else
13:     (l.(d.r)) ⇐ t;          (* decompose tree t             *)
14:     y ⇐ call pre((r.y));    (* traverse right subtree r     *)
15:     y ⇐ call pre((l.y));    (* traverse left  subtree l     *)
16:     y ⇐ (d.y)              (* add label d to list y        *)
17:   fi =? hd(y) 0̄;            (* head of list y is a leaf?    *)
18:   return y;
```

Fig. 3. Translation between infix expressions and Polish notation in R-WHILE.

to note that the assignment sets x to the value of e if the value of x is $\overline{nil}$, and sets x to $\overline{nil}$ if the values of x and e are equal; otherwise, it is undefined. In other words, a variable is updated or cleared depending on the original value of x. This definition ensures the reversibility of assignments.

No value is duplicated by a reversible replacement $q_1 \Leftarrow q_2$. Before the value constructed by q_2 is *matched* with q_1, all variables in q_2 are nil-cleared. Thus, the same variable may occur on both sides of a replacement (unlike an assignment).

Patterns play a central role in the construction and deconstruction of values, and are used in both ways (*e.g.*, reversible replacements). A *pattern* q is a variable x, a symbol $\overline{s}$, a pair of patterns $(q.q)$, or an invocation or inverse invocation of a procedure by call $f(q)$ or uncall $f(q)$, respectively. Patterns are linear (no variable occurs more than once in a pattern). The semantics of a procedure uncall is the inverse semantics of a procedure call. Procedures can only be invoked in patterns.

Expressions are conventional. An *expression* e is a variable x, a symbol $\overline{s}$, or the application of an operator, *i.e.*, constructor cons $(\cdot.\cdot)$, selectors head hd and tail tl, or equality test $=?$. The variables in a program are denoted by small letters, such as l, d, r, and symbols are overlined, such as $\overline{nil}$.

Example 1. There are many practical applications of translating infix expressions to Polish notation, and vice versa. Because this function is injective, it can be programmed cleanly in a reversible language and run in both directions.

In R-WHILE, infix expressions can be represented by full binary trees

$$tree ::= \overline{0} \mid (tree.(\overline{1}.tree)),$$

where symbols $\overline{0}$ and $\overline{1}$ stand for an operand (leaf) and an operator (inner label) in an expression, respectively. For simplicity, we only use these two symbols.

Figure 3 shows the recursive procedure *pre*, which reversibly translates an infix expression to a prefix expression (Polish notation) via a preorder traversal of the full binary tree t representing the infix expression. Procedure *pre* is called and uncalled in the two procedures *infix2pre* and *pre2infix* for translating to Polish notation, and vice versa. For example, the infix expression $t = ((\overline{0} \,.\, (\overline{1} \,.\, \overline{0})) \,.\, (\overline{1} \,.\, \overline{0}))$ translates to Polish notation $y = (\overline{1} \,.\, (\overline{1} \,.\, (\overline{0} \,.\, (\overline{0} \,.\, (\overline{0} \,.\, \overline{nil})))))$.

In *infix2pre*, the translation is invoked by a call to *pre* (line 2)

$$y \Leftarrow \mathsf{call}\ pre((t.\overline{nil})),$$

where the argument of the call is a singleton list $(t.\overline{nil})$ containing t, and the result is matched with the trivial pattern y, which binds the value to y. In *pre2infix*, the inverse computation of *pre* is invoked by an uncall of *pre* (line 6)

$$(t.\overline{nil}) \Leftarrow \mathsf{uncall}\ pre(y),$$

where y is the argument and t is picked from the resulting singleton list.

The body of *pre* is a reversible conditional if...fi (lines 10–17) with an entry test $=?\ t\ \overline{0}$ and an exit assertion $=?\ \mathsf{hd}(y)\ \overline{0}$. If t is a leaf $\overline{0}$, t is added to list y by $y \Leftarrow (t.y)$ (line 11). Otherwise, in the else-branch, *pre* calls itself recursively on the right and left subtrees r and l with the current list y (lines 14–15). The two subtrees and label d are selected from t by $(l.(d.r)) \Leftarrow t$. List y is constructed from right to left; thus, d is added after both subtrees are translated (line 16). The arity of all procedures is one; therefore, it is convenient to decompose the argument value by pattern $(t.y)$ already in the head of *pre* (line 9).

4 An Intrinsically Reversible Semantics

In this section, we illustrate the principle of reversible semantics by constructing a denotational semantics for R-WHILE with procedures using sets and partial injective functions. First, the domains of computation are constructed, followed by a semantic function for each syntactic category. While this approach yields a semantics for R-WHILE with procedures, for construction of such semantics for reversible programming languages in general, we stress the use of abstract concepts (*e.g.*, cartesian products, disjoint unions, traces, and fixed points), rather than the concrete realization of R-WHILE with procedures.

In the following, we use standard notation of denotational semantics [19], including brackets for semantic functions $[\![\cdot]\!]$, which show that the domain of the argument is syntax.

4.1 States and Values

We begin by constructing appropriate domains of computation for values and states. To achieve this, we assume that we are given an alphabet Λ of *symbols*, elements of which we denote using an overline, *e.g.*, $\overline{0}$, $\overline{1}$, and $\overline{nil}$. The set of values $\mathbb{V}$ is then constructed as the set of binary trees with elements from Λ at the leaves. More formally, this set can be constructed by the least fixed point of sets $\mathbb{V} = \mu X.\Lambda \oplus (X \otimes X)$. If t_1 and t_2 are such binary trees, we use the notation $t_1 \bullet t_2$ (read: "t_1 cons t_2") to mean the binary tree constructed from t_1 and t_2. A state associates each variable with a value. The set of states Σ can be constructed as finitely supported *colists* (*i.e.*, lists of infinite length) of values; that is, $\Sigma = \mathbb{V} \otimes \mathbb{V} \otimes \cdots$ (explicitly, this is constructed as the largest fixed point $\nu X.I \oplus (\mathbb{V} \otimes X)$). By associating each variable in the language (of which there are countably many) with a distinct index, a state is then precisely a description of the contents of all variables. In keeping with this principle, we write variables as x_1, x_2, x_3, etc. rather than as x, y, z etc. Note that the number of non-nil values in a state of a given program is finite.

4.2 Expressions

In irreversible languages, expressions are usually interpreted as partial functions of the signature $\Sigma \to \mathbb{V}$. Obviously, because there are multiple states resulting in the same value, such a function is not injective and cannot be an atomic function a in the metalanguage $\mathcal{L}$. Instead, expressions are interpreted as partial injective functions with signature

$$\Sigma \otimes \mathbb{V} \xrightarrow{\mathcal{E}[\![e]\!]} \Sigma \otimes \mathbb{V}.$$

Regardless of their syntactic form, expression interpretation is defined as

$$\mathcal{E}[\![e_1]\!](\sigma, v) = \begin{cases} (\sigma, \mathcal{E}'[\![e_1]\!]\sigma) & \text{if } v = \overline{nil} \\ (\sigma, \overline{nil}) & \text{if } v = \mathcal{E}'[\![e_1]\!]\sigma \neq \overline{nil} \\ \uparrow & \text{otherwise} \end{cases}$$

where $\mathcal{E}'[\![e]\!]\sigma \in \mathbb{V}$, given below, is understood to be the value of e in the state σ. When v in $\mathcal{E}[\![e_1]\!](\sigma, v)$ is $\overline{nil}$, the value of e_1 in σ is obtained. When v is equal to the value of e_1 in σ, $\overline{nil}$ is obtained. In both cases, σ is left unchanged. Otherwise, the meaning is undefined. The semantic function defines a *reversible update* [1] of the value argument, which also implies that it is self-inverse.

Concretely, $\mathcal{E}'$ is defined as follows, depending on the form of e:

$$\mathcal{E}'[\![x_i]\!]\sigma = v_i \quad \text{where } \sigma = (v_1, v_2, \ldots, v_i, \ldots)$$

$$\mathcal{E}'[\![\overline{s_1}]\!]\sigma = \overline{s_1}$$

$$\mathcal{E}'[\![(e_1.e_2)]\!]\sigma = \mathcal{E}'[\![e_1]\!]\sigma \bullet \mathcal{E}'[\![e_2]\!]\sigma$$

$$\mathcal{E}'[\![\mathsf{hd}(e_1)]\!]\sigma = \begin{cases} v_1 \text{ if } \mathcal{E}'[\![e_1]\!]\sigma = v_1 \bullet v_2 \\ \uparrow \text{ otherwise} \end{cases}$$

$$\mathcal{E}'[\![\mathsf{tl}(e_1)]\!]\sigma = \begin{cases} v_2 \text{ if } \mathcal{E}'[\![e_1]\!]\sigma = v_1 \bullet v_2 \\ \uparrow \text{ otherwise} \end{cases}$$

$$\mathcal{E}'[\![=? \ e_1 \ e_2]\!]\sigma = \begin{cases} \overline{nil} \bullet \overline{nil} \text{ if } \mathcal{E}'[\![e_1]\!]\sigma = \mathcal{E}'[\![e_2]\!]\sigma \\ \overline{nil} \quad \text{otherwise} \end{cases}$$

As such, the meaning of a variable in a state is given by its contents, and the meaning of a symbol is given by its direct representation in the alphabet Λ. The meaning of the cons of two expressions is given by the cons of their meanings, while the head (tail) of an expression takes the head (tail) of its meaning, diverging if not of this form. The meaning of equality test returns distinct values indicating whether the two expressions have the same value. Obviously, more operators can be added to this list.

A non-injective function is often used in the definition of an injective function in the context of reversible computation. Above, $\mathcal{E}[\![e]\!]$, a reversible update defined using non-injective $\mathcal{E}'[\![e]\!]$, is injective for any e. Because $\mathcal{E}[\![e]\!]$ is not defined exclusively in terms of the metalanguage, we regard it as defining an atomic function a of $\mathcal{L}$.

4.3 Patterns

As patterns may include procedure invocation, the meaning of a pattern depends on the program context ϕ in which it is interpreted. Patterns in a program context are all interpreted as partial injective functions with signature

$$\Sigma \xrightarrow{\mathcal{Q}[\![q]\!]\phi} \Sigma \otimes V.$$

In particular, note that this signature allows patterns to perform state alternations. Indeed, patterns may have side effects (here, in the form of altering the store). They should be regarded as a means to prepare a given value in a state, in such a manner that may alter the state it began with. Pattern interpretation is defined as follows, depending on the form of q:

$$\mathcal{Q}[\![x_i]\!]\phi(\sigma) = ((v_1, \ldots, v_{i-1}, \overline{nil}, \ldots), v_i) \quad \text{where } \sigma = (v_1, \ldots, v_{i-1}, v_i, \ldots)$$

$$\mathcal{Q}[\![\text{call } f_i(q_1)]\!]\phi(\sigma) = (\sigma', (\kappa_i^\dagger \circ \phi \circ \kappa_i)(v)) \quad \text{where } (\sigma', v) = \mathcal{Q}[\![q_1]\!]\phi(\sigma)$$

$$\mathcal{Q}[\![\text{uncall } f_i(q_1)]\!]\phi(\sigma) = (\sigma', (\kappa_i^\dagger \circ \phi^\dagger \circ \kappa_i)(v)) \quad \text{where } (\sigma', v) = \mathcal{Q}[\![q_1]\!]\phi(\sigma)$$

$$\mathcal{Q}[\![(q_1.q_2)]\!]\phi(\sigma) = (\sigma'', v_1 \bullet v_2)$$
$$\text{where } (\sigma', v_1) = \mathcal{Q}[\![q_1]\!]\phi(\sigma) \text{ and } (\sigma'', v_2) = \mathcal{Q}[\![q_2]\!]\phi(\sigma')$$

The meaning of a variable, as a pattern, is simultaneous extraction of its contents *and* clearing of the variable. A procedure call call $f_i(q_1)$ is interpreted as passing the value of q_1 to the i'th component of the program context ϕ, followed by extraction from the i'th component. As we discussed in Sect. 4.6, this corresponds precisely to invoking the i'th procedure. Uncalling of a procedure is handled analogously, but the *inverse* of the program context is used instead. Finally, the meaning of a cons pattern $(q_1.q_2)$ is as a kind of sequential composition: First, q_1 is executed, yielding a new state σ' and value v_1. Then, q_2 is executed in σ', yielding a final state σ'' and value v_2. The two values are then consed together, finally yielding the state σ'' and prepared value $v_1 \bullet v_2$. Recall that no variable occurs more than once in a pattern.

Alternatively, uncall can be defined using the inverted procedures instead of the inverse to the program context, $\phi^\dagger$, provided the inverted procedures are in ϕ. Addition of the inverse procedures to ϕ is discussed in Sect. 4.6.

4.4 Predicates

The predicate interpretation provides a different means of interpreting expressions for determining branching of control flow. They are interpreted as partial injective functions with signature

$$\Sigma \xrightarrow{\ \mathcal{T}[\![e]\!]\ } \Sigma \oplus \Sigma.$$

The definition is based on the convention that an expression interpreted as $\overline{nil}$ in a state σ is considered to be *false* in σ and *true* otherwise. The predicate interpretation of an expression e is defined as follows:

$$\mathcal{T}[\![e_1]\!](\sigma) = \begin{cases} \mathsf{inl}\ \sigma & \text{if } \mathcal{E}'[\![e_1]\!]\sigma \neq \overline{nil} \\ \mathsf{inr}\ \sigma & \text{otherwise} \end{cases}$$

As such, the predicate interpretation of e_1 sends the control flow to the first component if e_1 is considered true in the given state, and to the second component otherwise. As discussed in Sect. 4.5, this style allows straightforward interpretation of the *conditional execution* of commands. Here, inl and inr correspond to true and false in the semantics level, respectively.

4.5 Commands

Commands are interpreted as invertible state transformations, *i.e.*, as partial injective functions with signature

$$\Sigma \xrightarrow{\ \mathcal{C}[\![c]\!]\phi\ } \Sigma.$$

Command interpretation is defined as follows, depending on the form of c:

$$\mathcal{C}[\![c_1; c_2]\!]\phi = \mathcal{C}[\![c_2]\!]\phi \circ \mathcal{C}[\![c_1]\!]\phi$$

$$\mathcal{C}[\![x_i \mathrel{\hat{=}} e_1]\!]\phi = (\mathcal{Q}[\![x_i]\!]\phi)^\dagger \circ \mathcal{E}[\![e_1]\!] \circ \mathcal{Q}[\![x_i]\!]\phi$$

$$\mathcal{C}[\![q_1 \Leftarrow q_2]\!]\phi = (\mathcal{Q}[\![q_1]\!]\phi)^\dagger \circ \mathcal{Q}[\![q_2]\!]\phi$$

$$\mathcal{C}[\![\text{if } e_1 \text{ then } c_1 \text{ else } c_2 \text{ fi } e_2]\!]\phi = \mathcal{T}[\![e_2]\!]^\dagger \circ (\mathcal{C}[\![c_1]\!]\phi \oplus \mathcal{C}[\![c_2]\!]\phi) \circ \mathcal{T}[\![e_1]\!]$$

$$\mathcal{C}[\![\text{from } e_1 \text{ do } c_1 \text{ loop } c_2 \text{ until } e_2]\!]\phi = \mathrm{Tr}\left((\mathcal{C}[\![c_2]\!]\phi \oplus \mathrm{id}) \circ \mathcal{T}[\![e_2]\!] \circ \mathcal{C}[\![c_1]\!]\phi \circ \mathcal{T}[\![e_1]\!]^\dagger \right)$$

Note the use of *inverses* to patterns and predicates in the above definition. The inverse to a predicate corresponds to its corresponding *assertion*, whereas the inverse to a pattern performs *state preparation* consuming (part of) a value (rather than, in the forward direction, *value preparation* consuming part of a state).

Pattern inverses are illustrated in both reversible assignments and pattern matching, each consisting of a value preparation (indeed, the expression interpretation can be regarded as *side-effect-free* value preparation), using the interpretation of patterns, followed by a state preparation using the inverse. Similarly, the interpretation of conditionals and loops relies on predicate inverses. In both cases, they serve as conditional join points, corresponding to an assertion that e_2 is expected to be true when coming from the **then** branch of the conditional (respectively from the *outside* of the loop), and false when coming from the *else* branch (respectively from the *inside* of the loop).

4.6   Procedures

As procedures use the local state only, procedure definitions are interpreted (in a program context) as partial injective value transformations, *i.e.*, partial injective functions of the form

$$\mathbb{V} \xrightarrow{\mathcal{P}[\![f]\!]\phi} \mathbb{V}.$$

To define the procedure interpretation, we need an injective helper function $\mathbb{V} \xrightarrow{\xi} \Sigma \otimes \mathbb{V}$ given by

$$\xi(v) = (\overrightarrow{o}, v),$$

where $\overrightarrow{o} = (\overline{nil}, \overline{nil}, \dots)$ is the state in which all variables are cleared (*i.e.*, they contain $\overline{nil}$). This *canonical state* is the initial computation state in which all procedures are executed. A procedure definition in the program context ϕ is interpreted as

$$\mathcal{P}[\![\mathsf{proc}\ f(q_1)\ c; \mathsf{return}\ q_2]\!]\phi = \xi^\dagger \circ \mathcal{Q}[\![q_2]\!]\circ\mathcal{C}[\![c]\!]\phi \circ (\mathcal{Q}[\![q_1]\!]\phi)^\dagger \circ \xi.$$

This definition should be read as follows: in the canonical state $\overrightarrow{o}$, the state described by the inverse interpretation of the input pattern q_1 is first prepared. Then, the body of the procedure is executed, yielding a new state that is then used to prepare a value as specified by interpretation of the output pattern q_2. At this point, the system *must* again be in the canonical state $\overrightarrow{o}$. If this is the case, $\overrightarrow{o}$ can then be discarded, leaving only the output value.

4.7   Programs

Finally, programs are interpreted as the meaning of their topmost defined procedure and, thus, are interpreted as partial injective functions of signature

$$\mathbb{V} \xrightarrow{\mathcal{M}[\![m]\!]} \mathbb{V}.$$

As procedures may be defined to invoke themselves as well as other procedures, we must wrap them in a fixed point, passing the appropriate program context ϕ to each procedure interpretation. This yields the interpretation

$$\mathcal{M}[\![f_1 \cdots f_n]\!]=\kappa_1^\dagger \circ (\mu\phi.\mathcal{P}[\![f_1]\!]\phi \oplus \cdots \oplus \mathcal{P}[\![f_n]\!]\phi) \circ \kappa_1.$$

Note the inner interpretation of procedures $f_1 \cdots f_n$ as a disjoint union $\mathcal{P}[\![f_1]\!]\phi\oplus \cdots \oplus\mathcal{P}[\![f_n]\!]\phi$: This gives one large partial injective function, which behaves identically to the partial injective functions $\mathcal{P}[\![f_i]\!]\phi$ when inputs are injected into the

i'th component, save for the fact that outputs (if any) are also placed in the i'th component. This behavior explains the need for injections κ_i and quasiprojections $\kappa_i^\dagger$ in the definition of procedure calls in Sect. 4.3.

The interpretation ($\mathcal{M}[\![\cdot]\!]$, $\mathcal{P}[\![\cdot]\!]\phi$, and $\mathcal{C}[\![\cdot]\!]\phi$) maps syntax to injective (value, store, ...) transformations (on stores, values). The injective (value, store, ...) transformations can be expressed in $\mathcal{L}$.

4.8 Use of Inverse Semantics

In conventional programming languages, programs are not guaranteed to be injective, program inversion requires a global analysis, and inverse interpretation requires additional overhead. However, owing to the formalization, programs in object languages formalized in $\mathcal{L}$ are always injective, program inversion can be achieved through a recursive descendent transformation, and inverse interpretation often has a constant time overhead only. The intrinsic properties of the metalanguage are extremely helpful in deriving rules for program inversion. For any command c, the *inverse semantics* $(\mathcal{C}[\![c]\!]\phi)^\dagger$ can be a composition of the semantics of its components and traces, which can be mechanically obtained from the properties of **PInj** [5]. For example, we have

$$(\mathcal{C}[\![q_1 \Leftarrow q_2]\!]\phi)^\dagger = ((\mathcal{Q}[\![q_1]\!]\phi)^\dagger \circ \mathcal{Q}[\![q_2]\!]\phi)^\dagger = (\mathcal{Q}[\![q_2]\!]\phi)^\dagger \circ \mathcal{Q}[\![q_1]\!]\phi,$$

for a reversible replacement and, hence, we obtain the inverse replacement

$$(\mathcal{C}[\![q_1 \Leftarrow q_2]\!]\phi)^\dagger = \mathcal{C}[\![q_2 \Leftarrow q_1]\!]\phi.$$

The right-hand sides of the semantic function of commands are mostly symmetric. Therefore, their inversion rules are obtained in a similar way. The only exception is the loop, which requires an additional identity $\mathrm{Tr}((f_1 \oplus \mathrm{id}) \oplus f_2) = \mathrm{Tr}(f_2 \oplus (\mathrm{id} \oplus f_1))$ in order to yield the inversion rule. A similar anti-symmetry appears in the operational semantics of the reversible language Janus [22], in which the inference rule for the loop can be either right or left recursive.

As regards the semantic function of patterns, the inverse semantics of the program context, $\phi^\dagger$, defines the meaning of a procedure uncall. The inverse semantics of procedures is equal to the semantics of inverted procedures. This yields an alternative formalization of the same meaning. First, the inverted procedures are added to the program context in addition to the original procedures:

$$\mu\phi. \ \mathcal{P}[\![f_1]\!]\phi \oplus \cdots \oplus \mathcal{P}[\![f_n]\!]\phi \oplus (\mathcal{P}[\![f_1]\!]\phi)^\dagger \oplus \cdots \oplus (\mathcal{P}[\![f_n]\!]\phi)^\dagger.$$

Given such an extended program context ϕ, the access to the inverse semantics $\kappa_i^\dagger \circ \phi^\dagger \circ \kappa_i$ in the pattern execution $\mathcal{Q}[\![\mathsf{uncall}\ f_i(q_1)]\!]\phi(\sigma)$ (Sect. 4.3) can be replaced by $\kappa_{i+n}^\dagger \circ \phi \circ \kappa_{i+n}$; i.e., the $n + i$'th function is accessed.

5 Related Work

Formal meaning has been assigned to reversible programming languages using well-established formalisms, such as operational semantics to the imperative language Janus [22], the functional language RFUN [20], and the concurrent languages [15], small-step operational semantics to the assembler language PISA [1], transition functions to the flowchart language RFCL [21], and denotational semantics to R-WHILE [7,8]. However, the reversibility of a language is not directly expressed by these formalisms. It is the language designer's responsibility to guarantee the reversibility and to show the inversion properties of each language. Notably, the semantics of R-WHILE was first expressed irreversibly [22]. Note also that the type and effects systems have been studied for reversible languages [12].

In this paper, the reversible elements of R-WHILE were composed via the meta-language $\mathcal{L}$ in a manner that preserved their reversibility. In previous work, compositional approaches to reversibility were applied in various guises, *e.g.*, in the diagrammatic composition of reversible circuits from reversible logic gates and reversible structured flowcharts from reversible control-flow operators [21]. Similarly, reversible Turing machines have been constructed from reversible rotary elements [16].

To give meaning to reversible languages by interpreters and translators is another operational approach to a semantics. Examples of similar applications include the realization of reversible interpreters [7,22], translation of the high-level language R to the reversible assembler language PISA [3], and mapping hardware descriptions in SyReC to reversible circuits [18]. A different approach involves the reversibilization of irreversible languages by extending the operational semantics via tracing, so as to undo program runs [10]. Alternatively, irreversible programs can be inverted by program inverters, *e.g.*, [6]. Reversible cellular automata may have non-injective local maps; However, if the local map is injective, the update by the global map is guaranteed to be reversible [14].

6   Conclusion

Reversible systems have reversible semantics. In this study, we built upon a semantic foundation intended to describe the semantics of reversible programming languages. Our approach was demonstrated through the full development of a formal semantics for the reversibly universal language R-WHILE. This allowed us to concisely formalize features representative of many reversible languages, including iteration, recursion, pattern matching, dynamic data structures, and access to a program's inverse semantics. The intrinsic properties of the meta-language were essential for achieving formal reversible semantics. Hence, we argued that this approach provides a strong basis for understanding and reasoning about reversible programs.

Further exploration of the best description of advanced object-oriented structures, combinators, or features for concurrency, and the potentially useful meta-language features, may be interesting. Some related challenges include the characterization of reversible heap allocation and concurrent reversible computations. However, further explanation of the practical feasibility of the metalanguage and its relationship to advanced reversible automata including nondeterminism, *e.g.*, [11], is necessary.

Acknowledgments. Support in the form of EU COST Action IC1405 is acknowledged. The third author is supported by JSPS KAKENHI Grant Number 18K11250.

References

1. Axelsen, H.B., Glück, R., Yokoyama, T.: Reversible machine code and its abstract processor architecture. In: Diekert, V., Volkov, M.V., Voronkov, A. (eds.) CSR 2007. LNCS, vol. 4649, pp. 56–69. Springer, Heidelberg (2007). https://doi.org/10. 1007/978-3-540-74510-5_9
2. Cockett, R., Lack, S.: Restriction categories III: colimits, partial limits and extensivity. Math. Struct. Comput. Sci. **17**(4), 775–817 (2007)
3. Frank, M.P.: Reversibility for efficient computing. Ph.D. thesis, MIT (1999)
4. Giles, B.: An investigation of some theoretical aspects of reversible computing. Ph.D. thesis, University of Calgary (2014)
5. Glück, R., Kaarsgaard, R.: A categorical foundation for structured reversible flowchart languages: Soundness and adequacy. Log. Methods Comput. Sci. **14**(3) (2018)
6. Glück, R., Kawabe, M.: Revisiting an automatic program inverter for Lisp. SIGPLAN Not. **40**(5), 8–17 (2005)
7. Glück, R., Yokoyama, T.: A minimalist's reversible while language. IEICE Trans. Inf. Syst. E100-D **100**(5), 1026–1034 (2017)
8. Glück, R., Yokoyama, T.: Constructing a binary tree from its traversals by reversible recursion and iteration. IPL **147**, 32–37 (2019)
9. Haghverdi, E.: A categorical approach to linear logic, geometry of proofs and full completeness. Ph.D. thesis, Carlton Univ. and Univ. Ottawa (2000)
10. Hoey, J., Ulidowski, I., Yuen, S.: Reversing parallel programs with blocks and procedures. In: Pérez, J.A., Tini, S. (eds.) Expressiveness in Concurrency, Structural Operational Semantics. Electronic Proceedings in TCS, vol. 276, pp. 69–86 (2018)
11. Holzer, M., Kutrib, M.: Reversible nondeterministic finite automata. In: Phillips, I., Rahaman, H. (eds.) RC 2017. LNCS, vol. 10301, pp. 35–51. Springer, Cham (2017). https://doi.org/10.1007/978-3-319-59936-6_3
12. James, R.P., Sabry, A.: Information effects. In: POPL, pp. 73–84. ACM (2012)
13. Kaarsgaard, R., Axelsen, H.B., Glück, R.: Join inverse categories and reversible recursion. J. Log. Algebr. Methods **87**, 33–50 (2017)
14. Kari, J.: Reversible cellular automata: from fundamental classical results to recent developments. New Gener. Comput. **36**(3), 145–172 (2018)
15. Kuhn, S., Ulidowski, I.: A calculus for local reversibility. In: Devitt, S., Lanese, I. (eds.) RC 2016. LNCS, vol. 9720, pp. 20–35. Springer, Cham (2016). https://doi. org/10.1007/978-3-319-40578-0_2
16. Morita, K.: Reversible computing and cellular automata – a survey. Theor. Comput. Sci. **395**(1), 101–131 (2008)
17. Selinger, P.: A survey of graphical languages for monoidal categories. In: Coecke, B. (ed.) New Structures for Physics. LNP, vol. 813, pp. 289–355. Springer, Heidelberg (2011). https://doi.org/10.1007/978-3-642-12821-9_4
18. Wille, R., Schönborn, E., Soeken, M., Drechsler, R.: SyReC: a hardware description language for the specification and synthesis of reversible circuits. Integration **53**, 39–53 (2016)
19. Winskel, G.: The Formal Semantics of Programming Languages: An Introduction. MIT Press, Cambridge (1993)
20. Yokoyama, T., Axelsen, H.B., Glück, R.: Towards a reversible functional language. In: De Vos, A., Wille, R. (eds.) RC 2011. LNCS, vol. 7165, pp. 14–29. Springer, Heidelberg (2012). https://doi.org/10.1007/978-3-642-29517-1_2

21. Yokoyama, T., Axelsen, H.B., Glück, R.: Fundamentals of reversible flowchart languages. Theor. Comput. Sci. **611**, 87–115 (2016)
22. Yokoyama, T., Glück, R.: A reversible programming language and its invertible self-interpreter. In: PEPM, pp. 144–153. ACM (2007)

Two-Way Quantum and Classical Automata with Advice for Online Minimization Problems

Kamil Khadiev[1,2(✉)] and Aliya Khadieva[2,3]

[1] Smart Quantum Technologies Ltd., Kazan, Russia
kamilhadi@gmail.com
[2] Kazan Federal University, Kazan, Russia
aliya.khadi@gmail.com
[3] University of Latvia, Riga, Latvia

Abstract. We consider online algorithms. Typically the model is investigated with respect to competitive ratio. In this paper, we explore two-way automata as a model for online algorithms. We focus on quantum and classical online algorithms. We show that there are problems that can be solved more efficiently by two-way automata with quantum and classical states than classical two-way automata in the case of sublogarithmic memory (sublinear size) even if classical automata get advice bits.

Keywords: Quantum computation · Online algorithms · Streaming algorithms · Online minimization problems · Two-way automata · Automata

1 Introduction

Online algorithms are a well-known computational model for solving optimization problems. The peculiarity is that the algorithm reads an input piece by piece and should return an answer piece by piece immediately, even if the answer can depend on future pieces of the input. The algorithm should return an answer for minimizing (maximizing) an objective function (the cost of the output). There are different methods to define the effectiveness of online algorithms [13,17], but the most standard is the competitive ratio [28,42]. Typically, online algorithms have unlimited computational power. At the same time, it is quite interesting to solve online minimization problems in the case of a big input stream such that the stream cannot be stored completely in the memory. As the algorithms, we can consider Turing machines with restricted memory or two-way automata with non-constant size (a number of states). In the paper, we focus on two-way automata. Streaming algorithms or one-way automata as online algorithms were considered in [9,14,26,30,34–36]. We focus on *quantum online algorithms*. This model was introduced in [35] and discussed in [1]. In the case of one-way

© Springer Nature Switzerland AG 2020
E. Sekerinski et al. (Eds.): FM 2019 Workshops, LNCS 12233, pp. 428–442, 2020.
https://doi.org/10.1007/978-3-030-54997-8_27

streaming algorithms, it is known that quantum online streaming algorithms can be better than classical ones [30, 35]. Another model that was considered by researchers is quantum online streaming algorithms with repeated test [45].

In this paper, we explore quantum online algorithms that have the only restriction on memory but have no restriction on access to already taken input variables. We mean two-way automata as online algorithms [33]. This model is more close to the general model of online algorithms comparing to online streaming algorithms or online streaming algorithms with repeated test. The question of comparing quantum and classical models was explored for streaming algorithms (OBDDs and one-way automata) [2–4, 6, 7, 21–25, 31, 32, 38, 39], and for two-way automata [8]. Our results use these ones as a base.

Moreover, we are interested in an *advice complexity* measure [12, 15, 16, 19, 20, 37]. In this case, an online algorithm gets some bits of advice about an input. A trusted *Adviser* sending these bits knows the whole input and has unlimited computational power. Deterministic and randomized online algorithms with advice are considered in [10, 27, 37]. If we consider online streaming algorithms with advice, then the quantum model can be better than classical ones [34–36]. We compare the power of quantum online algorithms and classical ones in the case of two-way automata. This question was not investigated before. Typically, term "Adviser" is used in online algorithms theory; and term "Oracle" in the case of other models. We use the "Black Hats Method" for constructing hard online minimization problems [34, 36]. We present problems for a separation between the power of quantum and classical two-way automata using this method. Suppose that algorithms use only $o(\log n)$ bits of memory ($n^{o(1)}$ states) in the case of exponential expected working time and $o\left((\log n)^{0.5-\alpha}\right)$ bits of memory ($n^{o\left((\log n)^{-(0.5+\alpha)}\right)}$ states) in the case of polynomial expected working time, where n is the length of an input, $0 < \alpha < 0.5$. For both cases (exponential and polynomial working time), we have two results:

(i) There is a special online minimization problem that has a two-way automaton with classical and quantum states with better competitive ratio than any two-way classical (probabilistic or deterministic) automata, even if the classical ones have a non-constant number of advice bits.

(ii) For the same problem, a two-way automaton with classical and quantum states has a better competitive ratio than any deterministic online algorithm with unlimited computational power has.

We consider problems that are based on "Black Hats Method" [34, 36]; *Palindrome* and *Unitary equality* languages from [8].

The paper is organized as follows. We present definitions in Sect. 2. Black Hats Method is described in Sect. 3. A discussion on two-way automata with quantum and classical states vs. classical ones is given in Sect. 4.

2   Preliminaries

An online minimization problem consists of a set $\mathcal{I}$ of inputs and a cost function. Each input $I \in \mathcal{I}$ is a sequence of requests $I = (x_1, \ldots, x_n)$.

Furthermore, a set of feasible outputs (or solutions) is associated with each I; an output is a sequence of answers $O = (y_1, \ldots, y_n)$. The cost function assigns a positive real value $cost(I, O)$ to a feasible input I and a feasible output O. For each input I, we call any feasible output O for I that has the smallest possible cost (i. e., that minimizes the cost function) an optimal solution for I. The goal is the searching for the optimal solution for I.

Let us define an online algorithm for this problem as an algorithm which gets requests x_i from $I = (x_1, \ldots, x_n)$ one by one and should return answers y_i from $O = (y_1, \ldots, y_n)$ immediately, even if an optimal solution can depend on future requests. **A deterministic online algorithm** A computes the output sequence $A(I) = (y_1, \ldots, y_n)$ such that y_i is computed from $x_1, \ldots, x_i$. We say that a deterministic online algorithm A is c-*competitive* if there exists a non-negative constant α such that, for every n and for any input I of size n, we have: $cost(I, A(I)) \leq c \cdot cost(I, Opt(I)) + \alpha$, where Opt is an optimal offline algorithm for the problem and c is the minimal number that satisfies the inequality. Also we call c the **competitive ratio** of A. If $\alpha = 0, c = 1$, then A is optimal.

An online algorithm A **with advice** computes an output sequence $A^\phi(I) = (y_1, \ldots, y_n)$ such that y_i is computed from $\phi, x_1, \ldots, x_i$, where ϕ is the message from the adviser, who knows the whole input. A is c-competitive with advice complexity $b = b(n)$ if there exists a non-negative constant α such that, for every n and for any input I of size n, there exists some ϕ such that $cost(I, A^\phi(I)) \leq c \cdot cost(I, Opt(I)) + \alpha$ and $|\phi| \leq b$; $|\phi|$ is a length of ϕ.

A randomized online algorithm R computes an output sequence $R^\psi(I) = (y_1, \ldots, y_n)$ such that y_i is computed from $\psi, x_1, \ldots, x_i$, where ψ is the content of the random tape, i. e., an infinite binary sequence, where every bit is chosen uniformly at random and independently of all the others. By $cost(I, R^\psi(I))$ we denote the random variable expressing the cost of the solution computed by R on I. R is c-competitive in expectation if there exists a constant $\alpha > 0$ such that, for every I, $\mathbb{E}\left[cost(I, R^\psi(I))\right] \leq c \cdot cost(I, Opt(I)) + \alpha$.

We use two-way automata for online minimization problems as online algorithms with restricted memory. Let us give definitions of automata.

A two-way deterministic automaton working on inputs of length/size $m \geq 0$ (2DA) D is a 6-tuple $D = (\Sigma, \Gamma, S, s_1, \delta, Result)$, where (i) Σ is an input alphabet; (ii) Γ is an output alphabet; (iii) $S = \{s_1, \ldots, s_d\}$ is the set of states (d can be a function in m), $s_1 \in S$ is the initial state; (iv) $Results : S \to \Gamma$ is a function that transforms a state to an output symbol; (v) $\delta : S \times \Sigma \to S \times \{\leftarrow, \downarrow, \rightarrow\}$ is a transition function. Any given input $u \in \Sigma^m$ is placed on a read-only tape with a single head as $\mathvarphi u_1 u_2 \ldots u_m \$\diamond$, where $u_i \in \Sigma$ is the i-th symbol of u, $\mathcal{c}$ is a left end marker and $\$, \diamond$ are right end markers. When D is in $s \in S$ and reads $u_i \in \Sigma$ on the tape, the automaton switches to state $s' \in S$ and updates the head position with respect to $a \in \{\leftarrow, \downarrow, \rightarrow\}$ if $\delta(s, u_i) \to (s', a)$. If $a = $ " $\leftarrow$ " (" $\rightarrow$ "), then the head moves one square to the left (the right), and, it stays on the same square, otherwise. The transition function δ must be defined to guarantee that the head never leaves $\mathcal{c}u\$\diamond$ during the computation.

Moreover, if the automaton reaches the second endmarker ⋄ in a state s, then D finishes the computation and returns $Result(s)$ as a result.

The probabilistic counterpart of 2DA, denoted 2PA, can choose from more than one transition in each step such that each transition is associated with a probability. Thus, 2PAs can be in a probability distribution over the deterministic configurations (the state and the position of the head forms a configuration) during the computation. The total probability must be 1, i.e., the probability of outgoing transitions from a single configuration must be 1. Thus, a 2PA returns some result for each input with some probability. For $v \in \Gamma$, a 2PA returns a result v for an input, with bounded-error if the 2PA returns the result v with probability at least $1/2 + \varepsilon$ for some $\varepsilon \in (0, 1/2]$.

Let us use these models for online minimization problems. A **2DA for online minimization problems** A computes the output sequence $A(I) = (y_1, \ldots, y_n)$ where y_i is a result of computation A on the input $\mathbb{¢}x_1, \ldots, x_i \$ \diamond$, such that A starts from a state s that is the final state for computing y_{i-1}, and the input head observes x_1. A **2PA**, a **2DA with advice** and a **2PA with advice for online minimization problems** have similar definitions, but with respect to definitions of corresponding models of online algorithms.

Let us define the quantum counterparts of the models. You can read more about quantum automata in [7, 8, 40]. Quantum devices manipulate quantum states. A quantum state can be described by a 2^q-dimensional vector from Hilbert space over the field of complex numbers. Here q is a number of quantum bits (qubits). A unitary transformation is applying $2^q \times 2^q$ (left) unitary matrices of complex numbers. Let us describe the measurement process. Suppose that an automaton is in a distribution of quantum states $|\psi\rangle = (v_1, \ldots, v_{2^q})$ before a measurement and measures the i-th qubit. Suppose states with numbers $a_1^0, \ldots, a_{2^{q-1}}^0$ correspond to the 0 value of the i-th qubit, and states with numbers $a_1^1, \ldots, a_{2^{q-1}}^1$ correspond to the 1 value of the qubit. Then the result of the measurement of the qubit is 1 with probability $pr_1 = \sum_{j=1}^{2^{q-1}} |v_{a_j^1}|^2$ and 0 with probability $pr_0 = 1 - pr_1$. If the algorithm measures z qubits on the j-th step, then it gets number $\gamma \in \{0, \ldots, 2^z - 1\}$ as a result of the measurement.

A **quantum online algorithm** Q computes the output sequence $Q(I) = (y_1, \ldots, y_n)$ such that y_i depends on $x_1, \ldots, x_i$. The algorithm uses quantum memory, and can apply unitary transformations to quantum memory and measure qubits several times during a computation. Note that a quantum computation is a probabilistic process. Q is c-competitive in expectation if there exists a constant $\xi \geq 0$ such that, for every I, $\mathbb{E}\left[cost(I, Q(I))\right] \leq c \cdot cost(I, Opt(I)) + \xi$.

Let us consider a **two-way automaton with quantum and classical states** (2QCA), which is a 9-tuple $M = (Q, S, \Sigma, \Gamma, \theta, \delta, v_1, s_1, Result)$, where (i) Q and S are sets of quantum and classical states respectively; (ii) θ and δ are quantum and classical transition functions; (iii) $v_1 \in Q$ and $s_1 \in S$ are initial quantum and classical states; (iv) Σ is an input alphabet and Γ is an output alphabet; (v) $Results : S \to \Gamma$ is a function that obtain output symbol by a state. The function θ specifies the evolution of the quantum portion of the internal state: for each pair $(s, x) \in S \times \Sigma$, $\theta(s, x)$ is an action to be performed on the quantum portion of the internal state of M. Each action $\theta(s, x)$ corresponds to either a unitary transformation or an orthogonal measurement. The function δ specifies the evolution of the classical part of M (i.e., the classical part of the internal state and the tape head). In a case $\theta(s, x)$ is a unitary transformation, $\delta(s, x)$ is an element of $S \times \{\leftarrow, \downarrow, \rightarrow\}$ specifying a new classical state and a movement of the tape head. In a case $\theta(s, x)$ is a measurement, $\delta(s, x)$ is a mapping from the set of possible results of the measurement to $S \times \{\leftarrow, \downarrow, \rightarrow\}$ (again specifying a new classical state and a tape head movement, this time one such pair for each outcome of the observation). It is assumed that δ is defined so that the tape head never moves left when scanning the left end-marker $\not{c}$, and never moves right when scanning the right end-marker $\diamond$. Other restrictions and behavior are similar to 2DA. We can define **2QCA for online minimization problems** in the same way as for 2DA for online minimization problems. The 2QCA model is similar to 2QCFA model from [8] but the size (the number of states) of 2QCA can depend on the length of the input m. The same difference between 2DA and 2DFA, 2PA and 2PFA.

In the paper we use the terminology for branching programs [43] and algorithms. We say that an automaton computes a Boolean function f_m if for any input X of length m, the automaton returns result 1 iff $f(X) = 1$. We say that an automaton has s bits of memory if it has 2^s states.

3   Two-Way Automata for Black Hats Online Minimization Problem

Let us describe the "black hats method" from [34, 36] that allows us to construct hard online minimization problems. In the paper we discuss a Boolean function f, but in fact we consider a family of Boolean functions $f = \{f_1, f_2, \ldots\}$, for $f_m : \{0, 1\}^m \to \{0, 1\}$. We use notation $f(X)$ for $f_m(X)$ if the length of X is m and it is clear from the context.

Suppose we have a Boolean function f and integers $k, r, w, t > 0$, where $k \bmod t = 0$. Then an online minimization problem $BH_{k,r,w}^t(f)$ is the following. We have k guardians and k prisoners. They stay one by one in a line like $G_1 P_1 G_2 P_2 \ldots$, where G_i is a guardian, P_i is a prisoner. The prisoner P_i has an input X_i of length m_i and computes a function $f_{m_i}(X_i)$. The prisoner paints his hat black or white with respect to the result 1 or 0. Each guardian wants to know the parity of a number of following black hats. So, G_i wants to compute $f_{m_i}(X_i) \oplus \cdots \oplus f_{m_k}(X_k)$. We split sequential guardians into t blocks. The cost of a block is r if all guardians of the block are right; and w, otherwise. Let us define the problem formally:

Definition 1 (Black Hats Method). *We have a Boolean function f. Then an online minimization problem $BH_{k,r,w}^t(f)$, for integers $k, r, w, t > 0$, where $k \bmod t = 0$, is the following. Suppose we have an input $I = (x_1, \ldots, x_n)$ and k integers $m_1, \ldots, m_k > 0$, where $n = \sum_{i=1}^{k}(m_i + 1)$. Let $I = 2\ X_1\ 2\ X_2\ 2\ X_3\ 2\ \ldots\ 2\ X_k$, where $X_i = (x_1^i, \ldots, x_{m_i}^i) \in \{0, 1\}^{m_i}$, for $i \in \{1, \ldots, k\}$. Let O be a sequence of answers that corresponds to the input I. Let $O' = (y_1, \ldots, y_k)$ be answer variables* *corresponding to input variables with value 2 (in other words, output variables for guardians). An answer variable y_j corresponds to an input variable x_{i_j}, where $i_j = j + \sum_{r=1}^{j-1} m_r$. Let $g_j(I) = \bigoplus_{i=j}^{k} f_{m_i}(X_i)$. We separate all answer variables y_i to t blocks of length $z = k/t$. The cost of the i-th block is c_i. Here $c_i = r$ if $y_j = g_j(I)$ for $j \in \{(i-1)z + 1, \ldots, i \cdot z\}$; and $c_i = w$, otherwise. The cost of the whole output is $cost^t(I, O) = c_1 + \cdots + c_t$.*

We can show that any 2DA using s bits of memory cannot solve $BH_{k,r,w}^t(f)$ if there is no 2DA computing the function f using s bits of memory.

Theorem 1. *Let s be a positive integer. Suppose a Boolean function f is such that no 2DA for f uses at most s bits of memory. Then there is no c-competitive 2DA for $BH_{k,r,w}^t(f)$ using s bits of memory, where $c < w/r$.*

Proof. Let us consider any 2DA A for the $BH_{k,r,w}^t(f)$ problem that uses at most s bits of memory. Suppose that A returns y_1 as an answer of the first guardian. Let us prove that there are two parts of the input $X_1^0, X_1^1 \in \{0,1\}^{m_1}$ such that A returns the same value y_2 for both, but $f(X_1^0) = 0, f(X_1^1) = 1$. Assume that there is no such triple (y_2, X_1^0, X_1^1). Then, we can construct a 2DA A' that uses s bits of memory and has the following property: $A'(X_1') = A'(X_1'')$ iff $f(X_1') = f(X_1'')$, for any $X_1', X_1'' \in \{0,1\}^{m_1}$. The automaton A' emulates the automaton A. Therefore, A' computes f or $\neg f$. In the case of $\neg f$, we can construct A'' such that $A''(X_1) = \neg A'(X_1)$. It is a contradiction with the claim of the theorem. By the same way, we can show existence of similar triples (y_{i+1}, X_i^0, X_i^1) for $i \in \{2, \ldots, k\}$. Let us choose $\sigma_i = y_i \oplus 1 \oplus \bigoplus_{j=i+1}^{k} \sigma_j$, for $i \in \{1, \ldots, k\}$. Let us consider an input $I_A = 2X_1^{\sigma_1} 2 \ldots 2X_k^{\sigma_k}$. An optimal offline solution is $(g_1, \ldots, g_k)$ where $g_i = \bigoplus_{j=i}^{k} \sigma_j$. Let us prove that $g_i \neq y_i$ for each $i \in \{1, \ldots, k\}$. We have $\sigma_i = y_i \oplus 1 \oplus \bigoplus_{j=i+1}^{k} \sigma_j$. Therefore, $y_i = \sigma_i \oplus 1 \oplus \bigoplus_{j=i+1}^{k} \sigma_j = 1 \oplus \bigoplus_{j=i}^{k} \sigma_j = 1 \oplus g_i$, so $y_i = \neg g_i$. Hence, all answers are wrong and $cost^t(I_A, A(I_A)) = tw$. So the competitive ratio c cannot be less than $tw/(tr) = w/r$. $\square$

The similar result holds for probabilistic two-way automata.

Theorem 2. *Let s be a positive integer. Suppose a Boolean function f is such that no 2PA uses at most s bits of memory and computes f with bounded error. Then there is no c-competitive in expectation 2PA using s bits of memory and solving $BH_{k,r,w}^t(f)$ with bounded error, where $c < 2^{-z} + (1 - 2^{-z})w/r$.*

Proof (Sketch). The proof is similar to deterministic case but we can guess unknown bits with probability 0.5. $\square$

There is a bound on the competitive ratio in the case of unlimited computational power for a deterministic online algorithm.

Theorem 3 ([34])

Claim 1. There is no c-competitive deterministic online algorithm A computing $BH_{k,r,w}^t(f)$, for $c < \left(\lfloor (t+1)/2 \rfloor \cdot w + (t - \lfloor (t+1)/2 \rfloor) \cdot r\right)/(tr)$.

Claim 2. There is no c-competitive deterministic online algorithm A for $BH^1_{k,r,w}(f)$, for $c < w/r$.

Theorem 4. *Let us consider a Boolean function f. Suppose we have a 2QCA R that computes f with bounded error ε using s classical bits and s quantum bits of memory, where $0 \le \varepsilon < 0.5$. Then there is a 2QCA A for $BH^t_{k,r,w}(f)$ that uses at most $s + O(1)$ classical bits and at most $s + 1$ quantum bits of memory, and has expected competitive ratio $c \le \left(0.5(1 - \varepsilon)^{z-1} \cdot (r - w) + w\right)/r$.*

Proof. Let us present the 2QCA A:

Step 1. The automaton A guesses y_1 with equal probabilities and stores it in a qubit $|p\rangle$: the automaton initializes the qubit $|p\rangle = \frac{1}{\sqrt{2}}|0\rangle + \frac{1}{\sqrt{2}}|1\rangle$. Then A measures $|p\rangle$ and returns a result of the measurement as y_1.

Step 2. The automaton reads X^1 and computes $|p\rangle$ as a result of CNOT or XOR of $|p\rangle$ and $R(X^1)$, where $R(X^1)$ is the result of computation for R on the input X^1, i.e. $|p\rangle \to |p \oplus R(X^1)\rangle$. The automaton A uses a register $|\psi\rangle$ of s qubits for processing X^1. Then the automaton returns a result of a measurement for $|p\rangle$ as y_2. After that A measures all qubits of $|\psi\rangle$ and sets $|\psi\rangle$ to $|0 \ldots 0\rangle$.

Step i. The automaton reads X^{i-1} and computes $|p\rangle \to |p \oplus R(X^{i-1})\rangle$. A uses the same register $|\psi\rangle$ on processing X^{i-1}. Then A returns a result of the measurement for $|p\rangle$ as y_i. The A measures $|\psi\rangle$ and sets $|\psi\rangle$ to $|0 \ldots 0\rangle$.

Step k. The automaton reads and skips X^k. It does not need these variables, because it guesses y_1, and using this value it can obtain $y_2, \ldots, y_k$ without X^k.

Let us compute a cost of the output for this automaton. Let us consider a new cost function $cost'(I, O)$. For this function, a "right" block costs 1 and a "wrong" block costs 0. So, $cost^t(I, O) = (r-w) \cdot cost'(I, O) + tw$. Let us compute $\mathbb{E}\left[cost'(I, O)\right]$. We recall that the problem has k guardians, t blocks and $z = k/t$.

Firstly, let us compute p_i the probability that block i is a "right" block (costs 1). Let $i = 1$. So, if the i-th block is "right", then all $z - 1$ prisoners inside the block return right answers and a guess of the first guardian is right. A probability of this event is $p_1 = 0.5 \cdot (1 - \varepsilon)^{z-1}$.

Let $i > 1$. If the i-th block is "right", then two conditions should be true: (i) All $z - 1$ prisoners inside the block should return right answers. (ii) If we consider a number of preceding guardians that return wrong answers plus 1 if the preceding prisoner has an error. Then this number should be even.

The probability of the first condition is $(1 - \varepsilon)^{z-1}$. Let us compute the probability of the second condition. Let $E(j)$ be the number of errors before the j-th guardian. It is a number of errors for the previous prisoners plus 1 if the guess of the first guardian is wrong. Let $F(j)$ be a probability that $E(j)$ is even. Therefore $1 - F(j)$ is a probability that $E(j)$ is odd. If there is an error in a computation of the $(j - 1)$-th prisoner, then $E(j - 1)$ should be odd. If there is no error for the $(j - 1)$-th prisoner, then $E(j - 1)$ should be even. Therefore, $F(j) = \varepsilon(1 - F(j - 1)) + (1 - \varepsilon)F(j - 1) = F(j - 1)(1 - 2\varepsilon) + \varepsilon$. Note that the guess of the first guardian is right with probability 0.5. Therefore, $F(1) = 0.5$.

So, $F(j) = F(j-1)(1-2\varepsilon) + \varepsilon = F(j-2)(1-2\varepsilon)^2 + (1-2\varepsilon)\varepsilon + \varepsilon = \dots$
$= F(j-j+1)(1-2\varepsilon)^{j-1} + (1-2\varepsilon)^{j-2}\varepsilon + \dots + (1-2\varepsilon)\varepsilon + \varepsilon = F(1) \cdot (1 - 2\varepsilon)^{j-1} + \varepsilon \sum_{l=0}^{j-2}(1-2\varepsilon)^l = \frac{(1-2\varepsilon)^{j-1}}{2} + \frac{1-(1-2\varepsilon)^{j-1}}{2} = 0.5$.

Hence, $p_i = 0.5 \cdot (1-\varepsilon)^{z-1}$.

Finally, let us compute the expected cost:
$\mathbb{E}\left[cost'(I, A(I))\right] = \sum_{i=1}^{t}\left(p_i \cdot 1 + (1-p_i)\cdot 0\right) = \sum_{i=1}^{t} p_i = 0.5 \cdot (1-\varepsilon)^{z-1} \cdot t$.
Therefore, $\mathbb{E}\left[cost^t(I, A(I))\right] = 0.5 \cdot (1-\varepsilon)^{z-1} \cdot t(r-w) + tw$.

Let us compute the expected competitive ratio c:
$c \leq \left(0.5 \cdot (1-\varepsilon)^{z-1} \cdot t(r-w) + tw\right)/(tr) = \left(0.5 \cdot (1-\varepsilon)^{z-1} \cdot (r-w) + w\right)/r$ □

Let us consider the model with advice. In the following properties of $BH_{k,r,w}^t(f)$ problem, we show that if the model has not enough memory, then the problem can be interpreted as the "String Guessing, Unknown History" $(2-SGUH)$ problem from [11]. The problem is the following. On each step, an algorithm should guess the next input bit. The following result for the $2-SGUH$ is known:

Lemma 1 ([11]). *Consider an input string of length k for $2-SGUH$, for some positive integer k. Any online algorithm that is correct in more than αk characters, for $0.5 \leq \alpha < 1$, needs to read at least $(1 + (1-\alpha)\log_2(1-\alpha) + \alpha\log_2\alpha) k$ advice bits.*

Using this result for $2-SGUH$, we can show the following properties of $BH_{k,r,w}^t(f)$ problem with respect to two-way automata with advice for online minimization problems.

Theorem 5. *Let s be a positive integer. Suppose a Boolean function f is such that no 2DA uses at most s bits of memory and computes f. Then there is no c-competitive 2DA that uses $s - b$ bits of memory and b advice bits, and solves $BH_{k,r,w}^t(f)$, where $c < (hr + (t-h)w)/(tr)$, $h = \lfloor v/z \rfloor$, $z = k/t$, v is such that $b = (1 + (1 - v/k)\log_2(1 - v/k) + (v/k)\log_2(v/k)) k$, $0.5 \cdot k \leq v < k$.*

Proof. Let us prove the following claim by induction. If the automaton gets b advice bits, then there is an input such that at least $k - b$ prisoners return wrong answers. Let us consider different cases. The case of $b = k$ is next. Then the adviser can send $(g_1, \dots, g_k)$, for $g_i = \bigoplus_{j=i}^{k} f(X^j)$. So, The automaton returns right answers for all guardians. The case of $b = 0$ is next. It is a case of no advice that is described in Theorem 1.

The general case is next. Assume that the claim is proven for any pair (b'', k') such that $b'' \leq b$, $k' \leq k$ and at least one of these inequalities is strict. We focus on the first prisoner. Assume that there is an input $X^1 \in \{0,1\}^{m_1}$ for the first prisoner such that this prisoner cannot compute an answer with bounded error. Then we use this input and get a situation for $(k-1, b)$. In that case, $k - b - 1$ prisoners are wrong. Also, the first one is wrong by assumption.

Assume that the automaton always can compute an answer with a bounded error for the first prisoner. So we can describe the process of communication with the adviser as follows: the adviser separates all possible inputs into 2^b non-overlapping groups $G_1, \ldots, G_{2^b}$. After that, he sends a number of the group to the automaton, the group is such that it contains the current input. Then the automaton A processes the input with the knowledge that an input can be only from this group. Let us consider three sets of groups: $I_0 = \{G_i : \forall \sigma \in \{0,1\}^{m_1}$ such that σ is an input for the first prisoner and $f(\sigma) = 0\}$, $I_1 = \{G_i : \forall \sigma \in \{0,1\}^{m_1}$ such that σ is an input for the first prisoner and $f(\sigma) = 1\}$, $I_{10} = \{G_1, \ldots, G_{2^b}\} \backslash (I_1 \cup I_0)$. Let $|I_a| \neq 0$, for some $a \in \{0,1\}$. If $|I_a| \leq 2^{b-1}$, then we take any input from any group $G \in I_a$ as X^1. Hence, we have at most 2^{b-1} possible groups for the adviser that distinguish inputs of the next guardians. These groups can be encoded using $b-1$ bits, and we get the situation $(k-1, b-1)$. The claim is true for this situation. If $|I_a| > 2^{b-1}$, then we take any input from any group $G \notin I_a$ as X^1. Hence, we have at most 2^{b-1} possible groups for the adviser and the same situation. The claim is true for this case.

Let $|I_0| = |I_1| = 0$. Suppose that the automaton can solve the problem using s' bits of memory, where $s' < s - b$. We can simulate the work of the automaton with advice using the automaton B with the following structure. B has two parts of memory: M_1 of b bits and M_2 of s' bits. Suppose that the adviser initialized M_1 by advice bits. Then B invokes A depends on the value of M_1 and advice bits. So, B can simulate the work of A, the automaton B uses $s' + b < s$ bits of memory and computes f. It is a contradiction with the claim of the theorem.

Therefore, the only way to compute the result for the first prisoner is sending answer as one advice bit. So, we have the situation for $k - 1$ prisoners and $b - 1$ advice bits. So, it means, that for the algorithm the problem is the same as the *String Guessing Problem with Unknown History*$(2-SGUH)$ from [11]. Due to Lemma 1, if we want to get v right answers for guardians, then we need $b = \left(1 + (1 - \frac{v}{k}) \log_2(1 - \frac{v}{k}) + \frac{v}{k} \log_2 \frac{v}{k}\right) k$.

Because of properties of the cost function, the best case for the algorithm is getting right results about all guardians of a block. Hence, the algorithm can get $h = \lfloor v/z \rfloor$ full blocks and cost for each of them will be r, for $z = k/t$. Other blocks have at least one "wrong" guardian, and these blocks cost w. Therefore, we can construct an input such that it costs $\lfloor v/z \rfloor \cdot r + (t - \lfloor v/z \rfloor)w$, for $b = \left(1 + (1 - \frac{v}{k}) \log_2(1 - \frac{v}{k}) + \frac{v}{k} \log_2 \frac{v}{k}\right) k$. Hence, the algorithm is c-competitive for $c \geq \frac{\lfloor v/z \rfloor \cdot r + (t - \lfloor v/z \rfloor)w}{tr}$, $b = \left(1 + (1 - \frac{v}{k}) \log_2(1 - \frac{v}{k}) + \frac{v}{k} \log_2 \frac{v}{k}\right) k$. $\quad\square$

We have a similar situation in a probabilistic case. We use a function $\delta_x : \mathbb{R} \to \{0,1\}$ in the claim of the following theorem: $\delta_x = 1$ iff $x \neq 0$.

Theorem 6. *Let s be a positive integer. Suppose a Boolean function f is such that no 2PA uses at most s bits of memory and computes f. Then there is no c-competitive in expectation 2PA that uses $s - b$ bits of memory and b advice bits, and solves $BH_{k,r,w}^t(f)$ with bounded error, where $c \geq (hr + \delta_u \cdot (2^{u-z}r + (1 - 2^{u-z})w) + (t - h - \delta_u)(2^{-z}r + (1 - 2^{-z})w))/(tr)$, for $h = \lfloor v/z \rfloor, z = k/t, u = v - hz$, v is such that $b = (1 + (1 - v/k) \log_2(1 - v/k) + (v/k) \log_2(v/k)) k, 0.5k \leq v < k$.*

The idea of the proof is similar to the proof of Theorem 5, but here we can guess all "unknown" guardians with probability 0.5.

4   Application

Let us discuss applications of Black Hats Method. We present examples of problems that allow us to show benefits of quantum computing.

Exponential Expected Working Time. Let us consider exponential expected working time for two-way automata. In this case, we analyze the *palindrome* Boolean function. The Boolean function $Pal : \{0,1\}^m \to \{0,1\}$ is the following. $Pal(X) = 1$ if $X = X^R$; and $Pal(X) = 0$, otherwise. Here $X = (x_1, \ldots, x_m)$, $X^R = (x_m, \ldots, x_1)$ is a reversed X. It is known that there is a 2QCFA that recognizes the palindrome language [8]. 2QCFA is 2QCA with a constant size of memory. At the same time, we can show a lower bound for 2PA that is based on lower bounds from [5,18,29,37,41]. Therefore, we have the following results:

Lemma 2. *The following two claims are true: 1. There is a 2QCA that uses quantum and classical memory of constant size that works in exponential expected time and computes Pal with bounded error. 2. No 2PA uses $o(\log n)$ bits of memory that works in exponential expected time and computes Pal with bounded error, where n is the length of the input.*

Proof. The first claim follows from the result for the language version of *Pal* [8], let us prove the second claim. It is known from [18,29] that if a 2PA recognize a language or computes a Boolean function f, then the following property holds: $N(f) \le (C_1 \cdot \log T)^{C_2 \cdot d^2 \log_2 d}$, where $C_1, C_2 = const$, T is expected time, d is the size (the number of states) of the automaton. $N(f)$ is a number of Myhill-Nerode classes in a language version and the number of subfunctions in a Boolean functions version. The number of subfunctions is analogue of number of Myhill-Nerode classes, you can read more in [37,43,44]. Additionally, it is easy to see that $N(Pal) \ge 2^{n/2}$.

The memory of the automaton is $o(\log n) = o(0.5 \log n - \log \log n)$. Therefore, $d = o(\sqrt{n/(\log n)^2}) = o\left(\frac{\sqrt{n/(\log n)}}{\log(n/\log n)}\right)$. Hence $d^2 \log d = o(n/\log n)$. If T is exponential, then we can replace $C_1 \log T$ by $C_3 \cdot n$ for some constant C_3. Finally, we obtain that $(C_1 \cdot \log T)^{C_2 \cdot d^2 \log_2 d} = 2^{o(n)} < 2^{n/2}$. Therefore, by lower bounds [18,29], 2PAs with $o(\log n)$ bits of memory cannot compute the function.   □

Let us consider the $BHPal_{k,r,w}^t = BH_{k,r,w}^t(Pal)$ problem. Recall that $BH_{k,r,w}^t(f)$ is a black hat problem for k guardians, t blocks of guardians, the cost r for a right answer of a block, the cost w for a wrong answer of a block, $z = k/t$ and $k \bmod t = 0$. Let us discuss the properties of the $BHPal_{k,r,w}^t$ problem:

Theorem 7. *Suppose $P^t = BHPal_{k,r,w}^t$, $t \in \{1, \ldots, k\}$, $k = (\log_2 n)^{O(1)}$, v is such that $b = (1 + (1 - v/k)\log_2(1 - v/k) + (v/k)\log_2(v/k))k$, $0.5k \le v < k$, all automata work in exponential expected time; then*

1. *There is no c-competitive 2DA that uses $s = o(\log n)$ bits of memory and b advice bits, and solves P^t, where $c < C_1 = w/r$, $b = o(z/\log z)$.*
2. *There is no deterministic online algorithm with unlimited computational power computing P^1 that is c-competitive, for $c < C_1 = w/r$.*
3. *There is no c-competitive in expectation 2PA that uses $o(\log n)$ bits of memory and solves P^t, where $c < C_3 = 2^{-z} + (1 - 2^{-z})w/r$.*
4. *There is no c-competitive 2DA that uses $s = o(\log n)$ bits of memory and b advice bits, and solves P^t, where $c < C_2 = \frac{hr+(t-h)w}{tr}$, $h = \lfloor v/z \rfloor$.*
5. *No 2PA uses $s = o(\log n)$ bits of memory, b advice bits and solves P^t that is c-competitive in expectation for $h = \lfloor v/z \rfloor$, $u = v - hz$,*
   $$c < C_4 = \frac{hr+\delta_u \cdot (2^{u-z}r+(1-2^{u-z})w)+(t-h-\delta_u)(2^{-z}r+(1-2^{-z})w)}{tr}.$$
6. *There is a 2QCA Q that uses a constant number of classical and quantum bits of memory and solves P^t. The algorithm Q has expected competitive ratio $c \leq ((1 - \varepsilon)^{z-1} \cdot 0.5 \cdot (r - w) + w)/r < C_1, C_2, C_3, C_4$, for some $\varepsilon: 0 < \varepsilon < 0.5$.*

Proof. Let us consider Claim 1 of the theorem. Due to Lemma 2, no 2DA with $o(\log n)$ computes P^t. Hence, because of Theorem 5, Claim 1 is true. Claim 2 follows from Theorem 3. Let us consider Claim 3 of the theorem. Due to Lemma 2, no 2PA with $o(\log n)$ computes P^t with bounded error. Therefore, because of Theorem 2, Claim 3 is true. Claim 4 follows from Lemma 2 and Theorem 5. Claim 5 follows from Lemma 2 and Theorem 6. Claim 6 follows from Lemma 2 and Theorem 4.   □

This theorem gives us the following important results. (i) There is a 2QCA with a constant size of memory for $BHPal_{k,r,w}^1$ that has a better competitive ratio than any 2DA or 2PA with sublogarithmic memory and sublogarithmic number of advice bits (Claims 1, 3, 4, 5 and 6 of Theorem 7); any deterministic online algorithm without restriction on memory (Claims 2 and 6 of Theorem 7). (ii) If we increase the number of advice bits for 2DA or 2PA for $BHPal_{k,r,w}^t$, then the competitive ratio becomes smaller, in the case of sublogarithmic memory and $1 < t \leq k/2$. At the same time, the competitive ratio is still larger than for a 2QCA (Claims 4, 5 and 6 of Theorem 7).

Polynomial Expected Working Time. Let us consider the polynomial expected working time for two-way automata. For this case, we analyze the UEQ Boolean function. The Boolean function $UEQ : \{0,1\}^m \to \{0,1\}$ is the following. $UEQ(X) = 1$ iff $\#_1(X) = \#_0(X)$, where $\#_j(X)$ is the number of symbols j in X. It is known that there is a 2QCFA that recognizes the language version of UEQ in polynomial time [8]. At the same time, we can show a lower bound that is based on lower bounds from [18, 29, 37]. So, we have the next result.

Lemma 3. *The following two claims are true. 1. There is a 2QCA that uses quantum and classical memory of constant size that works in exponential expected time and computes UEQ with bounded error. 2. No 2PA uses $o\left((\log n)^{0.5-\alpha}\right)$ bits of memory that works in polynomial expected time and computes UEQ with bounded error, where n is the length of input, $0 < \alpha < 0.5$.*

Proof. The first claim follows from [8], the proof of the second claim is similar to the proof of Lemma 2.   □

Let us consider the $BHUEQ^t_{k,r,w} = BH^t_{k,r,w}(UEQ)$ problem. Recall that the problem is a black hat problem for k guardians, t blocks of guardians, the cost r for a right answer of a block, the cost w for a wrong answer of a block, $z = k/t$ and $k \bmod t = 0$. Let us discuss the properties of the $BHUEQ^t_{k,r,w}$ problem:

Theorem 8. *Suppose* $P^t = BHUEQ^t_{k,r,w}$, $t \in \{1, \ldots, k\}$, $k = (\log_2 n)^{O(1)}$, v *is such that* $b = (1 + (1 - v/k) \log_2(1 - v/k) + (v/k) \log_2(v/k)) k$, $0.5k \le v < k$, *all automata work in polynomial expected time,* $0 < \alpha < 0.5$; *then*

1. *There is no c-competitive 2DA that uses* $s = o\left((\log n)^{0.5-\alpha}\right)$ *bits of memory and* b *advice bits, and solves* P^t, *where* $c < C_1 = w/r$, $b = o(z/\log z)$.
2. *There is no deterministic online algorithm with unlimited computational power computing* P^1 *that is c-competitive, for* $c < C_1 = w/r$.
3. *There is no c-competitive in expectation 2PA that uses* $o\left((\log n)^{0.5-\alpha}\right)$ *bits of memory and solves* P^t, *where* $c < C_3 = 2^{-z} + (1 - 2^{-z})w/r$.
4. *There is no c-competitive 2DA that uses* $s = o\left((\log n)^{0.5-\alpha}\right)$ *bits of memory and* b *advice bits, and solves* P^t, *where* $c < C_2 = \frac{hr+(t-h)w}{tr}$, $h = \lfloor v/z \rfloor$.
5. *No 2PA using* $s = o\left((\log n)^{0.5-\alpha}\right)$ *bits of memory,* b *advice bits and solving* P^t *that is c-competitive in expectation for* $h = \lfloor v/z \rfloor$, $u = v - hz$,
   $$c < C_4 = \frac{hr + \delta_u \cdot (2^{u-z}r + (1-2^{u-z})w) + (t-h-\delta_u)(2^{-z}r + (1-2^{-z})w)}{tr}.$$
6. *There is a 2QCA Q that uses a constant number of classical and quantum bits of memory and solves* P^t. *The algorithm Q has expected competitive ratio* $c \le ((1 - \varepsilon)^{z-1} \cdot 0.5 \cdot (r - w) + w)/r < C_1, C_2, C_3, C_4$, *for some* ε: $0 < \varepsilon < 0.5$.

Proof. The proof is similar to the proof of Theorem 7. The claims follow from Lemma 3 and all theorems from Sect. 3.   □

This theorem gives us the following important results: (i) There is a 2QCA for $BHUEQ^1_{k,r,w}$ with constant size of memory and polynomial expected time that has a better competitive ratio than any 2DA or 2PA with the size of memory less than $o\left(\sqrt{\log_2 n}\right)$ and the number of advice bits less than $o\left(\sqrt{\log_2 n}\right)$, and works in polynomial time (Claims 1, 3, 4, 5 and 6 of Theorem 8); any deterministic online algorithm without restriction on memory (Claims 2 and 6 of Theorem 8). (ii) If we increase the number of advice bits for 2DA or 2PA for $BHUEQ^t_{k,r,w}$, then the competitive ratio becomes smaller, in the case of sublogarithmic memory and $1 < t \le k/2$. At the same time, the competitive ratio is still larger than for a 2QCA (Claims 4, 5 and 6 of Theorem 8).

Acknowledgements. This work was supported by Russian Science Foundation Grant 19-71-00149.

References

1. Ablayev, F., Ablayev, M., Khadiev, K., Vasiliev, A.: Classical and quantum computations with restricted memory. In: Böckenhauer, H.-J., Komm, D., Unger, W. (eds.) Adventures Between Lower Bounds and Higher Altitudes. LNCS, vol. 11011, pp. 129–155. Springer, Cham (2018). https://doi.org/10.1007/978-3-319-98355-4_9
2. Ablayev, F., Ambainis, A., Khadiev, K., Khadieva, A.: Lower bounds and hierarchies for quantum memoryless communication protocols and quantum ordered binary decision diagrams with repeated test. In: Tjoa, A.M., Bellatreche, L., Biffl, S., van Leeuwen, J., Wiedermann, J. (eds.) SOFSEM 2018. LNCS, vol. 10706, pp. 197–211. Springer, Cham (2018). https://doi.org/10.1007/978-3-319-73117-9_14
3. Ablayev, F., Gainutdinova, A., Karpinski, M., Moore, C., Pollett, C.: On the computational power of probabilistic and quantum branching program. Inf. Comput. **203**(2), 145–162 (2005)
4. Ablayev, F., Gainutdinova, A., Khadiev, K., Yakaryılmaz, A.: Very narrow quantum OBDDs and width hierarchies for classical OBDDs. In: Jürgensen, H., Karhumäki, J., Okhotin, A. (eds.) DCFS 2014. LNCS, vol. 8614, pp. 53–64. Springer, Cham (2014). https://doi.org/10.1007/978-3-319-09704-6_6
5. Ablayev, F., Khadiev, K.: Extension of the hierarchy for k-OBDDs of small width. Russ. Math. **53**(3), 46–50 (2013)
6. Ambainis, A., Yakaryılmaz, A.: Superiority of exact quantum automata for promise problems. Inf. Process. Lett. **112**(7), 289–291 (2012)
7. Ambainis, A., Yakaryılmaz, A.: Automata and quantum computing. Technical report 1507.01988, arXiv (2015)
8. Ambainis, A., Watrous, J.: Two-way finite automata with quantum and classical states. Theoret. Comput. Sci. **287**(1), 299–311 (2002)
9. Becchetti, L., Koutsoupias, E.: Competitive analysis of aggregate max in windowed streaming. In: Albers, S., Marchetti-Spaccamela, A., Matias, Y., Nikoletseas, S., Thomas, W. (eds.) ICALP 2009. LNCS, vol. 5555, pp. 156–170. Springer, Heidelberg (2009). https://doi.org/10.1007/978-3-642-02927-1_15
10. Böckenhauer, H.-J., Hromkovič, J., Komm, D., Královič, R., Rossmanith, P.: On the power of randomness versus advice in online computation. In: Bordihn, H., Kutrib, M., Truthe, B. (eds.) Languages Alive. LNCS, vol. 7300, pp. 30–43. Springer, Heidelberg (2012). https://doi.org/10.1007/978-3-642-31644-9_2
11. Böckenhauer, H.J., Hromkovič, J., Komm, D., Krug, S., Smula, J., Sprock, A.: The string guessing problem as a method to prove lower bounds on the advice complexity. Theoret. Comput. Sci. **554**, 95–108 (2014)
12. Boyar, J., Favrholdt, L., Kudahl, C., Larsen, K., Mikkelsen, J.: Online algorithms with advice: a survey. ACM Comput. Surv. **50**(2), 19 (2017)
13. Boyar, J., Irani, S., Larsen, K.S.: A comparison of performance measures for online algorithms. In: Dehne, F., Gavrilova, M., Sack, J.-R., Tóth, C.D. (eds.) WADS 2009. LNCS, vol. 5664, pp. 119–130. Springer, Heidelberg (2009). https://doi.org/10.1007/978-3-642-03367-4_11
14. Boyar, J., Larsen, K.S., Maiti, A.: The frequent items problem in online streaming under various performance measures. Int. J. Found. Comput. Sci. **26**(4), 413–439 (2015)
15. Böckenhauer, H.-J., Komm, D., Královič, R., Královič, R., Mömke, T.: On the advice complexity of online problems. In: Dong, Y., Du, D.-Z., Ibarra, O. (eds.) ISAAC 2009. LNCS, vol. 5878, pp. 331–340. Springer, Heidelberg (2009). https://doi.org/10.1007/978-3-642-10631-6_35

16. Dobrev, S., Královič, R., Pardubská, D.: How much information about the future is needed? In: Geffert, V., Karhumäki, J., Bertoni, A., Preneel, B., Návrat, P., Bieliková, M. (eds.) SOFSEM 2008. LNCS, vol. 4910, pp. 247–258. Springer, Heidelberg (2008). https://doi.org/10.1007/978-3-540-77566-9_21

17. Dorrigiv, R., López-Ortiz, A.: A survey of performance measures for on-line algorithms. SIGACT News **36**(3), 67–81 (2005)

18. Dwork, C., Stockmeyer, L.J.: A time complexity gap for two-way probabilistic finite-state automata. SIAM J. Comput. **19**(6), 1011–1123 (1990)

19. Emek, Y., Fraigniaud, P., Korman, A., Rosén, A.: Online computation with advice. In: Albers, S., Marchetti-Spaccamela, A., Matias, Y., Nikoletseas, S., Thomas, W. (eds.) ICALP 2009. LNCS, vol. 5555, pp. 427–438. Springer, Heidelberg (2009). https://doi.org/10.1007/978-3-642-02927-1_36

20. Emek, Y., Fraigniaud, P., Korman, A., Rosén, A.: Online computation with advice. Theoret. Comput. Sci. **412**(24), 2642–2656 (2011)

21. Gainutdinova, A.F.: Comparative complexity of quantum and classical OBDDs for total and partial functions. Russ. Math. **59**(11), 26–35 (2015). https://doi.org/10.3103/S1066369X15110031

22. Gainutdinova, A., Yakaryılmaz, A.: Unary probabilistic and quantum automata on promise problems. In: Potapov, I. (ed.) DLT 2015. LNCS, vol. 9168, pp. 252–263. Springer, Cham (2015). https://doi.org/10.1007/978-3-319-21500-6_20

23. Gainutdinova, A., Yakaryılmaz, A.: Nondeterministic unitary OBDDs. In: Weil, P. (ed.) CSR 2017. LNCS, vol. 10304, pp. 126–140. Springer, Cham (2017). https://doi.org/10.1007/978-3-319-58747-9_13

24. Gainutdinova, A., Yakaryılmaz, A.: Unary probabilistic and quantum automata on promise problems. Quantum Inf. Process. **17**(2), 1–17 (2017). https://doi.org/10.1007/s11128-017-1799-0

25. Gavinsky, D., Kempe, J., Kerenidis, I., Raz, R., de Wolf, R.: Exponential separations for one-way quantum communication complexity, with applications to cryptography. In: STOC 2007, pp. 516–525 (2007)

26. Giannakopoulos, Y., Koutsoupias, E.: Competitive analysis of maintaining frequent items of a stream. Theoret. Comput. Sci. **562**, 23–32 (2015)

27. Hromkovic, J.: Design and Analysis of Randomized Algorithms: Introduction to Design Paradigms (2005)

28. Karlin, A.R., Manasse, M.S., Rudolph, L., Sleator, D.D.: Competitive snoopy caching. In: 27th Annual Symposium on FOCS 1986, pp. 244–254. IEEE (1986)

29. Khadiev, K., Ibrahimov, R., Yakaryılmaz, A.: New size hierarchies for two way automata. Lobachevskii J. Math. **39**(7), 997–1009 (2018)

30. Khadiev, K., Khadieva, A.: Quantum automata for online minimization problems. In: Ninth Workshop on NCMA 2017 Short Papaers, pp. 25–33. Institute fur Computersprachen TU Wien (2017)

31. Khadiev, K., Khadieva, A.: Reordering method and hierarchies for quantum and classical ordered binary decision diagrams. In: Weil, P. (ed.) CSR 2017. LNCS, vol. 10304, pp. 162–175. Springer, Cham (2017). https://doi.org/10.1007/978-3-319-58747-9_16

32. Khadiev, K., Khadieva, A.: Quantum online streaming algorithms with logarithmic memory. Int. J. Theor. Phys. (2019). https://doi.org/10.1007/s10773-019-04209-1

33. Khadiev, K., Khadieva, A.: Two-way quantum and classical machines with small memory for online minimization problems. In: International Conference on Micro- and Nano-Electronics 2018. Proceedings of SPIE, vol. 11022, p. 110222T (2019)

34. Khadiev, K., Khadieva, A., Kravchenko, D., Rivosh, A., Yamilov, R., Mannapov, I.: Quantum versus classical online streaming algorithms with logarithmic size of memory. Lobachevskii J. Math. (2019). (in print). arXiv:1710.09595
35. Khadiev, K., Khadieva, A., Mannapov, I.: Quantum online algorithms with respect to space and advice complexity. Lobachevskii J. Math. **39**(9), 1210–1220 (2018)
36. Khadiev, K., Ziatdinov, M., Mannapov, I., Khadieva, A., Yamilov, R.: Quantum online streaming algorithms with constant number of advice bits. arXiv:1802.05134 (2018)
37. Komm, D.: An Introduction to Online Computation: Determinism, Randomization, Advice. Springer, Heidelberg (2016). https://doi.org/10.1007/978-3-319-42749-2
38. Le Gall, F.: Exponential separation of quantum and classical online space complexity. In: SPAA 2006, pp. 67–73. ACM (2006)
39. Sauerhoff, M., Sieling, D.: Quantum branching programs and space-bounded nonuniform quantum complexity. Theoret. Comput. Sci. **334**(1), 177–225 (2005)
40. Say, A.C.C., Yakaryılmaz, A.: Quantum finite automata: a modern introduction. In: Calude, C.S., Freivalds, R., Kazuo, I. (eds.) Computing with New Resources. LNCS, vol. 8808, pp. 208–222. Springer, Cham (2014). https://doi.org/10.1007/978-3-319-13350-8_16
41. Shepherdson, J.C.: The reduction of two-way automata to one-way automata. IBM J. Res. Dev. **3**, 198–200 (1959)
42. Sleator, D.D., Tarjan, R.E.: Amortized efficiency of list update and paging rules. Commun. ACM **28**(2), 202–208 (1985)
43. Wegener, I.: Branching Programs and Binary Decision Diagrams: Theory and Applications. SIAM, Philadelphia (2000)
44. Yablonsky, S.V.: Introduction to Discrete Mathematics: Textbook for Higher Schools. Mir Publishers, Moscow (1989)
45. Yuan, Q.: Quantum online algorithms. UC Santa Barbara. Ph.D. thesis (2009)

Quotients and Atoms of Reversible Languages

Hellis Tamm[✉]

Department of Software Science, Tallinn University of Technology, Tallinn, Estonia
hellis@cs.ioc.ee

Abstract. We consider several reversible finite automaton models which
have been introduced over decades, and study some properties of their
languages. In particular, we look at the question whether the quotients
and atoms of a specific class of reversible languages also belong to that
class or not. We consider bideterministic automata, reversible deterministic finite automata (REV-DFAs), reversible multiple-entry DFAs
(REV-MeDFAs), and several variants of reversible nondeterministic finite
automata (REV-NFAs). It is known that the class of REV-DFA languages is strictly included in the class of REV-MeDFA languages. We
show that the classes of complete REV-DFA languages and complete
REV-MeDFA languages are the same. We also show that differently from
the general case of a REV-DFA language, the minimal DFA of a complete REV-DFA language is a complete REV-DFA. We also show that
atoms of any regular language are accepted by REV-NFAs with a single
initial and a single final state.

1 Introduction

Reversibility of finite automata has been a subject of study for several
decades [1,5,6,12,13], and recently there has been renewed interest in this topic
[2,7,8,10,11]. Over the decades, several different reversible finite automata models have been introduced. Although injectivity is required by most models, the
number of initial and final states varies between different models.

A very restricted model of a reversible deterministic finite automaton (DFA)
with one initial and one final state (also called *bideterministic* automaton) was
considered in [1,13–15]. Reversible DFAs (REV-DFAs) – with one initial and
multiple final states – were recently a research subject in [7]. Reversible multiple-
entry deterministic automata (REV-MeDFAs) (with multiple initial and multiple
final states) have been studied in [12,13]. All these models of reversible automata
differ in their computational power, and they accept strict subclasses of regular
languages. For example, it is known that the class of REV-DFA languages is
strictly included in the class of REV-MeDFA languages [7,8]. Also, in the general
case, the minimal DFA of a REV-DFA language is not a REV-DFA.

This work was supported by the Estonian Ministry of Education and Research insti-
tutional research grant IUT33-13.

E. Sekerinski et al. (Eds.): FM 2019 Workshops, LNCS 12233, pp. 443–455, 2020.
https://doi.org/10.1007/978-3-030-54997-8_28

However, we show that the classes of complete REV-DFA languages and complete REV-MeDFA languages are the same. Also, we show that the minimal DFA of a complete REV-DFA language is a complete REV-DFA.

Recently, reversibility in the nondeterministic finite automaton (NFA) model was considered in [8], where an NFA has one initial state. It was shown in [8] that reversible NFAs with a sole initial state are more powerful than reversible DFAs, but still cannot accept all regular languages.

However, a model of NFA with multiple initial states is well known and has been widely considered in the literature. We consider a reversible NFA with multiple initial states and observe that this automaton model can accept any regular language.

We study some properties of the left quotients and the atoms of the languages accepted by different reversible automaton models mentioned above. Especially, we look at the question whether the quotients and the atoms of a specific class of reversible languages also belong to that class or not.

The paper is organized as follows. Section 2 provides definitions and notation for automata, languages, quotients, and atoms of regular languages. In Sect. 3, we present definitions of reversible automata and some known results about their language classes. In Sect. 4, we start our research about quotients and atoms of reversible languages in the bideterministic case, and in Sect. 5, we continue our study of reversible DFAs. Section 6 is devoted to reversible multiple-entry DFAs, and we give a particular consideration to the case of complete reversible MeDFAs in Sect. 6.1. Finally, in Sect. 7, we study several classes of reversible NFAs: we consider reversible NFAs with multiple initial states (REV-NFAs), with a single initial state (REV-SeNFAs), and with a single initial and a single final state (REV-SeSfNFAs). We show that atoms of any regular language are accepted by REV-SeSfNFAs. Since any regular language is a union of some of its atoms, we make an observation that every regular language is accepted by a union of REV-SeSfNFAs.

2   Automata, Languages, Quotients, and Atoms

A *nondeterministic finite automaton (NFA)* is a quintuple $\mathcal{N} = (Q, \Sigma, \delta, I, F)$, where Q is a finite set of *states*, Σ is a finite non-empty *alphabet*, $\delta : Q \times \Sigma \to 2^Q$ is the *transition function*, $I \subseteq Q$ is the set of *initial states*, and $F \subseteq Q$ is the set of *final states*. We extend the transition function to functions $\delta' : Q \times \Sigma^* \to 2^Q$ and $\delta'' : 2^Q \times \Sigma^* \to 2^Q$, using δ for all these functions. The *left language* of a state q of $\mathcal{N}$ is the set of words $w \in \Sigma^*$ such that $q \in \delta(I, w)$, and the *right language* of a state $q \in Q$ is the set of words $w \in \Sigma^*$ such that $\delta(q, w) \cap F \neq \emptyset$. A state is *unreachable* if its left language is empty. A state is *empty* if its right language is empty. An NFA is *trim* if it has no empty or unreachable states. The *language accepted* by an NFA $\mathcal{N}$ is $L(\mathcal{N}) = \{w \in \Sigma^* \mid \delta(I, w) \cap F \neq \emptyset\}$. Two NFAs are *equivalent* if they accept the same language.

A *strongly connected component (SCC)* of an NFA $\mathcal{N}$ is a maximal subautomaton $\mathcal{N}' = (Q', \Sigma, \delta, I \cap Q', F' \cap Q')$ of $\mathcal{N}$, with $Q' \subseteq Q$, such that for every

$p, q \in Q'$ there are words $u, v \in \Sigma^*$ such that $q \in \delta(p, u)$ and $p \in \delta(q, v)$. An NFA $\mathcal{N}$ is *strongly connected* if it has only one SCC.

An NFA $\mathcal{N}$ is a *multiple-entry deterministic finite automaton* (MeDFA) if $|\delta(q, a)| \leqslant 1$ for every state $q \in Q$ and $a \in \Sigma$.

A MeDFA $\mathcal{N}$ is a *deterministic finite automaton* (DFA) if $|I| = 1$.

A MeDFA (or DFA) $\mathcal{N}$ is *complete* if $|\delta(q, a)| = 1$ for every $q \in Q$ and $a \in \Sigma$, otherwise it is *incomplete*. It is well known that for every regular language there is a unique complete/incomplete minimal DFA.

An NFA $\mathcal{N}$ can be *determinized* by the well-known subset construction, resulting in a complete DFA $\mathcal{N}^D$ where only subsets (including the empty subset) reachable from the initial subset of $\mathcal{N}^D$ are used.

The *reverse* of $\mathcal{N}$ is the NFA $\mathcal{N}^R = (Q, \Sigma, \delta^R, F, I)$, where $q \in \delta^R(p, a)$ if and only if $p \in \delta(q, a)$ for $p, q \in Q$ and $a \in \Sigma$.

One can also use a *trimming* operation on $\mathcal{N}$, deleting all unreachable and empty states from $\mathcal{N}$ together with the incident transitions, yielding a trim NFA $\mathcal{N}^T$.

The *left quotient*, or simply *quotient*, of a language L by a word $w \in \Sigma^*$ is the language $w^{-1}L = \{x \in \Sigma^* \mid wx \in L\}$. We note here the fact that left quotients of L correspond to the states of the minimal DFA of L.

An *atom* of a regular language L with quotients $K_0, \ldots, K_{n-1}$ is any non-empty language of the form $\widetilde{K_0} \cap \cdots \cap \widetilde{K_{n-1}}$, where $\widetilde{K_i}$ is either K_i or $\overline{K_i}$, and $\overline{K_i}$ is the complement of K_i with respect to Σ^* [3]. An atom is *initial* if it has L (rather than $\overline{L}$) as a term; it is *final* if it contains ε. There is exactly one final atom, the atom $\widehat{K_0} \cap \cdots \cap \widehat{K_{n-1}}$, where $\widehat{K_i} = K_i$ if $\varepsilon \in K_i$, and $\widehat{K_i} = \overline{K_i}$ otherwise. If $\overline{K_0} \cap \cdots \cap \overline{K_{n-1}}$ is an atom, then it is called the *negative* atom, all the other atoms are *positive*. Thus atoms of L are regular languages uniquely determined by L; they define a partition of Σ^*. Every quotient K_i is a (possibly empty) union of atoms.

We also note that atoms are the classes of the *left congruence* $_L\equiv$ of L defined as follows: for $x, y \in \Sigma^*$, $x_L\equiv y$ if for every $u \in \Sigma^*$, $ux \in L$ if and only if $uy \in L$ [9].

Let $A = \{A_0, \ldots, A_{m-1}\}$ be the set of atoms of L, let I_A be the set of initial atoms, and let A_{m-1} be the final atom. The *átomaton* of L is the NFA $\mathcal{A} = (A, \Sigma, \alpha, I_A, \{A_{m-1}\})$ where $A_j \in \alpha(A_i, a)$ if and only if $A_j \subseteq a^{-1}A_i$, for all $A_i, A_j \in A$ and $a \in \Sigma$. It was shown in [3] that the atoms of L are the right languages of the states of the átomaton, and that the reverse NFA of the átomaton is the minimal DFA of the reverse language L^R of L.

We will use the next theorem which is a slightly modified version of the result by Brzozowski [4]:

Theorem 1. *If an NFA $\mathcal{N}$ has no empty states and $\mathcal{N}^R$ is a DFA, then $\mathcal{N}^D$ is a minimal DFA.*

3   Reversible Automata and Languages

Let L be a regular language and let $\mathcal{N} = (Q, \Sigma, \delta, I, F)$ be an NFA accepting L. A state $q \in Q$ of $\mathcal{N}$ is *reversible* if for any $a \in \Sigma$ there is at most one state $p \in Q$ such that $q \in \delta(p, a)$. An NFA $\mathcal{N}$ is *reversible* if all of its states are reversible, and it is said that $\mathcal{N}$ is a reversible NFA (REV-NFA). We note that $\mathcal{N}$ is a REV-NFA if and only if $\mathcal{N}^R$ is a MeDFA. If L is accepted by a REV-NFA, then L is called a REV-NFA language. Similarly, we define a reversible DFA (REV-DFA) together with REV-DFA languages, and a reversible MeDFA (REV-MeDFA) and REV-MeDFA languages. A reversible DFA with a single final state is also called *bideterministic* (Bi-DFA) because its reverse automaton is a DFA. We also consider reversible *single-entry* NFAs (REV-SeNFA) (that is, REV-NFAs with a single initial state), and REV-SeNFAs with a single final state (REV-SeSfNFA).

All the classes of reversible languages mentioned above have different expressive powers. Let the family of languages accepted by some type X of automata be denoted by $\mathcal{L}(X)$ and let REG denote the class of regular languages. The following strict inclusions were shown in [8] (although some of them have been known earlier): $\mathcal{L}$(Bi-DFA) $\subset$ $\mathcal{L}$(REV-DFA) $\subset$ $\mathcal{L}$(REV-MeDFA) $\subset$ REG, and $\mathcal{L}$(REV-DFA) $\subset$ $\mathcal{L}$(REV-SeNFA) $\subset$ REG. Also, it was shown in [8] that the language classes $\mathcal{L}$(REV-SeNFA) and $\mathcal{L}$(REV-MeDFA) are not comparable.

While NFAs and single-entry NFAs accept the same class of languges – regular languages –, the classes of languages accepted by REV-NFAs and REV-SeNFAs are not the same. In Sect. 7 we will observe that any regular language is accepted by a REV-NFA, that is, $\mathcal{L}$(REV-NFA) = REG. We will also show that the strict inclusion $\mathcal{L}$(REV-SeSfNFA) $\subset$ $\mathcal{L}$(REV-SeNFA) holds, and we will argue that although both REV-DFA and REV-SeSfNFA languages are subclasses of REV-SeNFA languages, they are not comparable.

We also note that Bi-DFA languages are clearly a proper subclass of REV-SeSfNFAs.

4   Bideterministic Languages

A Bi-DFA is a reversible DFA with a single final state. It is not difficult to see that any Bi-DFA is a minimal DFA. Indeed, let $\mathcal{D}$ be a Bi-DFA of a language L. By Theorem 1, the complete minimal DFA of L is isomorphic to the DFA $\mathcal{D}^{RDRD}$. If $\mathcal{D}$ is complete, then $\mathcal{D}^{RDRD} = \mathcal{D}$, and $\mathcal{D}$ is a complete minimal DFA. If $\mathcal{D}$ is incomplete, then $\mathcal{D}^{RDRDT} = \mathcal{D}$, and $\mathcal{D}$ is an incomplete minimal DFA.

Moreover, it has been shown in [15] that a Bi-DFA is a unique minimal NFA of its language.

There is a result in [3] that a language L is a complete Bi-DFA language if and only if the átomaton of L is isomorphic to the minimal DFA of L. Since the quotients of a language are the right languages of the states of the minimal DFA, and the atoms are the right languages of the átomaton, we can state the following:

Proposition 1. *A language is a complete Bi-DFA language if and only if its atoms are equal to its quotients.*

We also observe that for a complete Bi-DFA language, there is no empty quotient and all the atoms are positive.

For an incomplete Bi-DFA language, there exists an empty quotient and a negative atom. However, the following still holds for the general case:

Proposition 2. *A language is a Bi-DFA language if and only if its positive atoms are equal to its non-empty quotients.*

Proposition 3. *The non-empty quotients and positive atoms of a Bi-DFA language are Bi-DFA languages.*

Proof. If we take any state of a Bi-DFA as the only initial state, we get a Bi-DFA for the corresponding quotient/atom of the original Bi-DFA language.   □

Proposition 4. *The quotients of any Bi-DFA language are pairwise disjoint.*

Proof. Follows from Proposition 2 and from the fact that atoms of any language are pairwise disjoint.   □

5   Languages with a Reversible DFA

In this section we consider languages with a reversible DFA (REV-DFA languages).

Example 1. Consider a unary cyclic language L which has a minimal DFA $\mathcal{D} = (Q, \{a\}, \delta, q_0, F)$, where $Q = \{q_0, \ldots, q_{n-1}\}$ and $\delta(q_i, a) = q_{i+1}$ for $i = 0, \ldots, n-2$, and $\delta(q_{n-1}, a) = q_0$. Since $\mathcal{D}$ is reversible, L is a REV-DFA language.

Languages with a reversible DFA have been studied by Holzer, Jakobi and Kutrib [7], who showed that for the general case of a REV-DFA language, the minimal DFA is not necessarily reversible. They had the following result:

Theorem 2. *Let $\mathcal{D} = (Q, \Sigma, \delta, q_0, F)$ be a trim minimal DFA of a language L. The language L is accepted by a reversible DFA if and only if there do not exist states $p, q \in Q$, a letter $a \in \Sigma$, and a word $w \in \Sigma^*$ such that $p \neq q$, $\delta(p, a) = \delta(q, a)$, and $\delta(q, aw) = q$.*

Proposition 5. *All non-empty quotients of a REV-DFA language are REV-DFA languages.*

Proof. Let L be a REV-DFA language and let $\mathcal{D} = (Q, \Sigma, \delta, q_0, F)$ be a reversible DFA of L. It is known that for every non-empty quotient K_i of L, there is some state q_i of $\mathcal{D}$ and the corresponding DFA $\mathcal{D}_i = (Q, \Sigma, \delta, q_i, F)$, such that $K_i = L(\mathcal{D}_i)$. Clearly, any such DFA $\mathcal{D}_i$ is also reversible, implying that every non-empty quotient K_i is a REV-DFA language.   □

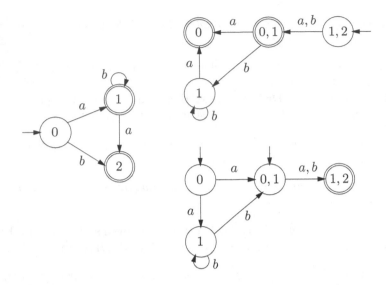

Fig. 1. A REV-DFA $\mathcal{D}$ (left); $\mathcal{D}^{RDT}$ (top right); $\mathcal{D}^{RDTR}$ (bottom right)

Proposition 6. *The reverse of a complete (incomplete) REV-DFA is a complete (incomplete) REV-MeDFA (with a single final state).*

Proof. Let $\mathcal{D} = (Q, \Sigma, \delta, q_0, F)$ be a reversible DFA, either complete or incomplete. If we interchange the initial and final states of $\mathcal{D}$, and reverse the transitions of $\mathcal{D}$, then the resulting automaton $\mathcal{D}^R$ is a REV-MeDFA (with a single final state). Since the number of transitions of $\mathcal{D}$ is $|Q||\Sigma|$ if $\mathcal{D}$ is complete, and less than that otherwise, and the same applies to $\mathcal{D}^R$, we conclude that $\mathcal{D}^R$ is complete if and only if $\mathcal{D}$ is complete. $\square$

It is known that the class of REV-MeDFA languages strictly includes REV-DFA languages [7,8]. The following example shows that the reverse of a REV-DFA language – which is accepted by a REV-MeDFA with a single final state – does not necessarily have a reversible DFA, and that the atoms of a REV-DFA language are not REV-DFA languages:

Example 2. Consider a reversible DFA $\mathcal{D}$ of the language $L = ab^* + ab^*a + b$, shown in Fig. 1 on the left. When this DFA is reversed, determinized, and trimmed, we know by Theorem 1 that the resulting DFA $\mathcal{D}^{RDT}$ is the (incomplete) minimal DFA of L^R (on the top right). One can see that this DFA contains a "forbidden pattern" of Theorem 2: $\delta'(\{1\}, b) = \delta'(\{1, 2\}, b) = \{1\}$, and $\delta'(\{1\}, b\varepsilon) = \{1\}$, where δ' is the transition function of $\mathcal{D}^{RDT}$. Therefore the language L^R cannot be accepted by a reversible DFA. The trim átomaton of L is isomorphic to the NFA $\mathcal{D}^{RDTR}$ (on the bottom right). One can verify that the right language $b^*b(a + b)$ of the state $\{1\}$ of $\mathcal{D}^{RDTR}$ does not have a REV-DFA, by computing the minimal DFA of this language and applying Theorem 2 again. Thus, the corresponding atom is not a REV-DFA language.

6   Languages with a Reversible MeDFA

In this section we study properties of the languages accepted by a reversible MeDFA. REV-MeDFAs and their languages have been studied, for example, by Pin [13] and Lombardy [12], who used the terms "reversible automaton" and "reversible language". Some characterizations of REV-MeDFA languages have been established in [13]. In [12], a method to compute a REV-MeDFA from the minimal DFA of a REV-MeDFA language was presented.

We note that a reversible MeDFA is not necessarily complete. If the complete version of a REV-MeDFA involves an empty state, then it is not reversible.

A REV-MeDFA may consist of one or more connected components which are themselves REV-MeDFAs.

In [13] the following property of a REV-MeDFA language was presented:

Proposition 7. *A language is accepted by a REV-MeDFA if and only if it is a finite union of Bi-DFA languages.*

Also, it is clear that the following statement holds:

Proposition 8. *The reverse language of a REV-MeDFA language is a REV-MeDFA language.*

When we determinize a REV-MeDFA, the resulting DFA is not necessarily reversible (otherwise the classes of REV-MeDFA and REV-DFA languages would be the same). Figure 2 shows a REV-MeDFA $\mathcal{M}$ and the DFA $\mathcal{M}^{DT}$, obtained from $\mathcal{M}$ by determinization and removing the empty state. This DFA is not reversible.

Proposition 9. *The quotients of a REV-MeDFA language are REV-MeDFA languages.*

Proof. Let L be a REV-MeDFA language and let $\mathcal{M}$ be a REV-MeDFA accepting L. Clearly, any quotient of L is a union of right languages of some states of $\mathcal{M}$. For any state of $\mathcal{M}$, its right language is accepted by a REV-DFA, and the union of these languages is a REV-MeDFA language.   □

However, atoms of a REV-MeDFA language are not necessarily REV-MeDFA languages, as we will see by the next example. The following proposition is a slightly modified version of a property of a REV-MeDFA language presented by Pin [13] (originally, Pin [13] had $xu^+y \subset L$ instead of $xu^+y \subseteq L$):

Proposition 10. *If L is a REV-MeDFA language, then for every $x, u, v \in \Sigma^*$, $xu^+y \subseteq L$ implies $xy \in L$.*

Example 3. Consider the language $L = a^* \cup b^*$. This language is a REV-MeDFA language, as can be seen by a REV-MeDFA $\mathcal{M}$ of Fig. 2. The states of the determinized and trimmed version $\mathcal{M}^{DT}$ of $\mathcal{M}$ correspond to the non-empty quotients of L. The quotients of L are $K_0 = \varepsilon^{-1}L = a^* \cup b^*$, $K_1 = a^{-1}K_0 = a^*$,

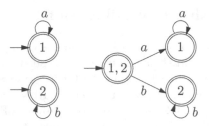

Fig. 2. A REV-MeDFA $\mathcal{M}$ (left) and the DFA $\mathcal{M}^{DT}$ (right)

$K_2 = b^{-1}K_0 = b^*$, and the empty quotient $K_3 = b^{-1}K_1 = a^{-1}K_2 = \emptyset$. The positive atoms of L are $A_0 = K_0 \cap K_1 \cap \overline{K_2} \cap \overline{K_3} = a^*a$, $A_1 = K_0 \cap \overline{K_1} \cap K_2 \cap \overline{K_3} = b^*b$, $A_2 = K_0 \cap K_1 \cap K_2 \cap \overline{K_3} = \varepsilon$, and there is also the negative atom $A_3 = \overline{K_0} \cap \overline{K_1} \cap \overline{K_2} \cap \overline{K_3} = \Sigma^*(ba^*a \cup ab^*b)$. By Proposition 10, the atom $A_0 = a^*a$ is not a REV-MeDFA language because $\varepsilon a^+ \varepsilon \subseteq A_0$, but $\varepsilon\varepsilon \notin A_0$. Similarly, one can verify that A_1 and A_3 are not REV-MeDFA languages.

6.1   Languages with a Complete Reversible MeDFA

In this section we study properties of the languages accepted by a complete reversible MeDFA.

First, similarly to the general case of REV-MeDFA languages, we can state the following proposition for the subclass of complete REV-MeDFA languages:

Proposition 11. *A language is accepted by a complete REV-MeDFA if and only if it is a finite union of complete Bi-DFA languages.*

A complete REV-MeDFA may consist of one or more connected components. Clearly, every connected component of a complete REV-MeDFA is itself a complete REV-MeDFA.

Proposition 12. *Any connected complete REV-MeDFA is strongly connected.*

Proof. Let $\mathcal{M}$ be a connected complete REV-MeDFA. Let us suppose that $\mathcal{M}$ is not strongly connected, that is, $\mathcal{M}$ consists of at least two strongly connected components. Because $\mathcal{M}$ is connected, every SCC of $\mathcal{M}$ is connected to some other SCC by either an incoming or outgoing transition. Consider any SCC C_i of $\mathcal{M}$. Because of complete reversibility, every state of C_i has $|\Sigma|$ incoming and $|\Sigma|$ outgoing transitions. If no state of C_i would have any incoming transition from any other SCC of $\mathcal{M}$, then every outgoing transition from every state of C_i would have to go into some state of C_i, or otherwise there would be a state of C_i with less than $|\Sigma|$ incoming transitions. Therefore, because C_i is connected to some other SCC by an incoming or outgoing transition, we conclude that C_i has an incoming transition from some SCC C_h as well as an outgoing transition to some SCC C_j, where $C_h \neq C_i$ and $C_j \neq C_i$. Since every SCC of $\mathcal{M}$ has this property and the number of SCCs is finite, we conclude that there are at least two SCCs which are strongly connected, a contradiction.   □

Proposition 13. *The reverse of a complete REV-MeDFA is a complete REV-MeDFA.*

Proof. Let $\mathcal{M}$ be a complete REV-MeDFA. If we interchange the initial and final states of $\mathcal{M}$ and reverse the transitions of $\mathcal{M}$, then the resulting automaton $\mathcal{M}^R$ is also a complete REV-MeDFA. □

Proposition 14. *The result of applying determinization to a complete REV-MeDFA is a complete REV-DFA.*

Proof. Let $\mathcal{M} = (Q, \Sigma, \delta, I, F)$ be a complete REV-MeDFA, and let us determinize it to get $\mathcal{M}^D$. First, we can see that every state s of $\mathcal{M}^D$ is a subset of Q with exactly $|I|$ elements in it.

Let the DFA $\mathcal{M}^D$ have n states. We show that every state of $\mathcal{M}^D$ is reversible. Let s be a state of $\mathcal{M}^D$ and $a \in \Sigma$. Because $\mathcal{M}$ is complete and reversible, there is a unique set $s' \subseteq Q$ with $|s'| = |s|$, such that $\delta(s', a) = s$, implying that the state s can have at most one incoming transition by a. Since the total number of transitions of $\mathcal{M}^D$ is $n|\Sigma|$, we conclude that every state of $\mathcal{M}^D$ has exactly one incoming transition with every symbol. Thus, $\mathcal{M}^D$ is a complete REV-DFA. □

As a consequence of Proposition 14, we can state the following theorem:

Theorem 3. *The classes of complete REV-MeDFA languages and complete REV-DFA languages are the same.*

Proposition 15. *The minimal DFA of a complete REV-MeDFA language is a complete REV-DFA.*

Proof. Let L be a complete REV-MeDFA language and let $\mathcal{M}$ be a complete REV-MeDFA of L. By Theorem 1, the minimal DFA of L is isomorphic to the DFA $\mathcal{M}^{RDRD}$. By Propositions 6, 13, and 14, the DFA $\mathcal{M}^{RDRD}$ is a complete REV-DFA. □

Corollary 1. *The minimal DFA of a complete REV-DFA language is a complete REV-DFA.*

Proposition 16. *The quotients of a complete REV-MeDFA language are complete REV-DFA languages.*

Proof. Let L be a complete REV-MeDFA language, and let $\mathcal{D}$ be the minimal DFA of L. By Proposition 15, $\mathcal{D}$ is a complete REV-DFA. Since any complete REV-DFA is connected and belongs to the class of complete REV-MeDFAs, we know by Proposition 12 that $\mathcal{D}$ is strongly connected. That is, every state of $\mathcal{D}$ is reachable from any other state of $\mathcal{D}$. Therefore, if we take any state of $\mathcal{D}$ as the initial state, we still get a complete REV-DFA. Thus, the right language of any state of $\mathcal{D}$ – a quotient of L – is a complete REV-DFA language. □

Proposition 17. *The átomaton of a complete REV-MeDFA language is a complete REV-MeDFA.*

Proof. Let L be a complete REV-MeDFA language. By Proposition 13, the reverse language L^R is also accepted by a complete REV-MeDFA. By Proposition 15, the minimal DFA of L^R is a complete REV-DFA, and by Proposition 6, the reverse automaton of the latter – the átomaton of L – is a complete REV-MeDFA.   □

Proposition 18. *The atoms of a complete REV-MeDFA language are complete Bi-DFA languages.*

Proof. Let L be a complete REV-MeDFA language, and let $\mathcal{A}$ be the atomaton of L. By Proposition 17, $\mathcal{A}$ is a complete REV-MeDFA. Since an atomaton is the reverse of a minimal DFA of the reverse language, $\mathcal{A}$ is connected, and by Proposition 12, $\mathcal{A}$ is strongly connected. Therefore, if we take any state of $\mathcal{A}$ as the only initial state, we get a complete REV-DFA with a single final state – a complete Bi-DFA. Thus, the right language of any state of $\mathcal{A}$ – an atom of L – is a complete Bi-DFA language.   □

7 Languages with a Reversible NFA

In this section we consider a class of languages accepted by a reversible NFA (REV-NFA). First, we make the following observation:

Proposition 19. *The átomaton of any regular language is a REV-NFA.*

Proof. The átomaton of a regular language is a REV-NFA (with a single final state), because its reverse automaton is the minimal DFA (of the reverse language).   □

Corollary 2. *The class of REV-NFA languages is equal to the class of regular languages.*

A subclass of REV-NFAs having a single initial state has been studied in [8]. We call such an NFA a reversible *single-entry* NFA (REV-SeNFA). In [8] it was shown that the class of REV-SeNFA languages is strictly included in the class of regular languages, implying that REV-SeNFA languages form a strict subclass of REV-NFA languages.

Example 4. Consider the language $L = c(a^* + b^*)$. The trim minimal DFA of L is shown in Fig. 3 on the left. One can see that this DFA does not meet the conditions of Theorem 2, therefore there is no REV-DFA for L. The trim átomaton of L is shown in Fig. 3 on the right. Since the átomaton has a single initial state, one can conclude that L is a REV-SeNFA language (in fact, it is a REV-SeSfNFA language). However, the quotient language $c^{-1}L = a^* + b^*$ does not have a REV-SeNFA as argued in [8].

As a consequence of Example 4, we can state the following two propositions:

Proposition 20. *Quotients of a REV-SeNFA language are not necessarily REV-SeNFA languages.*

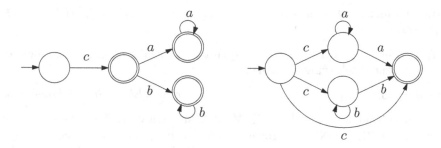

Fig. 3. Trim minimal DFA (left) and trim átomaton (right) of $L = c(a^* + b^*)$

Proposition 21. *Quotients of a REV-SeSfNFA language are not necessarily REV-SeNFA languages.*

Next, we will take a closer look at REV-SeNFAs with a single final state.

Proposition 22. *A language L is a REV-SeSfNFA language if and only if the átomaton of L has a single initial state.*

Proof. Let L be accepted by a REV-SeSfNFA $\mathcal{N}$. Then the reverse automaton $\mathcal{N}^R$ of $\mathcal{N}$ is a DFA with a single final state. This implies that the minimal DFA of L^R has a single final state. Therefore, the átomaton of L has a single initial state.

Conversely, if the átomaton of L has a single initial state, then it is a REV-SeSfNFA. ☐

The class of REV-SeNFA languages includes the REV-SeSfNFA languages as a strict subclass. An example of a REV-SeNFA language which does not have a REV-SeSfNFA, is the language $a^*(a + b + \varepsilon)$. Indeed, one can verify that this language is accepted by a REV-SeNFA, but does not have a REV-SeSfNFA because its átomaton has two initial states.

The following holds:

Proposition 23. *Atoms of any regular language are REV-SeSfNFA languages.*

Proof. Let L be a regular language and let $\mathcal{A} = (A, \Sigma, \delta, I_A, \{A_m\})$ be its atomaton. By Proposition 19, $\mathcal{A}$ is a REV-NFA. Now, for every atom A_i of L, we can form the NFA $\mathcal{A}_i = (A, \Sigma, \delta, \{A_i\}, \{A_m\})$ that accepts the language A_i. Some states of $\mathcal{A}_i$ may be unreachable, so we can also trim it. Clearly, $\mathcal{A}_i^T$ is a REV-SeSfNFA. ☐

Proposition 23 shows that atoms – which are building blocks of regular languages –, belong to a strict subclass of regular languages. Since any quotient of a regular language is a union of atoms, the following holds:

Proposition 24. *Quotients of a regular language are unions of REV-SeSfNFA languages.*

Also, every regular language L is equal to its initial quotient $\varepsilon^{-1}L$, therefore we can make the following corollary:

Corollary 3. *Every regular language is a union of REV-SeSfNFA languages.*

We note that although both REV-DFA and REV-SeSfNFA languages are subclasses of REV-SeNFA languages, they are not comparable. For example, the language $a + aa + b$ is in the class of REV-DFA languages (its incomplete minimal DFA is reversible), but by Proposition 22, it is not accepted by a REV-SeSfNFA. And the language a^*a is in the class of REV-SeSfNFA languages as can be verified by Proposition 22, but by Theorem 2, it is not accepted by any REV-DFA.

We also note that bideterministic languages are clearly a proper subclass of REV-SeSfNFA languages.

References

1. Angluin, D.: Inference of reversible languages. J. ACM **29**(3), 741–765 (1982)
2. Axelsen, H.B., Holzer, M., Kutrib, M.: The degree of irreversibility in deterministic finite automata. Int. J. Found. Comput. Sci. **28**(5), 503–522 (2017)
3. Brzozowski, J., Tamm, H.: Theory of átomata. Theor. Comput. Sci. **539**, 13–27 (2014)
4. Brzozowski, J.: Canonical regular expressions and minimal state graphs for definite events. In: Proceedings of the Symposium on Mathematical Theory of Automata. MRI Symposia Series, vol. 12, pp. 529–561. Polytechnic Press, Polytechnic Institute of Brooklyn, N.Y. (1963)
5. García, P., de Parga, M.V., López, D.: On the efficient construction of quasi-reversible automata for reversible languages. Inf. Process. Lett. **107**(1), 13–17 (2008)
6. Héam, P.: A lower bound for reversible automata. ITA **34**(5), 331–341 (2000)
7. Holzer, M., Jakobi, S., Kutrib, M.: Minimal reversible deterministic finite automata. Int. J. Found. Comput. Sci. **29**(2), 251–270 (2018)
8. Holzer, M., Kutrib, M.: Reversible nondeterministic finite automata. In: Phillips, I., Rahaman, H. (eds.) RC 2017. LNCS, vol. 10301, pp. 35–51. Springer, Cham (2017). https://doi.org/10.1007/978-3-319-59936-6_3
9. Iván, S.: Complexity of atoms, combinatorially. Inform. Process. Lett. **116**, 356–360 (2016)
10. Lavado, G.J., Pighizzini, G., Prigioniero, L.: Minimal and reduced reversible automata. J. Autom. Lang. Combin. **22**(1–3), 145–168 (2017)
11. Lavado, G.J., Pighizzini, G., Prigioniero, L.: Weakly and strongly irreversible regular languages. In: Proceedings 15th International Conference on Automata and Formal Languages, AFL 2017, Debrecen, Hungary, 4–6 September 2017, pp. 143–156 (2017)
12. Lombardy, S.: On the construction of reversible automata for reversible languages. In: Widmayer, P., Eidenbenz, S., Triguero, F., Morales, R., Conejo, R., Hennessy, M. (eds.) ICALP 2002. LNCS, vol. 2380, pp. 170–182. Springer, Heidelberg (2002). https://doi.org/10.1007/3-540-45465-9_16

13. Pin, J.-E.: On reversible automata. In: Simon, I. (ed.) LATIN 1992. LNCS, vol. 583, pp. 401–416. Springer, Heidelberg (1992). https://doi.org/10.1007/BFb0023844
14. Tamm, H.: On transition minimality of bideterministic automata. In: Harju, T., Karhumäki, J., Lepistö, A. (eds.) DLT 2007. LNCS, vol. 4588, pp. 411–421. Springer, Heidelberg (2007). https://doi.org/10.1007/978-3-540-73208-2_38
15. Tamm, H., Ukkonen, E.: Bideterministic automata and minimal representations of regular languages. Theor. Comput. Sci. **328**(1–2), 135–149 (2004)

SASB 2019 - 10th International Workshop on Static Analysis and Systems Biology

SASB 2019 Organizers' Message

The 10th International Workshop on Static Analysis and Systems Biology (SASB 2019) was held on October 8th, 2019 at Porto, Portugal. SASB 2019 was co-located with SAS 2019 (26th Static Analysis Symposium), both being part of the 3rd World Congress on Formal Methods.

The workshop SASB aims at promoting discussions and collaborations between biologists (modelers), computer scientists and applied-mathematicians. The workshop targets biological networks and executable models of biological systems, focusing on their formal specification and static analysis. A special emphasis is given to rule-based or process-algebraic languages that have the advantage of compact representation and provide a robust tool for systems and synthetic biology as well as a good base for molecular programming languages.

This year, five papers have been selected according to a rigorous refereeing process. The selected papers were presented at the workshop together with two invited presentations by Anne Siegel (CNRS, IRISA, Université Rennes 1, France) and Miguel P. Rocha (Universidade do Minho, Portugal). The post-proceedings include two out of the five workshop contributions. Fifteen Program Committee members helped to provide at least three reviews of the submitted contributions.

Further details on SASB 2019 are featured on the website: http://sat.inesc-id.pt/sasb2019/.

We are very grateful to the SAS General Chair Bor-Yuh Evan Chang, and to the FM'19 Workshop and Tutorial Chairs Emil Sekerinski and Nelma Moreira, for making this workshop possible. Also to Jérôme Feret for his advice and help on the organization and managing of SASB. We also would like to thank the Program Committee. We thank as well our contributing authors and our invited speakers Anne Siegel and Miguel P. Rocha.

November 2019

Pedro T. Monteiro
Jean Krivine

Organization

Lea Popovic	Concordia University, Canada
Verena Wolf	Saarland University, Germany
David Šafranek	Masaryk University, Czech Republic
Tatjana Petrov	University of Konstanz
Jérôme Feret	Inria, France
Luca Cardelli	Microsoft, UK
Ashutosh Gupta	TIFR, India
John Bachman	Harvard University, USA
Loïc Pauleve	CNRS/LRI, France
Heinz Koeppl	TU Darmstadt, Germany

Nicola Paoletti	Stony Brook University, USA
Hans-Michael Kaltenbach	ETH Zurich, Switzerland
Natasa Miskov-Zivanov	University of Pittsburgh, USA
Eugenio Cinquemani	Inria, France
Thomas Sauter	University of Luxembourg

Bayesian Verification of Chemical Reaction Networks

Gareth W. Molyneux$^{(\boxtimes)}$, Viraj B. Wijesuriya, and Alessandro Abate

Department of Computer Science, University of Oxford, Oxford OX1 3QD, UK
{gareth.molyneux,viraj.wijesuriya,alessandro.abate}@cs.ox.ac.uk

Abstract. We present a data-driven verification approach that determines whether or not a given chemical reaction network (CRN) satisfies
a given property, expressed as a formula in a modal logic. Our approach
consists of three phases, integrating formal verification over models with
learning from data. First, we consider a parametric set of possible models
based on a known stoichiometry and classify them against the property
of interest. Secondly, we utilise Bayesian inference to update a probability distribution of the parameters within a parametric model with
data gathered from the underlying CRN. In the third and final stage, we
combine the results of both steps to compute the probability that the
underlying CRN satisfies the given property. We apply the new approach
to a case study and compare it to Bayesian statistical model checking.

1 Introduction

Constructing complete models of biological systems with a high degree of accuracy is a prevalent problem in systems and synthetic biology. Attaining full
knowledge of many existing biological systems is impossible, making their analysis, prediction, and the designing of novel biological devices an encumbrance.
In this work, we integrate the use of probabilistic model-based analysis techniques with a data-based approach via Bayesian inference. Chemical Reaction
Networks (CRNs) [22] provide a convenient formalism for describing various biological processes as a system of well-mixed reactive species in a volume of fixed
size. This methodology allows for the construction of an accurate model from
the data to verify that the underlying data-generating system satisfies a given
formal property. Thus, by verifying the properties of the model, we can assert
quantitatively whether the underlying data generating system satisfies a given
property of interest. We leverage model analysis by means of formal verification,
namely quantitative model checking [6]. The end result is the computation of
a probability, based on the collected data, that the underlying system satisfies
a given formal specification. If the obtained probability is closer to either one
or zero, we can confidently draw an assertion on the satisfaction of the property over the underlying biological system. On the other hand, with a moderate

Gareth Molyneux acknowledges funding from the University of Oxford, the EPSRC &
BBSRC Centre for Doctoral Training in Synthetic Biology (grant EP/L016494/1).

© Springer Nature Switzerland AG 2020
E. Sekerinski et al. (Eds.): FM 2019 Workshops, LNCS 12233, pp. 461–479, 2020.
https://doi.org/10.1007/978-3-030-54997-8_29

probability value, a decision on the experimental setup or on the models needs to be made: we can either collect more data from the experiments, or propose alternative models and start the procedure once more. The proposed approach is different from statistical model checking (SMC) [1], in that standard SMC procedures require target systems with fully known models: these are also in general too large for conventional probabilistic model checkers (PMC) [6]. Alternative SMC procedures can also work with unknown models, provided that one is able to produce fully observable traces. Our work instead targets partially known systems that produce noisy observations at discrete points in time, which are commonplace in biology: these systems are captured by a parametric model class with imperfect knowledge of rates within a known stoichiometry. The new approach comprises of three phases. First, we propose a parametric model of a given, partially known biological system, and perform parameter synthesis [20] to determine a set of parameters over the parametric models that relates to models verifying the given property. This is performed via PRISM [20,21]. The second phase, executed in parallel with the first, uses Bayesian inference to infer posterior distributions over the likely values of the parameters, based on data collected from the underlying partially known and discretely observed system. In the third phase, we combine the outputs from the two phases to compute the probability that the model satisfies the desired property, which results in an assertion on the satisfaction of the property over the underlying biological system.

Related Work. CRNs have been utilised to model biological systems both deterministically [3] and stochastically [67] via the chemical master equation [30]. We use continuous-time Markov chains [42] (CTMCs) to model CRNs. Both probabilistic model checking approaches [5,44] and statistical model checking approaches [1] have been applied in many areas within biology [45,46,70] with tools such as PRISM [47], providing crucial support to perform procedures for continuous-time Markov chains such as parameter synthesis [18,20,38]. Bayesian inference [16,19] techniques have long been applied to biological systems [49]. In particular, we focus on inferring the kinetic parameters of the CRNs [17,60,66]. Exact inference is difficult due to the intractability of the likelihood function. Sampling techniques such as particle Markov chain Monte Carlo [33,34] and likelihood-free methods [52,58] such as approximate Bayesian computation [63,65] have been utilised to circumvent intractable likelihoods. Inferring parameters and formally verifying properties using statistical model checking for deterministic models is considered in [36]. Computing probability estimates using data produced by an underlying stochastic system, driven by external inputs to satisfy a given property, is considered in [37]. The integration of the parameter synthesis problem and Bayesian inference is considered for discrete-time Markov chains in [54] with the extension to actions for Markov decision processes in [55]. In [54], the authors consider exact parameter inference for a discrete state, discrete time system that consists of a handful of states with fully observed, continuous data. In our work, the data considered are discretely observed data points produced by a single simulation from a continuous-time

Markov chain given the true parameters, which is then perturbed by noise and we pursue likelihood free inference in the form of approximate Bayesian Computation [11,61]. Our approach is then compared to a Bayesian approach to statistical model checking [41,71].

The problem of learning and designing continuous-time Markov chains subject to the satisfaction of properties is considered in [14] meanwhile the model checking problem is reformulated to a sequential Bayesian computation of the likelihood of an auxiliary observation process in [51]. Directly related work is presented in [13]; a Bayesian statistical algorithm was developed that defines a Gaussian Process (GP) [57] over the parameter space based on a few observations of true evaluations of the satisfaction function. The authors build upon the idea presented in [14] and define the satisfaction function as a smooth function of the uncertain parameters of a given CTMC, where this smooth function can be approximated by a GP. This GP allows one to predict the value of the satisfaction probability at every value of the uncertain parameters from individual model simulations at a finite number of distinct parameter values. This model checking approach is incorporated into the parameter synthesis problem considered in [15] which builds upon the parameter synthesis problem defined in [21], but differs with the incorporation of the model checking approach presented in [13] and an active learning step being introduced to adaptively refine the synthesis. Model construction and selection via Bayesian design is presented in [7,8,69].

The rest of the paper is as follows. In Sect. 2, we cover the necessary background material required for our framework. In Sect. 3, we introduce our framework, covering parameter synthesis, Bayesian inference and the probability calculation techniques required. In Sect. 4, we consider the application of this framework to a case study and compare our framework to Bayesian statistical model checking [71]. We conclude with a discussion of our work and possible extensions.

2 Background

2.1 Parametric Continuous-Time Markov Chains

We work with discrete-state, continuous-time Markov chains [42].

Definition 1 (Continuous-time Markov Chain). *A continuous-time Markov chain (CTMC) $\mathcal{M}$ is a tuple $(\mathcal{S}, \boldsymbol{R}, AP, L)$, where;*

- *$\mathcal{S}$ is a finite, non-empty set of states,*
- *s_0 is the initial state of the CTMC,*
- *$\boldsymbol{R} : \mathcal{S} \times \mathcal{S} \to \mathbb{R}_{\geq 0}$ is the transition rate matrix, where $\boldsymbol{R}(s, s')$ is the rate of transitioning from state s to state s',*
- *$L : \mathcal{S} \to 2^{AP}$ is a labelling function mapping each state, $s \in S$, to the set $L(s) \subseteq AP$ of atomic propositions AP, that hold true in s.*

The transition rate matrix $\mathbf{R}$ governs the dynamics of the overall model. A transition between states s and s' can only occur if $\mathbf{R}(s, s') > 0$ and $s \neq s'$, in which case, the probability of triggering the transition within a time t is $1 - e^{-t\mathbf{R}(s,s')}$. If $s = s'$, $\mathbf{R}(s, s) = -E(s) = -\sum_{s' \in \mathcal{S}} \mathbf{R}(s, s')$, where $E(s)$ is defined as the exit rate from s. The time spent in state s before a transition is triggered is exponentially distributed by the exit rate, $E(s)$. We define a sample trajectory or path of a CTMC as follows.

Definition 2 (Path of a CTMC). *Let $\mathcal{M} = (\mathcal{S}, \mathbf{R}, AP, L)$ be a CTMC. A path ω of $\mathcal{M}$ is a sequence of states and times $\omega = s_0 t_0 s_1 t_1 \ldots$, where for all $i = 0, 1, 2, \ldots, n,$, $s_i \in \mathcal{S}$ and $t_i \in \mathbb{R}_{\geq 0}$, is the time spent in state s_i.*

Parametric continuous-time Markov chains (pCTMCs) extend the notion of CTMCs by allowing transition rates to depend on a vector of model parameters, $\boldsymbol{\theta} = (\theta_1, \theta_2, ..., \theta_k)$. The domain of each parameter θ_k is given by a closed real interval describing the range of possible values, $[\theta_k^\perp, \theta_k^\top]$. The parameter space Θ is defined as the Cartesian product of the individual intervals, $\Theta = \times_{\tilde{k} \in \{1, ..., k\}} [\theta_{\tilde{k}}^\perp, \theta_{\tilde{k}}^\top]$, so that Θ is a hyperrectangular set.

Definition 3 (Parametric CTMC). *Let Θ be a set of model parameters. A parametric Continuous-time Markov Chain (pCTMC) over $\boldsymbol{\theta}$ is a tuple $(\mathcal{S}, \mathbf{R}_{\boldsymbol{\theta}}, AP, L)$, where:*

- *$\mathcal{S}, s_0, AP$ and L are as in Definition 1, and*
- *$\boldsymbol{\theta} = (\theta_1, \ldots, \theta_k)$ is the vector of parameters, taking values in a compact hyperrectangle $\Theta \subset \mathbb{R}_{>0}^k$,*
- *$\mathbf{R}_{\boldsymbol{\theta}} : \mathcal{S} \times \mathcal{S} \to \mathbb{R}[\boldsymbol{\theta}]$ is the parametric rate matrix, where $\mathbb{R}[\boldsymbol{\theta}]$ denotes a set of polynomials over the reals $\mathbb{R}$ with variables θ_k, $\boldsymbol{\theta} \in \Theta$.*

Given a pCTMC and a parameter space Θ, we denote with $\mathcal{M}_\Theta$ the set $\{\mathcal{M}_{\boldsymbol{\theta}} | \boldsymbol{\theta} \in \Theta\}$ where $\mathcal{M}_{\boldsymbol{\theta}} = (\mathcal{S}, \mathbf{R}_{\boldsymbol{\theta}}, AP, L)$ is the instantiated CTMC obtained by replacing the parameters in $\mathbf{R}$ with their valuation in $\boldsymbol{\theta}$. We restrict the rates to be polynomials, which are sufficient to describe a wide class of biological systems [29].

2.2   Properties - Continuous Stochastic Logic

We aim to verify properties over pCTMCs. To achieve this, we employ the time-bounded fragment of *continuous stochastic logic* (CSL) [4,44].

Definition 4. *Let ϕ be a CSL formula interpreted over states $s \in \mathcal{S}$ of a pCTMC $\mathcal{M}_{\boldsymbol{\theta}}$, and φ be a formula over its paths. The syntax of CSL is given by*

$$\phi := true \mid a \mid \neg\phi \mid \phi \wedge \phi \mid \phi \vee \phi \mid P_{\sim p}[\varphi]$$

$$\varphi := X\phi \mid \phi U^{[t,t']}\phi \mid \phi U\phi,$$

where $a \in AP$, $\sim \in \{<, \leq, \geq, >\}$, $p \in [0, 1]$, and $t, t' \in \mathbb{R}_{\geq 0}$.

$P_{\sim p}[\varphi]$ holds if the probability of the path formula φ being satisfied from a given state meets $\sim p$. Path formulas are defined by combining state formulas through temporal operators: $X\phi$ is true if ϕ holds in the next state, $\phi_1 U^I \phi_2$ is true if ϕ_2 holds at all time points $t \in I$ and ϕ_1 holds for all time points $t' < t$. We now define a *satisfaction function* to capture how the satisfaction probability of a given property relates to the parameters and the initial state.

Definition 5 (Satisfaction Function). *Let ϕ be a CSL formula, $\mathcal{M}_\theta$ be a pCTMC over a space Θ, $s \in \mathcal{S}$, s_0 is the initial state, and $Path^{\mathcal{M}_\theta}(s_0)$ is the set of all paths generated by $\mathcal{M}_\theta$ with initial state s_0. Denote by $\Lambda_\phi : \theta \rightarrow [0,1]$ the satisfaction function such that $\Lambda_\phi(\theta) = Prob\left(\{\omega \in Path^{\mathcal{M}_\theta}(s_0) \models \varphi\} \,|\omega(0) = s_0\right) \sim p$.*

That is, $\Lambda_\phi(\theta)$ is the probability that a pCMTC $\mathcal{M}_\theta$ satisfies a property ϕ, $\mathcal{M}_\theta \models \phi$.

2.3 Stochastic Modelling of Chemical Reaction Networks

Semantics for continuous-time Markov chains include states that describe the number of molecules of each species and transitions which correspond to reactions that consume and produce molecules. These reactions are typically parameterised by a set of kinetic parameters that dictate the dynamics of the overall network and it is these parametric CRNs that we will turn our focus towards:

Definition 6 (Parametric Chemical Reaction Network). *A parametric Chemical Reaction Network (pCRN) $\mathcal{C}$ is a tuple $(M, \boldsymbol{X}, W, \mathcal{R}, \boldsymbol{v})$ where*

- *$M = \{m_1, \ldots, m_n\}$ is the set of n species;*
- *$\boldsymbol{X} = (X_1, ..., X_n)$ is a vector where each X_i represents the number of molecules of each species $i \in \{1, ..., n\}$. $\boldsymbol{X} \in W$, with $W \subseteq \mathbb{N}^N$ the state space;*
- *$\mathcal{R} = \{r_1, \ldots, r_k\}$ is the set of chemical reactions, each of the form $r_j = (\boldsymbol{v}_j, \alpha_j)$, with $\boldsymbol{v}_j$ the stoichiometry vector of size n and $\alpha_j = \alpha_j(\boldsymbol{X}, \boldsymbol{v}_j)$ is the propensity or rate function.*
- *$\boldsymbol{v} = (v_1, \ldots, v_k)$ is the vector of (kinetic) parameters, taking values in a compact hyper-rectangle $\Upsilon \subset \mathbb{R}^k$.*

Each reaction j of the pCRN can be represented as

$$r_j : u_{j,1}m_1 + \ldots + u_{j,n}m_n \xrightarrow{\alpha_j} u'_{j,1}m_1 + \ldots + u'_{j,n}m_n, \tag{1}$$

where $u_{j,i}$ $(u'_{j,i})$ is the amount of species m_i consumed (produced) by reaction r_j. The stoichiometric vector $\mathbf{v}_j$ is defined by $\mathbf{v}_j = \mathbf{u}'_j - \mathbf{u}_j$, where $\mathbf{u}_j = (u_{j,1}, \ldots, u_{j,n})$ and $\mathbf{u}'_j = (u'_{j,1}, \ldots, u'_{j,n})$.

A pCRN can be modelled as a pCTMC if we consider each state of the pCTMC to be a unique combination of the number of molecules. That is, if we denote $\mathbf{X}(t_i)$ as the number of molecules of each species at a given time, t_i, then the corresponding state of the pCTMC at time t_i is $s_i = \mathbf{X}(t_i)$. In fact, pCTMC semantics can be derived such that the transitions in the pCTMC correspond to reactions that consume and produce molecules, by defining the rate matrix as:

$$\mathbf{R}(s_i, s_j) = \sum_{j \in \zeta(s_i, s_j)} \alpha_j(s_i, v_j) = \sum_{j \in \zeta(s_i, s_j)} v_j g_j(s_i), \tag{2}$$

where $\zeta(s_i, s_j)$ denotes all the reactions changing state s_i into s_j and α_j is the propensity or rate function defined earlier and the propensity, α_j, often takes the form $\alpha_j(s_i, v_j) = v_j g_j(s_i)$, where $g_j(s_i)$ is the combinatorial factor that is determined by the number of molecules in the current state, s_i and the type of reaction j. It is clear to see that this new pCTMC is governed by the kinetic rate parameters, v, thus, $\mathcal{M}_v$ is the pCTMC that models the pCRN and for the rest of this paper, with a slight abuse in notation, we will let $\mathcal{M}_\theta$ be the pCTMC that represents a pCRN where θ are the kinetic rate parameters. Now the vector of kinetic parameters is defined as $\theta = (\theta_1, \ldots, \theta_k)$, where $\theta \in \Theta$ and $\Theta \subset \mathbb{R}^k$.

2.4   Bayesian Inference

When constructing mathematical models to describe real applications, statistical inference is performed to estimate the model parameters from the observed data. Bayesian inference [16] is performed by working either with or without a parametric model and experimental data, utilising the experimental data available to approximate the parameters in a given model and to quantify any uncertainties associated with the approximations. It is of particular interest to the biological community to constrain any uncertainty within the model parameters (or indeed the model itself) by using the observed data of biological systems. Moreover, when one is working with obstreperous stochastic models, noisy observations may add another layer of uncertainty. A plethora of literature is focused on the problem of Bayesian inference in stochastic biochemical models [60,65,67], let alone stochastic models [19]. Bayesian methods have been used extensively in the life sciences for parameter estimation, model selection and even the design of experiments [26,49,50,59,63,64].

Given a set of observations or data, D, and a model governed by θ, the task of Bayesian inference is to learn the true parameter values given the data and some existing prior knowledge. This is expressed through Bayes' theorem:

$$p(\theta|D) = \frac{p(D \mid \theta)p(\theta)}{p(D)}. \tag{3}$$

Here $p(\theta|D)$ represents the *posterior* distribution, which is the probability density function for the parameter vector, θ, given the data, D; $p(\theta)$ is the *prior* probability distribution which is the probability density of the parameter vector before considering the data; $p(D|\theta)$ is the *likelihood* of observing the data given a parameter combination; and $p(D)$ is the *evidence*, that is, the probability of observing the data over all possible parameter valuations. Assumptions about the parameters are encoded in the prior meanwhile assumptions about the model itself are encoded into the likelihood. The evidence acts as a normalisation constant and ensures the posterior distribution is a proper probability distribution. To estimate the posterior probability distribution, we will utilize Monte Carlo techniques.

3   Bayesian Verification

The main problem we address in this work is as follows. Consider a real-life, data generating biological system **S**, where we denote the data generated by the system as D and we are interested in verifying a property of interest, say ϕ. Can we use this obtained data and the existing knowledge of the model to formally verify a given property over this system, **S**?

Here on, we will be considering this problem using chemical reaction networks to describe biological systems. We assume that we have sufficient knowledge to propose a parametric model for the underlying system, which in this case is a pCTMC denoted by $\mathcal{M}_\theta$. We define the property of interest, ϕ, in CSL and we also assume that we are able to obtain data, D, from the underlying system. There are three aspects to the Bayesian Verification framework: parameter synthesis [20,21], Bayesian inference [16,19,52] and a probability or credibility interval calculation [16]. We shall discuss the data we work with and these methods in detail later. Given a model class $\mathcal{M}_\theta$ and a property of interest, ϕ, we first synthesise a set of parameter valuations $\Theta_\phi \subseteq \Theta$. If we were to choose a vector of parameters θ' such that $\theta' \in \Theta_\phi$, then the paths or traces generated from the induced pCTMC, $\mathcal{M}_{\theta'}$ would satisfy the property of interest with some probability, which we denote as $\mathcal{M}_{\theta'} \models \phi$. We learn the parameters of interest by inferring them from the data via Bayesian inference, to provide us with a posterior distribution, $p(\theta|D)$. Once we have this posterior distribution and a synthesised set of parameter regions, Θ_ϕ we integrate the posterior probability distribution over these regions to obtain a probability on whether the underlying data generating system satisfies the property or not. The full procedure is illustrated in Fig. 1.

3.1   Parameter Synthesis

Given a parametric model class $\mathcal{M}_\theta$ and a property ϕ defined in CSL, we synthesise parameter regions that satisfy ϕ using the approach introduced in [21]. We will focus on the threshold synthesis problem. Note that solutions to the threshold synthesis problem may sometimes lead to parameter points that are left undecided, that is, parameter points that either do or do not satisfy the property with a given probability bound, $\sim p$. Let us define this problem formally.

Definition 7 (Threshold Synthesis). *Let $\mathcal{M}_\theta$ be a pCTMC over a parameter space Θ, ϕ a CSL formula, $\sim p$ a threshold where $p \in [0,1]$, $\sim \in \{\leq, <, >, \geq\}$ and $\mathcal{E} > 0$ be a volume tolerance. The threshold synthesis problem is finding a partition $\{\mathcal{T}, \mathcal{U}, \mathcal{F}\}$ of Θ such that:*

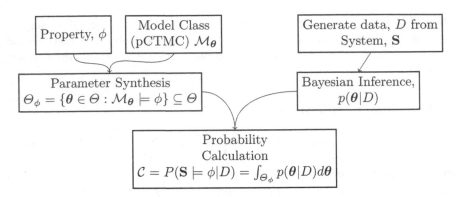

Fig. 1. Bayesian verification framework.

1. $\forall \boldsymbol{\theta} \in \mathcal{T}.\ \Lambda_\phi(\boldsymbol{\theta}) \sim p;$ and
2. $\forall \boldsymbol{\theta} \in \mathcal{F}.\ \Lambda_\phi(\boldsymbol{\theta}) \nsim p;$ and
3. $vol(\mathcal{U})/vol(\Theta) \leq \mathcal{E}$

where $vol(A)$ is the volume of A.

The goal of parameter synthesis is to synthesise the set of all possible valuations for which the model class $\mathcal{M}_\theta$ satisfies the property ϕ:

$$\Theta_\phi = \{\boldsymbol{\theta} \in \Theta\ :\ \mathcal{M}_\theta \models \phi\}. \tag{4}$$

We define the region $\Theta_\phi \subseteq \Theta$ as the feasible set of parameters. Parametric model checking capabilities of the tool introduced in [21] is leveraged to perform parameter synthesis over the CTMC constructed from a given pCRN.

3.2   Bayesian Inference for Parametric CTMC

In this section, we discuss the application of Bayesian inference for parametric CTMCs to infer unknown model parameters. Inferring parameters from pCTMCs is a widely studied problem in the realms of biology [17,28,34,35, 60,63,65–67]. The focus of our work here will be on performing inference over noisy time series data that has been observed a finite number of times at discrete points in time.

Partially Observed Data. Let us consider the case where the data D consists of Q observations of the CRN state vector at discrete points in time, $\tilde{t}_1, \tilde{t}_2, \ldots, \tilde{t}_Q$. Let $D = [\mathbf{Y}(\tilde{t}_1), \mathbf{Y}(\tilde{t}_2), \ldots, \mathbf{Y}(\tilde{t}_Q)]$, where $\mathbf{Y}(\tilde{t}_i) \in \mathbb{R}^N$ represents an observation of the molecule count sample $\mathbf{X}(\tilde{t}_i)$, which has a corresponding state s_i in the pCTMC. It is common to incorporate uncertainty in these observations with the use of additive noise [60,67],

$$\mathbf{Y}(\tilde{t}_i) = \mathbf{OX}(\tilde{t}_i) + \boldsymbol{\xi}, \tag{5}$$

where $\mathbf{O}$ is a $O \times n$ matrix, $\mathbb{R}^{O \times n}$ and $\boldsymbol{\xi}$ is a $O \times 1$ vector of independent Gaussian random variables. The observation vectors $\mathbf{Y}(\tilde{t}_i)$, are $O \times 1$ vectors where $O \leq n$, which reflects the fact that only a sub-set of chemical species of $\mathbf{X}(t_i)$ are observed. For this work, $\mathbf{O} = \mathbf{I}$, where $\mathbf{I}$ is an $n \times n$ identity matrix, recalling that n is the number of different chemical species. Due to both the nature of data we are working with and the intractability of the chemical master equation [30] that determines the likelihood, we turn away from working with the analytical likelihood to consider likelihood free methods [52,65]. Two popular classes of likelihood-free inference methods available are pseudo-marginal Markov chain Monte Carlo [2] and Approximate Bayesian Computation (ABC) [11,61]. In our work, we utilise ABC to infer parameters of our model. Not only do ABC methods allow working with highly complicated models with intractable likelihoods to be investigated, but also ABC methods are very intuitive and easy to implement - it has proven to be an invaluable tool in the life sciences [9,11,48,63]. To deploy ABC methods, we need to be able to simulate trajectories from a given model of interest, which in our case is a pCTMC, and require a discrepancy metric, $\rho(D, \tilde{\mathbf{X}})$, where $\tilde{\mathbf{X}} = (\tilde{\mathbf{X}}(\tilde{t}_1), \dots, \tilde{\mathbf{X}}(\tilde{t}_M))$ is the vector of simulated data generated through the model that consists of M reactions. This discrepancy metric provides a measure of distance between that of the experimental data and the simulated data and this simulated data will form the basis of our Bayesian inference technique. After calculating $\rho(D, \tilde{\mathbf{X}})$, we accept the traces where $\rho(D, \tilde{\mathbf{X}}) \leq \epsilon$, where ϵ is the discrepancy threshold. This leads to a modification of the original Bayes theorem

$$p(\boldsymbol{\theta} | \rho(D, \tilde{\mathbf{X}}) \leq \epsilon) = \frac{p(\rho(D, \tilde{\mathbf{X}}) \leq \epsilon \mid \boldsymbol{\theta}) p(\boldsymbol{\theta})}{p(\rho(D, \tilde{\mathbf{X}}) \leq \epsilon)}. \tag{6}$$

For the prior probability distribution, $p(\boldsymbol{\theta})$, we will assume a uniform prior over the possible parameter set, $\boldsymbol{\theta}$. By being able to produce simulations from the model, we are able to perform inference for the parameters of interest, subject to data D. The discrepancy threshold ϵ determines the level of approximation - as $\epsilon \to 0$, $p(\boldsymbol{\theta} \mid \rho(D, \tilde{\mathbf{X}}) \leq \epsilon) \to p(\boldsymbol{\theta}|D)$. In practice, Equation (6) can be treated as an exact posterior under the assumption of model and observation error when $\epsilon \to 0$ [68]. Picking an appropriate discrepancy metric is a challenge in itself [61] as the choice in discrepancy metric can lead to bias. The discrepancy metric used in our work is defined by

$$\rho(D, \tilde{\mathbf{X}}) = \left[\sum_{i=1}^{Q} (\mathbf{Y}(\tilde{t}_i) - \tilde{\mathbf{X}}(\tilde{t}_i))^2 \right]^{1/2}, \tag{7}$$

Clearly for any $\epsilon > 0$, ABC methods produce biased results and this bias should be considered in any subsequent results we obtain, especially for any Monte Carlo estimate. In order to estimate integrals such as the expected mean and covariance, which is necessary for the posterior probability distribution, we must be able to generate samples, $\boldsymbol{\theta}^{(i)}$ from the posterior. A summary of different methods available to obtain these samples can be found in [65] along with a detailed discussion on every method. We will be focusing on the approximate Bayesian computation sequential Monte Carlo (ABCSeq) approach [10,62,63]. The idea behind the ABCSeq approach is to use sequential importance resampling to propagate m samples, called particles, through a sequence of $R + 1$ ABC posterior distributions defined through a sequence of discrepancy thresholds, $\epsilon_0, \epsilon_1, \ldots, \epsilon_R$, with $\epsilon_r > \epsilon_{r+1}$, for $r = 0, 1, \ldots, R - 1$, for a number of R thresholds and $\epsilon_0 = \infty$. The method is presented in Algorithm 1.

Algorithm 1. ABCSeq Algorithm

1: Initialize threshold sequence $\epsilon_0 > \cdots > \epsilon_R$
2: Set $r = 0$
3: **for** $i = 1, \ldots, m$ **do**
4:     Simulate $\theta_i^{(0)} \sim p(\theta)$ and $\tilde{\mathbf{X}} \sim p(\tilde{\mathbf{X}}|\theta_i^{(0)})$ until $\rho(D, \tilde{\mathbf{X}}) < \epsilon_1$
5:     $w_i = 1/m$
6: **end for**
7: **for** $r = 1, \ldots, R - 1$ **do**
8:     **for** $i = 1, \ldots, m$ **do**
9:         **while** $\rho(D, \tilde{\mathbf{X}}) > \epsilon_r$ **do**
10:             Pick θ_i^* from the previously sampled $\theta_i^{(r-1)}$ with corresponding probabilities $w_i^{(r-1)}$, draw $\theta_i^{(r)} \sim K_r(\theta_i^{(r)}|\theta_i^*)$ and $\tilde{\mathbf{X}} \sim p(\tilde{\mathbf{X}}|\theta_i^{(r)})$
11:         **end while**
12:         Compute new weights as

$$w_i^{(r)} \propto \frac{p(\theta_i^{(r)})}{\sum_{i=0}^m w_i^{(r-1)} K_r(\theta_i^{(r)}|\theta_i^{(r-1)})}$$

13:         Normalize $w_i^{(r)}$ subject to $\sum_{i=0}^m w_i^{(r)}$
14:     **end for**
15: **end for**
16: **return** final particles, $\theta^{(R-1)}$

In Algorithm 1, $K_r(\cdot|\cdot)$ is a conditional density that serves as a transition kernel to move sampled parameters and then appropriately weight the accepted values, which are the parameter valuations which produce trajectories sufficiently close to the data. In the context of real-valued parameters, which we consider here, $K_r(\theta^*|\theta)$ is taken to be a multivariate normal distribution centred near θ. There are many adaptive schemes to increase the accuracy and the speed of ABCSeq [12,24], which vary from the choice of kernel [25], $K_r(\cdot|\cdot)$ to adapting the discrepancy threshold [56]. We implement the proposed kernel densities presented in [12] and chose an adaptive discrepancy threshold such that $\epsilon_{r+1} = median(\rho_r)$, where ρ_r is the vector of all accepted distances for each particle, calculated in line 9 of Algorithm 1. However, a larger number of particles, m, is required than the desired number of independent samples from the ABC posterior with discrepancy threshold ϵ. For our implementation, we set a maximum number of iterations in the loop in line 3 of Algorithm 1 to avoid infinite loops, and we return the particles of the previous sampled parameters if this were to be the case.

3.3 Probability Computation

In the final phase of our approach, a probability estimate is computed corresponding to the satisfaction of a CSL specification formula ϕ by a system of interest such that $\mathbf{S} \models \phi$. To calculate the probability that the system satisfies the specified property, we require two inputs - the posterior distribution over the whole set of kinetic parameters, $\boldsymbol{\theta}$, discussed in Sect. 3.2, and the feasible set of parameters that have been calculated in Sect. 3.1:

Definition 8. *Given a CSL specification ϕ and observed data D from the system* $\mathbf{S}$, *the probability that* $\mathbf{S} \models \phi$ *is given by*

$$\mathbb{C} = P(\mathbf{S} \models \phi \mid D) = \int_{\Theta_\phi} p(\boldsymbol{\theta} \mid D) d\boldsymbol{\theta}, \tag{8}$$

where Θ_ϕ denotes the feasible set of parameters. We estimate this integral with the use of Markov chain Monte Carlo (MCMC) methods focusing on the slice sampling technique [53].

4 Results

Experimental Setup. All experiments have been run on an Intel(R) Xeon(R) CPU E5-1660 v3 @ 3.00 GHz, 16 cores with 16 GB memory. We work with partially observed data of the type discussed in Sect. 3.2. Data is of the form $\mathbf{Y}(\tilde{t}_i) = \mathbf{X}(\tilde{t}_i) + \boldsymbol{\xi}$, where in the case of noisy observations, the additive noise for each observation j will be given by, $\xi_j \sim \mathcal{N}(0, \sigma)$ and $\sigma = 2$. The data generating system, $\mathbf{S}$ will in fact be a pCTMC with a chosen combination of parameters, of which we consider two. The first combination, $\boldsymbol{\theta}_\phi \in \Theta_\phi$, have been chosen such that $\mathcal{M}_{\boldsymbol{\theta}_\phi} \models \phi$, that is, the pCTMC model $\mathcal{M}_{\boldsymbol{\theta}_\phi}$, governed by $\boldsymbol{\theta}_\phi$, satisfies the property of interest. The second combination we choose are the parameters given by $\boldsymbol{\theta}_{\neg\phi} \in \Theta \setminus \Theta_\phi$, such that $\mathcal{M}_{\boldsymbol{\theta}_{\neg\phi}} \not\models \phi$. We will consider the scenario where we have both noisy and noiseless observations. To summarise, we have instances where we observe either 10 or 20 data points per species, which can be either noisy or noiseless and working with data that has been produced by either $\mathcal{M}_{\boldsymbol{\theta}_\phi}$ or $\mathcal{M}_{\boldsymbol{\theta}_{\neg\phi}}$. To ensure the inference does not depend on the initialisation of the ABCSeq technique, we ran 10 independent batches with 1000 particles each and calculated the corresponding weighted means and variance of the batches to derive the inferred mean and credibility intervals. The ABCSeq method produces sampled particles from the posterior probability distribution, which we use to calculate the mean, $\boldsymbol{\mu}$ and the covariance, $\boldsymbol{\Sigma}$, of the kinetic parameters. We assume the parameters are independent of each other, thus the nondiagonal elements of the covariance matrix are equal to 0. The inferred parameters $\tilde{\boldsymbol{\theta}}$ is thus described by a multivariate normal distribution $\tilde{\boldsymbol{\theta}} \sim \mathcal{N}(\boldsymbol{\mu}, \boldsymbol{\Sigma})$.

The Bayesian statistical model checking method [41] approach collects sample trajectories from the system, and then determines whether the trajectories satisfy a given property and applies statistical techniques, such as calculation of credibility intervals and hypothesis testing, to decide whether the system satisfies the property or not with a degree of probability.

4.1   Case Study: Finite-State SIR Model

We take into account the stochastic epidemic model [43], known alternatively as the SIR model. Epidemiological models of this type behave largely in the same way as CRNs [21]. The model describes the epidemic dynamics of three types, the susceptible group (S), the infected group (I), and recovered group of individuals (R). The epidemic dynamics can be described with mass action kinetics:

$$S + I \xrightarrow{k_i} I + I, \; I \xrightarrow{k_r} R. \tag{9}$$

Whenever a susceptible individual S encounters an infected individual I, the susceptible individual becomes infected with the rate k_i and infected individuals recover at rate k_r. Letting S, I and R represent chemical species instead of groups of individuals, this epidemiological model is the same as a CRN. From now on we treat the SIR model as a CRN. This CRN is governed by the parameters $\theta = (k_i, k_r)$, where each state of the CTMC describes the combination of the number of molecules for each species. The problem we consider is as follows. We assume that initially there are 95 molecules of species S, 5 molecules of species I and 0 molecules of species R, thus, the initial state is $s_0 = (S_0, I_0, R_0) = (95, 5, 0)$. We wish to verify the following property, $\phi = P_{>0.1}[(I > 0)U^{[100,150]}(I = 0)]$, i.e. whether, with a probability greater than 0.1, the chemical species I dies out strictly within the interval of $t = 100$ and $t = 150$ seconds. The data is produced by both $\mathcal{M}_{\theta_\phi}$ and $\mathcal{M}_{\theta_{\neg\phi}}$, where $\theta_\phi = (0.002, 0.05)$ and $\theta_{\neg\phi} = (0.002, 0.18)$.

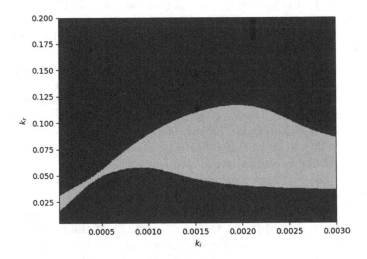

Fig. 2. Synthesised Parameter regions are shown here. The feasible set of parameters, $\mathcal{T}$, is shown in yellow (lighter colour), meanwhile the infeasible set of parameters, $\mathcal{F}$, is shown in blue (darker colour) $\Theta_{\neg\phi}$, with the undecided areas (if any) shown in white, the set $\mathcal{U}$. (Color figure online)

In the first phase of our method, we synthesise the feasible set of parameters, Θ_ϕ. For the parameter synthesis technique used in our work [20,21], we define parameter bounds and we confine our parameters to the set $\Theta = [k_i^\perp, k_i^\top] \times [k_r^\perp, k_r^\top] = [5 \times 10^{-5}, 0.003] \times [0.005, 0.2]$. The results of the parameter synthesis is shown in Fig. 2 and took a total of 3096 seconds (51.6 min) to compute. The second phase of our approach involves learning the kinetic parameters from data, D, via the ABCSeq method introduced in Sect. 3.2. To showcase the accuracy of our method, we consider different data scenarios. We take into account observed data where the observations are either distorted or not by additive noise, and the aforementioned two cases but with additional observed data points. A full list of different data scenarios and corresponding inferred parameters can be seen in Table 1. As expected, if we observe more, noiseless data points then our inferred parameters converge to the true parameters, $\boldsymbol{\theta}_\phi$ or $\boldsymbol{\theta}_{\neg\phi}$. The accuracy decreases drastically for data produced by the model $\mathcal{M}_{\boldsymbol{\theta}_{\neg\phi}}$. This is due to the largely uninformative observations as the samples reach steady state. To increase accuracy, more observations should be taken during the transient period of the model.

Bayesian SMC requires multiple simulated trajectories over a given model $\mathcal{M}_\theta$ to determine whether $\mathcal{M}_\theta \models \phi$. The issue with Bayesian SMC is that it considers a single instance of parameters, $\boldsymbol{\theta}^0$ and produces multiple simulations and statistically verifies whether the property is satisfied or not. When inferring parameters, we compute a probability distribution over the set of inferred parameters. If this distribution were to have a high variance, one would need to sample many parameters from the posterior distribution to sufficiently cover the space of the parameter probability distribution and then produce simulations for Bayesian SMC to evaluate each instantiation of the parameters. Meanwhile in our approach, we would only need to integrate the posterior distribution $p(\boldsymbol{\theta}|D)$ over the feasible parameter set Θ_ϕ to obtain a probability whether this property is satisfied or not. Bayesian SMC is illustrated in Fig. 3. For both Bayesian SMC and our method, we first had to infer the parameters to obtain a posterior probability distribution, which in this case, is a bivariate normal distribution. For Bayesian SMC, we sampled 100 independent evaluations of the parameters, and produced 1000 simulations for each evaluation to determine the probability that the model, $\mathcal{M}_\theta$, satisfies the property of interest. The sampled parameters are represented by the points represented by circles in Fig. 3, meanwhile the 95% credibility interval for the inferred parameters are represented by the black ellipses. The computation time for the Bayesian SMC approach was 756 seconds (12.6 min). With our approach, we simply need to integrate the bivariate normal distribution over the feasible parameter regions over the parameter regions to obtain the values in Table 1, and we do this numerically via slice sampling [53]. Both our technique and Bayesian SMC are in agreement, but for the Bayesian SMC approach we would require a larger number of sampled parameters to verify whether or not the entire posterior probability distribution lies in

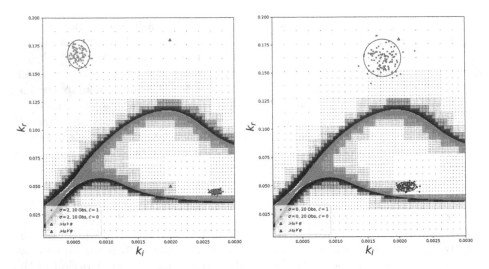

Fig. 3. Bayesian statistical model checking is performed over the inferred parameters for the case with 10 noisy observations on the left figure and for the case with 20 noiseless observations on the right figure. Dark blue (left figure) and green points (right figure) represent the probability values of 1 meanwhile the purple (left figure) and red points (right figure) represent probability values of 0. The parameters chosen to produce the data are represented by the cyan and orange triangles. The black elliptical lines represent the 95% credibility intervals of the inferred posterior distribution. The yellow (or blue) points represent the parameter valuation regions that satisfy ($\mathcal{T}$) (or don't satisfy, $\mathcal{F}$) the property. (Color figure online)

these feasible regions. Despite the fact that the parameter synthesis for the whole region takes longer to compute, the exhaustive parameter synthesis technique provides us a picture of the whole parameter space which is useful for further experiments and can be done entirely offline. For our multivariate slice sampler, we heuristically chose the number of samples to be 10000 and the scale estimates for each parameter, ν_i was chosen to be $\nu_i = 2$, with the initial value of the slice equal to the mean of the inferred posterior probability distribution. For further details on multivariate slice sampling (which leads to the credibility calculation given in Table 1), see [53]. For convergence results with statistical guarantees, we refer the reader to [23] meanwhile if interested in obtaining an upper bound on the probability calculated, we refer to [40]. Both the inference and Bayesian SMC techniques break down if simulating traces for CRNs is costly. Fortunately, there is ongoing research on approximation techniques that sacrifice the accuracy of Gillespie's algorithm for speed (such as the classical tau-leaping method [31]). For alternative approximation techniques, see [39,65] for more details.

Table 1. We have four different data scenarios to produce the data. Data within each of these datasets is produced given a combination of parameters that satisfy the property of interest, $\theta_\phi = (0.002, 0.05)$ and those that do not satisfy the property of interest $\theta_{\neg\phi} = (0.002, 0.18)$, (with or without additive noise $\sigma = 2$). We integrate the corresponding posterior distribution to give us the probability in column 5.

Inferred parameters					
Data	True par.	Mean	Std. dev.	Prob.	Comp. time (s)
10 Obs. with Noise	θ_ϕ	$\mu_{k_i} = 0.0027$	$\sigma_{k_i} = 4.7 \times 10^{-5}$	1	11791
		$\mu_{k_r} = 0.0451$	$\sigma_{k_r} = 0.0012$		
	$\theta_{\neg\phi}$	$\mu_{k_i} = 0.0006$	$\sigma_{k_i} = 8.7 \times 10^{-5}$	0	75
		$\mu_{k_r} = 0.1676$	$\sigma_{k_r} = 0.0063$		
20 Obs. with Noise	θ_ϕ	$\mu_{k_i} = 0.0022$	$\sigma_{k_i} = 0.0001$	0.9901	10840
		$\mu_{k_r} = 0.0468$	$\sigma_{k_r} = 0.0036$		
	$\theta_{\neg\phi}$	$\mu_{k_i} = 0.0015$	$\sigma_{k_i} = 0.0002$	0	3256
		$\mu_{k_r} = 0.1620$	$\sigma_{k_r} = 0.0104$		
10 Obs without Noise	θ_ϕ	$\mu_{k_i} = 0.0019$	$\sigma_{k_i} = 8.8 \times 10^{-5}$	0.9969	7585
		$\mu_{k_r} = 0.0549$	$\sigma_{k_r} = 0.00514$		
	$\theta_{\neg\phi}$	$\mu_{k_i} = 0.0015$	$\sigma_{k_i} = 0.0001$	0	3802
		$\mu_{k_r} = 0.1565$	$\sigma_{k_r} = 0.0074$		
20 Obs. without Noise	θ_ϕ	$\mu_{k_i} = 0.0021$	$\sigma_{k_i} = 7.3 \times 10^{-5}$	1	15587
		$\mu_{k_r} = 0.0487$	$\sigma_{k_r} = 0.0020$		
	$\theta_{\neg\phi}$	$\mu_{k_i} = 0.0017$	$\sigma_{k_i} = 0.0001$	0	5194
		$\mu_{k_r} = 0.1630$	$\sigma_{k_r} = 0.0084$		

5   Conclusions and Further Work

We have presented a data-driven approach for the verification of CRNs modelled as pCTMCs. The framework proposed integrates Bayesian inference and formal verification and proves to be a viable alternative to Bayesian SMC methods. We demonstrate how to infer parameters using noisy and discretely observed data using ABC and with the inferred posterior probability distribution of the parameters at hand, we calculate the probability that the underlying data generating system satisfies a property by integrating over the synthesised feasible parameter regions. Thus, given data from an underlying system, we can quantitatively assert whether properties of the underlying system are satisfied or not. Our method differs from that of typical Bayesian SMC as we calculate a single probability value with respect to the entire posterior distribution, meanwhile with Bayesian SMC, we would have to sample a sufficient amount of parameter values to cover the posterior distribution, thereon generate traces to determine whether a property is satisfied or not. Future work consists of integrating both learning and verification further as is done in [15] to improve the scalability of the parameter synthesis, working with different model classes such as stochastic differential equations [27,32] and models with actions, as is done in [55].

References

1. Agha, G., Palmskog, K.: A survey of statistical model checking. ACM Trans. Model. Comput. Simul. **28**(1), 6:1–6:39 (2018)
2. Andrieu, C., Roberts, G.O., et al.: The pseudo-marginal approach for efficient monte carlo computations. Ann. Stat. **37**(2), 697–725 (2009)
3. Angeli, D.: A tutorial on chemical reaction network dynamics. Eur. J. Control **15**(3), 398–406 (2009)
4. Aziz, A., Sanwal, K., Singhal, V., Brayton, R.: Verifying continuous time Markov chains. In: Alur, R., Henzinger, T.A. (eds.) CAV 1996. LNCS, vol. 1102, pp. 269–276. Springer, Heidelberg (1996). https://doi.org/10.1007/3-540-61474-5_75
5. Baier, C., Haverkort, B.R., Hermanns, H., Katoen, J.: Model-checking algorithms for continuous-time Markov chains. IEEE Trans. Softw. Eng. **29**(6), 524–541 (2003)
6. Baier, C., Katoen, J.: Principles of Model Checking. MIT Press, Cambridge (2008)
7. Barnes, C.P., Silk, D., Sheng, X., Stumpf, M.P.: Bayesian design of synthetic biological systems. Proc. Natl. Acad. Sci. **108**(37), 15190–15195 (2011)
8. Barnes, C.P., Silk, D., Stumpf, M.P.: Bayesian design strategies for synthetic biology. Interface Focus **1**(6), 895–908 (2011)
9. Beaumont, M.A.: Approximate bayesian computation in evolution and ecology. Annu. Rev. Ecol. Evol. Syst. **41**, 379–406 (2010)
10. Beaumont, M.A., Cornuet, J.M., Marin, J.M., Robert, C.P.: Adaptive approximate bayesian computation. Biometrika **96**(4), 983–990 (2009)
11. Beaumont, M.A., Zhang, W., Balding, D.J.: Approximate bayesian computation in population genetics. Genetics **162**(4), 2025–2035 (2002)
12. Bonassi, F.V., West, M., et al.: Sequential monte carlo with adaptive weights for approximate Bayesian computation. Bayesian Anal. **10**(1), 171–187 (2015)
13. Bortolussi, L., Milios, D., Sanguinetti, G.: Smoothed model checking for uncertain continuous-time Markov chains. Inf. Comput. **247**(C), 235–253 (2016)
14. Bortolussi, L., Sanguinetti, G.: Learning and designing stochastic processes from logical constraints. In: Joshi, K., Siegle, M., Stoelinga, M., D'Argenio, P.R. (eds.) QEST 2013. LNCS, vol. 8054, pp. 89–105. Springer, Heidelberg (2013). https://doi.org/10.1007/978-3-642-40196-1_7
15. Bortolussi, L., Silvetti, S.: Bayesian statistical parameter synthesis for linear temporal properties of stochastic models. In: Beyer, D., Huisman, M. (eds.) TACAS 2018. LNCS, vol. 10806, pp. 396–413. Springer, Cham (2018). https://doi.org/10.1007/978-3-319-89963-3_23
16. Box, G., Tiao, G.: Bayesian Inference in Statistical Analysis. Wiley Classics Library. Wiley, Hoboken (1973)
17. Boys, R.J., Wilkinson, D.J., Kirkwood, T.B.: Bayesian inference for a discretely observed stochastic kinetic model. Stat. Comput. **18**(2), 125–135 (2008)
18. Brim, L., Češka, M., Dražan, S., Šafránek, D.: Exploring parameter space of stochastic biochemical systems using quantitative model checking. In: Sharygina, N., Veith, H. (eds.) CAV 2013. LNCS, vol. 8044, pp. 107–123. Springer, Heidelberg (2013). https://doi.org/10.1007/978-3-642-39799-8_7
19. Broemeling, L.: Bayesian Inference for Stochastic Processes. CRC Press, Boca Raton (2017)
20. Ceska, M., Dannenberg, F., Paoletti, N., Kwiatkowska, M., Brim, L.: Precise parameter synthesis for stochastic biochemical systems. Acta Inf. **54**(6), 589–623 (2014)

21. Češka, M., Pilař, P., Paoletti, N., Brim, L., Kwiatkowska, M.Z.: PRISM-PSY: precise GPU-accelerated parameter synthesis for stochastic systems. In: Chechik, M., Raskin, J.-F. (eds.) TACAS 2016. LNCS, vol. 9636, pp. 367–384. Springer, Heidelberg (2016). https://doi.org/10.1007/978-3-662-49674-9_21

22. Cook, M., Soloveichik, D., Winfree, E., Bruck, J.: Programmability of chemical reaction networks. In: Condon, A., Harel, D., Kok, J., Salomaa, A., Winfree, E. (eds.) Algorithmic Bioprocesses, pp. 543–584. Springer, Heidelberg (2009). https://doi.org/10.1007/978-3-540-88869-7_27

23. Cowles, M.K., Carlin, B.P.: Markov chain monte carlo convergence diagnostics: a comparative review. J. Am. Stat. Assoc. **91**(434), 883–904 (1996)

24. Del Moral, P., Doucet, A., Jasra, A.: An adaptive sequential monte carlo method for approximate Bayesian computation. Stat. Comput. **22**(5), 1009–1020 (2012)

25. Filippi, S., Barnes, C.P., Cornebise, J., Stumpf, M.P.: On optimality of kernels for approximate Bayesian computation using sequential Monte Carlo. Stat. Appl. Genet. Mol. Biol. **12**(1), 87–107 (2013)

26. Galagali, N., Marzouk, Y.M.: Bayesian inference of chemical kinetic models from proposed reactions. Chem. Eng. Sci. **123**, 170–190 (2015)

27. Gardiner, C.: Stochastic Methods: A Handbook for the Natural and Social Sciences, vol. 13, 4th edn. Springer, Heidelberg (2009)

28. Georgoulas, A., Hillston, J., Sanguinetti, G.: Unbiased Bayesian inference for population Markov jump processes via random truncations. Stat. Comput. **27**(4), 991–1002 (2017)

29. Gillespie, D.T.: Exact stochastic simulation of coupled chemical reactions. J. Phys. Chem. **81**(25), 2340–2361 (1977)

30. Gillespie, D.T.: A rigorous derivation of the chemical master equation. Phys. A **188**(1), 404–425 (1992)

31. Gillespie, D.T.: Approximate accelerated stochastic simulation of chemically reacting systems. J. Chem. Phys. **115**(4), 1716–1733 (2001)

32. Gillespie, D.T.: The chemical Langevin equation. J. Chem. Phys. **113**(1), 297–306 (2000)

33. Golightly, A., Wilkinson, D.J.: Bayesian sequential inference for stochastic kinetic biochemical network models. J. Comput. Biol. **13**(3), 838–851 (2006)

34. Golightly, A., Wilkinson, D.J.: Bayesian parameter inference for stochastic biochemical network models using particle markov chain monte carlo. Interface Focus **1**(6), 807–820 (2011)

35. Golightly, A., Wilkinson, D.J.: Bayesian inference for Markov jump processes with informative observations. Stat. Appl. Genet. Mol. Biol. **14**(2), 169–188 (2015)

36. Gyori, B.M., Paulin, D., Palaniappan, S.K.: Probabilistic verification of partially observable dynamical systems. arXiv preprint arXiv:1411.0976 (2014)

37. Haesaert, S., den Hof, P.M.J.V., Abate, A.: Data-driven and model-based verification: a Bayesian identification approach. CoRR abs/1509.03347 (2015)

38. Han, T., Katoen, J.P., Mereacre, A.: Approximate parameter synthesis for probabilistic time-bounded reachability. In: 2008 Real-Time Systems Symposium, pp. 173–182 (2008)

39. Higham, D.J.: Modeling and simulating chemical reactions. SIAM Rev. **50**(2), 347–368 (2008)

40. Hoeffding, W.: Probability inequalities for sums of bounded random variables (1962)

41. Jha, S.K., Clarke, E.M., Langmead, C.J., Legay, A., Platzer, A., Zuliani, P.: A Bayesian approach to model checking biological systems. In: Degano, P., Gorrieri, R. (eds.) CMSB 2009. LNCS, vol. 5688, pp. 218–234. Springer, Heidelberg (2009). https://doi.org/10.1007/978-3-642-03845-7_15

42. Karlin, S., Taylor, H., Taylor, H., Taylor, H., Collection, K.M.R.: A First Course in Stochastic Processes, vol. 1. Elsevier Science, Amsterdam (1975)

43. Kermack, W.: A contribution to the mathematical theory of epidemics. Proc. R. Soc. Lond. A: Math. Phys. Eng. Sci. 115(772), 700–721 (1927)

44. Kwiatkowska, M., Norman, G., Parker, D.: Stochastic model checking. In: Bernardo, M., Hillston, J. (eds.) SFM 2007. LNCS, vol. 4486, pp. 220–270. Springer, Heidelberg (2007). https://doi.org/10.1007/978-3-540-72522-0_6

45. Kwiatkowska, M., Thachuk, C.: Probabilistic model checking for biology. In: Software Safety and Security. NATO Science for Peace and Security Series - D: Information and Communication Security. IOS Press (2014)

46. Kwiatkowska, M., Norman, G., Parker, D.: Probabilistic model checking: advances and applications. In: Drechsler, R. (ed.) Formal System Verification, pp. 73–121. Springer, Cham (2018). https://doi.org/10.1007/978-3-319-57685-5_3

47. Kwiatkowska, M., Norman, G., Parker, D.: PRISM 4.0: verification of probabilistic real-time systems. In: Gopalakrishnan, G., Qadeer, S. (eds.) CAV 2011. LNCS, vol. 6806, pp. 585–591. Springer, Heidelberg (2011). https://doi.org/10.1007/978-3-642-22110-1_47

48. Kypraios, T., Neal, P., Prangle, D.: A tutorial introduction to Bayesian inference for stochastic epidemic models using approximate Bayesian computation. Math. Biosci. 287, 42–53 (2017). 50th Anniversary Issue

49. Lawrence, N.D., Girolami, M., Rattray, M., Sanguinetti, G. (eds.): Learning and Inference in Computational Systems Biology. MIT Press, Cambridge; London (2010)

50. Liepe, J., Filippi, S., Komorowski, M., Stumpf, M.P.H.: Maximizing the information content of experiments in systems biology. PLoS Comput. Biol. 9(1), 1–13 (2013)

51. Milios, D., Sanguinetti, G., Schnoerr, D.: Probabilistic model checking for continuous-time Markov chains via sequential Bayesian inference. In: McIver, A., Horvath, A. (eds.) QEST 2018. LNCS, vol. 11024, pp. 289–305. Springer, Cham (2018). https://doi.org/10.1007/978-3-319-99154-2_18

52. Murphy, K.P.: Machine Learning - A Probabilistic Perspective. Adaptive Computation and Machine Learning Series. MIT Press, Cambridge (2012)

53. Neal, R.M.: Slice sampling. Ann. Statist. 31(3), 705–767 (2003)

54. Polgreen, E., Wijesuriya, V.B., Haesaert, S., Abate, A.: Data-efficient Bayesian verification of parametric Markov chains. In: Agha, G., Van Houdt, B. (eds.) QEST 2016. LNCS, vol. 9826, pp. 35–51. Springer, Cham (2016). https://doi.org/10.1007/978-3-319-43425-4_3

55. Polgreen, E., Wijesuriya, V.B., Haesaert, S., Abate, A.: Automated experiment design for data-efficient verification of parametric Markov decision processes. In: Bertrand, N., Bortolussi, L. (eds.) QEST 2017. LNCS, vol. 10503, pp. 259–274. Springer, Cham (2017). https://doi.org/10.1007/978-3-319-66335-7_16

56. Prangle, D., et al.: Adapting the ABC distance function. Bayesian Anal. 12(1), 289–309 (2017)

57. Rasmussen, C.E.: Gaussian processes in machine learning. In: Bousquet, O., von Luxburg, U., Rätsch, G. (eds.) ML -2003. LNCS (LNAI), vol. 3176, pp. 63–71. Springer, Heidelberg (2004). https://doi.org/10.1007/978-3-540-28650-9_4

58. Revell, J., Zuliani, P.: Stochastic rate parameter inference using the cross-entropy method. In: Češka, M., Šafránek, D. (eds.) CMSB 2018. LNCS, vol. 11095, pp. 146–164. Springer, Cham (2018). https://doi.org/10.1007/978-3-319-99429-1_9
59. Sanguinetti, G., Lawrence, N.D., Rattray, M.: Probabilistic inference of transcription factor concentrations and gene-specific regulatory activities. Bioinformatics **22**(22), 2775–2781 (2006)
60. Schnoerr, D., Sanguinetti, G., Grima, R.: Approximation and inference methods for stochastic biochemical kinetics: a tutorial review. J. Phys. A: Math. Theor. **50**(9), 093001 (2017)
61. Sisson, S.A., Fan, Y., Beaumont, M.: Handbook of Approximate Bayesian Computation. Chapman and Hall/CRC, Boca Raton (2018)
62. Sisson, S.A., Fan, Y., Tanaka, M.M.: Sequential monte carlo without likelihoods. Proc. Natl. Acad. Sci. **104**(6), 1760–1765 (2007)
63. Toni, T., Welch, D., Strelkowa, N., Ipsen, A., Stumpf, M.P.: Approximate bayesian computation scheme for parameter inference and model selection in dynamical systems. J. R. Soc. Interface **6**(31), 187–202 (2008)
64. Vanlier, J., Tiemann, C.A., Hilbers, P.A., van Riel, N.A.: Optimal experiment design for model selection in biochemical networks. BMC Syst. Biol. **8**(1), 20 (2014)
65. Warne, D.J., Baker, R.E., Simpson, M.J.: Simulation and inference algorithms for stochastic biochemical reaction networks: from basic concepts to state-of-the-art. J. R. Soc. Interface **16**(151), 20180943 (2019)
66. Wilkinson, D.J.: Parameter inference for stochastic kinetic models of bacterial gene regulation: a Bayesian approach to systems biology. In: Proceedings of 9th Valencia International Meeting on Bayesian Statistics, pp. 679–705 (2010)
67. Wilkinson, D.: Stochastic Modelling for Systems Biology, 2nd edn. Chapman & Hall/CRC Mathematical and Computational Biology, Taylor & Francis (2011)
68. Wilkinson, R.D.: Approximate Bayesian computation (ABC) gives exact results under the assumption of model error. Stat. Appl. Genet. Mol. Biol. **12**(2), 129–141 (2013)
69. Woods, M.L., Leon, M., Perez-Carrasco, R., Barnes, C.P.: A statistical approach reveals designs for the most robust stochastic gene oscillators. ACS Synth. Biol. **5**(6), 459–470 (2016)
70. Zuliani, P.: Statistical model checking for biological applications. Int. J. Softw. Tools Technol. Transfer **17**(4), 527–536 (2015)
71. Zuliani, P., Platzer, A., Clarke, E.M.: Bayesian statistical model checking with application to Stateflow/Simulink verification. Formal Methods Syst. Des. **43**, 338–367 (2013)

Nested Event Representation for Automated Assembly of Cell Signaling Network Models

Evan W. Becker[1]([✉]), Kara N. Bocan[1], and Natasa Miskov-Zivanov[1,2,3]

[1] Department of Electrical and Computer Engineering, University of Pittsburgh, Pittsburgh, USA
{ewb12,knb12,nmzivanov}@pitt.edu
[2] Department of Bioengineering, University of Pittsburgh, Pittsburgh, USA
[3] Department of Computational and Systems Biology, University of Pittsburgh, Pittsburgh, USA

Abstract. The rate at which biological literature is published far outpaces the current capabilities of modeling experts. In order to facilitate the automation of model assembly, we improve upon methods for converting machine reading output obtained from papers studying intracellular networks into discrete element rule-based models. We introduce a graph representation that can capture the complicated semantics found in machine reading output. Specifically, we focus on extracting change-of-rate information available when network elements are found to inhibit or catalyze other interactions (nested events). We demonstrate the viability of this approach by measuring the prevalence of these nested events in cancer literature, as well as the success rates of two machine readers in capturing them. Finally, we show how our algorithm can translate between machine reading output and the new graphical form. By incorporating these more detailed interactions into the model, we can more accurately predict cellular dynamics on a broad scale, leading to improvements in experimental design and disease treatment discovery.

Keywords: Machine reading · Text mining · Cell signaling networks · Automated model generation

1 Introduction

Modeling summarizes relevant information about a system and allows researchers to make inferences about behavior, find knowledge gaps, and construct new experiments. In the field of systems biology, researchers have often used qualitative graphical models, with cellular components represented as nodes (e.g., proteins, genes, chemicals), and interactions between these components as edges (e.g., phosphorylation, transcription) [1,2]. These models are highly interpretable and suitable for conveying the information about complex signaling pathways and feedback loops. Tools such as Cytoscape [3], OmicsNet [4,5], REACTOME [6], and STRING [7] have been designed to automatically visualize biological networks as graphs. However, experts must manually input information for each

© Springer Nature Switzerland AG 2020
E. Sekerinski et al. (Eds.): FM 2019 Workshops, LNCS 12233, pp. 480–499, 2020.
https://doi.org/10.1007/978-3-030-54997-8_30

interaction into these tools, a process that becomes impractical for extremely large networks. The tools that provide graphical model representations are also highly variable (e.g., different naming conventions, allowable interactions), making it difficult for researchers to share and extend.

Adding functions in nodes or on edges of graphical models enables model simulation, which can in turn provide detailed predictions about system dynamics. Compared to graphs, these models require many more parameters to be carefully selected. Typically, parameters are harder to find as well, often leading to tedious searches through specialized databases and experimental data. Sometimes, parameter values are not available at all, and in such cases parameterization techniques must be used to estimate them.

To solve the problem of automating both the model network assembly and the parameterization, attempts have been made to standardize the language of scientific discourse itself. Languages such as SBML (systems biology markup language) [8], CellML [9], BioNetGen (BNGL) [10], and Kappa [11] have been proposed and utilized to various extents for the communication of biological systems. However, these standards are often hard to directly interpret by humans and still require manual modification, either directly or through an interface. Moreover, natural language remains the most efficient way for researchers to summarize and distribute their findings. As there is currently no universal method for interpreting scientific text, models are often entirely constructed and parameterized by hand from the information in literature, leading to limitations in scope and accuracy [12]. The high rate of scientific publication further emphasizes the need for a standardized representation, which would also facilitate the automation of model assembly from publications.

First step in the automated assembly of models from scientific texts requires reliable machine reading engines. The field of natural language processing (NLP) focuses on tasks such as machine translation, information retrieval, text summarization, question answering, information extraction, and opinion mining [13]. As NLP techniques have moved from purely syntactic interpretations to deeper semantic understanding, the opportunity now exists to automate model generation. Two NLP systems (also called machine readers) built with this goal in mind are REACH [14] and TRIPS [15]. INDRA (Integrated Network and Dynamical Reasoning Assembler) is an example of a system currently being developed to automatically process machine reading output into models. INDRA utilizes domain specific "statements" to represent detailed information about interactions that are extracted from scientific papers by machine readers such as REACH or TRIPS. For biological applications, dozens of unique statement classes are instantiated with attributes such as location, mutation, residue. As INDRA aims to assemble event (biochemical reaction) rule-based models [16] and continuous ODE models, these statements must be very detailed. This requirement complicates the process of mapping NLP extractions to INDRA statements.

On the other hand, discrete element rule-based models have been shown to efficiently simulate biological systems, without the need for a complex parameterization process [12,17,18]. This highly canonical representation lends itself well to an automated assembly process, as demonstrated in [19], where the BioRECIPES format was proposed as an intermediate representation between

NLP system output and discrete element rule-based models. BioRECIPES is a tabular format where one row corresponds to one model element, listing the available structured information about that element, and each column represents one of the attributes of either a model element or the element's influence set. This format is easy to read and extend by both machines and humans. Having this intermediate representation is useful for aggregating data from multiple NLP sources, verifying the accuracy of extractions, and filtering the information to be used for constructing the executable model. Furthermore, as shown previously, various biological motifs (phosphorylation, translocation, transcription, binding, etc.) are easily represented using the BioRECIPES format [19,20].

Here we define a *nested event* to be any direct interaction between two events occurring in natural language. We also define a *regulating nested event* as a subtype of the nested event in which one event is modified by the other (e.g., an increase in activation). This type of interaction stands in contrast to a nested event in which one event serves as a causal input to another event (e.g., phosphorylation causes activation). The regulating nested event is the type of interaction that we are specifically focusing on in this work. A statement containing a regulating nested event would typically suggest a change in rate for an ODE model.

While enabling straightforward automated translation of simple biological interactions into executable models, the translation of nested events from reading output to the BioRECIPES format is still done manually. Being able to automatically capture this more complicated information (when available) would enable faster assembly and parameterization of models that will allow for more accurate simulation of system dynamics. To this end, the contributions of the work presented here include:

1. We propose a *new data structure* to extend the BioRECIPES representation format and enable more effective representation of nested events.
2. We introduce an algorithm to *automatically translate* biological nested events from available machine reading output into the new data structure.
3. We *evaluate* the accuracy of NLP systems at *extracting nested events* and demonstrate our algorithm's function on reading examples processed through REACH and TRIPS/DRUM systems.

2   Background

2.1   Discrete Element Rule-Based Models

Since we are especially interested in the cause and effect relationships between system components (instead of just correlations), we model connections between elements as directed. In other words, the set of all regulators influencing one element is called an *influence set* [1,21,22], and the overall model network is referred to as an *influence network*. All the information essential for studying such influence networks can be expressed using the BioRECIPES representation format [19].

Furthermore, the influence network models can also be translated from the BioRECIPES format into a graph representation. In graphical form, influences are represented with signed edges, which imply either an increase or decrease in value of the regulated node (illustrated with an arrow and bar, respectively). Edges are always directed toward a single child node but can have multiple parent nodes (directed hyperedge, see Fig. 1(left)) joined by logical operators. This formalism is extremely useful for its scalability and interpretability.

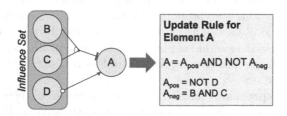

Fig. 1. (Left) Graphical visualization of a BioRECIPES influence set. Elements B and C are joined together with an AND rule (illustrated with an arc), while element D is inverted (illustrated with an unfilled circle). Positive and negative regulators can then be combined into a discrete update rule (right).

From both the BioRECIPES and the graphical format described above, one can automatically generate *executable models* in which each model element is assigned a variable and a regulatory function called *element update rule*. In discrete executable models, variable values correspond to the activation, strength, or quantity levels of the corresponding element. A special case of discrete models are logical models that assume only two values (0 and 1) for all variables and logic operations (AND, OR, NOT) between variables. While our methodology is applicable more generally to models with discrete variables and algebraic operations, for simplicity, we will use logical model examples in this paper (e.g., Fig. 1(right)).

When models are created from the information extracted from literature, both qualitative information about biological mechanisms of interactions and quantitative information about levels of activity or amount are incorporated, resulting in *discrete element rule-based models*. These models can be directly used to study the system dynamics and the behavior of its components in time, through simulations and model checking. The simulation is done by changing element states over time according to their update rules. Here, we use DiSH (Discrete, Stochastic, Heterogeneous) simulator, which offers several different schemes for updating element states, including simultaneous (deterministic, all elements are updated at the same time, based on their update rule and previous state), random-order sequential (elements update one at a time based on a probability distribution), and ranked sequential (elements or groups of elements updated in a predefined order) [14].

2.2   Established Motifs

In their initial paper on biological motifs, Sayed et al. [20] explored mapping gene expression, receptor activation, and translocation interactions to the BioRECIPES format. Later, the list of motifs was expanded to include complexes, activation/inhibition type events, and nested events [19]. A brief overview of these motifs is provided below, including the motif for simple biochemical interactions.

The **Simple Interaction** motif represents posttranslational modification events (phosphorylation, acetylation, methylation, dephosphorylation, ubiquitination, demethylation), as well as increase amount and decrease amount events. In Fig. 2(a), we show an example of phosphorylation, which is represented in the BioRECIPES format as positive regulation, unless it is explicitly stated that it is a negative regulation.

The **Gene Expression** motif represents a chain of elements, a gene, and its corresponding mRNA and protein. As illustrated in Fig. 2(b), in the BioRECIPES format, gene transcription is represented as positive regulation of mRNA X by gene X, and translation is represented as positive regulation of protein X by mRNA X.

The **Receptor Activation** motif includes three elements, an inactive (present) receptor, activated receptor, and ligand that binds to the receptor to activate it. In the BioRECIPES format, this is represented as the active receptor form being positively regulated by the presence of inactive receptor form and the ligand (AND rule). In the graphical representation, this motif is mapped to a hypergraph, as shown in Fig. 2(c).

The **Translocation** motif includes two versions of the same element at two different locations (e.g., protein in nucleus and protein in cytoplasm). In the BioRECIPES format, as shown in Fig. 2(d), this is represented as the version of element in the original ("from") location positively regulating the version of element in the final ("to") location.

The **Binding** motif is represented in the BioRECIPES format using multiple elements, that is, each individual component of a complex being formed has a corresponding model element, as shown in Fig. 2(e). If element X is facilitating the binding of A and B into a complex, then this regulation is included in the update rule of A as B AND X, and in the update rule for B as A AND X.

The **Regulation by Complex** motif is used when an element Y is regulated by a complex consisting of elements A and B. In the BioRECIPES format, this regulation is included in the update function for Y as A AND B. The graph representation of this motif is also shown in Fig. 2(e), on the right side of the graph.

The **Nested Interaction** motif, as defined in Sect. 1, represents regulation of activation or inhibition, that is, the situations when interactions between elements are themselves being regulated. An example of such motif, where protein A increases dephosphorylation of protein Y by protein X is shown in Fig. 2(f).

2.3   Machine Reading Engines

Representation format of machine reading output varies widely across readers, and even from application to application. Popular methods for representing knowledge about natural language include first order logic, default logic, production rules, semantic networks, and Bayesian networks [13]. The two readers analyzed in this work both produce outputs that can be considered semantic networks. They mainly consist of *event nodes* (indicating a type of change over time) and *entity nodes* (objects from text that can be distinctly identified). A set of predefined relations (*semantic roles*) link the nodes together.

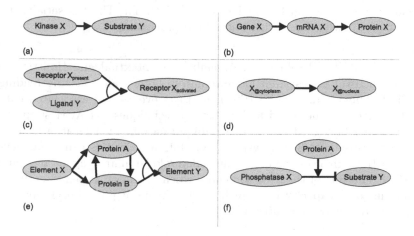

Fig. 2. Established motifs: (a) Simple Interaction motif: phosphorylation example, kinase X and substrate Y; (b) Gene Expression motif; (c) Receptor Activation motif, both ligand and receptor are necessary to activate receptor, illustrated with an arc; (d) Translocation motif, example of translocation of element X from cytoplasm to nucleus; (e) Binding and Regulation by Complex motifs, example of complex formation, and regulation of other elements by that complex; (f) Nested Interaction motif, example of protein A catalyzing dephosphorylation of Y by X, illustrated here by an edge ending at another edge.

TRIPS and Logical Form Graphs: The TRIPS (The Rochester Interactive Planner System) parser is a broad-coverage semantic parser that produces *logical forms* from natural language [15]. The logical form is a semantic notation that captures the meaning of a sentence and consists of a set of terms from the ontology that describe events, relations and entity types, all linked together by semantic roles. Two of the most useful semantic roles for our application describe how entities relate to events, either through an instigative role (AGENT) or an altered role (AFFECTED). In graphical form, terms are represented by nodes and roles by edges as seen in Fig. 3(a).

Since one of our modeling aims is to enable representation of causal relations, we need evidence of an object changing in response to another. Therefore, transitive and telic verbs are mainly of interest, and other semantic roles included in TRIPS such as neutral, formal, and experiencer are ignored. While roles such as modality are important for differentiating between putative relations and factual statements, their interpretation is outside the scope of this work.

TRIPS extends its parser for specific applications such as cellular biology (DRUM parser) [24]. Extensions include different cost minimization functions for sentence structure and custom named entity recognition (NER) mappings. With a few extraction rules for each class of event (phosphorylation, increase, decrease, etc.), TRIPS can then select relevant information to pass on to the user, called the extraction knowledge base (EKB). The EKB is serialized into XML format, allowing for further automated processing.

REACH: REACH (Reading and Assembling Contextual and Holistic Mechanisms from Text) is a system for automated, large-scale machine reading of biomedical papers [14]. Like TRIPS, it extracts events and associated entities through a series of rule-based and statistical techniques. REACH supports 12 types of simple biological events (e.g., ubiquitination, translocation), and can also detect nested events (catalysis and inhibition). Entities can be associated with events through a controlling or controlled role (similar to agent and affected in TRIPS). The role of theme is to denote when an entity is being modified by the event in some capacity (e.g., pRb, is the theme of phosphorylation in the sentence "CDK4 phosphorylates pRb").

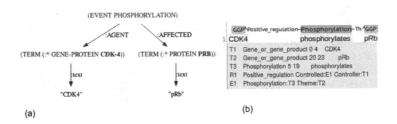

(a)   (b)

Fig. 3. Examples of machine reader outputs for "CDK-4 phosphorylates pRb": (a) Extractions from TRIPS (EKB); (b) REACH output shown using the online Bio Visualizer tool [21].

3   Methods

In this section, we propose a representation for regulating nested events and discuss its general use cases. We also provide an outline of a recursive algorithm that can automatically convert nested events from machine reading output into this new representation format.

3.1   Intermediate Nodes

While the six motifs shown in Fig. 2 allow us to represent a wide variety of biological networks, the nested interaction, as depicted in Fig. 2(e), cannot be immediately represented in a typical graph data structure. This stems from the fact that a standard graph (consisting of element nodes containing links to other nodes) has no way to represent regulation of an edge [23]. This incompatibility makes it challenging for nested events found in NLP extractions to be automatically translated into the BioRECIPES format. One can model nested events by creating implicit notations for hyperedges (see Fig. 2, parts (c) and (e)) but this format is not amenable to extension, since it is difficult to add new regulators to the hyperedge once created. The regulator notation used in the tabular format may be difficult to interpret by human readers without additional visualization software, especially when other logical operators are combined with nested notation. An example of such situation is illustrated in Fig. 4.

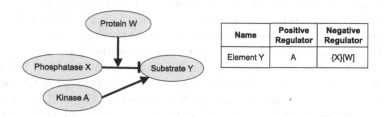

Fig. 4. Graphical representation where an edge ends in another edge instead of a node (left), and the same interaction represented using the BioRECIPES tabular notation (right). In this example, protein W increases the rate of dephosphorylation by phosphatase X. This complex interaction is represented by a bracketed notation.

To accurately model regulating nested events, we extend the graphical representation with an *intermediate node*, and a new type of influence termed *fixed regulation*. The intermediate node represents the biological event being modified and is regulated by this event's agent. This fixed regulation means that the child node's value directly tracks the parent node's value (this can be thought of as 0th order function as opposed to 1st order rate function that we see with positive and negative regulation). Additionally, the event is also positively or negatively regulated by the controlling event's agent. The intermediate node can then regulate other elements in the same manner as any other node in the graph. In the intermediate node template in Fig. 5(a), the influence of element B on the intermediate node is of a fixed regulation type, that is, when B's value is high, so is the intermediate node's value.

The proposed structure provides a few key advantages over previous representations. First, the intermediate node is compatible with all operations allowed by the BioRECIPES format, and therefore, can be used by tools that automatically extend models from literature, such as the method presented in [18]. Second, intermediate nodes are highly amenable to extension. Special cases of regulating nested events often occur when the regulated event is underspecified, that is, when the regulated event is missing either an agentive or affected role. Here, we propose mappings that maximize the information conserved and allow for additional information about the interaction to be added at a later time.

3.2   Underspecified Nested Events

We list here several types of underspecified nested events. The first type occurs when the modified event is missing an affected entity. An example sentence for which this situation applies is: "A inhibits phosphorylation by B". Though we do not know B's target, we can assume from the text that B acts as a kinase. Therefore, we create an intermediate node, as shown in Fig. 5(b). Later, if we process the sentence, "B phosphorylates C", we can simply run a check for existing intermediate nodes and extend our graph with node C.

Likewise, if our modified event is missing an agent, we can still include an intermediate node as a placeholder. When an agent is introduced in later extractions, another check of existing intermediate nodes is run, and the graph is extended, as shown in Fig. 5(c). Since an element can have multiple agents for the same event (for example multiple kinases), multiple extensions can occur in stages (Fig. 5(d)).

A standard event can also be extended into a nested interaction. For the example shown in Fig. 5(e), if an extraction is given describing, "A increases the effect of B on C", and if we already have extracted the event "B phosphorylates C", we can run a check for all events involving B and C. When the phosphorylation is found, we can consolidate the two into a fully specified nested event.

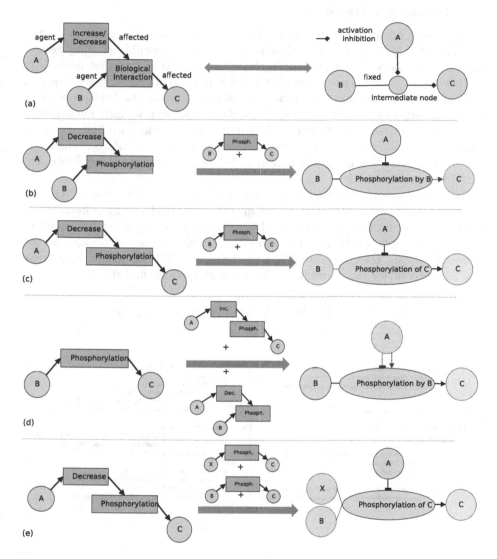

Fig. 5. Representation and extension of nested events, from machine reading output to the BioRECIPES format. (a) An event and entity graph, similar to TRIPS logical form (left), and the corresponding template graph for the BioRECIPES format, including an intermediate node (right); (b) Example of an interaction missing an affected role, extracted from "A inhibits phosphorylation by B", and an extension with the new sentence "B phosphorylates C" (new node and influence are shown in grey on the right); (c) Example of an interaction missing an agent role, "A inhibits phosphorylation of C", and an extension with the same sentence as in (b); (d) Extension of the underspecified nested event with two new sentences: "B phosphorylates C" and "X phosphorylates C"; (e) Example of extending a simple interaction into a nested interaction, due to extraction from "A increases the effect of B on C" or "A decreases the effect of B on C".

3.3   Translation Algorithm

In our main translation function (from machine reading output to the BioRECIPES format), for each element found in the machine reading extractions we can check if that element is the affected child of an event node. If it is, then we call a recursive function to add a new regulator to that element's influence set. The function to add the new influence first checks if the event modifying our target element is itself being modified. If so, then we have encountered a regulating nested event structure. To handle this situation, we first create an intermediate node and assign the event agent as its fixed regulator. Then, the add-influence function is called again to add a new regulator to the influence set of the intermediate node.

If instead our original event is not being modified, we have a standard event. In this case, the event agent is added into the target element's influence set. Before this occurs however, we can also run a check on existing intermediate nodes to determine whether we can add information to an underspecified nested event. If we can, then we consolidate the two BioRECIPES graph structures. The pseudocode for our translation algorithm is provided in Table 1.

Table 1. Pseudocode for the overall translation algorithm.

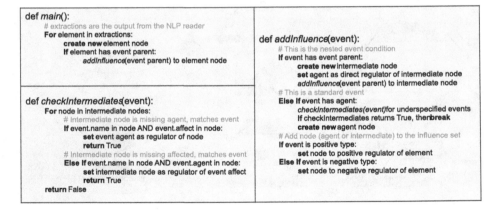

4   Results

We conducted several experiments to estimate the prevalence of nested events in biological literature (specifically, focusing on cancer cells), and to evaluate our translation algorithm. For the extraction and analysis of nested events from papers, manual processing was done by an expert, and we also used the web API's provided by REACH[1] and TRIPS[2]. The translation algorithm is implemented in Python and run on an Intel core i7 processor. The time to translate each paper was on the order of a few seconds.

---

[1] http://trips.ihmc.us/parser/api.html.

[2] http://agathon.sista.arizona.edu:8080/odinweb/api/nxml.

4.1   Prevalence of Nested Events

We selected from PubMed [26–33] eight highly cited papers studying cancer cells and reviewed them manually in order to find nested events. This list of found nested events was then compared to the number of nested event extractions processed by the REACH and TRIPS reading engines. The selected papers provided more than 1000 sentences to use for classification. While machine readers can read and output orders of magnitude more sentences, this would be impractical for a human expert reader, who could still process 1000 sentences in a relatively reasonable amount of time (approx. 15 h).

Each regulating nested event (consisting of multiple events taken from a single sentence) was counted as a single instance. The prevalence of nested events in each of these papers is presented in Fig. 6(a). Both the prevalence of regulating nested events in literature, as well as the precision and recall rates of the two NLP readers analyzed here vary widely from paper to paper. On average however, prevalence was recorded at 32.7%, with the lowest occurrence seen at 11%. This suggests that a significant amount of information may be available in the form of nested events. In Fig. 6(b), detailed prevalence data is shown for two of the papers [24, 25], including the percentage of extracted events that REACH and TRIPS classified as nested events (regardless of accuracy).

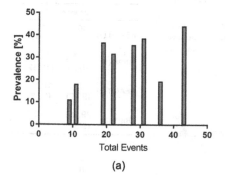

	Manual Count	REACH Extractions	TRIPS Extractions
Paper 1 PMC1403772	19% (32/167)	6.9% (5/72)	7.3% (24/333)
Paper 2 PMC1289294	31% (58/185)	8.9% (12/135)	11% (31/274)

(a)   (b)

Fig. 6. Prevalence of nested events in literature: (a) Percentage of events manually classified as nested during a review of eight PubMed papers. Average prevalence of nested events was found to be 32.7% (65/199); (b) Extractions captured as nested events from two [26, 27] of the eight PubMed papers, manual count gives the true prevalence of nested events out of all sentences in each paper, while REACH and TRIPS columns give the percentage of events extracted that were classified as nested.

When presenting the accuracy metrics of the two NLP readers, an important distinction is to be drawn between the *classification* (i.e., identifying if an event is of the type) of nested events and the *capture* (i.e., accurately representing the specific semantic structure) of nested events. Both readers had high precision when simply tasked with classifying sentences containing nested events (REACH had 82.4% and TRIPS had 87.3%, see Appendix Table 2). In Fig. 7(a), the capture rates of the two readers are compared graphically. The manual column gives the breakdown of nested events (manual true positive) and non-nested events (manual true negative), while the next two columns depict the nested extractions captured correctly (machine true positive) and those captured incorrectly (machine false positive). The precision and recall metrics were computed assuming the manual true positive and true negative classification as ground truth, with precision computed as (machine true positive)/(machine true positive + machine false positive) and recall computed as (machine true positive)/(manual true positive). The two metrics, illustrated in Fig. 7(b), based on the literature sample that we used, provide an estimate of accuracy of each reader in capturing nested events.

TRIPS was observed to pick up on complicated syntax better and generally had better recall, especially when simply identifying text which contained nested events. However, both systems suffered from variable precision when capturing the full information from the nested events. REACH performed best in situations where nested events took on a typical inhibit/activate phosphorylation paradigm, which explains why it performed well on the second paper (whose focus was a drug inhibiting the phosphorylation of a cancer related protein).

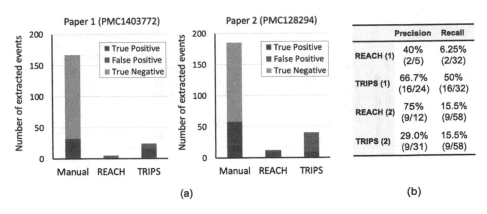

Fig. 7. (a) Total nested events as a fraction of all events (manual), compared to nested event extractions from both readers. (b) Precision and recall rates for nested events extracted from PMC1403772 (Paper 1) and PMC128294 (Paper 2) by REACH and TRIPS/DRUM systems.

4.2   Reading Examples

We conducted further analysis of the reading output accuracy from the first paper (PMC1403772) [26], and the following examples illustrate correct and incorrect nested event extractions. For interpretability purposes, the serialized output in JSON (JavaScript Object Notation) format from REACH has been converted into a graphical format similar to TRIPS logical form. See Appendix Tables 3, 4, 5, and 6 for full output.

Entity Recognition Issue. The first example, shown in Fig. 8, demonstrates a common situation in which phosphorylation is being catalyzed or inhibited. REACH processes this text correctly. The TRIPS extraction demonstrates a correct chain of events (inhibition of phosphorylation) but fails to properly capture Notch-IC as an agent due to errors in entity recognition (did not view Notch-IC as a form of Notch). This mistake could be easily rectified by using the Text-Tagger functionality to extend the TRIPS/DRUM ontology [24].

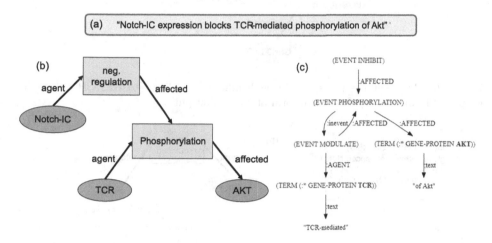

Fig. 8. (a) The sentence processed through machine reading, (b) REACH output in graphical form, and (c) the logical form of TRIPS output.

Underspecified Nested Event Example. In the example shown in Fig. 9, while AKT can most likely be thought of as a direct, negative regulator of GSK3β, the extraction still captures all relevant information without making unnecessary assumptions. Both readers successfully extract this event. This is an underspecified nested event, since no agent is assigned to transcription. Once converted to BioRECIPES format, an agent could be added at a later time.

Complex Syntax Issue. As observed in Valenzuela-Escárcega et al. [14], mistranslating complex syntax is the most common error made by the REACH system. For the example shown in Fig. 10, while REACH picks up on the inner event consisting of GSK3β phosphorylating N-IC, it also mistakenly detects that GSK3 regulates the phosphorylation event as well. TRIPS, on the other hand, can pick up on this complex example correctly, assuming that the term N-IC is changed to Notch.

4.3   Translation of Examples

For the examples in Fig. 8 and Fig. 9, the corresponding graphical representation including the intermediate node is shown in Fig. 11. The third "complex syntax"

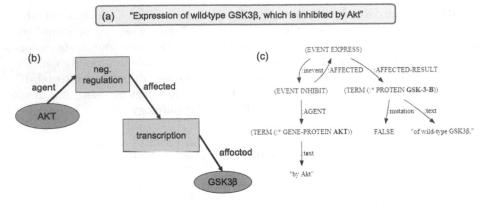

Fig. 9. (a) The sentence processed through machine reading, (b) REACH output in graphical form, and (c) the logical form of TRIPS output.

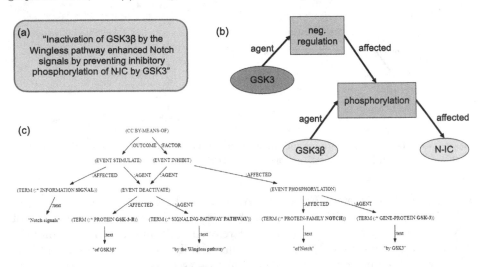

Fig. 10. (a) The sentence processed through machine reading, (b) REACH output in graphical form, and (c) the logical form of TRIPS output.

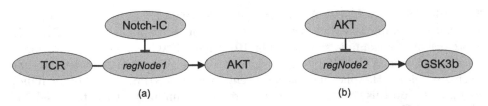

Fig. 11. Graphical visualization of the BioRECIPES influence set for the nested event example. (a) Here, regNode1 is the intermediate node representing the phosphorylation event. (b) In the translation of the second example, no fixed regulator of the transcription event is present.

example is not shown because it contains an event as an input, whose translation will be addressed in our future work.

In all cases where the NLP readers correctly extracted nested events, the reading output was converted successfully into the extended BioRECIPES format. Most of the incorrect extractions observed occurred when information was missing from the nested event (typically the agent of the regulating event), meaning conversion to the BioRECIPES format would not introduce false information into the model. This observation was supported by both readers' high precision in classifying nested events. In other words, it is unlikely that a sentence not containing a nested event type would be extracted as one. REACH and TRIPS both were found to capture nested events that the other did not, suggesting that the two could be used in a complementary fashion to maximize the collected useful information.

Often a researcher uses nested events to refer to indirect interactions between elements in the model. For example, when the authors in [27] mention, "serum-stimulated phosphorylation of p70S6K and 4EBP1," the element "serum," may not directly interact with the kinases of the mentioned proteins, but instead promote the pathway leading to the phosphorylation event. A future direction for this work could be to investigate methods of resolving these "causal short-circuits" by favoring direct interactions over those of intermediate nodes in the model. Using a standardized data structure creates opportunities for other graph analysis techniques such as clustering and network embedding [34], which will also be explored in future work.

Representing these second order interactions as a cascade of two first order events also provides the opportunity to simulate system dynamics more accurately. If intermediate nodes were simulated in the executable model like a normal element, its activation level over time could represent the "strength" of interaction between the nodes that it connects.

5   Conclusion

In this paper, we presented our work on a new data structure that can be used to extend the BioRECIPES representation format, and which enables biological nested events to be efficiently captured from scientific literature into models. This modelling extension was applied to papers from the PubMed database that had been run through TRIPS and REACH reading systems. Our results emphasize the fact that a significant portion of events extracted from literature is of the nested event type, all of which (when processed correctly by machine reading) were successfully translated into the BioRECIPES format and element influence sets. As NLP systems continue to improve, we anticipate that the number and accuracy of extracting complex biological interactions from published literature will keep increasing, thus highlighting the importance of efficient automated translation of this information into models. In turn, such rapid and accurate model evolution, will guide experts to new discoveries in disease diagnosis and treatment.

Acknowledgements. This work was partially supported by DARPA award W911NF-17-1-0135, and by the Swanson School of Engineering and the Office of the Provost at the University of Pittsburgh. The authors would like to thank Dr. Cheryl Telmer of the Molecular Bio-sensor and Imaging Center at Carnegie Mellon University for her constructive feedback.

Appendix

Table 2. Precision and recall rates for nested event CLASSIFICATION from PMC1403772 (1) and PMC128294 (2) by REACH and TRIPS/DRUM systems.

	REACH (1)	TRIPS (1)	REACH (2)	TRIPS (2)
Precision	60% (3/5)	95.8% (23/24)	91.7% (11/12)	80.6% (25/31)
Recall	9.38% (3/32)	71.9% (23/32)	19.0% (11/58)	43.1% (25/58)

Table 3. Example 1 reading output from REACH: "Notch-IC expression blocks TCR-mediated phosphorylation of Akt".

Event Text	Event Type	Controlled	Controller	Theme
Notch-IC expression blocks TCR-mediated phosphorylation of Akt	regulation	(EVENT) *TCR-mediated phosphorylation of Akt*	(ENTITY) Notch-IC	
TCR-mediated phosphorylation of Akt	regulation	(EVENT) *phosphorylation of AKT*	(ENTITY) TCR	
phosphorylation of AKT	protein-modification			(ENTITY) AKT

Table 4. Example 2 reading output from REACH: "Expression of wild-type GSK3β, which is inhibited by Akt".

Event Text	Event Type	Controlled	Controller	Theme
expression of wild-type GSK3β, which is inhibited by Akt	regulation	(EVENT) *expression of wild-type GSK3*	(ENTITY) AKT	
expression of wild-type GSK3	transcription			(ENTITY) GSK3

Table 5. Example 3 reading output from REACH "Inactivation of GSK3β by the Wingless pathway enhanced Notch signals by preventing inhibitory phosphorylation of N-IC by GSK3".

Event Text	Event Type	Controlled	Controller	Theme
inactivation of GSK3β by the Wingless pathway enhanced Notch signals by preventing inhibitory phosphorylation of N-IC by GSK3	regulation	(EVENT) GSK3β by the Wingless pathway enhanced Notch signals by preventing inhibitory phosphorylatio n of N-IC	(ENTITY) GSK3	
GSK3β by the Wingless pathway enhanced Notch signals by preventing inhibitory phosphorylation of N-IC	regulation	(EVENT) Phosphorylatio n of N-IC	(ENTITY) GSK3	
phosphorylation of N-IC	protein modification			(ENTITY) N-IC

Table 6. Example 4 reading output from REACH: "Akt construct was sufficient to potentiate the ability of pN1-IC to drive CBF1-dependent reporter".

Event Text	Event Type	Controlled	Controller	Theme
AKT construct was sufficient to potentiate the ability of pN1-IC to drive CBF1-dependent reporter	activation	(ENTITY) CBF1-dependent reporter	(ENTITY) AKT	

References

1. Shcuster, S., Fell, D.A., Dandekar, T.: A general definition of metabolic pathways useful for systematic organization and analysis of complex metabolic networks. Nat. Biotechnol. **18**(3), 326–332 (2000). https://doi.org/10.1038/73786
2. Pawson, T., Scott, J.: Protein phosphorylation in signaling - 50 years and counting. Trends Biochem. Sci. **30**(6), 286–290 (2005). https://doi.org/10.1016/j.tibs.2005.04.013
3. Shannon, P.: Cytoscape: a software environment for integrated models of biomolecular interaction networks. Genome Res. **13**, 2498–2504 (2003)
4. Zhou, G., Xia, J.: Using OmicsNet for network integration and 3D visualization. Curr. Protoc. Bioinform. **65**(1) (2018). https://doi.org/10.1002/cpbi.69

5. Zhou, G., Xia, J.: OmicsNet: a web-based tool for creation and visual analysis of biological networks in 3D space. Nucleic Acids Res. **46**(1) (2018). https://doi.org/10.1093/nar/gky510

6. Fabregat, A., et al.: The reactome pathway knowledgebase. Nucleic Acids Res. **46**(1), D649–D655 (2017)

7. Szklarczyk, D., et al.: STRING v10: protein-protein interaction networks, integrated over the tree of life. Nucleic Acids Res. **43**(1), D447–D452 (2014)

8. Hucka, M., et al.: The systems biology markup language (SBML): a medium for representation and exchange of biochemical network models. Bioinformatics **19**, 524–531 (2003)

9. Cuellar, A.A., Lloyd, C.M., Nielsen, P.F., Bullivant, D.P., Nickerson, D.P., Hunter, P.J.: An overview of CellML 1.1, a biological model description language. Simulation **79**, 740–747 (2003)

10. Harris, L.A., et al.: BioNetGen 2.2: advances in rule-based modeling. Bioinformatics **32**, 3366–3368 (2016)

11. Boutillier, P., et al.: The Kappa platform for rule-based modeling. Bioinformatics **34**(13), i583–i592 (2018). https://doi.org/10.1093/bioinformatics/bty272

12. Albert, R., Wang, R.S.: Discrete dynamic modeling of cellular signaling networks. Methods Enzymol. **467**, 281–306 (2009)

13. Cambria, E., White, B.: Jumping NLP curves: a review of natural language processing research. IEEE Comput. Intell. Mag. **9**, 48–57 (2014)

14. Valenzuela-Escárcega, M.A., et al.: Large-scale automated machine reading discovers new cancer-driving mechanisms. Database **2018** (2018). bay098, https://doi.org/10.1093/database/bay098

15. Allen, J.F., Teng, C.M.: Broad coverage, domain-generic, deep semantic parsing. In: AAAI Workshop on Construction Grammars, Stanford, CA (2017)

16. Lopez, C.F., Muhlich, J.L., Bachman, J.A., Sorger, P.K.: Programming biological models in Python using PySB. Mol. Syst. Biol. **9**, 646–646 (2014)

17. Sayed, K., Kuo, Y.-H., Kulkarni, A., Miskov-Zivanov, N.: DiSH simulator: capturing dynamics of cellular signaling with heterogeneous knowledge. In: 2017 Winter Simulation Conference (2017)

18. Sayed, K., Bocan, K.N., Miskov-Zivanov, N.: Automated extension of cell signaling models with genetic algorithm. In: 40th Annual International Conference of the IEEE Engineering in Medicine and Biology (2018). https://doi.org/10.1109/embc.2018.8513431

19. Sayed, K., Telmer, C.A., Butchy, A.A., Miskov-Zivanov, N.: Recipes for translating big data machine reading to executable cellular signaling models. In: Nicosia, G., Pardalos, P., Giuffrida, G., Umeton, R. (eds.) MOD 2017. LNCS, vol. 10710, pp. 1–15. Springer, Cham (2018). https://doi.org/10.1007/978-3-319-72926-8_1

20. Sayed, K., Telmer, C.A., Miskov-Zivanov, N.: Motif modeling for cell signaling networks. In: 8th Cairo International Biomedical Engineering Conference, Cairo (2016)

21. Miskov-Zivanov, N., Marculescu, D., Faeder, J.R.: Dynamic behavior of cell signaling networks. In: Proceedings of the 50th Annual Design Automation Conference (2013). https://doi.org/10.1145/2463209.2488743

22. Miskov-Zivanov, N.: Automation of biological model learning, design and analysis. In: Proceedings of the 25th Edition on Great Lakes Symposium on VLSI (2015). https://doi.org/10.1145/2742060.2743765

23. Klamt, S., Haus, U., Theis, F.: Hypergraphs and cellular networks. PLoS Comput. Biol. **5**(5) (2009). https://doi.org/10.1371/journal.pcbi.1000385

24. Allen, J.F., Bahkshandeh, O., de Beaumont, W., Galescu, L., Teng, C.M.: Effective broad-coverage deep parsing. In: Thirty-Second AAAI Conference on Artificial Intelligence, New Orleans, LA (2018)
25. Valenzuela-Escárcega, M.A., Hahn-Powell, G., Surdeanu, M., Hicks, T.: A domain-independent rule-based framework for event extraction. In: Proceedings of ACL-IJCNLP 2015 System Demonstrations (2015). https://doi.org/10.3115/v1/p15-4022
26. Mckenzie, G., et al.: Cellular Notch responsiveness is defined by phosphoinositide 3-kinase-dependent signals. BMC Cell Biol. 7(1), 10 (2006). https://doi.org/10.1186/1471-2121-7-10
27. Tichelaar, J.W., Zhang, Y., Leriche, J.C., Biddinger, P.W., Lam, S., Anderson, M.W.: Increased staining for phospho-Akt, p65/RELA and cIAP-2 in pre-neoplastic human bronchial biopsies. BMC Cancer 5(1), 1–13 (2005)
28. Westphal, S., Kalthoff, H.: Apoptosis: targets in pancreatic cancer. Mol. Cancer 2(6), 6 (2003)
29. Pym, A.S., Saint-Joanis, B., Cole, S.T.: Effect of katG mutations on the virulence of myco-bacterium tuberculosis and the implication for transmission in humans. Infect. Immun. 70, 4955–4960 (2002)
30. Bockstaele, L., Coulonval, K., Kooken, H., Paternot, S., Roger, P.P.: Regulation of CDK4. Cell Div. 1(25) (2006)
31. Peiro, S.: Snail1 transcriptional repressor binds to its own promoter and controls its expression. Nucleic Acids Res. 34, 2077–2084 (2006)
32. Salvioli, S., Sikora, E., Cooper, E.L., Franceschi, C.: Curcumin in cell death processes: a challenge for CAM of age-related pathologies. Evid.-Based Complement. Altern. Med. 4, 181–190 (2007)
33. Miakotina, O.L., Goss, K.L., Snyder, J.M.: Insulin utilizes the PI 3-kinase pathway to inhibit SP-A gene expression in lung epithelial cells. Respir. Res. 3, 26 (2002)
34. Pavlopoulos, G.A., et al.: Using graph theory to analyze biological networks. BioData Mining 4(1) (2011). https://doi.org/10.1186/1756-0381-4-10

TAPAS 2019 - 10th Workshop on Tools for Automatic Program Analysis

TAPAS 2019 Organizers' Message

This volume contains the post-proceedings of the Tenth Workshop on Tools for Automatic Program AnalysiS (TAPAS 2019), held on 8 October 2019 in Porto, Portugal, as part of the Third World Congress on Formal Methods.

The series of Workshops on Tools for Automatic Program AnalysiS are intended to promote discussions and exchanges of experience between users of static analysis tools, and specialists in all areas of program analysis design and implementation. Previous workshops were held in Perpignan, Venice, Deauville, Seattle, Munich, Saint-Malo, Edinburgh, New York, and Freiburg.

The Program Committee (PC) received 16 submissions by authors from 12 countries. Each paper was evaluated using a multi-phase review process. In the first phase, each paper received independent reviews from 3 PC members. Then, a meta-review was supervised by the PC chair, to reach a consensus. 7 submissions were accepted for presentation:

- *PrideMM: Second Order Model Checking for Memory Consistency Models*, by Simon Cooksey, Sarah Harris, Mark Batty, Radu Grigore and Mikolas Janota;
- *fkcc: the Farkas Calculator*, by Christophe Alias;
- *Experiments in Context-Sensitive Incremental and Modular Static Analysis in CiaoPP (Extended Abstract)*, by Isabel Garcia-Contreras, Jose F. Morales and Manuel V. Hermenegildo;
- *Boost the Impact of Continuous Formal Verification in Industry*, by Felipe R. Monteiro, Mikhail R. Gadelha and Lucas Cordeiro;
- *Handling Heap Data Structures in Backward Symbolic Execution*, by Robert Husák, Jan Kofron and Filip Zavoral;
- *AuthCheck: Program-state Analysis for Access-control Vulnerabilities*, by Goran Piskachev, Tobias Petrasch, Johannes Späth and Eric Bodden;
- *Leveraging Highly Automated Theorem Proving for Certification*, by Deni Raco, Bernhard Rumpe and Sebastian Stüber.

The authors additionally notified whether their submission was also accepted for publication as part of the current post-proceedings, or whether it needed to be significantly updated, or resubmitted.

In addition, the program also featured 3 invited talks, shared with the 8th International Workshop on Numerical and Symbolic Abstract Domains (NSAD 2019):

- *Transforming Development Processes of Avionics Software with Formal Methods*, by Pascal Lacabanne (Airbus, France);
- *Establishing Sound Static Analysis for Integration Verification of Large-Scale Software in Automotive Industry* by Bernard Schmidt (Bosch, Germany);
- *Some thoughts on the design of abstract domains*, by Enea Zaffanella (University of Parma, Italy).

Finally, revised versions of some of the presented papers were submitted after the workshop, and the reviews of the PC were updated accordingly. These post-proceedings enclose the four regular contributions to TAPAS 2019 selected for formal publication, as well as the abstracts of two invited talks. The abstract of the third invited talk may be found in the post-proceedings of NSAD 2019.

We would like to thank everyone involved in the organization of the workshop. We are very thankful for the members of the Program Committee for their evaluation work, and for all the discussions on the organization of the event. We would like to give a particular acknowledgment to the Organizing Committees of the FM Week and the Static Analysis Symposium (SAS), in particular José Nuno Oliveira (FM General Chair), Nelma Moreira and Emil Sekerinski (FM Workshop and Tutorial Chairs), Bor-Yuh Evan Chang (SAS PC Chair), and Antoine Miné (SAS PC member), for their great support to the organization of satellite events such as TAPAS 2019. We would also like to thank Patrick Cousot for giving us the opportunity to organize TAPAS 2019.

Finally, we would also like to thank the authors and the invited speakers for their contributions to the program of TAPAS 2019, as well as Springer for publishing these post-proceedings.

December 2019   David Delmas

Organization

Program Committee Chair

David Delmas   Airbus, France

Steering Committee

Bor-Yuh Evan Chang   University of Colorado Boulder, USA
Francesco Logozzo   Facebook, USA
Anders Moeller   Aahrus University, Denmark
Xavier Rival   Inria, France

Program Committee

Fausto Spoto   Università di Verona, Italy
Caterina Urban   Inria, France
Franck Vedrine   CEA LIST, France
Jules Villard   Facebook, UK
Jingling Xue   University of New South Wales, Australia
Tomofumi Yuki   Inria, France
Sarah Zennou   Airbus, France

Invited Talks

Transforming Development Processes
of Avionics Software with Formal Methods

Pascal Lacabanne

Airbus Operations S.A.S., 316 route de Bayonne, 31060 Toulouse Cedex 9,
France
Pascal.Lacabanne@airbus.com

Abstract. The safety and correctness of of avionics software products is paramount, especially for safety-critical software. It is thus developed against stringent international regulations (DO-178). Nonetheless, the size and complexity of avionics software products have grown exponentially in the four last decades. Legacy methods, based on informal designs, testing and intellectual analysis, have been shown to scale poorly, as opposed to some formal techniques. Airbus have therefore been transforming the development processes of avionics software, taking advantage from sound formal formal methods to preserve safety, while improving cost-efficiency. The talk will report on this transformation.

Establishing Sound Static Analysis for Integration Verification of Large-Scale Software in Automotive Industry

Bernard Schmidt

Robert Bosch GmbH, Renningen, 70465 Stuttgart, Germany
Bernard.Schmidt@de.bosch.com

Abstract. Safety-critical embedded software has to satisfy stringent quality requirements. For example, one such requirement, imposed by the relevant safety standard (ISO26262), is that no critical run-time errors must occur. In the last years, we introduced sound static analysis methods and tools in the development process for large-scale software with several million lines of code. They are used to prove highly automated the absence of run-time errors especially caused by integration. The talk will report on this experience and give an outlook about future challenges.

PrideMM: Second Order Model Checking
for Memory Consistency Models

Simon Cooksey[1]([✉]), Sarah Harris[1], Mark Batty[1], Radu Grigore[1],
and Mikoláš Janota[2]

[1] University of Kent, Canterbury, UK
{sjc205,seh53,mjb211,rg399}@kent.ac.uk
[2] IST/INESC-ID, University of Lisbon, Lisbon, Portugal

Abstract. We present PrideMM, an efficient model checker for second-order logic enabled by recent breakthroughs in quantified satisfiability solvers. We argue that second-order logic sits at a sweet spot: constrained enough to enable practical solving, yet expressive enough to cover an important class of problems not amenable to (non-quantified) satisfiability solvers. To the best of our knowledge PrideMM is the first automated model checker for second-order logic formulae.

We demonstrate the usefulness of PrideMM by applying it to problems drawn from recent work on memory specifications, which define the allowed executions of concurrent programs. For traditional memory specifications, program executions can be evaluated using a satisfiability solver or using equally powerful ad hoc techniques. However, such techniques are insufficient for handling some emerging memory specifications.

We evaluate PrideMM by implementing a variety of memory specifications, including one that cannot be handled by satisfiability solvers. In this problem domain, PrideMM provides usable automation, enabling a modify-execute-evaluate pattern of development where previously manual proof was required.

1 Introduction

This paper presents PrideMM, an efficient model checker for second-order (SO) logic. PrideMM is used to automatically evaluate tests under the intricate memory specifications[1] of aggressively optimised *concurrent* languages, where no automated solution currently exists, and it is compared to existing tools over a simpler class of memory specifications.

We argue that SO logic is a sweet spot: restrictive enough to enable efficient solving, yet expressive enough to extend automation to a new class of memory specifications that seek to solve open problems in concurrent language design. PrideMM enables a modify-execute-evaluate pattern of memory-specification development, where changes are quickly implemented and automatically tested.

---

[1] The paper uses the term 'memory specification' instead of 'memory (consistency) model', and reserves the word 'model' for its meaning from logic.

© Springer Nature Switzerland AG 2020
E. Sekerinski et al. (Eds.): FM 2019 Workshops, LNCS 12233, pp. 507–525, 2020.
https://doi.org/10.1007/978-3-030-54997-8_31

Memory specifications define what values may be read in a concurrent system. Current evaluators rely on ad hoc algorithms [3,6,14] or satisfiability (SAT) solvers [40]. However, flaws in existing language memory specifications [5]—where one must account for executions introduced through aggressive optimisation—have led to a new class of memory specifications [20,22] that cannot be practically solved using existing ad hoc or SAT techniques.

Many memory specifications are definable in $\exists$SO in a natural way and one can simulate them using SAT solvers. We demonstrate this facility of PrideMM for a realistic C++ memory specification [24], reproducing previous results [39,40]. But, some memory specifications are naturally formulated in higher-order logic. For example, the Jeffrey-Riely specification (J+R) comes with a formalisation, in the proof assistant Agda [11], that clearly uses higher-order features [20]. We observed that the problem of checking whether a program execution is allowed by J+R can be reduced to the model checking problem for SO. From a program execution, one obtains an SO structure $\mathfrak{A}$ on an universe of size n, and then one asks whether $\mathfrak{A} \models$ JR$_n$, where

$$\mathsf{JR}_n := \exists X \left(\mathsf{TC}_n(\mathsf{AeJ}_n)(\emptyset, X) \wedge \mathsf{F}(X) \right)$$

$$\mathsf{AeJ}_n(P,Q) := \begin{cases} \mathsf{sub}^1(P,Q) \wedge \mathsf{V}(P) \wedge \mathsf{V}(Q) \wedge \\ \forall X \left(\mathsf{TC}_n(\mathsf{AJ})(P,X) \to \exists Y \left(\mathsf{TC}_n(\mathsf{AJ})(X,Y) \wedge \mathsf{J}(Y,Q) \right) \right) \end{cases}$$

We will define precisely these formulae later (Sect. 5.4). For now, observe that the formula JR$_n$ is in $\exists\forall\exists$SO. In practice, this means that it is not possible to use SAT solvers, as that would involve an exponential explosion. That motivates our development of an SO model checker. It is known that SO captures the polynomial hierarchy [27, Corollary 9.9], and the canonical problem for the polynomial hierarchy is quantified satisfiability. Hence, we built our SO model checker on top of a quantified satisfiability solver (QBF solver), QFUN [17].

The contributions of our work are as follows:

1. we present a model checker for SO, built on top of QBF solvers;
2. we reproduce known simulation results for traditional memory specifications;
3. we simulate a memory specification (J+R) that is a representative of a class of memory specifications that are out of the reach of traditional simulation techniques.

2   Overview

Figure 1 shows the architecture of our memory-specification simulator. The input is a litmus test written in the LISA language, and the output is a boolean result. LISA is a programming language that was designed for studying memory specifications [1]. We use LISA for its compatibility with the state-of-the-art memory-specification checker Herd7 [3]. We transform the input program into an event structure [41]. The memory-specification generator (MSG) produces an SO formula. We have a few interchangeable MSGs (Sect. 5). For some memory specifications (Sect. 5.1, Sect. 5.2, Sect. 5.3), which Herd7 can handle as well, the formula is in fact fixed and does not depend at all on the event structure. For other memory specifications (such as Sect. 5.4), the MSG might need to look at certain characteristics of the structure (such as its size). Finally, both the second-order structure and the second-order formula are fed into a solver, giving a verdict for the litmus test.

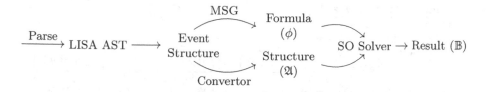

Fig. 1. From a LISA test case to a Y/N answer, given by the SO solver.

We are able to do so because of a key insight: relational second-order logic represents a sweet-spot in the design space. On the one hand, it is expressive enough such that encoding memory specifications is natural. On the other hand, it is simple enough such that it can be solved efficiently, using emerging QBF technology.

2.1   Memory Specifications

A *memory specification* describes the executions allowed by a shared-memory concurrent system; for example, under *sequential consistency* (SC) [25] memory accesses from all threads are interleaved and reads take their value from the most recent write of the same variable. Processor speculation, memory-subsystem reordering and compiler optimisations lead mainstream languages and processors to violate SC, and we say such systems exhibit *relaxed concurrency*. Relaxed concurrency is commonly described in an *axiomatic* specification (e.g. SC, ARM, Power, x86, C++ specifications [3]), where each program execution is represented as a graph with memory accesses as vertices, and edges representing program structure and dynamic memory behaviour. A set of axioms permit some execution graphs and forbid others.

Figure 2 presents a *litmus test*—a succinct pseudocode program designed to probe for a particular relaxed behaviour—together with an execution graph and an axiom. We shall discuss each in turn.

The test, called *LB+ctrl*, starts with x and y initialised to 0, then two threads concurrently read and conditionally write 1 back to their respective variables. The outcome $r_1 = 1 \land r_2 = 1$ (1/1) is unintuitive, and it cannot result from SC: there is no interleaving that agrees with the program order and places the writes of 1 before the reads for both x and y.

In an axiomatic specification, the outcome specified by the test corresponds to the execution graph shown in Fig. 2. Initialisation is elided, but the read and

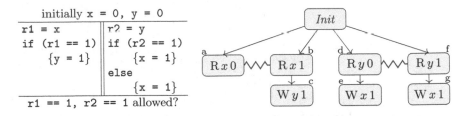

initially x = 0, y = 0

r1 = x	r2 = y
if (r1 == 1)	if (r2 == 1)
{y = 1}	{x = 1}
r1 == 1, r2 == 1 allowed?	

$a: \mathrm{R}\,x\,1$ $c: \mathrm{R}\,y\,1$
$\downarrow po$ rf $\downarrow po$ acyclic($po \cup rf$)
$b: \mathrm{W}\,y\,1$ rf $d: \mathrm{W}\,x\,1$

Fig. 2. LB+ctrl, an axiomatic execution of it, and an axiom that forbids it.

initially x = 0, y = 0

r1 = x	r2 = y
if (r1 == 1)	if (r2 == 1)
{y = 1}	{x = 1}
	else
	{x = 1}
r1 == 1, r2 == 1 allowed?	

Fig. 3. LB+false-dep and the corresponding event structure.

write of each thread is shown with *po* edges reflecting program order and *rf* edges linking writes to reads that *read from* them. The axiom of Fig. 2 forbids the outcome 1/1 as the corresponding execution contains a cycle in $po \cup rf$. The SC, x86, Power and ARM specifications each include a variant of this axiom, all forbidding 1/1, whereas the C++ standard omits it [6] and allows 1/1.

MemSAT [39] and Herd7 [3] automatically solve litmus tests for axiomatic specifications using a SAT solver and ad hoc solving respectively, but not all memory specifications fit the axiomatic paradigm.

Axiomatic Specifications Do Not Fit Optimised Languages. Languages like C++ and Java perform dependency-removing optimisations that complicate their memory specifications. For example, the second thread of the LB+false-dep test in Fig. 3 can be optimised using common subexpression elimination to r2 = y; x = 1;. On ARM and Power, this optimised code may be reordered, permitting the relaxed outcome 1/1, whereas the syntactic control dependency of the original would make 1/1 forbidden. It is common practice to use syntactic dependencies to enforce ordering on hardware, but at the language level the optimiser removes these *false* dependencies.

The memory specification of the C++ standard [15] is flawed because its axiomatic specification cannot draw a distinction between the executions leading to outcome 1/1 in LB+ctrl and LB+false-dep: to see that the dependency is false, one must consider more than one execution path, but axiomatic specifications judge single executions only [5].

Event Structures Capture the Necessary Information. A new class of specifications aims to fix this by ordering only real dependencies [12,20,22,31]. With a notable exception [22], these specifications are based on *event structures*, where all paths of control flow are represented in a single graph. Figure 3 presents the event structure for LB+false-dep. Program order is represented by arrows ($\rightarrow$). Conflict ($\mathsf{\sim\!\!\sim}$) links events where only one can occur in an execution (the same holds for their program-order successors). For example, on the left-hand thread, the load of x can result in a read of value 0 (event a) or a read of value 1 (event b), but not both. Conversely, two subgraphs unrelated by program-order or conflict, e.g. $\{a, b, c\}$ and $\{d, e, f, g\}$, represent two threads in parallel execution.

It should be clear from the event structure in Fig. 3 that regardless of the value read from y in the right-hand thread, there is a write to x of value 1; that is, the apparent dependency from the load of y is false and could be optimised away. Memory specifications built above event structures can recognise this pattern and permit relaxed execution.

The Jeffrey and Riely Specification. J+R is built above event structures and correctly identifies false dependencies [20]. Conceptually, the specification is related to the Java memory specification [29]: in both, one constructs an execution stepwise, adding only memory events that can be *justified* from the previous steps. The sequence captures a causal order that prevents cycles with real dependencies. While Java is too strong, J+R allows writes that have false dependencies on a read to be justified before that read. To do this, the specification recognises confluence in the program structure: regardless of the execution path, the write will always be made. This search across execution paths involves an alternation of quantification that current ad hoc and SAT-based tools cannot efficiently simulate. However, the problem is amenable to QBF solvers.

2.2   Developing SC in SO Logic

The SC memory specification can be expressed as an axiomatic model [3] using *coherence order*, a per-variable total order of write events. An execution is allowed if there exists a reads-from relation rf and a coherence order co such that the transitive closure of $rf \cup co \cup (rf^{-1}; co) \cup po$ is acyclic. Here, po is the (fixed) program-order relation, and it is understood that co and rf satisfy certain further axioms. In our setting, we describe the sequentially consistent specification as follows. We represent rf and co by existentially-quantified SO arity-2 variables Y_{rf} and Y_{co}, respectively. For example, to say $(x, y) \in co$, we use the formula $Y_{co}(x, y)$. The program order po is represented by an interpreted arity-2 symbol $<$. Then, the SO formula that represents $rf \cup co \cup (rf^{-1}; co) \cup po$ is

$$\mathsf{R}(y, z) \; := \; Y_{rf}(y, z) \lor Y_{co}(y, z) \lor \exists x \left(Y_{rf}(x, z) \land Y_{co}(x, y) \right) \lor (y < z)$$

The definition from above should be interpreted as a macro expansion rule: the left-hand side $\mathsf{R}(y, z)$ is a combinator that expands to the formula on right-hand side. To require that the transitive closure of R is acyclic we require that there exists a relation that includes R, is transitive, and irreflexive:

$$\exists Z \left(\mathsf{sub}^2(\mathsf{R}, Z) \land \mathsf{trans}(Z) \land \mathsf{irrefl}(Z) \right)$$

The combinators sub^2, trans, irrefl are defined as one would expect. For example, $\mathsf{sub}^2(P, Q)$, which says that the arity-2 relation P is included in the arity-2 relation Q, is $\forall xy \, (P(x, y) \rightarrow Q(x, y))$. In short, the translation from the usual formulation of memory specifications into the SO logic encoding that we propose is natural and almost automatic.

To represent programs and their behaviours uniformly for all memory specifications in Sect. 5, we use event structures. These have the ability to represent an overlay of potential executions. Some memory specifications require reasoning about several executions at the same time: this is a salient feature of the J+R memory specification.

Once we have the program and its behaviour represented as a logic structure $\mathfrak{A}$ and the memory specification represented as a logic formula ϕ, we ask whether the structure satisfies the formula, written $\mathfrak{A} \models \phi$. In other words, we have to solve a model-checking problem for second-order logic, which reduces to QBF solving because the structure $\mathfrak{A}$ is finite.

3   Preliminaries

To introduce the necessary notation, we recall some standard definitions [27]. A (finite, relational) *vocabulary* σ is a finite collection of *constant symbols* $(1, \ldots, \mathbf{n})$ together with a finite collection of *relation symbols* $(\mathsf{q}, \mathsf{r}, \ldots)$. A (finite, relational) *structure* $\mathfrak{A}$ over *vocabulary* σ is a tuple $\langle A, Q, R, \ldots \rangle$ where $A = \{1, \ldots, n\}$ is a finite set called *universe* with several distinguished relations $Q, R, \ldots$ We assume a countable set of *first-order variables* $(x, y, \ldots)$, and a countable set of *second-order variables* $(X, Y, \ldots)$. A *variable* α is a first-order variable or a second-order variable; a *term* t is a first-order variable or a constant symbol; a *predicate* P is a second-order variable or a relation symbol. A (second-order) *formula* ϕ is defined inductively: (a) if P is a predicate and $t_1, \ldots, t_k$ are terms, then $P(t_1, \ldots, t_k)$ is a formula[2]; (b) if ϕ_1 and ϕ_2 are formulae, then $\phi_1 \circ \phi_2$ is a formula, where $\circ$ is a boolean connective; and (c) if α is a variable and ϕ is a formula, then $\exists \alpha \, \phi$ and $\forall \alpha \, \phi$ are formulae. We assume the standard satisfaction relation $\models$ between structures and formulae.

The logic defined so far is known as relational SO. If we require that all quantifiers over second-order variables are existentials, we obtain a fragment known as $\exists$SO. For example, the SC specification of Sect. 2.2 is in $\exists$SO.

The Model Checking Problem. Given a structure $\mathfrak{A}$ and a formula ϕ, determine if $\mathfrak{A} \models \phi$. We assume that the relations of $\mathfrak{A}$ are given by explicitly listing their elements. The formula ϕ uses the syntax defined above.

Combinators. We will build formulae using the combinators defined below. This simplifies the presentation, and directly corresponds to an API for building formulae within PrideMM.

---

[2] We make the usual assumptions about arity.

$$\mathsf{sub}^k(P^k, Q^k) := \forall \vec{x} \left(P^k(\vec{x}) \rightarrow Q^k(\vec{x}) \right) \qquad \mathsf{id}(x, y) := (x = y)$$
$$\mathsf{eq}^k(P^k, Q^k) := \forall \vec{x} \left(P^k(\vec{x}) \leftrightarrow Q^k(\vec{x}) \right) \qquad \mathsf{inv}(P^2)(x, y) := P^2(y, x)$$
$$\mathsf{seq}(P^2, Q^2)(x, z) := \exists y \left(P^2(x, y) \wedge Q^2(y, z) \right) \qquad \mathsf{irrefl}(P^2) := \forall x \, \neg P^2(x, x)$$
$$\mathsf{inj}(P^2) := \mathsf{sub}^2 \left(\mathsf{seq}(P^2, \mathsf{inv}(P^2)), \mathsf{id} \right) \qquad \mathsf{or}(\mathsf{R}, \mathsf{S})(x, y) := \mathsf{R}(x, y) \vee \mathsf{S}(x, y)$$
$$\mathsf{trans}(P^2) := \mathsf{sub}^2 \left(\mathsf{seq}(P^2, P^2), P^2 \right) \qquad \mathsf{maybe}(\mathsf{R})(x, y) := \mathsf{or}(\mathsf{id}, \mathsf{R})(x, y)$$

$$\mathsf{acyclic}(P^2) := \exists X^2 \left(\mathsf{sub}^2(P^2, X^2) \wedge \mathsf{trans}(X^2) \wedge \mathsf{irrefl}(X^2) \right)$$
$$\mathsf{TC}_0(\mathsf{R}) := \mathsf{eq}^1$$
$$\mathsf{TC}_{n+1}(\mathsf{R})(P^1, Q^1) := \mathsf{eq}^1(P^1, Q^1) \vee \exists X^1 \left(\mathsf{R}(P^1, X^1) \wedge \mathsf{TC}_n(\mathsf{R})(X^1, Q^1) \right)$$

By convention, all quantifiers that occur on the right-hand side of the definitions above are over fresh variables. Above, P^k and Q^k are arity-k predicates, x and y are first-order variables, and R and S are combinators.

Let us discuss two of the more interesting combinators: acyclic and TC. A relation P is acyclic if it is included in a relation that is transitive and irreflexive. We remark that the definition of acyclic is carefully chosen: even slight variations can have a strong influence on the runtime of solvers [18]. The combinator TC for bounded transitive closure is interesting for another reason: it is higher-order—applying an argument (R) relation in each step of its expansion. By way of example, let us illustrate its application to the subset combinator sub^1.

$$\mathsf{TC}_1(\mathsf{sub}^1)(P, Q)$$
$$= \mathsf{eq}^1(P, Q) \vee \exists X \left(\mathsf{sub}^1(P, X) \wedge \mathsf{TC}_0(\mathsf{sub}^1)(X, Q) \right)$$
$$= \begin{cases} \forall x_1 \left(P(x_1) \leftrightarrow Q(x_1) \right) \vee \\ \exists X \left(\forall x_2 \left(P(x_2) \rightarrow X(x_2) \right) \wedge \mathsf{eq}^1(X, Q) \right) \end{cases}$$
$$= \begin{cases} \forall x_1 \left(P(x_1) \leftrightarrow Q(x_1) \right) \vee \\ \exists X \left(\forall x_2 \left(P(x_2) \rightarrow X(x_2) \right) \wedge \forall x_3 \left(X(x_3) \leftrightarrow Q(x_3) \right) \right) \end{cases}$$

In the calculation above, P, Q and X have arity 1.

4   So Solving Through QBF

From a reasoning perspective, SO model-checking is a highly non-trivial task due to quantifiers. In particular, quantifiers over relations, where the size of the search-space alone is daunting. For a universe of size n there are 2^{n^2} possible binary relations, and there are 2^{n^k} possible k-ary relations.[3]

A relation is uniquely characterised by a vector of Boolean values, each determining whether a certain tuple is in the relation or not. This insight lets us formulate a search for a relation as a SAT problem, where a fresh Boolean variable is introduced for any potential tuple in the relation. Even though the translation is exponential, it is a popular method in finite-model finding for first-order logic formulae [13, 33, 38].

---

[3] Finding constrained finite relations is NEXP-TIME complete [26].

However, in the setting of SO, a SAT solver is insufficient since the input formula may contain alternating quantifiers. We tackle this issue by translating to quantified Boolean formulae (QBF), rather than to plain SAT. The translation is carried out in three stages.

1. each interpreted relation is in-lined as a disjunction of conjunctions over the tuples where the relation holds;
2. first-order quantifiers are expanded into Boolean connectives over the elements of the universe, i.e. $\forall x \phi$ leads to one conjunct for each element of the universe and $\exists x \phi$ leads to one disjunct for each element of the universe;
3. all atoms now are ground and each atom is replaced by a fresh Boolean variable, which is inserted under the same type of quantifier as the atom.

For illustration, consider the formula $\exists X \forall Y \forall z \left(Y(z) \rightarrow X(z) \right)$ and the universe $A = \{1, 2\}$. The formula requires a set X that is a superset of all sets. Inevitably, X has to be the whole domain. The QBF formulation is $\exists x_1 x_2 \forall y_1 y_2 \left((y_1 \rightarrow x_1) \wedge (y_2 \rightarrow x_2) \right)$. Intuitively, rather than talking about a set, we focus on each element separately, which is enabled by the finiteness of the universe. Using QBF enables us to arbitrarily quantify over the sets' elements.

PrideMM enables exporting the QBF formulation into the QCIR format [21], which is supported by a bevy of QBF solvers. However, since most solvers only support prenex form, PrideMM, also additionally prenexes the formula, where it attempts to heuristically minimise the number of quantifier levels.

The experimental evaluation showed that the QFUN solver [17] performs the best on the considered instances, see Sect. 6. While the solver performs very well on the J+R litmus tests, a couple of instances were left unsolved. Encouraged by the success of QFUN, we built a dedicated solver that integrates the translation to QBF and the solving itself. The solver represents the formula in dedicated hash-consed data structures (the formulae grow in size considerably). The expansion of first-order variables is done directly on these data structures while also simplifying the formula on the go. The solver also directly supports non-prenex formulation (see [19] for non-prenex QBF solving). The solver applies several preprocessing techniques before expanding the first-order variables, such as elimination of relations that appear only in positive or only in negative positions in the formula.

5   Memory Specification Encodings

In this section, we show that many memory specifications can be expressed conveniently in second-order logic. We represent programs and their behaviours with event structures: this supports the expression of axiomatic specifications such as C++, but also the higher-order specification of J+R. For a given program, its event structure is constructed in a straightforward way: loads give rise to mutually conflicting read events and writes to write events [20]. We express the constraints over event structures with the following vocabulary, shared across all specifications.

Vocabulary. A memory specification decides if a program is allowed to have a certain behaviour. We pose this as a model checking problem, $\mathfrak{A} \models \phi$, where $\mathfrak{A}$ captures program behaviour and ϕ the memory specification. The vocabulary of $\mathfrak{A}$ consists of the following symbols:

- arity 1:`read`, `write`, `final`
- arity 2: $\leq$, `conflict`, `justifies`, `sloc`, $=$

Sets `read` and `write` classify read and write events. The symbol `final`, another set of events, identifies the executions that exhibit final register states matching the outcome specified by the litmus test.

Events x and y are in program order, written $x \leq y$, if event x arises from an earlier statement than y in the program text. We have `conflict`(x, y) between events that cannot belong to the same execution; for example, a load statement gives rise to an event for each value it might read, but an execution chooses one particular value, and contains only the corresponding event. We write `justifies`(x, y) when x is a read and y is a write to the same memory location of the same value. We have `sloc`(x, y) when x and y access the same memory location. Identity on events, $\{\, (x, x) \mid x \in A \,\}$, is denoted by $=$.

Configurations and Executions. We distinguish two types of sets of events. A *configuration* is a set of events that contains no conflict and is downward closed with respect to $\leq$; that is, X is a configuration when $\mathsf{V}(X)$ holds, where the V combinator is defined by

$$\mathsf{V}(X) := \begin{cases} \forall x \forall y \left((X(x) \wedge X(y)) \rightarrow \neg\texttt{conflict}(x, y) \right) \\ \wedge\, \forall y \left(X(y) \rightarrow \forall x\, ((x \leq y) \rightarrow X(x)) \right) \end{cases}$$

We say that a configuration X is an *execution of interest* when every final event is either in X or in conflict with an event in X; that is, X is an execution of interest when $\mathsf{F}(X)$ holds, where the F combinator is defined by

$$\mathsf{F}(X) := \mathsf{V}(X) \wedge \forall x \left(\begin{array}{l} (\texttt{final}(x) \wedge \neg X(x)) \rightarrow \\ \exists y\, (\texttt{conflict}(x, y) \wedge \texttt{final}(y) \wedge X(y)) \end{array} \right)$$

Intuitively, we shall put in `final` all the maximal events (according to $\leq$) for which registers have the desired values.

Notations. In the formulae below, X will stand for a configuration, which may be the execution of interest. Variables Y_{rf}, Y_{co}, Y_{hb} and so on are used to represent the relations that are typically denoted by rf, co, hb, ... Thus, X has arity 1, while Y_{rf}, Y_{co}, Y_{hb}, ... have arity 2.

In what follows, we present four memory specifications: sequential consistency (Sect. 5.1), release–acquire (Sect. 5.2), C++ (Sect. 5.3), and J+R (Sect. 5.4). The first three can be expressed in $\exists$SO (and in first-order logic). The last one uses both universal and existential quantification over sets. For each memory specification, we shall see their encoding in second-order logic.

5.1 Sequential Consistency

The SC specification allows all interleavings of threads, and nothing else. It is described by the following SO sentence:

$$\mathsf{SC} := \exists X \, Y_{co} \, Y_{rf} \left(\mathsf{F}(X) \wedge \mathsf{co}(X, Y_{co}) \wedge \mathsf{rf}(X, Y_{rf}) \wedge \mathsf{acyclic}(\mathsf{R}(Y_{co}, Y_{rf})) \right)$$

Intuitively, we say that there exists a coherence order relation Y_{co} and a reads-from relation Y_{rf} which, when combined in a certain way, result in an acyclic relation $\mathsf{R}(Y_{co}, Y_{rf})$. The formula $\mathsf{co}(X, Y_{co})$ says that Y_{co} satisfies the usual axioms of a coherence order with respect to the execution X; and the formula $\mathsf{rf}(X, Y_{rf})$ says that Y_{rf} satisfies the usual axioms of a reads-from relation with respect to the execution X. Moreover, the formula $\mathsf{F}(X)$ asks that X is an execution of interest, which results in registers having certain values.

$$\mathsf{co}(X, Y_{co}) := \begin{cases} \mathsf{trans}(Y_{co}) \, \wedge \\ \forall xy \left(\begin{array}{c} (X(x) \wedge X(y) \wedge \mathtt{write}(x) \wedge \mathtt{write}(y) \wedge \mathtt{sloc}(x,y) \wedge (x \neq y)) \\ \leftrightarrow (Y_{co}(x,y) \vee Y_{co}(y,x)) \end{array} \right) \end{cases}$$

$$\mathsf{rf}(X, Y_{rf}) := \begin{cases} \mathsf{inj}(Y_{rf}) \wedge \mathsf{sub}^2(Y_{rf}, \mathtt{justifies}) \, \wedge \\ \forall y \left((\mathtt{read}(y) \wedge X(y)) \rightarrow \exists x \, (\mathtt{write}(x) \wedge X(x) \wedge Y_{rf}(x,y)) \right) \end{cases}$$

When X is a potential execution and Y_{co} is a potential coherence-order relation, the formula $\mathsf{co}(X, Y_{co})$ requires that the writes in X for the same location include some total order. Because of the later condition that $\mathsf{R}(Y_{co}, Y_{rf})$ is acyclic, Y_{co} is in fact required to be a total order per location. When X is a potential execution and Y_{rf} is a potential reads-from relation, the formula $\mathsf{rf}(X, Y_{rf})$ requires that Y_{rf} is injective, is a subset of $\mathtt{justifies}$, and relates all the reads in X to some write in X.

The auxiliary relation $\mathsf{R}(Y_{co}, Y_{rf})$ is the union of strict program-order ($<$), reads-from (Y_{rf}), coherence-order (Y_{co}), and the from-reads relation:

$$\mathsf{R}(Y_{co}, Y_{rf})(y, z) := (y < z) \vee Y_{co}(y,z) \vee Y_{rf}(y,z) \vee \exists x \left(Y_{co}(x,z) \wedge Y_{rf}(x,y) \right)$$

5.2 Release–Acquire

Release–Acquire is a simple relaxed memory specification, which is represented straightforwardly in SO logic. It is captured by the formula RA using the vocabulary established in the definition of SC:

$$\mathsf{RA} := \exists X \, Y_{co} \, Y_{rf} \left(\begin{array}{c} \mathsf{F}(X) \wedge \mathsf{co}(X, Y_{co}) \wedge \mathsf{rf}(X, Y_{rf}) \wedge \mathsf{acyclic}(Y_{co}) \\ \wedge \exists Y_{hb} \left(\begin{array}{c} \mathsf{sub}^2(<, Y_{hb}) \wedge \mathsf{sub}^2(Y_{rf}, Y_{hb}) \wedge \mathsf{trans}(Y_{hb}) \\ \wedge \mathsf{irrefl}(Y_{hb}) \wedge \mathsf{irrefl}(\mathsf{seq}(Y_{co}, Y_{hb})) \\ \wedge \mathsf{irrefl}(\mathsf{seq}(\mathsf{inv}(Y_{rf}), \mathsf{seq}(Y_{co}, Y_{hb}))) \end{array} \right) \end{array} \right)$$

The existential SO variable Y_{hb} over-approximates a relation traditionally called happens-before.

5.3 C++

To capture the C++ specification in SO logic, we follow the Herd7 specification of Lahav et al. [24]. Their work introduces necessary patches to the specification of the standard [6] but also includes fixes and adjustments from prior work [4,23]. The specification is more nuanced than the SC and RA specifications and requires additions to the vocabulary of $\mathfrak{A}$ together with a reformulation for efficiency, but the key difference is more fundamental. C++ is a *catch-fire* semantics: programs that exhibit even a single execution with a data race are allowed to do anything—satisfying every expected outcome. This difference is neatly expressed in SO logic:

$$
\mathsf{CPP} := \exists X\, Y_{co}\, Y_{rf}\, Y_{\alpha\beta} \left(\begin{array}{l} \mathsf{co}(X, Y_{co}) \wedge \mathsf{rf}(X, Y_{rf}) \wedge \mathsf{hb}(Y_{\alpha\beta}, Y_{rf}) \\ \wedge\, \mathsf{M}(Y_{\alpha\beta}, Y_{co}, Y_{rf}) \wedge (\mathsf{F}(X) \vee \mathsf{C}(Y_{\alpha\beta}, Y_{rf})) \end{array} \right)
$$

The formula reuses $\mathsf{co}(X, Y_{co})$, $\mathsf{rf}(X, Y_{rf})$ and $\mathsf{F}(X)$ and includes three new combinators: $\mathsf{hb}(Y_{\alpha\beta}, Y_{rf})$, $\mathsf{M}(Y_{\alpha\beta}, Y_{co}, Y_{rf})$ and $\mathsf{C}(Y_{\alpha\beta}, Y_{rf})$. $\mathsf{hb}(Y_{\alpha\beta}, Y_{rf})$ constrains a new over-approximation, $Y_{\alpha\beta}$, used for building a transitive relation. $\mathsf{M}(Y_{\alpha\beta}, Y_{co}, Y_{rf})$ captures the conditions imposed on a valid C++ execution, and is the analogue of the conditions applied in SC and RA. $\mathsf{C}(Y_{\alpha\beta}, Y_{rf})$ holds if there is a race in the execution X. Note that the expected outcome is allowed if $\mathsf{F}(X)$ is satisfied or if there is a race and $\mathsf{C}(Y_{\alpha\beta}, Y_{rf})$ is true, matching the catch-fire semantics.

New Vocabulary. C++ *Read-modify-write* operations load and store from memory in a single atomic step: a new rmw relation links the corresponding reads and writes. C++ *fence* operations introduce new events and the set fences identifies them. The programmer annotates each memory access and fence with a *memory order* parameter that sets the force of inter-thread synchronisation created by the access. For each choice, we add a new set: na, rlx, acq, rel, acq-rel, and sc.

Over-Approximation in Happens Before. The validity condition, $\mathsf{M}(Y_{\alpha\beta}, Y_{co}, Y_{rf})$, and races $\mathsf{C}(Y_{\alpha\beta}, Y_{rf})$, hinge on a relation called *happens-before*. We over-approximate transitive closures in the SO logic for efficiency, but Lahav et al. [24] define happens-before with nested closures that do not perform well. Instead we over-approximate a reformulation of happens-before that flattens the nested closures into a single one (see Appendix A).

We define a combinator for happens-before, $\mathsf{HB}(Y_{\alpha\beta}, Y_{rf})$, that is used in $\mathsf{M}(Y_{\alpha\beta}, Y_{co}, Y_{rf})$ and $\mathsf{C}(Y_{\alpha\beta}, Y_{rf})$. It takes as argument an over-approximation of the closure internal to the reformed definition of happens-before, $Y_{\alpha\beta}$. $\mathsf{hb}(Y_{\alpha\beta}, Y_{rf})$ constrains $Y_{\alpha\beta}$, requiring it to be transitive and to include the conjuncts of the closure, α and β below.

$$\mathsf{HB}(Y_{\alpha\beta}, Y_{rf}) := \mathsf{or}(<, \mathsf{seq}(\mathsf{maybe}(<), \mathsf{sw}_{\mathsf{begin}}(Y_{rf}), Y_{\alpha\beta}, \mathsf{sw}_{\mathsf{end}}(Y_{rf}), \mathsf{maybe}(<)))$$

$$\alpha(Y_{rf}) := \mathsf{seq}(\mathsf{sw}_{\mathsf{end}}(Y_{rf}), \mathsf{maybe}(<), \mathsf{sw}_{\mathsf{begin}}(Y_{rf}))$$

$$\beta(Y_{rf}) := \mathsf{seq}(Y_{rf}, \mathtt{rmw})$$

$$\mathsf{hb}(Y_{\alpha\beta}, Y_{rf}) := \begin{cases} \mathsf{trans}(Y_{\alpha\beta}) \\ \wedge \, \mathsf{sub}^2(\mathsf{id}, Y_{\alpha\beta}) \wedge \mathsf{sub}^2(\alpha(Y_{rf}), Y_{\alpha\beta}) \wedge \mathsf{sub}^2(\beta(Y_{rf}), Y_{\alpha\beta}) \end{cases}$$

5.4 Jeffrey–Riely

The J+R memory specification is captured by a sentence JR_n, parametrised by an integer n. Unlike the formulae we saw before, JR_n makes use of three levels of quantifiers ($\exists\forall\exists$), putting it on the third level of the polynomial hierarchy. We begin by lifting[4] $\mathtt{justifies}$ from events to sets of events P and Q:

$$\mathsf{J}(P, Q) := \forall y \left(\begin{array}{l} (\neg P(y) \wedge Q(y) \wedge \mathtt{read}(y)) \\ \rightarrow \exists x \, (P(x) \wedge \mathtt{write}(y) \wedge \mathtt{justifies}(x, y)) \end{array} \right)$$

$$\mathsf{AJ}(P, Q) := \mathsf{J}(P, Q) \wedge \mathsf{sub}^1(P, Q) \wedge \mathsf{V}(P) \wedge \mathsf{V}(Q)$$

We read J as 'justifies', and AJ as 'always justifies'. Next, we define what Jeffrey and Riely call 'always eventually justify'

$$\mathsf{AeJ}_n(P, Q) := \begin{cases} \mathsf{sub}^1(P, Q) \wedge \mathsf{V}(P) \wedge \mathsf{V}(Q) \wedge \\ \forall X \left(\mathsf{TC}_n(\mathsf{AJ})(P, X) \rightarrow \exists Y \left(\mathsf{TC}_n(\mathsf{AJ})(X, Y) \wedge \mathsf{J}(Y, Q) \right) \right) \end{cases}$$

The size of the formula $\mathsf{TC}_n(\mathsf{AeJ}_m)(P, Q)$ we defined above is $\Theta(mn)$. In particular, it is bounded. Finally, we let[5]

$$\mathsf{JR}_n := \exists X \left(\mathsf{TC}_n(\mathsf{AeJ}_n)(\emptyset, X) \wedge \mathsf{F}(X) \right)$$

and ask solve the model checking problem $\mathfrak{A} \models \mathsf{JR}_n$. Since the formulae above are in MSO, it is sufficient to pick $n := 2^{|A|}$. Since all bounded transitive closures include the subset relation, they are monotonic, and it suffices, in fact, to pick $n := |A|$. For actual solving, we will use this observation.

6 Evaluation

We evaluate our tool in the context of Herd7 [3], which is a standard tool among memory specification researchers for building axiomatic memory specifications. No similar tool exists for higher-order event structure based memory specifications.

---

[4] Our definition of J is different from the original one [20]: we require that only new reads are justified, by including the conjunct $\neg P(y)$. Without this modification, our solver's results disagree with the hand-calculations reported by Jeffrey and Riely; with this modification, the results agree.

[5] The symbol $\emptyset$ denotes the empty unary relation, as expected.

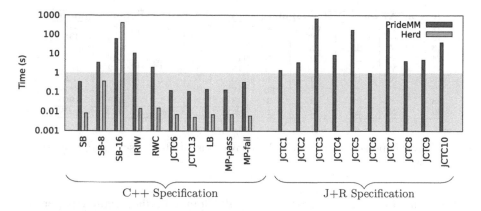

Fig. 4. Comparison of PrideMM's performance in contrast to Herd7 [3].

6.1   Comparison to Existing Techniques

In Fig. 4 we compare the performance and capabilities of PrideMM to Herd7, the de facto standard tool for building axiomatic memory specifications. Herd7 and PrideMM were both executed on a machine equipped with an Intel i5-5250u CPU and 16 GB of memory. We choose not to compare our tool to MemSAT [39], as there are more memory specifications implemented for Herd7 in the CAT language [2] than there are for MemSAT.

Performance. Notably Herd7's performance is very favourable in contrast to the performance of PrideMM, however there are some caveats. The performance of PrideMM is largely adequate, with most of the standard litmus tests taking less than 2 s to execute. $y \leq 1s$ is highlighted on the chart. We find that our QBF technique scales better than Herd7 with large programs. This is demonstrated in the SB-16 test, a variant of the "store buffering" litmus test with 16 threads. The large number of combinations for quantifying the existentially quantified relations which are explored naïvely by Herd7 cause it to take a long time to complete. In contrast, smarter SAT techniques handle these larger problems handily.

Expressiveness. We split the chart in Fig. 4 into 2 sections, the left-hand side of the chart displays a representative subset of common litmus tests showing PrideMM's strength and weaknesses. These litmus tests are evaluated under the C++ memory specification. Note that these include tests with behaviour expected to be observable and unobservable, hence there being two MP bars. The C++ memory specification is within the domain of memory specifications that Herd7 can solve, as it requires only existentially quantified relations.

The right-hand half of the chart is the first 10 Java causality test cases run under the J+R specification, which are no longer expressible in Herd7. PrideMM solves these in reasonable time, with most tests solved in less than

Prob.	SAT	caqe (s)	qfun (s)	qfm (s)	Prob.	SAT	caqe (s)	qfun (s)	qfm (s)
1	N	⊥	610	**2**	10	Y	⊥	36	**10**
2	N	⊥	23	**2**	11	Y	⊥	598	**335**
3	Y	⊥	⊥	**222**	13	Y	1	1	1
4	Y	⊥	**2**	5	14	Y	⊥	**29**	33
5	Y	⊥	78	**51**	15	Y	⊥	512	**157**
6	N	5	4	**1**	16	N	⊥	⊥	**12**
7	Y	⊥	280	**56**	17	N	⊥	39	311
8	N	⊥	**2**	**2**	18	N	⊥	359	**190**
9	N	⊥	2	1	#17		#2	#15	#17

Fig. 5. Solver approaches for PrideMM on Java causality test cases. ⊥ represents time-out or mem-out.

10 min. Our J+R tests replicate the results found in the original paper, but where they use laborious manual proof in the Agda proof assistant, PrideMM validates the results automatically (Fig. 5).

6.2   QBF vs SO Solver Performance

PrideMM enables emitting the SO logic formulae and structures directly for the SO solver, or we can convert to a QBF query (see Sect. 4). This allows us to use our SO solver as well as QBF solvers. We find that the SO solver affords us a performance advantage over the QBF solver in most of the Java causality test cases, where performance optimisations for alternating quantification are applicable.

We include the performance of the QBF solvers CAQE and QFUN, the respective winners of the CNF and non-CNF tracks at 2017's QBFEVAL competition [32]. Our QBF benchmarks were first produced in the circuit-like format QCIR [21], natively supported by QFUN. The inputs to CAQE were produced by converting to CNF through standard means, followed by a preprocessing step with Bloqqer [7].

We can also emit the structures and formulae as an Isabelle/HOL file, which can then be loaded into Nitpick [8] conveniently. We found that Nitpick cannot be run over the C++ specification or the J+R specification, timing out after 1 hr on all the litmus tests.

7   Related Work

We build on prior work from two different areas—relaxed memory specifications, and SAT/QBF solving: the LISA frontend comes from the Herd7 memory-specification simulator [3], the MSGs implement memory specifications that have been previously proposed [20, 24], and the SO solver is based on a state-of-the-art QBF solver [17].

There is a large body of work on finite relational model finding in the context of memory specifications using Alloy [16]. Alloy has been used to compare memory specifications and find litmus tests which can distinguish two specifications [40], and has been used to synthesise comprehensive sets of tests for a specific memory specification [28]. Applying SAT technology in the domain of evaluating memory specifications has been tried before, too. MemSAT [39] uses Kodkod [38], the same tool that Alloy relies on to do relational model finding. MemSynth [10] uses Ocelot [9] to embed relational logic into the Rosette [37] language. Our results are consistent with the findings of MemSAT and MemSynth: SAT appears to be a scalable and fast way to evaluate large memory specification questions. Despite this, SAT does not widen the class of specifications that can be efficiently simulated beyond ad hoc techniques.

There is work to produce a version of Alloy which can model higher-order constructions, called Alloy* [30], however this is limited in that each higher order set requires a new signature in the universe to represent it. Exponential expansion of the sets quantified in the J+R specification leaves model finding for J+R executions intractable in Alloy* too.

While Nitpick [8] can model higher order constructions, we found it could not generate counter examples in a reasonable length of time of the specifications we built. There is work to build a successor to Nitpick called Nunchaku [34], however, at present Nunchaku does not support higher order quantification. Once Nunchaku is more complete we intend to output to Nunchaku and evaluate its performance in comparison to our SO solver.

There is a bevy of work on finite model finding in various domains. SAT is a popular method for finite model finding in first-order logic formulae [13,33]. There are constraint satisfaction-based model finders, e.g. the SEM model finder [42], relying on dedicated symmetry and propagation. Reynolds et al. propose solutions for finite model finding in the context of SMT [35,36] (CVC4 is in fact used as backend to Nunchaku).

8   Conclusion

This paper presents PrideMM, a case study of the application of new solving techniques to a problem domain with active research. PrideMM allows memory specification researchers to build a new class of memory specifications with richer quantification, and still automatically evaluate these specifications over programs. In this sense we provide a Herd7-style modify-execute-evaluate pattern of development for higher-order memory specifications that were previously unsuitable for mechanised model finding.

Acknowledgments. This work was supported by national funds through FCT — Fundação para a Ciência e a Tecnologia with reference UID/CEC/50021/2019 and the project INFOCOS with reference PTDC/CCI-COM/32378/2017. The work was supported by the European Regional Development Fund under the project AI&Reasoning (reg. no. CZ.02.1.01/0.0/0.0/15_003/0000466).

Appendix A   Reformulation of Happens Before

Lahav et al. [24] define happens before, hb, in terms of *sequenced before* sb, the C++ name for program order, and *synchronises with*, sw, inter-thread synchronisation. Their rf and rmw relations match Y_{rf} and rmw in our vocabulary. Fixed sequences of memory events initiate and conclude synchronisation, and these are captured by sw_{begin} and sw_{end}. In the definition below, semicolon represents forward relation composition.

$$\text{sw} := \text{sw}_{begin}; (\mathbf{rf}; \mathbf{rmw})^*; \text{sw}_{end}$$

$$\mathbf{hb} := (\mathbf{sb} \cup \text{sw})^+$$

For efficiency we over-approximate transitive closures in the SO logic, but the nesting over-approximation that follows from the structure of $\mathbf{hb}$ does not perform well. Instead we over-approximate a reformulation of $\mathbf{hb}$.

$$\mathbf{hb'} := \mathbf{sb} \cup (\mathbf{sb}^?; \text{sw}_{begin}; ((\text{sw}_{end}; \mathbf{sb}^?; \text{sw}_{begin})) \cup (\mathbf{rf}; \mathbf{rmw}))^*; \text{sw}_{end}; \mathbf{sb}^?)$$

By unpacking the definition of sw, the reformulation flattens the nested closures into a single one. The closure combines fragments of happens before where at the start and end of the fragment, a synchronisation edge has been initiated but not concluded. Within the closure, the synchronisation edge can be concluded and a new one opened, or some number of read-modify-writes can be chained together with $\mathbf{rf}$.

We explain the definition of $\mathbf{hb'}$ by considering the number of sw edges that constitute a particular $\mathbf{hb}$ edge. If a $\mathbf{hb}$ edge contains no sw edge, then because $\mathbf{sb}$ is transitive, the $\mathbf{hb}$ edge must be a single $\mathbf{sb}$ edge. Otherwise, the $\mathbf{hb}$ edge is made up of a sequence of one or more sw edges with $\mathbf{sb}$ edges before, between and after some of the sw edges. The first sw edge is itself a sequence of edges starting with sw_{begin}. This is followed by any number of $\mathbf{rf}; \mathbf{rmw}$ edges. At the end of the sw edge there are two possibilities: this edge was the final sw edge, or there is another in the sequence to be initiated next. The first conjunct of the closure, $\text{sw}_{end}; \mathbf{sb}^?; \text{sw}_{begin}$ captures the closing and opening of sw edges, the second captures the chaining of read-modify-writes. The end of the definition closes the final sw edge with sw_{end}.

References

1. Alglave, J., Cousot, P.: Syntax and analytic semantics of LISA (2016). https://arxiv.org/abs/1608.06583
2. Alglave, J., Cousot, P., Maranget, L.: Syntax and analytic semantics of the weak consistency model specification language CAT (2016). https://arxiv.org/abs/1608.07531
3. Alglave, J., Maranget, L., Tautschnig, M.: Herding cats: modelling, simulation, testing, and data mining for weak memory. ACM Trans. Program. Lang. Syst. **36**(2), 7:1–7:74 (2014). https://doi.org/10.1145/2627752. http://doi.acm.org/10.1145/2627752

4. Batty, M., Donaldson, A.F., Wickerson, J.: Overhauling SC atomics in C11 and OpenCL. In: Proceedings of the 43rd Annual ACM SIGPLAN-SIGACT Symposium on Principles of Programming Languages, POPL 2016, St. Petersburg, FL, USA, 20–22 January 2016, pp. 634–648 (2016). https://doi.org/10.1145/2837614. 2837637. http://doi.acm.org/10.1145/2837614.2837637
5. Batty, M., Memarian, K., Nienhuis, K., Pichon-Pharabod, J., Sewell, P.: The problem of programming language concurrency semantics. In: Vitek, J. (ed.) ESOP 2015. LNCS, vol. 9032, pp. 283–307. Springer, Heidelberg (2015). https://doi.org/ 10.1007/978-3-662-46669-8_12
6. Batty, M., Owens, S., Sarkar, S., Sewell, P., Weber, T.: Mathematizing C++ concurrency. In: Proceedings of the 38th ACM SIGPLAN-SIGACT Symposium on Principles of Programming Languages, POPL 2011, Austin, TX, USA, 26–28 January 2011, pp. 55–66 (2011). https://doi.org/10.1145/1926385.1926394. http://doi. acm.org/10.1145/1926385.1926394
7. Biere, A., Lonsing, F., Seidl, M.: Blocked clause elimination for QBF. In: Bjørner, N., Sofronie-Stokkermans, V. (eds.) CADE 2011. LNCS (LNAI), vol. 6803, pp. 101–115. Springer, Heidelberg (2011). https://doi.org/10.1007/978-3-642-22438-6_10
8. Blanchette, J.C., Nipkow, T.: Nitpick: a counterexample generator for higher-order logic based on a relational model finder. In: Kaufmann, M., Paulson, L.C. (eds.) ITP 2010. LNCS, vol. 6172, pp. 131–146. Springer, Heidelberg (2010). https://doi. org/10.1007/978-3-642-14052-5_11
9. Bornholt, J., Torlak, E.: Ocelot: a solver-aided relational logic DSL (2017). https:// ocelot.memsynth.org/
10. Bornholt, J., Torlak, E.: Synthesizing memory models from framework sketches and litmus tests. In: Proceedings of the 38th ACM SIGPLAN Conference on Programming Language Design and Implementation, PLDI 2017, Barcelona, Spain, 18–23 June 2017, pp. 467–481 (2017). https://doi.org/10.1145/3062341.3062353. http://doi.acm.org/10.1145/3062341.3062353
11. Bove, A., Dybjer, P., Norell, U.: A brief overview of agda – a functional language with dependent types. In: Berghofer, S., Nipkow, T., Urban, C., Wenzel, M. (eds.) TPHOLs 2009. LNCS, vol. 5674, pp. 73–78. Springer, Heidelberg (2009). https:// doi.org/10.1007/978-3-642-03359-9_6
12. Chakraborty, S., Vafeiadis, V.: Grounding thin-air reads with event structures. PACMPL 3(POPL), 70:1–70:28 (2019). https://dl.acm.org/citation.cfm? id=3290383
13. Claessen, K., Sörensson, N.: New techniques that improve MACE-style finite model finding. In: Proceedings of the CADE-19 Workshop: Model Computation - Principles, Algorithms, Applications (2003)
14. Gray, K.E., Kerneis, G., Mulligan, D.P., Pulte, C., Sarkar, S., Sewell, P.: An integrated concurrency and core-ISA architectural envelope definition, and test oracle, for IBM POWER multiprocessors. In: Proceedings of the 48th International Symposium on Microarchitecture, MICRO 2015, Waikiki, HI, USA, 5–9 December 2015, pp. 635–646 (2015). https://doi.org/10.1145/2830772.2830775. http:// doi.acm.org/10.1145/2830772.2830775
15. ISO/IEC: Programming languages - C++. Draft N3092, March 2010. http://www. open-std.org/jtc1/sc22/wg21/docs/papers/2010/n3092.pdf
16. Jackson, D.: Alloy: a lightweight object modelling notation. ACM Trans. Softw. Eng. Methodol. 11(2), 256–290 (2002). https://doi.org/10.1145/505145.505149. http://doi.acm.org/10.1145/505145.505149

17. Janota, M.: Towards generalization in QBF solving via machine learning. In: AAAI Conference on Artificial Intelligence (2018)
18. Janota, M., Grigore, R., Manquinho, V.: On the quest for an acyclic graph. In: RCRA (2017)
19. Janota, M., Klieber, W., Marques-Silva, J., Clarke, E.: Solving QBF with counterexample guided refinement. Artif. Intell. **234**, 1–25 (2016). https://doi.org/10.1016/j.artint.2016.01.004
20. Jeffrey, A., Riely, J.: On thin air reads towards an event structures model of relaxed memory. In: Proceedings of the 31st Annual ACM/IEEE Symposium on Logic in Computer Science, LICS 2016, pp. 759–767. ACM, New York (2016). https://doi.org/10.1145/2933575.2934536. http://doi.acm.org/10.1145/2933575.2934536
21. Jordan, C., Klieber, W., Seidl, M.: Non-CNF QBF solving with QCIR. In: AAAI Workshop: Beyond NP. AAAI Workshops, vol. WS-16-05. AAAI Press (2016)
22. Kang, J., Hur, C., Lahav, O., Vafeiadis, V., Dreyer, D.: A promising semantics for relaxed-memory concurrency. In: Proceedings of the 44th ACM SIGPLAN Symposium on Principles of Programming Languages, POPL 2017, Paris, France, 18–20 January 2017, pp. 175–189 (2017). http://dl.acm.org/citation.cfm?id=3009850
23. Lahav, O., Giannarakis, N., Vafeiadis, V.: Taming release-acquire consistency. In: Proceedings of the 43rd Annual ACM SIGPLAN-SIGACT Symposium on Principles of Programming Languages, POPL 2016, St. Petersburg, FL, USA, 20–22 January 2016, pp. 649–662 (2016). https://doi.org/10.1145/2837614.2837643. http://doi.acm.org/10.1145/2837614.2837643
24. Lahav, O., Vafeiadis, V., Kang, J., Hur, C., Dreyer, D.: Repairing sequential consistency in C/C++11. In: Proceedings of the 38th ACM SIGPLAN Conference on Programming Language Design and Implementation, PLDI 2017, Barcelona, Spain, 18–23 June 2017, pp. 618–632 (2017). https://doi.org/10.1145/3062341.3062352. http://doi.acm.org/10.1145/3062341.3062352
25. Lamport, L.: How to make a multiprocessor computer that correctly executes multiprocess programs. IEEE Trans. Comput. **28**(9), 690–691 (1979). https://doi.org/10.1109/TC.1979.1675439. https://doi.org/10.1109/TC.1979.1675439
26. Lewis, H.R.: Complexity results for classes of quantificational formulas. J. Comput. Syst. Sci. **21**(3), 317–353 (1980). https://doi.org/10.1016/0022-0000(80)90027-6. http://www.sciencedirect.com/science/article/pii/0022000080900276
27. Libkin, L.: Elements of Finite Model Theory. Springer, Heidelberg (2004). https://doi.org/10.1007/978-3-662-07003-1
28. Lustig, D., Wright, A., Papakonstantinou, A., Giroux, O.: Automated synthesis of comprehensive memory model litmus test suites. In: Proceedings of the Twenty-Second International Conference on Architectural Support for Programming Languages and Operating Systems, ASPLOS 2017, pp. 661–675. ACM, New York (2017). https://doi.org/10.1145/3037697.3037723. http://doi.acm.org/10.1145/3037697.3037723
29. Manson, J., Pugh, W., Adve, S.V.: The Java memory model. In: Proceedings of the 32nd ACM SIGPLAN-SIGACT Symposium on Principles of Programming Languages, POPL 2005, Long Beach, California, USA, 12–14 January 2005, pp. 378–391 (2005). https://doi.org/10.1145/1040305.1040336
30. Milicevic, A., Near, J.P., Kang, E., Jackson, D.: Alloy*: a general-purpose higher-order relational constraint solver. In: ICSE (2015)

31. Pichon-Pharabod, J., Sewell, P.: A concurrency semantics for relaxed atomics that permits optimisation and avoids thin-air executions. In: Proceedings of the 43rd Annual ACM SIGPLAN-SIGACT Symposium on Principles of Programming Languages, POPL 2016, St. Petersburg, FL, USA, 20–22 January 2016, pp. 622–633 (2016). https://doi.org/10.1145/2837614.2837616

32. QBF Eval 2017. http://www.qbflib.org/event_page.php?year=2017

33. Reger, G., Suda, M., Voronkov, A.: Finding finite models in multi-sorted first-order logic. In: Creignou, N., Le Berre, D. (eds.) SAT 2016. LNCS, vol. 9710, pp. 323–341. Springer, Cham (2016). https://doi.org/10.1007/978-3-319-40970-2_20

34. Reynolds, A., Blanchette, J.C., Cruanes, S., Tinelli, C.: Model finding for recursive functions in SMT. In: Olivetti, N., Tiwari, A. (eds.) IJCAR 2016. LNCS (LNAI), vol. 9706, pp. 133–151. Springer, Cham (2016). https://doi.org/10.1007/978-3-319-40229-1_10

35. Reynolds, A., Tinelli, C., Goel, A., Krstić, S.: Finite model finding in SMT. In: Sharygina, N., Veith, H. (eds.) CAV 2013. LNCS, vol. 8044, pp. 640–655. Springer, Heidelberg (2013). https://doi.org/10.1007/978-3-642-39799-8_42

36. Reynolds, A., Tinelli, C., Goel, A., Krstić, S., Deters, M., Barrett, C.: Quantifier instantiation techniques for finite model finding in SMT. In: Bonacina, M.P. (ed.) CADE 2013. LNCS (LNAI), vol. 7898, pp. 377–391. Springer, Heidelberg (2013). https://doi.org/10.1007/978-3-642-38574-2_26

37. Torlak, E., Bodik, R.: A lightweight symbolic virtual machine for solver-aided host languages. In: Proceedings of the 35th ACM SIGPLAN Conference on Programming Language Design and Implementation, PLDI 2014, pp. 530–541. ACM, New York (2014). https://doi.org/10.1145/2594291.2594340. http://doi.acm.org/10.1145/2594291.2594340

38. Torlak, E., Jackson, D.: Kodkod: a relational model finder. In: Grumberg, O., Huth, M. (eds.) TACAS 2007. LNCS, vol. 4424, pp. 632–647. Springer, Heidelberg (2007). https://doi.org/10.1007/978-3-540-71209-1_49

39. Torlak, E., Vaziri, M., Dolby, J.: MemSAT: checking axiomatic specifications of memory models. In: Proceedings of the 31st ACM SIGPLAN Conference on Programming Language Design and Implementation, PLDI 2010, pp. 341–350. ACM, New York (2010). https://doi.org/10.1145/1806596.1806635

40. Wickerson, J., Batty, M., Sorensen, T., Constantinides, G.A.: Automatically comparing memory consistency models. In: Proceedings of the 44th ACM SIGPLAN Symposium on Principles of Programming Languages, POPL 2017, Paris, France, 18–20 January 2017, pp. 190–204 (2017). http://dl.acm.org/citation.cfm?id=3009838

41. Winskel, G.: Event structures. In: Brauer, W., Reisig, W., Rozenberg, G. (eds.) ACPN 1986. LNCS, vol. 255, pp. 325–392. Springer, Heidelberg (1987). https://doi.org/10.1007/3-540-17906-2_31

42. Zhang, J., Zhang, H.: SEM: a system for enumerating models. In: Proceedings of the Fourteenth International Joint Conference on Artificial Intelligence, IJCAI, pp. 298–303. Morgan Kaufmann (1995). http://ijcai.org/Proceedings/95-1/Papers/039.pdf

Fkcc: The Farkas Calculator

Christophe Alias[(✉)]

CNRS, ENS de Lyon, Inria, UCBL, Université de Lyon, Lyon, France
Christophe.Alias@ens-lyon.fr
http://foobar.ens-lyon.fr/fkcc

Abstract. In this paper, we present FKCC, a scripting tool to prototype program analyses and transformations exploiting the affine form of
Farkas lemma. Our language is general enough to prototype in a few
lines sophisticated termination and scheduling algorithms. The tool is
freely available and may be tried online via a web interface. We believe
that FKCC is the missing chain to accelerate the development of program
analyses and transformations exploiting the affine form of Farkas lemma.

Keywords: Farkas lemma · Scripting tool · Termination · Scheduling

1 Introduction

Many program analyses and transformations require to handle conjunction of
affine constraints C and C' with a universal quantification as $\forall x : x \models C \Rightarrow x \models C'$. For instance, this appears in loop scheduling [6,7], loop tiling [2], program
termination [1] and generation of invariants [3]. Farkas lemma – affine form –
provides a way to get rid of that universal quantification, at the price of introducing quadratic terms. In the context of program termination and loop scheduling,
it is even possible to use Farkas lemma to turn universally quantified quadratic
constraints into *existentially quantified affine constraints*. This requires tricky
algebraic manipulations, not easy to applied by hand, neither to implement.

In this paper, we propose a scripting tool, FKCC, which makes it possible
to manipulate easily Farkas lemma to benefit from those nice properties. More
specifically, we made the following contributions:

- A general formulation for the resolution of equations $\forall x : S(x) = 0$ where S is
  summation of affine forms including Farkas terms. So far, this resolution was
  applied for specific instances of Farkas summation. This result is the basic
  engine of the FKCC scripting language.
- A scripting language to apply and exploit Farkas lemma; among polyhedra,
  affine functions and affine forms.
- Our tool, FKCC, implementing these principles, available at http://foobar.ens-
  lyon.fr/fkcc. FKCC may be downloaded and tried online *via* a web interface.
  FKCC comes with many examples, making it possible to adopt the tool easily.

© Springer Nature Switzerland AG 2020
E. Sekerinski et al. (Eds.): FM 2019 Workshops, LNCS 12233, pp. 526–536, 2020.
https://doi.org/10.1007/978-3-030-54997-8_32

This paper is structured as follows. Sect. 2 presents the affine form of Farkas lemma, our resolution theorem, and explains how it applies to compute scheduling functions. Then, Sect. 3 defines the syntax and outlines informally the semantics of the FKCC language. Section 4 presents two complete use-cases of FKCC. Finally, Sect. 5 concludes this paper and draws future research perspectives.

2 Farkas Lemma in Program Analysis and Compilation

This section presents the theoretical background of this paper. We first introduce the affine form of Farkas lemma. Then, we present our theorem to solve equations $S(\boldsymbol{x}) = 0$ where S is a summation of affine forms including Farkas terms. This formalization will then be exploited to design the FKCC language.

Lemma 1 (Farkas Lemma, affine form). *Consider a convex polyhedron $\mathcal{P} = \{\boldsymbol{x}, \ A\boldsymbol{x} + \boldsymbol{b} \geq 0\} \subseteq \mathbb{R}^n$ and an affine form $\phi : \mathbb{R}^n \to \mathbb{R}$ such that $\phi(\boldsymbol{x}) \geq 0$ $\forall \boldsymbol{x} \in \mathcal{P}$.*
Then: $\exists \boldsymbol{\lambda} \geq \boldsymbol{0}, \lambda_0 \geq 0$ such that:

$$\phi(\boldsymbol{x}) = {}^t\boldsymbol{\lambda}(A\boldsymbol{x} + \boldsymbol{b}) + \lambda_0 \quad \forall \boldsymbol{x}$$

Hence, Farkas lemma makes it possible to remove the quantification $\forall \boldsymbol{x} \in \mathcal{P}$ by encoding directly the positivity over $\mathcal{P}$ into the definition of ϕ, thanks to the Farkas multipliers $\boldsymbol{\lambda}$ and λ_0. In the remainder, *Farkas terms* will be denoted by: $\mathfrak{F}(\lambda_0, \boldsymbol{\lambda}, A, \boldsymbol{b})(\boldsymbol{x}) = {}^t\boldsymbol{\lambda}(A\boldsymbol{x} + \boldsymbol{b}) + \lambda_0$. We now propose a theorem to solve equations $S(\boldsymbol{x}) = 0$ where S involves Farkas terms. The result is expressed as a conjunction of affine constraints, which is suited for integer linear programming:

Theorem 1. *Consider a summation $S(\boldsymbol{x}) = \boldsymbol{u} \cdot \boldsymbol{x} + v + \sum_i \mathfrak{F}(\lambda_{i0}, \boldsymbol{\lambda}_i, A_i, \boldsymbol{b}_i)(\boldsymbol{x})$ of affine forms, including Farkas terms. Then:*

$$\forall \boldsymbol{x} : \ S(\boldsymbol{x}) = 0 \quad \textit{iff} \quad \begin{cases} \boldsymbol{u} + \sum_i {}^tA_i\boldsymbol{\lambda}_i = \boldsymbol{0} \ \wedge \\ v + \sum_i (\boldsymbol{\lambda}_i \cdot \boldsymbol{b}_i + \lambda_{0i}) = 0 \end{cases}$$

Proof. We have:

$$S(\boldsymbol{x}) = {}^t\boldsymbol{x}\left(\sum_i {}^tA_i\boldsymbol{\lambda}_i\right) + \sum_i (\boldsymbol{\lambda}_i \cdot \boldsymbol{b}_i + \lambda_{0i}) + \boldsymbol{u} \cdot \boldsymbol{x} + v$$

$$= {}^t\boldsymbol{x}\left(\boldsymbol{u} + \sum_i {}^tA_i\boldsymbol{\lambda}_i\right) + v + \sum_i (\boldsymbol{\lambda}_i \cdot \boldsymbol{b}_i + \lambda_{0i})$$

$S(\boldsymbol{x}) = \boldsymbol{\tau} \cdot \boldsymbol{x} + \tau_0 = 0$ for any $\boldsymbol{x}$ iff $\boldsymbol{\tau} = \boldsymbol{0}$ and $\tau_0 = 0$. Hence the result. $\square$

Application to Scheduling. Consider the polynomial product kernel depicted in Fig. 3.(a). Farkas lemma and Theorem 1 may be applied to compute a *schedule*, this is a way to reorganize the computation of the program to fulfill various criteria (overall latency, locality, parallelism, etc). On this example, a schedule may be expressed as an *affine form* $\theta : (i, j) \mapsto t$ assigning a *timestamp* $t \in \mathbb{Z}$ to each iteration (i, j). This way, a schedule *prescribes* an execution order $\prec_\theta :=$ $\{((i, j), (i', j')) \mid \theta(i, j) < \theta(i', j')\}$. Figure 3.(b) illustrates the order prescribed by the schedule $\theta(i, j) = i$: a sequence of vertical wave fronts, whose iterations are executed in parallel.

A schedule must be positive everywhere on the set of *iteration vectors* $\mathcal{D}_N = \{(i, j) \mid A^{\,t}(i, j, N) + \boldsymbol{b}\}$ (referred to as *iteration domain*). In general, the iterations domains are parametrized (typically by the array size N) and the schedule may depends on N. Hence we have to consider vectors (i, j, N) instead of (i, j):

$$\theta(i, j, N) \geq 0 \quad \forall (i, j) \in \mathcal{D}_N \tag{1}$$

Applying Farkas lemma, this translates to:

$$\exists \lambda_0 \geq 0, \boldsymbol{\lambda} \geq 0 \quad \text{such that} \quad \theta(i, j, N) = \mathfrak{F}(\lambda_0, \boldsymbol{\lambda}, A, \boldsymbol{b})(i, j, N) \tag{2}$$

Moreover, a schedule must *satisfy the data dependencies* $(i, j) \to (i', j')$. $\to$ is generally expressed as a Presburger relation [8], in turned *abstracted* as a rational convex polyhedron Δ_N containing the correct vectors (i, j, i', j') and sometimes false positives. Here again, $\Delta_N = \{(i, j, i', j') \mid C^{\,t}(i, j, i', j', N) + \boldsymbol{d} \geq 0\}$ is parametrized by structure parameter N. This way, the correctness condition translates to:

$$\theta(i', j', N) > \theta(i, j, N) \quad \forall (i, j, i', j') \in \Delta_N \tag{3}$$

Note that $\theta(i', j', N) > \theta(i, j, N)$ is equivalently written as the positivity of an affine form over a convex polyhedron: $\theta(i', j', N) - \theta(i, j, N) - 1 \geq 0$. Applying Farkas lemma:

$$\exists \mu_0 \geq 0, \boldsymbol{\mu} \geq 0 \text{ such that } \theta(i', j', N) - \theta(i, j, N) - 1 = \mathfrak{F}(\mu_0, \boldsymbol{\mu}, C, \boldsymbol{d})(i, j, i', j', N)$$

Substituting θ using Eq. (2), this translates to $S(i, j, i', j', N) = 0$, where $S(i, j, i', j', N)$ is defined as the summation:

$$\mathfrak{F}(\lambda_0, \boldsymbol{\lambda}, A, \boldsymbol{b})(i', j', N) - \mathfrak{F}(\lambda_0, \boldsymbol{\lambda}, A, \boldsymbol{b})(i, j, N) - \mathfrak{F}(\mu_0, \boldsymbol{\mu}, C, \boldsymbol{d})(i, j, i', j', N) - 1$$

Since $-\mathfrak{F}(\lambda_0, \boldsymbol{\lambda}, A, \boldsymbol{b}) = \mathfrak{F}(-\lambda_0, -\boldsymbol{\lambda}, A, \boldsymbol{b})$, we may apply Theorem 1 to obtain a system of affine constraints with $\lambda_0, \boldsymbol{\lambda}, \mu_0, \boldsymbol{\mu}$. Linear programming may then be applied to find out the desired schedule [2, 7]. The same principle might be applied in *termination analysis* to derive a ranking function [1], this will be developed in Sect. 4.

3   Language

This section specifies the input language of FKCC and outlines informally its semantics. Figure 1 depicts the input syntax of FKCC. Keywords and syntax program ::= (**parameters** = { p, ..., p };)? instruction; ...; instruction;

instruction ::= object | id := object | **lexmin** polyhedron | **lexmax** polyhedron | **set** id

object ::= polyhedron | affine_form | affine_function

polyhedron ::=
  [p, ..., p] -> { [v, ..., v] : inequation **and** ... **and** inequation }
| polyhedron * ... * polyhedron
| **solve** affine_form = 0
| **define** affine_form **with** v
| **keep** v, ..., v **in** polyhedron
| **find** id, ..., id **s.t.** affine_form = 0

affine_form ::= leaf_affine_form | leaf_affine_form [+-] ... [+-] leaf_affine_form

leaf_affine_form ::=
  { [v, ..., v] -> expression }
| **positive_on** polyhedron
| leaf_affine_form . affine_function
| int
| int * leaf_affine_form

affine_function ::= { [v, ..., v] -> [expression, ..., expression] }

Fig. 1. Fkcc syntax

sugar are written with **verbatim** letters, identifiers with *italic* letter and syntactic categories with roman letters. Among identifiers, p is a parameter, v is a variable (typically a loop counter) and id is an FKCC identifier.

Program, Instructions, Polyhedra. An FKCC program consists of a sequence of instructions. There is no other control structure than the sequence. An instruction may assign an FKCC object (polyhedron, affine form or affine function) to an FKCC identifier, or may be an FKCC object alone. In the latter, the FKCC object is streamed out to the standard output. Also, we often need to compute the lexicographic optimum of a polyhedron, typically to pick an optimal schedule. FKCC uses *parameteric integer linear programming* [5] *via* the Piplib library. The result is a discussion on the parameter value:

```
parameters := {N};
lexmin [N] -> {[i,j]: 0 <= i and i <= N and 0 <= j and j <= N};
```

would give:

```
if(N >= 0)
  {
    [] -> {[0,0]}
  }
```

```
else
 {
   (no solution)
 }
;
```

Note that structure parameters *must* be declared with the **parameters** construct. When no parameters are involved, the **parameters** construct may be omitted. To ensure the compatibility with ISCC [10] syntax, the parameters of a polyhedron *may* be declared on preceding brackets **[N] -> ....** This is purely optional: FKCC actually does not analyze this part. The instruction **set** *id* emits id := to the standard output. This makes it possible to generate ISCC scripts for further analysis. Finally, the set intersection of two polyhedra P and Q is obtained with P*Q.

Affine Forms. An affine form may be defined as a *Farkas term*:

```
iterations := [] -> {[i,j,N]: 0 <= i and i <= N and 0 <= j and j <= N};
theta := positive_on iterations;
```

If **iterations** is $\{x \mid Ax + b \geq 0\}$, then **theta** is defined as $\mathfrak{F}(\lambda_0, \lambda, A, b)$ where λ_0 and λ are fresh positive variables. In that case, the polyhedron is *never* parametrized: the *parameters must be handled as variables*. In particular, do not name variables with identifiers declared as parameters with **parameters :=**, as they would be treated as parameters whatever the context. Affine forms might be summed, scaled and composed with *affine functions*, typically to adjust the input dimension:

```
to_target := {[i,j,i',j',N]->[i,j,N]};
to_source := {[i,j,i',j',N]->[i',j',N]};
sum := theta.to_target - 2*theta.to_source + 1 + {[i,j,i',j',N] -> 2*i-i'};
```

In a summation of affine forms, affine forms must have the same input dimension. Also, a constant (1) is automatically interpreted as an affine form (**[i,j,i',j',N] -> 1**). Affine forms may also be stated explicitly (**{[i,j,i',j',N] -> 2*i-i'}**). The terms of the summation are simply separated with + and -, no parenthesis are allowed.

Resolution. The main feature of FKCC is the resolution of equations $S(x) = 0$ where S is a summation of affine forms including Farkas terms. This is obtained with the instruction **solve**:

```
solve sum = 0;
```

The result is a polyhedron with Farkas multipliers (obtained after applying Theorem 1):

```
[] -> {[lambda_0,lambda_1,lambda_2,lambda_3,lambda_4] :
      (2+lambda_0)+(-1*lambda_1) >= 0 and (-2+(-1*lambda_0))+lambda_1 >= 0 and
      lambda_2+(-1*lambda_3) >= 0 and (-1*lambda_2)+lambda_3 >= 0 and
      (-1*lambda_1)+(-1*lambda_3) >= 0 and lambda_1+lambda_3 >= 0 and
      (-1+(-2*lambda_0))+(2*lambda_1) >= 0 and (1+(2*lambda_0))+(-2*lambda_1) >= 0 and
      (-2*lambda_2)+(2*lambda_3) >= 0 and (2*lambda_2)+(-2*lambda_3) >= 0 and
      1+(-1*lambda_4) >= 0 and -1+lambda_4 >= 0 and lambda_4 >= 0 and
      lambda_0 >= 0 and lambda_1 >= 0 and lambda_2 >= 0 and lambda_3 >= 0 and
      lambda_4 >= 0 and lambda_0 >= 0 and lambda_1 >= 0 and lambda_2 >= 0 and lambda_3 >= 0};
```

At this point, we need to recover the coefficients of our affine form `theta` in terms of λ (`lambda_0,lambda_1,lambda_2,lambda_3`) and λ_0 (`lambda_4`). Observe that $\mathtt{theta}(x) = \mathfrak{F}(\lambda_0, \lambda, A, b)(x) = {}^t\lambda Ax + \lambda \cdot b + \lambda_0$. If the coefficients of `theta` are written: $\mathtt{theta}(x) = \tau \cdot x + \tau_0$, we simply have: $\tau = {}^t\lambda A$ and $\tau_0 = \lambda \cdot b + \lambda_0$. This is obtained with `define`:

```
define theta with tau;
```

The result is a conjunction of definition equalities, gathered in a polyhedron:

```
[] -> {[lambda_0,lambda_1,lambda_2,lambda_3,lambda_4,tau_0,tau_1,tau_2,tau_3] :
       ((-1*lambda_0)+lambda_1)+tau_0 >= 0 and (lambda_0+(-1*lambda_1))+(-1*tau_0) >= 0 and
       ((-1*lambda_2)+lambda_3)+tau_1 >= 0 and (lambda_2+(-1*lambda_3))+(-1*tau_1) >= 0 and
       ((-1*lambda_1)+(-1*lambda_3))+tau_2 >= 0 and (lambda_1+lambda_3)+(-1*tau_2) >= 0 and
       (-1*lambda_4)+tau_3 >= 0 and lambda_4+(-1*tau_3) >= 0};
```

The first coefficients `tau_k` define τ, the last one defines the constant τ_0. On our example, `theta(i,j,N) = tau_0*i + tau_1*j + tau_2*N + tau_3`. Now we may gather the results and eliminate the λ to keep only τ and τ_0:

```
keep tau_0,tau_1,tau_2,tau_3 in ((solve sum = 0)*(define theta with tau));
```

The result is a polyhedron with the solutions. Here, there are no solutions: the result is an empty polyhedron. All these steps may be applied once with the `find` command:

```
find theta s.t. sum = 0;
```

The coefficients are automatically named `theta_0`, `theta_1`, etc with the same convention as `define`. We point out that `define` *choose fresh names* for coefficients (e.g. `tau_4`, `tau_5` on the second time with ''tau'') whereas `find` *always choose the same names*. Hence `find` would be prefered when deriving separately constraints on the same coefficients of `theta`. `find` may filter the coefficients for several affine forms expressed as Farkas terms in a summation:

```
find theta_S,theta_T s.t.
  theta_T.to_target - theta_S.to_source - 1
    - (positive_on dependences_from_S_to_T) = 0;
```

This is typically used to compute schedules for programs with multiple assignments (here S and T with dependences from iterations of S to iterations of T). Finally, note that `keep tau_0,tau_1,tau_2,tau_3 in P;` projects P on variables `tau_0,tau_1,tau_2,tau_3`: the result is a polyhedron with integral points of coordinates (`tau_0,tau_1,tau_2,tau_3`). This way, the order in which `tau_0,tau_1,tau_2,tau_3` are specified to `keep` impacts directly a further lexicographic optimization.

4   Examples

This section shows how FKCC might be used to specify in a few lines termination analysis and loop scheduling.

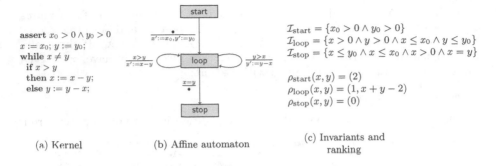

assert $x_0 > 0 \wedge y_0 > 0$
$x := x_0;\ y := y_0;$
while $x \neq y$
  if $x > y$
  then $x := x - y;$
  else $y := y - x;$

$\mathcal{I}_{\text{start}} = \{x_0 > 0 \wedge y_0 > 0\}$
$\mathcal{I}_{\text{loop}} = \{x > 0 \wedge y > 0 \wedge x \leq x_0 \wedge y \leq y_0\}$
$\mathcal{I}_{\text{stop}} = \{x \leq y_0 \wedge x \leq x_0 \wedge x > 0 \wedge x = y\}$

$\rho_{\text{start}}(x, y) = (2)$
$\rho_{\text{loop}}(x, y) = (1, x + y - 2)$
$\rho_{\text{stop}}(x, y) = (0)$

(a) Kernel   (b) Affine automaton   (c) Invariants and ranking

Fig. 2. Termination example

4.1   Termination Analysis

Consider the example depicted on Fig. 2. The program computes the gcd of two integers x_0 and y_0 (a). It is translated to an affine automaton (b) (also called integer interpreted automaton), in turn analyzed to check the termination (c): does the program terminates for *any* input (x_0, y_0) satisfying the precondition $x_0 > 0 \wedge y_0 > 0$?

This problem is – as most topics in static analysis – undecidable in general. However, we may conclude when it is possible to derive statically an abstraction precise enough of the program execution. In [1], we provide a termination algorithm based on the computation of a *ranking*. A ranking is an application $\rho_{\text{label}} : \mathbb{Z}^n \to (\mathcal{R}, \prec)$ which maps each reachable state of the automaton $\langle label, \boldsymbol{x} \rangle$ to a *rank* belonging to well-founded set. On our example a reachable state could be $\langle loop, (x : 3, y : 3, x_0 : 3, y_0 : 6) \rangle$ after firing the initial transition and the right transition.

The ranking is decreasing on the transitions: for any transition $\langle label, \boldsymbol{x} \rangle \to \langle label', \boldsymbol{x}' \rangle$, we have: $\rho_{\text{label}'}(\boldsymbol{x}') \prec \rho_{\text{label}}(\boldsymbol{x})$. Since ranks belong to a well founded set, there are – by definition – no infinite decreasing chain of ranks. Hence infinite chains of transitions from an initial state never happen.

On [1], we provide a general method for computing a ranking of an affine automaton. Our ranking is *affine per label*: $\rho_{\text{label}}(\boldsymbol{x}) = A_{label}\boldsymbol{x} + b_{label} \in \mathbb{N}^p$. Figure 2.(c) depicts the ranking found on the example. Ranks ordered with the lexicographic ordering $\ll$, the well-founded set is $(\mathbb{N}^p, \ll)$. This means that, by decreasing order, **start** comes first (2), then all the iterations of **loop** (1), and finally **stop** (0). The transitions involved to compute those constants are the transitions from **start** to **loop** and the transitions from **loop** to **stop**. Then, transitions from **loop** to **loop** (left, denoted τ_1 and right, denoted τ_2) are used to computed the second dimension of ρ_{loop}. *In the remainder, we will focus on the computation of the second dimension of ρ_{loop} $(x + y - 2)$ from transitions τ_1 and τ_2.* We will write $\rho_{\text{loop}}(\boldsymbol{x})$ for $\rho_{\text{loop}}(\boldsymbol{x})[1]$ to simplify the presentation.

Positivity on Reachable States. The ranking must be positive on reachable states of **loop**. The set of $\boldsymbol{x}$ such that $\langle loop, \boldsymbol{x} \rangle$ is reachable from an initial state is called the *accessibility set* of loop. In general, we cannot compute it – this is the undecidable part of the analysis. Rather, we compute an over-approximation thanks to linear relation analysis [4,9]. This set is called an *invariant* and will be denoted by $\mathcal{I}_{\text{loop}}$. Figure 2.(c) depicts the invariants on the program. All the challenge is to make the invariant close enough to the accessibility set so a ranking can be computed. In FKCC, the assertion $x \models \mathcal{I}_{\text{loop}} \Rightarrow \rho_{\text{loop}}(x) \geq 0$ translates to:

```
I_loop := [] -> {[x,y,x0,y0]: x>0 and y>0 and x <= x0 and y <= y0};
rank := positive_on I_loop;
```

Decreasing on Transitions. Now it remains to find a ranking decreasing on transitions τ_1 and τ_2. We first consider τ_1. The assertion $x \models \mathcal{I}_{\text{loop}} \wedge x > y \Rightarrow \rho_{\text{loop}}(x - y, x, x_0, y_0) < \rho_{\text{loop}}(x, y, x_0, y_0)$ translates to:

```
tau1 := [] -> {[x,y,x0,y0]: x>y};
s1 := find rank s.t. rank - (rank . {[x,y,x0,y0]->[x-y,y,x0,y0]}) - 1
                     - positive_on (tau1*I_loop) = 0;
```

Similarly we compute a solution set s2 from τ_2 and $\mathcal{I}_{\text{loop}}$. Finally, the ranking is found with the instruction `lexmin (s1*s2);`, which outputs the result:

```
[] -> {[1,1,0,0,-2]};
```

This corresponds to the dimension $x + y - 2$.

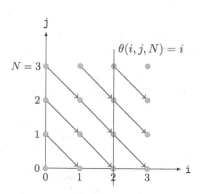

```
for i := 0 to N
  for j := 0 to N
    c[i+j] := c[i+j] + a[i]*b[j];
```

(a) Product of polynomials   (b) Iterations and schedule

Fig. 3. Scheduling example

4.2 Scheduling

Figure 3 depicts an example of program (a) computing the product of two polynomials specified by their array of coefficients a and b, and the iteration domain with the data dependence across iterations (b) and an example schedule θ prescribing a parallel execution by vertical waves, as discussed in Sect. 2.

Positivity. Similarly to the ranking, the positivity condition (1) translates to:

```
iterations := [] -> { [i,j,N]: 0 <= i and i <= N  and 0 <= j and j <= N};
dependence := [] -> { [i,j,i',j',N]: 0 <= i and i <= N  and 0 <= j and
                        j <= N and 0 <= i' and i' <= N  and 0 <= j' and
                        j' <= N and i+j = i'+j' and i<i'};
```

```
# theta(i,j,N) >= 0 for any iteration (i,j,N)
theta := positive_on iterations;
```

Correctness. We enhance the correctness condition (2) by making it possible to *select* the dependence to satisfy. For each dependence class d, we use a 0-1 variable ϵ_d. Here we have a single dependence class from S to S, so have only one 0-1 variable ϵ:

$$\theta(i', j', N) \geq \theta(i, j, N) + \epsilon \quad \forall (i, j, i', j') \in \Delta_N$$

On the ranking example, we would have four classes ($i = start \rightarrow loop, \tau_1, \tau_2, e = loop \rightarrow stop$). This makes it possible to choose which dependence class is satisfied ($\epsilon_d = 1$) or just respected ($\epsilon_d = 0$). This is the way multidimensional schedules are built [7]: on the termination example we would have $\epsilon_i = \epsilon_e = 1, \epsilon_{\tau_1} = \epsilon_{\tau_2} = 0$ for the first dimension, then $\epsilon_{\tau_1} = \epsilon_{\tau_2} = 1$ for the second dimension. Here it is kind of artificial, since we have a single dependence. However, the presentation generalizes easily to several dependence classes. This translates as:

```
parameters := {inv_eps,eps};

to_target := {[i,j,i',j',N]->[i',j',N]};
to_source := {[i,j,i',j',N]->[i,j,N]};

# s -> t ==> theta(s) <= theta(t) + eps, 0 <= eps <= 1
theta_correct := solve (theta . to_target) - (theta . to_source)
                  + {[i,j,i',j',N] -> -1*eps}
                  - (positive_on dependence) = 0;
theta_def := define theta with theta;
eps_correct := [] -> {[i]: 0 <= eps and eps <= 1 and inv_eps = 1-eps};
```

Here is the trick: parameters are forbidden to define Farkas terms; however parameters are perfectly allowed in summation. In that case, **the resolution interprets parameters as constants**. Hence the trick to set ϵ as a parameter and to put it in the summation by declaring an explicit affine form `{[i,j,i',j',N] -> -1*eps}`. We then keep the definition of theta coefficients in terms of Farkas multipliers (`theta_def`) and the domain of ϵ (`eps_correct`).

Optimality. We seek a schedule θ with a minimal latency $\ell(\theta)$ (number of steps). When θ is an affine form, $\ell(\theta)$ may be bounded by an affine form $L(N)$ of the structure parameters [6]: $\ell(\theta) \leq L(N)$. This means that:

$$\forall (i, j) \in \mathcal{D}_N : \quad \theta(i, j, N) \leq L(N)$$

Which is, again, completely Farkas compliant. It remains to express $L(N)$, which have to be positive provided $\mathcal{D}_N$ is not empty i.e. $N \geq 0$. This translates to:

```
# L(N) >= 0 on the parameter domain
latency := positive_on ([] -> {[N]: N >= 0});

# theta(i,j,N) <= L(N)
theta_bounded := solve (latency . {[i,j,N] -> [N]}) - theta
                       - (positive_on iterations) = 0;
bound_def := define latency with latency;
```

Finally, it remains to gather the constraints (positivity, correctness, optimality) to obtain the result:

```
lexmin (keep inv_eps,latency_0,latency_1,theta_0,theta_1,theta_2,theta_3,eps
        in theta_correct*theta_def*eps_correct*theta_bounded*bound_def);
```

By priority order, we want to (i) maximize the dependence satisfied (minimize inv_eps), then (ii) to minimize the latency (L(N) = latency_0*N + latency_1). This amounts to find the lexicographic minimum with variables ordered as (inv_eps,latency_0,latency_1). Note that eps and inv_eps are parameters. Adding them to the variable list of keep has the effect to turn them to counters eps_counter and inv_eps_counter. We obtain the following result, pretty printed using the -pretty option:

```
theta_0 = 0
theta_1 = -1
theta_2 = 1
theta_3 = 0
latency_0 = 1
latency_1 = 0
eps_counter = 1
inv_eps_counter = 0
```

Hence $\theta(i,j,N) = N - j$, $L(N) = N$ and the dependence was satisfied (eps_counter = 1).

5 Conclusion

In this paper, we have presented FKCC, a scripting tool to prototype program analyses and transformations using the affine form of Farkas lemma. The script language of FKCC is powerful enough to write in a few lines tricky scheduling algorithms and termination analysis. The object representation (polyhedra, affine functions) is compatible with ISCC, a widespread polyhedral tool featuring manipulation of affine relations. FKCC provides features to generate ISCC code, and conversely, the output of ISCC might be injected in FKCC. This will allow to take profit of both worlds.

We believe that scripting tools are mandatory to evaluate rapidly research ideas. So far, Farkas lemma-based approaches were locked by two facts: (i) applying by hand Farkas Lemma is nearly impossible and (ii) implementing an analysis with Farkas lemma is usually tricky, time consuming and highly bug prone. With FKCC, computer scientists are now freed from these constraints.

References

1. Alias, C., Darte, A., Feautrier, P., Gonnord, L.: Multi-dimensional rankings, program termination, and complexity bounds of flowchart programs. In: Cousot, R., Martel, M. (eds.) SAS 2010. LNCS, vol. 6337, pp. 117–133. Springer, Heidelberg (2010). https://doi.org/10.1007/978-3-642-15769-1_8
2. Bondhugula, U., Hartono, A., Ramanujam, J., Sadayappan, P.: A practical automatic polyhedral parallelizer and locality optimizer. In: Proceedings of the ACM SIGPLAN 2008 Conference on Programming Language Design and Implementation, Tucson, AZ, USA, 7–13 June 2008, pp. 101–113 (2008). https://doi.org/10.1145/1375581.1375595
3. Colón, M.A., Sankaranarayanan, S., Sipma, H.B.: Linear invariant generation using non-linear constraint solving. In: Hunt, W.A., Somenzi, F. (eds.) CAV 2003. LNCS, vol. 2725, pp. 420–432. Springer, Heidelberg (2003). https://doi.org/10.1007/978-3-540-45069-6_39
4. Cousot, P., Halbwachs, N.: Automatic discovery of linear restraints among variables of a program. In: 5th ACM Symposium on Principles of Programming Languages (POPL 1978), Tucson, pp. 84–96, January 1978
5. Feautrier, P.: Parametric integer programming. RAIRO Recherche Opérationnelle 22(3), 243–268 (1988)
6. Feautrier, P.: Some efficient solutions to the affine scheduling problem. Part I. one-dimensional time. Int. J. Parallel Program. 21(5), 313–348 (1992). https://doi.org/10.1007/BF01407835
7. Feautrier, P.: Some efficient solutions to the affine scheduling problem, part II: multi-dimensional time. Int. J. Parallel Prog. 21(6), 389–420 (1992)
8. Feautrier, P., Lengauer, C.: Polyhedron model. In: Padua, D. (ed.) Encyclopedia of Parallel Computing, pp. 1581–1592. Springer, Boston (2011). https://doi.org/10.1007/978-0-387-09766-4
9. Gonnord, L.: Accélération abstraite pour l'amélioration de la précision en Analyse des Relations Linéaires. Ph.D. thesis, Université Joseph Fourier - Grenoble (2007)
10. Verdoolaege, S.: Counting affine calculator and applications. In: First International Workshop on Polyhedral Compilation Techniques (IMPACT 2011), Charmonix, France (2011)

Handling Heap Data Structures in Backward Symbolic Execution

Robert Husák[✉], Jan Kofroň, and Filip Zavoral

Faculty of Mathematics and Physics, Charles University, Prague, Czech Republic
{husak,zavoral}@ksi.mff.cuni.cz, jan.kofron@d3s.mff.cuni.cz

Abstract. Backward symbolic execution (BSE), also known as weakest precondition computation, is a useful technique to determine validity of assertions in program code by transforming its semantics into boolean conditions for an SMT solver. Regrettably, the literature does not cover various challenges which arise during its implementation, especially when we want to reason about heap objects using the theory of arrays and to use the SMT solver efficiently. In this paper, we present our achievements in this area. Our contribution is threefold. First, we summarize the two most popular state-of-the-art approaches used for BSE, denoting them as *disjunct propagation* and *conjunct combination*. Second, we present a novel method for modelling heap operations in BSE using the theory of arrays, optimized for incremental checking during the analysis and handling the input heap. Third, we compare both approaches with our heap handling implementation on a set of program examples, presenting their strengths and weaknesses. The evaluation shows that conjunct combination is the most efficient variant, exceeding the straightforward implementation of disjunct propagation in an order of magnitude.

Keywords: Backward symbolic execution · Weakest precondition ·
Heap data structures · Input heap · Theory of arrays

1 Introduction

Symbolic execution is an established technique to explore semantics of programs, create tests with high code coverage and discover bugs [2]. To achieve that, it systematically explores the state space of the program reachable from the entry point, transforming the possible execution paths into boolean constraints. These constraints are usually passed to an SMT solver to determine the reachability of the corresponding paths. To reason about objects on the heap, several of the practically-usable tools [6,18] use the theory of arrays [10], which can be handled by the most of the state-of-the-art SMT solvers [8].

If we are not interested in the exploration of the whole program and we want to inspect only one particular problematic place instead, we can use the *backward* variant of symbolic execution, sometimes referred to also as the *weakest precondition* analysis [7,9]. As its name suggests, backward symbolic execution starts at the assertion of our interest and traverses the execution direction backwards. If it manages to reach the entry point and find an assignment satisfying the path

© Springer Nature Switzerland AG 2020
E. Sekerinski et al. (Eds.): FM 2019 Workshops, LNCS 12233, pp. 537–556, 2020.
https://doi.org/10.1007/978-3-030-54997-8_33

constraints, it can provide us with a valuable test case. Otherwise, if no under-approximation is used and the assertion violation is proved to be unreachable, it is validated.

As we can see, each run of backward symbolic execution can be very expensive in terms of resources. However, the information it provides is potentially very detailed and useful for detecting the causes of errors. Therefore, it is important to use it in an appropriate context. There is a plethora of techniques which use some kind of abstraction, enabling them to efficiently analyse large programs for the cost of introducing false positives [11,15,17]. Backward symbolic execution can be then used only at the places where these techniques found potential errors in order to examine them further. For example, the authors of Snugglebug were able to verify 29 of 38 feasible *null* dereference exceptions found by FindBugs [11] in a Java codebase of 750 kLOC [7]. Another usage of backward symbolic execution is to run it in an interactive fashion, enabling programmers to gather as much information about a specific program error as possible [12].

Although backward symbolic execution can be indeed very useful, it is not as popular in the literature as the forward variant. Therefore, many important design considerations and potential complications have to be rediscovered during each implementation. For example, when calling an SMT solver multiple times, it is often efficient for the subsequently analysed conjunctions to share a common prefix. As we illustrate in Sect. 2, that complicates the way to handle the constraints, because we then should not alter the existing ones, only add new ones. We tackle this problem and other issues in our contributions:

1. We summarize the existing algorithms commonly used for backward symbolic execution in Sect. 3.
2. We present a novel way to transform heap operations into boolean constraints in Sect. 4. These transformations fit into the mentioned algorithms and utilize performance enhancements of the state-of-the-art SMT solvers.
3. We compare the performance of all the presented approaches on a set of code examples in Sect. 5.

In Sect. 6, we compare our approach to the most important papers and tools related to our work, while Sect. 7 concludes.

2   Problem

All the issues related to implementing a backward symbolic execution tool stem from its very nature. Forward symbolic execution starts with a fixed set of symbolic input variables and all the gradually constructed constraints can be essentially build from them. With backward symbolic execution, the situation is different, as the set of input variables constantly changes according to the variables encountered along the way. Every time a variable is read, it is added to this set; every time it is assigned to, it is removed from it.

Listing 1.1: Sample C# code to demonstrate symbolic execution

```csharp
1  void ScalarExample(int a) {
2      int b = 1;
3      int c = 2;
4      Debug.Assert(a != b);
5  }
6
7  void HeapExample1(Node a) {
8      a.next = new Node();
9      Node b = a.next;
10     Debug.Assert(a != b);
11 }
12
13 void HeapExample2(Node a) {
14     Node b = a.next;
15     Node c = new Node();
16     Debug.Assert(b != c);
17 }
```

We will illustrate the approaches on a simple method `ScalarExample` in Listing 1.1. The forward variant starts with a symbolic variable a assigned to a, at lines 2 and 3 it then assigns 1 to b and 2 to c. When it comes to the assertion a != b at line 4, it interprets it using the known values and negates the expression to discover any error inputs, resulting in a simple condition $a = 1$. The backward variant starts directly at the assertion, creating a condition $a = b$, where a and b are the input variables corresponding to their symbolic variables a and b, respectively. As the condition is not dependent on c in any way, it can safely skip its assignment at line 3. Next, the assignment of 1 into b at line 2 must effectively remove it from the set of input variables and replace it by 1 in the condition, resulting again in $a = 1$. Although this simple example does not demonstrate any significant differences, things become more complicated when heap operations and various efficiency optimizations are involved.

Constantly Changing Input Heap: The rule with the constantly changing set of input variables applies to the input heap as well. Moreover, its analysis gets more complicated, because the objects from the input heap might get intertwined with the ones created during the analysed program run. Consider the assertion a != b on the line 10 in Listing 1.1. At first, the objects in the input heap might be possibly referenced by both a and b. The field read at line 9 causes b to be loaded from the current input heap. However, we cannot assume that the loaded reference is from the input heap as well, because it can always be assigned an explicitly allocated object, as at line 8. Therefore, we need to provide a way to correctly distinguish between the input heap and the explicitly allocated objects and to enable their various interactions.

Incremental Solving: There are many usage scenarios of SMT solvers where we need to call them successively on similar formulas. E.g., in the case of symbolic execution, we might want to explore two independent code branches sharing the same prefix. Therefore, a modern SMT solver can be usually used incrementally, with the possibility to cache certain knowledge between subsequent calls. To add and remove assertions, they offer two useful mechanisms: an *assertion stack* and *assumptions*. The former enables us to use a stack-based system of scopes containing the particular assertions, with the ability to destroy all the data of the topmost scope while retaining the remaining ones. The latter works by adding every assertion a in the form of $l \implies a$, where l is a literal specified later during each call of the solver. Because we want to utilize these features to optimize our SMT calls, it is important that we construct the formulas in a proper way, possibly combining the strengths of both techniques.

3   Backward Symbolic Execution

3.1   Notation

Let us clarify the terminology and semantics of various formulas and symbols used in this paper. If we speak about a *function* or *mapping* $g : A \rightarrow B$, it is understood as a partial function, hence defined on the subset of its domain A. If $g(a)$ for $a \in A$ is not defined, we denote it as $g(a) = undef$. The function $g[a \rightarrow b]$ is defined to be the same as g, except for it maps a to b. This notation can be generalized for a set: $g[\{a_1, ..., a_n\} \rightarrow b] = g[a_1 \rightarrow b]...[a_n \rightarrow b]$.

As to the formalism used for SMT queries, many-sorted first-order logic is used. Because the meaning of *sort* in logic corresponds to the meaning of *type* in computer science, we will use these two names interchangeably, according to the context. The *signature* $\Sigma = (\mathcal{S}, \mathcal{F}, \mathcal{P})$ comprises a set of *sorts* $\mathcal{S}$, a set of *function symbols* $\mathcal{F}$ and a set of *predicate symbols* $\mathcal{P}$. Symbolic variables Σ_v, terms Σ_t, atoms Σ_a, and formulas Σ_f are derived from the signature, using the standard recursive way. A formula $\varphi[a/b]$ is constructed by replacing all the occurrences of a in φ by b. The function FRESH_{Σ_v} retrieves a symbolic variable not yet used in any context. In general, for any domain A, FRESH_A retrieves a variable $a \in A$, which is not yet used in the analysis.

Let C be a set of classes contained in the analysed program. For each class $c \in C$, there is a corresponding set F_c containing all its fields. All the fields in the program are contained in $F = \bigcup_{c \in C} F_c$. To enable working with reference symbolic variables, we introduce a set of reference sorts $R = \{\sigma_c \mid c \in C\} \subset \mathcal{S}$. As an instrument to reason about types of fields and variables, we use function $t : V \cup F \rightarrow \mathcal{S}$. $F_{t(v)}$ as an abbreviation for F_c where $\sigma_c = t(v)$. Reference fields F_R and value fields F_V are defined as follows:

$$F_R = \{f \in F \mid t(f) \in R\} \qquad F_V = F \setminus F_R$$

Analogicaly, reference and value variables:

$$V_R = \{v \in \Sigma_v \mid t(v) \in R\} \qquad V_V = \Sigma_v \setminus V_R$$

Note that the sorts R representing reference variables are used only to ease formal description of heap operations. They are effectively replaced by functions on arrays and integers, as we describe in Sect. 4. All the reference variables are expected to point to objects on the heap, there is no notion of low-level pointers and of accessing stack variables by references.

To reason about a certain program, we expect it to be given as a control flow graph (CFG). Each node n contains at most one operation $n.op$ and each edge $e = (n_1, \psi_e, n_2)$ is marked with a condition ψ_e. The possible operations follow: scalar assignment of term $v_t \leftarrow_s t$, reference assignment $v_t \leftarrow_r v_r$, reference comparison assignment[1] $v_t \leftarrow (v_r^1 = v_r^2)$, new object creation $v_t \leftarrow_r \mathbf{new}\ T$, field read $v_t \leftarrow v_r.f$ and field write $v_r.f \leftarrow v_v$. Note that the last two operations can occur both for reference and variable fields, in some cases we denote it by $\leftarrow_r$ and $\leftarrow_s$, respectively. Assertions are modelled as edges to special nodes.

To keep the scope limited, this paper does not directly address handling loops, interprocedural analysis or recursion. In order to evaluate our approach on programs of smaller size, we use a simple preprocessor for CFGs, which unwinds the loops for a given number of iterations. To handle interprocedural calls, we plan to extend it to handle inlining of the procedures up to a certain level of recursive calls. We are aware that this approach is underapproximate and does not scale well on larger programs. In order to mitigate this issue, we will inspire from the existing tools which were able to efficiently extend backward symbolic execution into an interprocedural analysis. Snugglebug uses directed call graph construction and tabulation, enabling it to explore the call graph lazily and reuse certain summaries obtained for each procedure [7]. ALTER combines backward and forward symbolic execution to combine method summaries, utilizing interpolant computation to learn from infeasible paths [16].

3.2 Algorithm

Whereas in forward symbolic execution we usually want to reasonably spread our analysis among the state space to achieve high code coverage [2], backward symbolic execution often works by gathering summaries towards the entry point [1,7]. At least in the intraprocedural case it is a natural approach, as we are interested in finding a feasible path between the entry node and the target node.

An overall algorithm structure is shown in Fig. 1. Given a target node n_{trg}, it traverses cfg backwards towards the entry node and gathers useful information along the way. The information is stored in the $states$ associative array. In the beginning, because we expect cfg to be acyclic, we can sort its nodes according to their topological order in the reversed cfg, skipping those not reachable from n_{trg}. This way, when processing a node, we are sure that the dependent nodes were already processed. For each node, we gather the states of the directly adjacent nodes and their corresponding edge conditions into $deps$. MERGE is a core function

---

[1] We did not put reference comparison directly in the edge conditions so that we can describe its processing later in the unified manner with the other heap operations, see Sect. 4.

BSE(*cfg*, n_{trg})

1: var *states*: *node* → *state*
2: *states*[n_{trg}] ← state representing *true*
3: **for all** node *n* in *cfg* sorted by reverse dependency on n_{trg} **do**
4:     var *deps* ← {(ψ_e, n_{dep}, *states*[n_{dep}]) | edge (*n*, ψ_e, n_{dep}) in *cfg*}
5:     *states*[*n*] ← MERGE(*n*, *deps*)
6:     **if** DoSolve() ∧ Solve(GetCondition(*states*, *n*)) = *UNSAT* **then**
7:         *states*[*n*] ← state representing *false*
8: **return** *states*

Fig. 1. Backward symbolic execution algorithm

responsible for inferring the state of a given node according to its dependencies. DoSolve is a heuristic returning *true* for the entry node and possibly also during the exploration so that certain infeasible parts get pruned. GetCondition is used to gather the condition corresponding to a given state, returns false if n_{trg} is unreachable from that node. Eventually the algorithm retrieves all the computed states. The caller can then extract interesting pieces of information from it, such as a possible input driving the execution towards n_{trg}.

state: formula in DNF

MergeDisj(*n*, *deps*)

1: var *merged* ← disjunction of {ψ_e ∧ *d* | *d* disjunct in φ, (ψ_e, n_{dep}, φ) ∈ *deps*}
2: **return** ProcessOperationDisj(Simplify(*merged*), *n*.op)

ProcessOperationDisj(*state*, v_t ←$_s$ *t*)

1: **return** *state*[v_t / *t*]

GetConditionDisj(*states*, *n*)

1: **return** *states*[*n*]

Fig. 2. Backward symbolic execution implementation using disjunct propagation

In the literature, we have identified two main possible implementations of this algorithm. The first, listed in Fig. 2, is based on formulas in DNF and their propagation in the form of disjuncts [7]. MergeDisj merges the disjunctions in all the dependent nodes and enhances them by their corresponding edge conditions, simplifying the resulting formula by Simplify and passing it to ProcessOperationDisj. Simplify applies various techniques of reducing a disjunction size while maintaining its semantics. ProcessOperationDisj handles an assignment v_t ←$_s$ *t* by replacing the target variable v_t by the term *t* representing its value, GetConditionDisj simply returns the disjunction for the given node. Heap operations and the implementation of GetCondition for heaps is described in Sect. 4.

state: (node condition ψ_n, *vers*: $V_V \rightarrow \mathbb{N}$, *heap*)

MERGECONJ(n, *deps*)

1: var *mergedVers* $\leftarrow$ merge *vers* in *deps* to get the highest of each entry
2: (var *mergedHeap*, var *heapJoinConds*) $\leftarrow$ MERGEHEAPS(*heaps* in *deps*)
3: var ψ_{join} $\leftarrow$ disjunction of
   {versioned $\psi_e \wedge c_{n_{dep}} \wedge$ JOINVERS(*vers*, *mergedVers*) $\wedge$ *heapJoinCond* for *heap*
   | $(\psi_e, n_{dep}, \psi_{n_{dep}}, vers, heap) \in deps$}
4: (var ψ_{op}, var *finalVers*, var *finalHeap*) $\leftarrow$ PROCESSOPERATIONCONJ(*mergedVers*, *mergedHeap*,
   n.op)
5: **return** $(c_n \implies \psi_{join} \wedge \psi_{op}$, *mergedVers*, *mergedHeap*)

PROCESSOPERATIONCONJ(*vers*, *heap*, $v_t \leftarrow_s t$)

1: **if** *vers*[v_t] = *undef* **then**
2:    **return** (*true*, *vers*, *heap*)
3: **else**
4:    var *oldVer* $\leftarrow$ *vers*[v_t]
5:    var *newVers* $\leftarrow$ *vers*[$v_t \rightarrow$ *oldVer* + 1, {unknown variables in t} $\rightarrow$ 0]
6:    **return** ($v_t^{oldVer} = t$ versioned by *newVers*, *newVers*, *heap*)

GETCONDITIONCONJ(*states*, n)

1: **return** $c_n \wedge$ conjunction of $\psi_{n'}$ where n' is reachable from n

Fig. 3. Backward symbolic execution implementation using conjunct combination

In Fig. 3, the other implementation is listed [1]. Instead of propagating a set of disjuncts to the entry node, it associates each node n with a condition ψ_n describing its semantics and control flow. As seen in GETCONDITIONCONJ, to reason about the whole path, we can pass a conjunction of these conditions to an SMT solver, which enables an efficient incremental usage. Since we can reason about mutable variables, our state contains also a map *vers* containing a version number for each encountered program variable. Unlike the previous case, we need to store certain information about a symbolic heap in each state; the details will be provided in Sect. 4.

MERGECONJ works as follows. Each node n is associated with a propositional variable c_n to express that the control flow reached it. The condition ψ_n is an implication with c_n on the left side. The right side consists of two parts: a join condition ψ_{join} and an operation condition ψ_{op}. The purpose of ψ_{join} is to model the branching of the control flow by creating a disjunction on the edge conditions where each disjunct redirects the flow to the corresponding $c_{n_{dep}}$ and possibly synchronizes the variable versions of the dependent nodes using JOIN-VERS. An operation condition, created by PROCESSOPERATIONCONJ, handles an assignment by making the given variable under its current version equal to the given term and associating the variable with a new version. Notice that if v_t has not been encountered so far, we can safely ignore the operation. Heap operation handling is described in Sect. 4, including the merging of heaps.

As we can see, each implementation is connected with certain advantages and disadvantages. The disjunct propagation approach is based on maintaining sets of disjuncts and simplifying them, while the operations are handled as term substitutions. As a result, the final condition can be potentially much simpler than in the other case, because it does not contain any helper variables representing various versions and SIMPLIFY can help to get rid of various repetitive patterns. On the other hand, if the simplification is not successful enough, the size of the resulting formula can be exponential with respect to the number of calls to MERGE. Furthermore, it cannot fully utilize incremental SMT solvers, as they work by adding immutable conjuncts to an assertion stack. The conjunction combination case is able to use them efficiently and the generated condition size is usually linear with respect to the number of the analysed nodes, which is redeemed by the presence of helper variables.

Although in this work, the implementations are handled as two separate techniques, we plan to pursue a way to efficiently combine them, using the best features of both. Creating simple procedure summaries might be crucial for developing an efficient interprocedural algorithm, whereas utilizing an incremental SMT solver might help with exploring large program state.

4   Modelling Heap Using Array Theory

4.1   Main Idea

The array theory enables SMT solvers to reason about heap memory in forward symbolic execution and concolic execution [6,18]. Its axioms, in addition to those of theory of uninterpreted functions, follow [4]:

$$\forall a, i, j \ (i = j \Rightarrow read(write(a, i, v), j) = v)$$

$$\forall a, i, j \ (i \neq j \Rightarrow read(write(a, i, v), j) = read(a, j))$$

$$\forall a, b \ (\forall i(read(a, i) = read(b, i)) \Leftrightarrow a = b)$$

As we can see, array theory generalises the operations of the array data structure, with the only difference being the immutability of the array variables. In the forward variant of symbolic execution, a common approach is to associate an array with each defined field and represent all the references by integers [18]. Reading a value from an instance can be then naturally modelled by using the *read* operation on the corresponding reference and array. Writing a value is similarly performed by using the *write* operation to produce a new version of the particular array. To ensure that different allocations of new objects do not reference the same object, we can use an internal counter and increment it every time an allocation is performed (allocation site counting) [3]. To denote *null* references, 0 is used.

All these principles can be directly adopted for backward symbolic execution as well [7]. However, to our knowledge there is a serious problem not sufficiently tackled in the literature. If we do not analyse a program from its very start, we expect that there are existing objects on the heap, prior to the entry point, where the analysis begins from, being called the input heap. Therefore, each reference can point either to an object located in the input heap, to *null*, or to an object allocated explicitly during the analysis. The problem is that if we do not constrain the references from the input heap to be distinct from the explicitly allocated objects, the SMT solver might produce a model where the references from those two distinct groups are equal.

Consider the method `HeapExample1` in Listing 1.1. Apart from the instance created at line 8, there is also an instance passed as the parameter a. Because this instance was created before the method call, we must assert that it is distinct from the former. Otherwise, an SMT solver might create an invalid model where $a = b$, so the input heap contains a reference to the explicitly created instance before it even exists.

Furthermore, all the references from a in the beginning of the method must point either to *null* or to other input heap instances. In method `HeapExample2`, we can see the reason. If we do not constrain the reference loaded from a.next in any way, the SMT solver can create a model where $b = c$.

A natural approach used in our solution is to restrict all the input heap objects to be represented as negative integers. In the case of forward symbolic execution, we can remember the first version of the variable representing each field and then constrain it whenever we access it from any reference. In `HeapExample1`, we start with an input reference $a \leq 0$ and an array variable $next^0$ representing the field `next` in the beginning. At line 8 we assert $next^1 = write(next^0, a, 1)$, making $next^1$ the current version of the field. Nevertheless, when we access the field at line 9, we can retrospectively add a constraint $read(next^0, a) \leq 0$, making a.next from the input heap either to be *null* or to reference another object from the input heap. As we only add constraints and never alter the existing ones, this approach is naturally efficient for incremental solving.

When trying to using this approach in backward symbolic execution, we encounter a major problem. Because the view of the input heap continues to change as the analysis proceeds backwards, we cannot use any single version of the array variable representing the given field. For example, if we decide to set the input heap constraint at line 9 as $read(next^0, a) \leq 0$, we prevent a.next to be assigned any explicitly created instance, which exactly happens at line 8.

As we explain below, we tackle this problem by creating a helper "input" array variable for each field and firmly asserting its equality with the current field variable version only when explicitly checking the condition. A similar solution is created also for the reference variables, as they face the same issue.

4.2   Operation Definitions

The implementation of heap operation handling for the disjunct propagation algorithm from Fig. 2 is shown in Fig. 4. To mark symbolic variables corresponding to reference variables and fields, we use the s superscript. For a reference variable v, v^s represents a symbolic integer variable; for a field f, f^s represents a symbolic array variable indexed by integers. The value sort of f^s is $t(f)$ if $f \in F_V$, integer otherwise. The semantics of a reference variable v is as follows.

If $v^s = 0$, v is *null*; therefore, $null^s = 0$. If $v^s > 0$, v references an object explicitly created during the analysed part of the program. Otherwise, if $v^s < 0$, v references an object in the input heap, i.e., it is created in the not yet analysed code.

PROCESSOPERATIONDISJHEAP(*state, op*)

1: **switch** *op* **do**
2:     **case** $v_t \leftarrow_r v_v$
3:         **return** $state[v_t^s / v_r^s]$
4:     **case** $v_t \leftarrow (v_1 = v_2)$
5:         **return** $state[v_t / (v_1^s = v_2^s)]$
6:     **case** $v_t \leftarrow_r$ new T
7:         **return** $state[v_t^s / \text{FRESH}_{N^+}()]$
8:     **case** $v_r.f \leftarrow v_v$
9:         **return** $state[f^s / write(f^s, v_r^s, \text{SYMB}(v_v))] \wedge v_r^s \neq 0$
10:    **case** $v_t \leftarrow_s v_r.f$
11:        **return** $state[v_t / read(f^s, v_r^s)] \wedge v_r^s \neq 0$
12:    **case** $v_t \leftarrow_r v_r.f$
13:        **return** $state[v_t^s / read(f^s, v_r^s)] \wedge v_r^s \neq 0 \wedge read(f^{in}, v_r^s) \leq 0$

GETCONDITIONDISJHEAP(*states, n*)

1: var *inputRefs* ← gather reference symbolic variables in *states*[*n*]
2: **return** $states[n] \wedge \bigwedge_{f \in F_R} f^s = f^{in} \wedge \bigwedge_{v \in inputRefs} v \leq 0$

Fig. 4. Heap operation modelling in the disjunct propagation approach from Fig. 2

We can see that assignments, comparisons and new object creations are implemented as simple replacements of the corresponding target variables in the existing formula. FRESH_{N_+} ensures that each created object is represented by a distinct number. A field write replaces all the occurrences of the given field array variable f^s by an expression that writes the given value v_v to f^s on the index given by the instance v_r. Because v_v can be either a reference variable or a scalar value (term), we use a helper function SYMB which optionally adds the s superscript if $v_v \in V_R$. Because the operation would not have been executed if v_r was *null*, we also add the condition $v_r^s \neq 0$.

When reading a value from a field, we distinguish between the scalar case $\leftarrow_s$ and the reference case $\leftarrow_r$. In the scalar case, we just replace the read variable by the formula representing array read and assert that v_r is not *null*. In the reference case, we also need to handle the aforementioned problems with input heap. Therefore, for each field f, we create also a helper symbolic array variable f^{in}, which is never rewritten during any operation. By adding $read(f^{in}, v_r^s) \leq 0$ we ensure that any read from the input heap using v_r will always either be *null* or reference an input heap object. These variables are then used in GETCONDITIONDISJHEAP, where we associate all the constraints gathered for them with their corresponding fields. We also identify all the input heap references and constrain them to be ≤ 0 as well.

As we can see from the algorithms in Fig. 2 and Fig. 4, the disjunct propagation approach is straightforward to implement and the condition transformations directly correspond to the operations. However, its efficiency heavily depends on the implementation of formula handling, especially their substitution and simplification. The best results are supposed to be obtained by a custom implementation which reflects all the requirements of the particular project [7]. It is also possible to reuse existing solutions, for example the efficient algorithms for terms in Z3 using its API [8].

Nevertheless, even with the best implementation possible, the conditions in certain programs can grow beyond a reasonable complexity, where every term substitution or simplification consumes too many resources. Therefore, we will now focus on the implementation of heap operations in Fig. 5 for the conjunct combination based algorithm shown in Fig. 3. Although the semantics regarding fields as array variables and references as integer variables remains the same, there are several differences, making the operations more complex. Because each condition is associated with the semantics of a single node and we cannot manipulate conditions for the already processed nodes, we are not allowed to use term substitution. Instead, we utilize a version-based mechanism similar to the implementation of assignment in PROCESSOPERATIONCONJ, where the version of the given variable is incremented and its equality with the particular term is added to the condition.

As a result, each node is also associated with a symbolic heap (η, α). The environment η contains all the current input heap reference variables and maps each of them either to 0 or to an integer symbolic variable. In the beginning of the analysis, η contains only the mapping from $null$ to 0. The field version map α associates each field $f \in F$ with a non-negative integer representing the current version of its array symbolic variable. If $\alpha[f] = i$, the variable is denoted f^i. Initially, all fields have the version 0.

Let us proceed to the semantics of PROCESSOPERATIONCONJHEAP. The reference assignment $v_t \leftarrow_r v_v$ distinguishes three cases. If we have not yet encountered v_t, it is not contained in η and we are not interested in any value assigned to it. Otherwise, if we do not know v_v, we associate it with variable[2] $\eta[v_t]$. If both v_t and v_v are known, we must assert the equality of their symbolic variables. Eventually, in any case, we must remove v_t from η, because by being assigned to it was effectively removed from the set of input heap references. When comparing two references v_1 and v_2, we use helper function INIT, which associates them in η with fresh symbolic integer variables, if they are not already present there. Then, the scalar assignment of boolean term $\eta[v_t] = \eta[v_v]$ to v_t is performed, updating the version of v_t in $vers$ accordingly. A new object creation is again modelled only if we have encountered the target reference variable v_t before. Its symbolic integer variable $\eta[v_t]$ is asserted to be equal with a fresh positive number and v_t is removed from η. A field write $v_r.f \leftarrow v_v$ needs to manipulate α by incrementing the version of f and using its two distinct versions

---

[2] We expect that $null$ cannot be on the left side of the assignment.

heap: (environment $\eta : V_R \rightarrow \{0\} \cup \Sigma_v$, field versions $\alpha : F \rightarrow \mathbb{N}^0\}$

PROCESSOPERATIONCONJHEAP(*vers*, (η, α), *op*)

1: var $\varphi \leftarrow true, vers' \leftarrow vers, \eta' \leftarrow \eta, \alpha' \leftarrow \alpha$
2: **switch** *op* **do**
3:     **case** $v_t \leftarrow_r v_v$
4:       **if** $\eta[v_t] \neq undef$ **then**
5:         **if** $\eta[v_v] = undef$ **then**
6:           $\eta' \leftarrow \eta[v_v \rightarrow \eta[v_t], v_t \rightarrow undef]$
7:         **else**
8:           $\eta' \leftarrow \eta[v_t \rightarrow undef]$
9:           $\varphi \leftarrow \eta[v_t] = \eta[v_v]$
10:     **case** $v_t \leftarrow (v_1 = v_2)$
11:       $\eta' \leftarrow \text{INIT}(\eta, v_1, v_2)$
12:       $vers' \leftarrow vers[v_t \rightarrow vers[v_t] + 1]$
13:       $\varphi \leftarrow v_t^{vers[v_t]} = (\eta'[v_1] = \eta'[v_2])$
14:     **case** $v_t \leftarrow_r \text{new } T$
15:       **if** $\eta[v_t] \neq undef$ **then**
16:         $\eta' \leftarrow \eta[v_t \rightarrow undef]$
17:         $\varphi \leftarrow \eta[v_t] = \text{FRESH}_{\mathbb{N}^+}()$
18:     **case** $v_r.f \leftarrow v_v$
19:       $\eta' \leftarrow \text{INIT}(\eta, v_r, v_v)$
20:       $\alpha' \leftarrow \alpha[f \rightarrow \alpha[f] + 1]$
21:       $\varphi \leftarrow (f^{\alpha[f]} = write(f^{\alpha'[f]}, \eta'[v_r], \text{SYMB}(\eta', v_v))) \wedge (\eta'[v_r] \neq 0)$
22:     **case** $v_t \leftarrow_s v_r.f$
23:       $\eta' \leftarrow \text{INIT}(\eta, v_r)$
24:       $vers' \leftarrow vers[v_t \rightarrow vers[v_t] + 1]$
25:       $\varphi \leftarrow (v_t^{vers[v_t]} = read(f^{\alpha[f]}, \eta'[v_r]) \wedge \eta'[v_r] \neq 0)$
26:     **case** $v_t \leftarrow_r v_r.f$
27:       $\eta' \leftarrow \text{INIT}(\eta, v_r)$
28:       $\varphi \leftarrow (\eta'[v_r] \neq 0)$
29:       **if** $\eta[v_t] \neq undef$ **then**
30:         **if** $v_t = v_r$ **then**
31:           $\eta' \leftarrow \eta'[v_r \rightarrow \text{FRESH}_{\Sigma_v}()]$
32:         **else**
33:           $\eta' \leftarrow \eta'[v_t \rightarrow undef]$
34:         $\varphi \leftarrow \varphi \wedge (\eta[v_t] = read(f^{\alpha[f]}, \eta'[v_r]) \wedge read(f^{in}, \eta'[v_r]) \leq 0)$
35: **return** $(\varphi, vers', (\eta', \alpha'))$

GETCONDITIONCONJHEAP(*states*, *n*)

1: var *inputRefs* $\leftarrow$ gather symbolic variables in η of the heap in *states*[*n*]
2: **return** GETCONDITIONCONJ(*states*, *n*) $\wedge \bigwedge_{f \in F_R} f^{\alpha[f]} = f^{in} \wedge \bigwedge_{v \in inputRefs} v \leq 0$

Fig. 5. Heap operation modelling in the conjunct combination approach from Fig. 3

to express the write. Note that due to the backward approach of our analysis, the version being written to is the current one.

Again, a field read operation is the most complicated one to model. In both scalar and reference cases, we use INIT to ensure that there is a symbolic integer variable corresponding to v_r, constrain it not to be equal to *null* by $\eta'[v_r] \neq 0$ and use *read* to model the read of the field from the heap. In the scalar case $\leftarrow_s$, we must also handle the assignment into v_t by increasing its version in *vers*. In the reference case $\leftarrow_r$, when we are interested in the reference stored in v_t, we also use the helper f^{in} array variable enabling us to constrain the input heap later in GETCONDITIONCONJHEAP. Note that we also explicitly handle the situation when $v_t = v_r$ in order not to accidentally remove v_r from the environment. MERGEHEAPS uses the same version map merging as MERGECONJ utilizing JOINVERS. To merge environments with two or more distinct values corresponding to one reference variable, it is suitable to randomly pick one of them and constrain all the others to point to it. In the algorithm, we must avoid introducing unintentional aliases in the resulting environment.

4.3 Example

To demonstrate the operations on a real-life example, let us examine the assertion in Fig. 6, which corresponds to inspecting the reachability of the node n_{13} in the CFG. Notice that the heap operations from the code were decomposed into the atomic ones, producing helper variables such as tv, tn or rnv.

The solution using the disjunct propagation approach is depicted in Table 1. Each row captures the current state of the condition computed for it, starting

```
1   class Node {
2       public int val;
3       public Node next;
4
5       public Node AddSmaller(int v) {
6           Node n = new Node();
7           n.val = v;
8           Node r;
9           if (v < this.val) {
10              n.next = this;
11              r = n;
12          } else {
13              n.next = this.next;
14              this.next = n;
15              r = this;
16          }
17          Assert(r.val <= r.next.val);
18          return r;
19      }
20  }
```

(a) C# code

(b) CFG

Fig. 6. Sample C# code with heap objects and the corresponding CFG

Table 1. The verification of the assertion in Fig. 6 using disjunct propagation

n_{13}	$true$
n_{12}	$rv > read(val, rn) \wedge rn \neq 0$
n_{11}	$rv > read(val, read(next, r)) \wedge read(next, r) \neq 0$ $\wedge read(next^{in}, r) \leq 0 \wedge r \neq 0$
n_{10}	$read(val, r) > read(val, read(next, r)) \wedge read(next, r) \neq 0$ $\wedge read(next^{in}, r) \leq 0 \wedge r \neq 0$
n_9	$read(val, this) > read(val, read(next, this)) \wedge read(next, this) \neq 0$ $\wedge read(next^{in}, this) \leq 0 \wedge this \neq 0$
n_8, n_7, n_6	$read(val, this) > read(val, n) \wedge n \neq 0$ $\wedge read(next^{in}, this) \leq 0 \wedge this \neq 0$
n_5	$read(val, n) > read(val, read(next, n)) \wedge read(next, n) \neq 0$ $\wedge read(next^{in}, n) \leq 0 \wedge n \neq 0$
n_4	$read(val, n) > read(val, this) \wedge this \neq 0$ $\wedge \, read(next^{in}, n) \leq 0 \wedge n \neq 0$
n_3	$(v \geq read(val, this) \wedge read(val, this) > read(val, n) \wedge n \neq 0$ $\wedge \, read(next^{in}, this) \leq 0 \wedge this \neq 0)$ $\vee \, (v < read(val, this) \wedge read(val, n) > read(val, this) \wedge this \neq 0$ $\wedge \, read(next^{in}, n) \leq 0 \wedge n \neq 0)$
n_2	$(v \geq read(write(val, n, v), this) \wedge read(write(val, n, v), this) > v \wedge n \neq 0$ $\wedge \, read(next^{in}, this) \leq 0 \wedge this \neq 0)$ $\vee \, (v < read(write(val, n, v), this) \wedge v > read(write(val, n, v), this) \wedge this \neq 0$ $\wedge \, read(next^{in}, n) \leq 0 \wedge n \neq 0)$
n_1, n_0	$(v \geq read(write(val, 1, v), this) \wedge read(write(val, 1, v), this) > v$ $\wedge \, read(next^{in}, this) \leq 0 \wedge this \neq 0)$ $\vee \, (v < read(write(val, 1, v), this) \wedge v > read(write(val, 1, v), this) \wedge this \neq 0$ $\wedge \, read(next^{in}, 1) \leq 0)$

from n_{13} and going backwards to n_0. The table is divided into four blocks according to the shape of the CFG. To simplify the notation, we do not use the s superscripts to denote symbolic variables, as all the variables in the condition are symbolic. Instead, they are differentiated by their font, as the program variables from the CFG use a monospaced one.

Since the reachability from n_{13} to n_{13} is trivial, the condition starts with $true$. Next, to reach it from n_{12}, the condition $rv > rnv$ is added and the field read is performed, replacing rnv with $read(val, rn)$ and ensuring that rn is not $null$. The next read into rn is a reference one; therefore, $read(next^{in}, r) \leq 0$ is added. The helper variable rv is replaced by its semantics in n_{10}. Notice that if we called GETCONDITIONDISJHEAP at this point, the condition $next = next^{in} \wedge r \leq 0$ would be temporarily added, ensuring that the input heap consisting of r is separated from the objects potentially created during the analysis.

Table 2. The verification of the assertion in Fig. 6 using conjunct combination

n_{13}	$c_{13} \implies true$	$\eta_{13} = \{(null, 0)\}$
		$\alpha_{13} = \{(\text{next}, 0), (\text{val}, 0)\}$
n_{12}	$c_{12} \implies c_{13} \wedge rv > rnv \wedge rnv = read(val^0, rn) \wedge rn \neq 0$	$\eta_{12} = \eta_{13}[\text{rn} \to rn]$
n_{11}	$c_{11} \implies$	$\eta_{11} = \eta_{12}[\text{rn} \to undef]$
	$\quad c_{12} \wedge rn = read(next^0, r) \wedge r \neq 0 \wedge read(next^{in}, r) \leq 0$	
n_{10}	$c_{10} \implies c_{11} \wedge rv = read(val^0, r) \wedge r \neq 0$	$\eta_{10} = \eta_{11}[\text{r} \to r]$
n_9	$c_9 \implies c_{10}$	$\eta_9 = \eta_{10}[\text{r} \to undef, \text{this} \to r]$
n_8	$c_8 \implies c_9 \wedge next^0 = write(next^1, r, n) \wedge r \neq 0$	$\eta_8 = \eta_9[\text{n} \to n]$
		$\alpha_8 = \alpha_{13}[\text{next} \to 1]$
n_7	$c_7 \implies c_8 \wedge next^1 = write(next^2, n, tn) \wedge n \neq 0$	$\eta_7 = \eta_8[\text{tn} \to tn]$
		$\alpha_7 = \alpha_8[\text{next} \to 2]$
n_6	$c_6 \implies$	$\eta_6 = \eta_7[\text{tn} \to undef]$
	$\quad c_7 \wedge tn = read(next^2, r) \wedge r \neq 0 \wedge read(next^{in}, r) \leq 0$	
n_5	$c_5 \implies c_{10}$	$\eta_5 = \eta_{10}[\text{r} \to undef, \text{n} \to r]$
n_4	$c_4 \implies c_5 \wedge next^0 = write(next^1, r, this) \wedge r \neq 0$	$\eta_4 = \eta_5[\text{this} \to this]$
		$\alpha_4 = \alpha_{13}[\text{next} \to 1]$
n_3	$c_3 \implies$	$\eta_3 =$
	$\quad ((c_4 \wedge v < tv \wedge next^1 = next^2 \wedge r = n)$	$\{(null, 0), (\text{this}, this), (\text{n}, n)\}$
	$\quad \vee (c_6 \wedge v \geq tv \wedge r = this))$	$\alpha_3 = \{(\text{next}, 2), (\text{val}, 0)\}$
	$\quad \wedge tv = read(val^0, this) \wedge this \neq 0$	
n_2	$c_2 \implies c_3 \wedge val^0 = write(val^1, n, v) \wedge n \neq 0$	$\alpha_2 = \alpha_3[\text{val} \to 1]$
n_1	$c_1 \implies c_2 \wedge n = 1$	$\eta_1 = \eta_3[\text{n} \to undef]$
n_0	$c_0 \implies c_1$	

In n_9, the last node of the **else** branch, the assignment $r \leftarrow_r$ **this** causes the replacement of r by *this*. After the field write in n_8, $read(write(next, this, n), this)$ is simplified to n. Notice that now *next* is not a part of the formula and *this* and n are already constrained not to be *null*, so the operations in n_7 and n_6 do not have any effects. The semantics of the positive **if** branch is similar, as it replaces r by n and then reduces both occurrences of $read(next, n)$ to *this*.

Node n_3 merges the disjuncts from nodes n_6 and n_4, adds their respective conditions and performs the replacement of tv by $read(val, this)$. By the assignment **n.val** $\leftarrow_s$ **v** in n_2, we reduce $read(val, n)$ to v. The creation of new object in n_1 replaces n by 1 in both disjuncts, simplifying away the conditions $n \neq 0$. Finally, the condition for n_0 enhanced with input heap handling is passed to the SMT solver, proving the assertion by returning *UNSAT*.

Table 2 shows how the conjunct combination variant works. As its name suggests, the assertions created for all the relevant nodes are combined using conjunction. In order to determine the reachability from n_1, we must combine all the conditions in the table. Notice that for each node n_i, there exist an environment η_i, a field version map α_i and a helper c_i to express that the control flow reached it.

The semantics of the operations is the same as in the former case, but the construction is different. In general, η_i and α_i keep track of the symbolic variables which represent the current versions of references and fields, respectively. As we can see in n_8, n_7, n_4 and n_2, every field read causes the corresponding α_i to create another version of its corresponding array symbolic variable. Whenever we read an unknown reference, we create a symbolic integer variable for it, such as in the case of η_{12}. As soon as that reference is being assigned to, we forget it, e.g. in η_{11}.

Let us have a look on the assignments in n_9 and n_5. The former one causes all the usages of `this` in the `else` branch to be represented by r, whereas the latter one does the same in the positive `if` branch for `n`. Their versions are properly united after being merged in n_3.

We can see that in our simple example, the formula resulting from disjunct propagation is much shorter than the one from conjunct combination. However, in case of larger programs with more branches, the number of disjuncts can grow in an exponential manner if we do not simplify them efficiently.

5   Evaluation

We implemented the techniques into a development version of AskTheCode, an open-source tool for backward symbolic execution of C# code, which uses Z3 as the SMT solver. In order to compare the efficiency of the aforementioned approaches, we prepared a simple program which can be parametrized so that its complexity and validity of the assertions can vary. *Degree counting*(a, b) is an algorithm receiving a linked list as the input. Each of its nodes contains an additional reference to another node and the algorithm calculates for each node its in-degree: the number of nodes referencing it. The assertion fails if it encounters a node whose in-degree is greater than its zero-based index in the list and also greater than a given number a. The second parameter b specifies the number of loop unwindings, i.e., the number of nodes inspected from the start of the list. As a result, the assertion is refutable if and only if $a + 2 \leq b$. Increasing b produces a larger CFG with also potentially more complicated conditions, but the counterexample might be easier to find due to a larger number of paths corresponding to it.

The execution time of analysis of each input variant is shown in Table 3[3]. Notice that there are multiple approaches both to disjunct propagation *Disj* and to conjunct combination *Conj*. Because we considered creating a custom implementation of term simplification and efficient representation too complex, we decided to use the well-optimized terms available in the API of Z3. *Disj*$_{Set}$ uses a set of Z3 terms to represent the disjuncts in each state. Their uniqueness is ensured by the hash consing implemented in Z3. The simplification is

---

[3] We conducted the experiments on a desktop with an Intel Core i7 CPU and 6 GB RAM.

Table 3. Performance evaluation, the times are in milliseconds

Test case	$Disj_{Set}$	$Disj_{Z3}$	$Disj_{Comb}$	$Conj_{Never}$	$Conj_{Always}$	$Conj_{Loops}$
Degree counting (0, 3)	298	775	668	18	55	20
Degree counting (1, 3)	302	773	688	21	60	26
Degree counting (2, 3)	284	752	675	15	59	20
Degree counting (1, 4)	2062	1225	791	31	119	46
Degree counting (2, 4)	2075	1152	822	43	121	53
Degree counting (3, 4)	1949	874	754	25	115	32
Degree counting (2, 5)	13334	1856	1287	91	242	102
Degree counting (3, 5)	13381	1947	1360	85	232	99
Degree counting (4, 5)	13226	1764	1125	40	246	50
Degree counting (3, 6)	81282	4728	4052	200	469	219
Degree counting (4, 6)	80853	4566	4214	161	427	178
Degree counting (5, 6)	80915	3116	2364	62	390	78

performed for each term separately. On the other hand, $Disj_{Z3}$ represents each state using a Z3 term; merging is performed by creating a disjunction of all the terms in the dependent nodes. $Disj_{Comb}$ is a combination of the two approaches. A state is represented as a Z3 term set, but the merging is performed by creating a disjunction term and putting it as a single item of the set. In $Conj_{Never}$, DoSolve always returns *false*, so no intermediate calls of the SMT solver are performed. An opposite extreme is $Conj_{Always}$, where DoSolve always returns *true*. In $Conj_{Loops}$, *true* is returned only for entry nodes of loops. The underlying solver is used incrementally, which enables it to reuse the information gained during the previous checks.

The results show that for our problem, conjunct combination was more efficient than disjunct propagation. The best times were obtained for $Conj_{Never}$, where the SMT solver was called only once at the very end of the analysis. However, in case of more complicated examples where an early check may prevent the analysis from inspecting large regions of code, the incremental usage of the SMT solver might be useful. The results of $Conj_{Always}$ show that it is unnecessary and inefficient to call it on every operation, as it causes an overhead of more than 250% on average. Instead, when we carefully select the nodes where to perform these additional checks like we did in $Conj_{Loops}$, the overhead is less than 25% on average.

We believe that implementing a custom well-optimized simplifier will lead a substantial performance improvement of disjunct propagation, as achieved in the case of Snugglebug [7]. However, writing such a simplifier might be a challenging feat, whereas the utilization of incremental solving can efficiently move the problem to a well-optimized SMT solver.

6 Related Work

The disjunct propagation approach originates from Snugglebug [1], a tool using weakest preconditions to assess the validity of assertions in Java code. Snugglebug uses the algorithm for intraprocedural analysis, utilizing a custom-made simplifier over the propagated disjuncts. For interprocedural analysis, various other methods are used, such as directed call graph construction or tabulation. The SMT solver is utilized only at the entry point, as many infeasible paths are rejected using the simplifier. The conjunct combination approach is used in UFO [1] as the under-approximation subroutine. UFO, however, does not handle heap objects.

Microsoft Pex [18] is a tool generating unit tests for .NET programs using dynamic symbolic execution. It executes the program with concrete inputs and observes its behaviour, using the Z3 SMT solver to generate new inputs steering the execution to uncovered parts of the code. It also uses the array theory to model heap operations, but the way it works with the input heap is different from our pure symbolic approach.

KLEE [6] is a symbolic virtual machine utilizing the LLVM [13] infrastructure, used mainly for C and C++ projects. It uses array theory not only to reason about heap operations, but also about pointers, low-level memory accesses, etc. This differs from our approach, because we target only higher level languages with reference semantics, without the usage of pointers. Furthermore, KLEE does not support running symbolic execution backwards.

Symbolic execution tools JBSE [5] and Java StarFinder (JSF) [14] both employ lazy initialization to reason about heap objects, which lazily enumerates all the possible shapes of the heap. They differ by the languages used for specification of the heap objects' invariants. Whereas JBSE uses custom-made HEX, JSF utilizes separation logic. Although we use a different approach for the core of the heap operations, taking heap invariants into account might help us to prune infeasible paths and save resources.

7 Conclusion

In this paper, we focused on the task of demand-driven program analysis by studying methods of efficiently implement backward symbolic execution. We identified two main approaches used for the core algorithm, namely disjunct propagation and conjunction combination. The former one has the benefit of easier implementation and creating potentially simpler conditions passed to an SMT solver, while the latter one is more predictable in terms of the resulting condition size and can better utilize incremental SMT solvers. To handle heap operations in both approaches, we use the theory of arrays, paying attention to properly handle the notion of an input heap throughout the analysis. The evaluation on our code examples shows that the effort put into the implementation of the conjunct combination approach is reasonable, because its results exceeded the straightforward implementation of disjunct propagation in an order of magnitude.

Due to the narrow focus of this work, the application of our technique is currently limited mainly by the inability to soundly handle loops, interprocedural calls and recursion. Our future work will mainly focus on removing these limitations by exploring the possibilities of computing and reusing procedure summaries, possibly learning from infeasible paths using interpolants. We will build on our knowledge of how disjunct propagation and conjunct combination perform in different circumstances, combining them to reach a valuable synergy.

Acknowledgements. This work was supported by the project PROGRESS Q48, the Czech Science Foundation project 17-12465S and the grant SVV-2017-260451.

References

1. Albarghouthi, A., Gurfinkel, A., Chechik, M.: From under-approximations to over-approximations and back. In: Flanagan, C., König, B. (eds.) TACAS 2012. LNCS, vol. 7214, pp. 157–172. Springer, Heidelberg (2012). https://doi.org/10.1007/978-3-642-28756-5_12
2. Baldoni, R., Coppa, E., D'elia, D.C., Demetrescu, C., Finocchi, I.: A survey of symbolic execution techniques. ACM Comput. Surv. (CSUR) **51**(3), 50 (2018)
3. Bjørner, N.: Engineering theories with Z3. In: Yang, H. (ed.) APLAS 2011. LNCS, vol. 7078, pp. 4–16. Springer, Heidelberg (2011). https://doi.org/10.1007/978-3-642-25318-8_3
4. Bradley, A.R., Manna, Z.: The Calculus of Computation: Decision Procedures with Applications to Verification. Springer, Heidelberg (2007). https://doi.org/10.1007/978-3-540-74113-8
5. Braione, P., Denaro, G., Pezzè, M.: JBSE: a symbolic executor for java programs with complex heap inputs. In: Proceedings of the 2016 24th ACM SIGSOFT International Symposium on Foundations of Software Engineering, pp. 1018–1022. ACM (2016)
6. Cadar, C., Dunbar, D., Engler, D.: Klee: unassisted and automatic generation of high-coverage tests for complex systems programs. In: Proceedings of the 8th USENIX Conference on Operating Systems Design and Implementation, OSDI 2008, pp. 209–224. USENIX Association, Berkeley (2008). http://dl.acm.org/citation.cfm?id=1855741.1855756
7. Chandra, S., Fink, S.J., Sridharan, M.: Snugglebug: a powerful approach to weakest preconditions. SIGPLAN Not. **44**(6), 363–374 (2009). http://doi.acm.org/10.1145/1543135.1542517
8. De Moura, L., Bjørner, N.: Z3: an efficient SMT solver. In: Ramakrishnan, C.R., Rehof, J. (eds.) TACAS 2008/ETAPS 2008. LNCS, vol. 4963, pp. 337–340. Springer, Heidelberg (2008). https://doi.org/10.1007/978-3-540-78800-3_24. http://dl.acm.org/citation.cfm?id=1792734.1792766
9. Dinges, P., Agha, G.: Targeted test input generation using symbolic-concrete backward execution. In: 29th IEEE/ACM International Conference on Automated Software Engineering (ASE), Västerås, Sweden. ACM, 15–19 September 2014
10. Goel, A., Krstić, S., Fuchs, A.: Deciding array formulas with frugal axiom instantiation. In: Proceedings of the Joint Workshops of the 6th International Workshop on Satisfiability Modulo Theories and 1st International Workshop on Bit-Precise Reasoning, SMT 2008/BPR 2008, pp. 12–17. ACM, New York (2008). http://doi.acm.org/10.1145/1512464.1512468

11. Hovemeyer, D., Pugh, W.: Finding bugs is easy. SIGPLAN Not. **39**, 92–106 (2004). https://doi.org/10.1145/1028664.1028717
12. Husák, R., Kofroň, J., Zavoral, F.: AskTheCode: interactive call graph exploration for error fixing and prevention. Electron. Commun. EASST **77** (2019). https://doi.org/10.14279/tuj.eceasst.77.1109. InterAVT 2019
13. Lattner, C., Adve, V.: LLVM: a compilation framework for lifelong program analysis & transformation. In: Proceedings of the International Symposium on Code Generation and Optimization: Feedback-directed and Runtime Optimization, CGO 2004, pp. 75–86. IEEE Computer Society, Washington, DC (2004). http://dl.acm.org/citation.cfm?id=977395.977673
14. Pham, L.H., Le, Q.L., Phan, Q.S., Sun, J., Qin, S.: Testing heap-based programs with java starfinder. In: Proceedings of the 40th International Conference on Software Engineering: Companion Proceedings, pp. 268–269. ACM (2018)
15. Sagiv, M., Reps, T., Wilhelm, R.: Parametric shape analysis via 3-valued logic. ACM Trans. Program. Lang. Syst. **24**(3), 217–298 (2002). https://doi.org/10.1145/514188.514190. http://doi.acm.org/10.1145/514188.514190
16. Sinha, N., Singhania, N., Chandra, S., Sridharan, M.: Alternate and learn: finding witnesses without looking all over. In: Madhusudan, P., Seshia, S.A. (eds.) CAV 2012. LNCS, vol. 7358, pp. 599–615. Springer, Heidelberg (2012). https://doi.org/10.1007/978-3-642-31424-7_42
17. Sridharan, M., Chandra, S., Dolby, J., Fink, S.J., Yahav, E.: Alias analysis for object-oriented programs. In: Clarke, D., Noble, J., Wrigstad, T. (eds.) Aliasing in Object-Oriented Programming. Types, Analysis and Verification. LNCS, vol. 7850, pp. 196–232. Springer, Heidelberg (2013). https://doi.org/10.1007/978-3-642-36946-9_8
18. Tillmann, N., De Halleux, J.: Pex–white box test generation for.NET. In: Beckert, B., Hähnle, R. (eds.) TAP 2008. LNCS, vol. 4966, pp. 134–153. Springer, Heidelberg (2008). https://doi.org/10.1007/978-3-540-79124-9_10

AuthCheck: Program-State Analysis for Access-Control Vulnerabilities

Goran Piskachev[1]([✉]), Tobias Petrasch[2], Johannes Späth[1], and Eric Bodden[1,3]

[1] Fraunhofer IEM, Paderborn, Germany
{goran.piskachev,johannes.spaeth}@iem.fraunhofer.de
[2] BCG Platinion, Berlin, Germany
petrasch.tobias@bcgplatinion.com
[3] Paderborn University, Paderborn, Germany
eric.bodden@upb.de

Abstract. According to security rankings such as the SANS Top 25 and the OWASP Top 10, access-control vulnerabilities are still highly relevant. Even though developers use web frameworks such as Spring and Struts, which handle the entire access-control mechanism, their implementation can still be vulnerable because of misuses, errors, or inconsistent implementation from the design specification. We propose AuthCheck, a static analysis that tracks the program's state using a finite state machine to report illegal states caused by vulnerable implementation. We implemented AuthCheck for the Spring framework and identified four types of mistakes that developers can make when using Spring Security. With AuthCheck, we analyzed an existing open-source Spring application with inserted vulnerable code and detected the vulnerabilities.

Keywords: Static analysis · Access-control · Authentication · Authorization · Web systems · Security

1 Introduction

With increasing popularity and amount of processed data, web applications are attractive targets for attackers. The access-control vulnerabilities are still ones of the most relevant as rankings show. For instance, five of the SANS Top 25[1] most dangerous vulnerabilities are related to access-control. On the OWASP Top 10[2] ranking, on place two is *broken authentication* vulnerability and on place five is *broken authorization* vulnerability.

Nowadays, web frameworks are heavily used by software developers [19]. Modern frameworks, such as Spring[3] and Struts.[4] provide mechanism for access-control making developers' implementation effort smaller. At runtime, the actual

---

[1] https://cwe.mitre.org/top25/.
[2] https://www.owasp.org/index.php/Top_10-2017_Top_10.
[3] https://spring.io/.
[4] https://struts.apache.org/.

© Springer Nature Switzerland AG 2020
E. Sekerinski et al. (Eds.): FM 2019 Workshops, LNCS 12233, pp. 557–572, 2020.
https://doi.org/10.1007/978-3-030-54997-8_34

access-control checks of such mechanism are performed within frameworks' code via dynamic verification, hereby software developers do not need to write customized access-control code and implementation bugs are avoided.

Instead of writing access-control code manually, frameworks allow software developer to specify the access rules via framework specific APIs. Spring, for instance, provides a fluent interface with specification language SpEL [3] combined with Java annotations to allow the specification of access rules.

However, implementing the access-control rules using the frameworks' APIs according to a design specifications, created by the software architect, remains a challenging task. In practice, it is often the case that these specifications are informally defined. In the implementation, the access-control is often a combination of annotations of methods, a configuration class, and a set of permission groups for the resources of the system (i.e., URI). The resulting access-control of the implementation easily diverges from the design specification and the application may accidentally grant an unauthorized user access to confidential data.

In this paper, we propose a typestate-inspired analysis for detecting three access-control vulnerabilities:

- *CWE-306* missing authentication [8] - The system does not perform an identity check on a request to a resource which by design should be accessed only be identified requests.
- *CWE-862* missing authorization [9] - The system does not perform a check whether an authenticated request has the correct rights to access a resource.
- *CWE-863* incorrect authorization [7] - The system performs an authorization check on the resources, but this check is wrong.

Our static analysis uses *finite state machines* (FSMs) of each vulnerability to track the authorization state of the program. The state changes are triggered by method calls that authorize the user or access a critical resource along the control flow paths.

The main contributions of this paper are:

- AUTHCHECK: a program-state analysis for access-control vulnerabilities,
- an implementation of AUTHCHECK for the Spring Security framework,
- a running example and four typical errors in Spring Security, and
- a case study on a real-world open source application demonstrating the applicability of the implementation.

The following section introduces our running example within the Java Spring framework. In Sect. 3, we provide background information and definitions for the AUTHCHECK approach, which is then introduced in Sect. 4. Implementation details are discussed in Sect. 5. A case study and limitations are discussed in Sect. 6.

2   Running Example

As a running example we consider a minimal web-application that helps a user to organize her tasks. An anonymous user browsing the web application must only see the web applications version number. A user that is authenticated can view tasks assigned to herself. An administrator (group *ADMIN*) can create new tasks for a particular user.

Table 1 details the design specification of the web-application's REST-API [10]. The specification maps the URI of an incoming request to the actual API method which shall be invoked to process the incoming request. Table 1 additionally details the permissions required for each request. A software architect specifies these requirements and hands them to a software developer.

Table 1. Specification resources and access rules in the running example

HTTP	URI	Resource	Description	Access rule
GET	/version	version()	Returns application's version	No rule
GET	/profile	profile()	Returns user profile	Authenticated
GET	/task	retrieveAll()	Returns list of all tasks	*USER* or *ADMIN*
POST	/task	create()	Creates new task	*ADMIN*

Spring-Based Implementation. The software developer uses the Spring framework [1] to implement the software as specified. Spring provides a security component [2] that ships with a mechanism for access-control of resources. Spring handles requests from users via chain of filters (chain of responsibility design pattern [11]). The requests are matched and processed based on their URIs.

```
1  public class WebSecurityConfig extends
       WebSecurityConfigurerAdapter {
2  @Override
3  protected void configure(HttpSecurity http) throws
       Exception {
4  http.csrf().disable().sessionManagement()
5  .sessionCreationPolicy(SessionCreationPolicy.STATELESS)
6  .and().authorizeRequests()
7  .antMatchers(HttpMethod.GET, "/version").permitAll()
8  .antMatchers(HttpMethod.GET,
       "/task").access("hasAnyRole('USER', 'ADMIN')")
9  .antMatchers(HttpMethod.CREATE, "/task").hasRole("USER")
10 .antMatchers(HttpMethod.GET,
       "/profile").authenticated().and().httpBasic();
11 }}
```

Listing 1.1. Resource and access-control configuration of the running example implemented with Spring Security

Listing 1.1 shows the implementation of Table 1 using Spring Security. By the use of a fluent interface the developer can implement the chain of filters that is applied upon each incoming request at runtime. Each filter is created through the method `antMatcher(..)` defined by the HTTP method and the URI of the resources which that filter can process. The `permitAll()` method allows any request to access the resource. The `authenticated(..)` method creates a filter that restricts the incoming request to the one where the user is authenticated. The `hasRole(..)` method allows access to the resource by any request that has the role of the specified group. The `access(...)` method evaluates the specified argument which has to be defined in the *Spring Expression Language (SpEL)* [3], and when evaluated to true, allows the corresponding request to access the resource.

The implementation in Listing 1.1 has inconsistency with the specification in Table 1. The software developer erroneously allowed basic users (*USER*) to create new tasks as opposed to restricting the action to *ADMIN*s only. AUTHCHECK detects the deviation from the specification automatically.

3   Background and Definitions

3.1   Typestate Analysis and Program-State Analysis

Typestate analysis [20] is a data-flow analysis that can detect invalid states of objects from the code being analyzed. The analysis uses specification of all possible states of the object, typically expressed as *final state machine (FSM)*. For example, using the *FSM* of the type *java.io.FileWriter*, in a given program, the analysis can report if any object of type *java.io.FileWriter* is not closed at the end of the program. Another example is CogniCrypt [13], a typestate analysis for detecting API misuses of cryptographic libraries.

To detect access-control vulnerabilities, such as *CWE-306* [8], *CWE-862* [9], and *CWE-863* [7], we designed a program-state [5,12] analysis. Similar to the typestate analysis, the program-state analysis uses *FSM* to track the states, not of single objects, but the state of the program. Figure 1 shows the *FSM* that models the program states when detecting *CWE-306*. Based on our running example (Sect. 2), the *acm()* (authentication-critical method) is replaced by one of the resources, e.g. *profile()*. The legal states are *NA* (not authenticated) and *A* (authenticated). The *init()* transition models the entry point of the analysis, which in this case is the arrival of a request from a user. If the request is for the resource *profile()*, the application has to make sure that the call to the method *authenticate()* from Spring was successfully called before. This is modeled by the transition with label *authenticate()*. If this transition was fired, the state of the *FSM* will be changed from *NA* to *A*. In case, the implementation of the application does not contain a call to the method *authenticate()*, when the resource *profile()* is requested, the *FSM* will go to the state *CWE-306*, which models an illegal state and this can be reported.

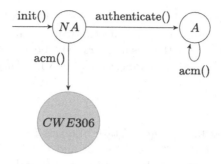

Fig. 1. *FSM* for missing authentication *CWE-306*

3.2 Definitions

Before we introduce the AuthCheck approach (Sect. 4), we define the term *web application*. In the following, we introduce the required terms. A user is a client program, e.g. web browser, that can send requests to the server. An authorization group is a boolean characteristic of a user with a unique name and access rights. A user can belong to more authorization groups. The set of all authorization groups G in a given system is finite.

The function *userGroups*: $U \rightarrow Pow(G)$ maps each user $u \in U$ to the authorization groups. $Pow(G)$ is the power set of G. We define the help function *hasRole*: $U \times G \rightarrow \mathbb{B}$, that expresses whether a user u belongs to an authorization group g: $hasRole(u, g) := g \in userGroups(u)$

Each user that is authenticated in the system belongs to the special authorization group ANONYMOUS.

Authorization formula is a boolean formula a, formed by the function *hasRole*, *true*, *false*, and the operators $\vee, \wedge, \neg$.

Definition 1. *Resource*
An authentication and authorization critical resource is a 4-tuple $r = (m, p, s, a)$, where m is an HTTP method, p is a URI, s is a method signature, and a is an authorization formula that defines the access rule of the resource. Access to the resource is given when a is evaluated to true for a request of a user u. Users identify each resource with the URI p and the HTTP method m. The corresponding method in the system is identified by the signature s.

Definition 2. *Web application*
A web application W, is a pair $W = (R, G)$, where R is a set of resources and G is a set of authorization groups.

Example. The web application from Sect. 2 has the authorization groups *ADMIN*, for administrators and *USER*, for basic users. By default, it also has the *ANONYMOUS* group. Thus, $G = \{ANONYMOUS, ADMIN, USER\}$. The set of resources has 4 elements (Table 1). The first resource is defined as $r_1 = (GET, /version, Stringversion\ (), a_1)$, where $a_1(u) = true$.

We consider a user u with $userGroups(u) = \{ANONYMOUS, USER\}$. If this user requests the resource r_1, the access will be allowed because $a_1(u) = true$. However, a request to the resource r_4 will be denied because $a_4(u) = hasRole(u, ANONYMOUS) \wedge hasRole(u, ADMIN) = false$.

4   Approach

We present AUTHCHECK, a program-state analysis for detecting three access-control vulnerabilities, *CWE-306*, *CWE-862*, and *CWE-863*. The analysis uses a call graph of the program (detailed in Subsect. 5.2) and an *access-control specification model (ACSM)*, like the one in Table 1. *ACSM* is defined as a web application $S = W_S$, where $W_S = (R_S, G_S)$ (Definition 2). *ACSM* can be created manually by software architects or automated from requirements and design specifications. Either way, we assume that the following information is available: resource API, URI, and access rule, that is aware of the authorization groups in the system.

AUTHCHECK checks whether the call graph confirms the *ACSM* by checking each path from the call graph (Algorithm 1). To extract all paths, the depth first search *DFS* algorithm is used. AUTHCHECK uses a predefined *FSM* for each vulnerability, e.g. Fig. 1. Algorithm 2 shows the tracking of each path with the *FSM*. The *FSM* starts in the initial state (e.g. *NA* in Fig. 1) and for each node of the path a new state of the *FSM* is calculated (line 4 in Algorithm 2). If an error state is reached (e.g. *CWE-306* in Fig. 1), a new vulnerability will be reported.

For each path, the function *DetectVuln* is called which is defined by Algorithm 2. *DetectVuln* uses the *FSM* to analyse the path.

Algorithm 1. Check the call graph against vulnerabilities

1: **function** CHECKCALLGRAPH($CallGraph, FSM$)
2:     $Paths \leftarrow DFS(CallGraph)$
3:     $Vul \leftarrow \emptyset$
4:     **for each** $p \in Paths$ **do**
5:         $Vul \leftarrow Vul \cup \text{DETECTVULN}(p, FSM)$
6:     **return** Vul

The complexity of Algorithm 1 is $\mathcal{O}(|V| + |E| + |P| \cdot T(\text{DETECTVULN}))$, where V is the number of nodes, E is the number of edges, and P is the number of paths in the call graph. In *DetectVuln*, every node of the path is analyzed, resulting in $\mathcal{O}(|P|)$. The worst case path is the one with all nodes from the call graph $|V|$. Additionally, the number of paths in the worst case is $|E|$. Thus, the total complexity of Algorithm 1 is

$$\mathcal{O}(|V| + |E| + |P| \cdot |V|) = \mathcal{O}(|V| + |E| + |V| \cdot |E|) = \mathcal{O}(|V| \cdot |E|)$$

In the following, we discuss the three the *FSM* used by AUTHCHECK.

Algorithm 2. Checking each path against vulnerabilities

1: **function** DᴇᴛᴇᴄᴛVᴜʟɴ($Path, FSM$)
2:     $v \leftarrow FSM{\rightarrow}init()$
3:     **for each** $n \in Path$ **do**
4:         $v \leftarrow FSM{\rightarrow}nextState(n)$
5:         **if** $v \in FSM.ERROR\_STATES$ **then**
6:             **return** new $Vulnerability(v)$
7:     **return** $\emptyset$

Missing Authentication. A program is vulnerable to *CWE-306* when an authentication-critical method (*acm()*) can be accessed by user that has not been authenticated before. AᴜᴛʜCʜᴇᴄᴋ models this vulnerability as shown in Fig. 1. Authentication critical methods are all resources that in the *ACSM* have an access rule that requires authentication. The error state in Fig. 1 is reached when an authentication-critical method is processed next in a given path and the current state of the *FSM* is *NA* (not authorized). In this case, the program-state analysis will create a vulnerability (Algorithm 2, line 8).

Missing Authorization and Incorrect Authorization. *CWE-862* occurs in a given program when a non-authorized user u can request an authorization-critical method (*azcm()*). If the user is authorized but the belonging group g does not confirm the access rule for that authorization-critical method as specified in the *ACSM* ($hasRole(u, g) = false$), then incorrect authorization occurs (*CWE-863*). Figure 2 shows the *FSM* that AᴜᴛʜCʜᴇᴄᴋ uses to model *CWE-862* and *CWE-863*. The transitions with the label *azcm()* without an argument denote calls to an authorization-critical method when the user is not authorized. When there is an argument g, the user has been authorized and the belonging group is being checked. This happens in state *A2*. When the user's group evaluates to true the self transition of state *A2* is fired, otherwise the transition to state *CWE-863* is fired. AᴜᴛʜCʜᴇᴄᴋ performs a group hierarchy check.

Strategies for Detecting Critical Methods. The transitions *acm()* in Fig. 1 and *azcm()* in Fig. 2 denote an authentication-critical and authorization-critical method. These methods correspond to the resources defined in the *ACSM*. In the following, we discuss AᴜᴛʜCʜᴇᴄᴋ's strategies for detecting these methods in the call graph.

In the case of *CWE-306*, the authentication-critical methods are detected by iterating the set of all resources R from the *ACSM* for each method M that is currently processed in the path.

Algorithm 3 shows the AᴜᴛʜCʜᴇᴄᴋ strategy to identify the authorization-critical methods in the call graph for *CWE-862*. When checking the *CWE-862*, each method M currently processed in the path is classified as authorization-critical if the method is contained in the *ACSM* as a resource and its access rule is not a tautology (i.e. the rule can be evaluated to false for at least one input combination). The evaluation of the authorization formula depends on the

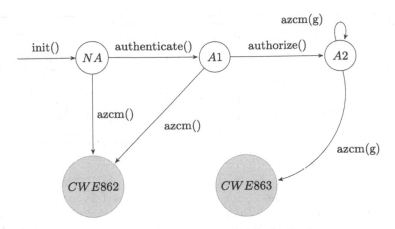

Fig. 2. *FSM* for missing authorization *CWE-862* and incorrect authorization *CWE-863*

Algorithm 3. Identifying methods as authorization-critical

1: **function** ISMETHODAUTHORIZATIONCRITICAL(R, s')
2:     **for each** $r \in R$ **do**
3:         **if** $r_s = s'$ *and* r_a *is not tautology* **then**
4:             **return** *true*
5:     **return** *false*

---

number of relevant authorization groups used in the authorization formula. For the calculation, all possible combinations $\forall\, g \in Pow(G')$ of relevant authorization groups G' must be evaluated.

Algorithm 4 shows the AUTHCHECK strategy to identify the authorization-critical methods in the call graph. For each resource in the *ACSM*, it checks whether its signature matches the signature of the method M currently processed in the call graph. In addition, the authorization formulas are checked. The runtime depends on the number of relevant authorization groups. For the calculation, all possible combinations $\forall\, g \in Pow(G')$ of relevant authorization groups G' must be evaluated for tautology check.

5   Spring Security AUTHCHECK

We implemented the AUTHCHECK concept from Sect. 4, as a Java application that checks the implementation of a given Java Spring Security application and a given *ACSM*. We used the Soot framework [14] for the analysis. In the following, we discuss the architecture of our implementation, the insights of the call graph construction, and the four typical developer's mistakes with Spring Security that AUTHCHECK can detect. Our implementation is available on Github [18].

Algorithm 4. Identifying methods as authorization-critical and group-belonging

---
1: **function** ISMETHODAUTHORIZATIONCRITICAL(R, s', a')
2:     **for each** $r \in R$ **do**
3:         **if** $r_s = s'$ and $eval(r_a) = eval(a')$ **then**
4:             **return** *true*
5:     **return** *false*

5.1 Architecture

The AUTHCHECK tool follows a pipeline architecture, since it consists of several sequential phases that work on shared artifacts. Our AUTHCHECK implementation consists of 3 phases:

1. *Call graph construction*: parses the code, the Spring Security configuration, and annotations, and constructs the call graph,
2. *Call graph update*: patches missing edges into the call graph based on Spring Security configuration,
3. *CWE analysis*: analyzes the call graph against *CWE-306*, *CWE-862*, and *CWE-863* based on Sect. 4.

Figure 3 shows the meta-model of the components of the tool's architecture. The root class is the *Analysis* that contains all components. The *Phase* can process objects of type *Artifact*. This separation of the processes into *Phases* and data into *Artifacts*, makes the architecture extensible. One can easily add or remove *Phases* and *Artifacts*. *Phases* can be even executed in parallel if they are not dependent. In our implementation, the call graph instance, *FSMs*, and *ACSM* are defined as artifacts. The final results of the analysis are stored in a *Result* object which can be presented via *Presenter* object. Our tool has one presenter, that generates HTML pages (see Sect. 6 and Figure 5). In this architecture new phases can be added easily. Furthermore, new types of vulnerabilities can be created as *FSM* and added as artifacts in the analysis.

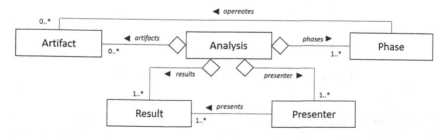

Fig. 3. UML class diagram of AUTHCHECK implementation for Spring Security

5.2   Call Graph Construction

Phase 1 constructs the call graph using the class hierarchy algorithm and extracts the Spring Security configuration needed in phase 2 to complete the missing edges in the call graph due to reflection. The extracted information is prepared according to Definition 2. Each critical method is annotated with its URI and HTTP method. This is transferred together with the signature of the method into a resource according to the Definition 1.

The Spring Security configuration is extracted from the program using an intraprocedural analysis. A special case is the method *access(a)*, which can take as an input a *SpEL* formula. For this, we use the Spring mechanism to evaluate the string values containing the *SpEL* formula.

An authorization formula is assigned to a resource when the defined filter matches the method and the URI. If multiple authorization formulas are applied to a resource, they are associated with a logical AND ($\wedge$).

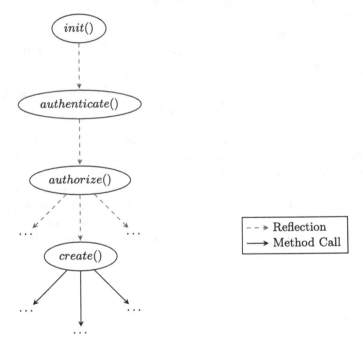

Fig. 4. Incomplete call graph due to reflection

The extracted information is stored as web application (Definition 2). Then, in phase 2, the missing edges are added to the call graph according to Algorithm 5. The algorithm gets the extracted web application W_J and generated call graph *CallGraph*. For each resource, it is checked whether the Spring Framework performs an authorization check, authentication check, or no access check.

Accordingly, an edge is created to the critical method from the *authorize()*, *authenticate()*, or *init()* methods as shown in Fig. 4. We use this three method calls which are sufficient to model the call stack in Spring. We identified them using dynamic traces we produced from our running example.

Algorithm 5. Adding missing edges in the call graph

1: **function** CREATEMISSINGEDGES($W_J = (R_J, G_J), CallGraph$)
2:     **for each** $r \in R_J$ **do**
3:         **if** ISMETHODAUTHORIZATIONCRITICAL(R_J, r_{sig}) **then**
4:             $CallGraph \rightarrow addEdgeFromAuthorize(r_{sig})$
5:         **else if** *isMethodAuthenticationCritical*(R_J, r_{sig}) **then**
6:             $CallGraph \rightarrow addEdgeFromAuthenticate(r_{sig})$
7:         **else**
8:             $CallGraph \rightarrow addEdgeFromInit(r_{sig})$

5.3 Developers' Mistakes

As demonstrated in Listing 1.1, the access-control rules in Spring Security are specified with the SpEL fluent interface. With this approach, we foresee two factors that can lead to inconsistencies of the implementation and the intended design. First, the developer should be familiar with the domain specific language SpEL in order to specify the *antMatchers* correctly, i.e. in the correct order. Second, the string values of some arguments are not parsed and automatically checked. Based on that and the information we found in the MITRE database[5] for access-control CWEs, we identified 4 mistakes that developers can make when using Java Spring Security.

Missing or Wrong Authentication Rule: The developer forgets to include the authentication filter *authenticated()* for the URI of a particular resource in the configuration or uses the filter *permitAll()* to incorrectly allow access to all users. However, in the specification model, the resource requires valid authentication. If no filter is specified, this is equivalent to the filter *permitAll()*. As a result, any user without authentication is able to request this resource. The error causes the security vulnerability missing authentication *CWE-306*.

Missing Authorization Rule: The developer forgets to include one of the authorization filters *hasRole(role)* or *access(rule)* for the URI of a particular resource. However, according to the *ACSM*, the resource requires a valid authorization. The filter *authenticated()* leads to the same error because it only checks the authentication of the user. Depending on the filter used, either all users or only authenticated users are able to request this resource. The error causes the security vulnerability of missing authorization *CWE-862*.

---

[5] https://cwe.mitre.org.

Incorrect Authorization Rule: The developer incorporates an authorization filter *hasRole(role)* or *access(rule)* for the URI of a certain resource, but a wrong authorization formula is used. As a result, a user without the required access rights is able to request this resource. The error causes the security problem of incorrect authorization *CWE-863*.

Method Call with Higher Access Rights: The developer creates a correct configuration for the resource, but in a deeper layer of the application, a call to a method is created that requires higher access rights and therefore should not be called by the user. The error causes the security problem of incorrect authorization *CWE-863*.

We implemented an extended version of the running example from Sect. 2 that includes the four mistakes and serves as a test scenario for our implementation. It is available under [18]. The tool generates a HTML page with all vulnerabilities detected. Figure 5 shows a detected *CWE-306* in our running example, including the path and description for solving the issue.

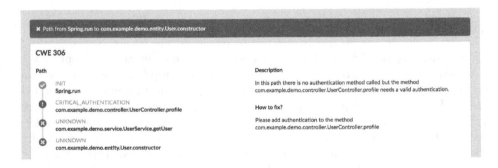

Fig. 5. Screenshot from AUTHCHECK generated output with *CWE-306*

6 Case Study

We used the open-source project *FredBet*[6] to perform a case study in which we apply our analysis on a real-world application.

6.1 FredBet

The web application *FredBet* is a football betting system developed with Java Spring Boot and Spring Security. FredBet offers the possibility to initiate an online football bet with several users. In addition to the betting, the web application offers statistics about the matches, rankings, a profile management, and

---

[6] https://github.com/fred4jupiter/fredbet.

many other features. The application is actively developed since 2015 and as of October 2019, its repository has more than 1300 commits.

FredBet contains 37 resources. The access-control mechanism is implemented via 22 Spring Security controllers organized in hierarchical structure where the root controller is *MatchController*. There are 28 permission types used to define 4 authorization groups.

Since we have access only to the implementation and no design specification is available from which we can infer an *ACSM*, we decided to create the *ACSM* based on the implementation. Then, we ran AUTHCHECK for all controllers successfully. As expected no errors were reported. The analysis took 71.9 s, running on a machine with 8 GB RAM and i5-6200U CPU (2,3 GHz).

To evaluate whether real-world applications with known vulnerabilities will be correctly analyzed by AUTHCHECK, we made some modifications in *Fred-Bet* to introduce vulnerabilities. As implemented in *FredBet*, any request that is authenticated by the *MatchController* is authenticated for all other controllers. This is defined by the code line 61 in the file WebSecurityConfig.cs, *http.authorizeRequests().anyRequest().authenticated();*. By commenting out this line of code we are introducing *CWE-306* vulnerability. To introduce *CWE-862*, it was easier to make a change in the *ACSMs*. In particular, we chose the *UserProfileController* which contains four resources: *changeUsername*, *changeUsernamePost*, *changePassword*, and *changePasswordPost*. As implemented, these four resources can be accessed by any authorized user. We made a change by changing the authorization expressions for *changeUsername* and *changePassword* to *hasAuthority('PERM$_A$DMINISTRATION')*. This allows only users from the *PERM_ ADMINISTRATION* group to be able to change usernames and passwords. In total, we introduced five errors. Further details on them and how to run the analysis we documented on github[7] where we hosted our analysis code [18].

6.2 Limitations

When applying AUTHCHECK to FredBet, we realized that the specification scope in Spring Security is much broader than the available official documentation [2]. There are multiple ways to specify the same configuration information. For example, a developer can specify an URI for a given class containing critical methods. This URI is then concatenated to the URIs of the critical methods it contains. Also, the annotations can have different formats or even some can be skipped, like the HTTP method, which in such case, a default value *GET* will be considered by the framework. Then, the configuration of the *antMatchers* (see Listing 1.1) can have different parameters.

In the implementation of AUTHCHECK, the parser has a full support for the language constructs that are part of the official documentation as well as all corner cases that we found in the FredBet application. This does not guarantee

---

[7] https://github.com/secure-software-engineering/authcheck/blob/master/Evalu-ation_ With_ FredBet/Evaluation.md.

a full coverage of the specification scope of Spring Security and one may need to do further extensions to the parser for other corner cases that we are not aware of. However, these extensions are only technical and does not change the concepts presented in this paper.

Since Spring is written in Java, developers can specify dynamically constructed calls even for the fluent chain of method calls. This is statically hard to analyze and our approach does not address it. For that reason false alarms can occur.

7 Related Work

Security vulnerabilities caused by the misuses of access-control mechanisms have been investigated by Dalton et al. [6]. The approach examines access-control problems by analyzing the flow of user credentials within the web application. In contrast to AUTHCHECK, their approach is dynamic and can not be used for early detection of the vulnerabilities.

Sun et al. [21] introduced a static analysis approach for the detection of access-control vulnerabilities. They assume that the source code contains implicit documentation of intended accesses. From this, sitemaps for different authorization groups are generated and checked whether forced browsing can happen. Another static analysis specific for access-control of XML documents was introduced by Murata et al. [16]. They use XPath representation for the access-control rules and XQuery for specifying the requests. The analysis checks all paths defined by the query against the XPath rules. Naumovich et al. [17] proposed a static analysis for Java EE applications where the resources are security fields from the Java Beans objects.

In the area of model checking, few approaches address the access-control protocols [15,22]. In these approaches, the focus is to validate the message communication of the defined protocols. Similarly, Alexander et al. applied model checking to verify the authentication mechanism in the communication of a set of interacting virtual machines [4].

8 Conclusion and Future Work

Even though sophisticated Java web frameworks, such as Spring, provide secure mechanism for access-control of resources, for many developers using the APIs and the configuration specifications correctly, can be challenging. Thus, these misuses may cause access-control vulnerabilities in the code. In this paper, we presented AUTHCHECK, a static analysis, that tracks the program-state to detect the vulnerabilities *CWE-306*, *CWE-862*, and *CWE-863*. Based on *finite state machine* specification of each vulnerability, AUTHCHECK checks each path. We implemented the approach on top of the Soot framework and applied it to one open-source project on which we detected four types of errors that were previously inserted in the existing application.

We plan to evaluate the precision of AuthCheck in cooperation with industry to overcome the problem of the open-source projects of not having a design specification on which we can check the implementation against. Additionally, in future the choice of the call graph algorithm should be evaluated.

Acknowledgement. We thank Abdul Rehman Tareen for extending the initial version of the tool to support all Spring annotations needed for complete analysis of the FredBet application. We also thank the reviewers for the constructive feedback and proposals for improving this paper. This research was partially supported by the Software Campus Program of the German Ministry of Education and Research and the research project "AppSecure.nrw - Security-by-Design of Java-based Applications" funded by the European Regional Development Fund (ERDF-0801379).

References

1. Spring framework, java spring. https://spring.io/projects. Accessed 9 Mar 2019
2. Spring framework, java spring security. https://spring.io/guides/topicals/spring-security-architecture. Accessed 9 Mar 2019
3. Spring framework, spring expression language. https://docs.spring.io/spring/docs/5.0.5.RELEASE/spring-framework-reference/core.html. Accessed 12 Mar 2019
4. Alexander, P., Pike, L., Loscocco, P., Coker, G.: Model checking distributed mandatory access control policies. ACM Trans. Inf. Syst. Secur. **18**(2), 6:1–6:25 (2015)
5. Ball, T., Rajamani, S.K.: The slam project: debugging system software via static analysis. In: Proceedings of the 29th ACM SIGPLAN POPL, POPL 2002, pp. 1–3. ACM, New York (2002)
6. Dalton, M., Kozyrakis, C., Zeldovich, N.: Nemesis: preventing authentication and access control vulnerabilities in web applications. In: Proceedings of USENIX, SSYM 2009, pp. 267–282. USENIX Association, Berkeley (2009)
7. Enumeration, C.C.W.: Incorrect authorization. https://cwe.mitre.org/data/definitions/863.html. Accessed 12 Mar 2019
8. Enumeration, C.C.W.: Missing authentication for critical function. https://cwe.mitre.org/data/definitions/306.html. Accessed 12 Mar 2019
9. Enumeration, C.C.W.: Missing authorization. https://cwe.mitre.org/data/definitions/862.html. Accessed 12 Mar 2019
10. Fielding, R.T.: Architectural styles and the design of network-based software architectures. Ph.D. thesis, University of California, Irvine (2000)
11. Gamma, E., Vlissides, J., Johnson, R., Helm, R.: Design Patterns CD: Elements of Reusable Object-Oriented Software. Addison-Wesley Longman Publishing Co. Inc., Boston (1998)
12. Henzinger, T.A., Jhala, R., Majumdar, R., Sutre, G.: Software verification with BLAST. In: Ball, T., Rajamani, S.K. (eds.) SPIN 2003. LNCS, vol. 2648, pp. 235–239. Springer, Heidelberg (2003). https://doi.org/10.1007/3-540-44829-2_17
13. Krüger, S., Späth, J., Ali, K., Bodden, E., Mezini, M.: CrySL: an extensible approach to validating the correct usage of cryptographic APIs. In: ECOOP, pp. 10:1–10:27 (2018)
14. Lam, P., Bodden, E., Lhotak, O., Hendren, L.: The soot framework for java program analysis: a retrospective. In: Cetus Users and Compiler Infrastructure Workshop (CETUS 2011), October 2011

15. Marrero, W., Clarke, E., Jha, S.: A model checker for authentication protocols. In: Rutgers University (1997)
16. Murata, M., Tozawa, A., Kudo, M., Hada, S.: XML access control using static analysis. ACM Trans. Inf. Syst. Secur. **9**(3), 292–324 (2006)
17. Naumovich, G., Centonze, P.: Static analysis of role-based access control in J2EE applications. SIGSOFT Softw. Eng. Notes **29**(5), 1–10 (2004)
18. Petrasch, T., Piskachev, G., Spaeth, J., Bodden, E.: Authcheck spring implementation. https://github.com/secure-software-engineering/authcheck/
19. del Pilar Salas-Zárate, M., Alor-Hernández, G., Valencia-Garca, R., Rodríguez-Mazahua, L., Rodríguez-González, A., Cuadrado, J.L.L.: Analyzing best practices on web development frameworks: the lift approach. Sci. Comput. Program. **102**, 1–19 (2015)
20. Strom, R.E.: Mechanisms for compile-time enforcement of security. In: Proceedings of the 10th ACM SIGPLAN POPL, pp. 276–284. ACM, New York (1983)
21. Sun, F., Xu, L., Su, Z.: Static detection of access control vulnerabilities in web applications. In: Proceedings of USENIX. USENIX Association, Berkeley (2011)
22. Xu, Y., Xie, X.: Modeling and analysis of authentication protocols using colored petri nets. In: Proceedings of the 3rd ASID, ASID 2009. IEEE Press, Piscataway (2009)

Author Index

Printed in the United States
by Bookmasters

Printed in the United States
By Bookmasters